PRESIDENTIAL PARTIES

The Dorsey Series in Political Science

PRESIDENTIAL PARTIES

John H. Kessel

Department of Political Science
The Ohio State University

1984
THE DORSEY PRESS
Homewood, Illinois 60430

ISBN 0-256-03103-7

Library of Congress Catalog Card No. 83–73705

Printed in the United States of America

1 2 3 4 5 6 7 8 9 0   MP   1 0 9 8 7 6 5 4

For Maggie

PREFACE

The American Constitution did not envision political parties, but American political parties have been shaped by the Constitution. The parties have occupied constitutional crevices and filled constitutional lacunae. In the exercise of power, both executive parties and legislative parties have been molded by the responsibilities assigned to those branches of government. As competitors for power, parties have developed ways of selecting nominees and conducting election campaigns. Consequently, one cannot make meaningful statements about "the Democratic party" or "the Republican party." Since party activities are carried on in four different institutional domains, meaningful statements are limited to what Republicans or Democrats are doing in one of these settings. To understand American politics, therefore, we must understand executive politics *and* legislative politics *and* nomination politics *and* electoral politics. And if we want to understand citizen response, we must be able to speak of their attitudes and behavior as well.

A second requisite to understanding—and one certainly not unique to American politics—is the use of methodological power to wrest new insights from reluctant data. It is the combination of method and substance that is important here. There are fascinating intellectual challenges in method alone, but unless the analysis is directed to real political questions, one lives in a closed intellectual world. And it is easy to be drawn to the fascinating realm of political maneuver, but unless one gets beyond substance, no advances in understanding result. The combination of substance and method may be awkward and imperfect, but it is essential. As V. O. Key expressed it: "Method without

substance may be sterile, but substance without method is only fortui-
tously substantial."

These two beliefs—that one must master politics in all four institutional domains and address both substantive and methodological problems—combine into a view of how one should write about American
politics. But, alas, time tempers ambition. The last data (interviews
with Reagan staff members and a few interviews on Capitol Hill) were
not collected until the summer of 1982. A fair amount of writing had
been done earlier. About two thirds of the material on nominations,
elections, and citizen behavior had been published in an earlier edition
of *Presidential Campaign Politics.* The first two chapters were drafted
in the late summer of 1981. But all of the writing on executive politics,
legislative politics, and the analyses of 1980 nomination politics, campaign strategies, and citizen behavior were done in the last half of
1982 and during 1983. I am quite conscious of analyses left undone,
and criticisms that I have not been able to take into account, but I
wanted to get the book published in 1984 while the analyses were
still fresh, and there were limits to what could be done in the time
available.

My argument is that *why* something happens is sometimes explained
by internal structure, sometimes by external structure, and sometimes
by both. *When* it happens is explained by the temporal pattern of
the acting unit. I would like to say a word about each of these three
organizing categories.

The analysis of internal structure is now reasonably straightforward.
I began using this in *The Goldwater Coalition,* published in 1968. My
thinking about this has evolved a little. Certainly the agreement scores
and CLUSTER analysis that allows me to determine the existence of
issue groups rather than assert their existence is an advance, but I
have used nested concepts to determine aggregative properties before.
Temporal patterns have become more important in my thinking. When
I wrote the analyses of nomination and electoral politics, I began with
temporal patterns. I wanted to use them to introduce material as well
as to focus attention on the patterns themselves. By the time I was
writing about executive and legislative politics, the temporal patterns
were full chapters that were carrying more of the analysis. I am least
satisfied with the development of external structure. It is not a question
of whether context matters. It does. The problem is that once you
begin to consider environmental effects on the acting unit, *everything*
becomes a potential cause. The difficulties are to distinguish the most
important external effects from all those that are somewhat important,
and then to demonstrate that these environmental considerations are
having some impact on the acting unit. I think that I have been able
to show this at the end of Chapter 5 with the time use data, and in
Chapter 14 in the section on cognitive interaction with the informational

environment, but I am less content with the other discussion of external structure.

In any case, I have done what I could do with these ideas. Now it is up to the reader to judge how useful they are.

John H. Kessel

Columbus, Ohio
February 17, 1984

ACKNOWLEDGMENTS

Any book such as this requires a lot of help, and it has been offered to me. I have been extremely fortunate in having colleagues at Ohio State with strong research orientations. Those whose work overlaps most with my own—Herbert Asher, Aage Clausen, Randall Ripley, and Herbert Weisberg—have been more than generous with their time and counsel when I have come to them with questions and puzzlements. Thomas Boyd, Thomas Jackson, Bruce Moon, Barbara Norrander, Stephen Shaffer, Evelyn Small, Gerald Stacy, Kenneth Town, and Steven Yarnell have all been responsible in one way or another for analyses that appear between these covers. Thomas Boyd made particularly important contributions to Chapters 4, 7, and 15, Barbara Norrander to Chapter 15, Stephen Shaffer to Chapters 10 and 15, and Steven Yarnell did so for Chapter 10.

Ohio State University granted me professional leave during 1980–1981 which allowed me time to gather material on the 1980 general election campaign and to conduct White House interviews. The American Enterprise Institute for Public Policy Research gave me a Washington base by welcoming me as a Visiting Scholar. I profited from the many insights of knowledgeable colleagues there, and—as a glance at the bibliography will attest—from the high-quality literature that AEI has been producing. The National Science Foundation has supported my research with three grants, GS-2660, GS-35084, and SES-80-24079, to collect and analyze data on presidential politics. And the Earhart Foundation gave me a fellowship research grant that allowed me to devote Winter Quarter 1983 to full-time writing. I am deeply appreciative of all this support.

I should like to thank Richard Hofstetter for allowing me to use his 1972 surveys of political activists and voters, and Aage Clausen for making available the data from his analysis of the 95th Congress. Doris Graber, Jeane Kirkpatrick, and Herbert Weisberg allowed me to use some of their data. The Election Studies of the Survey Research Center/Center for Political Studies were made available through the Inter-University Consortium for Political and Social Research. Neither the individual scholars nor the Consortium are responsible for the interpretation I put on their data.

Richard McKelvey was kind enough to send his probit analysis program, and Forrest Nelson and John Aldrich (the latter on repeated occasions) helped me understand how to use probit analysis. Herbert Weisberg helped remove a block from the OSIRIS CLUSTER program so a large input matrix could be used, rewrote a section of the CLUSTER program to assure that each case would end up in the cluster with which it was most closely associated, and coached me on the use of the MDSCAL program. James Ludwig wrote programs to calculate agreement scores from raw data, and to use matrices of such scores as input to CLUSTER programs. In addition to general gratitude to the authors of the OSIRIS and SPSS programs, a special word of thanks ought to go to Norman Nie and his SPSS colleagues for the COMPUTE (and other similar) statements that allow nonprogrammers to manipulate data to meet particular needs.

The Polimetrics Laboratory at Ohio State under three Directors, Richard Hofstetter, Stuart Thorson, and Kristi Andersen, and its invaluable systems programmer, James Ludwig, has been of continuing assistance in maintaining and running these programs and other needed software. A couple of years ago, Kristi Andersen encouraged me to begin using the computer as a text-editor, and this book was written from a computer terminal. This was possible because Kristi, Stuart Thorson, James Ludwig, and other friendly people in the Polimetrics Laboratory were good enough to help me understand SCRIPT, SYSPAPER, and WYLBUR.

Kristi Andersen, Richard Fenno, and Fred Greenstein all offered helpful reactions as plans for this book were being made. Samuel Patterson read the entire manuscript, and offered continuing encouragement and sensible advice. John Bibby read all but the part on executive politics, and gave much helpful counsel. Steven Brown, Allan Cigler, Philip Converse, William Crotty, Richard Fenno, Lyman Kellstedt, Paul Light, Richard Niemi, Steven Rosenstone, Norman Thomas, and Herbert Weisberg all read the parts of the book that corresponded to their own fields of specialization, and offered their usual expert guidance. If I did not have the time or wit to take advantage of all their help, the fault is mine, not theirs.

Finally, and above all, my thanks to Maggie for all the love and understanding she has shared with me since 1954.

John H. Kessel

CONTENTS

PART ONE

EXPLANATION

CHAPTER 1

THE NATIONAL ENERGY ACT
OF 1978

*Congress gave President Carter the most important domestic
victory of his presidency at dawn Sunday when it finally
approved his energy program after 18 months of bitter
legislative battles. After meeting all night to finish its work
in its rush to adjourn the 95th Congress, the House voted
231 to 168 to adopt the energy bill at the moment the rising
sun began to tint the autumn leaves on the Capitol grounds.*

Los Angeles Times, October 16, 1978, p. 1

There are many reasons for wanting to understand American politics.
As citizens, we all need enough information to follow the activities
of our government and to cast intelligent votes. Many who are drawn
to politics want to know enough about strategy and maneuvering to
participate themselves. Some are fortunate enough not to have lost
their childhood curiosity, and continue to prize knowledge in its own
right. But whatever the reason for wanting understanding, political science should provide it.

The above quotation focuses on one class of events it is important
to understand. In our indirect system of government, policy choices
are not made immediately by the citizenry. Officials elected by them
actually decide whether the government should regulate some activity,
should conduct research on some topic, or should confer benefits on
some class of persons, and how all this should be financed. The House
vote at dawn confirmed that the government would adopt certain energy
policies.

Actually the more suspenseful vote had come the preceding Friday afternoon when the House had adopted a procedural motion (without which the bill would almost certainly have been defeated) by a single vote, 207 to 206. This was the climax of a legislative struggle that had begun 18 months earlier when President Carter submitted the legislation. Indeed, since the legislation dealt with the decontrol of natural gas prices, it resolved a question that had been on the congressional agenda since 1949. America consumes more energy than any other nation on earth. Consequently energy production and distribution are major questions of national policy.

Many different things might be explained here. One might take the legislation as a single undifferentiated event, and then ask what impact it had on American society. An historian concerned with a much broader time span might want to ask why the question of energy prices had been on the public agenda for much of the 20th century. But we want to explain the series of events culminating in the passage of the legislation. To do so, we want to focus on the actors, the groups, and the coalitions involved. Specifically, we want to ask: Why did the Carter administration make the proposals it did? How were these proposals modified by the House and the Senate? And why was the ultimate bill able to obtain the support of a winning coalition?

A SKETCH OF THE PROCESS

The Carter Administration Proposals

Newly elected President Jimmy Carter made two decisions that were to shape his most important policy proposal.[1] One was to charge James R. Schlesinger with the responsibility for putting together an energy plan. The other was to promise that this plan would be submitted to Congress within 90 days of his inauguration. Together these decisions determined the kind of energy package the administration would submit, and the fate that awaited it on Capitol Hill. What lay behind them?

In meetings following the 1976 election, Jimmy Carter found James Schlesinger to be a compatible advisor. Carter's and Schlesinger's habits of thought were different, but both preferred "rational" planning to political bargaining. Schlesinger, a Harvard summa cum laude with a Ph.D. in economics, was much more at home thinking about abstract economic mechanisms than in the give-and-take of politics. In the Nixon administration, he had been successively in the Office of Management

---

[1] There is an extensive literature, both about energy politics in general, and the Carter proposals in particular. This account draws upon Cochran (1981), *Congressional Quarterly* (1979), Jones (1979), Malbin (1980), Malbin (1983), Nivola (1979), and Sinclair (1981) in addition to newspaper and magazine accounts and my own interviews.

and Budget, chairman of the Atomic Energy Commission, director of the Central Intelligence Agency, and secretary of defense. President Ford had replaced him as defense secretary, reportedly because of Schlesinger's differences with Henry Kissinger (which would have nothing to do with the Carter energy plan) and because he lacked rapport on Capitol Hill (which would have a lot to do with what happened to the Carter energy plan). Few doubted that Schlesinger had the intellect to fashion a comprehensive plan, but it was said that he tended to be arrogant and inflexible in defending his plans.

In setting an early deadline, President Carter was following advice Richard Neustadt had given some years earlier in *Presidential Power:*

> [A president] needs means of putting pressure on himself, of imposing new deadlines on himself, to come to grips with those things he would want to make his own if he were free to interfere and pick and choose at will. Deadlines self-imposed are no less helpful to a president than tangible details. The one informs his mind, the other arms his hand. (1960, p. 156)

More recent scholars, Paul Light (1980) and Valerie Bunce (1981) among them, have stressed the importance of a new president getting off the mark quickly if he is going to accomplish anything. Thus there were good reasons for Jimmy Carter to set an action-forcing deadline for his energy advisor and himself.

Mr. Schlesinger assembled a staff of 15 on the second floor of the Old Executive Office Building, an ornate Victorian structure just west of the White House. This staff came from two principal sources. Seven of the staff members, including Alvin L. Alm and John O'Leary, were longtime associates of Schlesinger's. Most of the others had worked on energy questions for liberal Democrats. Roger Colloff had worked for Vice President Mondale when Mondale was in the Senate; Deborah Gottheil came from Representative Toby Moffett of Connecticut; Leslie Goldman from Senator Adlai Stevenson of Illinois; Robert Nordhouse from the staff of the House Commerce Committee; and S. Douglas Freeman came from the Ford Foundation where he had directed an energy study calling for a coordinator with sufficient power to implement a coherent national energy policy. Most of the staff members were relatively young, and since their experience was in the public sector rather than business, they tended to rely on governmental mechanisms. Michael Malbin has written that the staff members had three key beliefs: "(1) domestic oil and gas production inevitably would decline sharply in the not-too-distant future, (2) conservation therefore represented the best short-term strategy for decreasing dependence on imports, and (3) conservation through governmental intervention was preferable to market-induced conservation through price" (1983, p. 222).

The shared attitudes of a group are always important in forecasting that group's actions. In the case of this staff, the attitudes were particularly important because James Schlesinger insisted that they work by themselves. This is not to say that there was *no* contact with persons outside the group. It is to say that other officials with vital interests in the program, such as the secretaries of the treasury and transportation and the chairman of the Council of Economic Advisors, were kept in the dark. Further, this was an energy plan to be presented *to* the Congress, not one to be prenegotiated through consultation with key members before legislation was sent to the Hill. Cabinet members were able to make a few changes around the edges at a meeting in early April, but the staff's plan remained essentially intact.

This meant that many people were surprised, and not always pleasantly, when the plan was unveiled. For example, on October 19, 1976, candidate Carter had written to the Governors of Oklahoma, Louisiana, and Texas: "I will work with the Congress, as President Ford has been unable to do, to deregulate new natural gas." This letter was given wide publicity. Carter carried Louisiana and Texas by narrow margins, but deregulation of "new" natural gas was not a part of the Carter energy plan.

The problem Carter planners had to address was American overdependence on oil and natural gas. Because these fuels once had been abundant, and because government policies had kept their prices low, consumption had shifted so that by the mid-70s oil and natural gas supplied three quarters of American energy. What was needed were measures that would conserve energy, increase the cost of oil and natural gas so they would not be used uneconomically, and accomplish these goals without an economic shock that would crush individuals and without providing further fuel for an already rampant inflation.

The Schlesinger plan had three major components. First, there was a series of conservation measures: tax credits for home insulation, mandatory energy efficiency standards for home appliances, a tax on gas-guzzling cars, authority to force industry conversion to more abundant supplies of coal, and a tax on industrial and utility use of oil or natural gas. Second, to deal with too-cheap oil, the price of domestic oil was to be allowed to rise (through a complicated formula) to the price of world oil, a crude-oil equalization tax was to take the resulting profits and rebate them through the income tax, and a standby gasoline tax was to be put into effect if conservation goals were not being met. The third element was a gradual increase in the cost of natural gas between 1978 and 1985. Through a method called incremental pricing (developed by Schlesinger staffer Leslie Goldman when he was working for Senator Stevenson), the increased costs were to be borne by industry until the cost of natural gas reached a price equivalent to that of oil, after which the increased costs would be split between industrial and residential consumers. The focus was therefore on conservation. The plan contained direct conservation measures, and aimed at further conservation through a gradual increase in the cost of oil, and a gradual increase in the cost of natural gas.

In an interview shortly after he presented his plan to Congress, President Carter said:

> Had I another 30 days on the energy package, there would not have been a substantial difference in what we proposed. . . . I believe Dr. Schlesinger has done a superb job in putting together a package that is, in its totality, fair and equitable and well balanced. . . . So, I have got to see it go through Congress as an entire package.

But reflecting at the end of the Carter administration, one of his chief legislative aides said:

> I think the single most critical decision on passing the National Energy Act was that it had to be sent up by April 20, 1977. If it hadn't been for that, we'd have still been talking about what to propose. But having said that, it also forced all kinds of decisions into time frames that did not allow thorough discussion, that did not allow working through them, rather than having them worked through after you've sent them up.

As already noted, there was good reason to use a short deadline as a stimulus to action. But when that was combined with secrecy that kept information about the plan away from others who had vital interests in it, the effect was to stimulate opposition to the plan rather than enlist support.

Action by the House of Representatives

The reception given the Carter proposals in the House was shaped by skepticism and strong leadership. The skepticism came from a developing administration reputation for vacillation. President Carter had abruptly withdrawn a proposal for a $50 tax rebate *after* congressional supporters had gone to some lengths to line up votes for it. Many congressmen, especially conservatives who favored decontrol of natural gas prices, saw the switch from the campaign pledge of decontrol as another example of administration unpredictability.

The strong leadership was provided by House Speaker Thomas P. (Tip) O'Neill. O'Neill pledged to work for the speedy passage of the President's energy bill. To this end, he had created a special ad hoc committee to handle it. The creation of such a supercommittee had been resisted by the standing committees that ordinarily would have handled the legislation, but O'Neill worked out a compromise. The five standing committees would be represented on the ad hoc committee, and the legislation would be referred to the standing committees first. The standing committees, however, were given short deadlines in which to complete their work; and the ad hoc committee was to put the pieces into a single bill, and get the bill to the floor in time for action before the August recess. All this was done.

The White House legislative liaison men worked particularly closely with two representatives at the committee stage, John Dingell of Michigan and Joe Waggoner of Louisiana. Dingell usually voted with a large group of liberals that was the core of the House Democratic party. Coming from Dearborn, Michigan, he favored low fuel prices to keep cars on the road and to heat his constituents' homes. Waggoner voted with a group of traditional southern Democrats. He came from a fuel-producing state, and thus favored higher prices to help his constituents. Although he was not a senior member of the Ways and Means Committee, he was regarded as shrewd. Furthermore, anytime he could think of a way to get four or five other Democrats to vote with him (and if the Republicans voted as a bloc on the same side), he could beat the committee leadership. Consequently, the Carter administration and the House leadership wanted to keep Dingell and Waggoner happy.

The House is too complex, and the voting coalitions are too fragile, to suggest that any two representatives held the key to House action. The tendencies represented by Dingell and Waggoner did, however, point to a division in the Democratic party between liberals who wanted to hold fuel costs down and conservatives who wanted to increase the profits for producers. Because of this division, two changes were introduced at the committee stage. One made the energy bill more palatable to liberals; the other made it more palatable to conservatives. The incremental pricing feature for natural gas was altered to make the energy package more attractive to individual natural gas consumers. As originally written, increased costs were to be borne by industry until the prices of natural gas and oil were equivalent. Afterward the higher costs were to be split between industrial and residential customers. This was rewritten to leave the entire cost burden on industry. The change that made the package more attractive to producers was proposed by Robert Eckhardt of Texas. This expanded the definition of "newly discovered" natural gas, so that much more gas would be eligible for the higher prices to be paid for "new" gas. This was ultimately adopted on the floor of the House (with the support of the ad hoc energy committee), and won over a number of votes that otherwise would have been for deregulation.

Once the energy bill cleared the ad hoc energy committee and was headed for the floor, Speaker O'Neill introduced another innovation: Speaker's task forces to line up Democratic votes (Sinclair, 1981). The task forces worked with data, compiled by Robert Eckhardt of Texas and Andrew Maguire of New Jersey, which identified likely voting patterns. Individuals then contacted representatives whose votes were likely to be crucial, explaining provisions and soliciting their support. Three task forces were organized for particular amendments, and the administration position was sustained on these amendments by an average majority of 25 votes.

One crucial vote concerned deregulation of natural gas prices. This was rejected by a margin of 199 to 227, with 210 of the votes against deregulation coming from Democrats and only 17 from Republicans. The Democrats split along ideological lines with liberals against deregulation, moderates splitting, and conservatives voting for deregulation. Most Republicans were for deregulation; only liberal Republicans voted for continued regulation.

An even closer call came on a motion by Republican Congressman William Steiger of Wisconsin to delete the crude-oil equalization tax. No task force had been set up on this (although one did work on a related amendment that would have used crude-oil equalization tax funds to provide incentives for further production). The Steiger amendment was rejected by a vote of 203 to 219. The split among Democrats was essentially the same as on gas deregulation. Liberals opposed the Steiger amendment; conservatives supported it; the moderates were split. The reason for the closer vote was that all but three Republicans supported the Steiger amendment.

Only one important provision of the Carter energy bill—the standby gasoline tax—was defeated on the House floor. Otherwise, the major provisions survived; and on final passage the bill had a comfortable 244 to 177 majority. But a number of consequential things had taken place. First, the bill had been modified to pick up additional support. Second, the bill had been supported by a coalition normally seen on legislation dealing with economics. Most liberal and moderate Democrats supported the Carter administration; many conservative Democrats and most Republicans were opposed. Third, the margins by which the crucial provisions were passed were not large. Fourth, these narrow margins had been achieved though some very hard work on the part of an able House Democratic leadership team.

Action by the Senate

Several circumstances suggested the Senate might act differently. First, because of the constitutional requirement for equal representation by the states, the South and West enjoyed slightly larger representation in the upper house. Second, a major supporter of the energy producers, Russell Long of Louisiana, exercised great power as chairman of the Senate Finance Committee.[2] Third, party leadership in the Senate is much weaker than in the House. Senate Majority Leader Robert Byrd

---

[2] The Carter White House, generally naive about Capitol Hill, seemed to be unaware of Senator Long's influence. At one White House meeting early in 1977, Senator Long said, "Perhaps I had better introduce myself. My name is Russell Long. I am chairman of the Senate Finance Committee."

was not in a position to hold the Democratic party together as Speaker O'Neill had done in the House. Fourth, Senator Byrd followed a multibill strategy. Whereas Speaker O'Neill wanted a single energy bill, and created a special ad hoc committee to produce it, Senator Byrd left each piece of the energy package to its own fate. Thus, some bills were referred to the Energy and Natural Resources Committee, chaired by Washington's Henry Jackson who was generally supportive of the administration, and other bills to the Finance Committee, chaired by Russell Long.

The most important element handled by the Energy and Natural Resources Committee was the deregulation of natural gas, but committee action was ineffectual because of a split within the committee. The committee rejected a proposal by Republican Senator Dewey Bartlett of Oklahoma for immediate decontrol of natural gas (except that under contract) by a vote of 6 to 12. But then the committee deadlocked 9 to 9 on a motion by Republican Senator Clifford Hansen of Wyoming to phase out regulation of "new" natural gas within five years. In view of the deadlock, the Committee sent the bill to the Senate floor without a recommendation.

Democratic Senators Metzenbaum of Ohio and Abourezk of South Dakota, both strong opponents of deregulation, tried to prevent a vote with a filibuster. Vice President Mondale and Senator Byrd, feeling that the filibuster was just delaying Senate action, cooperated to end it, and the decision came on October 4. The vote was on an amendment offered by Senators Pearson (R, Kans.) and Bentsen (D, Tex.). Their amendment called for immediate decontrol for "new" onshore natural gas and phased decontrol over a five-year period for offshore natural gas, and it changed the incremental pricing arrangement back so residential customers would have priority *until* the cost of natural gas was equivalent to that of oil. The Pearson-Bentsen amendment passed 50 to 46. Northern Democrats voted 5 to 35 against, with the only favorable votes coming from border and mountain states senators. Southern Democrats voted 11 to 8 in favor with most of the votes against the amendment coming from South Atlantic states that were not energy producers. The Republicans voted 34 to 3 in favor, the opponents being Senators Case of New Jersey, Javits of New York, and Brooke of Massachusetts. As in the House, this was a modified party-line vote typical of economic issues. The difference was that the liberal and moderate Democrats had won a narrow victory in the House, while the Republicans and conservative Democrats won a narrow victory in the Senate.

The Finance Committee did not recommend any of the proposals for new taxes that had been referred to them. On September 20, the committee voted 11 to 5 against the proposed tax on gas-guzzler cars. Six days later, they removed the economic heart of the Carter program, the crude-oil equalization tax, by a vote of 10 to 6.[3] And on October 6, the Finance Committee voted 14 to 4 against the tax on utility use of oil or natural gas. In place of these taxes that were intended to inhibit the use of oil and natural gas, the committee recommended tax credits intended to stimulate energy production and conservation. These recommendations were passed by the full Senate by a 52 to 35 margin.

Conference

The Conference Committee is the device by which the House and Senate reconcile differences in versions of bills that have passed the two chambers. The conferees are senior members who have been intimately involved in the legislation. The conferees are expected to fight for the version of the bill that passed their own chamber but, at the same time, resolve differences so the legislation will be acceptable to both the House and the Senate.

Consider the problem facing the conferees on the energy package. There were some relatively uncontroversial portions (for example, tax credits for home insulation) that had passed both houses, and were certain to be approved. But the House and Senate had adopted totally opposed policies on the major provisions. The House bill called for continued control of natural gas prices; the Senate wanted decontrol. The House bill contained a crude-oil equalization tax that would hold down consumption by making oil more expensive; the Senate bill called for tax credits to stimulate both production and conservation.

Furthermore, there were narrow margins in each chamber. Only 53 percent of the representatives (who voted) wanted to continue control of natural gas prices, and only 52 percent of the senators wanted decontrol. There was a somewhat greater consensus in the Senate on tax policy. Only 52 percent of the representatives wanted the crude-oil equalization tax, whereas 61 percent of the senators did not want it.

Given the best will in the world, there was no compromise that was going to be completely acceptable to majorities in both chambers. In addition, Russell Long had gained instructions from the Senate that gave him considerable flexibility on the tax question—and he had made it clear that he was not going to bargain seriously on tax matters until he was satisfied about the deregulation of natural gas. So, unless progress could be made on the very difficult question of natural gas deregulation, only the few noncontroversial portions of the package would survive the congressional labyrinth.

---

[3] Russell Long did try to revive this tax, with the funds to be used to stimulate fuel production rather than for tax rebates as President Carter had proposed. He was unsuccessful.

For several months, the conferees got nowhere. There were at least two problems. One dealt with the arcane provision known as incremental pricing. The House version protected residential customers by placing the entire burden of "new" natural gas on industry. The Senate version protected residential customers from higher prices only until the cost of natural gas rose to the price level of home heating oil. The problem with the House version was that it would ultimately make oil a cheaper fuel for industry, and give industry an incentive to shift away from natural gas. One natural gas supplier calculated that after seven years, they would not have *any* industrial customers left. At that point, the "protected" residential customers would find that they had to pay the entire cost. For whatever reason, this argument was too subtle for many representatives to understand. The negotiations were protracted because it took a long time to get a practicable incremental pricing formula back into the bill.

An even more basic problem was that the Senate conferees were divided among themselves. For some time, nine senators were in favor of deregulation, and nine were opposed. Moreover, three liberal Democrats (Abourezk of South Dakota, Metzenbaum of Ohio, and Durkin of New Hampshire) were opposed to anything that resembled deregulation. This ruled out a strategy based on holding the Democrats together, and implied that a moderate coalition would have to be constructed from a group of northern Democrats willing to entertain some form of deregulation, and groups of southern Democrats and Republicans willing to consider something less than immediate deregulation.

Such a shaky coalition began to emerge in March 1978. It consisted of six Democrats and three Republicans, four of whom had been opponents of deregulation and five of whom had been proponents of deregulation.[4] Negotiators reached tentative agreement with members of the House on April 21, and this was finally confirmed at a meeting of all the House and Senate conferees on May 24. The votes were barely there: 10 to 7 among the senators and 13 to 12 among the representatives. Even so, Senator Jackson said, "We have been able to merge our differences for the first time in 30 years," and Representative Dingell announced, "I'm going back and try to sell this proposal to my colleagues."

What the conferees agreed on was essentially phased-in decontrol. Price controls were to be extended to all categories of natural gas, but controls on "new" natural gas were to expire on January 1, 1985. The economic impact of this was to be softened by a number of provisions, including a satisfactorily worded incremental pricing formula. As Pietro Nivola explained:

---

[4] The sudden death of Senator Lee Metcalf in January meant that nine was now a majority of the Senate conferees.

In order to entice Republican support, the compromise had to involve "deregulation" at some point. But to hold the votes of most Senate Democrats, and to keep the House conferees from bolting, any deregulation had to be hedged with qualifications like a protracted phase-in, incremental pricing to the burner tip, and multiple categorization of gas, designed in part to ensure that only the "right" sorts of gas would be decontrolled. . . . *The alternatives were drastically limited:* if the 95th Congress were to emit any natural gas legislation whatsoever, the May compromise (or something very like it) was almost certainly the only prospect. (1979, p. 35)

The conference on taxes was separate. Because of Russell Long's insistence on a natural gas settlement first, the conferees did not even meet between December 7, 1977, and July 13, 1978, and they did not finish their work until October 12, 1978. The crude-oil equalization tax and the tax on utility use of oil and natural gas were dropped, but the tax on gas-guzzling cars was included in the final legislation.

The Conference Report was not ready until July 31. This was the most complex single piece of legislation ever passed by Congress, and the staff had a lot of work to do. With the passage of time between the end of May and early August, however, some of the original supporters of the natural gas compromise decided they would not sign. For example, Senator J. Bennett Johnston, who had in fact written most of the compromise, felt he could not sign because he was a candidate for reelection from Louisiana. And in the House of Representatives, conservatives Joe Waggoner and Charles Wilson (D, Tex.) and liberal Henry Reuss (D, Wis.) had backed off. Two more liberals, James Corman (D, Calif.) and Charles Rangel (D, N.Y.), were persuaded to sign during a personal meeting with President Carter, and Charles Wilson's signature was affixed to the document after an all-night meeting in the White House that involved Vice President Mondale and James Schlesinger, among others. The touch-and-go nature of all this turned out to be an accurate forecast of what would happen to the Conference Report as it went back to the House and Senate for final approval.

Senate and House Approval

Under an agreement between Senate Majority Leader Byrd and House Speaker O'Neill, the bill was to go first to the Senate, where each portion would be voted on separately, and then to the House, where it would be voted on as a whole. This was in keeping with Byrd's preference for a multiple-bill strategy, and O'Neill's desire for a single-bill strategy. The bill was a far cry from what the administration had introduced more than a year earlier. It now called for phased-in deregulation of natural gas rather than continued regulation; the major taxes had been removed; only the noncontroversial portions had survived intact. Even so, it was vulnerable. Southern Democrats and Republicans thought it didn't give the gas and oil companies enough incentive; northern Democrats thought it gave the oil companies too much. Russell Long was rounding up conservative Democratic votes against it; Minority Leader Howard Baker was rounding up Republican votes against it; Edward Kennedy was rounding up liberal Democratic votes against it. Subject to attack by both liberals and conservatives, the bill was in danger of being chewed to death from both ends.

At this juncture, the White House finally did some very effective lobbying. Anne Wexler, who had been brought to the White House to build public support for legislative priorities believed there was no substitute for one-on-one communication. Large groups were brought to the East Room to be briefed by the President and other administration leaders. As she explained it:

> If a senator has a problem on a piece of legislation that we badly want, we can go to him and say, "Senator, we'd certainly like you to consider this bill. One of the things we'd like to do is to invite people from your state in to hear about it. . . . Would you give us a list of people you think would benefit by understanding the legislation?"

In this way, persons presumably influential with the senator would hear such administration spokesmen as Robert Strauss. "It no longer makes a difference," Strauss argued, "whether the bill is a C- or an A+. Certainly it is better than a zero, and it must pass." James Schlesinger was also said to have been persuasive in these sessions. After they went back home, these influential citizens might well repeat the arguments to others, and thus build home state support for wavering senators. Meanwhile, the senators themselves were hearing directly from Strauss, Schlesinger, Vice President Mondale, and President Carter.

When the Senate took up the bill in September, the results of the White House effort showed. The crucial vote came on a motion by Howard Metzenbaum to recommit (in effect, defeat) the Conference Report provisions on natural gas deregulation. The Metzenbaum motion was defeated by a vote of 39 to 59. The administration had been particularly successful with Democrats. Only two more southern Democrats joined their colleagues from the producing states; and only a dozen northern Democrats, all liberals, joined Metzenbaum. There was a 21 to 15 Republican majority favoring recommittal, but considering normal Republican support for private enterprise, this was hardly lopsided either. The final Senate vote on natural gas was virtually the same. Only five senators shifted their positions from the Metzenbaum motion in one direction or the other, and the bill passed 57 to 42.

Whether a moderate coalition could be put together to pass the Conference Report in the House was a close question. In the Senate, many of the conservatives and moderates who had voted for the Pearson-Bentsen amendment continued to support the legislation thereafter. But in the House, the 1977 energy legislation had been passed by a more liberal coalition. Many Frostbelt liberals felt they could not countenance higher heating bills for their constituents, and such persons were more numerous in the House than in the Senate.

In the judgment of Speaker O'Neill (and opponents of the bill as well), it would be easier to pass a single energy bill than to pass all of the sections one at a time. Under the latter procedure, the natural gas bill would probably be defeated, and that would scuttle the whole compromise that had been so laboriously worked out with the Senate. In the House, legislation (including any Conference Report) comes to the floor under a rule, granted by the Rules Committee, that stipulates the length and terms of the debate. The leadership sought a rule specifying that there would be one vote on the entire energy package. At first, this failed in the Rules Committee by an 8 to 8 tie vote, but a retiring member was prevailed upon to change his mind, and the single-bill rule was passed by the committee.

The rule came to the floor on October 13, just two days before the session was supposed to end.[5] The rules themselves must be approved by the House. Technically, the vote is only procedural. The House is agreeing to consider a particular bill in a particular way. Practically, the vote is substantive. In the case at hand, all recognized that the best opportunity to defeat the bill was to defeat the rule. The outcome could not have been closer. The vote in favor of the motion by Richard Bolling was 207 to 206. The only issue groups casting solid votes were liberal Democrats and conservative Republicans, all of whom voted against. As compared to the closest vote in the summer of 1977, the Steiger motion on the crude-oil equalization tax, 48 Democrats switched to oppose the Bolling motion and 28 switched to support it. The defections were all liberal. They came from such states as California, New York, Massachusetts, Ohio, Michigan, Wisconsin, and Minnesota. The new Democratic support came primarily from the South, from such states as Alabama, Georgia, Oklahoma, and Texas. Only the Louisiana delegation cast a solid vote against the Bolling motion. The Oklahomans and Texans voting for the Bolling motion might well have preferred immediate decontrol, but given a practical choice between the Senate-House compromise and no bill at all, they supported the compromise.[6]

This should have led to final passage, but one more hurdle remained. The House could not take up the Conference Report until the Senate

---

[5] Since 1978 was a congressional election year, members were anxious to wind up and get back home to campaign.

[6] The Democratic leadership was probably helped by the fact that this was a procedural motion. Individual representatives are generally more apt to support their leaders on a decision to consider a bill in one way rather than another.

had approved all parts of it, and the Senate had not yet passed the Conference Report on taxes. And on Saturday morning, the date Congress was scheduled to adjourn, Senator Abourezk began a filibuster. He hoped that if he held things up in the Senate, liberal Democratic allies in the House would get a chance to vote for an alternative to the Conference Report. He was finally convinced that this longing was futile, but not until after midnight.

So it was that the House of Representatives began debating the National Energy Act of 1978 at 2:45 on Sunday morning. The vote finally came at dawn. The vote passed by the comfortable margin of 231 to 168 because 34 Republicans who had opposed the Bolling motion voted for the bill on final passage. Most of the issue groups that normally vote together were split. Only moderate Democrats were united in favor of the bill, and only conservative Republicans were united in opposition. But if it is true that this compromise was the only energy legislation that could have passed the 95th Congress, then it follows that a moderate coalition was the only one capable of bringing it through the final stages of the legislative labyrinth.

WHAT THIS EXPLANATION DOES NOT TELL US

All explanations are selective, and therefore partial. Given limited time to devote to any topic, one must choose what to include. Usually, explanations that generalize over many cases are preferred to those that are case specific. Since much legislation can be understood as coalition behavior, we have paid more attention to the coalitions that formed than to all the particulars of this bill. And in general, parsimonious explanations are preferred over complex ones. But to arrive at a reasonably simple explanation, many factors must be omitted. It is therefore as important to understand what an explanation does *not* tell you as it is to grasp what an explanation does enable you to comprehend. In this sketch of the passage of the National Energy Act of 1978, any number of important considerations were simply left out.

To begin with, our analysis is confined to the Carter administration and the 95th Congress. This excludes a good deal of relevant history. Previous administrations all had energy policies of one kind or another. Indeed, policies based on relatively cheap oil and natural gas dated from times when America could produce most of what it needed from apparently plentiful domestic sources. And Jimmy Carter was the third president whose administration had produced an energy plan after the Arab oil embargo of 1973; Richard Nixon and Gerald Ford had also addressed the same problems. In the just-completed 94th Congress, the House had voted for continued control of natural gas prices, and the Senate had adopted a Pearson-Bentsen amendment calling for decontrol. (If the Carter administration's original plan had been designed to appeal to Congress rather than reflecting the attitudes of the Schlesinger staff, it is hard to say what it would have contained. Whether the administration had chosen continued control *or* decontrol, it would have been recommending a policy that had just been rejected by *one* of the houses of Congress.) Nor did the evolution of energy policy end in 1978. In 1979, President Carter began the decontrol of crude-oil prices, and the 96th Congress passed a windfall profits tax on some of the resulting profits. In 1981, President Reagan removed the remaining controls from crude-oil prices, and the 97th Congress changed the tax structure once again.

We have not dealt with the merits of President Carter's national energy plan. We simply reported its main features, and then described how certain features were altered by legislative action. Yet some of the congressional resistance to the administration plan was because it had been subjected to considerable criticism. Several independent agencies—the Office of Technology Assessment, the Congressional Research Service of the Library of Congress, the General Accounting Office, the Congressional Budget Office, and the University Council on Natural Resources of the University of Texas—issued critical analyses. Many of these reports argued that if the Carter administration's announced goals were accepted, then the program was inadequate to meet them.

We have not dealt with interest groups. There was intensive lobbying activity in connection with this legislation. But it is difficult to say what impact this lobbying had. There were many disagreements among the lobbyists themselves, even among supposedly unified groups such as the "gas and oil lobby." The interests of the gas producers (those who own the wells from which the gas is extracted) were not the same as those of the gas suppliers (who sell the gas to the local utility, which sells it to individual customers). The producers profit from high prices; but the suppliers are subject to state regulation, and can raise their prices only if granted a rate increase by state agencies. High prices at the wellhead do not help suppliers squeezed between high prices charged by the producers and the low rates permitted them by state regulatory commissions. A similar point can be made about the divergence of interests among oil companies. Many of the giant companies were in a position to shift profits from one division to another and so were relatively little affected by continued controls, while many smaller companies were quite directly affected and hence opposed controls. Therefore Exxon, Shell, and Mobil chose not to fight the Carter energy plan, while Sun Oil, Conoco, and Marathon did so.

We have seen a little of the activity of a few leading senators and representatives. Thus we saw that Senators Howard Metzenbaum and James Abourezk and Congressman John Dingell favored continued regulation of natural gas prices, while Senator Russell Long and Congress-

man Joe Waggoner preferred removal of controls. We noted some of
the efforts of Speaker of the House O'Neill and Senate Majority Leader
Byrd to shepherd the energy package through their chambers, and of
Senate Minority Leader Baker to round up Republican votes in opposition to the legislation. But even if the few sentences devoted to these
half-dozen senators and three congressmen had been adequate to describe their attitudes and activities, there were 94 senators and 432
representatives who were not discussed. In order to explain a vote
of 207 to 206 (i.e., the Bolling motion), one has to account for the attitudes
of 413 representatives, as well as the forces that moved them in one
direction or another. General statements that moderate Democrats
voted for a motion, or that conservative Republicans voted against
it, are accurate as far as they go, but all one can do with such statements
is to set forth a general pattern.

It is not that these factors—history, substantive merits, interest group
activity, all of the individual members of the House and Senate, and
other matters[7] —were considered and rejected as having little to do
with the legislation. They had a good deal to do with the outcome.
The reason for their exclusion was just that one cannot include everything in any explanation.

We were also unable to make statements about relative influence
of the factors we did consider. At least implicitly, a number of reasons
were given why senators and representatives voted pro or con. Democrats were more likely to support a Democratic administration; Republicans to oppose. Legislators tended to support their constituents' interests: Those from fuel-producing regions wanted high prices for fuel;
those from consuming regions wanted the opposite. Ideology played
a part: Other things being equal, liberals were more likely to trust
governmental mechanisms, while conservatives preferred to rely on
the market. When these factors tended in the same direction, there
was no difficulty in applying this explanation. A liberal Democrat from
a fuel-consuming region was likely to vote for continued price controls.
A conservative Republican from a producing region was apt to vote
for decontrol. But when these motives conflicted (as with a liberal
Republican from a district containing both producers and consumers),
it is harder to make a guess about what the representative might do.
In order to disentangle the relative importance of partisan motivations,
constituency interests, and ideology, we would need measures of each
of these that could be related to the legislators' votes. Such measures
were not at hand.

---

[7] For example, Michael Malbin argues that President Carter's rhetoric failed to "con-
nect his program to the passions and beliefs around which Americans can be rallied"
(1983, p. 239).

WHAT THIS EXPLANATION DOES TELL US

To begin with, attention was called to several individuals who played crucial roles in developing and passing this legislation. James Schlesinger, Tip O'Neill, John Dingell, Joe Waggoner, Russell Long, and a number of others shaped the National Energy Act of 1978 in important ways. Space did not permit much discussion of any of these people, but the explanation provides at least a hint of their activities and some of the reasons for them.

The sketch called our attention to group activity. The staff assembled by James Schlesinger to draft the energy bill was relatively young. Most members were drawn from the public sector. Their attitudes—that oil and gas production would decline, that conservation was the best strategy to deal with this, and that conservation should be induced by government action—would have been significant in any case, but they were more significant because they were shared attitudes. The staff members reinforced one another's views, and they moved as a group in the same direction. The reactions of the different issue groups in the Congress—incompletely characterized as conservative Republicans, moderate Democrats, and so forth—were important in determining legislative reaction to the Schlesinger group's plan.

Coalition activity was a central element in the explanation. In 1977, the supporting coalitions were composed of groups of liberal Democrats and moderate Democrats. The opposing coalitions were made up of groups of conservative Democrats and Republicans. These are the normal coalitions in economic management.[8] The supporting coalition won a narrow victory in the House, and the opposing coalition won a narrow victory in the Senate. There was a shift to quite different coalitions on the Conference Committee and on subsequent votes in 1978. In 1978, moderate Democrats and those responsive to party leaders supported the legislation. They were opposed by groups of doctrinaire liberals and conservatives. Some Republicans joined the supporting coalitions in the Senate and on final passage in the House, but almost all Republicans were in the opposing coalition on the critical Bolling motion.

Both the Schlesinger group and the legislative coalitions were reacting to external audiences as well as to their colleagues in the same institutions. The executive branch had to obtain the cooperation of the legislative branch, and vice versa. The Carter administration had to have congressional support to get the legislation through, and the Democrats in both chambers were more likely to suppport it because it came from a Democratic president. At the same time, legislators

---

[8] The normal coalitions differ from one policy area to another. This will be discussed in Chapter 7.

were reacting to constituents—and in 1978, the Carter White House (through the outreach operation coordinated by Anne Wexler) was trying to convince constituents so they might influence legislators in turn.

This explanation called attention to the formal structure of the Senate and the House. We saw some of the differences between the two chambers—for example, the much stronger leadership position of the Speaker in the House of Representatives as compared with the Senate majority leader. In the House itself, the ad hoc energy committee, the Speaker's task forces, and the Rules Committee all played important roles. The Conference Committee was unusually prominent because of the deep differences between the House and the Senate. And given the importance of legislative structure, the persons holding key positions inevitably influenced the outcome. Russell Long's chairmanship of the Senate Finance Committee placed him in a position to hold up any legislation he did not like. Richard Bolling's position as a senior member of the House Rules Committee enabled him to work for the passage of the kind of energy bill the leadership wanted.[9]

There were several very close votes. Between the introduction of the legislation and final passage 18 months later, there were the Steiger motion, the tie vote in the Senate Energy Committee, the votes of the House and Senate conferees, an initial tie vote by the House Rules Committee, and the vote on the Bolling motion. Few pieces of legislation have this many tie votes and single-vote margins, but all have to pass the same scrutiny. This need to pass several stages points to another generalization about the legislative process. The advantage in legislation always belongs to those on the defensive. Blocking a bill at *any* stage is sufficient to defeat it. The sponsors need to figure out how to get it past *every* stage.

In addition to the patterns of support and opposition (the individuals, groups, and coalitions) and the formal structure of the House and the Senate, we saw two or three instances of the importance of timing. The first was the action-forcing 90-day deadline that President Carter set to get something before Congress for its consideration. The legislative process itself was, of course, sequential. The difficulties in the Conference Committee were a result of what the House and the Senate *already* had done. The strongest example of the importance of temporal factors was the passage of the bill at the very end of the 95th Congress. Senator Abourezk's only hope of success with his last-day filibuster was that proponents would compromise because time was about to expire. The tactic would have been futile in the middle of May. Some-

---

[9] Bolling's position was a little unusual. He did not yet chair the committee, but the chairman, James Delaney, was 77 years old and less forceful than Bolling. Bolling became rules chairman at the beginning of the 96th Congress.

thing of the same thing could be said about supporters of the legislation. Since many of them were held together by the thought that this was their only chance to get an energy bill, it was important that no time remained for further bargaining. The congressional tempo means that tactics that would be useless at one point in a session become the only possible tactics at another.

Summary

Substantively, we have reviewed the crucial steps in one extraordinarily complex piece of legislation. The energy plan that was submitted emphasized conservation stimulated by government intervention. This moved through the House substantially intact because of the leadership of Speaker O'Neill, and the support of a moderate-liberal coalition. In the Senate, conservatives were able to delete the major taxes and the regulation of natural gas. After a protracted deadlock, a compromise was struck calling for phased-in deregulation, almost no taxes, and some noncontroversial provisions. This was sustained by moderates in the Senate, and barely so by moderates in the House of Representatives.

Conceptually, we learned something about a few of the leading actors, saw the importance of shared attitudes in the Schlesinger group, and took note of a number of instances of coalition activity on crucial votes in the House and the Senate. We were able to see advantages given to liberals and moderates in the House, and conservatives in the Senate, by positions of power that enabled leaders to manipulate rules of the game to promote their ends. We got a glimpse of the importance of time, especially at the beginning and end of the process. Finally, there were a number of considerations whose influence we were not able to appraise, and we were not able to rank the relative importance of the factors we did consider.

CHAPTER 2

PARTICIPATION IN THE 1980 ELECTION

Voters in Virginia, Maryland and the District of Columbia are expected to turn out in average numbers today despite cloudy skies, scattered showers and gloomy feelings about the 1980 presidential election. . . . Virginia's election chief predicts a 78 percent turnout, compared with official predictions of a 72.5 percent turnout in Maryland and 60 percent in the District. Nationwide turnout is expected to be about 50 percent, but officials caution that the figures cannot be contrasted directly since they are calculated against different bases.

Washington Post, November 4, 1980, p. 1

Voting is the central act of citizenship, the means of choosing one officeholder over another and thereby indicating preferences for the direction of public policy. Yet, before choosing who to vote for, citizens must decide whether to cast a ballot at all. In 1980, slightly fewer citizens cast ballots for president than in 1976. Using comparable figures for both years, 53.9 percent of the voting-age population voted for president in 1980 as compared to 54.4 percent four years earlier. The 1980 turnout was, however, nearly 10 points lower than 1960, when 63.1 percent had voted for president. What do we know about turnout? Who is more likely to vote, and who is less likely to vote? In the light of this knowledge, does the decline in turnout since 1960 represent a dangerous trend, or is it something that should have been expected?

In this chapter, we shall analyze reported turnout using 1980 survey data collected by the University of Michigan Center for Political Studies.

Seventy-one percent of the respondents told interviewers they had voted. (Note that this is higher than the 53.9 percent figure in the preceding paragraph. Later in the chapter, we shall want to ask why reported turnout is higher than actual turnout.) Because of its importance, turnout has been studied extensively (Kelley, Ayers, & Bowen, 1967; Verba & Nie, 1972; Rosenstone & Wolfinger, 1978; Wolfinger & Rosenstone, 1980; Shaffer, 1981; Abramson & Aldrich, 1982; Patterson & Caldiera, 1983; and *many* more), and the factors associated with variations in turnout are reasonably well known. There were some small surprises when the 1980 data were analyzed, but the tendency to vote or abstain could be predicted reasonably well.

DETERMINANTS OF TURNOUT

Political Interest.   The most important factor associated with turnout in 1980 was in many ways the most obvious: interest in politics. Fully twice as many very interested persons cast ballots as did the uninterested. Only 44 percent of those who said they were "not much interested" in the campaign reported voting as compared to 74 percent who were "somewhat interested" and 90 percent of those who were "very interested." When an action is voluntary, interest is apt to play a large role in a citizen's decision about it. Interested citizens find it easy to schedule their time so they can vote; the uninterested find they are just too busy to go around to the polls.

A greater interest in politics leads one to scan the environment constantly for more information about politics. Thirty-one percent of the very interested had high levels of information about the 1980 campaign as opposed to only 4 percent of the uninterested. Sixty percent of the very interested said they had read a good many newspaper articles about the campaign as opposed to only 10 percent of the uninterested. Greater information in turn stimulates further interest, and both make it more likely that the citizen will choose to engage in politics. Political interest is also quite dependent on the extent of education. Among those with grade school backgrounds, 42 percent said they were not much interested, and only 29 percent said they were very interested. Among those holding college degrees, only 8 percent were not much interested, and 39 percent said they were very interested.

Level of Information.   In speaking of the tendency for the interested to acquire more information about politics, we've already pointed to the second determinant of turnout: information level. The reported turnout level is 44 percent among those with very low information, 64 percent among those with average-minus information levels, 82 percent for average-plus information levels, 88 percent for high information, and 100 percent for very high information.[1] Obviously, the more citizens know about politics, the easier it is to sort through all the choices from president to county commissioner, and the more motivation they have to vote.

As has already been pointed out, interest and information level are quite dependent on one another. Information level is also strongly associated with education. Those with modest educational backgrounds are overrepresented among the less informed, and those with educational advantages are overrepresented in the high information levels. There is also a link between information levels and partisanship. Strong partisans are more likely to know more about politics, and Republicans are better informed than Democrats. Nine percent of the Democrats were in the low-information category as compared to 5 percent of the Republicans, and 16 percent of the Democrats were in the high-information category as compared to 24 percent of the Republicans.

Political Efficacy.   An explanation that is frequently given for declining turnout is alienation. As a result of Vietnam and Watergate, it is argued, citizens feel a sense of distance and estrangement from the government. The two most widely used measures that tap these attitudes are "trust in government" and "political efficacy." The trust-in-government index measures whether citizens have confidence in the national government or are cynical about it. Political efficacy reflects whether citizens feel they can have an impact on the political process. However, trust in government is *not* related to turnout. Political efficacy is.

Political efficacy is a concept introduced in the early 1950s to account for a citizen's own sense of competence and effectiveness. Campbell, Gurin, and Miller designed four questions to measure this attitude (1954, pp. 187–94). Careful studies during the 1970s (Converse, 1972; Balch, 1974; McPherson, Welch, & Clark, 1977) showed that these questions were measuring two different attitudes. Disagreement with statements such as "Sometimes politics and government seems so complicated that a person like me can't really understand what's going on" were tapping the respondents' subjective competence, their self-perception of their *own* capacity to participate in the political process. Disagreement with other statements such as "I don't think public officials really care much what people like me think" were getting at governmental responsiveness, the respondent's sense of the likelihood that political institutions would be attentive to citizens' preferences. Therefore the Center for Political Studies began to use two different measures: internal efficacy to get at subjective competence, and external efficacy to measure governmental responsiveness. Internal efficacy scores have

---

[1] These information levels are defined in Chapter 14.

been relatively stable, while external efficacy scores dropped during the 1968–74 Vietnam-Watergate period.

Turnout is associated with external efficacy. In 1980, only 64 percent of those with the lowest external efficacy scores reported voting as compared to 85 percent of those with the highest external efficacy scores. External efficacy is also associated with education, information level, and interest in politics. Those who are most educated, most informed, and most interested are most likely to think the government is responsive. And given this belief that their political acts are effective, they are more likely to vote.

Age. Propensity to vote is very dependent on age. The reported turnout in 1980 was 51 percent for the 18- to 24-year-olds, 69 percent for those 25 to 39, 79 percent for those 40 to 60, 82 percent for those 61 to 75, and 67 percent for those over 75. Postelection media comments often lament the failure of college students to vote. These criticisms rather miss the point. When compared with others in the same age bracket, college students have very high turnout rates, but young adults are the least likely of all age groups to vote.

The reason that younger persons are less likely to vote is that they are less concerned with society in general. This is the stage when they are occupied with a number of life choices. At this time, they are choosing spouses and hunting for jobs; many are completing educations. All of these choices are individual, so it is not surprising that young adults are preoccupied with themselves. Once these choices are made, once they find positions in the adult world, participation rates in politics (and other social ventures) begin to go up.

Turnout continues to increase across the adult life span until it is slowed by the circumstances of old age. Even then, the over-75-year-olds are about as likely to vote as the 25- to 39-year-olds. They never drop back to the 18- to 24-year-old level. Among the reasons for this are the facts that political interest continues to increase across all age groups, and that the oldest citizens are likely to be the strongest partisans. If it were not for their more limited educations, and for differences in sex and marital status, the oldest age group would be likely to have the very highest turnout rate.

Education. The final determinant of turnout is education. The significant break points appear to be whether the citizen has gone beyond high school (regardless of the kind of post-high school training) and whether or not a college degree has been obtained. For those with only a high school diploma (or less), the reported turnout rate is 58 percent. Of those with post-high school educations, 77 percent say they have voted, and the turnout rate jumps to 91 percent with those who have at least a bachelor's degree.

The reasons for the impact of education are not hard to find. Those who have gone to college are more likely to understand abstract arguments. Consequently, if rival presidential candidates are basing their appeals on different economic philosophies, a high school dropout might hear just so many words. A college graduate, however, could perceive a real difference, and hence see a real choice to be made. Furthermore, there are registration requirements to be met before one votes. To one accustomed to filling out forms for bursars, registrars and other college authorities, registering to vote is trivial. Registration requirements pose much more substantial barriers to those with limited educations. Finally, education is strongly associated with interest, information level, and external efficacy, all of which are determinants of voting in their own right.

The Relative Importance of the Determinants of Turnout

Of the five factors associated with voting, four are significantly associated with each other. Only age is not. Increasing age is significantly associated with increasing political interest, but age is not related to either external efficacy or information level, and since opportunities for advanced education are of relatively recent origin, age is negatively associated with education. Otherwise, all the determinants are related to each other. If you increase education, you also increase interest, information level, and external efficacy. This same statement applies to any combination of these four variables.

If all these factors are related to turnout, and if they are all related to each other, what is their relative impact on turnout? For example,

FIGURE 2-1
Relative Importance of Turnout Determinants

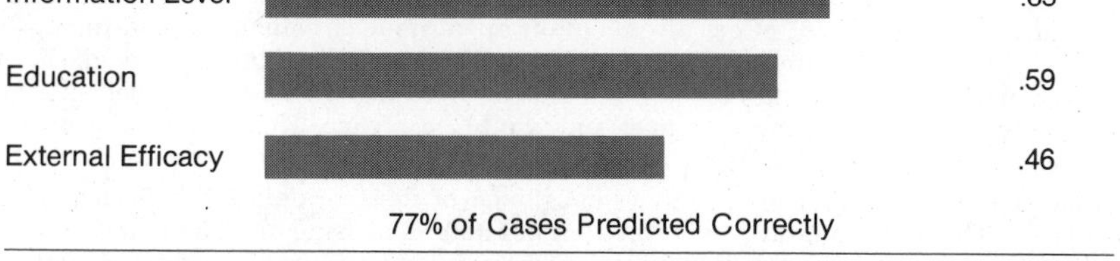

Determinant		Importance MLE*
Political Interest		.74
Age		.70
Information Level		.65
Education		.59
External Efficacy		.46

77% of Cases Predicted Correctly

The higher the value of the Maximum Likelihood Estimate, the more important the determinant. For further information, see the box entitled "Maximum Likelihood Estimate = Best Guess" in Chapter 15.

Data Source: 1980 CPS Election Study.

if we say that political interest is the most important determinant of turnout, how do we know that interest is having this effect? How do we know that it is not, say, education that is producing this increased tendency to vote? To answer such questions, we need to move from bivariate analysis to multivariate analysis. Bivariate analysis shows us how two variables, one a presumed cause and the other a presumed effect, are related to each other, but it neglects the effects of all other variables on this relationship. Multivariate analysis, however, employs statistical controls for the effects of other variables. Thus, multivariate analysis tells us how strongly turnout is affected by increasing political interest, while simultaneously controlling for the effects of information level, external efficacy, age, and education.[2]

We have used a form of multivariate analysis known as probit analysis. The results are shown in Figure 2–1.[3] All five factors are important, but there is a clear gradation in impact. Among the cognitive factors, interest in politics is slightly more important than information level. Age is a more important personal characteristic than education, although again both are important. External efficacy is the least consequential consideration.

WHAT THIS EXPLANATION DOES NOT TELL US

This explanation is just as selective as the sketch of the passage of the National Energy Act in the preceding chapter. The limits are different, but it is equally important to know what is included and what is not. In this instance, we have a limited number of cases. Some potential causes are not in the data set. We are looking at turnout in one country. Our data come from a single year. Each of these facts places limits on our explanation.

Our analysis of turnout rests on 1,407 persons who told interviewers from the Center for Political Studies that they did or did not vote.[4] This means that we can detect effects when there is sufficient variation

---

[2] For further discussion of bivariate analysis and multivariate analysis, see the box entitled "Bivariate Analysis = Association between Two Things" in Chapter 14 and the box entitled "Maximum Likelihood Estimate = Best Guess" in Chapter 15.

[3] The probit solution shown in Figure 2-1 rests on a single equation. This means that we can show the *direct* effect of each independent variable on turnout, but not the *total* effect. The direct effect of education on turnout is estimated, controlling for the effects of interest, information, external efficacy, and age. The total effect of education, however, would also include the *indirect* effects of education acting through interest, information, external efficacy, and age, and would be higher. This should be borne in mind while reading the discussion about the relative importance of the determinants.

[4] The statements about the relative importance of the five determinants depend on 1,168 cases. The probit analysis program does not handle missing data, and an additional 239 cases were lost because data were missing on one or more of the independent variables.

across those cases. For example, there were 335 who said they were not much interested in the campaign, 606 who said they were somewhat interested, and 418 who said they were very interested. This enabled us to detect the effect of political interest on turnout. But we could not make statements about the effect of the electoral laws in, say, Idaho or Montana because there were far too few cases to note any variation between these states.

Raymond Wolfinger and Steven Rosenstone (1980) have analyzed the 88,105 cases available from the 1972 Census Bureau Current Population Survey which contains questions on registration and turnout. They also found age and education to be of overriding importance among demographic variables. But the much larger number of cases allowed them to pick up variations that could be traced to electoral law:

> Four registration provisions were found to present significant barriers to citizens voting: early closing dates, irregular closing hours, no Saturday or evening registration, and no absentee registration. The costs of registration do not fall equally on everyone. Those with the least education—who are least able to cope with the bureaucratic hurdles of registration—are most affected by these provisions. (p. 88)

Wolfinger and Rosenstone estimated that if all states had permissive laws regarding these four provisions, 1972 turnout would have been increased 9 percent.

While we could estimate the impact upon turnout of all the variables included in the data set, there was nothing we could do to determine the impact of possible causes not in the data set. In a study of state-level turnout in gubernatorial elections in 1978 and 1980, Samuel Patterson and Gregory Caldeira found that political efforts, especially campaign spending, have a significant effect on turnout. "Variations in spending represent variations in campaigning effort," they write. "Candidates and parties spend money to advertise, canvass, hold rallies, promote, conduct polls, and otherwise endeavor to get out the vote. Campaign spending pays off very impressively in increased turnout at the polls" (1983, p. 684). Patterson and Caldeira argue that with some exceptions (such as Kramer, 1971) political mobilization has been too often overlooked as an explanation of turnout. There is merit to their argument, but since campaign spending was not included in the data set, we could not use it as an independent variable and determine what impact it had in 1980.

Since we have focused on turnout in an American election, we have not been able to comment on variations in turnout resulting from cross-national differences in laws and cultures. There are countries that require voting. Ivor Crewe (1981) reports that the six democracies with the highest turnout rates—Australia, the Netherlands (until 1967), Venezuela, Austria, Italy, and Belgium—all have some form of compulsory voting. Since turnout in the Netherlands fell from 95 percent during the 1945-67 period when they required voting to 84 percent in the post-1970 period when they abandoned the requirement, compulsory voting laws apparently do make a difference in turnout.

One puzzle in cross-national studies is how much weight to put on cultural and institutional factors, such as a close correspondence between social divisions and party divisions or a system of proportional representation, and how much to put on individual factors, such as political interest or age. Crewe suggests that institutional factors may be more important when they work to facilitate voting.

> In the presence of such institutional incentives to vote as a close align-
> ment between partisan and social divisions, automatic registration, a
> PR system, a competitive party system, and the administrative facilitation
> of voting, individual-level factors will be overridden. (1981, p. 260)

When institutional arrangements inhibit voting, on the other hand, then individual factors become more important. Since the United States has relatively complex requirements for registration, this would explain why the U.S. has a low turnout in comparison to other countries, and why so much of the variation in American turnout can be accounted for on the basis of individual factors.

Finally, our explanation is static. All the data come from a single year. We can make some inferences by asking what has been happening to the five determinants of turnout over time, but we cannot *directly* address the question of why turnout has been declining over a series of elections. For this purpose, a time-series analysis is necessary.

There have been two good studies that focused on *changes* in independent variables, and asked how much of the decline in turnout could be accounted for by these changes. Stephen Shaffer (1981) found that 86 percent of the decline (among nonsoutherners 21 or older) could be explained by changes in education, newspaper reliance, age, political efficacy, and partisan intensity. Paul Abramson and John Aldrich (1982) were able to explain about two thirds of the decline in presidential turnout among whites by pointing to changes in political efficacy and partisan intensity.[5]

We can make some *inferences* by asking what has happened to our five determinants of turnout. The level of education has been increasing, and this has prevented turnout from declining even more than it has. Information levels have remained relatively constant. Political interest has fluctuated from election to election, declining a bit in the one-sided elections of 1956, 1972, and 1980. External efficacy dropped sharply from 1968 (when it was first measured) through 1974,

---

[5] It should not be forgotten that the 1960 turnout was the highest since 1920. Whenever a time series reaches a high point, there is only one direction it can go—down.

and has declined very slightly since. Thus both political interest and external efficacy have made some contribution to the drop in turnout. The changing age distribution clearly has depressed turnout in the last two decades, because of the extension of the vote to the 18- to 21-year-old group, and because the very large post-World War II generation has been at an age when they are least likely to vote. No one can forecast what will happen to political interest and political efficacy during the coming years, but turnout ought to begin to edge upward again as the large postwar generation matures and both age and education exert positive effects.

WHAT THIS EXPLANATION DOES TELL US

While there are limits to this explanation, it is still quite strong. To begin with, the probit solution presented in Figure 2-1 predicts 77 percent of the cases correctly. An ability to predict[6] three out of four cases correctly may not seem terribly impressive, but this is a 20 percent improvement over a null model,[7] and actually quite a good prediction rate for turnout.

The careful reader will have noticed that the percentages for reported turnout are quite high. For instance, the reported turnout rates for high school graduates, post-high school, and college graduates are 58 percent, 77 percent, and 91 percent, respectively. How can this be when the overall turnout is 52.9 percent?[8] The reason is the difference between the known *population parameter,* 52.9 percent, and the *sample estimate,* 71.4 percent, obtained from the survey. One must always be concerned with errors in sample estimates, but this is particularly important with reports of voting and nonvoting. Surveys normally produce substantial overestimates of turnout.

There are several reasons for the discrepancy between the population parameter and the survey estimate. To begin with, the population parameter *underestimates* the true turnout. This 52.9 percent figure results from dividing the number of *votes cast for president* by the *1980 voting-age population*. There are sources of error in both the numerator and denominator. There are people who vote, but not for presi-

---

[6] Actually, this is known as "postdiction" because it is after the fact. Both prediction and postdiction are important in science because the ability to classify cases correctly tells you how satisfactory your explanation is.

[7] A null model indicates what your prediction would have been if you had no information at all. In this instance, you would have predicted that 100 percent would vote. Since the sample estimate is that 71.4 percent voted, this means that 28.6 percent of the null model predictions would be wrong. With the probit estimate, only 23 percent of the prediction would be wrong. According to a formula suggested by Weisberg (1978), this would be a 20 percent improvement.

[8] The 53.9 percent figure mentioned earlier in the chapter was calculated in a way to be comparable with the 1976 turnout figure.

dent. The voting-age population includes prisoners, mental patients, and others ineligible to vote. If the ratio were all those who voted at all to the genuinely eligible, the turnout figure would be closer to 60 percent (Plissner & Mitofsky, 1981). Another problem is the nature of the population that is surveyed. The survey population excludes students living in dormitories, persons living on military reservations, and residents of rooming houses and retirement homes. While these persons are eligible to vote, they are less likely to do so. Therefore their exclusion from the survey population inflates the survey estimate (Wolfinger & Rosenstone, 1980, Appendix A).

Then there are reporting errors. These occur in both directions, although much the larger proportion of errors are made by nonvoters who say they have cast ballots. While respondents have no special reason to deceive an interviewer about their occupations, respondents often feel they should have voted, and tell the interviewer that a vote was cast when it was not. This tendency to claim to have voted is strongest among those who are most aware of the social desirability of having voted, the college educated.

A careful study of the validity of turnout reports in 1976 (Weisberg, 1979) yielded an estimate that 17 percent of the voting reports were inaccurate. This has two implications. Since 83 percent of the reports are valid, we can use them to analyze turnout. At the same time, the 17 percent looms large, especially when compared to the 23 percent total of incorrect predictions. The relation between prediction and errors is not so simple that we can say anything such as 17 out of every 23 errors were caused by false reports of voting. It is clear, however, that misreports of voting set an upper limit on the predictive accuracy that we can expect. In this perspective, a multivariate solution that calls 77 percent of the cases correctly is quite good.

A second strength of this explanation is that it allows us to make statements about the relative importance of the causes. While many have argued that citizens are not voting because they are alienated, the probit analysis reveals that political interest is much more important than external efficacy. Similarly, we saw that both age and education were important, but the direct effect of age is slightly more important than that of education. This ability to rank the causes lends precision to our explanation.

A third strength is that the explanation not only includes the five determinants, but it excludes other possible causes. Bivariate analysis showed that there were 10 variables in the data set that were significantly associated with turnout. In addition to the factors already discussed, these included partisan intensity (whether one thinks of himself as a strong Democrat or Republican rather than an independent), internal efficacy (the citizen's subjective sense of competence to deal with politics), region (whether one lives in the South), reliance on newspapers for news of the campaign, and the perceived closeness of the presidential contest. Being a strong partisan, having a high sense of internal efficacy, living outside the South, reading newspapers, and believing the election would be close were all associated in the bivariate analysis with a greater tendency to vote. All these factors have been associated with turnout in other studies, but none were significantly associated with turnout in this multivariate analysis when statistical controls were in place for the effects of the five more important determinants.

It was mildly surprising to find that party identification and region were not significantly related to turnout in 1980. This may have been due to changes over time. (There are now fewer Strong Partisans than there were in the 1950s and the early 1960s.[9] Recently southern turnout has been increasing while nonsouthern turnout has been declining.) And it may be because the multivariate solution has controlled for variables, such as interest and education, through which party identification and region were linked to turnout.

In summary then, our explanation allows us to say that variation in turnout is due to five specific factors rather than some equally plausible considerations, to state the relative importance of the five factors, and to predict 77 percent of the cases correctly.

DIFFERENCES AND SIMILARITIES IN
EXPLANATIONS

DIFFERENCES IN EXPLAINING LEGISLATION AND PARTICIPATION

Many of the differences between our explanations of the National Energy Act of 1978 and turnout in the 1980 presidential election are to be found in the strengths of the latter. As we just saw, we have an accurate and parsimonious prediction of whether individual citizens cast ballots. To correctly predict 77 percent of the cases, we needed to have information on only five variables. There is no comparable prediction that could have been made in the spring of 1977 about what Congress was likely to do with the Carter energy program. To be sure, assertions were made that Congress would do this or that, but these are very different from accurate forecasts.

In the case of turnout, we could exclude a number of plausible causes—party identification, region, internal efficacy, and so on. We could do so because these variables were not significantly related to turnout in 1980 when tested in a multivariate model. With the legislative

---

[9] See Chapter 16 for a discussion of this change.

example, a number of considerations—the merits of the proposal, interest group activity, and so on—were simply excluded. For all we know,
their influence on congressional action was greater than some of the
things we did examine.

We are also in a position to account for the relative importance of
the five causes of turnout. The probit solution allows us to say, for
example, that political interest is slightly more important than age,
and much more important than external efficacy. We cannot make
similar statements about whether Russell Long's being from Louisiana,
or being relatively conservative, or being an experienced parliamenta-
rian was more important in determining his behavior. Nor can we say
if Russell Long's actions or Robert Byrd's actions were more consequential in influencing the Senate.

These differences *do not mean that the explanation of turnout is
better* than the explanation of why the energy act was passed, but
we *do have a stronger explanation* of participation in three important
respects. The reasons *why* we are able to provide a stronger explanation are to be found in vital differences in *what* we are trying to explain.
One obvious difference is that an election is a single event, while passage of a bill embraces a whole series of events. Once an election
has taken place and, say, 55 percent of the electorate has voted, the
explicandum (the fact that needs to be explained) is in hand. But as
we saw, once the energy bill passed the House of Representatives, it
moved to a very different reception in the Senate. One stage does
not forecast another, and the *explicanda* (the facts that need to be
explained) include what happened at each and every stage.

Another distinction is that turnout rests on a simple dichotomous
choice. There are only two possibilities. A citizen either votes or does
not. The choices involved in legislation are more involved. In the case
of natural gas pricing, one begins with the possibilities of controls
continued indefinitely, some form of eventual decontrol, or immediate
decontrol. However that is decided, there is the question of which
natural gas should be decontrolled, all natural gas or only "new" natural
gas. If decontrol is limited to "new" natural gas, does this include
new wells drilled in existing fields, new wells at some stated distance
from already producing wells, or only newly discovered natural gas?
And so on. And then the legislator must decide what approximation
of his or her most preferred position (based on some combination of
the preceding choices) is most likely to pass, and what to do to advance
that possibility. This list of examples could be greatly extended, but
it should be clear that the single decision to be made by the citizen
is limited to two alternatives, while many of the decisions to be made
by legislators involve multiple alternatives.

Still another fundamental difference is to be found in the *levels of*

explanation. Turnout is explained on the *individual* level. A high turnout or a low turnout results from solitary citizens making their own
decisions about whether or not to vote. If we can explain why one
person chooses to vote or abstain, and repeat that over and over for
a representative sample of voters, that's all there is to it. The legislative
program devised by the Schlesinger staff, however, calls for a *group*
level explanation, and the acting units in the House and Senate were
coalitions. In order to explain group behavior, we must account for
the aggregation of individuals into groups, and show how their attitudes
reinforce one another. In order to deal with coalitions, we must show
how the issue groups made up of moderate Republicans, conservative
Democrats, and all the rest, came together to provide a majority in
favor of a given policy. Because one must begin with individual-level
behavior (for example, why a Michigan liberal favors decontrol while
a Louisiana conservative favors decontrol), and then work up to the
coalition level, an explanation on the coalition level has more packed
into it than one on the individual level.[10]

A final difference between turnout and the energy bill is that measures exist for turnout and its determinants that allow us to use statistical analyses. In large part, **the measures are available because of the
preceding simplicities: a single event, one dichotomous choice, and individual-level explanation.** Since there are fewer elements to account
for, it is easier to develop measures for each one. This does not mean
we have more accurate information about turnout than about legislation. As we saw, there was a good deal of measurement error in the
self-reports of turnout. In contrast, we had very accurate information
about congressional voting on the energy bill. We know exactly which
207 representatives voted for the Bolling motion, and which 206 representatives voted against. And the lack of measures for all the elements
affecting the energy bill emphatically does not mean that measures
could not be devised, given wit enough and time. It means only that
the list of possible causes of turnout is shorter, and it has therefore
been more practicable to develop measures for them. The major point,
however, remains. **The existence of measures is a vital difference in
the explanations of the two phenomena because the measures allow
us to use statistical analyses. The statistics, in turn, allow us to say
that certain plausible causes are not significantly related to turnout,
and to rank those that are related in order of importance.**

---

[10] It is possible, of course, to have very simple explanations on any level by just
making holistic statements about the acting units on that level. Statements about an
"imperial presidency," for example, presumably account for much presidential behavior,
on the ground that certain phenomena are to be expected when an imperial presidency
exists. This is a very weak form of explanation.

This is the central point. We are able to provide stronger explanations of simple events because it is easier to do so. Complex events can be explained, but they present more elements to be accounted for, and therefore require a great deal more work. It is not an intrinsic difference between turnout and legislation that inhibits understanding of the latter, but its greater complexity. Indeed, if we cut out a single roll call vote from a legislative sequence so that we need only explain whether individual representatives voted pro or con, there are models that account for this behavior just as satisfactorily as turnout. But every time we move from a single event to a series of events, from a dichotomous choice to multiple alternatives, or from a less-inclusive level of analysis to a more-inclusive level, the explanation becomes more complex. Science begins by understanding simple phenomena, and builds on this to comprehend more complex phenomena.

SIMILARITIES IN EXPLAINING LEGISLATION AND PARTICIPATION

As is true of all explanations, both of these accounts are partial. They are limited so they can be set forth compactly, and because each has a chosen focus. For example, both of these try to account only for what happened. Why did citizens cast ballots for president in November 1980? Why did Congress pass a particular energy bill in October 1978? Neither explanation raised normative questions. One could certainly argue that the level of turnout was bad because many citizens felt that it didn't make any difference how they voted, or argue that it was good because many voters were contented enough to feel they didn't have to vote. Similarly, one could argue that eventual decontrol of natural gas was bad because many poor citizens could not afford to pay their heating bills, or that it was good because governmental regulations distort market forces. We did not explore these questions because they lie outside the foci of our explanations.

A second common element is that both explanations were limited by the availability of data. We did not detect any influence of interstate variation in legal requirements for registration, although Wolfinger and Rosenstone have done so. We have no reason to doubt their findings. It is simply that our data set had too few cases to pick up interstate variation, and no explicit information on legal requirements, so we could not detect this influence. And we know that Representatives James Corman and Charles Rangel met with President Carter before they decided to sign the Conference Report, but we do not know what was discussed. It is possible that the President appealed to their patriotism, or their loyalty to the Democratic party, or that he indicated his willingness to support some project of interest to the congressmen.

We just don't know, and no amount of analytical ingenuity can compensate for missing information.[11]

The focus of both explanations was on particular acting units. With turnout, the acting units were individuals. In most cases concerning legislation, the acting units were coalitions. Part of the explanation for the behavior of the acting units came from their component parts. Thus, individuals with high political interest and more extensive education were more likely to vote. A coalition made up of liberal Democrats and moderate Republicans was more likely to vote for governmental action to keep fuel prices down. A coalition made up of conservative Democrats and conservative Republicans was more likely to vote to let market forces determine prices.

The acting units were presented in context, and part of the explanation for their behavior was found in that context. We saw that individuals with a high level of information, or a strong belief in external efficacy, were more likely to vote. But a person's information level is dependent on how rich the informational environment is, and an individual's external efficacy score is dependent on whether the political system is viewed as responsive. Thus, when we note the influence of information level or external efficacy, we are seeing some contextual effects.

When the energy bill was introduced in the House, the liberal-moderate coalition was strengthened by Speaker O'Neill's creation of an ad hoc committee to coordinate it, and Speaker's task forces to provide arguments for wavering members. The conservative coalition prevailed in the Senate, in part, because of the lack of an equally strong leader in that body, and because of the influence of Russell Long as chairman of the Senate Finance Committee. In both of these instances, the composition of the coalitions was quite similar, but context made a good deal of difference.

A third element common to both explanations is the importance of time. Time is important to turnout through the operation of registration laws. If a state requires that voters be registered 30 days prior to the election, citizens whose attention is not arrested by politics until the last week in October will find they are too late to get their names on the rolls. A similar effect results from the length of time that polls are open on election day. A state that closes the polling places at 6 p.m. makes it more difficult to vote after work than one that allows ballots to be cast until 9. But by far the strongest temporal

---

[11] Every explanation is also limited by the theories with which the analyst is familiar. An economist or an historian would be likely to interpret the same facts differently than I would. A useful rule to detect the limits of any explanation is to ask yourself *what* the analyst is trying to explain, *what data* are available, and *which theories* the analyst is using.

effect is age. Younger citizens are much less likely to vote than those
who have established themselves in their communities and have become aware of the consequences of politics in their own lives.

We saw repeated instances of the importance of time in the actions
of the protagonists on both sides of the energy bill. President Carter
set a short deadline in order to get something before Congress to consider. Speaker O'Neill hurried the bill through the House so there would
be enough time to get the legislation over the more difficult hurdles
in the Senate. Conferees on both sides delayed action, hoping to negotiate changes that would make the legislation more favorable. At the
very end, Senator Abourezk launched a filibuster in a vain attempt
to wrest further advantages, but the House leadership proved more
determined and more skillful in their estimate of what could be accomplished in the dying hours of a Congress.

THE ELEMENTS OF EXPLANATION

American political parties, in the sense of "all Republicans" or "all
Democrats," do not exist except as abstractions. There are ideas that
the parties are said to favor. Republicans proclaim their belief in free
enterprise, and Democrats point to programs that benefit "the common
man." Both the Republicans and the Democrats have histories in which
they take pride. But if one tries to observe "whole parties," there is
nothing to see. Whether the focus is on citizens (such as Republican
voters) or on a complex political unit (such as a Democratic coalition
in the House of Representatives), there is a specific set of actors in a
specific institutional domain. These are the the living elements of American political parties whose behavior can be observed, and which de-
serve our attention. In this book, we will focus on party activity in
four institutional domains—executive politics, legislative politics, nomination politics, and electoral politics—and on citizen response to these
activities. In order to explain these things, we shall use three components of our explanations of 1980 turnout and the 1978 energy act:
internal structure, external structure, and *time.*

INTERNAL STRUCTURE

The idea of internal structure follows from an observation made
by Herbert Simon (who won a Nobel Prize in economics for his work
on decision making):

> Complexity in any body of phenomena has generally led to the construc-
> tion of specialized theories, each dealing with the phenomena at a particu-
> lar 'level.' Levels are defined by specifying certain units as the object

of study and by stating the propositions of theory in terms of intra-unit behavior and inter-unit behavior. (Compare the sequence of elementary particle-atom-molecule in physics and the sequence: gene-chromosome-nucleus-cell-tissue-organ-organism in biology.) (1952, pp. 1030-31)

Levels of analysis may thus be understood as nested concepts. The unit on any particular level is made up of smaller components from a less-inclusive level. The same unit is also contained within a larger unit on a more-inclusive level. Atoms are made up of elementary particles, and are contained within molecules. Similarly, groups are made up of individuals, and are contained within coalitions.

On the *individual level of analysis, the internal structure is the actor's cognitive structure,* specifically the citizen's (or activist's) cognitive map of the political world. The most general measure is *information level,* how much the citizen knows. More specific bits of information are organized into *attitudes,* valenced cognitions about political objects. The valence may be positive, neutral, or negative. The objects may be quite specific (such as Ronald Reagan or a particular economic policy) or rather diffuse (such as politics in general). If a citizen's cognitions about these objects were positive, neutral, and negative, respectively, we would say that the citizen had positive views about Ronald Reagan, was neutral about the economic policy, and felt negatively about politics in general.

Since attitudes may be positive, neutral, or negative, one is led to theories of *cognitive consistency.* For example, if a person was a Democrat, had positive views about the Democratic candidate, about the record of the last Democratic president, and wanted more welfare programs, we would say that this person's views were consistent when measured against a partisan criterion. If, on the other hand, a Democrat preferred the Republican candidate and the Democratic party's position on issues, we would say that there was an attitude conflict.

Not all attitudes are of equal importance. At one time, candidates' trustworthiness may get more attention; at another, foreign policy may be dominant. Politics itself may be quite visible in one person's cognitive landscape, and remote from the concerns of another. These variations in the relative prominence of attitude objects are referred to as *salience* and *centrality.* If the situation calls attention to the attitude object—for example, if some dramatic foreign event leads to greater news coverage—we would say that international involvement has become more salient. If the attitude object is of more enduring concern, as with a person who is more interested in politics than business or art, then we would say that politics is more central to this person. If an attitude object is more salient, or central, or both, then attitudes about that topic will be more important in the citizen's cognitive structure.

Just as cognitive structure forms the internal structure for the individual citizen, so citizens themselves are part of the internal structure for coalitions. Not all citizens are members, only those sufficiently involved to be regarded as political activists. For our purposes, a *coalition will be understood as having three analytical levels,* each with its own sets of attitudes and behavior. At the first level, there is the *activist,* a citizen who is active in politics. The activist's attitudes are a set of valenced cognitions about political objects. (Here the definition simply picks up the internal structure for individuals.) The set of behaviors includes those appropriate to executive politics, legislative politics, nomination politics, or electoral politics, depending on the domain in which the citizen is active. The concept on the next level is the *group,* which is defined as a set of activists. The group attitudes are shared attitudes on such topics as the group's goals, norms, and environment. The group behaviors are those that fall into a reasonably stabilized pattern of interaction. A *coalition* is composed of a set of groups. The most important coalition attitudes are those that fall into the intersection of the sets of attitudes of member groups. Coalition behaviors need not be overtly coordinated, but the member groups are dependent on each other for achievement of the coalition goals.

The level on which analysis focuses depends on the institutional domain. In executive politics, the dominant actor is obviously an individual, the president. Within the White House, therefore, the analysis focuses on the president, his immediate advisors, and staff groups supporting them. In nomination politics, the campaign may begin with the candidate and two or three very close aides. If the campaign prospers, this small group is enveloped by others, and by the time of the convention a successful candidate will be supported by a coalition made up of many groups of delegates. In both legislative politics and electoral politics, analysis normally focuses on coalitions because no individual or group is powerful enough to win alone. In general, we shall be interested in coalitions, but the characteristics of executive and nomination politics place some limits on this.[12]

The social sciences have developed rich theories of individual behavior, group behavior, and coalition behavior, and we shall want to take advantage of them. But there are also implications that flow directly from our use of nested concepts. A coalition is not just a collection of individuals. Rather, one must consider the groups to which the activists belong, understand how the shared attitudes of the groups modify individual behavior, and consider which coalitions could be constituted

---

[12] Given the definitions of a group as a set of actors, and a coalition as a set of groups, we can consider the acting units in executive politics and early nominating politics to be coalitions whose sets have very few members. However, it is more important to remember the differences between the institutional domains than to understand how the definitions can be defended.

from the existing groups. During the 95th Congress, for example, there were eight issue groups among the Democrats.[13] Four were liberal. The Dominant group was the largest and included most of the leadership. The next two were Liberals. The only difference between them was that one favored abortion while the other opposed it. Both groups were more ideological than the Dominant group. The proabortion Liberals in particular were regarded as knee-jerk liberals by other Democrats. The fourth group, Neoliberals, tended to be younger, and to shade their liberalism with a little more skepticism about government control of the economy. These four issue groups all opposed the Steiger amendment to kill the crude oil equalization tax in 1977, but they split on the Bolling motion to vote on the 1978 energy bill as one package. The Dominant group and the Neoliberals, both a trifle more moderate, voted to support Bolling, while the two groups of Liberals opposed. Thinking about coalitions in this way suggests where tensions are apt to develop, and thus helps to understand coalition behavior.

EXTERNAL STRUCTURE

External structure is harder to define than internal structure. It potentially includes *all* the more-inclusive levels of analysis, and *all* the constraints that somehow delimit and shape the behavior of the acting unit. It would certainly be fair to include all the external causes of activity in this category, but this would include so much as to be analytically useless. Therefore we need to limit the concept to the activities designed to reach those external audiences whose support or understanding is crucial to the success of the activity, and to those rules and contextual features that delimit this much smaller set of behaviors.[14]

The *external structure for the citizen consists of the informational environment and the citizen's opportunity for political participation.* The notion of an informational environment is that a person is surrounded at all times by a number of information sources. These include television, radio, newspapers, magazines, books, and all of the persons and things that one can see or listen to. As the citizen comes in contact with these sources, whether sitting at home reading a newspaper or walking into a campaign rally, information is absorbed from them. The citizen's opportunities for participation range all the way from such effortless things as simply absorbing information or voting to quite demanding activities such as contacting a government official or cam-

---

[13] Much more information about these groups may be found in Chapter 7.

[14] External structure corresponds to what has been variously called contextual or institutional properties, or environmental constraints, except that temporal effects are separated out for distinct treatment.

paigning. The citizen may take part in any of these activities as he
or she sees fit.

Internal and external structure are intimately dependent on one another. As Daniel J. Levinson puts it:

> An essential feature of human life is the *interpenetration* of self and
> world. Each is inside the other. Our thinking about the one must take
> account of the other. The interpenetration of self and world has been
> beautifully portrayed by Arthur Miller in his plays and essays. . . . "Soci-
> ety is inside man and man is inside society, and you cannot even create
> a truthfully drawn psychological entity on the stage until you understand
> his social relations and their power to make him what he is and to prevent
> him from being what he is not. The fish is in the water and the water
> is in the fish." (1977, p. 47)

Such interpenetration can certainly be seen in individual political
activity. Citizens' cognitive structures are the result of all the information they have absorbed and organized, whether from a forgotten civics
book read 30 years earlier or a newscast seen that very day. Citizens'
attitudes, in turn, are linked to votes and other forms of political participation. To the extent that the citizen cares about politics and is involved
in it, further information is acquired—and so the cycle continues. Thus
the question *why* a citizen takes a particular action depends on both
internal structure and external structure, on both the citizen's attitudes
and the opportunities for participation.

On the coalition level, **external structure depends on the institutional
domain in which the coalition is active.** For example, since legislative
approval of the energy bill was required, activities to influence Congress
were part of the external structure of the Carter executive coalition.
The same could be said of the outreach activities that contacted interest
groups in the hope of reaching swing votes on Capitol Hill. From the
point of view of the House coalitions, external structure would include
the contacts with interest groups, the executive branch, and the Senate
that helped to shape the legislation, as well as those House rules that
advantaged and/or inhibited the coalitions in their efforts to pass or
defeat an energy bill. So long as our acting unit is coalition-in-institution, the external structure will shift as our attention moves from one
institutional domain to another.

TIME

An individual's attitudes or activity level, or both, may fluctuate
or remain stable. Fluctuation, if it occurs, is likely to follow two general
patterns. One is the *life cycle;* the other is the *temporal pattern of
whatever institution* the citizen is in contact with. We have already
seen how voting increases sharply as citizens move from young adult-

hood to middle life. What is perhaps less appreciated is the relative frequency with which American citizens can vote. As Ivor Crewe summarizes:

> No country can approach the United States in the frequency and variety of elections. . . . No other country elects its lower house as often as every two years, or its president as frequently as every four years. No other country popularly elects its state governors *and* town mayors; no other has as wide a variety of nonrepresentative offices (judges, sheriffs, attorneys general, city treasurers, and so on) subject to election. Only one other country (Switzerland) can compete in the number and variety of local referendums; only two others (Belgium and Turkey) hold party "primaries" in most parts of the country. (1981, p. 232)

Confronted with this multitude of elections, a person who is concerned about politics is likely to exhibit stable attitudes and stable behavior. A person with little political information or interest, on the other hand, tends to show quite irregular behavior—not bothering to vote in many instances and swinging unpredictably between parties when a ballot is cast.

On the coalition level, the temporal pattern depends on the institutional domain. As we shall see, nomination politics has four characteristic phases. It begins with Early Days, the period just prior to delegate selection when plans are being made, organizations assembled, and funds raised. Next comes Initial Contests, the first primaries when large fields of contenders are being winnowed down. The third stage is Mist Clearing, the point at which the identity of the serious contenders is known. Finally comes the Convention, which brings the ratification of all that has gone before. Each institution has such a temporal pattern, and as our attention passes from executive politics to legislative politics to nomination politics to electoral politics, we shall review each in turn.

Internal Structure, External Structure, and Time

On the individual level, both internal structure and external structure may change over time. This may take the form of a slow evolution as a well-informed person in a rich informational environment extracts new bits of data, or it may take place quite suddenly as persons normally unconcerned have their attention arrested by some dramatic development. The net of such changes, when multiplied by all of the citizens who make up an electorate, is that new political possibilities constantly emerge as one-time political certainties recede into the past.

On the coalition level, the identity of the activists who are the "elementary particles" of a coalition changes rather slowly in legislative politics and electoral politics; but in executive politics wholesale

change takes place at the beginning of each new administration. Nomination politics is a little more complex. If a candidate has run before,
many of the leaders are drawn from previous campaigns, but four out
of five delegates have not been to the preceding national convention.
The external structure, the rules of the game and the external audiences
for any particular institution, also tends to change rather slowly. The
result is that the behavior of coalitions in any one institution tends
to evolve relatively slowly over time due to the constraining effect of
a slowly changing external structure.

In this book we shall be concerned with the activities of the parties
that can be observed—specific coalitions in specific institutional settings—and in the citizens' responses to these initiatives. Our general
argument will be that *why* a coalition or an individual takes a particular
action will sometimes be explained by internal structure, sometimes
by external structure, and sometimes by both. *When* the action is taken
will be explained by the applicable temporal pattern.

Summary

Substantively, we saw that turnout in the 1980 election was determined by political interest, age, information level, education, and external efficacy. The pattern was similar to explanations of turnout in other
elections. Because of the importance of age and education, if other
factors remain constant, turnout should begin to edge upward again
in future elections.

Conceptually, we were able to do some things we could not achieve
in the explanation of energy legislation. We were able to exclude a
number of other plausible causes as not being significantly related,
and we were able to rank the five causes in order of their importance.
We were able to do this because the properties of the action being
explained—a single event, dichotomous choice, and individual-level
behavior—meant that measures had been developed that permitted
statistical analysis.

While a stronger explanation can presently be adduced on the individual level, there is a general pattern of explanation that can be used
on both the individual and coalition levels. This is based on internal
structure, external structure, and time. We shall use this approach to
analyze executive politics, legislative politics, nomination politics, electoral politics, and citizens' responses thereto, and it is to this task
that we now turn.

PART TWO

EXECUTIVE POLITICS

CHAPTER 3

THE ALLOTTED TIME

"All the world's a stage," Shakespeare asserts, "and all the men and women merely players: They have their exits and their entrances." The exits and the entrances of our presidents are fixed in the Constitution. Unless fate intervenes, once a president-elect has taken the oath of office, he has exactly four years at the center of our political system. If reelected, four more. But then the power and responsibilities pass to another. Not only that, but the constitutionally ordained calendar means the proximity of the president's exit and entrance shapes the power that can be effectively exercised and the behavior of those involved in presidential politics. For executive politics, in common with other political institutions, moves through several stages. It is useful to distinguish between *Transition, Midterm Election, a Maturing Administration, Reelection, a Mature Administration,* and *Retirement.*

THE STAGES OF A PRESIDENCY

TRANSITION

Either of two dates can be used as the beginning of modern presidential transitions. One is March 2, 1932. The other is November 4, 1952. On March 2, 1932, Senator George W. Norris, the great reformer from Nebraska, introduced the 20th Amendment to the Constitution. This "lame-duck" amendment eliminated a session of Congress following the November election, and specified that henceforth the terms of senators and congressmen would begin at noon on January 3, and the terms of the newly elected president and vice president would begin on January 20. Because the Roosevelt and Truman years followed the adoption of this amendment in 1933, it was not until 1952 that a president-elect was required to assemble a new administration under this revised time table.

Until the adoption of the 20th Amendment, presidents-elect were given more time to pick up the reins of government. Because the presidential term did not begin until March 4, they had more than half again as much time to choose the persons they wanted to join the administration. And Congress did not meet until the first Monday in December, so the new president and his colleagues had more than a year between the election and the first meeting of Congress[1] in which to decide what legislation to seek, what budget allocations should be made, and so forth. After his election in 1952, Dwight Eisenhower had only 76 days until his inauguration, and Congress had been in session for more than two weeks before the inaugural ball was over. So, too, with the Kennedy, Nixon, Carter, Reagan, and future transitions.

The formal transfer of power does indeed take place at noon on January 20. At that moment, the predecessor feels an enormous relief, and the responsibilities of the successor begin. But in a larger sense, the inaugural ceremony is a holiday, an interruption in the real process of transition that goes forward for a much longer time period. The behavior that marks the transition stage—selection of key personnel, planning, and learning—begins with the election, but it goes on long after the inaugural ceremony, and it is to that longer process that we ought to pay attention. Richard Neustadt, who began calling attention to the importance of temporal factors many years ago, argues that, in this larger sense, transition

> stretches on until about the time, two years after election, when the "new" administration has experienced both sessions of a Congress along with friends and adversaries overseas, and begins to see the shape of events, hence commitments, that will dominate the presidential term. (1980, p. 217)

Valerie Bunce has written that the honeymoon period (by which she means the first year of an administration) "is a time of great optimism and openness" (1981, p. 19). But, she goes on, both of these characteristics rest on the naiveté of the incoming administration. When looked at closely, the transition stage has the double possibility of serious failure and unusual accomplishment. We will want to return to this double possibility shortly, but first we need to know a bit more about personnel selection.

Personnel Selection

Jimmy Carter won the 1976 election and Ronald Reagan won the 1980 election, and thereby the Democratic party won the 1976 election

---

[1] The president could summon a special session of Congress to meet earlier, but this would be at *his* choice, and the agenda would be limited to topics of *his* choosing.

and the Republican party won the 1980 election. The principal way the parties affected public policy during the ensuing terms was through the selection of Democrats to hold office during the Carter administration and Republicans to hold office during the Reagan administration. But these were not just any Democrats or any Republicans. The ability of the incoming administration to select persons who will be effective administrators and committed to the new president's values does much to determine the success of the administration.

It took Dwight Eisenhower 28 days after the election to pick his cabinet members. Succeeding presidents-elect have taken longer. The elapsed time from election until the last cabinet appointment was 40 days for John Kennedy in 1960, 36 days for Richard Nixon in 1968, 51 days for Jimmy Carter in 1976, and 64 days for Ronald Reagan when the last appointment was not announced until January 7, 1981. The point here is not that one administration has moved more swiftly than another, but the process has been taking longer and longer. The implication is that it must be growing more difficult, and that is indeed the case.

Four things complicate the selection of ranking appointees. One is the increasing number of complex jobs. A second is an attempt to find people who have the skills and are loyal to the president. Third, once selections have been tentatively made, they must be cleared on Capitol Hill with those who will confirm them. And fourth, there are FBI investigations of the designees' past careers for any evidence of wrongdoing or possible conflict of interest. Even this short list makes the process seem too neat and sequential. The real selection process is a swirling tangle of individual ambition and political promotion, in the center of which those closest to the new president try to guard his interests.

Hugh Heclo (1978) argues that "issue networks" composed of persons who follow particular policies and share a common base of information are becoming increasingly important. These are complex, and activity in one part of an issue network may often stimulate activity in another.

> For example, there is no single health policy network but various sets of people knowledgeable and concerned about cost-control mechanisms, insurance techniques, nutritional programs, prepaid plans, and so on. At any one time, those expert in designing a nationwide insurance system may seem to be operating in relative isolation, until it becomes clear that previous efforts to control costs have already created precedents that have to be accommodated in any new system, or that the issue of federal funding for abortion has laid land mines in the path of any workable plan. (p. 104)

More and more, there is a corresponding need for political executives to be able to deal with the issue networks germane to their departments. Therefore, Heclo says, cabinet members tend to come from (or to have moved among) "four great estates: academia, corporate business and

the law, the government bureaucracy, and . . . elective politics." Take
the Defense Department. Eisenhower's first defense secretary was president of General Motors, Kennedy's was president of Ford, Nixon's
was a senior Republican congressman from Wisconsin,[2] Carter's was
president of the California Institute of Technology, and Reagan's was
an executive with the Bechtel Corporation. Obviously, there is some
variation from one administration to the next. If one takes the immediate pregovernmental position (and ignores movement from, say, law
to government to business), four of Carter's initial appointees came
from academic life, none from government, five from corporate business
and law, and three from elective politics. None of Reagan's initial appointees came from academia, two came from (state) government, nine
from business and legal positions, and two from elective politics. The
Reagan administration had much closer connections to business than
the Carter administration, but all of the appointees in both administrations had some acquaintance with the relevant issue networks.[3]

When John Kennedy was working on his transition, he said he
thought that he had met everyone in the United States as a candidate,
but when he came to look for cabinet members, he knew only a few
politicians. To aid him, Kennedy set up a task force headed by brother-
in-law Sargent Shriver to seek appointees with the desired qualities
of excellence, toughness, industry, and "being on the same wave
length." The Carter personnel search was given the acronym TIP for
Talent Inventory Process. Many of the TIP recommendations were set
aside when the cabinet members were, for all practical purposes, given
freedom to select their own subordinates. Perhaps the most thorough
modern search was conducted in the Reagan transition under the direction of E. Pendleton James. James brought experience to his task, having
worked in the Nixon administration's personnel office, after which he
had headed his own executive recruitment agency in California. He
had been asked by Edwin Meese (chief of staff during the campaign
and head of the Reagan transition team) some months earlier to begin
work on what an incoming administration would need to do. By election
day, key positions had been identified and lists of potential appointees
were ready.

To select the cabinet members, James served as staff for the "Kitchen
Cabinet," a group of Reagan confidants most of whom were California
executives. After discusing possible appointees, this group produced

---

[2] Nelson Polsby (1978) has argued that cabinet members may be divided into specialists, those who are client-oriented, and generalists, and that Richard Nixon tended to
choose generalists because of his distrust of government.

[3] This is true even if the contacts were largely adversarial. Interior Secretary James
Watt, with prior background in law and government, had been president of the Mountain
States Legal Foundation. Many of the law suits he had filed were opposed by environmen-
tal interests, but Watt certainly was familiar with the issues.

short lists of four to seven possibilities for each cabinet post. These
short lists were considered at smaller meetings of Reagan, a group
of his closest political associates,[4] and James. Ronald Reagan himself
made the final selections, usually reflecting the consensus of the meetings (Mackenzie, 1981b).

While selection of cabinet members is the most visible part of personnel recruitment, it is only the beginning. There are a considerable number of positions to be filled, and all manner of political sponsors send
names to the recruiters.[5] As soon as they are selected, the new cabinet
members become sponsors themselves. Ed Meese told all the Reagan
cabinet members that the White House would be making the choices
in concert with the James personnel selection process. But quite frequently, there was a race in which the cabinet members tried to get
their preferences into the clearance process first.

The personnel recruiters and the new cabinet members had a common interest in finding people with the skills to do the job (a qualification which itself admits of widely differing interpretation). But other
clearances were called for once they agreed on a name. First, there
was a political clearance on loyalty to the conservative political goals
of the new president. The people who rendered this judgment were
three longtime Reagan aides: political advisor Lyn Nofziger, domestic
advisor Martin Anderson, and foreign policy advisor Richard Allen.
Their clearest criterion for loyalty to Reagan was having worked for
his nomination and election. At the same time, Counsel Fred Fielding[6]
would ask the FBI to do a name check to find out if the nominee had
ever been in any trouble with the law. If no political objections were
raised (there often were; see the box on Christopher Cross), then James
would clear the name at a meeting with James Baker, Mike Deaver,
and Ed Meese, President Reagan's ranking aides. In the Reagan administration, therefore, a personnel decision represented the agreement
of (or at least no objections encountered from) the personnel office,
the cabinet member, campaign aides, and the senior White House staff,
as well as a preliminary legal check.

Once a White House decision had been made on the nominee, the
legislative liaison team would check around Capitol Hill to find out
if there was any consequential opposition. Here it is important to remember that senators and congressmen have been sponsors to begin
with. In the nature of things, they are not going to prevail every time
they suggest someone, but if their wishes are ignored too often, they

---

[4] George Bush, Edwin Meese, James Baker, Michael Deaver, William Casey, Paul
Laxalt.

[5] One estimate was that 8,000 resumes arrived in the first three weeks after the election.

[6] All of the principals moved from transition headquarters to the White House after
the inauguration, Fielding as Counsel to the President.

THE CASE OF CHRISTOPHER CROSS

Some sense of the pulling and tugging that takes place in the contest over appointments can be seen in the instance of Christopher T. Cross. Cross had known Terrell Bell, the new secretary of education, since the early 1970s when both were together in the Department of Health, Education and Welfare. After Bell had been selected, Cross had sent him a couple of memoranda suggesting some issues that needed attention. Then on January 29, nine days *after* the inauguration, Bell told Cross he would like him to be undersecretary of education. Kitchen Cabinet members were not acquainted with Cross, but mutual acquaintances and Bell assured them that Cross was a Republican and knowledgeable about education. On January 31, Bell met with Pendleton James, and the two of them agreed on Cross as undersecretary. In early February, Cross was interviewed and assured that everything was set.

Later the same morning the personnel office contacted Cross, told him some questions had been raised, and asked him to provide information on his 1980 campaign involvement and a list of persons who could testify about his politics and ability. Then on February 10, the personnel office told Cross that his nomination had been vetoed. At this point, some congressmen and senators who had known Cross as a staff member of the House Education and Labor Committee made phone calls, and Cross's name came off the black-list by February 12. Friday the 13th brought another phone call telling Cross that he had again been vetoed, and still another from a White House friend saying he was still "alive." After another week of suspense, Secretary Bell told Cross that he had finally been vetoed at a White House meeting on February 19.

In this particular case, the contest was between persons who wanted Cross because of his background in educational politics, and others who thought that he was insufficiently conservative, but it illustrates two more general points. One is that senior appointments are contests between powerful sponsors, who not only have individuals in mind, but often different notions about relevant skills. The other is that the decision not to appoint Cross was not made until a full month after the new administration took office. With all the clearances that are necessary, personnel decisions take a long time (Cross, 1981).

can become very unhappy. (Over the course of a congressional career, they can prevail often enough to seed the bureaucracy with protégés. One reason a "powerful senator" is powerful is because many in the executive branch have been placed there by the senator.) Sometimes, too, senators will oppose a nominee because they prefer a different policy than they think the administration will follow. But if there was no significant legislative opposition to a prospective nominee, then

Pendleton James would take the name to President Reagan (Mackenzie, 1981b).

The final steps were a full field check by the FBI, and investigation by the White House Counsel's office to make sure there were no conflict-of-interest problems. The FBI's full field investigation involves dozens of interviews with the nominee's acquaintances around the country. The conflict-of-interest study is also time-consuming. The rules were tightened up after Watergate, and closer scrutiny is now in order. Finally, after all of this is done, the nominee's name is formally submitted.

There was a time when names came principally from congressional and party sources, and there was someone at the party's National Committee who handled patronage. Each of the present clearances has been added for good reason. Dwight Eisenhower began FBI investigations to make sure that any untoward information was discovered before an appointment was made, and not in some later scandal. John Kennedy started a personnel office in the White House to help get qualified persons.[7] The orgy of spending in the 1972 campaign (which was one of the things that made Watergate possible) led to tighter conflict-of-interest requirements. But the clearances are sequential, and each one of them lengthens the queue through which every name must go. This, in turn, extends the Transition stage for every administration.

The Likelihood of Early Failure

The men who took power with the Kennedy administration were proud. They had won the nomination in the face of substantial skepticism, and not a little opposition, from leaders of the Democratic party. They had been able to retire the myth that no Catholic could be elected president. John Kennedy had been the youngest elected president in American history.[8] Coming after Eisenhower, they liked to compare themselves to the Lincoln administration taking over after the ineffectual Buchanan. Less than three months later came the abortive invasion attempt by Cuban exiles at the Bay of Pigs, later described by ranking Kennedy aide Theodore Sorenson as "the worst disaster of this disaster-filled period, the incident that showed John Kennedy that his luck and his judgment had human limitations" (1965, p. 329).

Richard Neustadt focuses on this danger in a chapter entitled "Hazards of Transition:" "In this Bay of Pigs affair the new regime's decision-making showed two striking features, ignorance and hopefulness. The ignorance was tinged with innocence, the hopefulness with arrogance"

---

[7] Sometimes the office has been headed by professional personnel recruiters, sometimes not.

[8] Theodore Roosevelt was younger when he took office, but he succeeded from the vice presidency on McKinley's death.

(1980, p. 223). Ignorance is easy to understand in a new administration. If senior advisors have been preoccupied with the campaign for the presidency, the chances are they haven't dealt with Congress, with the bureaucracy, and with foreign powers. As a result, they are slow to pick up cues that would be readily apparent later in an administration. Further, they don't know each other very well yet, and don't have a good sense of who has what kind of skill.

The hopefulness stems in large part from their campaign experience. For instance, Kennedy aides could remember very well how Democrats had said that no Catholic could be elected president, how Harry Truman had openly asked Kennedy if he was ready to be president, how many people had believed that John Kennedy would never be able to match Richard Nixon in a debate—and they remembered that all of these challenges had been overcome. What would be more natural than a belief that doubts expressed in the White House would likewise turn out to be less than fatal? The result, Neustadt argues, is that questions that should have been raised about the Bay of Pigs plan presented by the CIA were not, and a high price was paid for this understandable combination of ignorance and hopefulness.

These two characteristics are likely to be present at the beginning of any presidency. While subsequent administrations have been spared the embarrassment of military defeat, there have been similar episodes that Neustadt calls "piglets." One of these was Gerald Ford's attempt to halt inflation with WIN (for Whip Inflation Now) buttons. Another was Jimmy Carter's mishandling of the charges against Bert Lance in his first year in office. In this case, the problem resulted partly from a failure to look closely enough at one of the trusted insiders (Lance was virtually alone in having a close personal tie to Carter), and partly from an inability to sense how the media and other Washington denizens would react to stories of interest-free loans from Lance's Georgia bank to a favored few. Little more than a month after President Carter had told a national television audience, "Bert, I'm proud of you," Lance was on his way back to Georgia.

Another prime example of a piglet, I think, was the economics[9] of the tax cut bill passed in the first year of the Reagan administration. Supply-side economists argued that a massive tax cut would stimulate the economy. Here was certainly a combination of ignorance and hopefulness, reinforced by the deeply ingrained optimism of Ronald Reagan himself. The immediate result of a massive cut in revenue turned out to be a massive deficit, which would have been bad enough in any case because of the deep 1981–82 recession. When Martin Feldstein

---

[9] It is very important here to distinguish the untested economics from the legislative and communications strategies with which the economic package was sold to Congress. The legislative and communication strategists certainly *were* experienced, and showed great skill.

arrived in Washington 18 months later as the new Chairman of the Counsel of Economic Advisors, he said that supply-side economics had been decisively proven wrong.

Early failure is not an inevitable part of transition, but the possibility of failure is. It is hard to avoid hopefulness amid a mood of a new beginning, and in the absence of a sense of limits, easy promises and excessive rhetoric are likely to be heard. Nor is this limited to the White House. Transition is precisely the time when public expectations of the new president are at their highest, and the hopefulness, heightened rhetoric, and public anticipations all feed on one another. All the more reason that students of the presidency should remember that this is the season of the easy misstep.

The Possibility of Substantial Accomplishment

In modern times, there have been three presidents who dominated Congress during their first year after their elections: Franklin Roosevelt in 1933, Lyndon Johnson in 1965, and Ronald Reagan in 1981. Somehow these presidents were able to use the golden early hours of their administrations to make a mark on public policy.[10] How did this come about? One clue, and a hint about the general possibility of accomplishment during transition, comes from the work of Paul Light. He argues that there are two policy cycles. "The first might be called the *cycle of decreasing influence*. It is based on declines in presidential capital, time and energy." At the outset of an administration, a president has the most capital. He has just won election; he is likely to have the most receptive Congress as well as that containing the largest number of his partisans; his standing with the public is high. These resources are going to disappear with the passage of time, and are of most benefit to a president immediately after he takes office. Light's "second pattern in presidential resources might be called the *cycle of increasing effectiveness*." This assumes, as Neustadt's analysis assumes, that both the president and his staff are going to gain in experience, and that this increased experience is going to give them greater skill in maneuvering on a political terrain (Light, 1982, pp. 36–37).

Now, what happens to this argument if one assumes instead that a new president recruits experienced aides who are knowledgeable about Washington? This implies some already skilled staff members who may be able to move fast enough to take advantage of the new president's high political standing before this capital is dissipated by the passage of time. Just this happened at the beginning of the Reagan administration. Chief of Staff James Baker had been under secretary

---

[10] Of course, one might disagree with the wisdom of the New Deal, the Great Society, or supply-side economics, but that is another matter.

of commerce in the Ford administration before directing the Ford reelection campaign. Legislative liaison head Max Friedersdorf had represented the Nixon administration on the Hill and had been in charge during the Ford administration. Communications chief David Gergen had been head speechwriter at the end of the Nixon administration, and head of the Office of Communications in the Ford administration. There were some other experienced Reagan aides,[11] but these were particularly important because of their key roles in legislative and communications strategies.

The incoming Reagan administration also profited from planning, some of it by David Gergen who was head of the transition team for the White House, and some of it by the Richard Wirthlin/Richard Beal team that had developed much of the 1980 campaign strategy. They had looked at the initial periods of five newly elected presidents, and had drawn three lessons. The first was that a presidential image is formed during the first weeks. The second was that the central theme of a presidency emerges during this initial period. The third was the danger of early failure that we have already discussed. Feeling that these first weeks would set the tone of the whole administration, they sought every opportunity for President Reagan to display his upbeat personality, took any number of steps to keep the issue focus on the President's economic package, and repeatedly reminded the President about the need for early caution in the light of his predecessor's problems (Drew, 1981a).

There is another point to be made about the possible success that awaits a newly elected president who is able to move swiftly. Paul Light has examined the success of president's legislative proposals for Kennedy through Carter. He found that initiatives that got to Congress in the January-March period were enacted at a 72 percent rate as compared to 39 percent for those that got to the Hill in the second quarter of the year, and 25 percent for the last half of the year. Ninety-four percent of the 1965 Johnson proposals were transmitted during the first three months as compared to 76 percent of the (much shorter) Kennedy agenda in 1961, 33 percent of the 1977 Carter proposals, and only 12 percent of the 1969 Nixon bills (1982, pp. 44–45). Johnson benefited by some special circumstances. He had been in office since late

---

[11] Stephen Hess, speaking at a Princeton University Conference on the Reagan Presidency, pointed out that one can go through the Reagan appointees almost at random and pick out three traits: born since 1941, experience in the Nixon or Ford administrations, and coming back into government service at least at the assistant secretary level. Such experienced personnel were not available to Eisenhower because of the twenty years Roosevelt and Truman were in power, and not available to Nixon because of the advanced age of many Eisenhower appointees. But they constitute a core of experience that can now be called upon. Further, there are a good many comparable Democrats who served in the Carter administration who would be available to a Democratic administration if one should come to power in 1985 or 1989.

1963, had realized that he would be reelected as soon as Goldwater was nominated in 1964, had begun then to get his legislative program ready, and had lopsided Democratic majorities in both houses. But most important of all was his long experience with Congress. He had come to Washington as a congressional assistant in 1931, and had been a congressman, senator, and senate majority leader prior to his election to the vice presidency. He knew long before it dawned on his critics that the time he had in which to take advantage of his 1964 landslide was limited, and he had to move as swiftly as possible. Toward the end of his administration, President Johnson reflected:

> You've got to give it all you can that first year. Doesn't matter what kind of majority you come in with. You've got just one year when they treat you right and before they start worrying about themselves. . . . That's why I tried. Well, we gave it a hell of a lick, didn't we? (McPherson, 1972, p. 268)

MIDTERM ELECTION

In the typical administration, there is substantial inexperience, and much of the first year is one long learning period. This learning continues, but by the beginning of the second year, White House staff members will be doing some things that have been done before: one State of the Union Message usually has been delivered; one budget has been submitted to Congress; and so forth. Moreover, while some of the president's legislative program will have been passed during the first year, more bills submitted during the first year eventually get passed during the second, third, and fourth years.

William Cable, chief House liaison during the Carter administration, recalled: "I think there is a flow in an administration where you (first) set out your agenda, and then you work through the next couple of years, the two middle years, trying to enact (it)." The process of trying to obtain favorable legislative action, Cable explained, "has a sort of pace to it because the Congress has an artificial two-year cycle in the middle of the term. It is artificial from the president's standpoint, but it is a very real deterrent in that it is a time line to work against." Artificial or not, different things happen on Capitol Hill and in the White House once the midterm election looms on the horizon. We need to know what these things are.

Perhaps the most important thing in the minds of the members of the House is that all of them (except for those who are retiring) are running for reelection. The same is true of a third of the senate. Hence decisions about votes are made more and more with election considerations in mind. Sometimes this leads the congressman or senator to cast votes with the party in order to sharpen an issue which they want to debate before the voters. Sometimes it means that constituency needs are given greater prominence. But it certainly means that the legislator thinks more as a candidate, and less as a supporter of the administration who has an abstract interest in voting with the president.

As a consequence of the individual member's concern with reelection, politically difficult matters are often kept off the floor (or away from Congress altogether) during the months preceding an election. One good example of this was President Reagan's National Commission on Social Security Reform, which was instructed to bring in its report after the 1982 election. It was understood both in the White House and on Capitol Hill that something had to be done to address the financial problems of the social security system, but it was also assumed that little could be done until the 1982 election was over and the 1984 election was still some time away.

The administration may begin to think that it might do well enough in the midterm election so as to have a more favorable Congress in the next session. The record of history is that this almost never happens,[12] but if little progress is being made with the present Congress, there's always the feeling that it can't be much worse, and it might be better.

This seemed to have happened to the Nixon administration with respect to the elections of 1970. Both the House and the Senate were Democratic. Relatively little Nixon legislation was moving through Congress; and the Senate, especially after the Cambodian incursion in the spring of 1970, debated and narrowly passed amendments limiting the President's freedom of action in the Vietnamese conflict. The Democratic margin in the House was deemed to be too large for any real chance of a Republican takeover, but there was some hope of capturing the Senate. A number of House Republicans were encouraged to give up their House seats and run for the Senate: Lowell Weicker in Connecticut, Robert Taft in Ohio, Bill Brock in Tennessee, William Cramer in Florida, Clark MacGregor in Minnesota, and George Bush in Texas. President Nixon campaigned in 23 states, and Vice President Agnew in 29.

This meant that the administration was willing to give up some of the ablest legislators in the House in the hope of taking control of the Senate. And with the President spending a lot of time on the hustings in the fall, he was not in the Oval Office, so many decisions were simply put on hold until after the election. In this case, the administration's gamble did not pay off. The Democrats retained control of both houses. But hope springs eternal. In 1981, some in the Reagan administration were talking about taking over the House in 1982. By 1982, more realism was setting in, and Reagan administration efforts were directed at restricting their losses.

---

[12] 1934 was the last time.

When does the Transition stage end and the Midterm Election stage begin? There isn't a fixed date, and the two processes overlap at least to some extent. Appointees are still accumulating experience well into the second year, and members facing tight races will begin to focus on their reelection very early. It is really a question of the point when the midterm election concern becomes dominant. This concern becomes visible earlier to those who are working more closely with Congress.

Kenneth Duberstein, chief congressional liaison in the Reagan administration, said that in 1982 that point came in early February:

> I can't pinpoint a certain date for you, or a certain issue, but I think it was toward the beginning of February. It was after the State of the Union, but before or right around the time that the budget was presented. [It was then that I was] starting to gear myself intellectually to an upcoming campaign, to a much more difficult session because it was an election year.

On the other hand, Richard Beal, director of the Reagan Office of Planning and Evaluation, put the date about the first of June.

> In late spring, the election is still far enough away that it is not beating on your door yet. A lot of people are running around saying, "You guys don't think enough about politics," but the consideration is not the election, just the political environment. Then it switches into, "Well, the election is just 120 days away," and then you move into that more specific phase.

A MATURING ADMINISTRATION

Whatever problems there may be in fixing the passage from Transition to Midterm Election, there is no doubt that the third year allows a glimpse of the administration in mature form. The effects of two years of experience ought to have taken hold. A newly elected Congress is back in town. Their next election—and the president's—is 22 months away. The presence of experience and the absence of immediate partisan considerations are reasons given by Richard Neustadt for the third year being a "key year . . . in the search for signs of pattern (and) clues to conduct" (1968, p. 199). It was in the third year, for example, that John Kennedy made the American University speech that led to the test ban treaty with the Soviet Union, and sent Congress the proposals that resulted in the historic Civil Rights Act of 1964.[13]

The argument that an administration differs as it matures depends

---

[13] While Neustadt, and to a lesser extent Paul Light, emphasize the possibility of accomplishment because of accumulated experience, Valerie Bunce calls her post-honeymoon stage "The Midterm Time of Troubles." "In place of harmony within the Executive Branch, one finds conflict which is both ideological and bureaucratic" (1981, p. 27).

on the effects of experience, of learning. Just how does an administration learn? And why should we expect this to alter its behavior?

A lot of learning takes place on the individual level. Individuals discover things about each other. They learn who to approach to get answers, and as their circles of acquaintance widen, it becomes less necessary to go through intermediaries. For example, Lynn Daft, an agricultural economist who was a member of the Carter Domestic Policy Staff, said that the change he had noticed had to do with White House staff members

> getting to know one another and making judgments as to what certain individuals have to offer, where they can be most effective. I'm not from Georgia or from the campaign. Before this I'd been a careerist in the public service. Not the typical person coming in. So I knew almost no one in this organization when I came in. And it takes time, I'd say at least a couple of years, for these relationships to evolve. That includes the president getting to know, not a lot about me, but something about me and what I could be called upon to do.

One result of people knowing each other is that they know who can (and who cannot) provide needed information. This knowledge enables them to act much more swiftly. Claudia Townsend, an associate press secretary who dealt with the press corps on a day-to-day basis, spoke about how her job had changed:

> My job in particular is often a chore of trying to get information very quickly. When I first came to this job, I had a hard time getting stuff done, particularly as quickly as I wanted. As I got to know people and became friendly with [them], it made all the difference in the world. You get your phone calls answered first. People trust you and tell you what you want to know because they know you'll exercise some discretion with what you've just heard.

Dan Tate, who was in charge of Senate liaison for Carter, spoke about the efficiency of knowing a number of different people who could provide information he needed.

> I now know, for example, that if I have a problem with the handicapped, I don't have to make half a dozen telephone calls to the Department of Health and Human Services, getting passed from one person to the next over there to find the right individual with whom I have to speak. Now I can go, if necessary, to the secretary herself. If I choose not to deal with the Department at all, I can go to the person on the Domestic Policy Staff who has responsibility for programs involving the handicapped. Or I could go to the Office of Management and Budget, to the director, to the deputy director, or the associate director who has responsibility for that particular program. In other words, I don't have to thrash around in the thicket as I did before.

Not having to thrash around in the political thicket is probably as good a short definition as can be found for the effects of experience.

What was taking place was, in an important sense, group learning. It was not simply that Lynn Daft or Claudia Townsend or Dan Tate got to know some other people, but that their colleagues also knew them and trusted them, so there came to be open and easy communication. And as group learning takes place, members of the administration spot procedural problems. One of the least organized units at the beginning of the Carter administration was the Office of Congressional Liaison. While it never gained the skill of the Reagan legislative liaison team, it did make some real improvements. In late 1977, Bill Cable and Dan Tate reviewed the situation of the Carter program on the Hill. As Cable recalled:

> One of the most interesting documents we produced was an estimate of the time required for Congress to pass the bills that were then before them, if a bill did get to the floor, how much time it would take on the floor. Making assumptions that proved to be more accurate in the overall than they were in the specific, we came to the conclusion that if Congress did nothing but act on half of the major legislative items that we'd asked them to do, they would consume all of the legislative days that were left.

That piece of paper, Cable said, proved to be a very useful argument. Without even entering into the question of the merits of individual bits of legislation (which meant they were able to avoid a lot of intra-staff dispute), they were able to argue successfully that some kind of priority list was needed. Thereafter a priority list was negotiated among the National Security Council staff, the Domestic Policy Staff, the legislative liaison staff, and other relevant units. It went to the President as a memo from Vice President Mondale. "That was a major asset to us," Domestic Policy chief Stuart Eizenstat said, "in how we allocated our time and how we allocated the President's time."

Robert Thomson, deputy director of the Carter legislative liaison office, said that early in the administration there had been a problem with vetoes of bills that had been passed on the Consent Calendar.[14] Occasionally, the Office of Legislative Reference in OMB (the unit that checks with government agencies to ascertain their views about whether a bill should be signed or vetoed) would recommend a veto, and President Carter would do so. As Thomson explained:

> Consequently we had a bill that was passed on the Consent Calendar in the House, passed without a dissenting vote in the Senate, come down here [and be vetoed]. . . . The Congress would scream, or particularly

---

[14] The Consent Calendar is a procedure used by Congress to pass bills to which no one objects. As a practical matter, these are usually minor bills that are important to very few members.

the affected members would scream, because they didn't feel they had been given proper notice that the President himself and the White House itself felt badly about the bill. . . . What we did was to have OMB put together a troublesome-bills list early on in the [session] and kept that list updated as we went along. . . . What we tried to do was to get the agencies, or in some cases the White House itself, involved in working out the problems with the bill. . . . We had far fewer of those types of confrontations in the last years, I think, than we did in the first two years.

Along with particular procedures that were devised to handle specific problems came a measure of general staff integration. Early in the Carter administration, the President had an early morning meeting with Frank Moore, the head of legislative liaison, and then a late morning meeting with press secretary Jody Powell. Powell discovered that he was going to the earlier congressional liaison session because of his need to find out firsthand what was happening on the Hill, so the two meetings were combined to save time. Jody Powell continued:

Then we began to expand it to include other senior staff members including the chief of staff and others as need required. The vice president's office was also always represented. And those became a sort of daily session with the boss, both so he knew what we were about, and we knew from him the sort of things that a staff needs to know. It also gave us a chance, along with him, just to chew over matters that didn't necessarily require a decision that day, but which he would need to know about or be kept current on, so that when he did have to make a decision, he was not operating in a vacuum.

Zbigniew Brzezinski said that the Carter staff became more systematized when Jack Watson became chief of staff. (This did not happen until the fourth year, when Hamilton Jordan left to run Carter's reelection campaign.) Brzezinski explained:

It started being more like a joint staff. Until then it was a series of separate entities. I suspect [the reason for the change] was more Watson's management skills, but I think the President recognized the need for a more integrated staff, and so did the key principals, Wexler, Cutler, Powell, and Eizenstat. This helped pull things together to a greater extent than was the case during the first two or so years.

The reputation of the Carter White House never caught up with the early criticism for disorganization, but the accumulated experience and organizational adjustments had improved its effectiveness by the latter part of the Carter administration. Similar learning brings greater skill to any administration as it matures.

REELECTION

As every recent president has entered his fourth year in the White House, he has decided that he ought to run for relection. The only 20th century presidents who were eligible to run for another term, but who declined to do so—Calvin Coolidge in 1928, Harry Truman in 1952, and Lyndon Johnson in 1968—had been vice presidents who had succeeded to the presidency on the death of their predecessors, and had served for longer than four years themselves. Presidents seeking reelection have been defeated—William Howard Taft in 1912, Herbert Hoover in 1932, Gerald Ford in 1976, and Jimmy Carter in 1980—but none with just a single term has voluntarily given up the office. And when the president is an active candidate for reelection, institutional behavior is perceptibly different.

Any number of things are not done that would take place in a third or fifth year of an administration. When Gerald Ford was a candidate for renomination and reelection in the summer of 1976, the State Department was not taking steps to normalize relations with the People's Republic of China. No efforts were being made to resume talks with the Soviet Union leading toward conclusion of a second strategic arms limitation treaty. Although diplomats could see how such a treaty could be concluded, the Ford administration was under attack by conservative Republicans for insufficient firmness toward the Soviet Union. In deference to the Jewish vote, the State Department had suspended the search for a more even-handed approach to the Middle East. Domestically, the Occupational Safety and Health Administration had announced that they would not promulgate any more job safety regulations. The Ford administration did not seem anxious to find a new head for the Equal Employment Opportunity Commission. And when the White House did move, there was often partisan opposition. For example, when they proposed a reform of regulatory agencies, Democratic Representative John Moss of California said that nothing should be done "until we can get the views of an elected president" (Weaver, 1976).[15] In holding up Ford proposals in expectation of a change in administration, Democrats were emulating Republican senators who held up Lyndon Johnson's nomination of Abe Fortas as chief justice in 1968 in the hope that Nixon would win and be able to choose a more conservative chief justice.

It is more difficult to pass any legislation during a reelection year for two reasons. First, legislative leaders are just as loath to put members in positions where they have to cast politically difficult votes as they are before a midterm election. For instance, the leaders had let

---

[15] I should like to thank Edward Tufte for calling my attention to these examples.

it be known early in 1976 that they would not bring any abortion or gun control measures to the floor. But beyond this, Congress is in session for a shorter time. They take two long summer recesses, one for each party's convention, and then, of course, they adjourn earlier in the fall to permit the members to get back home to campaign.

There is a considerable reallocation of talent in a reelection year, as many members of the administration give their greatest attention to the election. In 1980, 9 percent of the names in the "Carter/Mondale Yellow Pages" (the campaign staff telephone directory) had been listed in the White House telephone directory. The shift of personnel from the White House to the campaign staff, though, is selective. Most of the people who went over to the campaign came from the political side of the White House: from Hamilton Jordan's, Tim Kraft's, and the Congressional Liaison offices. Of legislative liaison personnel we have already encountered, Bill Cable spent the fall out in Illinois, and Robert Thomson was in charge of the campaign in Washington. We will meet Les Francis, Tom Donilon, and Ronna Freiberg in the chapters on nomination and electoral politics. All of them came from the legislative liaison staff. People did not move from the Domestic Policy Staff, the NSC staff, or the OMB staff. There were two reasons for this difference: the differential effects of the Hatch Act, and the political skills that had led to the White House appointments on the political units in the first place.

Obviously, many of those still on the White House staff are concerned with the election. For example, press secretary Jody Powell was carrying more of a workload than a press secretary normally would, because he was so close to the President. This redefined the role of Ray Jenkins, an experienced newsman who had joined the press staff in the fall of 1979. "Generally speaking, I just try to take as much work as I can off of Jody Powell. . . . Whenever the President traveled during the campaign, Jody traveled with him, and we had to have someone here in the White House press office and that was me." David Rubenstein, who was the deputy to chief domestic advisor Stuart Eizenstat, traveled with the President on all his domestic trips "because I made myself into the expert on local issues as well as what the President's current positions were. He needed to have somebody traveling with him all the time who knew what his positions were and could tell him what he should say or shouldn't say."

David Aaron, Zbigniew Brzezinski's deputy on the NSC staff, was also drawn deeply into the campaign. Foreign policy was being debated in the campaign, and professionals in the State and Defense Departments were reluctant to join in because of the political context. Political leaders, the President, Vice President Mondale, Robert Strauss, and others could and did defend their record; but there was also a need for special foreign policy expertise. As Aaron recounted his experience:

This NSC itself is forbidden to participate in these things, and we are very scrupulous about that. This placed an enormous burden on me because Zbig for various reasons didn't want to speak out. That left one person in the White House who knew anything about the subject. I ended up having to work day and night on the platform . . . and in the campaign . . . there were sort of minidebates around the country on foreign policy. So I would appear on TV and go to Texas, New York, Boston, Chicago, and so forth.

There are some people on the White House staff with less to do during a reelection year. In the main, these are persons with policy responsibilities who are forbidden to campaign, and who must await instructions from political masters who are preoccupied with the campaign. But whether particular individuals are up to their eyebrows in politics or waiting for things to return to the pattern of a nonelection year, the presidency is different when the president is a candidate.

The Reelection stage of an administration has been lengthened in recent years by two developments. One has been the lengthening of nomination politics. The visible campaigning in the Early Days stage of nomination politics has been starting earlier and earlier. The January 1976 caucuses in Iowa were the first major event of the 1976 campaign. In November 1979, there was a straw poll on 1980 preferences at the Florida Democratic convention. And in January 1983, there was a straw poll on 1984 preferences at the California Democratic convention. The other development has been an increasing tendency to challenge an incumbent president for his own party's nomination. Lyndon Johnson was challenged in 1964 by George Wallace, Richard Nixon in 1972 by John Ashbrook and Pete McCloskey, and, of course, Gerald Ford and Jimmy Carter faced very serious challenges from Ronald Reagan and Edward Kennedy, respectively. The impact of these developments is to lengthen the Reelection stage of the presidency. This, in turn, shortens the opportunity available to the Maturing Administration. The third year is not the only chance for accomplishment, but it is one of the better. And since we ought to seek statesmanship in our presidents, it does not bode well to shorten the periods during which they can give their principal attention to public policy.

A MATURE ADMINISTRATION

A splendid opportunity for accomplishment should come in the fifth year[16] *if* the president is reelected with a decent majority and *if* his own party has reasonable majorities in both the House and the Senate.

---

[16] And as much of the sixth year as is available until congressional attention shifts to yet another midterm election.

By this time, the administration should have the benefit of four years of experience, and be able to move swiftly to get their proposals before sympathetic legislators. In Light's language, the cycle of influence ought to have been renewed by the election, and the cycle of effectiveness ought to have been buoyed by a full term's learning.

Unfortunately, we do not have any recent examples of this situation. When Richard Nixon was sworn in for his second term, he faced a Democratic Congress, as did Dwight Eisnhower when he was sworn in for his second term. (In considering what is "normal," it helps to remember that for 20 of the last 40 years, presidents have been constrained by having Congress, or just the House in Reagan's case, controlled by their political opponents.) Since Franklin Roosevelt's administration, only Harry Truman and Lyndon Johnson have been reelected with Congresses controlled by fellow partisans.

Some idea of the possibilities can be gained from the discussion of Lyndon Johnson's "Transition." This was a first year only in a very special sense. Johnson would have been likely to do well with Congress in any case because of his extensive experience on the Hill. But in 1965, he had the advantages of his own landslide victory and large Democratic majorities in both houses, *and* he was in the White House during 1964 so he had a full legislative program ready to lay before Congress right away. The result was that he was able to pass bills that had been sought unsuccessfully by other Democrats for a full generation.

Even if they are favored with a sympathetic legislature, Mature Administrations are hampered in other ways. There is a fair amount of personnel turnover. A majority of Eisenhower's original cabinet was gone by 1957, and none of Nixon's original cabinet members stayed in their posts through 1973. Getting persons who are at the peaks of non-governmental careers to drop things and come to Washington is harder than when the president was first elected, so there are recruiting difficulties. This is not all bad, of course. An inability to bring in outsiders means a greater tendency to promote from within, and this capitalizes on their experience. But lack of fresh blood also means fewer new ideas, thus increasing the already strong probability that a second-term administration will stay in policy paths developed during the first term.

The same lack of freshness limits an administration's ability to accomplish things. Congress and the public already know the actors. To say that they are jaded would be a trifle too strong, but the familiar often lacks fascination. Network television, for example, covered Amy Carter's first day in a Washington grade school in 1977. How much interest would there have been with her continuation in junior high school in 1981? Of greater substantive importance, legislators and other politicians have well-developed attitudes toward the administration's policies, and can react very quickly. And those within the administration know the political opposition that their proposals are likely to engender. The naivete of the first year is gone, but the exhilarating feeling that all things are possible has disappeared along with it.

RETIREMENT

Retirement comes to an administration instantly or gradually, but always after an election. For a one-term presidency, it comes with the incumbent's defeat. For a two-term presidency, it comes after the final midterm election. Retirement for a one-term presidency doesn't require much description because it is so brief. It lasts only for the 11-week period from election to the inauguration of the next president. Its chief characteristic is the loss, not of all power, but of virtually all power that requires the cooperation of someone else. With a new president about to be sworn in, those other actors who have any hope of working successfully with the next administration will want to spend their political capital in a way that will bring rewards over the next four years.

A two-term administration gradually begins to wind down after the election of the last Congress with which it will deal. All of the representatives and two thirds of the senators have now been chosen in an election in which the president was not a candidate. Even if the president has been sufficiently skilled (and sufficiently lucky) to have been able to maintain his public popularity into the closing years of his administration, he has not displayed his prowess at the polls lately. Many of the political resources of the administration have been expended, and other politicians have begun to think about the next administration.

The problems of recruiting personnel from outside the government become quite severe. With only a year or so left, who wants to leave their business, sell their home, and move to Washington? It was said that some 70 persons were considered or approached about the secretaryship of defense by the Eisenhower administration before Thomas S. Gates was promoted from secretary of the navy. This rumor may well have been exaggerated, but Dwight Eisenhower was the only modern American president to be able to entice all of his original cabinet choices to Washington (Hess, 1976, p. 60), and the defense post is one of the prime portfolios in any administration. What does this imply about the ability of a more typical administration to recruit a deputy assistant secretary?

As a consequence of recruiting difficulties, the Retirement stage of an administration is dominated by promotion from within. And if the persons promoted have been with the administration for six or seven years, they are likely to be more than a trifle weary. There are relatively

few people who are able to respond to the many demands made upon
political executives without losing a measure of vitality.

This is not to imply that an administration in its closing years is
incapable of decisive action. In 1951, Harry Truman summarily fired
General Douglas MacArthur to underscore presidential control of
American policy. And in 1959, a single, forceful Eisenhower speech
was enough to win passage of the Landrum-Griffin Labor-Management
Act from a Democratic Congress over the opposition of Speaker Sam
Rayburn and Senator John Kennedy. But it is accurate to say that the
Retirement stage is seldom marked by major new initiatives. The stan-
dard fare is continued advocacy of the familiar.

The administration still gives attention to public business in the
final weeks after the election, but for many the first order of private
business is compiling résumés, while the few who are closing out their
careers along with the administration are making final plans for retirement. Offices become crowded with transfer files full of papers, most
of which are to be shipped off to a future presidential library. And
finally the permanent government takes over. The erstwhile powerful
are reminded that they must turn over their passes, and be out of
the White House and Executive Office Building by noon on January
20.

"Beginnings and *endings* are different," Stephen Hess has told us.
And no one has better summed up the mood at the close of an administration. The term seems much longer to someone who has not been
part of the administration. The president finds that his time

> was largely consumed by crises and the demands of others, bargaining
> with congressmen, feuds, small symbolic acts, worrying about getting
> reelected, finding people for jobs and getting rid of them (usually by
> "kicking them upstairs"), approving budgets that he could only change
> around the edges. He never really "ran" the government as he had ex-
> pected. Rather, the president found that his job was to try to keep the
> social fabric intact; to keep the peace if possible; to defend the nation
> from aggressors; to maintain the nation's place in the world, even by
> force; to attempt to balance economic growth and stability; and at best
> to make some new initiatives that history books would record as his.
> (Hess, 1976, p. 26)

THE ANNUAL POLICY CYCLE

In addition to these long-term stages that arise from the electoral
calendar, there is an annual cycle of policy development and advocacy.
This cycle is anchored in January by constitutional and statutory requirements that the president deliver State of the Union, Budget, and
Economic Messages. The main thrust of the president's legislative program is defined by these three documents. The preceding months are

devoted to getting them ready, and the succeeding months to trying to persuade Congress to adopt the program they outline.

It is slightly misleading to refer to this as an annual cycle. The same events do take place at about the same time each year, but the full policy cycle lasts longer than a year. The cycle begins with the spring budget review process, an early look at the budget the president will submit to the Congress the following January. The spring review forms the basis for letters that are sent to the agencies in June giving them instructions for preparing their requests for the next budget. The agency requests arrive in early September, and are scrutinized during the fall as OMB puts together the budget they will recommend to the president. The September-to-January budget review is a process that is well known in OMB. "It is very easy to make sure that everything gets evaluated in a budgetary context," explained Donald Moran, associate OMB director in the Reagan administration. "The real challenge is also to keep in focus and have some mechanism to follow through with the issues that arise out of cycle."

In the opinion of Charles Schultze, chairman of Carter's Council of Economic Advisors and Lyndon Johnson's budget director, the "period between October and the end of the year is the most active in terms of policy recommendations because . . . the budget is put together then [and that] encapsulates a lot of it." Moreover, the Council of Economic Advisors is working on the Economic Report, and legislative proposals are at least being blocked out. All of these are dependent on one another. Writing the Economic Report is the occasion for an economic forecast which, together with the tax rates, indicates how much revenue will be available for the budget. The budget, in turn, must make provision for any new legislative proposals. Without funding provisions, legislators will conclude that the administration is not taking the proposals seriously.

At the same time the budget decisions are nearing the president's desk, outreach units are in contact with other actors on the Washington political scene. Anne Wexler, head of the Carter administration's Office of Public Liaison, explained the activities of her unit:

> Most of our activities between October and January in any given calendar year are devoted to meetings with interest groups, understanding their priorities for the upcoming budget that is then being decided upon. Being sure that we have narrowed down the concerns of the people who are most involved with the budget can mean anything from defense to urban policy. And we are making sure the President understands what those concerns are, and is prepared to deal with the trade-offs that have to go with the final budget decisions.

The Domestic Policy Staff was centrally involved in shaping legislative proposals. Staff members here saw a clear distinction between pulling legislative proposals together, and working in behalf of these proposals before Congress. Associate director Simon Lazarus commented:

> I would say that from November through February, we were involved really in making the decisions as to what was going to be our agenda for the coming year on the Hill, and after that between February and November we participated in the management of the bills that we decided to support. The main thrust of our work was legislative, so there was a very clear divide between these two parts of the year.

His boss, Stuart Eizenstat, agreed:

> Toward the end of one calendar year and at the beginning of the next, you're doing more policy development, drafting of legislation, getting ready for the congressional session. That never really stops; there is always something going on. But once you move into spring, and we've got most of our proposals up there, it then becomes one in which I would go up and explain our proposals.

Once the president has delivered his State of the Union, Budget, and Economic Messages, and the remaining decisions have been made about the content of the legislative program, the focus shifts to Capitol Hill. Most White House units are involved in advocacy of administration programs, but the unit with special responsibility for this is the Congressional Liaison office. The congressional year now tends to begin with a budgetary focus because of the First Budget Resolution. "The First Budget Resolution is not binding by law," Robert Thomson explained, "but nevertheless, the decisions that are made set the tone for the year, so if you want to get a particular series of cuts, it's essential that the first resolution reflect those so that people can bite the bullet" later on. Once that is passed in mid-May, attention swings to the authorizing committees, where substantive legislative proposals are being scrutinized, and this continues through the middle of the year. Toward the end of the year, Thomson continued, there is another shift:

> You're always involved in appropriations matters. More and more as time goes on, you have continuing resolutions because Congress is very reluctant to deal with controversial appropriations matters until the last minute. You always have a tax bill or two. For tactical reasons, they always like to delay; and inevitably as Congress winds down to a close, you have a key conference.

In a nonelection year, Congress may work until nearly Christmas eve— roughly 21 months after OMB began its spring budget review.

This annual cycle is a recurring feature of all administrations, but as outlined here, this is how the cycle looks from the White House during the third, fifth, and seventh years of a two-term cycle. The annual cycle takes place within the longer electoral cycle. During the first year, there are transition concerns. The new administration has time to do little more than adapt the preceding administration's budget to reflect their most urgent priorities. Even in 1981, when there were major alterations, the Reagan administration was still working with what was essentially the last Carter budget. (The incoming Office of Management and Budget officials did not even see the complete set of budget figures until after January 20.) During midterm election years, Congress adjourns in the fall so the members can get back home to campaign. If the president is campaigning, he and many of his senior aides will be unavailable to take part in decisions about budget and legislation, so these will be delayed until the latter part of November. And, of course, during a presidential election year, the need for reelection dominates everything else.

Summary

Every first-term presidency passes through the same stages. Transition is a search for men and women who can carry out the erstwhile candidate's promises, a longer learning period than the new appointees anticipated, and now and again a burst of exceptional activity if the newcomers are skilled enough to take advantage of recently demonstrated electoral support. Before they know it, it is time for a first Midterm Election. The Maturing Administration has another chance for accomplishment in the third year, and then the administration is catapulted back into the electoral area as the president seeks Reelection.

If the administration wins a second term, it somehow seems shorter. A Mature Administration certainly should have the skills for another attempt to guide Congress and the bureaucracy along the paths they prefer, but then comes another Midterm Election. In the final Retirement phase, the administration still holds center stage, but the spotlight slowly dims until it is time for another set of ambitious men and women to devote their energies to the service of the Republic.

In addition, there is an annual policy cycle that is fitted into the interstices of this longer electoral cycle. This begins with the development of budget and legislative proposals, and continues with their advocacy largely according to the demands of a congressional calendar. Nor is this all. As we will see in Chapter 5, there are policy areas that also have characteristic temporal patterns. Executive politics is governed by all three: the electoral pattern, the annual pattern, and the patterns of the several policy areas.

CHAPTER 4

INTERNAL STRUCTURES OF THE WHITE HOUSE

Of all the appointments a president makes, none are more important to the presidency than those to the White House staff.[1] White House staff appointments go to those who have been closest to the president. John Kennedy brought Theodore Sorenson, Kenneth O'Donnell, and Lawrence O'Brien with him; Lyndon Johnson appointed Walter Jenkins, George Reedy, and Bill Moyers; Richard Nixon relied heavily on H. R. Haldeman and John Erlichman; Gerald Ford brought Philip Buchan and William Seidman from Grand Rapids; Jimmy Carter put Hamilton Jordan and Jody Powell in central posts; Ronald Reagan located his long-time California aides Ed Meese and Mike Deaver close to the Oval Office. The White House staff also has been enriched by distinguished substantive expertise. McGeorge Bundy, Walt Rostow, Henry Kissinger, and Zbigniew Brzezinski were all well-known academics before they headed National Security Council (NSC) staffs. Arthur Burns, Walter Heller, and Martin Feldstein had distinguished reputations as economists before their appointments as chairmen of the Council of Economic Advisers (CEA).[2] In fact, it could be argued that the White House

---

[1] I am using "White House staff" to refer to the principal policymaking units serving the president. It includes the National Security Council staff, the Office of Management and Budget staff, Office of Policy Development (the domestic policy staff, which has had various names), and Council of Economic Advisers, although they are formally part of the larger Executive Office of the President. I am not including the Office of the First Lady, support services, scheduling, advance, or correspondence, although they are part of the White House Office itself. The former units have a good deal to do with policy; the latter do not.

[2] The persons just named may be typical of senior members of the White House staff, but they are atypical of the White House staff as a whole. The confidants were too close to the president, and the academics had professional reputations that were too eminent to be representative of most White House staff members.

staff works best when it has a good balance between confidants with whom the president feels comfortable, and substantive experts who can guide the president as he makes difficult policy decisions.

ACTIVISTS

On White House office walls are found commissions which read, "Reposing special trust and confidence in your integrity, prudence, and ability, I do appoint you . . . ," and are signed by the president. The phrases are at once ceremonial and meaningful. The first reference is to trust, and the White House staff works by an extension of trust. The president trusts those with whom he is working directly. They extend this trust to their own assistants. And ability is only one of three attributes that are given equal weight in the following phrase. The others are integrity, "adherence to a code of moral values," and prudence, "caution as to danger or risk." The president has granted the staff members great power, but the other side of this relationship is that the president's reputation depends on the staff members' "integrity, prudence, and ability."

The changes in background characteristics of White House staff members parallel changes in America in recent decades, particularly as regards education. If one goes back to Franklin Roosevelt's staff, nearly half of the staff members did not have bachelor's degrees.[3] For Truman through Johnson, over 80 percent had undergraduate degrees, and between one half and two thirds had advanced degrees. All of the Carter staff members were college graduates, and 86 percent had postbaccalaureate degrees. A single Reagan staffer lacked a college degree, and 63 percent had master's, law, or doctoral degrees. Five of the Carter aides had degrees from Georgia universities—Emory, Georgia, and Georgia State—and the Reaganites had degrees from Berkeley, Stanford, Southern California, UCLA, and Occidental, not to mention that splendid California effort to make education more broadly available, California State University, with one graduate each from San Jose, Modesto, and Fresno. But some 31 percent of the "Georgians" had at least one degree from Harvard, Yale, Princeton, Columbia, or MIT as did 28 percent of the "Californians." The proportion of Ivy League degrees is about the same as it was on the Roosevelt and Truman staffs, but much lower than on the Eisenhower, Kennedy, and Johnson staffs.

---

[3] The data for Roosevelt through Johnson come from Lacy (1967); those for the Carter and Reagan staffs come from my own interviews. Lacy's data refer to members of the White House Office. The Carter and Reagan data refer to roughly 28 members of the Carter staff (as defined in the preceding footnote), and roughly 38 members of the Reagan staff. The exact numbers vary a bit from one background factor to the next.

The average age of staff members dropped a full decade between Roosevelt and Reagan. On FDR's staff, it was 49.6. For each of the Truman, Eisenhower, Kennedy, and Johnson staffs, the mean age was between 44 and 46. The average Carter staffer was 38.7 years old, and the average Reagan staffer 40.0.

To the four great estates mentioned by Heclo as sources of cabinet members—academia, corporate business and the law, government, and elective politics—one and a half more must be added to describe the occupational background of staff members. The additional estate is that of journalism and advertising. The partial estate lies between universities and the government. It is comprised of consulting firms and think tanks such as the Brookings Institution and the American Enterprise Institute. From a White House perspective, this partial estate is more an adjunct of government. All of the staffers recruited from consultantships or think tanks had previous government experience. To some degree, this emerging occupation can be seen as a continuation of policy analysis when your friends are out of power.

The immediate occupational backgrounds of the Carter and Reagan staffs are shown in Table 4-1. The five and a half estates are all represented, but the Carter staffers were more likely to have been drawn from legal or governmental backgrounds, while the Reagan staffers were more likely to have been involved in public relations. The greater proportion of governmental background on the Carter staff is partly illusory. The Carter aides coming immediately from government were employed on Democratic staffs on the Hill during the Nixon-Ford years. Republicans did not have this opportunity during the Carter administration, so more of them worked for think tanks or as consultants. If these categories are added together, the Carter advantage in government experience remains, but it is not as great. The other great difference is the much larger number of Reagan staffers who were employed in journalism or advertising firms. In fact, if one looks through vitas

TABLE 4-1
Backgrounds of Carter and Reagan Staffs

Occupation	Carter Staff	Reagan Staff
Law	33%	21%
Business	4	10
Government	33	10
Consulting/ think tank	4	15
Academia	13	18
Journalism/ advertising	13	26

for all those who were in journalism at some time in their careers, the Reagan proportion goes up to 36 percent. The only other modern White House staff with anything approaching this proportion of journalists was Franklin Roosevelt's. The two recent presidents most often singled out for their skills as communicators chose to keep professional journalists close at hand.

What Table 4-1 does not show is the extent to which White House staff members have moved back and forth between these occupations. After Stuart Eizenstat graduated from Harvard Law School, for example, he first had a research job on Lyndon Johnson's White House staff, then a clerkship with a federal judge, then a partnership in an Atlanta law firm, and then was director of policy planning in the 1976 Carter campaign. David Aaron had been a foreign service officer for six years, then had worked for the Arms Control agency for four, then had spent four years working on three Senate staffs (including Walter Mondale's) before coming to the White House as deputy director of the NSC staff. Lyn Nofziger had been a reporter for 16 years before he joined Governor Reagan's staff in 1967, then had been on the Nixon legislative liaison staff, next the Republican National Committee staff, and since 1973 had alternated between political consultantships and Reagan campaigns. Dave Gergen began writing for his hometown *Durham Morning Herald* at 14, became managing editor of the *Yale Daily* as an undergraduate, took a cum laude degree at Harvard Law School, then joined the Nixon speechwriting staff, spent part of the Ford administration working for Treasury Secretary Simon and then went back to the Ford staff, and spent the Carter years in consulting and as a resident fellow at the American Enterprise Institute who helped to found *Public Opinion.* And so on. Occasionally, there will be a person with only one occupation, but more often there are shifts between law, government, journalism, universities, and politics. The common "occupation" is a late 20th century skill in handling information and symbol manipulation.

These background characteristics lead to another question. We are members of what Robert Lane has called "a knowledgeable society;" and in such a society, advanced education with attendant information and communication skills is not scarce. The pool of individuals who have similar backgrounds is much larger than the number of persons who end up on the White House staff. How are these particular persons chosen?

Recruitment

The individual who has been selected in any personnel process does not have as good an idea of why he or she has been chosen as the person who is doing the choosing, but often they have some idea.

Reagan staffers were asked about their own selection in the spring of 1981. No one instance was typical, but a few examples can provide some sense of how the selection process was working. There were a few longtime Reagan aides whose selection was nearly automatic. Robert Carleson, for example, had helped develop the California welfare program as Governor Reagan's welfare director, and then had become U.S. commissioner of welfare at the invitation of Caspar Weinberger. Carleson had been a senior policy adviser in the 1980 campaign, working principally with welfare issues. At the outset of the Reagan administration, he was appointed to the policy development staff, and put in charge of welfare and federalism issues.

The most important non California appointment was James Baker as chief of staff. He was frank to say he did not know why he had been selected as chief of staff, but added that he had heard the President was pleased with "what we organized [as] briefings for the debates, and the decision to go forward with the debates."

"I guess there's no school for this sort of thing," said Counsel Fred Fielding, "except experience." He had the advantage of having been deputy counsel during the Nixon administration. Shortly before the election, he had been asked to submit a paper outlining clearance procedures for security and conflict of interest for prospective nominees. "Then, after the election," Fielding continued, "I was asked if I would assist in the transition in the clearance process, getting the paper flow work done. So I originally and personally interviewed all the candidates for the cabinet. This could not be delegated to staff assistants. In the course of that, I got to know a lot of the people who were working for the President-elect."

Karna Small had known a number of Reagan aides when she had lived in San Francisco, where she had anchored television news programs from 1972 to 1978. She knew she was being considered because she "had a number of calls from people close to the President during the transition process saying, 'Do you want to come on board?' 'Would you consider coming on board?' " In early January, she was appointed deputy press secretary.

These explanations help, but don't answer all the questions about how appointments are made to the White House staff. The appointees had skills relevant to the positions for which they were being considered, and were known to senior staff members who were making the choices. The Reagan recruiters made unusual—and successful—efforts to find persons who agreed with Ronald Reagan's brand of conservatism (Mackenzie, 1981a; Penner and Heclo, 1983). This concern narrowed the pool of potential appointees from all Republicans with advanced educations and information handling skills. But there must have been others with similar qualifications and acquaintanceships. Why were they rejected, and these staff members selected? Without knowing who was considered and rejected, this question can't be answered, but we can at least say that no one[4] was appointed who had not worked with, or at least was known to, Reagan insiders.

Aspirations

What did the White House aides hope to accomplish by their active participation in executive politics? The answers of newly appointed Reagan staffers fell into two general categories. One type of ambition was defined largely by the position to which the staff member had been appointed. Murray Weidenbaum, the chairman of the Council of Economic Advisers, said simply that he wanted to help with the development of the administration's economic policies. Fred Fielding said, "I hope to accomplish the obvious, which is to have error-free judgment from a legal standpoint on the part of the executive branch, in particular the President." In these instances, the economist and the lawyer hoped to make appropriate use of their professional skills.

Others focused on the political goals of the new administration. Shannon Fairbanks, who was dealing with housing on the policy development staff, said, "I think the main goal I have is to accomplish what Ronald Reagan is seeking: a revolution that he not only spoke for and stood for, but was accepted by the voters. I hope to achieve his goals with regards to changing policies in economics and in the public policy and social policy spheres." There was some tendency for those with previous government experience to state more modest goals, and for those entering government for the first time to speak of the broad changes that they would bring about. Weidenbaum and Fielding had prior government experience; Fairbanks did not. Yet this was only a tendency. Powell Moore, who had been in the legislative liaison office in the Nixon and Ford administrations, and was the first head of Senate liaison on the Reagan staff, spoke of three goals:

> I hope to be part of a team that achieves a number of things. Number one, I want to restore strength to national defense so that we can help guarantee a more peaceful world. . . . Secondly, I want to see that the time is ripe to reduce the intrusion of the federal government into the daily lives of the American people. Thirdly, I would like to see . . . that the regulatory burden and the tax burden is reduced . . . to make America more productive, so that we have less inflation, less economic dislocation, and so that we have more work, more jobs, more prosperity, and a higher standard of living.

Altogether, there was a mix of wanting to do a good job in an individual sense, and a desire to advance the broad political goals of the administration.

---

[4] Or, more exactly, no one among those I interviewed.

ISSUE GROUPS

While the goals of individual staff members may hint at the direction in which an administration will move, they do not determine it. If the individual staff member is to accomplish anything, allies are needed.

In an often-quoted passage, Clark Clifford spoke about the efforts of like-minded liberals on the Truman White House staff to win the President to their point of view:

> The idea was that six or eight of us would try to come to an understanding among ourselves on what directions we would like the President to take on any given issue. Then quietly and unobtrusively, each in his own way, we would try to steer the President in that direction.
>
> Naturally, we were up against tough competition. Most of the cabinet and congressional leaders were urging Mr. Truman to go slow, to veer a little closer to the conservative line. . . .
>
> Well, it was two forces fighting for the mind of the President, that's what it really was. It was completely unpublicized, and I don't think Mr. Truman ever realized it was going on. But it was an unceasing struggle during those two years, and it got to the point where no quarter was asked and none given. (Anderson, 1968, p. 72)

In executive politics, this is the political reality that lies behind the theoretical discussion at the end of Chapter 2 about the need to isolate *groups* with shared attitudes about goals. Whether the aim is to employ the rich theories of group behavior in an explicitly political setting, or to understand the forces that are fighting for the mind of of the president, one is led to ask the same questions. What are the central tendencies with regard to policy—liberal, moderate conservative, or what? How do these central tendencies vary from one White House staff to the next? How do they vary from one policy area to another? Does an administration take, say, a moderate position in international affairs, a conservative posture in economics, and a liberal position on social benefits, or does it take a moderate conservative position across all policy areas? And once we know about the general thrust of a White House staff, we need to seek specific issue groups in order to understand the forces that are contending within these boundaries.

Data on the central policy tendencies of three administrations are given in Table 4-2. These summarize the attitudes of 16 members of the Nixon Domestic Council staff,[5] 30 members of the Carter White House staff, and 39 members of the Reagan White House staff. (For

---

[5] Including the Nixon staff members meant that a smaller set of attitude items had to be used. This did not appreciably change the estimates of the Carter and Reagan positions, however, and including the Nixon data adds perspective.

TABLE 4-2
Median Issue Positions of Three White House Staffs

Policy Area	Carter	Nixon	Reagan
International involvement	Moderate Liberal (4.1)	Moderate Conservative (3.4)	Moderate Conservative (2.7)
Economic management	Moderate (3.1)	Conservative (2.0)	Conservative (1.3)
Social benefits	Moderate (3.6)	Moderate Conservative (3.3)	Conservative (1.9)
Civil liberties	Moderate Liberal (5.1)	Conservative (2.2)	Conservative (1.4)
Agriculture	Moderate (4.0)	Moderate Conservative (2.8)	Conservative (2.1)

Note: The figures in parentheses are median positions on scales that vary between 1 and 7. In general a high score (7) represents a dove position in international involvement, and a willingness to use government power and resources in the domestic policy areas. A low score (1) represents the opposite.

The convention followed for substantive interpretations of the scale scores was: values from 1 to 2.4, conservative; 2.5 to 3.4, moderate conservative; 3.5 to 4.5, moderate; 4.6 to 5.5, moderate liberal; 5.6 to 7, liberal. This classification is nothing more than an aid to understanding and should not be taken as a precise denotation. (The Carter staff classifications are one category more liberal in international involvement and economic management because they had higher median scores when responding to a more complete set of questions.)

For further information, see Appendix A-4.1.

further information on what these scores represent, see Appendix A-4.1.) Not surprisingly, in view of the White House staffs being compared, the Carter staff was the most liberal of the three in every policy area, and the Reagan staff the most conservative. Looking at the absolute positions of each staff, the Carter staff was moderate liberal or moderate in each policy area; the Nixon staff was moderate conservative or conservative in each policy area; and the Reagan staff was conservative in every area but one. But there were also interesting variations on each staff across policy areas. The two Republican administrations took their most conservative positions in economics, and their economic postures were only a shade more conservative than their feelings about civil liberties. The Carter staff took its most liberal stand, by a wide measure, in civil liberties. Consequently there was the greatest difference in the policy tendencies of the administrations on civil liberties. On the other hand, all three staffs tended toward moderation on international matters, with the result that there was the least difference in this policy area. The Nixon staff was halfway between the Carter staff and the Reagan staff on international involvement. On social benefits, the Nixon staff median was actually closer to the Carter position than to the Reagan position. To call the Carter administration moderate, and the Nixon and Reagan administrations both conservative—statements that are frequently made—is approximately accurate, but only that.

The Carter Issue Structure.   There are two basic steps to the analysis that is used to discover issue groups in a population. First one calculates agreement scores between each pair of individuals. These are calculated in such a way that a score of 0 indicates that they have the amount of agreement one would expect by chance, and a score of 1.0 indicates that the two persons have responded in identical ways to every single question.[6] Then these agreement scores are used as input to a cluster program that groups the individuals so they are associated with the others with whom they have the highest average agreement scores. If a particular person's score is not high enough to represent agreement with any of the issue groups, then that person is treated as an isolate. Further details of this procedure are given in Appendix A-4.3, but the procedure does produce groups whose members have common views on public policy.

When agreement scores were calculated for the Carter White House staff, the mean agreement score turned out to be .31. This means that the similarity of attitudes on the Carter staff was 31 percent beyond what one would expect by chance. As we will see in Chapter 10, this is the level of agreement that existed among all Democratic activists in 1972. In other words, if one had selected a staff randomly from all campaign activists, the same level of agreement should have existed. This is more agreement than would be found among all Democratic voters, and of course much more agreement than among a general population, but it represents rather little consensus.

The extent of disagreement among Carter aides became apparent when the agreement scores were put into the cluster analysis. Using the same cutting points employed in the cluster analyses in later chapters, *every single person turned out to be an isolate.* This came about because of a program parameter that stipulates a minimum value that must exist between at least one pair of cases before a cluster will begin to form. The concrete meaning of no issue groups is that *not a single pair* of Carter staffers had an agreement score high enough to begin this process.

In order to find issue groups on the Carter staff, it was necessary to lower this parameter to allow clusters to begin to form. When this was done, three issue groups were found. Nine staff members could be called "Social Moderates," seven "Social Liberals," seven "Thrifty Libertarians," and there were still seven isolates. These names—Social Moderates, Social Liberals, and Thrifty Libertarians—suggest, but do

---

[6] Further information about the agreement scores is given in Appendix A-4.2.

TABLE 4-3
Positions of Carter Issue Groups by Policy Area

Policy Area	Social Moderates	Social Liberals	Thrifty Libertarians
International involvement	Moderate (4.3)	Moderate (4.5)	Moderate Liberal (4.7)
Economic management	Moderate (4.0)	Moderate (4.2)	Moderate Conservative (3.1)
Social benefits	Moderate Conservative (3.0)	Moderate Liberal (5.1)	Moderate Liberal (5.0)
Civil liberties	Moderate Liberal (4.8)	Moderate (4.3)	Liberal (5.9)
Natural resources	Conservative (2.9)	Moderate Conservative (2.4)	Conservative (3.1)
Agriculture	Conservative (2.0)	Moderate Liberal (5.3)	Moderate Liberal (4.7)

Note: The figures in parentheses are median positions on scales that vary between 1 and 7. In general a high score (7) represents a dove position in international involvement, and a willingness to use government power and resources in the domestic policy areas. A low score (1) represents the opposite.

For the convention followed in giving substantive interpretation to these scores, see the explanation at the bottom of Table 4-2.

For further information, see Appendix A-4.3.

not fully describe,[7] the issue preferences of the groups shown in Table 4-3. The Social Moderates were Chief of Staff Jack Watson, Press Secretary Jody Powell, National Security Assistant Zbigniew Brzezinski, CEA Chairman Charles Schultze, Kitty Schirmer who had moved from the Domestic Policy Staff to the OMB staff, Robert Thomson of the Legislative Liaison staff, and David Rubenstein, Simon Lazarus, and Lynn Daft of the Domestic Policy Staff. The Social Liberals were Stuart Eizenstat, Bert Carp, and Al Stern of the Domestic Policy Staff, Bill Cable and Dan Tate of Legislative Liaison, and Ray Jenkins and Claudia Townsend of the Press Office. The Thrifty Libertarians were Anne Wexler who headed the Office of Public Liaison, Intergovernmental Affairs chief Eugene Eidenberg, David Aaron and Robert Hunter of the NSC

---

[7] The "full" name of the Thrifty Libertarians would be "the group that takes a moderate conservative position on economic management, a moderate liberal position on social benefits, and a liberal position on civil liberties." The shorter name "Thrifty Libertarians" reflects the *distinctive* characteristics of the group, but can do no more. The most accurate descriptions of the groups are the median scores presented in Table 4-3.

staff, Staff Director Alonzo McDonald, Staff Secretary Rick Hutcheson, and Erica Ward of the Domestic Policy Staff.

The proximity of the individual staff members' issue positions is suggested by Figure 4-1, a plot of the issue agreement structure of the Carter staff. This figure results from an analysis known as multidimensional scaling. Some details about the procedure are given in Appendix A-4.4, but the essential point is that it produces a spatial analysis in which individuals with the greatest agreement with each other are located closest together, and those with the greatest disagreement are located farthest apart. The same agreement scores were used as input to the multidimensional scaling as were used with the cluster program, so the multidimensional scaling plot can be used to help understand

FIGURE 4-1
Issue Agreement Structure of Carter White House Staff Members

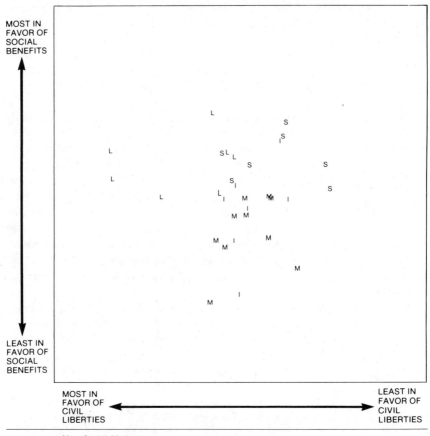

M = Social Moderate
S = Social Liberal
L = Thrifty Libertarian
I = Isolate

the issue groups. In Figure 4-1, M stands for a Social Moderate, S for
a Social Liberal, L for a Thrifty Libertarian, and I for an isolate who
is not a member of any group. The vertical dimension represents one's
position on social benefits. The higher the location on that dimension,
the more one favors social programs, and the lower, the more one
opposes them. The horizontal dimension represents civil liberties. The
farther to the left one is located in Figure 4-1, the more one takes
libertarian positions; the farther to the right, the less emphasis is given
to civil liberties.[8] The Social Moderates took a more conservative position on social benefits than either the Social Liberals or the Thrifty
Libertarians who tended to agree on this issue. The Thrifty Libertarians,
on the other hand, took more liberal positions on civil liberties. The
Social Moderates were slightly more liberal on this question than the
Social Liberals,[9] though they were much closer to them than to the
Thrifty Libertarians.

The preferences of the issue groups by policy area are shown in
Table 4-3. There are significant differences in four policy areas: economic management, social benefits, civil liberties, and agriculture. The
Social Moderates were less likely than the others to think that taxes
should be cut. They took moderate liberal positions on civil rights,
but they had relatively conservative postures on social programs, and
quite conservative positions on support of farm income. The Social
Liberals were willing to see taxes cut, took moderate positions on civil
rights, but tended to be supportive of social programs. The Thrifty
Libertarians had relatively conservative economic views, but were as
supportive of social programs as the Social Liberals, and were more
likely to champion civil liberties than either of the other two groups.

There was no issue group that consistently took the most conservative (or the most liberal) position across the disputed policy areas.
On economic management, the Thrifty Libertarians were the most conservative. On social benefits, the Social Moderates had the most conservative posture. And on civil liberties, it was the Social Liberals who
were relatively conservative. All in all, the Carter issue structure was
rather chaotic.

The Reagan Issue Structure.   As we saw, the Carter White House
was the most liberal of the three, and the Reagan White House the
most conservative. An even more striking difference emerged between
the disagreement on the Carter staff and the similarity of outlook on
the Reagan staff. The mean agreement score for the Carter White House

---

[8] There are other dimensions that reflect positions in other policy areas. Figure 4-1
is part of a seven-dimension solution, so there are five more dimensions that reflect
other differences. The need to go to a seven-dimension solution to find something interpretable says something about the extent of disagreement on the Carter staff.

[9] Here again we see the inability of any simple name (in this case, Social Liberals)
to capture the full complexity of policy positions.

staff was .31, but the mean agreement score for the Reagan White House staff was .53. And if one of the 39 cases is dropped, then the average score rises to .55. The issue consensus in the Reagan White House was substantially greater than that in the Carter White House.

The most dramatic difference between the Carter and Reagan staffs emerged when the cluster program was used to detect issue groups within the staff. When this was done with the Carter staff using normal parameters, not a single pair of staff members had an agreement score high enough to begin forming a group. With the Reagan staff, the results were precisely the opposite. One large group emerged that included 32 of the 39 staff members for whom data were available. The average agreement score within this one big issue group was .58, not all that much higher than the consensus for the total staff, but certainly high in any absolute sense.[10] In order to find issue groups smaller than virtually the entire Reagan staff, it was necessary to do the opposite of what had been done in the analysis of the Carter staff. In that case, one of the parameters had been lowered to allow groups to begin to form. With the Reagan staff, parameters had to be raised. This had the effect of producing issue groups whose rates of interpersonal agreement were still higher, and when this was done, three groups were formed. (For further information about the cluster analysis, see Appendix A-4.3.)

One group of 11 could be called Unalloyed Conservatives. A second 10 member group was made up of Domestic Conservatives. And there were 6 who could be regarded as Altruistic Conservatives. (This leaves a dozen isolates—members of no issue group—but that is a consequence of having created such exclusive issue groups.) The Unalloyed Conservatives included James Baker, Assistant for Cabinet Affairs Craig Fuller, Assistant for Political Affairs Lyn Nofziger,[11] Media Relations Director Karna Small, Robert Carleson, Danny Boggs, Shannon Fairbanks, and Dennis Kass (all of the Office of Policy Development [OPD]) and James Miller and Donald Moran of the Office of Management and Budget. The Domestic Conservatives were Ed Meese, Mike

---

[10] The Nixon Domestic Council staff was also midway between the Carter and Reagan White House staffs in the extent of their agreement. The mean agreement score on this Nixon staff was .40. The cluster analysis produced a single issue group, but only 56 percent of the Nixon staffers were members as compared to 82 percent of the Reagan aides who were members of their issue group.

[11] There is a continual turnover of personnel on the White House staff. Let me give two examples of this from the Reagan administration. My interviews were conducted in the spring of 1981. At that time, I asked if I might come back for a more extended interview in the summer of 1982. Of the 30 people I interviewed in 1981, 7 were in different positions, and another 10 were gone from the White House altogether when I returned in the summer of 1982. Between the summer of 1982 and the end of 1983, William Clark, Elizabeth Dole, Kenneth Duberstein, Edwin Harper, Murray Weidenbaum, and Richard Williamson—all high-ranking advisors—had departed. The positions given in the text for individuals are those they held at the time I interviewed them.

Deaver, David Stockman, Office of Policy Development Director Edwin
Harper, Intergovernmental Relations Director Richard Williamson, Senate Liaison head Powell Moore, Edwin Gray and Michael Uhlmann
of the Office of Policy Development, Wayne Valis of the Office of Public
Liaison, and Speechwriter Aram Bakshain. The Altruistic Conservatives were Congressional Liaison head Kenneth Duberstein, Deputy
Press Secretary Larry Speakes, Counsel Fred Fielding, Deputy Counselor Robert Garrick, Deputy OPD Director Roger Porter, and Office
of Administration head John Rogers.

Figure 4-2 presents a multidimensional plot of the issue agreement
structure of the Reagan staff. C stands for an Unalloyed Conservative,
D for a Domestic Conservative, A for an Altruistic Conservative, and

FIGURE 4-2
Issue Agreement Structure of Reagan White House Staff Members

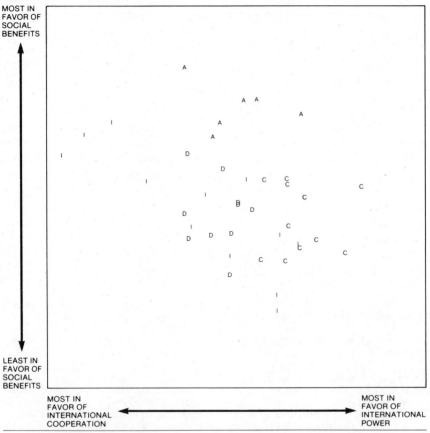

C = Unalloyed Conservative
D = Domestic Conservative
A = Altruistic Conservative
I = Isolate

I for an isolate who was not a member of any group. In this particular plot, the horizontal dimension represents preferences on international involvement. Positions to the left indicate a preference for policies based more on international cooperation; positions to the right a preference to base foreign policy more on an assertion of national power. The vertical dimension concerns social benefits. Higher locations on this dimension indicate a moderate posture on social welfare; lower positions an opposition to social benefit programs. The Unalloyed Conservatives, located to the lower right of this issue space, preferred to base international policies on American power, and were opposed to social programs. The Domestic Conservatives, located to the left of the Unalloyed Conservatives on the international dimension, were more disposed to cooperation in foreign policy, but were as opposed to domestic social programs as the Unalloyed Conservatives. The Altruistic Conservatives, located higher on the social dimension, thought that *a few* social programs were desirable. On international matters, the group tendency was about the same as that of the Domestic Conservatives, but individual members were spread over a wider range.

The preferences of the groups in each issue area—shown in Table 4-4—revealed slight variations on the essential conservatism of the Reagan White House. The central question was whether the govern-

TABLE 4-4
Positions of Reagan Issue Groups by Policy Area

Policy Area	Unalloyed Conservatives	Domestic Conservatives	Altruistic Conservatives
International involvement	Conservative (2.1)	Moderate (3.8)	Moderate (3.1)
Economic management	Conservative (1.6)	Conservative (1.6)	Conservative (1.9)
Social benefits	Conservative (1.6)	Conservative (2.1)	Conservative (2.3)
Civil liberties	Conservative (1.8)	Conservative (2.3)	Conservative (2.2)
Natural resources	Conservative (1.5)	Conservative (1.6)	Conservative (1.8)
Agriculture	Conservative (1.8)	Conservative (2.1)	Moderate Liberal (5.5)

Note: The figures in parentheses are median positions on scales that vary between 1 and 7. In general a high score (7) represents a dove position in international involvement, and a willingness to use government power and resources in the domestic policy areas. A low score (1) represents the opposite.

For the convention followed in giving substantive interpretation to these scores, see the explanation at the bottom of Table 4-2.

For further information, see Appendix A-4.3.

ment should engage in any new programs[12] at all. With the Unalloyed Conservatives, the only favored government activity was defense spending. Their posture was one of resolute opposition to any more government. The real difference between the Unalloyed Conservatives and the Domestic Conservatives came in international involvement. The Domestic Conservatives took moderate positions on foreign aid, and were more likely than either of the other groups to emphasize the need to try to get along with the Soviet Union. There were some very slight differences between the Unalloyed and Domestic Conservatives on domestic programs, but nothing substantial. The Altruistic Conservatives believed in the same underlying conservatism, but were significantly more likely to think aid programs should be continued. The strongest differences between them and the other two groups came on help to foreign countries and maintenance of farm income. The Altruistic Conservatives were also less likely to want to cut health and education programs.

IMPLICATIONS

The very different degrees of consensus on the Carter and Reagan staffs carry quite different implications for the formation of executive coalitions. Take the most liberal Carter group in each of the disputed policy areas. In economic management, the Social Liberals were very close to the Social Moderates, and would have found it easy to coalesce with them in favor of a middle-of-the-road economic policy. But the Thrifty Libertarians would have opposed them on spending questions as would a number of isolates. On social programs, the Social Liberals would have found it easy to coalesce with the Thrifty Libertarians, but this combination would have been opposed by Social Moderates and many isolates. On civil liberties matters, the Thrifty Libertarians were distinctly more liberal than the other two groups, and would have been opposed by both. We could look at other possible combinations, but the conclusion would remain the same. There was so much disarray in issue preferences that it would have been very difficult for any combination of issue groups to form a winning coalition in the Carter White House.

In the Reagan White House, on the other hand, the issue consensus was so high that it was *unnecessary* to bother with coalition formation. Virtually everyone belonged to the single large issue group (identified by the cluster program using normal parameters), and this controlled the general posture on policy.

---

[12] Coming to power after the New Deal, Fair Deal, and Great Society meant, of course, that the Reagan administration inherited a very substantial level of government activity. In most cases, their actions took the form of slowing the rate of program growth, or continuing programs at reduced levels of funding, not program elimination.

In any case, there are two factors in the White House that constrain coalition formation. One is the president himself. Pure coalition theory assumes that there is no dictator, that is, no single individual who can determine an outcome by his action alone (Luce & Raiffa, 1957, p. 338; Riker, 1962, p. 257; Hinckley, 1981, p. 77). In the White House, however, the president manifestly is a dictator in the sense that his decisions *do* determine outcomes. Therefore, in executive politics, the focus is necessarily more on the president, and on the relation of other actors to him, than on coalition formation as such.

The other consideration is the existence of an organizational matrix that channels the activities of the staff members. In the next sections of this chapter, we shall be describing communications structures and influence structures. We can speak of these as structures in the same sense that the issue preferences form a structure: that is, they can be measured at a point in time, and the resulting pattern can be described. But to understand the dynamic relation of the three structures to each other in a White House context, it would be better to think of *a flow of information*, and *a flow of influence,* both *within a well-defined organizational matrix.* The *advancement of issue preferences* by staff members is affected by the flow of information and influence within the organizational matrix.

There are at least three possible ties between the issue groups, the influence structure, and the organizational matrix that would link group activity to policy decisions. The first would be if all, or most, issue group members were concentrated in certain organizational units. If almost all of the members of Issue Group One were on the OMB staff, almost all the members of Issue Group Two were on the NSC staff, almost all the members of Issue Group Three were on the Domestic Policy staff, and so on, then the conditions would be present for a straight organizational fight. Policy preferences would be reinforced by organizational loyalties; each unit would make decisions they controlled in a manner satisfactory to themselves; the president would be forced to arbitrate continual interunit disputes. The second possibility would occur if almost all of the most *influential* staff members belonged to one issue group. The combined individual skills of the members would then allow that issue group to be dominant. The third logical possibility is that a single issue group is so extensive that there is "a White House point of view."

The third possibility—that there is an effective issue consensus throughout the staff—is the simplest. It clearly applies to the Reagan staff, but is clearly inapplicable to the Carter staff. The first possibility—concentration of issue group members in particular organizational units—does not apply to the Carter staff either. (If you look back at the assignments of the members of the three issue groups, you will find that the groups were spread across various units.) This leaves open the possibility that one issue group included almost all of the more influential members of the Carter staff. We can check that presently when we look at information about the distribution of influence, but first we need to take a look at the communication links that tie a White House staff together.

COMMUNICATION STRUCTURES

Communication is crucial to any organization, and especially so in the White House. If the presidency is to be responsive to the political environment in which it is situated, then the White House staff should be scanning that environment constantly to pick up cues from congress-men, bureaucrats, interest group leaders, and other relevant actors. If several organizational units—for example, the domestic staff, the legis-lative liaison staff, and OMB—are all concerned with a decision, there must be some means of consultation between them. If the decision is sufficiently important to go to the president, there must be a flow of information from staff units to the Oval Office. Once a decision has been made, it must be communicated to those within and without the White House who have to implement it. Consequently, knowing about the communications structure tells something about the decision-mak-ing pattern within the White House, and how the White House is linked to the larger political environment.

Information about the communication structures was picked up by asking White House aides: "Which persons do you spend the most time with getting your own work done?" Asking about communications in this way summons up some amalgam of the interpersonal contacts of each White House staff member. It therefore allows us to trace informal communications as well as those that flow through regular channels.

No job is "typical" on the White House staff. Everyone's responsibili-ties are to some degree unique, and each staff member's contacts there-fore give them a unique perspective. We can get something of the flavor of the differing jobs, and the communication possibilities that go with these jobs by looking at a few of the answers to the question, "Which persons do you spend the most time with getting your own work done?"

Claudia Townsend was an associate press secretary who was in charge of the downstairs press room in the Carter White House. In this job, she was dealing constantly with the press corps "regulars." To the question about those with whom she spent time, she replied simply: "Rex (Granum, a deputy press secretary), I guess, and the folks immediately out here who are always on the phone and who are always asking you questions all day long." When asked if there was anyone else on the White House staff, she continued: "No, not really. I deal with people as I need them, but most of what goes on here revolves around Jody (Powell) and the reporters who are right here. Other people I will call as I need to."

James Thomson was a member of the National Security Council staff in the Carter administration. A physics Ph.D., he spent most of his time dealing with defense concerns. He spoke at much greater length:

> I spend most of my time with Robert Blackwell who is the European guy here; I did until recently with Fritz Ermarth who was one of my colleagues in this cluster, that is, in the defense area; with Roger Molander who was also in this area; with Marshall Brennen who's got the Soviet desk here. In the State Department with David Doepper who's the deputy director of the Bureau of Political-Military Affairs; with his boss, Reginald Bartholomew who is the director, but to a much lesser extent; with Alan Holmes who is the deputy assistant secretary for European affairs. In the Defense Department with Robert Komer, the undersecretary for policy; with David Gifford, the undersecretary for I.S.A.; Walter Slocum, the deputy undersecretary for policy; Lynn Davis, the assistant deputy undersecretary for policy. Having gone through those people, I spend a lot of time working with their Office Directors: with Lou Bench, who directs the nuclear policy in the Pentagon; with Richard Derelick, who directs the MDFR Office in the Pentagon; with Charles Thomas, who directs regional political affairs in the State Department; with David Klinnert, who is an assistant deputy director of the Arms Control Agency; Lucas Fisher who is one of his office directors; Jim Timbe who is his deputy. I'm going to . . . I don't want to get too far down because I've got all the people who work under them. I'm a 20 to 30 phone call a day guy.

Joseph Wright came to the government with 15 years of management experience. From 1976 to 1981, he had been president of the credit card subsidiary of Citicorp. He had become deputy secretary of commerce at the beginning of the Reagan administration, and then moved to OMB as the deputy director in the early spring of 1982. Joe Wright explained his time use this way:

> Within OMB it would obviously be Dave Stockman, though I don't spend most of my time with Dave. We hit each other with half sentences, and then we both go and do our own thing, which is the way the director and the deputy director should work. They shouldn't spend a lot of time together because if that one box [the management unit consisting of director and deputy director] is going to really, truly expand its ability to handle decisions, it should not spend a lot of time in the same room. So I would say that maybe I spend only an hour a day with Dave Stockman, and that's broken up into 10 different pieces.
>
> I spend most of my time with our associate directors. The program associate directors are Bill Schneider, Annelise Anderson, Ken Clarkson,

and Fred Khedouri. The management is Hal Steinberg. The deregulation or regulatory compliance is Chris DeMuth. Then within the staff here, David Gerson handles all the administrative and project tracking systems. Larry Kudlow does the economics, and Don Moran does all the legislative and budget. These are the primary people I spend my time with.

Then I would say I spend most of my time with Ed Harper of the Office of Policy Development and/or his people, but more with him than his people. Dick Darman and Craig Fuller. Of the Big Four over there right now, I spend most of my time with Ed Meese. Then, as needed, with Fred Fielding, the counsel, and David Gergen and Larry Speakes. And quite a bit of time with Ken Duberstein and Bobby Thompson on the legislative. That's it.

Three and a half years after his graduation from law school, David Rubenstein had become deputy to Stuart Eizenstat, the head of Carter's Domestic Policy Staff. He said: "I spend the most time with Stu and Bert Carp, Stuart's other deputy, and then the relevant members of our own staff. Frank Moore's staff. Anne Wexler's staff. Jody Powell and his staff people. For the last year or so, a lot of the political people who have been involved in the campaign."

Michael Deaver had been close to Reagan since the 1960s, when Reagan was Governor of California. His formal White House title was deputy chief of staff, but he handled the President's personal and travel arrangements, and functioned less formally as friend, troubleshooter, and guardian of the President's time. He said that the people he spent the most time with were:

Baker. Clark. My own personal staff, which is Sittman and McManus and the two secretaries. The scheduling office. The President's own personal staff; I would say Dave Fisher there. The advance operation. The press office; I would say Gergen and Speakes. I would say Rosebush and Muffy Brandon in the First Lady's office. I would say Darman and Fuller in Baker's and Meese's operations, and Clark directly on the NSC.

These answers varied a good deal, as most of the answers did. The typical answer was probably closer in length to those given by Claudia Townsend or Mike Deaver than the unusually detailed responses of James Thomson or Joe Wright. (Thomson's and Wrights's answers are valuable because they are long enough to suggest a little of the work pattern of the National Security Council and the Office of Management and Budget.) But together these answers tell us something about communications within the White House staff.

To begin with, the examples move progressively closer to the president. Staff members who are closer to the president are involved in different patterns than those who are not. Those distant from the president are more apt to be handling a specialized assignment, and to be in contact with others with similar substantive concerns. Those close to the president are more apt to be generalists, and to be dealing with other senior staffers.

Second, notice the extent to which Claudia Townsend and James Thomson were dealing with "outsiders" rather than other members of the White House staff. Townsend said she spent her time with the reporters "who are always asking you questions all day long," and Thomson was in constant contact with officials in the State and Defense departments. These patterns are typical of those in "external" White House units. They are just as busy as other staff members, but they are relatively isolated from the internal communication network because they are so involved in providing links to other elements of the political environment.

Third, most of the internal communication takes place within one's own organizational unit. For instance, Joe Wright began by talking about his colleagues in the Office of Management and Budget. And Mike Deaver spoke about his immediate staff, and the advance office, the scheduling office, and the First Lady's office, all of which report to him.

Finally, most unit heads are so busy that they have assistants of their own, who attend meetings on their behalf and can be reached when their bosses are busy. David Rubenstein played this role for Stuart Eizenstat. And even Mike Deaver, who certainly got his phone calls returned, said that he dealt frequently with Richard Darman and Craig Fuller in Baker's and Meese's operations. These people, in effect, accumulate information, which they then review with their superiors when they are free. If they have any skills, being located at such critical junction points in the communication network makes them important. And as we shall presently see, Rubenstein, Darman, and Fuller were all very influential.

The full network of relationships between White House staff members can be analyzed by arraying the communication data in matrix form. A simple communication network is shown in Figure 4-3. The arrow diagram at the top of the figure (technically, a directed graph) shows the relationships between four persons, Ken, Linda, Mike, and Nan. A person at the foot of an arrow can send a message in one stage to the person at the head of that arrow. Thus, Ken can send a message to either Linda or Mike since he is linked to both. Similarly, Linda can send messages to either Mike or Nan. Mike, however, can send messages only to Nan, and Nan can send messages only to Ken.

The same information that is in the arrow diagram is presented in the one-stage communication matrix. Here, a cell entry of 1 indicates the presence of a communication channel, and a 0 indicates its absence. For example, since Ken can send messages to Linda and Mike in one

FIGURE 4-3
Simple Communication Network

Simple Communication Network

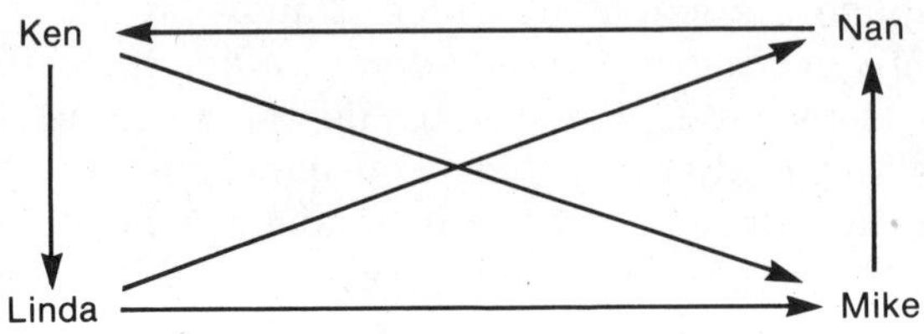

	Ken	Linda	Mike	Nan
Ken	0	1	1	0
Linda	0	0	1	1
Mike	0	0	0	1
Nan	1	0	0	0

One-Stage Communication Matrix

	Ken	Linda	Mike	Nan
Ken	0	0	1	2
Linda	1	0	0	1
Mike	1	0	0	0
Nan	0	1	1	0

Two-Stage Communication Matrix

stage, 1s appear in the Linda and Mike columns of Ken's row, and 0s appear in the other two cells in that row. The row sums therefore give the number of persons to whom a message can be sent in one stage, and the column sums give the number of messages that can be received. In this simple example, the arrow diagram and the matrix are alternate ways of presenting identical information. In a large communication network, however, one must use the matrix form because there would be so many arrows running between communication partners that a directed graph would be too dense to read.

So far we have been talking about one-stage communication. Two-stage communication takes place if, for example, Mike tells Nan something in one stage, and Nan then passes the message along to Ken in a second-stage. Note that this *assumes* that whatever a communication partner is told will be passed along to another communication partner. An important advantage of the matrix presentation is that one can determine a two-stage communication matrix by taking the square of

TABLE 4-5
Second-Stage Carter Communication Matrix Reduced

Staff Unit Sending Messages	Staff Unit Receiving Messages						
	NSC	Econo- mists	Domes- tic	Press	Legis- lative	Unit Heads	Total
NSC	1.00	.44	1.45	0	.67	.60	4.16
Economists	1.56	8.60	10.50	.89	7.25	3.09	31.89
Domestic	1.33	3.50	10.86	2.54	7.20	2.92	28.35
Press	1.00	.89	3.63	4.25	2.00	1.00	12.77
Legislative	.57	0	3.80	1.71	5.33	2.22	13.63
Unit heads	1.00	1.45	6.62	3.80	5.33	6.50	24.70
Total	6.46	14.88	36.86	13.19	27.78	16.33	115.5

a one-stage communication matrix.[13] A two-stage matrix appears at the bottom of Figure 4-3. The meaning of the cell entries is the same, except that they may now be higher than one because more than one two-stage path may exist between communication partners. The "0 0 1 2" entries in Ken's row mean that there is no path through which he can communicate with himself (i.e. feedback) in two stages, no path through which he can communicate with Linda in two stages, one path (through Linda) that allows two-stage communication with Mike, and two paths (one through Linda and one through Mike) that allow two-stage communication with Nan. The reader can confirm that the square of the one-stage matrix does give the two-stage possibilities by comparing the entries in the other rows with the arrow diagram at the top of Figure 4-3.

Table 4-5 presents a *second*-stage communication network for the Carter White House.[14] Since the most important things about White House staff communication relate to organizational units, the matrix has been reduced so the cell entries represent the number of messages being sent within or between units. Take, for example, the entries in the "Economists" row. The first number, 1.56, represents the relative number of messages sent (in two stages) from the economists to the NSC staff; the second cell entry, 8.60, reflects the volume of communication among the economists themselves; the third, 10.50, the volume of communications from the economists to the Domestic Policy Staff. Thus

---

[13] Similarly, one can determine a three-stage communication matrix by taking the cube of the one-stage matrix, a four-stage matrix by raising it to the fourth power, and so on.

[14] By looking at the second-stage network, we do not lose much information from the first-stage network, and we see some things that are not obvious in the first-stage network.

we know that there are many more messages being exchanged among the economists than sent by them to the NSC staff, but that a few more are going to the domestic staff than are being exchanged among the economists. (Further information about these communication matrices may be found in Appendix A-4.5.)

The matrix tells us several things about the communication structure in the Carter White House. First of all, there was a rough division between units that were part of a common internal communication network, and those whose attention was focused elsewhere. The units that made up the internal network were concerned with the development and passage of domestic legislation: the economists, the Domestic Policy Staff, the Office of Congressional Liaison, and the heads of other relevant units. The two units involved in external networks were the National Security Council staff and the press office. The differences between these two communication networks echo the different work patterns of David Rubenstein (who was involved in the internal network), and James Thomson and Claudia Townsend (whose time was spent with foreign policy specialists and journalists, respectively).

Once we pass this gross division, there is a very clear ordering to the intensity of communications between the units. In every case save one, the greatest frequency of contact was with the Domestic Policy Staff. This is reflected in the large entries in the Domestic column in Table 4-5. The next greatest concentration of communication was within each unit. (There was a difference here between first-stage and second-stage communication. In first-stage communication, the largest volume of communication was within organizational units.) The third target of messages was the legislative liaison staff. Thereafter the pattern becomes less clear until we reach the National Security Council staff which was the most isolated.

Table 4-6 presents a second-stage communication matrix for units

TABLE 4-6
Second-Stage Reagan Communication Matrix, Reduced

Staff Unit Sending Messages	Staff Unit Receiving Messages							
	NSC	Econo-mists	OPD	Coordi-nators	Press	Legis-lative	Unit Heads	Total
NSC	1.25	1.33	2.00	4.50	2.00	2.57	1.11	14.76
Economists	0	6.00	4.33	10.75	2.86	2.29	2.22	28.45
OPD	1.00	8.67	9.75	14.00	4.55	3.36	3.69	45.30
Coordinators	0	2.00	2.50	13.50	3.71	3.14	2.22	27.07
Press	0	.57	1.27	8.57	3.67	1.67	1.50	17.25
Legislative	0	2.00	3.09	6.29	.67	1.33	1.25	14.63
Unit heads	.22	3.78	4.00	14.22	3.50	4.00	2.40	32.12
Total	2.47	24.35	26.94	71.83	20.96	18.64	14.39	179.58

on the Reagan White House staff.[15] Comparison of the Carter and Reagan networks shows important differences and, once these are taken into account, an overall similarity. The most important difference was that there simply was more communication in the Reagan White House, more than half again as much. This can be seen by comparing the grand sums which appear in the lower right hand corners of the two tables. The number for the Reagan White House was 179.58; the comparable total for the Carter White House was only 115.5. The principal reason for the greater number of communication links in the Reagan White House was the existence of central coordinators—Jim Baker, Ed Meese, Mike Deaver, Dick Darman, and Craig Fuller—who did not have counterparts in the Carter White House.[16] Messages in the Reagan White House were going upward from lower-ranking staffers to the coordinators. When one looks at the individual data summarized in Table 4-6, it becomes very clear how much of the communication was flowing to the coordinators and the unit directors. The three highest column totals (that is, number of messages received) were: Ed Meese, 95; Craig Fuller, 86; and Jim Baker, 79. Mike Deaver's total was 55. Of the 10 highest scores, 8 belonged to assistants to the President, and 2 (the 8th and 9th) to deputy assistants to the President. The communication structure in the Reagan White House was centralized and hierarchical.

Another important difference involved the legislative liaison staffs. The Carter legislative staff received the second largest number of messages, ranking behind only the domestic policy staff. This was not true in the Reagan communication structure. There were probably two reasons for this. One was that Ken Duberstein could manage affairs within the White House far more capably than Frank Moore. The other was the existence of a very important Reagan staff unit called the Legislative Strategy Group. This was chaired by Jim Baker, and its agendas were drawn up by Dick Darman. Its members included Ed Meese, Mike Deaver, Craig Fuller, and Ken Duberstein (with others invited depending on the subject matter). Its meetings were very brief, and were focused on making legislative strategy decisions on a limited number of topics. With such a mechanism for making decisions, the legislative liaison staff was free to spend its time making contacts

---

[15] Most of the units are organizational entities, but three need a bit of clarification. The coordinators are four top staff members: James Baker, Ed Meese, Mike Deaver, and Craig Fuller. Press does not include anyone in the press secretary's office, but refers to David Gergen, speechwriter Aram Bakshian, and Karna Small, whose responsibilities include handling the out-of-town press. The Unit Heads are not a unit at all, but instances where I interviewed only a single person (in all but one case, the person in charge) from a unit. This was also the case with Unit Heads in the Carter analysis.

[16] Chief of Staff Jack Watson and Staff Secretary Rick Hutcheson had similar responsibilities, but were far less prominent than Baker, Meese, Deaver, Darman, and Fuller in the Reagan White House.

on Capitol Hill. In the absence of such a group in the Carter White
House, the legislative staff was drawn much more deeply into negotiations on the content of the Carter legislative program.

In the two communication structures, there are also some less consequential differences that seem to reflect variations in the standings
of units on the Carter and Reagan staffs. For example, economists
(principally OMB) received more messages in the Reagan White House,
where budget considerations were more important. But otherwise, the
two communication structures show a lot of similarity. The Domestic
Policy Staff was centrally located in the Carter network. The Office
of Policy Development, the comparable staff in the Reagan White
House, was centrally located in that network. In both White Houses,
the National Security Council staff appeared to be the most isolated.

To sum up, both the similarities and the differences in communication
structures appear to follow from organizational factors. The persons
located close to the centers of the communication networks are those
with coordinating responsibilities, or those whose work requires a lot
of clearance with units whose duties overlap their own. Those who
seem isolated in this White House perspective are busy providing liaison—especially the NSC staff, and to a lesser extent the press and
legislative staffs—with external sets of actors.

INFLUENCE STRUCTURES

It is difficult to conceive of politics without influence. Whether one
considers a presidential candidate seeking votes, a legislative leader
trying to build a coalition behind some proposed legislation, or a convention delegate trying to get support from enough states to bring a
minority report to the floor, all are engaged in influence attempts. So,
too, in all the interpersonal contacts in the White House. Whether
staff members have come to the White House from the campaign, or
after scholarly study of foreign policy, they need to be able to influence
others to build support for the policies that they favor.

Person A can influence Person B in four different ways. First of
all, B may *identify* with A because B respects A, because A is a leader
of one of B's reference groups, or because B has been associated with
A in some common endeavors. Second, B may recognize A as an *expert*
in some area in which B wishes guidance. This need not involve A's
having any formal credentials, or even accurate knowledge about the
subject. To be sure, expertise is more easily exercised by someone
with both credentials and knowledge (as an M.D. who influences us
to take some medicine), but all that is really necessary is that B believe
that A is expert in the relevant subject matter. Third, there are the
sanctions which A can bring to bear. These can be either negative

sanctions, as the traffic ticket the policeman gives to the speeder, or positive sanctions, such as the promotion or raise that a boss can give to a favored employee. Finally, A may exercise *legitimate* influence over B because A holds some formal position that gives him or her authority over B. This legitimacy may come from an election, because of the law (as in the legitimate power of a judge hearing a case), or because A has been appointed to a position supervising B by someone having a right to do so.[17]

Data are available about White House staff members who were respected, were thought to be expert, were believed to be able to exercise the sanction of effective opposition, and who were in positions of legitimate authority over others. The resulting influence relationships have been analyzed through dominance matrices. Some details of these procedures are given in Appendix A-4.6, but the procedure is exactly analogous to the communication matrices discussed in the preceding section. The only differences are that we are considering influence relationships (as B respects A) rather than a communication link (B can receive a message from A), and since there are multiple bases of influence that can be exercised at the same time, the cell entries in a dominance matrix can take on values higher than one. Otherwise, the two types of matrices are analyzed in exactly the same way. Analyzing influence in this way allows us to answer two types of questions: How do the four bases of influence combine? And who is exercising how much influence?

It turned out that there was a "standard" pattern of influence. The modal pattern was for roughly half of the references about another staff member to concern respect, about 3 out of 10 to deal with sanctions, and about a fifth to be about expertise.[18] The comments about Carter aides Stuart Eizenstat, Jody Powell, and Lloyd Cutler all fell into this "typical" pattern. This was also the nature of comments made about top Reagan aides Jim Baker and Ed Meese. It was as though a measure of respect went along with positions of legitimate authority—unless the individuals managed to lose that respect through their own actions.

---

[17] Obviously, influence has been conceptualized in many different ways. In this instance, the analysis focuses on four *bases* of influence. Choosing these four bases of influence for analysis follows Simon, Smithburg and Thompson (1950), and Cartwright (1965). Simon and others speak of the authority of identification, the authority of confidence, the authority of sanctions, and the authority of legitimacy (pp. 188–201). Cartwright speaks of referent power, expert power, reward power, coercive power, and legitimate power (pp. 28–31). There is some difference in their discussions, but the only difference in their categories is that Cartwright distinguishes between reward power and coercive power whereas Simon and others consider these to be positive and negative sanctions.

[18] Legitimacy is not included here because the extent of legitimate influence exercised by a staff member depends on the number of other staff members they supervise. Since the present estimates are analyzed through dominance matrices, the extent of a person's legitimate influence depends on how many subordinates I interviewed.

A reputation for an ability to block proposed actions or for expertise, especially the latter, depended more on the individual.

The second way to gain influence was for a person to know what they were talking about.[19] This was the case with Charles Schultze and David Rubenstein on the Carter staff. Another economist said of Schultze, "With Charlie, the professional expertise is always decisive." Stuart Eizenstat said simply, "I think Charlie Schultze is the most informed man in the White House." David Rubenstein was looked to, especially by other junior staff members, as a source of general information. One aide said, "He always seems to have a wealth of knowledge about what's happening in the White House decision-making process, even down to the latest gossip about the White House staff. Rubenstein is always well informed. He and I talk a lot." Another staffer added, "David I rely on because he knows everthing about everything, and that's what I need. I don't want to make a whole bunch of individual phone calls."

Influence on the Reagan staff stayed closer to the standard model. None of the reputations of Reagan staff members rested as much on a single base of power as did those of several Carter aides. But within the Reagan White House, David Stockman, Richard Darman, and Ken Duberstein were regarded as being the best informed. Ed Harper, for example, said, "There's no question that David Stockman has a tremendous amount of expertise in a wide variety of areas. His stock-in-trade more than anybody else is substantive expertise." Speaking of Dick Darman, Mike Deaver said, "He's the brightest member of the White House staff, and works at keeping himself fully informed, sometimes to other people's chagrin." And Dave Gergen singled out Darman as one who was "enormously respected for his intelligence and shrewdness."

The third pattern of influence rested largely on respect. All but one of the persons who mentioned Carter Public Liaison head Anne Wexler said she was respected. As Wexler herself commented, "Those who have been together since before Carter was governor certainly have a different relationship than those of us who are latecomers to the Carter inner circle." She might have added that persons who merit respect have a way of building relationships. Over 70 percent of the references to Carter Chief of Staff Jack Watson said he was respected. On the Reagan staff, Dave Gergen drew the highest proportion of comments—over 60 percent—saying he was respected.

The final pattern of influence was unique to Hamilton Jordan. His reputation in the White House seemed to be different than it was with members of the Carter campaign staff, where his authority was unques-

---

[19] The "standard" model and the expertise model were the two patterns of influence that existed on the Nixon Domestic Council staff.

tioned. Over half of the comments about Jordan made reference to sanctions. No one else's influence in either the Carter or Reagan White House rested so much on his ability to stop things. Other senior staff members believed that Jordan was highly regarded by President Carter himself. They may have felt that he could convince the President, perhaps the ultimate sanction in staff politics. Some echo of this showed up on the Reagan staff. Of the comments about Baker, Meese, Deaver, and Clark, three eighths concerned sanctions as compared to only a fifth of the comments about other influential staff members. As already noted, leaders of the Reagan staff were more likely to employ several bases of influence. Even so, the opposition of those known to be close to the President gave greater cause for concern than opposition coming from a more typical staff member.

Table 4-7 presents findings on the total amount of power exercised by the most influential Carter staff members. The first-stage influence scores are the total number of times a person has been mentioned as being respected, expert, able to exercise sanctions, or in a position of legitimate authority over other staff members. These scores represent the total number of first-stage influence opportunities open to the individual.

Second-stage influence stands to first-stage influence exactly as second-stage communication stands to first-stage communication. A second-stage influence relationship is simply one in which A can influence B in one stage, B can influence C in one stage, and A can therefore influence C in two stages. The bases of influence may differ in the two stages. B may consider A to be an expert, and C may respect B. It is not necessary for C to have any contact with A; if A can work through B to influence C, that is sufficient. A nice description of second-stage influence was given by a member of the Carter Domestic Policy

TABLE 4-7
First- and Second-Stage Influence,
Carter Staff

	First-Stage Influence Score	Second-Stage Influence Score
Eizenstat	49	343
Powell	43	251
Jordan	16 (est.)	207 (est.)
Watson	18	162
Wexler	13	138
Brzezinski	23	136
Schultze	11	102
Cutler	13	93
McIntyre	11	90

Staff. In this instance the third person influenced was the President
of the United States.

> There's an important thing about working on this staff. You had a great
> deal of effective discretion if you were someone that Stuart trusted and
> you understood the way his mind worked, because he understood the
> way the President's mind worked and everyone out there knew that.
> Basically a person in my position (for reasons having nothing to do with
> a personal relation with the President, because I didn't have one) was
> in a position of being 90 percent likely to be able to convince the President.

The second-stage influence scores in Table 4-7 correspond to the number of opportunities Carter staff members had to influence other staff
members in two stages.

Whether measured by first-stage or second-stage influence scores,
Stuart Eizenstat and Jody Powell were by far the most influential members of the Carter staff. Eizenstat served as the link between those
whose concerns were primarily substantive, and those whose concerns
were more political. He said that Theodore Sorenson, a ranking Kennedy adviser, had told him when he assumed the job "that if I perform
the way he performed his somewhat comparable role, the policy specialists would think I was a politician, and the politicians would think
I was a policy specialist." Eizenstat went on to say that prediction
was not too far off. Jody Powell was much more than press secretary.
Because of his long personal tie to the President, other staff members
saw him as the best person to approach the President with news the
President had real need to hear. After Eizenstat and Powell, influence
dropped off in steps, first to Hamilton Jordan,[20] next to Jack Watson,
then to Anne Wexler and Zbigniew Brzezinski, and then to Charles
Schultze, Lloyd Cutler, and James McIntyre. Watson, Wexler, Brzezinski, Schultze, Cutler, and McIntyre all were persons of influence in
the Carter White House, but their power did not match Eizenstat's
or Powell's.[21]

Table 4-8 presents the first- and second-stage influence scores for
the ranking members of the Reagan staff. Chief of Staff James Baker

---

[20] An estimate for Jordan's influence is included even though he was not interviewed.
This is based on statements others made about him. The same procedure was used to
make estimates (which will appear in later tables) for William Clark, Richard Darman,
David Stockman, and Frank Moore. In Jordan's case, it is important to remember that
he had left the Carter White House staff to run the 1980 reelection campaign some six
months before the interviews.

[21] This allows us to answer the question raised earlier about the possibility that
the most influential staff members all belonged to one issue group. The Social Moderates
had some advantage because Powell, Watson, Brzezinski, and Schultze all belonged
to this issue group. The four most influential persons, however, belonged to three different
groups, and if one looks at the issue group membership of the next most influential
set of persons as well as those listed in Table 4-7, it appears that no one issue group
had a decisive advantage.

TABLE 4-8
First- and Second-Stage Influence,
Reagan Staff

	First-Stage Influence Score	Second-Stage Influence Score
Baker	54	292
Meese	39	291
Darman	28 (est.)	276 (est.)
Clark	31 (est.)	268 (est.)
Stockman	39 (est.)	262 (est.)
Fuller	14	254
Deaver	27	217
Harper	24	169
Williamson	5	140
Duberstein	14	125
Gergen	10	84

had the highest first-stage influence score of anyone on either the Carter or Reagan staffs. It is no exaggeration to say that he was highly regarded by virtually everyone on the Reagan White House staff. Counselor Edwin Meese did not have as high a first-stage influence score, but he and Baker had second-stage scores that should be regarded as identical.

One major difference between the Carter and Reagan influence structures is evident from the other second-stage influence scores in Table 4-8. Whereas Eizenstat, Powell and Jordan, were the only Carter staffers with scores over 200, there were seven Reagan aides with second-stage influence scores in that range: James Baker, Edwin Meese, Richard Darman, William Clark, David Stockman, Craig Fuller, and Michael Deaver. Moreover Edwin Harper, Richard Williamson, Kenneth Duberstein, and David Gergen also had substantial influence scores. At the upper levels of the Reagan staff, power was shared among a much larger number of people.

All of the persons listed in Tables 4-7 and 4-8 are senior staff members. What about other staff members? There were two important distinctions between the influence of senior staff members and that exercised by others. With but a few exceptions, the senior staff members had visible first-stage influence scores, and as Tables 4-7 and 4-8 indicate, this influence increased fairly substantially when second-stage influence was calculated. Lower-ranking aides did not begin with such high scores, and they did not always increase at the second-stage. On the Carter staff, the next highest first-stage scores were Bert Carp, deputy director of the Domestic Policy Staff, 8; David Aaron, deputy director of the NSC staff, 7; David Rubenstein, Stuart Eizenstat's deputy,

6; and Katherine (Kitty) Schirmer, associate OMB director for natural
resources, energy, and science, 6. But at the second-stage, some scores
went up, one remained the same, and some scores went down. The
second-stage scores for those just named were Carp, 5; Aaron, 16; Rubenstein, 44, and Schirmer, 3.[22] On the Reagan staff, the next highest
first-stage scores were Roger Porter, deputy OPD director, 10, and CEA
Chairman Murray Wiedenbaum, 5, and at the second-stage their scores
dropped to 5 and 1, respectively.

The reason for this difference between the senior staff and others
was that the extent of second-stage influence depends on *who* you
have your first-stage relationships with. If the persons who respect
you (or regard you as expert, or whatever) at the first-stage are influential themselves, that will produce second-stage influence. If the persons
with whom you have first-stage ties are not influential themselves,
then the influence comes to a dead end. This was exactly what was
happening with the senior staff and the subordinates. The senior staff
members tended to influence other senior staff members. Consequently
their influence was multiplied at the second-stage. Junior aides, on
the other hand, tended to influence other junior aides with the result
that they had little second-stage influence.

The second principal difference in influence structure between the
Carter and Reagan staffs also related to lower-ranking aides. A larger
number of junior Reagan aides were without any influence. On the
Carter staff, only 31 percent (of the staff members interviewed) were
without any first-stage influence, and that number increased to only
38 percent when second-stage influence was calculated. On the Reagan
staff, however, the uninfluential portion began at 52 percent for first-
stage influence, and rose to 59 percent for second-stage influence. With
more influential senior staff members but fewer influential junior aides,
the Reagan White House was in the position of having more battalion
commanders but fewer lieutenants.

THE ORGANIZATIONAL MATRIX

The alert reader will have noticed that many of the influential staff
members in the Carter and Reagan administrations held the same jobs.
Indeed, NSC directors Zbigniew Brzezinski and William Clark, domestic advisers Stuart Eizenstat and Edwin Harper, OMB directors James
McIntyre and David Stockman, and others in comparable leadership
positions did show up in Tables 4-7 and 4-8. This even extends to
the deputy assistant level. Bert Carp, David Rubenstein, and Roger

---

[22] Aside from Ruberstein and those named in Tables 4-7 and 4-8, the only persons
on either staff with second-stage scores higher than 20 were Carter Senate liaison Dan
Tate, 41, and Reagan Counsel Fred Fielding, 59.

Porter, deputy directors of the Domestic Policy Staff (and the corresponding Office of Policy Development), had relatively high influence scores. This raises the possibility that we haven't been measuring the individual attributes of respect or expertise at all, but only picking up the legitimacy and the opposition potential that comes from holding a senior post.

In order to assess the importance of the organizational units, each staff member was asked to judge the importance of a hypothetical recommendation received, knowing only that the recommendation came from a particular source, such as the Office of Management and Budget or the Office of Public Liaison. The answers to these questions have been used to compute organizational importance scores which appear in Table 4-9. Details on the calculation of these scores can be found in Appendix A-4.7, but the essential point is that a higher score means that the unit is more important, while a lower score means that the unit is less important.

It is evident that some organizational entities are much more consequential than others. The National Security Council staff, for example, is much more important than the Office of Public Liaison. After we learn a bit more about these units in the next chapter, we'll want to ask why these differences between units exist. For the moment, however, our concern is with the remarkable stability in organizational reputations across the two administrations. There are differences, the most visible of which is the greater importance of OMB in the Reagan White House. Reasons for this are not hard to find. The major domestic initiative of the administration was President Reagan's drive to cut domestic spending. Since budget questions dominated the Reagan administration, the greater importance of OMB is hardly surprising. But none of the differences between the Carter and Reagan staff units are significant. The measures of importance of four of the seven units are virtually identical—in spite of apparent differences in the skills of the

TABLE 4-9
Organizational Continuity on Two
White House Staffs

Organizational Unit	Carter Organizational Importance Score	Reagan Organizational Importance Score
NSC	52.2	54.9
Legislative	47.7	47.1
Domestic/OPD	46.0	36.6
OMB	42.3	55.3
CEA	34.5	26.1
Press	29.9	25.8
Public liaison	18.2	14.3

TABLE 4-10
Individual Differences on Two White House Staffs

Carter Head	Second-Stage Influence Score	Reagan Head	Second-Stage Influence Score
Brzezinski	136	Clark	268 (est.)
Moore	15 (est.)	Duberstein	125
Eizenstat	343	Harper	169
McIntyre	90	Stockman	262 (est.)
Schultze	102	Weidenbaum	1
Powell	251	Gergen	84
Wexler	138	Dole	0

staffs. And the only difference in the order of importance is that OMB moves from an effective tie for second to first. Otherwise, the ranking of importance is the same. All in all, there is very little change between the two administrations.

When the influence scores of the heads of these units are compared, as in Table 4-10, very considerable differences emerge between the Carter and Reagan staffs. William Clark and David Stockman were much more influential in the Reagan White House than Zbigniew Brzezinski and James McIntyre had been in the Carter White House. Stuart Eizenstat and Jody Powell were much more powerful figures in the Carter White House than Ed Harper and Dave Gergen in the Reagan White House. But the influence scores of the unit heads are not just free-floating in comparison with the relatively fixed measures of organizational importance. The importance of the organizational unit seems to establish an expected level for personal influence.[23] Take the mean influence scores of the heads of more-consequential and less-consequential units. The average influence score for the NSC and Domestic/OPD heads is 229. The average influence score for the press and Public Liaison heads is 118.[24] If one occupies one of the important staff positions, a measure of influence goes with it unless that is sacrificed through manifest incapacity. This seems to have happened with Frank Moore. On the other hand, if one is appointed to head a less-important unit, then some personal attribute is needed to transcend the relatively

---

[23] Looked at from the other direction, the personal reputation of the unit head seems to be making a slight contribution to organizational importance.

[24] The difference between the influence scores of the heads of consequential and inconsequential units would have been greater if the influence score of Larry Speakes, the head of the press secretary's office, had been used rather than communications head Dave Gergen. Speakes was not mentioned by anyone in the Reagan White House as influential, and so would have first- and second-stage influence scores of zero. This would have reduced the mean influence score of press secretaries and Public Liaison heads from 118 to 97.

weak organizational base. Jody Powell had a long-standing personal tie to President Carter, and was well regarded himself. Anne Wexler and Dave Gergen became influential, in both cases because of the respect in which they were held by colleagues. Elizabeth Dole apparently did not have such a special personal ability and, as the head of a less-important unit, was a nonperson on the Reagan White House staff. The organizational matrix sets the bounds within which the influence structure varies.

The constraining effect of the organizational matrix leads to a more general point. In this chapter, we have looked at issue structures, communication structures, and influence structures in the Carter and Reagan White Houses. Which changed the most between the two administrations, and which were the most stable? There seems to be a fairly clear ordering. The issue structures were the least stable, then the influence structures, and the communications structures were the most stable. The issue tendency of the Carter staff in most policy areas was moderate liberal, while that of the Reagan staff was conservative. There was an even wider difference on the extent of agreement. When normal parameters were employed with the cluster program, not a single pair of persons on the Carter staff had a high enough rate of agreement to begin forming an issue group. On the Reagan staff, a single issue group was formed that included over 80 percent of the staff members. There were differences between the two influence structures. As compared to the Carter influence structure, the Reagan influence structure was skewed in the direction of senior staff members, but there were also more senior members with high influence scores. The principal difference between the two communication structures was the greater volume of communications on the Reagan staff, which in turn was largely caused by the presence of a group of coordinators who were receiving messages from various units. Otherwise the communication structures were very similar.

It appears that the greater the personal component, the more variation from one administration to another. The greater the organizational component, the more stability. The issue structure is aggregated entirely from individual policy preferences. Organization makes some contribution to differences in influence since high-ranking aides are more likely to have high influence scores. Yet there is still a large personal component evident in the different scores of Carter and Reagan appointees in the same positions. There is a small personal element in communication structure, but both the similarities and differences between the Carter and Reagan administrations can be explained largely on the basis of organizational factors.

It is relatively obvious why the personal component should shift from one administration to another. Jimmy Carter appointed different people than were in the Ford White House. Ronald Reagan appointed different people from those in the Carter White House. And Reagan's successor will bring in yet another team. We should therefore expect to find change wherever it reflects individual attributes. But why should organizational factors change so slowly? This will be one focus of the next chapter, but the short answer is that the organization exists to provide links to the external political environment. As long as Congress, the bureaucracy, foreign countries, the American economy, and other groupings and entities with which the president must deal change rather slowly, the organizational linkage is going to change slowly. Every American president must do certain jobs, and in the next chapter, we will see how the institutionalized presidency helps him get them done.

Summary

In the late 20th century, the activists in executive politics tend to have advanced educations, to have moved among law, government, consulting, universities, politics, or public relations; and to have been selected because of prior experience and/or because they have contacts with persons close to the president-elect. They are likely to agree with their fellow appointees about public policy. There are obviously changes in the resulting issue preferences from one administration to the next, and (less obviously but perhaps more importantly) changes in the extent of this issue agreement. The communication in which the staff engages depends on their assignments. If their organizational unit is outward looking, they may spend full time providing liaison, but be relatively isolated from the rest of the White House. If they are concerned with policy development, or have a coordinating role, they may spend almost all their time in touch with other White House aides. The influence that individual staff members are able to exert is a function of personal attributes, the organizational unit to which they are assigned, and their seniority.

It is important to remember that these conclusions rest principally on two administrations. There are a number of possible structures that have not been observed. For example, we have not seen a White House with a liberal issue structure. We have not seen a staff in which one group of aides took a relatively liberal position across the whole set of policy areas, and another group took relatively conservative positions on the same issues. We have not seen a White House organized so that everything flowed to the president through a single chief of staff. So it is entirely possible that future research will revise our understanding. But it does appear that the structures that are aggregated from individual properties will continue to vary from administration to administration, while the organizational matrix will change rather slowly.

CHAPTER 5

EXTERNAL STRUCTURES OF THE WHITE HOUSE

What must a president do? What tasks must be accomplished in his name? These are complex questions, but the beginning of an answer comes with the realization that the White House is located in the middle of a political environment. Other political actors and institutions constrain a president. They arrest his attention by their actions, and shape the opportunities that are available to him. The president and his aides, in turn, initiate actions that will have an impact on their political milieu, while responding to the actions taken by others. There is a structure to these "outward-looking" actions. This structure can be understood in a number of ways, but one useful approach is to think of certain *policy areas* in which the president must be engaged, and certain *essential audiences* whose attention and support must be maintained.

THE POLICY AREAS

The principal policy actions of the modern presidency can be defined in terms of six policy areas. Each of these has a substantive content that gives it a name, but each is more than such familiar rubrics as "the politics of education" or "the politics of coal." Each of these policy areas contains a cluster of related policies rather than a single subject. Moreover, each policy area is further defined by characteristic behaviors, and by temporal patterns. They are not completely stable, and as with most behavioral phenomena, they represent tendencies rather than certainties. But these half-dozen policy areas can be seen in the presidencies since World War II, and they constitute an important part of the external structure of executive politics.[1]

International Involvement

The most important issue area is international involvement. More than any other area, the major activity here takes place within the executive branch. Many agencies take part in the traditional diplomacy of negotiation, and the newer diplomacy of foreign aid, arms sales, information exchange, and presidential travel. The armed forces provide strength for negotiating positions and, if all else fails, military power which can be committed to battle.

International involvement is an imperative policy area, one to which a president must respond. The degree of American involvement in world affairs can be seen in the speed with which foreign events crowd in on new presidents. President Ford had barely said "our long national nightmare is over" before he had to deal with a serious clash between Greece and Turkey over Cyprus. In his first news conference, President Carter called for a complete halt to all nuclear testing, and predicted speedy ratification of an arms limitation agreement which the Russians promptly rejected. President Reagan conferred with Chancellor Schmidt of Germany and Mexican President Lopez Portillo before even taking office, and his first official foreign visitor—Prime Minister Edward Seaga of Jamaica—symbolized concern with developments in the Caribbean area. This policy area tends to become more prominent in the second year than the first, and more so in the third year than the second, receding from presidential attention only when reelection concerns become paramount in the fourth year. If there is a second term, then international involvement is even more important in the second term than the first. This pattern suggests international responsibilities are sufficiently compelling that a president is drawn to national security affairs, whether he comes to office with the long experience in foreign policy of a Dwight Eisenhower, or whether he is as inexperienced on the foreign scene as Jimmy Carter or Ronald Reagan.

The politics of international involvement are primarily symbolic. Heads of foreign governments visit Washington and the president takes trips abroad. Speeches are given in which the rhetoric is harsh or gentle. Ambassadors are called home "for consultation." The United States and a few other nations boycotted the 1980 Olympic Games in Moscow. The MX missile is called "the peacekeeper." Even during the Cold War era, positive symbolic references—"America stands for the best hopes of mankind."—were far more frequent than recourse to military activity. This reflects limits to American resources as well as an obvious

---

[1] The policy areas were originally discerned in an analysis of State of the Union Messages delivered by Presidents Truman, Eisenhower, Kennedy, and Johnson (Kessel, 1974). Their continued existence was shown in an analysis of President Nixon's 1973 State of the Union Message (Kessel, 1977), and President Carter's 1979 message.

desire to avoid war. When measured against other policy areas, expenditures on national security have been very high. But when measured against the range of our international commitments, American resources are finite indeed. Therefore the majority of our actions must be symbolic.

Economic Management

The other imperative policy area in which presidents must take action is economic management. This deals not only with the obvious elements of fiscal and monetary policy, but also with employment, labor relations, and such economic infrastructure matters as transportation. While purely economic concerns are part of the activity pattern, this policy area is better conceptualized as resource management in a very broad sense.

International involvement and economic management are referred to as imperative policy areas because this is the way that presidents talk about them. The word *must* is used far more frequently when presidents are dealing with international or economic topics than with any of the other policy areas. Presidents feel they have no choice about providing jobs, protecting investments, or ensuring revenue for the government. And as we will see in Chapter 15, these two policy areas have the greatest impact on voting choice. As a Nixon aide once put it with only slight overstatement, "If you don't do well in foreign policy and economics, success in other matters doesn't help. But if you are successful in these two areas, then it doesn't make any difference what else you do."

Governmental activity in this area follows economic cycles rather than the election calendar. If the economy is faltering, then the White House is going to be concerned about rising unemployment, and falling tax receipts. If there is a serious problem with inflation, then a president feels called upon to try to slow down a rapidly rising cost of living. Another stimulus to presidential action comes from conflict between rival economic groupings. If the rivals are deadlocked, each has a desire to bring government in on its side.

The politics of economic management *tend* to be regulatory.[2] Rules

---

[2] The verb is deliberately emphasized here. The types of politics that can be associated with a policy area are allocative, regulatory, and symbolic. (The inclusive term, allocative, was used for both distributive and redistributive policies because of the difficulty in distinguishing between these Lowi-Salisbury categories. Symbolic was added because of Edelman's work on the importance of symbolic politics. It turned out that symbolic referred to a class of political activities that difffered from allocative and regulatory politics.) Each policy area is to some degree allocative *and* regulatory *and* symbolic. For example, while the politics of international involvement are *primarily* symbolic, foreign aid programs are allocative, and export-import rules and passport requirements are regulatory. What is being said here is that when economic management is compared with other policy areas, there is a larger element of regulatory politics in economic management. (The evidence for this is that the factor loading for regulatory politics is higher than that of allocative politics or symbolic politics.)

are promulgated; parties are told they may and may not do certain things. This may suggest why presidents prefer to avoid this policy area unless they are forced into it. U.S. Steel did not like it when President Kennedy told them that they should not raise prices; funeral directors fought proposed Federal Trade Commission regulations on Capitol Hill, and labor unions are quite unhappy when presidents invoke the "90-day cooling-off period" provision of the Taft-Hartley Act. Since presidents, in common with other politicians, would rather make friends than generate opposition, they hesitate to engage in regulation. They will take action in this policy area, but before they do so, the economic perils and adverse political consequences of inaction must be clear enough to outweigh the political costs.

Social Benefits

The third policy area is social benefits. Whereas economic management deals broadly with resource management on a national scale, social benefits focuses on individuals. If the macroeconomic winds are adverse, then the benefits that are conferred on individuals (actually, classes of individuals) may shelter them to some degree from harmful economic circumstances. When the entitlements go to middle-class citizens, as do many social security benefits, they may come to regard them as a right that should not be restricted by further government action. Whether the beneficiaries are rich or poor, housing programs, educational subsidies, aid to dependent children, medical benefits, veterans hospitals, and other similar programs would all be included in this policy area. Often a single population grouping is the object of such a program. They make what the administration regards as a legitimate claim, and the president asks Congress for legislation to confer a benefit on them.

The dominant tendency in this policy area is allocation. This is a popular business. If presidents run the risk of losing friends through regulation, it is relatively easy for them to make friends by distributing benefits. These political rewards help to explain why the government has tended to multiply entitlement programs over time.

The temporal pattern of social benefits follows from its utility in building political support. It is just the opposite of international involvement. The distribution of social benefits is primarily a first-term phenomenon. Attention to social benefits rises gradually, then becomes the *most* important concern during a president's fourth year in office. If reelected, presidential concern with this form of allocative politics is apt to drop sharply. Presidents tend to distribute largess when they have the greatest need to increase their own political support.

In recent administrations, economic management and social benefits have been increasingly associated with one another rather than remain-

TABLE 5-1
Presidential Policy Areas

Policy Area	Type of Politics	Importance	Imperative
International involvement	Symbolic	Major	Yes
Economic management	Regulatory	Major	Yes
Social benefits	Allocative	Major	No
Civil liberties	Symbolic and regulatory	Minor	No
Natural resources	Regulatory	Minor	No
Agriculture	Allocative	Minor	No

ing as distinct policy areas. A good bit of macroeconomic policy is allocative. For example, the joint effect of the 1981 Reagan tax cut and spending cuts was to give an advantage to middle- and upper-income groups at the expense of lower-income groups. There are also important aspects of social benefits that are regulatory. Occupational safety and health regulations are an example of this. A second reason for the increasing association of economic management and social benefits is that there are many issue groups, such as the Unalloyed Conservatives in the Reagan White House or the Social Liberals in the Carter White House who exhibit the same ideological posture in both policy areas. Those who take conservative positions on economic management and liberal positions on social benefits (or the other way round), thus keeping the policy areas distinct, are less numerous. Since the politics tend to be different and the temporal patterns are different, there is some analytic convenience in treating these separately, but they often blend together in real-world politics.

Civil Liberties

In the 1950s and 1960s, the area of civil liberties was dominated by the historic struggle for civil rights. In the 1970s and 1980s, efforts for gender equality have become prominent. All the while, this policy area has included the great constitutional guarantees of individual liberty, free speech, and due process, as well as the rights of society summed up in the injunction that the government shall ensure domestic tranquillity. However strident calls for "law and order" sometimes seem, they have their origin in the ancient effort to extend the king's peace.

It might seem redundant to refer to the politics of civil liberties as the politics of justice, but the concept of equity is essential to understanding this policy area. The tendency has been to rely on symbols and regulation in about equal measure. Regulations in such controver-

sial areas as civil rights are more easily accepted if they are understood
as more general rights of citizens, or understood as privileges granted
to all persons under the Constitution. Appeals to fairness on behalf
of all people are more likely to be honored if they are backed by the
force of law. Either regulation without symbolism, or symbolism without
regulation, is apt to be insufficient, but both together give some hope
of dealing with these delicate issues. The temporal pattern in this policy
area has been very slight, but it can be detected. Presidents have been
most apt to move in this policy area just after their elections, presumably because of commitments made in the course of their campaigns.

Natural Resources and Agriculture

The last two policy areas—natural resources and agriculture—can
be thought of as special cases of policy areas already described. Natural
resources is closely related to economics. If one thinks of the latter
in the broad sense of resource management, the relation is quite clear.
The issues that have recently animated this policy area—recreation
areas, pollution control, and energy needs—certainly are related to
population growth. The material we reviewed in Chapter 1 about the
Carter administration efforts to pass energy legislation, or more recent
reaction to various proposals made by Interior Secretary James Watt,
give something of the flavor of the strong reactions to regulatory politics.
The temporal pattern, sporadic attention as a function of long-range
developments, also resembles economic management.

The final policy area, agriculture, is a special case of the distribution
of social benefits. The beneficiary groups have been farmers, specifically those producing any of the six "basics": wheat, corn, dairy products, cotton, tobacco, and peanuts. These have not been the only agriculture programs, but the producers of the basics have been cushioned
against adversity by subsidies for half a century. The dominant temporal pattern has been long range with agriculture receding in importance
as farmers have become less numerous. The farmers may be effectively
challenged one day, but for the moment, the politics of agriculture
are quite stable because of all the supports that farmers built into
the political system during their decades of political power.

Pervasiveness of the Policy Areas.   Since the government is in the
business of making policy, examples of policy areas summarized in
Table 5-1 can be found throughout the political system. In the last
chapter, we saw issue groups in the Carter and Reagan administrations
that had distinctive outlooks on the behavior that was appropriate in
the policy areas. We shall see this again in issue groups in the House
and Senate that shape the legislative coalitions that can be formed,
and in issue groups in the electoral parties that influence the policies
advocated during election campaigns. Finally, we shall see that voters'

attitudes about appropriate actions in these policy areas has been very important in determining their presidential choices.

For the moment, though, we want to concentrate on implications for executive politics. Since actions in these policy areas constitute such a vital part of presidential activities, organizational arrangements have emerged to channel them. Essentially, there are three clusters of these. The two imperative policy areas, international involvement and economic management, have structures of their own. All the rest get lumped together in what the White House calls domestic policy. We shall look at each of these in turn.

INTERNATIONAL INVOLVEMENT

There are, I. M. Destler tells us, three views of the National Security Council. First, it is a committee of senior officials, some designated by law, others stipulated by the president. Second, it is a process through which the recommendations of the foreign policy community (the State Department, the Defense Department, the CIA, and, somewhat less importantly, the aid and information agencies) are coordinated, and decisions about international involvement are made. Third, it "has provided the umbrella for the emergence of a presidential foreign policy staff. The first of these was how its founders mainly saw it; the last is what it has most importantly become" (1975, p. 6).

Characteristics of Foreign Policy Decisions

Whatever the views of the 80th Congress that passed the National Security Act of 1947, it can be argued that presidents needed help in this policy area because of the nature of foreign policy decisions. There are at least five characteristics of many foreign policy decisions: *uncertainty*, "*value-complexity*," *crisis*, *strong governmental departments*, and *limited power for implementation*. Policymaking is difficult in the presence of any of these circumstances. Since many of the choices in international involvement are marked by several of them, this policy area presents real challenges to any chief executive.

Alexander George (1980) has made a careful study of the psychological effects of uncertainty, value-complexity, and crisis.[3] To begin with uncertainty, important chunks of information are likely to be missing when a president makes major international decisions. If Harry Truman ordered forces across the 38th parallel during the Korean War, would

---

[3] This discussion relies heavily on Alexander George's (1980) analysis of psychological aspects of decision making. His book should also be consulted as an example of policy-relevant theory.

China enter the war on the North Korean side? (They did.) If John Kennedy placed a "quarantine" around Cuba to prevent Russian ships from bringing supplies for the missiles that were being installed, would the Soviet vessels challenge the blockade and begin World War III? (They didn't.) Would the Iranians seize the American embassy and hold U.S. diplomats hostage if Jimmy Carter admitted the Shah to the United States for medical treatment? (They did.) Each of these possibilities was speculated upon, but the presidents had to make their decisions without the answers in hand. The psychological responses to such uncertainty include procrastination, "bolstering" (that is, viewing the situation so as to make one option seem more attractive than others), incrementalism, accepting a consensus about what is likely to happen, and relying on supposed historical analogies. All of these lead to a decision, but carry with them a high risk of failure.

Value-complexity, as George defines it, *"refers to the presence of multiple, competing values and interests that are imbedded in a single issue"* (1980, p. 26). Do we restrict the number of Japanese cars imported into the United States to protect the jobs of American auto workers at a time when many of them are out of work anyway? Or do we admit as many as the Japanese can manufacture, because we believe in a free market, and want American workers to be able to buy less-expensive automobiles? Do we support the British in the Falklands War because England is a traditional ally, and most of the Falkland residents want the islands to remain British? Or do we support the Argentinians because the United States has many vital ties in Latin America? In theory, one could come up with a creative solution which serves all of the conflicting interests, or one can act on the basis of clear-eyed judgments that one set of interests is more important than another. But there is a danger that in giving attention to one interest, a president may just ignore the harm being done to other, equally important interests.

A widely accepted definition of a crisis (Hermann, 1969) is that it combines three features: a high threat to important national values, a limited time for response, and surprise. The majority of international decisions are not crisis choices. Who shall be sent to Paris as the American ambassador? How large an information program should be conducted in Brazil? Should we sell aircraft to South Korea? None of these decisions are made under crisis conditions, but many of the most important decisions are. The seizure of the *Mayaguez* by the Khmer Rouge during the Ford administration, the occupation of the American embassy by Iranian students in the Carter administration, and the invasion of Lebanon by Israel when President Reagan was attending an economic summit meeting at Versailles all precipitated crisis decisions. The resulting stress may lead to cognitive rigidity, impaired perception, failure to pay attention to longer-term consequences of decisions, and a tendency to blame political opponents rather than focusing on a constructive response.

Beyond the psychological problems engendered by uncertainty, value-complexity, and crisis, there is the organizational fact of life that the State Department and Defense Department have an unusual measure of independence. Robert McNamera demanded the ability to appoint his own subordinates as a condition of accepting the Defense Department portfolio. Defense Secretary Melvin Laird was said to have instructed his aides that if the White House called with instructions, they were to reply that if President Nixon wanted such and such done, then the President should tell the Secretary of Defense. And Caspar Weinberger has fought a successful battle for increases in the defense budget in the face of huge budget deficits. This is not to say that presidents are unable to overrule their secretaries of state and defense, but it is to say that persons with the stature to do these jobs often insist on considerable latitude, and that coordinating their activities therefore requires more than normal effort.

Finally, there are very real limits to American ability to influence events overseas. In late 1973, OPEC quadrupled the price of petroleum (from $1.77 to $7 a barrel), and in spite of actions of the Nixon, Ford, and Carter administrations, it had quadrupled again by the end of the decade. The United States has been quite unable to persuade Japan to open its markets to American foodstuffs, although the cost of food in Japan is quite high. The Reagan administration was very opposed to the participation of Western European nations in the building of a natural gas pipeline from the Soviet Union, but when economic sanctions were imposed, the European countries went right ahead. In fact, the sanctions proved such an embarrassment that Secretary of State Schultz had to devote some effort to getting them lifted. The United States is not without influence overseas, but success in foreign policy depends on securing the agreement of foreign governments, not on enforcing American will.

These five characteristics do not exhaust the complexity of this policy area, but they do suggest the difficulty of presidential choice. As a National Security Council staff member put it: "Given the complexity of the choices—that they are choices between evils, that the clock is ticking while the choices are being made, that we are dealing with 150 sovereign countries over whom we have no authority, at least 10 to 12 of which are major powers—one must have strong central authority." A president in a constitutional system with shared powers may or may not be a strong central authority, but at a minimum he needs help in dealing with foreign affairs. This has been the imperative behind the emergence of the National Security Council as a presidential staff.

The Roles of the National Security Advisor

Alexander George (1972; 1980, chap. 11) has described six roles that have been played by assistants to the president for national security affairs. While the national security advisor is the actor for whom the roles are specified, most of the roles require substantial staff support, and thus suggest the activities of the NSC staff as well. The first is *custodian*, in which the assistant is enjoined by the president *not* to become an advocate of any option himself, but to act as a guardian of the process. The custodian should balance actor resources, strengthen weaker advocates, bring in new advisors to argue for unpopular options, set up new channels of information so the president is not dependent on a single channel, arrange for independent evaluation of options when necessary, and otherwise protect the quality of information reaching the president. Robert Cutler, Eisenhower's national security assistant, said that Eisenhower instructed him not to become an advocate. Eisenhower took a number of steps to ensure adequate intelligence. He was briefed both by the national security assistant, and by the staff secretary, Andrew Goodpaster (later commander of NATO forces as a four-star general), who was in constant contact with the secretaries of state and defense. When these did not produce the information he wanted, Eisenhower would send off memoranda asking quite precise questions. One to the secretary of defense, for example, asked eight specific questions about whether the United States could supply IRBMs to Greece, such as "Do we in fact have a firm plan for stationing IRBMs in Greece?" and "What additional sums for defense support and economic assistance would be requested of the Congress as a result of any such action?" Eisenhower concluded: "I do not want this memorandum widely circulated or worked on by junior staffs. . . . These matters involve high policy and so I should like this paper handled by the fewest possible people" (Greenstein, 1982, p. 135).

A second role is that of *enforcer,* who sees to it that policy decisions are being complied with. Since this involves monitoring, it is essentially a staff responsibility. In the Eisenhower administration, this was done by the Operations Coordinating Board, a group parallel to the National Security Council. In more recent administrations, this responsibility has been taken over by the NSC staff. If instructions have been issued to a negotiator, then staff members know from the cable traffic that the instructions are being followed. At other times, NSC staffers must devote a good deal of effort to this.

When McGeorge Bundy became national security assistant in the Kennedy administration, he recruited a talented staff of his own. This was consistent with a custodian's responsibility to give the president independent evaluations, but Bundy became an active *advisor,* which was quite a different role. One contemporary account said that

> The impression in Washington is that Bundy, as much as anyone, helped conceive and promote the program of restrained attacks upon North Vietnam as a way of preventing the collapse of South Vietnam; that Bundy, perhaps more than anyone else, persuaded the President not to fuss and fume about DeGaulle and not to ram the so-called multilateral nuclear force down the throats of unwilling allies. (Frankel, 1965, p. 32)

When the national security assistant becomes an advocate, there is conflict with the neutral role of custodian.

Another role that was added in the Bundy period was *operator.* Bundy was adept at working within the bureaucracy, but he also began making inspection trips to Vietnam. This role also continued with future national security assistants: Henry Kissinger being sent to Beijing to make secret preparations for Nixon's trip the following year; Kissinger's shuttle diplomacy between Middle Eastern capitals; Zbigniew Brzezinski at the Afghan border. Members of the NSC staff may also be given operational responsibilities. For example, David Aaron, Zbigniew Brzezinski's deputy, spoke regarding his negotiation about the installation of missiles in Europe.

> After Chancellor Schmidt made a speech in 1977, we had a big debate inside the government, and we came to the conclusion that we should make an effort to fill this gap in Europe—but before making any commitments, that I should go over and talk with various people very privately to see if we were going to get the requisite support for it. Others agreed that it was important for me to do it, in part because of the uncertainties that came out of the neutron bomb episode, because someone who represented the president *would have more credibility than someone who is just from Defense or State.* And that is how I ended up not just coordinating the activity back here but also dealing with it directly in Europe with the principal political leaders there. (emphasis added)

A fifth role for the national security assistant is that of *spokesman.* In part, this role grows out of the national security assistant's substantive expertise, and his knowledge of current negotiations. He knows what can and what cannot be said, and can judge what language will best convey the proper degree of pleasure or displeasure. McGeorge Bundy began playing this role, though at first on a background basis. He became increasingly prominent in the Johnson administration, as was his successor, Walt Rostow. The national security assistant who made the most of this role was, of course, Henry Kissinger. While most members of the Nixon administration were uncomfortable with the press, Kissinger spent a great deal of time on the telephone talking to reporters. His most famous briefing was on October 26, 1972, when

he began, "Ladies and gentlemen, we have now heard from both Viet-
nams, and it is obvious that the war that has been raging for 10 years
is drawing to a conclusion."

The sixth role for the national security assistant is *political watchdog
for the president's power stakes.* This has been the most recent of
the roles to emerge, and is based on the proximity of the NSC staff
to the president as compared to other agencies of government. The
State Department's distinctive expertise is in events in foreign countries. Therefore it is not unusual for State to conclude that the situation
in a particular country makes it unpropitious to press for agreement
at that time. The NSC staff, on the other hand, is quite aware of the
president's political need for accomplishments before he runs for reelection, and is therefore more likely to push for an agreement regardless
of circumstances in the foreign country. President Carter sensed that
Zbigniew Brzezinski was valuable to him as a watchdog. "I need Zbig
to speak out publicly," Mr. Carter said. "He can go after my enemies.
He can protect my flanks" (Gelb, 1980, p. 26).

The Reagan Test of a Strong National Security Advisor

It would be much too neat to suggest that the six roles had emerged
one after the other, or that each national security assistant inherited
all of the power of his predecessor and added some more himself.
On the contrary, there has been considerable variation in the way
presidents have chosen to work their advisors, and the way in which
national security assistants have organized their own staffs.[4] Still, it
is accurate to say that there has been a gradual increase in the number
of roles played by the national security assistant; that there is a conflict
between the assistant's custodian role and his roles as adviser and
operator; that as the number of roles has increased, so has the danger
of role overload; and that national security assistants have become
more and more powerful.

Henry Kissinger became so powerful that he eclipsed Secretary of
State William Rogers, and Zbigniew Brzezinski was a rival of Secretaries Cyrus Vance and Edmund Muskie. Mr. Brzezinski defined his responsibilities as "coordinating and integrating the work of the State
Department, Defense, and Central Intelligence, and also giving the President an independent policy perspective, thereby influencing the policy
choices he would make." He said that the areas in which he had the
greatest impact "were China normalization and expansion of the rela-

---

[4] In fact, there has been so much variation that analyses of the NSC staff tend to
degenerate into accounts of the NSC under President A, the NSC under President B,
the NSC under President C, and so forth.

tionship with China; strategic modernization both in terms of programming and doctrine; and the development of the regional security parameter for the Persian Gulf." He was playing all of the roles except that of a neutral custodian.

The Reagan administration, in effect, tested the need for a strong national security adviser in their first year. They came into office aware of the problems arising from clashes between strong national security advisors and secretaries of state. Furthermore, President Reagan wanted to have cabinet government, following his administrative practice as governor of California. Therefore Richard V. Allen, his first national security assistant was given reduced responsibilities, and instructed to report through Counselor Edwin Meese rather than being given direct access to the President. The experiment did not work. In less than a year, Richard Allen was out and had been replaced by William Clark. Clark was no foreign policy expert, but as a longtime Reagan aide, he had all the access to the President he wanted. Quite beyond Richard Allen's personal difficulties, the Reagan White House discovered they needed a strong national security advisor. It seems unlikely that the Allen experiment will be repeated soon.

In due course, the Reagan NSC staff resumed many of their normal activities. (While Judge Clark—so addressed because Governor Reagan had appointed him to the California Supreme Court—lacked foreign policy experience, almost all the NSC staff members did have such experience, and a number had served in several administrations.) Two roles were deemphasized: spokesman and custodian. Judge Clark made occasional public appearances and granted a few interviews, but much preferred to work quietly inside the White House. And in contrast to previous staffs, the Clark NSC staff did not undertake independent studies implied by that aspect of the custodian role of giving the president alternative policy choices. They did combine issues as they came from the agencies, reframed them, and put them in different perspectives, but independent initiation was virtually nonexistent.

The roles of advisor, enforcer, watchdog, and operator were all apparent. NSC staff members paid close attention to option papers, the lifeblood of the system. They checked with their contacts in the agencies, and with staff colleagues who had similar responsibilities. If others concurred, and this was indicated by attached concurrences, then the paperwork flowed upward to Judge Clark. Clark acted as an advocate for the views of the foreign policy community within the White House. Once a decision was made (the Clark NSC used national security decision directives to record this), then it became the job of the staff member with responsibility in that area to make sure it was being implemented. Given his long association with Ronald Reagan, Bill Clark was certainly watching out for the President's power stakes. And when Robert McFarlane, Judge Clark's principal deputy on the NSC staff, was given operating responsibilties as President Reagan's special Middle Eastern envoy in July 1983, he kept his NSC post. This was consistent with the developing tradition of using NSC staff as operators, and McFarlane remained in line to succeed Clark when the latter became secretary of the interior.

ECONOMIC MANAGEMENT

The Major Players

Just to the east of the White House stands the Treasury Building. Immediately to the west is the Executive Office Building. Built in the latter half of the 19th century, this gray stone structure houses many presidential agencies, including the Office of Management and Budget, and the much smaller Council of Economic Advisors. Several blocks off to the southwest, there is the Federal Reserve Building. There are many other government agencies that make economic policies—the Commerce Department, the Labor Department, the independent regulatory agencies, and so forth—but these four are the agencies most continuously involved with economic management. The Treasury Department, the Office of Management and Budget, and the Council of Economic Advisors are subject to presidential direction. The Federal Reserve System is independent—and in this sense more remote from the presidential cluster of agencies—but it is one of the major actors in the economic arena.

The Treasury is responsible for the revenue side of fiscal policy. While OMB draws up the budget, the Treasury must estimate where the revenues are going to come from. This means not only tax collection through the Internal Revenue Service, but policy judgments about the proper level of taxation, and support of tax legislation that has been sent to Congress. The department is also responsible for debt management, which among other things means that the Treasury seeks to borrow money on the most favorable terms. (Interest on the debt is more than 10 percent of the total budget.) And the Treasury is concerned with international finance, which means they must worry about balance-of-payments problems. In addition to the institutional responsibilities, the secretary is one of the most senior officials in an administration. George Humphrey, John Connally, and Donald Regan, for example, were among the strongest members of their administrations.

The Office of Management and Budget does many things on behalf of the president, but its most important fiscal responsibility is the preparation of the budget itself. There is almost no time that some budget decision is not being made. As Carter OMB director James McIntyre explained it:

> The budget process establishes a pattern of responsibilities. The budget is presented to the Congress in January, and you testify in February

and March. The Congress has to act by March 15. The authorizing committees have to make their recommendations to the budget committees. The
budget committees deliberate and make their first cut at the Budget Resolution by May 15. Then the appropriation committees begin acting by
late May or early June and into July. Then we have a July update required
by law, so we present that to the Congress in July. Then we begin hearings
on our midsession update in preparation for the Second Budget Resolution
that has to be completed by September 15, with the new fiscal year
beginning October 1. In the meantime, in the spring, we are involved
with the spring budget review process. We usually conclude that by
early June. Letters are sent out to the agencies telling them what we
want to look at in preparation for the next fiscal year's budget. We get
those in around the first of September, and then we begin the fall budget
review process, which we conclude in the middle of December.

Donald Moran, executive associate OMB director in the Reagan administration, said that in "the first two years of this administration, the
budget process has become a framework handling around 90 percent
of the major policies that get made." The budget process has been
important in all recent administrations. It is so central to OMB that
in order to concentrate on it, the agency long resisted recommendations
that it assume other management functions (Berman, 1979).

While the major responsibilities for fiscal policy are split between
the Treasury (taxing) and OMB (spending), monetary policy is controlled by the Federal Reserve System. (President Kennedy kept track
of the "Fed's" responsibility for monetary policy by remembering that
the middle initial of William McChesney Martin, then Federal Reserve
chairman, was M.) Monetary policy refers to the amount of money in
circulation, and how much it costs to borrow money. The Fed has
three methods of controlling the amount of money available. It buys
and sells "paper" (that is, Treasury notes and the like); it stipulates
the amount of money banks must hold back as a reserve; and it changes
the discount rate, the interest it charges banks, which in turn affects the
rate at which banks will lend money. By loosening these restrictions,
the Federal Reserve System can make more money available. This
allows economic expansion, but at the risk of inflation. By tightening
these restrictions, the Fed can inhibit inflation by causing higher interest
rates. While the Federal Reserve and the agencies subject to direct
presidential control are independent of each other, they are mutually
dependent. The monetary policies of the Fed are less likely to be successful if they are thwarted by the fiscal policies of an administration.
In turn, the cost of borrowing determined by the Federal Reserve directly affects the Treasury's debt management problems and the interest that is part of the budget.

The Council of Economic Advisors, it has been said, has a *client*
(the president) whom it advises, as opposed to the specific responsibili-

ties of the Treasury, OMB, and the Federal Reserve. "The bread-and-butter function of the job," Reagan CEA chairman Murray Weidenbaum said, "is monitoring and forecasting the national economy and evaluating apparent recent and prospective developments in the economy." In addition to formal forecasts and reports, the CEA chairman is a principal source of economic information for the president. As Carter CEA chairman Charles Schultze explained it:

> Every time a new important statistic comes out—I've never counted, but let's say there are 10 a month—I usually get them the night before, and give the President an advance indication of what they are, almost always accompanied by some interpretations. In other words, a running commentary on the state of the economy goes from me to him. These do not normally have policy suggestions, but are fairly obviously policy oriented. And I meet with the President one on one about every two weeks for a general session without a fixed agenda.

Each of the four agencies thus has a piece of the action without any one being able to dominate. Moreover, different types of persons tend to head the agencies, and therefore different interests are represented. Secretaries of the treasury are likely to be prominent businessmen: Michael Blumenthal had been chief executive of Bendix, and Donald Regan was chairman of Merrill, Lynch. The budget director is likely to be someone is personally close to the president, or is on the same ideological wave length and hence ready to implement the president's wishes. Bert Lance was Jimmy Carter's best friend in the administration, and David Stockman was ready to cut domestic spending for Ronald Reagan. The Federal Reserve chairman is likely to be someone such as Arthur Burns or Paul Volcker who has the respect of the national and international financial community. And the CEA has always been headed by a professional economist who is on the same side of the ideological fence as the president. Walter Heller, a liberal, served in the Kennedy administration, and Martin Feldstein, a conservative, in the Reagan administration.

Too much should not be made of these background characteristics. There is a lot of moving from one economic chair to another. George Schultz moved from OMB to the Treasury in the Nixon administration, and William Miller moved from the Federal Reserve to the Treasury during the Carter years. Carter CEA chairman Charles Schultze had been Lyndon Johnson's budget director, and Paul Volcker (appointed to the Federal Reserve by Carter and reappointed by Reagan) had been an assistant treasury secretary under Nixon. Still, there is some tendency for the treasury secretary to speak for business; the OMB director to echo the president; and the CEA chairman to speak as a professional economist. Something of the rivalry between businessman-politician John Connally and University of Michigan economist Paul McCracken (Nixon's CEA head) is reflected in the latter's comment on a Watergate book:

> In this book the then Secretary of the Treasury, Governor Connally, is reported to have told the President that my advice was a disaster. Now upon reflection I found that comment downright reassuring because advice that qualified as a disaster could hardly be called trivial or meaningless. Fortunately, as we all know, the free market economy was saved from disaster through price-and-wage controls and the Lockheed loan [both of which had been advocated by Secretary Connally].

When the 1984 Economic Report of the President (written by the CEA) was issued, Treasury Secretary Donald Regan told senators, "As far as I'm concerned, you can throw it away." CEA Chairman Martin Feldstein quipped, "I suppose that was just a throwaway line." This exchange was only one episode in a public disagreement between Regan and Feldstein over the urgency of dealing with the budget deficit, but Regan and Feldstein were by no means the first treasury secretary and OMB chairman to disagree over policy.

Even if responsibility were not so fragmented, the American economy would be difficult to manage for several reasons. First of all, economic growth, low unemployment, and stable prices are often brought about by different policies. Second, for fiscal or monetary policy to be effective, the policy ought to be in place in advance of economic developments. But *certain* information about the direction of the economy is not available until after the fact. For example, if inflation has been evident for, say, six months, will the next six months bring more inflation, or will it abate? Further inflation calls for one set of policies, declining inflationary pressure a different course of action. A similar problem is that political support for desirable economic policies may not be available until adverse developments are evident to much of the electorate, and then it may be too late. Finally, only some 23 percent of America's gross national product is spent by the federal government. Even allowing for the additional proportion spent by state and local governments, the *majority* of economic decisions are made in the private sector, and thus are beyond government control.

Means of Coordination

In the face of these difficulties, some means of coordination between the economic agencies is necessary if an administration is to have any hope of keeping its economic troops marching in approximately the same direction. A number of these means have developed, and most of them involve the Troika[5] composed of the Treasury secretary, OMB director, and CEA chairman. Informally, its origins go back to the Eisenhower administration, but the group was given a formal responsibility in the Kennedy administration. The Troika members, together with their agencies, were made responsible for preparing economic forecasts. The Treasury was responsible for estimating revenue; OMB for estimating expenditures; and CEA for taking both sets of estimates, together with other information about the American economy and preparing the forecast.

By the time of the Nixon administration, the Troika members were meeting once a week. (They usually met at the Cosmos Club—a private club to which many academics belong—but when John Connally entered the government, he announced that henceforth the meetings would be at the Treasury.) After Arthur Burns became chairman of the Federal Reserve, it was suggested that it would be useful to include him, and the Troika became the Quadriad when Burns was present. The Quadriad never became as useful a coordinating device as the Troika, at least in part for organizational reasons. The Fed chairman is in fact chairman of the Board of Governors of the Federal Reserve System. Many Fed decisions are made by the board, and many more by a larger group known as the Open Market Committee. The result is that the Fed chairman cannot speak for the board or committee. This has kept the relationship at arm's length, and of course, the Quadriad members may just disagree with each other on substantive grounds (Stein, 1981).

The Ford administration developed most of their economic proposals in a single forum: the Economic Policy Board (EPB). As a congressman with long experience on the Appropriations Committee, Ford had developed a real personal mastery of budget issues, and facing both double-digit inflation and the deepest recession in 40 years, his administration was compelled to face economic issues. The heart of the Economic Policy Board was an executive committee, and the core of this committee was the Troika plus L. William Seidman, a longtime Ford confidant who was assistant to the president for economic affairs. A fifth member, the executive director of the Council on International Economic Policy, was added because of concern with international economics; and then as the EPB developed into a major center of decision making, the secretaries of state, commerce, and labor were added to broaden the executive committee. In deference to the independence of the Federal Reserve, Fed chairman Arthur Burns was not formally a member of the

---

[5] The word is Russian and refers to a three-horse team. It was first used because of a Russian desire for three coequal secretaries general at the United Nations after Dag Hammarskjold's death. It was then used to describe the economic Troika, and has come to be used to refer to any group of three such as James Baker, Michael Deaver, and Edwin Meese in the Reagan White House.

EPB, but was invited to attend and often did so. Others attended when the subject matter made this appropriate.

The executive committee met "daily" (actually 351 times over 2¼ years) at 8:30 at the White House. Three items were on a typical day's agenda, two with background papers prepared in advance. After the executive committee meeting, an options paper would go to President Ford in which the competing arguments were carefully preserved. Ford himself, who liked to hear oral discussion of issues, met with the executive committee about once a week (more often than that in 1974–75, less frequently when campaigning for reelection). The Economic Policy Board was not the only locus of decisions, but it was the most important domestic forum during the Ford administration, and marked a high point in coordination of economic policy (Porter, 1980).[6]

The Carter administration was more loosely organized, and the President himself was less interested in economics. The Carter administration used an Economic Policy Group. At first this was attended by a number of cabinet members and staff assistants, but then was cut down to the Troika plus Domestic Policy head Stuart Eizenstat. When international economic matters were being discussed, the four were often joined by the undersecretary of state for economic affairs and by Henry Owen, another expert on international economic affairs. Others were also invited to join them as appropriate. The agenda was quite flexible. Once agreement was reached, a decision memorandum was sent to President Carter. It came from the Economic Policy Group rather than from any single member.

The Reagan administration has used several coordinating devices. As already noted, a lot of Reagan economic policy got decided in the budget process (or alternatively by the budget review board consisting of James Baker, Edwin Meese, and David Stockman). Another major locus was the Cabinet Council on Economic Affairs. The Reagan administration set up several cabinet councils because of the President's desire for cabinet government. The Council on Economic Affairs met much more frequently than other councils, and was important, according to executive secretary Roger Porter (who had a similar job on the Ford Economic Policy Board) "because it is the most regular continual forum that attracts most of the major players." Another major group might be called "Troika Plus." The "plus" in the Reagan administration

---

[6] Across time, there have been numerous boards, councils, and committees. These break down into two general types. There have been special-purpose groups, such as the Cost of Living Council that existed when the Nixon administration was using wage and price controls, and the Council on Wage and Price Stability that was concerned with inflation in the Ford and Carter administrations. There have also been larger cabinet committees, usually formed because some cabinet members thought they *ought* to be playing more of a role in economic policy. In practice, the most important groups are relatively small and include the Troika.

consisted of the secretary of commerce, the head of OPD, sometimes
the Federal Reserve chairman, and after he joined the administration,
Secretary of State George Schultz, who represented not only State's
interest in international economics, but his own personal experience
as a former labor secretary, OMB director, and treasury secretary.
This group met in the Treasury Secretary's office every Tuesday morning. A number of economic decisions were effectively made by the
Legislative Strategy Group, because it was composed of White House
heavyweights joined by Treasury Secretary Regan and OMB Director
Stockman when budget or tax policy was being discussed. The Troika
still developed forecasts. After these were developed by the career
staff (now known as T3) and the second-level agency heads (T2), the
Troika members (T1) would take the forecast to a meeting with Baker,
Deaver, Meese, Darman, and Fuller. Once they reached agreement,
the Troika, Baker, and Meese would present it to the President who
made the decision on what forecast he would accept. To say there
were several different forums (and there were more than mentioned
here) underestimates the degree of coordination. "What evolved in
the first two years of the Reagan administration," Penner and Heclo
write:

> was a working committee of the presidency, composed exclusively of
> senior staff, meeting on a continuous daily basis, and responsible for
> meshing day-to-day tactics with longer-term goals. To put it most baldly,
> their loyalty was to the idea of a successful Reagan presidency rather
> than to any particular economic theory or policy agenda, apart from a
> general commitment to government retrenchment. (1983, p. 40)

Continuing Economic Tasks

While economics embraces a great many things, the activities of
presidential advisors may be summarized as three continuing tasks.
The first of these is the forecasting formally assigned to the Troika.
The government is continuously making spending decisions. To know
how much there is to spend, one must know the expected revenue,
and given fixed rates of taxation (until Congress is willing to change
them), one must have economic forecasts to estimate the revenues.
But decisions about spending and taxes in turn affect the economy,
so all three are inextricably linked. Consequently the government is
permanently in the forecasting business, and the president's economic
advisors are constantly monitoring economic indicators.

The second task is to manage the political-economic cycle—if an
administration chooses to use economic techniques to bolster its political chances. Edward Tufte's analysis showed that "the United States
has experienced two types of political-economic cycles: a two-year

cycle of acceleration and deceleration in real disposable income, and a four-year presidential cycle of high unemployment early in the term followed by economic stimulation, increasing prosperity, and reduced unemployment late in the term" (1978, pp. 56–57). The increase in income in congressional election years doesn't take much skill. The payment of checks that are due in any case is simply speeded up. The presidential-year increase in prosperity, however, does require some macroeconomic intervention, and good advice is needed to do this effectively. Some administrations engage in this; some do not. The Eisenhower administration did not; and Richard Nixon, blaming this for his 1960 election defeat, made sure that his administration stimulated the economy in 1972. Gerald Ford decided against it in 1976. William Seidman explained that "he believed the country had been subjected to enough of that kind of manipulation and refused to go along with it one more time" (Reichley, 1981, p. 401). Economists, looking at the aftermath of the 1972 and 1976 decisions, would be likely to applaud Ford's choice. Presidents, being politicians, are likely to note Nixon's 1972 victory and Ford's 1976 defeat, and act accordingly.

The third task might be called fighting the administration's major economic battles. In many ways—especially in providing jobs—the American economy has been remarkably robust. The number of jobs increased from 45 million in 1940 to 100 million in 1981, an expansion sufficient to absorb the postwar baby boom and the many women who have begun to work in recent decades. But each recent administration has faced real economic problems. The Ford administration faced a severe recession and high inflation. The Carter administration had to deal with even worse inflation. The Reagan administration faced huge deficits caused by the simultaneous tax cut and increase in defense spending, and the deficits were made worse by the 1981–82 recession. These administrations were unable to fight their battles successfully,[7] but the effort required the attention of successive teams of economic advisors.

DOMESTIC POLICY

Domestic policy is more inclusive than either national security policy or economic policy. Whereas both national security and economics refer to single policy areas, domestic policy embraces social benefits, civil liberties, natural resources, and agriculture. The White House, often preoccupied with crises in the two imperative policy areas, sees domestic policy as everything (domestic) that's left over, something that can be handled by lawyers and generalists (Cronin, 1980, pp. 150–

---

[7] A case can be made that Ford policies were successful by January 1977. Inflation was down under 5 percent for 1976, and GNP increased 7.5 percent in the first quarter of 1977.

53). It was also the last major staff to be organized. At the close of the Eisenhower administration, domestic policy was being handled by Robert Merriam with the help of Douglas Price, and they also handled relations with the governors and mayors. In the Kennedy administration, it was taken care of by Theodore Sorenson with the aid of a staff of three, but Sorenson was also handling the jobs of counsel, speechwriter, and general policy coordination which involved some foreign policy and politics. The big jump in numbers came in the Johnson administration. There were four staff members handling some aspects of domestic policy—Bill Moyers, Harry McPherson, Joseph Califano, and Douglass Cater—and if their own staff members are counted, there were 20 persons involved, a tenfold increase since Eisenhower left office.

The formal organization of a Domestic Council staff came in 1970. Acting on the recommendations of an advisory council, President Nixon created a Domestic Council to coordinate domestic policy formulation, and reorganized the Budget Bureau as the Office of Management and Budget to act as the president's principal management arm.[8] The Domestic Council was retained by the Ford administration, renamed Domestic Policy Staff by the Carter administration, and renamed again as the Office of Policy Development (OPD) by the Reagan administration. These units were not identical, but they had very similar responsibilities. What were the domestic staffs doing?

Domestic Policy Tasks

Since all the rest of the government (other than the foreign and economic policy agencies) is involved in domestic policy, coordination is a central task. "This is a terribly important function," said Stuart Eizenstat, "perhaps the most important function of all. Any decision worth the president getting involved in almost inevitably involves two or more departments. And once you get more than one agency involved, you need some neutral court that doesn't have a turf consideration." Eizenstat's deputy Bert Carp commented: "The most important thing that we do is to take the mass of paper that pours in here from a bureaucracy which inevitably confuses length with persuasiveness, and boil it down into pieces of paper that a president might conceivably read."

Coordination, then, is the first essential function, and coordination

---

[8] It is likely that a domestic policy staff would have been created by whoever won the election in 1968. An advisory task force in the Johnson administration had recommended the creation of an Office of Program Development, and an Office of Program Coordination (for management). The recommendations were kept secret, and were to be implemented at the beginning of Johnson's next term in 1969. Hubert Humphrey, the 1968 Democratic nominee, had called for the creation of a National Domestic Policy Council in a speech given July 11, 1968.

implies enough condensation to give the president some hope of keeping up without being drowned in paper. But why should decisions go to the president? One reason is that in arguments between departments, cabinet officers often side with their departments. A Nixon aide re-counted his experience:

> I can sit right here in this room and watch a fight between the secretary of interior and the secretary of agriculture. According to the secretary of interior, a tree must be protected. According to the secretary of agricul-ture, a tree is a crop and should be harvested. What am I going to do? I can say, "Gentlemen, do you think this is really worth the president's time?" If they say yes, then I have no choice but to put an option paper in for the president. Because there are no other symbols of authority, if we have two cabinet officers differing with one another, someone else is going to have to decide.

The someone else often is the president, not because of the importance of the issue, but because the decision needs to be made by someone who outranks the disputing parties.

A very different reason for agencies to communicate with the presi-dent via the domestic staff is their belief that the president is more likely to agree if the domestic staff supports the agency. Particularly with the constrained resources of the last decade or so, agencies want all the help they can get. David Rubenstein spoke about departmental desires to enlist Stuart Eizenstat for this purpose:

> I would think that before a cabinet secretary ever makes a recommenda-tion, he will know what the interest groups want and will probably have a recommendation that's somewhat consistent with what they want. He will probably try to line up Stu to support his position because the general view was, rightly or wrongly, that if Stu Eizenstat supported their position, chances were they were going to win in front of the President. What they would try to do, knowing generally they couldn't get OMB to support their position, was that they would try to line Stu up, and get Stu to be the person who argued with OMB. Then when he couldn't get that far with OMB, he would take a hand in drafting a memo that would go to the President. He would make sure that his view and the agency's view was presented much more favorably than if OMB had drafted the memo, or if the agency had drafted the memo without Stuart's involve-ment, and OMB had put a cover memo on top that basically killed the position.

Of course, agencies are not the only actors who hope to use the leaders' ties to the president to make administration policy. A member of the Nixon staff was quite frank about his activities. "What I try to do is to develop policy that can be sold to Krogh, and if he buys it, sold to Ehrlichman as administration policy."

But, again, must all disputes between agencies go to the president? When staff members first come to the White House, they tend to think

that the most important thing they can do is to sort out issues for
the president to decide. They want to make sure that all options have
been explored, all of the benefits and risks presented, so that the president will make the choice with as complete information as possible.
In time, though, they discover that if every dispute goes to the president,
then the president isn't going to do anything besides settle arguments,
many of which are too inconsequential to be worth the president's
time. Furthermore, if every controversy goes to the president, the lines
of communication become so clogged that it is difficult to get things
that are truly important to the Oval Office for resolution. It is at this
point that the staff member begins to broker disputes short of the president. Settling controversies at a level lower than the president is a
second important task of the domestic staff.

Bert Carp explained this by comparing agencies to nations.

> Cabinet agencies have most of the characteristics of independent nations.
> They have their own territories, and their own flags. They communicate
> with each other basically in writing, and have long historic disagreements
> that stretch so far back that nobody knows where they began. And to
> a large extent, there is a kind of internal patriotism. Now sometimes
> when we get a couple of assistant secretaries over here so that they
> can say they took their case to the White House, they can find a way
> to agree. You know, the president doesn't really have to resolve these
> disputes which have their primary meaning to these territorial bureaucra-
> cies.

Whenever the domestic staff discovers a dispute that is not of presidential importance, they make an effort to resolve it at the staff level.[9]

A third function of the domestic staff is to maintain liaison with
the agencies. This is by no means a complete oversight or a full awareness of everything that is going on in the agencies. The staffs were
simply too small (26 for Nixon, 32 for Carter, 20 for Reagan) for that.
How liaison was maintained was left up to the staff members concerned. "My experience," said Simon Lazarus, who worked on government efficiency issues on the Carter staff, "and I think the experience
of the other key people on the staff was that they had a lot of real
discretion, that is to say discretion to evaluate what the trends were,
what cabinet officers' decisions ought to be given how much weight,
and so forth."

A lot of liaison comes from an agency desire to touch base to make

---

[9] It is on this point that Robert Merriam and Theodore Sorenson, who coordinated
domestic policy with very few aides, are critical. If a dispute can be resolved short of
the president, why bring it into the White House at all? "I think a large staff is a terrible
mistake," said Merriam. "Once you set up such a mechanism, it tends to suck things
into the White House. We tried to keep things out. We tried to ask: Why do we have
to decide this? Is this a presidential decision? Usually it was not." Both Merriam and
Sorenson made greater use of the Bureau of the Budget for domestic policy decisions.

sure that a proposed course of action is all right. Lynn Daft, the agricultural specialist on the Eizenstat staff, gave an example:

> I had a call from the under secretary of agriculture this morning on an issue that involves meat imports and action that they proposed to take. This is an issue that the President has recently touched; that Eizenstat has recently touched. And it comes to me in this vein: This is what we plan to do; these are the likely effects; does this sound ok to you? And my response is: Yes, it sounds fine, let's go ahead. I think they feel that it's fairly important to touch base with me and get my concurrence, but they recognize that I'm not really a decision maker.

Danny Boggs, who was handling energy, agriculture, and natural resources on the Reagan OPD staff, gave a virtually identical account. Much of his contact, he said

> tends to be a kind of consultative thing where a department or legislative affairs or somebody will call and say: We think we're going to do this; is there any problem with it? I would say that on those sorts of things I will be essentially giving advice that they will take because they respect my opinion, or saying: Shoot, I don't see any problem with that.

When he did smell a problem, Boggs said, he would raise questions, and then tell his boss that a department had called, and there might be a problem with such and such that they proposed to do.

A fourth function is program development, and more often than not, this means getting legislation ready to be sent to the Hill. Representatives of the agencies concerned are brought together for an extensive set of meetings. This was what happened when Nixon's 1969 Family Assistance Plan was being drafted.

> The President knew generally what he wanted on this. He set down general guidelines. He knew that if the current system was projected, it was going to go bust. It would bankrupt the system. I was the person who headed up the task force on this. I had assistant secretaries from Labor, HEW, someone from Budget, and one person from Moynihan's staff, and one person from Burns' staff. I don't mean to say that we did it all. We had departmental backup. We got figures from Labor, from HEW, from OEO. They had the best computer runs at the time, results of experiments, and so forth.

Stuart Eizenstat told of three-hour meetings involving assistant secretaries and assistant directors from the departments of Energy, Transportation, EPA, OMB, and his own staff while developing the energy legislation President Carter sent to Congress in 1979.

> I spent months of intensive meetings every night at five o'clock getting all the agencies together to try to work on what a next wave of energy legislation would look like. We sat down with the agencies and talked it through. We asked them to staff it out, and let the other agencies

see it. And ultimately we presented some decision packages for the President, an awful lot of which had been agreed on as a result of that process. These people were able to listen to each other and argue it out, and were able to resolve a lot at that stage. Once the President made his decisions, they were then put into legislative form. During this whole time, we were consulting with the Congress, and when we sent the legislation up, we continued that consultation.

This process stands in sharp contrast to the secret drafting of the 1977 energy package described in Chapter 1. Domestic aides generally argue that program development of this kind (and aside from the family assistance and energy legislation being more important, these descriptions are rather typical) has three effects. First, mutual participation by White House and agency personnel means that the president's political concerns and departmental expertise can both be incorporated. Second, the departments know that their views have at least reached the president. Therefore the chances of departmental support of the legislation are much greater. Third, eliciting congressional reaction early allows the legislation a chance of passage without being torn apart and rewritten on the Hill.

Variation across Administrations

There are many sources of variation across administrations, but four are worthy of note. They concern personalities, the relative importance of other White House units, administration priorities, and the decision-making styles of the presidents themselves. Taken together, these variations had the effect of making the domestic staffs somewhat less influential in the Ford and Reagan administrations.

After Gerald Ford had selected Nelson Rockefeller as vice president, both men were very hopeful that the Domestic Council, under Rockefeller's leadership, could be used to coordinate domestic policy. Ford did appoint a Rockefeller aide, James Cannon, to head the staff, but the initial hopes were not fulfilled. Rockefeller concluded that the Council was being used "to put out brushfires" (Reichley, 1981, p. 308), and lost interest. The Domestic Council was further weakened by Rockefeller's announced departure from the Ford ticket, and by divisions within a staff made up of some Nixon holdovers, some Rockefeller appointees, and some Ford appointees.

Martin Anderson, Reagan's principal domestic adviser in the 1976 and 1980 campaigns, was the first head of the Office of Policy Development, but was unable to build it into a strong unit. One of his aides recounted some problems:

> Marty was very much a house intellectual . . . someone more comfortable in dealing with ideas. . . . He was not particularly interested in managing. . . . There were some particular issues he got very interested in, draft

registration was one, the law of the sea was another. . . . He never
made use of the full staff. . . . There were four of us who worked directly
for Marty. For everyone else, there was less of a sense of direction,
and I know that some of the people expressed frustration to me.

We have already seen the principal rival unit in the Ford White
House. The Ford Economic Policy Board was influential, and handled
some of the work that otherwise might have gone to a domestic staff.
There are a number of influential units in the Reagan White House,
but the cabinet councils have a direct bearing on work of OPD. There
are six cabinet councils. That on economic affairs has been *by far*
the most active. Those on commerce and trade, and natural resources
and environment, have met about a third as often. The cabinet councils
on human resources, food and agriculture, and a newer council on
legal policy have met still less frequently. Each is chaired by the relevant cabinet member (for example, Treasury Secretary Regan chairs
the Cabinet Council on Economic Affairs); each has other cabinet officers as members, and, the appropriate staff member of OPD serves
as the executive secretary of each council.

Craig Fuller described the cabinet council process as a "triangle,
large at one side, with a larger number of people involved in the policy
formulation process. It continually narrows so you are left just prior
to the decision with the President meeting with eight or nine cabinet
officers, hearing their views as to which of the three or four options
he must decide from." The frequency of President Reagan's attendance
at the meetings varied from council to council, but overall he attended
about a third of the meetings during the first year. Michael Uhlmann,
the OPD aide who served as staff to the Council on Legal Policy, said
that the cabinet councils served two purposes. "First, this President
likes to hear the actual exchange of views of articulate people actively
involved in the decisions rather than merely reading memoranda on
the options. The second is to minimize friction between the White
House staff and the departments."

Martin Anderson's interest in a few projects, and the time required
to staff the cabinet councils, effectively defined OPD. Ed Harper, Anderson's successor, explained: "The situation I inherited was that when
the Office of Policy Development was created, it was seen more or
less as a project staff. Its only process responsibility was that of executive secretary to the various cabinet councils through which a number
of issues flowed." Harper hoped to gain more responsibility for OPD,
but by the time he left, and was succeeded by John V. Svahn in the
summer of 1983, OPD still had not emerged as a major force in the
Reagan administration.

The Nixon Domestic Council did produce environmental protection
legislation, revenue sharing, and a stillborn plan for government reorganization. The Carter Domestic Policy Staff began almost at once to

develop plans to implement Jimmy Carter's long list of campaign promises. In contrast, President Ford wanted to cut the growth of government
spending from 11 percent a year to 5.5 percent, and announced in January 1975, that there were to be no new programs except for energy.
Ronald Reagan, who declared in his inaugural address his intention
"to curb the size and influence of the federal government," was even
more averse to new federal programs.

A final difference was in the way the presidents decided things.
Ed Harper, who had been a member of Nixon's domestic staff as well
as head of Reagan's, described it this way:

> In the Nixon administration, policymaking was very hierarchical and
> authoritarian; and in the Reagan administration, it tends to be much
> more collegial. Obviously the President makes the final decision, but
> he enjoys hearing the issues discussed in kind of a free form with every-
> body having their say about it—whereas President Nixon, if he felt the
> issues were adequately staffed out, was comfortable making his own
> decision based on material that he had read.

In the Nixon administration, the option papers were thick notebooks
that the President would read, and return with his instructions. President Ford liked to hear discussions of his Economic Policy Board after
he had read briefing papers. The Carter administration called their
option papers presidential review memoranda. They were briefer than
the Nixon notebooks, but crammed with details about which agencies
favored which options from which President Carter had to decide. Carter, like Reagan, made his decisions after reading the documents. The
Reagan system uses two-page memoranda simply stating the pros and
cons of options, together with a box the President can check to provide
a record of what has been decided. (If the President has issued oral
instructions, then Craig Fuller sends a memorandum to the depart-
ment(s) concerned saying that the President wants to take certain
steps.) With Ford and Reagan, the papers were less important because
the presidents made their decisions after listening to advisors' views.
Presidents Nixon and Carter, however, made their decisions after reading, and the domestic staffs that controlled the paper flow into the
Oval Office were relatively stronger.

LINKS TO ESSENTIAL AUDIENCES

The staff units we have reviewed to this point—the NSC staff, the
various economic advisors, and the domestic staff—provide policy
coordination.[10] At the same time, they provide links to external group-

---

[10] There are other policy units, such as the Office of Science and Technology Policy,
the Council on Environmental Quality, and the Office of the U.S. Trade Representative,
but their concerns are more narrowly focused.

ings who administer the policies and are affected by them. For example, the NSC staff provides liaison between the White House and the State and Defense departments (and other foreign policy agencies), and thereby to the whole network of foreign governments and multinational agencies. But there are other external contacts needed for political viability regardless of the policies being pursued. The president must have support from Congress, the media (in order to reach the electorate), interest groups, and others so as to attain his policy goals. Conversely, representatives and senators want presidential support for their goals, and reporters need information about what the president is doing to write their stories. The president therefore needs staff units to provide liaison to external actors with whom he has continuous contact. The most important are the congressional liaison staff[11] and the press office.

CONGRESSIONAL LIAISON

Boundary Roles

A large green street sign hung on the office wall of William Cable, who was in charge of House liaison in the Carter administration. The sign had a double arrow on it. "Pennsylvania Avenue," it read, "Two Way Street." The sign had been a going away present to Cable from Speaker O'Neill when he had joined the White House staff. Cable said:

> I think that sign describes my job. I think if I do my job well, there is meaningful communication from both ends of Pennsylvania Avenue. I am as much a representative of the Congress within the policymaking in the President's office as I am a representative of the President on the Hill when I go to lobby for a legislative program that is sent up.

A more formal description of this relationship is that of a "boundary role," a concept from organizational theory used by Joseph Pika in his study of the legislative liaison office:

> Boundary role persons (BRPs) occupy formally designated positions within an organizational structure with responsibility to oversee exchanges between the organization and its environment. . . . Supervising relations with the environment gives BRPs an outward- rather than inward-looking orientation within the organization, which is sometimes described as placing them in a peripheral position both physically and psychologically in relation to their organizational colleagues. (1979, pp. 2–4)

Specifically, White House colleagues may hold legislative liaison staffers responsible for what happens on the Hill, while legislators

---

[11] As is true of the domestic staff, this unit has had a number of names. It was the Office of Congressional Relations in the Kennedy administration, the Office of Congressional Liaison in the Carter administration, and the Office of Legislative Affairs under Nixon, Ford, and Reagan.

may hold them responsible for decisions made by the White House. If they are able to cope with these diverse expectations, they may be effective two-way communicators. If not, they may be hampered by severe role conflict.

What Bill Cable said about liaison with the House for the Carter administration was echoed by David Swanson, a member of the Reagan Senate liaison staff:

> It is always thought that the primary role of a lobbyist is to convince the voting body that the proposals that the president is making have merit and should be adopted. We try to add another dimension to it; and that is, we spend as much time representing the situation in the House and the Senate in the councils here at the White House as we do representing the White House on the Hill.

When asked if that did not carry with it the danger of always being seen as an outsider, Swanson continued:

> It is a problem if you don't work both sides with integrity. All of us have worked at one time or another on the Hill; we all have professional relationships with members of the staff up there, so people do not see us as outsiders. They know us; they trust us. We have built that trust, and we are very careful with it. Down here, we feel as though we have had a chance to make our points, that we have been heard. Then once a decision has been made by the President, knowing that all issues have been raised, we have that much more reason to carry that message to the Hill. If we become a separate part within the White House itself, arguing strictly for the Senate, then we can't move either end of the avenue.

Gathering Information

A large part of the liaison job is routine.[12] Since their effectiveness depends so heavily on being able to accurately represent each side to the other, a fair amount of the staff's time is devoted to gathering intelligence. Bill Cable stressed that it is very important to give a congressman an answer that is quick, accurate, and definitive:

> Even if the answer is that it is the worst goddamned project that has ever been sent to the Department of X, that it has no merit, and that it will never be funded even if you try for the next 500 years, a guy is

---

[12] The White House legislative liaison staff is small. The Reagan staff, for example, was made up of 10 persons: Ken Duberstein, 5 aides who worked the House side, and 4 on the Senate side. Therefore a lot of liaison work is carried on by others. OMB's Office of Legislative Reference keeps continual track of all the bills, not just the few high-priority items being handled by the White House staff. Further, each department has their own staff. The Defense Department had over 200 legislative liaison staff members, and estimates of the number of persons involved in congressional liaison work ran as high as 1500. The White House staff coordinates the departmental liaison activity.

much happier with an accurate answer than he is with being jerked around for six or eight months, and then getting an answer that says all this time has been wasted anyway.

Needless to say, a member of Congress would rather get a positive answer. And if the representative or senator is a person of influence, the liaison aides go out of their way to see if that can't be arranged. Ken Duberstein commented that they would pick up a lot of ideas on the Hill which they would then put into policy channels and track. "Depending on who the congressman is, we make sure that one way or another they get a good response, and sometimes weigh in on their behalf." Dan Tate made a similar point about the importance of the person making the request:

> Let's say it's the chairman of the Finance Committee, and he wants a tax credit for something. Well, even though we are opposed to tax credits generally, we have to take into account that this is the chairman of the tax-writing committee. So I will call Stuart Eizenstat, Jim McIntyre, or the Secretary of the Treasury, and try to find out if there is any way we can accommodate him.

The Carter administration procedure known as the troublesome bills process—the procedure discussed in Chapter 3 wherein OMB would put together early in the session a list of bills that were likely to cause trouble, and that domestic policy staff, OMB, and legislative liaison personnel would review periodically to see what helpful action could be taken—was another information-gathering routine that was developed to prevent unpleasant surprises for members of Congress.

Of course, the essential bit of intelligence in any legislative operation is knowing the vote intent of the legislators. Carter Senate liaison Dan Tate constructed his vote count in five categories: committed for the president; leaning toward the president; undecided (or unknown); leaning against; and committed against. His efforts at persuasion were then concentrated on those leaning toward the president and the undecided, but he did not neglect those who were leaning against the president. The Reagan administration also concentrated on wavering members. Just before the crucial June 1981 procedural vote that allowed final passage of the Reagan budget, the President was given a list of members, whom he phoned from the West Coast. Max Friedersdorf said that it wasn't very difficult to put the list together:

> We've had enough votes now that the patterns are established. We know who on the Republican side and who on the Democratic side are vulnerable to switching for or against us. Our House staff of five members constantly monitors those House members to know if there's any slippage. The essential thing was that we had the correct intelligence on who was being ripped away by the Democrats, and who needed presidential shoring up. So we were able to give him the correct people to call.

Participation in Policymaking

The legislative liaison staff participates in policy in a number of ways. Not a few policies are made in on-the-spot decisions when the president's representatives are conferring with representatives or senators. Soon after he became President Kennedy's congressional liaison head, Lawrence O'Brien was in a meeting with Speaker Sam Rayburn and other legislators about the level and coverage of the minimum wage. As O'Brien recounted the situation, "Everyone in the room turned to me and said, well what's the President's view? Well, I wasn't going to pick up the phone and ask the President when I was in a better position at that moment to make a judgment perhaps than he was. It was up to me to do it, and I made the judgment" (Wayne, 1978, p. 148). Dan Tate discussed this kind of situation a little more generally.

> A senator or his staff person will say, "We don't think we are going to be able to help you on this particular issue because you haven't been helpful to us on a matter that we have been working on." Well, I have to make the decision. Can I commit to him to try to help him with the issue he's been working on? Sometimes I don't have much time to decide. Almost invariably, I'll know either that we are interested in it, but we just haven't devoted much manpower to it, and I'll say sure, we'll be happy to. Or I'll know that the issue is not an administration priority, or we may even be opposed to it, and I'll tell him no. In that respect, I'm announcing a policy decision based on what I believe our administration policy would be if we sat down and had a meeting over it.

Obviously, a more senior person has greater discretion to make on-the-spot decisions of this kind, but such judgments are reasonably common. The alternatives, after all, are to reveal that you don't know what administration policy is, or that you don't have authority to speak for the president. In either case, the legislator would be likely to stop dealing with the staff member, and bargain in the future with someone who could speak for the administration.

More serious matters, of course, must be worked out with others in the administration. How this is done depends on how the administration is organized. In the Carter White House, one major opportunity came during the annual priority setting that was begun in 1978 after Cable and Tate had demonstrated that the administration was submitting too much legislation for Congress to handle. The staff was involved in drafting this list well before it got to Vice President Mondale and President Carter. With the priority items, a strategy memorandum would be drafted either by a task force or by the person handling the bill. This would go to other White House units, and ultimately would be reviewed by the President. There was increasing use of task forces (such as the group that met with Stuart Eizenstat on the 1978 energy legislation) for the top-priority bills. Legislative liaison personnel were members of these task forces, as were persons from other units.

Strategy on less-consequential bills was devised by the liaison persons to whom they were assigned.

In the Reagan White House, much of the contact with other White House decision makers was handled by liaison head Ken Duberstein.[13] There were four decision forums in which Duberstein participated regularly. The 8 A.M. senior staff meeting normally devoted 5 to 10 minutes to events coming up on the Hill. Second, Duberstein (or an assistant) sat in on many of the cabinet council meetings. Third, there was the Monday luncheon attended by President Reagan and 10 ranking staff members. Typically, Duberstein would spend 10 minutes or so discussing legislation expected to come up in the next week to 10 days. And, probably most importantly, there was the Legislative Strategy Group (LSG). The LSG, chaired by Jim Baker with agendas drawn by Dick Darman, was composed of core senior staff; the other regulars were Ed Meese, Mike Deaver, and Craig Fuller. The meetings were short, and devoted to pressing tactical decisions. Jim Baker recalled one such meeting:

> Last week we had the Republican conferees on the Job Training Bill down here. They'd cut a deal with the House conferees they had not told us about, that watered down a little bit of the requirements that a certain percentage of that money of the job bill go to training and not be used for support services. They had to get back within an hour, and let the House conferees know whether or not the White House would support it, support the compromise, and everybody support the job training bill. We got the Labor Department in here, and we got the Office of Policy Development, and Duberstein's office, and convened a meeting of the Legislative Strategy Group in effect, and we came up with a decision.

The existence of the Legislative Strategy Group, whether meeting formally with an agenda, or on an immediate-need basis as in this example, gave the Reagan White House an ability to act swiftly and with authority.

Involving the Principals

The liaison process works best when there is no need for a liaison staff. When the principal actors on both sides deal directly with each other, the chance of inadvertent misrepresentation on either side is eliminated; and with the principals on both side making their own commitments, there is a better chance that the deals will hold in the face of subsequent maneuvering. For these reasons, there has been a regular weekly meeting ever since the late 1930s when Sam Rayburn suggested to James Roosevelt, then working as an aide to his father,

---

[13] We have already seen a consequence of this in the communication patterns in the last chapter. Carter aides had to work around the inept Frank Moore. Because of Duberstein's skill, other Reagan aides could spend more of their time on the Hill.

that it would be useful if the congressional leadership and the president could talk from time to time.

Obviously, the president and the congressional leaders can't handle all the business. There is too much of it, and that is why there is a liaison staff. But whenever they can, and certainly whenever the matter is important, the liaison staff tries to engage important actors on both sides. Bill Cable, for example, said:

> I'd rather have John Dingle be the author-sponsor-leader of my energy program than any other one person in the Congress. To the extent that he's wrapped up in it, and has embraced it, he uses a whole different set of relationships with members of Congress. The best lobbyist the president can have is the chairman or influential congressman who wants the same basic outcome. When you work together with him and his staff, you really get a much better product out of it in the long run.

M. B. Oglesby, Reagan's principal House liaison who succeeded Ken Duberstein as assistant to the president for legislative affairs, referred to the importance of the House Republican leadership:

> The story that really wasn't that widely reported was Bob Michel's unbelievable ability to hold Republicans together as a voting bloc on the issues. He and Trent Lott have become a very effective team, so that is our first base to touch. If it is a jurisdictional issue, we again go via our committee ranking people, and committee staff. . . . They're our lead people. And whether they agree, or don't agree, they're the ones that we always go to. We have to be very responsive to them and to their thoughts in terms of getting anything enacted into policy.

Pam Turner, Senate liaison head for Reagan, said the same thing. When working on a bill, she would go first to Majority Leader Howard Baker, then to the committee chairman, and then fan out a bit from there.

The president, of course, can often persuade persons no one else can persuade. President Carter was said to dislike personal bargaining with legislators, but he did become involved on occasion. For example, Senator John Glenn opposed the President on a question of supplying nuclear fuel to India, and the vote looked to be very close. The undecided senators had been contacted by both the secretary of state and the secretary of defense. The President was asked to make a few telephone calls, did so, and prevailed by a vote of 48 to 46.

President Reagan, on the other hand, has been constantly involved. Within an hour of the Reagan budget victory in May 1981, all House members who had voted with the President had letters on their desks, signed by Mr. Reagan, thanking them for their votes.[14] Another instance

---

[14] This says a good deal about the efficiency of the liaison operation. The letters obviously had to be prepared in advance, so this confirms Max Friedersdorf's statement (quoted above) about the accuracy of their intelligence. And some organization was necessary just to get the letters distributed so swiftly after the vote.

in which Ken Duberstein took great pride was sustaining a veto of a bill concerning strategic petroleum allocation. The bill had been sponsored by Senator James McClure, chairman of the Energy Committee. The administration had been opposed, and had gone to some effort to get their opposition on record. But at the same time, Senator McClure was promised that he would have a chance to make his case to the President before Mr. Reagan made up his mind about vetoing. McClure was invited to the White House, along with Representatives James Broyhill and Thomas Corcoran, Republican members of the House committee. Senator McClure thought the President should sign the legislation; the congressmen thought he should veto; there was a full discussion in which the legislators were given ample opportunity to state their cases. "When the President made his decision at Camp David on a Friday night," Duberstein recalled, "the first thing he did was to call Howard Baker and then Jim McClure, and explain why he was going to veto the bill, why he felt that the legislation was inconsistent with his philosophy." The administration had intended to sustain the veto in the House, but on the morning of the veto override vote in the Senate, with 11 votes on their side, they decided to try to sustain the veto in the Senate. The President, Senator Baker, Senator Tower, and the legislative liaison staff all worked to persuade senators on the grounds of supporting the President, and they were successful with a couple of votes to spare. In Duberstein's opinion, they were successful because lines of communication had been kept open. Other senators knew that Senator McClure had been listened to, and that President Reagan was personally involved.

Conditions of Presidential Leadership

When describing the functions of the liaison staff, it is tempting to infer that a skillful, well-organized liaison staff allows a president to lead Congress. Tempting, but wrong.[15] Charles O. Jones has repeatedly (1968, 1970, 1981a, 1983) reminded us that favorable conditions make political leadership possible, not the other way round. "Favorable political conditions, a full agenda, and a strongly motivated and interested president," Jones writes, combined to make Lyndon Johnson's Great Society legislation possible. "It is important to be reminded of this happy coincidence of factors when deciding whether to measure other presidents by the Johnson standard." (1983, p. 107)

One fundamental condition is the size of the president's party in the House and Senate. Lyndon Johnson had big Democratic majorities;

---

[15] Similarly, one should not infer that if all the Troika members are smart and get along with each other, the president will be spared any problems with inflation or unemployment, or that a smoothly running press operation will mean that a president will be favorably treated by the media. Good organization helps to cope with the political environment, but no staff arrangement controls what is happening in that environment.

Gerald Ford's Republican party was outnumbered 61 to 37 in the Senate
and 291 to 144 in the House. Another is the popularity of the president
with the electorate. A closely related question is whether a president
who has just won an election victory can get organized fast enough
to take advantage of that victory. Still another condition is the overlap
between the White House issue groups discussed in the last chapter,
and the issue groups in the House and Senate we will see in the next
chapter. If there is a coincidence of policy goals, cooperation is easily
achieved. To appreciate the importance of these conditions, it is well
to remember that Max Friedersdorf was head of the liaison staff in
both 1975 and 1981. The difference in results didn't mean that Friedersdorf was inept when working for Gerald Ford in 1975, or suddenly
talented when working for Ronald Reagan in 1981. It was just that
conditions were different.

MEDIA LIAISON

According to Jody Powell:

> There were various points when things would come along that absolutely
> dominated the news. No matter what else you might have to say, the
> people in the briefing room are only going to be interested in one thing.
> It might be a week, 10 days, or 2 weeks on Billy Carter and the Libyans.
> It might be for several months on Iran, or for several days on Three
> Mile Island. It might be a couple of weeks up on the mountain with
> the Sadat-Begin-Camp David thing.

One essential fact about White House news is that high-salience stories
of this kind occur sporadically, but the need for stories is continuous.
The television networks do not switch to their White House correspondents for them to stand in front of the West Wing and announce, "Nothing much happened today." Therefore regularly produced stories are
needed when there is an absence of high drama.[16]

The other essential fact about White House media relations is that
there are certain news organizations that are vastly more important
than others. *The Washington Post*, *The New York Times*, and *The
Wall Street Journal* are important because they are widely read in
Washington, and because they are often used as sources of stories
by others. The news magazines—*Time*, *Newsweek*, and *U.S. News &
World Report*—the wire services, AP and UPI, and the three television
networks are important because of their vast national audiences. These
news organizations make up the "inner ring" of prime consequence
in disseminating news (Hess, 1981, chap. 2; Grossman & Kumar, 1981,

---

[16] The "routine" stories are often more important. A briefing on the budget the president is submitting in January tells far more about administration policies than the antics
of a Billy Carter.

chap. 3). At the same time, there are a much larger number of other news organizations whose needs also require attention. Keeping these two divisions—the occasional salient stories versus the much larger number of regular stories, and the small number of inner-ring news organizations versus the much larger number of others—in mind is a good start in understanding how the White House is organized to transmit news.

Gathering Information

Just as legislative liaison staffers spend a lot of time acquiring information so they can accurately portray the administration position on the Hill, the press staff needs to know what is happening to be able to answer reporters' questions. The person who can do this best is the press secretary with a close personal relation to the president, such as James Hagerty[17] or Jody Powell. Powell said that he wanted to know things himself if he was going to be a primary source of information at a briefing.

> It was much easier for me to drop in on meetings because if the Joint Chiefs were sitting there, they didn't bat an eyelash if I walked in. . . . I could ask questions, not being involved in the details of policymaking, but viewing it a little bit from the outside. . . . The press office needs to be there in a way that allows you to grab the cabinet secretary on the way out the door if you need to, and say, "Listen, you said so-and-so, and I'm not sure if I understood you; but if that's what you said, then I wondered about so-and-so."

Even if one does not have the long relationship of a Jody Powell to his President, the structure of meetings allows the acquisition of a lot of information. Reagan communications director Dave Gergen participated in the 8 A.M. senior staff meeting, the Monday issues luncheon with President Reagan, learned a great deal through the Legislative Strategy Group, and had regular weekly meetings with the Office of Policy Development to discuss pending domestic events, and with representatives of NSC, State, Defense, and USIA to learn about pending foreign developments. Gergen aide Michael Baroody headed a separate research staff, and coordinated administration news by staying in touch with the departmental public affairs directors.

---

[17] As Greenstein (1982) makes clear, Eisenhower prized accurate information. Hagerty once said that Eisenhower complained privately that he had difficulty as a member of General MacArthur's staff because MacArthur never wanted to hear any bad news. When Hagerty had bad news to tell, he often began, "Mr. President, you remember that young major in the Philippines?" and Eisenhower would reply, "All right, what is it now?"

The Regulars

There are perhaps 2,000 reporters who have credentials allowing them access to the White House, but there are about 100 who show up at least every other day. The wire services, networks, and a few large papers keep someone at the White House all the time; others come and go. The typical regular has not been covering the White House very long.[18] The senior television correspondent in 1982 was Sam Donaldson, who had arrived in 1977. Many have been assigned to the White House because they covered the successful candidate during his campaign. "The practical effects of the presidential-campaign-to-the-White-House movement," writes Stephen Hess, "are that it ensures a press corps of high energy and low historical memory, and further accentuates politics as the touchstone that the press will use to explain the motivation of all presidential behavior" (1983, p. 9). Furthermore, the vast majority of the stories are about the president, not the presidency. Thus, the television story is about the president and first lady going out to the helicopter to fly to Camp David for the weekend, not about a discussion among economic advisors on tax policy. And when the tax policy is announced, the story is likely to be about whether Congress will enact it, not the economic consequences *if* the tax policy is adopted.

Since the regulars are writing about the president, their first stop is the "downstairs" press room. This office provides copies of the president's schedule, speeches, any announcements or press releases, as well as answers to a good many substantive questions. Claudia Townsend, in charge of the downstairs press room in the Carter administration, explained her activities:

> There is a large amount of routine. When you get an answer to a given question, the chances are good that that particular question is going to be asked a hundred times in a day. It's not necessary for Jody to answer it a hundred times. It's not necessary for me to, but it's necessary for somebody to make that information available, to talk about the president's schedule or any of the routine so that Jody and the folks upstairs only have to deal with the stuff that needs to get to them.

The principal source of regular information is the press secretary's daily briefing. As already indicated, a lot of the briefer's time during the morning is spent getting ready for the questions that are expected. The briefing itself is around noon. The Carter and Reagan administrations both experimented with alternating briefers: Press Secretary Jody Powell and Deputy Press Secretary Rex Granum for Carter, and Com-

---

[18] There are exceptions. Helen Thomas, the senior UPI correspondent, began in the Kennedy administration. In spite of her status, she has been seen taking time to give directions to a stranger, a refreshing sight in a world of self-important people.

munications Director Dave Gergen and Principal Deputy Press Secretary Larry Speakes[19] for Reagan. Both ended up with one principal briefer, Powell in the Carter administration and Speakes in the Reagan administration. Both Powell and Granum recognized that the press was going to want the information from Powell, and Powell enjoyed gathering the information and the subsequent exchange with the press. And the communications liaison in the Reagan White House was organized so that most of the day-to-day contact with the press was Speakes's area of responsibility.

Stars and Specialists

By the beginning of the Nixon administration, media liaison had outgrown the press secretary's office. As late as the Truman administration, the press secretary would tell reporters to look up a new appointee in *Who's Who* rather than providing biographical information (Grossman & Kumar, 1981, p. 129). But with each administration, the press secretary was providing more and more service to the regulars. This meant that there were things that were not being done, at least not being done very efficiently. These included planning, following the headline stories more closely, giving particular attention to the special needs of the inner-ring media, and giving the president a capacity to reach journalists outside of Washington. Therefore Nixon appointed Herbert Klein, his longtime press aide and editor of the *San Diego Union*, as director of communications. The theory was that the communications director would deal with grander questions of communications strategy while the press secretary concentrated on the day-to-day needs of the White House regulars. It didn't work out that way for a while. The position continued to exist in succeeding administrations; but for reasons that differed from one administration to another, the press secretary remained the principal media spokesman while the communications director handled auxiliary tasks. It was not until the Reagan administration that there was a communications director, David Gergen, who had the responsibilities originally envisaged.

Some of the communications director's time is spent with the stars of the inner ring. Gergen sees the network television correspondents two or three times a week on stories they are developing. He also deals with the network bureau chiefs. This will be done individually if, say, NBC calls with a request for an interview with the president. On other occasions, with fast-breaking news, for example, Gergen will call the pool chairman (a designation that rotates among the three network bureau chiefs every two months), and the pool chairman will

---

[19] The humane reason for this unusual title was the desire to let James Brady, so badly wounded in the March 1981 assassination attempt, keep the title of press secretary.

contact the other two bureau chiefs. Gergen also sets aside half an hour each week for each of the news magazines.

There are two types of stories handled by Gergen. First of all, he is concerned about the important issues that are in the headlines or on television each night. The other type of story that requires some special handling is one that goes beyond the president's activities. As Gergen explained, "I tend to pick up a lot of reporters who are looking for analysis-type pieces, feature pieces, or something more re- flective. They just want to sit down and talk about them." Especially when they begin to write about the presidency as an institution, they need to go beyond the press office. "They also try to see other people," Gergen added. "I'm not the only stop along the way."

A Gergen deputy, Karna Small, takes care of the non-Washington press. If there are questions that come from outside the capital, or from the specialized press, they go to her office. But a major part of her job is organizing press sessions for non-Washington groups. "If you want to get information out to the regulars," Small said, "you simply say there will be an announcement for sound and cameras in 10 minutes, and everybody go outside to the Rose Garden. This is very easy. You just walk outside. For the rest of the country, you either have to mail it out to them or bring them in; so we do a lot of both." She continued:

> For example, we would take a whole morning and invite in editors of newspapers with a circulation of 25,000 or more, plus news directors of major television and radio stations, say, in the Northeast. We will give them a whole morning of briefings with, say, Don Regan, Cap Wein- berger, Dave Stockman, whomever. Then we will take 75 or 80 plus a whole lot of camera crews over to the State Dining Room for lunch with the President. He would speak to them; have some brief remarks and take questions; and then they would be out the door by 1:30, and they could file their stories.

Getting the Story Out

All of the time and energy that goes into media liaison is not, of course, just a response to the insistent demands of the press corps. There is certain amount of this, but the White House is equally inter- ested in getting their stories out. There are so many channels that can be used, Dave Gergen said, that the decision about which one to employ is almost tactical in nature. In Claudia Townsend's view, the decision is based on what you're trying to get out, how hard it is to get a favorable hearing for it, and how hard it is to understand.

The best spokesman, all the press aides agreed, is the president. What he says is news by definition, and it will be covered. The question is whether the subject is of sufficient importance for the president to be personally involved. Once that question is answered affirmatively, David Gergen explained, "we first of all figure out what forum and on what basis he should speak, whether it should be something for the Rose Garden, a speech out on the road, a television speech at night, whatever it may be. That is the initial issue: how you are going to have the issue framed."

If a policy initiative is involved (for example, something that has been developed by the domestic staff) then regardless of presidential involvement, the press staff will organize a briefing. This will be conducted by subject matter experts, and typically is accompanied by fact sheets and background material. But as Claudia Townsend explained, there are two disadvantages to a briefing. One is that "you can open yourself up to hostile questions. Sometimes, a group of reporters talking to somebody will pick up off each other. And if it turns nasty, it can really get nasty." This hostile-crowd effect can be avoided by dealing with reporters in smaller groups. The other problem arises with a complex policy initiative. "You don't want to stand at the podium," Townsend continued, "and explain the whole thing for fear folks are only going to hear half of it, and not get the rest." In this not unusual situation, it is better to begin with a half-dozen writers for major papers who have appropriate specialties in economics or the environment or whatever. Then when their stories come out, stimulating questions by the rest of the press, a more general release can be arranged.

And, of course, there are a host of other methods that can be used. Statements by administration spokespersons, interviews with members of Congress, luncheons with a group of columnists who have been invited to the White House, appearances by White House staff members on the morning television programs or the Sunday talk shows, and so forth, are all available to the media staff.

The most important announcements often come in presidential speeches. And while the ability of Presidents Carter and Reagan to give speeches differed vastly, the process of speech preparation was not all that different.[20] One of the major questions, according to Hendrick Hertzberg and Aram Bakshain, who were principal speechwriters for Presidents Carter and Reagan, respectively, is whether the basic policy decisions have been made. If so, it is simply a matter of writing a speech announcing it; if not, then competing interests all try to get their point of view confirmed in the speech. The speechwriters first receive input from senior members of the administration concerned with the policy area in question. These are woven together into an initial draft which is circulated to the officials concerned and senior

---

[20] See also the discussion of campaign speechwriting, especially the distinction between principal, collaborator, and feeders, in Chapter 11.

members of the White House staff. Once their reactions have been obtained, and the draft adjusted accordingly,[21] it goes to the president for whatever changes he wants to make. At this point, Aram Bakshain explained, "Probably because he has spent more time working on speeches himself over the years, President Reagan is much more involved [than Presidents Nixon or Ford]. He has a better ear for phraseology and is just more interested in the writing process."

Speechwriters for several administrations have said that the State of the Union Message is the most complex speech to write, and normally the most important. Because of its consequence, all departments want to get something in. "The initial bidding and jockeying is always intense," said Bakshain. "The great task is to pare it down to the essentials, because you can only say so much in one speech or you just lose focus." Rick Hertzberg compared the process "to a great big family sitting around the dinner table, 15 or 16 children, with the father out of the room or perhaps phoning in once in a while." Once the speech gets to the president, a lot of the competition is resolved since anything the president doesn't want in the speech doesn't get in. What he chooses to include is consequential. The media pay attention, of course, as do many citizens. And both the legislative and executive branches give heed to the way in which the president chooses to set his agenda for the coming year.

OTHER LIAISON UNITS

This discussion of legislative liaison and media liaison by no means exhausts the White House units whose prime responsibility is to link the president with various publics. The Office of Public Liaison was established during the Ford administration, and has provided a White House point of contact for interest groups. Public Liaison was particularly important in the latter years of the Carter administration when the politically astute Anne Wexler to some degree compensated for the maladroit Frank Moore. Intergovernmental Relations provides ties to governors and mayors, links that served Jimmy Carter well in his campaign for renomination. There are presidential assistants for political affairs who maintain contacts with members of the president's party.[22] This has been headed by some important political figures, such

---

[21] The number of officials consulted and the number of drafts through which a speech goes vary depending on the subject matter and importance.

[22] Why not devote more attention to these persons in a book entitled *Presidential Parties?* This is a fair question, and there are two basic answers. One is that the office is quite small in comparison with the five units that were discussed. But more consequentially, White House staff members do not regard organized political parties as very important. The median importance score given by Carter staff members for Democratic party leaders was 10.0; the median importance score given by Reagan staff members

as Drake Edens in the Nixon administration and Lyn Nofziger at the beginning of the Reagan administration. And there are persons or offices that serve as contact points for groups of voters. (There were six persons working in the Carter administration's Office of Hispanic Affairs as compared with only two maintaining liaison with the United States Senate.) All of these units are referred to as "outreach" organizations by White House staffers, and any complete discussion of presidential liaison would have to include them. The reason for not paying further attention to these outreach units is not that they are inconsequential. It is rather that some limits must be placed on this discussion of external structure of executive politics, and I have chosen to focus on those units that I regard (and the White House staff also regards, to judge by the organizational importance scores) as more consequential.

THE CONTINUING PATTERN

Regardless of the particular responsibilities of a unit—to coordinate foreign policy, shepherd the administration's legislative program through the Congress, or whatever—all must devote time to some common tasks. The first of these is scanning the environment. For the policy units, this means monitoring agency activity to be fully aware of the ways ongoing programs are being administered. (For the legislative liaison staff, this means monitoring congressional activity, and for the press staff, monitoring the media to be fully aware of what's being written and said.) The second task is collecting information and developing long-range plans. The third is clarifying options among issues being presented for decision. The fourth is for the staff members themselves to make policy decisions or clarify administration priorities. Finally, there are "fire-engine" chores when there's a problem or answers are needed in a hurry.

Table 5-2 shows the extent of time devoted to these common tasks by members of the Carter and Reagan White House staffs. Collectively, they spent a fair amount of time on most of these activities. If these mean scores were rounded to integers, both staffs would have average scores of 3 on four of the five tasks, which means that they devoted a fair amount of time to the activity. Only fire-engine chores, an inescapable part of White House life, took a great deal of time.

There were a couple of discernible differences between the two

---

for Republican party leaders was 10.1. (In comparison with the scores reported in Table 5-3, these are quite low.) Very similar results for Republican party leaders were obtained from the Nixon Domestic Council staff.—Political parties have a very considerable impact on executive politics because of the policy views of the president, cabinet members, and senior White House staff, and their efforts to implement those policies. Political parties as organizations, however, are much less important in executive politics.

TABLE 5-2
Time Use by Carter and Reagan Staffs

Activity	Carter Staff	Reagan Staff
Monitoring activity	2.7	2.7
Information and planning	3.0	3.1
Clarifying options	3.3	2.9
Making decisions	3.0	2.6
Fire-engine chores	3.6	3.6

Note: Score of 4 = A great deal of time.
        Score of 3 = A fair amount of time.
        Score of 2 = Not too much time.
        Score of 1 = No time at all.

staffs. The Reagan staff spent less time clarifying options and making decisions than the Carter staff. (When the comparison is restricted to domestic staffs so that the Nixon staff can be included, the Carter and Nixon staffs were both spending much more time clarifying options than the Reagan staff.) But the time devoted to the other three tasks is identical or nearly so for both staffs, and *none* of the differences between the two staffs on any of the five tasks is significant. When the three domestic staffs are compared on time use, the *only* significant difference is on clarifying options, because of the greater time required to prepare the written documentation for Presidents Nixon and Carter. The pattern of activities is common across administrations.

Nor is this all. Carter and Reagan staff members were also asked about the amount of time they were devoting to each of the 6 policy areas, the amount of contact they had with 16 units (8 internal and 8 external), and, as we have already seen at the end of Chapter 4, the importance of the 16 units. There were 43 items in all on which the moderate Democratic and conservative Republican administration could have differed. Of the 43, there were significant differences on only 5 items. The Carter administration spent significantly more time on social benefits and natural resources, and the Carter staff had significantly more contact with the subcabinet. Reporters were regarded as significantly more important by the Reagan staff, but staff members spent significantly less time with them. There were another five items on which the staffs had differences that were noticeable, but not quite significant. For example, the cabinet was seen as more important, and the Council of Economic Advisers as less important, by the Reagan staff. But the major finding is that for 38 of the 43 possibilities—88 percent—there were no significant differences. Here we see clear evidence of the constraining effect of the organizational matrix.

Reasons for Stability

There are many hints about the stability of the organizational matrix in this chapter. Democratic domestic aide Lynn Daft told of an assistant secretary calling to touch base about some plans and ask, "Does this sound OK to you?" Republican domestic aide Danny Boggs told of an agency calling to touch base about some plans and ask, "Is there any problem?" When the Ford administration was departing in January, 1977, domestic aide Janet Brown received a call from a Sioux chief she had been helping. He was worried about losing his White House contact when Janet Brown left. She replied, "Louie, I got a name for you. Get a pencil. Eizenstat. E-I-Z-E-N-S-T-A-T" (Broder, 1980, p. 466). Governmental agencies do not need such coaching about who to call in the White House. They are quite accustomed to clearing their plans, and the newly arrived White House aides soon find themselves responding to the same clients who had been working with their predecessors.

This similarity of task is not limited to domestic staffs. Bill Cable (who headed liaison with the House in the Carter administration) and David Swanson (a member of the Reagan Senate liaison staff) used very similar language to speak of the dual job of representing the president on the Hill and at the same time trying to convey congressional views to others in the White House. This perception of a boundary role has also been found with legislation liaison staffs from the Kennedy, Johnson, Nixon, and Ford administrations (Pika, 1979). Similarly, the television networks want their evening stories and the news magazines their weekly columns from the White House whether the president's name is Ford or Carter or Reagan—or Smith or Jones or Black. Foreign governments do not begin or end on January 20 every fourth year. Their interests remain constant whether there is a Democrat or a Republican in office. Labor unions retain their hopes for better wages, and managers their desires for higher profits. In short, the organizational matrix is stable because the external structure is anchored in the political environment. That environment changes, of course, but the change is at a very slow rate, and the measured pace of that development means the tasks facing an incoming administration are nearly identical to those of its immediate predecessor.[23]

---

[23] Here tasks are being distinguished from policy goals which are often quite different from one administration to the next. We saw a good example of variation in policy goals early in Chapter 4 when we looked at the issue preferences of the Carter and Reagan administrations. The free-floating issue preferences are part of the internal structure; the stable set of tasks is part of the external structure.

Reasons for the Relative Importance of Staff Units

There are some important distinctions to be drawn in the external structure, but these are not differences between administrations. Rather they are differences among the staff units.[24] This leads us back to the question raised at the end of Chapter 4: How can we account for a ranking of the importance of staff units that runs from the National Security Council to the Office of Public Liaison?

The first thing that needs to be said is that there were no unimportant units. A score of 79 means extremely important; 44, very important; 10, moderately important; 5, of minor importance; and 1, of no importance. Therefore, what we need to explain is a ranking that says NSC ranks higher than very important; OMB, legislative liaison, and the domestic staff are bunched close to very important; CEA and the press staff are a little lower than very important; and public liaison ranks a little higher than moderately important. Collectively, the staff is not dismissing any of the units as trivial.

The first possible explanation is the quality of the staff members themselves. NSC and some of the economic posts, in particular, call for a degree of technical training that the liaison posts do not. But, as we saw at the end of Chapter 4, personal reputation seems to make a small contribution to organizational ranking, while organizational ranking makes a major contribution to personal influence. So this is no more than a partial explanation.

A second possibility is that the units handling the crucial questions in any administration will be more highly ranked. This would account for the continuing ascendancy of the NSC staff, and explain why OMB was more highly ranked in the Reagan White House, where cutting the budget was so important. Over time, it would mean that the units handling the imperative policy areas of international involvement and economic management would be more important.

A third factor is organizational. On a good many domestic questions, the domestic staff, OMB, CEA, legislative liaison staff, and public liai-

---

[24] There were 27 measures of time use: the amount of time devoted to each policy area, the amount of contact with other units, and the time devoted to the five tasks. When these responses are analyzed by staff assignment, there are 16 that show significant differences. Many of these are obvious in view of the responsibilities of the unit, but some are less so. For example, the media liaison and congressional liaison staffs both tend to pay more attention to international involvement, economic management, and social benefits. As external spokespersons, they have to know something about each of these major policy areas. The economists also follow international involvement and agriculture, both of which, of course, have economic consequences. The two tasks that show significant differences are monitoring activity and clarifying options. The press and legislative liaison staffs spend much more time scanning their environments than the NSC, economic, and domestic staffs do in monitoring the agencies. Conversely, the latter three units spend significantly more time clarifying options for presidential decision than do the liaison staffs.

son staff can all claim to have some degree of authority. In international affairs, on the other hand, the National Security Council staff does not have any institutional rival within the White House. Thus when foreign crises occur, an administration necessarily deals with them through the NSC staff. The common experience of living through crises forges bonds between the president, the NSC staff, and other senior members of the White House staff.

A fourth possible explanation has to do with others' knowledge of the subject matter handled by the various staffs. Most White House staffers have a good deal of contact with interest groups. Consequently, they need not stand in awe of an Office of Public Liaison that specializes in interest group contact. Something of the same case could be made with respect to the media. The staff members are well informed about what is happening within the administration. From their perspective, news coverage appears superficial, and errors in stories are easily spotted. This may decrease their respect for reporters and the press office a bit. The OMB, domestic, and legislative liaison staffs have somewhat more specialized knowledge. Given their information about the budget and likely developments in the agencies and on Capitol Hill, they are in the best position to assert that "There isn't room in the budget for that" or "If we send the bill up in that form, Congress won't pass it." And when it comes to the intellectual domain of the NSC staff—the history of various Burmese tribes who have never fully acknowledged Burman suzerainty, the impact of power conflicts within the Kremlin on negotiating opportunities, or the differences between Somalia and Ethiopia—members of other staffs don't know very much, and they *know* they don't know very much.

The final explanation may be the best. This has to do with the external groups the White House units are in touch with. We are in a position to test this because we have comparable data on external groups and the internal units.

Table 5-3 gives the ratings by the (combined) Carter and Reagan staffs for internal units, and for external groups when there was some

TABLE 5-3
Importance of Internal Units and External Groups

Internal Unit	"Grand Mean" Rating	External Group	Mean Rating
NSC	53.6	Cabinet	53.1
OMB	48.8		
Legislative	47.4	Congressmen	34.8
Domestic/OPD	41.3	Cabinet	53.1
CEA	30.3		
Press	27.9	Reporters	13.8
Public liaison	16.3	Interest groups	16.4

group outside the White House with which the internal unit was in continuous contact.[25] The relationship between the "grand mean" rating of the internal unit and the mean rating of the external group is very strong. Cabinet members and congressmen were highly regarded as were the units who were in contact with them. In fact, if one adopts Thomas Cronin's (1980, pp. 274–86) very useful distinction between an "inner cabinet" made up of the secretaries of state, defense, treasury, and the attorney general, and an "outer cabinet" consisting of all the rest, then one could account for the higher rating of the NSC staff (in comparison to the domestic staff) because they are in contact with the most important members of the cabinet.[26] Reporters and interest group spokesmen, on the other hand, are not highly regarded, and the same thing tends to be true of the internal units that deal with them. So it may well be that a message is seen as important because of whom it ultimately comes from, and not the identity of the unit that conveys the message. Whether or no, something of the prestige of external groups seems to rub off on the internal unit that provides liaison with them.

The Senior Staff

The other important distinction on the White House staff concerns the senior staff and the rest of the staff. The senior staff certainly includes all those with direct access to the president, but this is probably too restrictive a definition. There were only seven persons with this direct access at the end of the Carter administration, and four— James Baker, William Clark, Michael Deaver, and Edwin Meese—with walk-in privileges with President Reagan. We will use a little larger group, including those with central coordinating functions and the heads of the principal staff units.

Table 5-4 shows data on time use for senior staff members from the Carter and Reagan administrations, and nonsenior staff members from the Nixon, Carter, and Reagan administrations. There are two tasks which do not divide the staff along lines of seniority. Both senior and nonsenior staff members are devoting a fair amount of time to gathering information and planning, and to clarifying options. But monitoring agency activity is clearly left up to junior staff members in whatever time they can find for it (which probably means that not much of this is being done). And senior staff members spend much of their time on fireengine chores and decision making. Not only do ranking staffers have the authority to act, but it is often faster for senior mem-

---

[25] The proper external groups would probably have been "all government agencies" for OMB and "professional economists" for the Council of Economic Advisors.

[26] Members of the Reagan staff used the words Big Three or Big Four to refer to the Inner Cabinet.

TABLE 5-4
Time Use by Senior and Nonsenior Staffs

Activity	Senior Staff	Other Staff
Monitoring activity	2.3	2.7
Information and planning	3.1	2.9
Clarifying options	3.2	3.2
Making decisions	3.6	2.7
Fire-engine chores	3.9	3.4

Note: Score of 4 = A great deal of time.
        Score of 3 = A fair amount of time.
        Score of 2 = Not too much time.
        Score of 1 = No time at all.

bers to take care an emergency situation themselves than to explain it to someone else and then wait for the lower-ranking aide to act. Decision making takes significantly more time on the part of the ranking staff members than for their colleagues. (In fact, the time devoted to decision making is the only one of these five tasks that shows a significant difference between senior and junior when just the Reagan staff is considered.) It would be inaccurate to say the senior staff members are making most of the decisions, but they are making the more important decisions.

Staff Decision Making

Decisions are being made by White House staff members all the time. As has already been noted, staff members learn that it is impractical to refer everything to the president. And presidents know that much is being screened out. John F. Kennedy once told a group of correspondents:

> President Eisenhower said to me on January 19th [1961], "There are no easy matters that will ever come to you as president. If they are easy, they will be settled at a lower level.". . . The matters that come to you as president are always the difficult matters, and matters that carry with them large implications.

The important question, of course, is what decisions are being made at what level. Some sense of this can be suggested by a few examples. We'll look first at some choices made by those more remote from the president, then proceed gradually to choices made by his immediate assistants. At each level, we'll first look at some decisions made by Carter staff members, then at some decisions made by Reagan staff members.

Rex Granum, a deputy press secretary in the Carter administration, said he would decide whether to have open coverage (which allows the entire press corps to cover an event) or pooled coverage. He would decide whether to produce a full blown fact sheet for a bill the President was signing, or to have something sketchier and let the reporters depend on the President's comments for more information. He would refer a decision on whether to have a press conference in 10 days to Jody Powell, who in turn would confer with the President. Al Stern, an associate director of the Carter Domestic Policy Staff, mentioned a study of tax incentives for which he had picked agencies that were to participate. Once the program had been decided upon, he made several decisions on which responsibilities were going to be assigned to which agency, although one such question, on which there was agency disagreement, went all the way to the President. Robert Thomson, who had coordinating responsibilities in the Carter legislative liaison shop, said it would be up to him whether to send a letter to a representative warning him that a particular bill was in deep trouble, or whether or not to submit a legislative strategy memorandum to the President. The contents of such a memorandum would be reviewed by more senior legislative liaison personnel, and the choice of strategy would be up to the President.

Doug Bandow, a special assistant in the Reagan OPD, said that he had told OMB that he thought Selective Service should not be given $50,000 to study the system, because the larger question of whether there should be draft registration had not yet been decided, whereas the question of what position OPD should take on draft registration would be up to OPD head Martin Anderson. Bob Carleson, also a special assistant in OPD, said that if he were saying yes to a proposed course of action, he would decide that himself, but if he were saying no, and he thought the agency was going to appeal anyway, he would refer that up the line. Kenneth Clarkson, an associate director of OMB, mentioned making second-tier decisions once the general policy had been established. "For example," he continued, "block grants are an extremely effective way to carry out many of the basic thrusts of federalism. So if a decision involves the block grant principles, I make that decision."

Rick Hertzberg, Carter's head speechwriter, would decide which speechwriter would draft a particular speech, while the content of the speech would be decided by more senior persons. Eizenstat deputy David Rubenstein said the real issue he faced was whether something was important enough to take to the President. If there was disagreement, the tendency was to go to the President to prevent charges that decisions were being made by staff members.

> Let's say that somebody wanted to spend 30 million more for some project, and we could do it by simply adding it on the Hill in a conference. I call the Office of Management and Budget and say I think it's a good

idea to add the 30 million dollars for these reasons. If they agree, we would probably go ahead an do it and not tell the President, although I would probably tell Stuart to make sure he thought it was ok. But if that same thing came along (the congressman called and said he wanted to add 30 million dollars) and OMB said no, I would talk to Stuart about it. If he thought it was a good idea, we would go to the President, and say, "Congressman X wants this 30 million dollars. He's useful to us. OMB says no. What do you want to do?"

OMB deputy director Gil Omenn said he had made all but four decisions on the Department of Labor budget out of "hundreds of small decisions, a couple dozen big decisions, and a few really important decisions. In each of those four cases, we negotiated a figure, but thought the political implications important enough that they should go to the President. In each case, what came out was the negotiated figure."

John Rogers, deputy assistant for management in the Reagan White House, made most of the day-to-day decisions on personnel. Jim Baker had decided that the White House would take a 12 percent cut in the operating budget the first year, and another 4 percent cut the following year. Those cuts had implications for personnel; it was up to Rogers to implement them. By 1982 Donald Moran, executive associate director of OMB, was making decisions that David Stockman had been making in 1981—for example, whether or not to transmit a particular supplemental budget request to Congress or to delay it for the time being. Roger Porter, executive secretary of the Cabinet Council on Economic Affairs, and deputy director of OPD, made the Reagan administration decision on which amendments would be accepted or rejected for a targeted jobs tax credit bill. Porter also recalled:

> Yesterday I made a decision that I would prepare the paper, working with State and the National Security Council, and OMB and our own office with respect to whether or not the United States would join the African Development Bank. I wouldn't make [the] decision [based on the paper] on my own, but would take it to the Cabinet Council and ultimately to the President.

Anne Wexler, head of Carter's Office of Public Liaison, said that the President would decide how much of his time he was going to devote to working on a particular issue, but that she would make all the decisions having to do with developing a legislative strategy around the issue, and how her office was going to work on the issue. Chief of Staff Jack Watson said that he would clearly take any major appointment to President Carter, but "by contrast, the President has delegated to me the responsibility and authority for making a large number of appointments on behalf of the President to various commissions and boards and institutes." National Security Advisor Zbigniew Brzezinski commented that "a lot of the decisions in terms of communications to foreign leaders, or regarding the deployment of forces, or choices in our SALT negotiations were made by me on behalf of the President, though reported to the President. And, of course, the more basic decisions such as MX basing, China normalization, and so forth were made by the President."

Craig Fuller, Reagan's assistant for cabinet affairs, believed the decisions that he made himself were principally decisions about timing, and whether the quality of material bearing on a decision was such that it was ready to be forwarded to the President. Most of these decisions were made jointly with Deputy Chief of Staff Dick Darman, since Fuller got material from the cabinet and agencies, and Darman got parallel material from White House personnel. Counsel Fred Fielding gave an example that he saw as a straight legal issue, rather than a policy issue:

> During the first month, I reviewed the President's financial situation, and realized that he was getting a pension from the state of California. I researched it and decided in my own mind that the President was not violating the Constitution by taking that pension. About a month later, I sent a memo over to the Office of Legal Counsel [in the Justice Department] and they concurred.

When questions were raised about this many months later, the work had already been done. Chief of Staff James Baker said the decision after the ad hoc meeting of the Legislative Study Group about the job training bill (described earlier) was "pretty much mine to make" and that he had decided to agree with the Senate conferees. There was "only one route to go so as not to be put in the position of having to veto a big billion dollar jobs bill. So we ought to go for this, and embrace it now in time to get credit for it. In order to do that, we had very little lead time."

A GLANCE AT TWO PRESIDENTS'

DECISION STYLES

It's a risky business, says Richard Cheney, congressman from Wyoming and President Ford's chief of staff, to compare the White House to a legislative body:

> In a legislature, everybody gets a vote. Downtown in the White House, the President gets a vote, and the only people who get an opportunity to influence that vote are the ones he talks to, or who have a chance to get paper to him in advance. He's got sessions going on the side. The Economic Policy Board was the formal mechanism by which deci-

sions were moved up to the President. Informally, the President would often sit down with, say, Alan Greenspan, and have a long chat. That's where the decision got made instead of in the more formal, more visible kind of mechanism. There's only one vote cast, and it's in the Oval Office.

Richard Cheney's reminder is useful. In executive politics, the focus must ultimately return to the president himself.

As we have seen, presidents have continuing responsibilities for international involvement, economic management, and domestic policy, and must maintain support in Congress and the media to achieve their policy goals. How prepared have recent presidents been to assume these tasks? Dwight Eisenhower and Richard Nixon came to the presidency with long experience or real interest in foreign affairs. Harry Truman, Lyndon Johnson, and Gerald Ford all had views about domestic policies developed in long political careers.[27] Lyndon Johnson had been majority leader in the United States Senate, and Gerald Ford had been minority leader in the House of Representatives. Both knew the nuances of life on the Hill. Franklin Roosevelt had been editor of the *Harvard Crimson*; John Kennedy had prepared for a career as a journalist; and Ronald Reagan knew all about communication from a lifetime spent as a radio announcer, movie actor, and syndicated columnist. While none save Jimmy Carter arrived in the Oval Office without good grounding in at least one of the five areas, none came to the presidency with experience in all of them. In familiar areas, presidents are more confident; in new areas, they are necessarily more dependent on staff support. But regardless of the extent of prior experience, presidents make the crucial decisions themselves. How do they do this?

This question must be answered on the individual level, and really with a good deal more evidence than we have. Still, perhaps a little light can be cast on the subject by looking at the cases of the two presidents whose staffs have been described in these chapters. Jimmy Carter was certainly an intelligent man, but his cognitive style was based on a mastery of detail, and focusing on a single problem at a time. Mr. Carter recalled:

> It was my nature as an engineer to want to understand the details of an issue. For instance, when I negotiated the SALT agreement with Dobrynin, or Gromyko, or Brezhnev, I didn't have to turn around to Harold Brown or Brzezinski and say, "Will you explain this issue to me so I can negotiate the final, concluding point?"
>
> And when I was at Camp David with Begin and Sadat, I didn't have to trust Hal Saunders [an assistant secretary of state] or Cy Vance to

---

[27] "No president up to now," Herbert Stein reminds us, "has been an economist. . . . Like other adult Americans, presidents have certain information and certain ideas about the economy. . . . They also have a body of shibboleths about such things as free enterprise, balanced budgets, and full employment. But of economics as a science, or near science, they are likely to be innocent" (1981, p. 1).

tell me history of the Mideast, the exact delineation of the borders, or
how many people lived in certain areas, or what the Israeli and Egyptian
policies were. I understood these things because I had studied them.

As I studied as a naval officer, and as I studied as a governor, and
as I studied when I was getting the Carter warehouse started, I studied
for the presidency. (Sperling, 1983, p. 13)

Mr. Carter used these facts to make decisions. When he was making
his decision about whether to produce the B-1 aircraft in 1977, he went
over all of the review memoranda from State, Defense, NSC, and so
on, and extracted 47 arguments which he listed on a yellow legal pad.
Next President Carter assigned numerical values to each argument,
two points or five points depending on the force of the argument. Finally,
he added up the totals, and since there were more negative points
than positive, the decision went against building the B-1 (Smith, 1978,
p. 30). Orderly, inductive reasoning.

Jimmy Carter liked orderliness, and having certain people responsible for defined tasks. Domestic aide Si Lazarus observed that

> the relationships between the senior staff members were firmly fixed
> by Carter's unusual degree of immutability in the way he regarded them.
> In other words, Eizenstat was his basic resource on domestic policy. It
> never changed. Jody was obviously his resource in dealing with the press.
> Hamilton was his political seer. Brzezinski was for foreign policy. There
> was very little bureaucratic competition within the White House.

The irony was that, while President Carter liked decisions to flow
through proper channels, the system (that is, the staff arrangements
and Carter's cognitive style taken together) encouraged endless appeals. The channels that were visible inside were visible to other interested players. If you wanted money for a new program, you went in
through the Domestic Policy Staff, and if you wanted to cut spending,
you went in through OMB—and in either case, the paper flowed to
the President's desk.

There was another feature of the Carter cognitive style that had
important consequences, too. While the President liked to talk about
"comprehensive" solutions, his style of thinking was quite segmented.
James Fallows described this in a notable article, "The Passionless
Presidency":

> He holds explicit, thorough positions on every issue under the sun, but
> he has no large view of the relations between them, no line indicating
> which goals . . . will take precedence . . . when the goals conflict.
> Spelling out these choices makes the difference between a position and
> a philosophy, but it is an act that is foreign to Carter's mind. He is a
> smart man, but not an intellectual in the sense of liking the play of ideas,

of pushing concepts to their limits to examine their implications. . . . (Consequently) he fails to project a vision larger than the problem he is tackling at the moment (May 1979, pp. 42–43).

Now what about Ronald Reagan? How does he make up his mind? There is no one process, but a typical sequence begins with options papers. These are brief, initially not more than one or two pages. Dave Gergen explained:

> As he gets drawn into an issue, as he is spending more and more time on it, he becomes better acquainted with the details and he gets himself deeply immersed in it. But when, say, the subject of the Clean Air Act (first) comes up, he doesn't want a hundred page paper. This is not the way he deals with it. He would much prefer a sharp, plain, distilled document on that, and then if he wants more he will reach for it.

While the initial papers to reach him may be brief, there are enough of them that together they take a fair amount of presidential time. "He does spend a lot of time at his desk, largely in the residence," said Mike Deaver, "although I try to see that he gets 30 to 40 minutes, sometimes an hour, at his desk in the Oval Office, and another 30 to 40 minutes in the afternoon. I would say he probably spends another four hours a day reading materials."

The next stage in Ronald Reagan's personal decision making is likely to be a meeting. In this case, the options paper will have served the purpose of starting his thought processes, and alerting him to the issues to be discussed. The four senior staff members are likely to be the first to whom Ronald Reagan reveals his reactions to the papers. "After he has done his reading," Mike Deaver continued, "then he usually shares his thoughts or concerns or questions with Meese, Baker, Clark and myself, or maybe one or two of us, or all four." The President's reaction varies from one instance to another. "Sometimes," said Jim Baker, "he will come down from the residence after reading the options papers the night before with the decision pretty well made and tell us what it is. He will tell us how he is strongly leaning even before the meeting, before he hears the oral arguments."

At a meeting, President Reagan very much wants to hear all the arguments. "He happens to like the clash of voices in front of him," Dave Gergen commented. Mike Deaver said much the same thing. "He does not mind disagreements on philosophical points or details of strategy and that sort of thing. In fact, he somewhat thrives by having different views come together by hearing the opposing sides, and it seems to me that it helps his thinking process."

What is the President looking for in these discussions? First of all, Ronald Reagan wants to be sure that he is aware of the choice to be made. "He wants to be sure," explained Ed Meese, "that he has all of the available options and the pros and cons of those options. Then he will ask for background information to make sure that he has pretty much all the varying points of view. . . . What are the arguments (in favor and) against doing this, and what quarters are they likely to come from, that sort of thing." Second, President Reagan is interested in objections that are likely to be raised by other significant political actors. Meese continued:

> He is particularly interested in who else would have an objection if we took this course of action, or who would be in favor. For example, if something sounds good from a philosophical standpoint, he would want to know what the congressional objections will be so at least he knows before he makes a decision whether it's likely to be able to get through Congress. This will not stop it from going up because you can always change Congress's mind, or sometimes you can change it. But at least he wants to know what the obstacles are before we put it through.

A third concern which is sometimes raised has to do with the fairness of the proposal. "He wants to be sure that we are doing something that is fair to the people that might be affected by it." The last question has to do with political benefits. According to Meese, "his least concern is what is the political advantage or disadvantage in doing this. He will inquire into the political probabilities, can we generate public or congressional support, will this help us or hurt us at the polls, but the short-run political advantage is probably the lowest thing in his priorities."

After hearing the discussion in the wider group, President Reagan is likely to withdraw to his close circle of advisors. At times, said Jim Baker, "he will go to a meeting, hear the arguments, and take it under advisement. Sometimes he never asks us what we think." Often, though, he wants further discussion with his trusted confidants. "Many times," Baker continued, "he will say, what do you fellows think? And we will put in our two cents worth." Mike Deaver saw it the same way. "I think he makes his decisions, most of his decisions, in (the) much smaller area, relying heavily on the three or four of us who he spends most of his time with."

It seems noteworthy that on some occasions President Reagan will have his mind virtually made up after reading the initial paper—and at other times he will carefully inquire about the political terrain. What is critical in President Reagan's decision to follow his original disposition or to modify his plans because of a political assessment may be his principles and/or stereotypes.[28] If a suggestion triggers one of Rea-

---

[28] Defenders of President Reagan would be likely to say he is principled. Critics would be likely to say that he uses stereotypes. When the subject is Reagan's cognitive style, however, it doesn't make any difference. Whether his central beliefs are called principles or stereotypes, their effect on his thinking is the same.

gan's stereotypes, that determines his position. If the subject is novel, then the President may well be guided by political considerations. "He has always been flexible," Ed Meese has said, "where his principles were not involved." This could explain why President Reagan appears at times to be a conservative ideologue, and at other times to be a quite pragmatic politician.[29]

Summary

In this part of the book, we have analyzed the temporal pattern, the internal structure, and the external structure of executive politics. In Chapter 3, we saw that each administration tends to pass through the same stages: Transition, Mid-Term Election, Maturing, Reelection, Maturity, and Retirement. In Chapter 4, we reviewed the sources from which the players are recruited, the issue structures that arise from the preferences of White House staff members, the flow of information and personal influence within the White House, and the relative importance of the staff units in the organizational matrix.

In this chapter, we have learned about the continuing tasks that must be handled by any administration. There must be ways of handling problems as they arise in the policy areas. Organizationally, this has meant a National Security Council apparatus, some means of coordinating the several sources of economic advice, and a domestic staff. While these staffs are primarily concerned with policymaking, they also provide links between the president and the bureaucracy. Among the outreach units, we reviewed the responsibilities of the legislative liaison and media liaison staffs. While these staffs have their prime responsibility in providing links between the president and the political environment, they impinge on policymaking as they bring information about the views of other important actors. We saw that collectively, the amount of time spent on common tasks is similar across the two administrations, but there are significant differences from one staff unit to another, and between the senior staff and other staff members. Finally, we reviewed the cognitive styles of the two most recent presidents.

---

[29] I would like to thank Margaret Hermann for her help in arriving at this interpretation.

PART THREE

LEGISLATIVE POLITICS

CHAPTER 6

TEMPORAL PATTERNS OF LEGISLATIVE POLITICS

Two Impressions of Congress

Congress has been most visible when connected to the president. A presidential appearance for an address to a joint session of Congress produces a vastly larger television audience than normally follows legislative politics. This is one of the images that is engraved on the American consciousness. The doorkeeper announces, "Mr. Speaker. The President of the United States." The president enters, walks down the aisle to the applause of the members, mounts the rostrum, greets the Speaker and the vice president, is introduced by the Speaker, and begins his address.

An occasion when citizens watched television even more raptly came in July 1974, when the House Judiciary Committee met to consider recommending articles of impeachment for President Richard M. Nixon. High drama, this, but a setting that allowed the representatives to emerge as individuals, and gave citizens a sense of the quality of their legislators. There was Peter Rodino, a World War II veteran from Newark, to whom seniority had given the imposing task of chairing these proceedings. There were Democrats such as soft-voiced Robert Kastenmeier of Wisconsin; Robert Drinan, a Jesuit priest from Massachusetts; Barbara Jordan of Texas, whose deep voice and impressive speech gave her a commanding presence; Elizabeth Holtzman, a Harvard Law graduate from Brooklyn; Paul Sarbanes of Maryland, an erstwhile Rhodes Scholar; and Walter Flowers from an Alabama district where there was considerable support for President Nixon. The Republicans included Robert McClory from a suburban Chicago district, and Delbert Latta from Bowling Green, Ohio, both lawyers who were part of the midwestern core of the House Republican coalition; Charles Wiggens of California, another lawyer whose incisive mind and skillful presentation made him the President's ablest defender; and Tom Railsback of Illinois and William Cohen of Maine, who ultimately decided that they could not countenance abuse of power, even from a Republican president. There were more, 38 in all, and the majority had voted to recommend that the House impeach the President before Richard Nixon relinquished the office to Vice President Ford (White, 1975, chap. 12).

These events are hardly typical. A presidential address to a joint session of Congress takes place early in the year with the State of the Union Message, and at other times only when some very unusual development makes a presidential address desirable. And presidential impeachment has been considered only twice in American history. More importantly, the legislature is a separate branch of government. Tip O'Neill was the elected leader of the House Democrats, not Jimmy Carter; and Robert Byrd was the elected leader of the Senate Democrats. Robert Michel was the elected leader of the House Republicans, not Ronald Reagan; and Howard Baker was the elected leader of the Senate Republicans.

Still, it is as well to begin with these events. The State of the Union Message—the president's legislative program—defines much of his party's legislative program for that year. And the early 70s saw a number of developments that altered the structures and temporal patterns of legislative politics. In the 1974 election that followed Watergate, the Republican party suffered the worst defeat in its history. The 75 new Democrats who were sent to Washington played a crucial role in reforms that strengthened the Speaker and subcommittees, both at the expense of those chairing full committees. The new members formed a new members' caucus to advance their interests. Indeed, since they were somewhat more concerned with issues than their predecessors, the number of issue caucuses—the congressional steel caucus, the environmental study conference, the ad hoc congressional committee for Irish affairs, and so forth—increased from 8 in 1973 to 40 in 1980 (Loomis, 1981). And two months before the Nixon resignation, Congress had given final clearance to the Congressional Budget and Impoundment Control Act of 1974. The Budget Committee created by this act became a contender for congressional fiscal power against the tax committees (Ways and Means in the House; Finance in the Senate) and Appropriations Committees, and the congressional budget process reshaped the temporal pattern of legislative politics.

While some of the spate of congressional reform during the 1970s can be connected to Richard Nixon, still more was the culmination of criticism that had been heard for some time. Committee chairmen had been regarded as too independent of party leaders, and as too domineering of committee members. The combination of Tax committees and Appropriations Committees had not been able to prevent growing deficits (Schick, 1981a). And it has been shown that Congress is subject to one period of reform after another as it struggles to emphasize one or another of its multiple functions (Jones, 1982, chap. 15). The responsibility for legislation remained central, of course, but once these reforms were in place, neither the temporal pattern nor the structures (which will be discussed in the coming chapter) were what they had been before.

THE TEMPORAL PATTERN OF CONGRESS

At any one time, a great many things are going on in Congress. Some sizable fraction of the 100 senators and 435 representatives— and the more than 17,000 staff members—are engaged making laws, breathing life into ideas that may become laws one day, providing funds for governmental activities already authorized, giving voice to constituents' sentiments, providing service to these constituents by interceding with government agencies, and so on. During the week of April 18–22, 1977, 143 House committee and subcommittee meetings were held, as were 107 on the Senate side. The House was in session for 19 hours and 30 minutes during which time 307 public bills were introduced, and the Senate met for 24 hours and 29 minutes while senators introduced 79 public bills (Jones, 1982, chap. 2).

It is very difficult to condense all of this to any simple pattern. Just as in executive politics, several things must be considered. In executive politics, there are the basic stages of the electoral cycle, the annual policy cycle, and the temporal patterns that characterize the policy areas. In legislative politics, attention must be paid to four patterns: the five stages that mark the two-year electoral cycle of each Congress; the session-and-recess sequence that punctuates each calendar year; the congressional budget process; and the distinction between the two-year periodicity of a representative's life, and the six-year cycle of a senator's life.

THE STAGES OF A

CONGRESSIONAL SESSION

Each Congress lasts for two years. The First Congress met during 1789 and 1790. The 100th Congress will meet during 1987 and 1988. In recent years, the two years of each Congress have been divided into five stages: Organization; Legislative Preparation; Floor Action;

Election Awareness; and Closing Rush of Business. The first and last
are the most distinctive; the other three can be sketched, but not drawn
in bold relief.

ORGANIZATION

Congress begins with an election. The amount of time and effort
required to organize either chamber is a direct function of the disrup-
tiveness of the preceding election. Certain things occur during this stage.
Leaders must be elected by their parties. Committee assignments must
be made. Any rules changes for that particular Congress must be considered. All this must be done before attention can be devoted to the
legislative business to come. If relatively few members have been defeated, and no major leaders have retired, then both the issue coalitions
and institutional leaders of the last session are likely to continue. In
these circumstances, Organization takes place rather quickly and rou-
tinely. But if the existing equilibrium has been disturbed by a change
of political fortunes, then there are many committee assignments to
be made; the ratio of committee seats (between majority and minority
members) is open for renegotiation; and the stage may have been set
for a revolt against the defeated party's leadership. In these circumstances, Organization is likely to be more protracted.

House Leadership Selection

1946. 1958. 1964. 1974. When looking at the House elections since
World War II, these stand out. In any House election, the vast majority
of House members can expect to be reelected.[1] But if one takes the
average proportion returned in the elections of 1946, 1948 (which
marked a return from 1946), 1958, 1964, and 1974, the average is only
77.6 percent. The mean proportion of the previous House membership
reelected in all other postwar election is 84.8 percent. The 7.2 percent
difference may not look like much, but this translates into 31 more
new House members who have to be incorporated into the committee
structure, and it *may* suggest to members of the losing party that something has gone wrong that requires a change of leadership.

After each of these elections, something major happened. In 1946,
it was a switch in partisan control, the first Republican House since
1930. In 1948, a switch back to the Democrats. After the 1958 election,
the Republicans deposed their aging leader, Joseph Martin of Massachu-

---

[1] The mean proportion of House members reelected in the 1946–1982 elections was
83 percent (Ornstein, Mann, Malbin, and Bibby, 1982, Table 2-7). This is a more useful
figure for our purposes than the proportion seeking reelection who were successful (90.7
percent). The proportion of total House membership reelected also reflects decisions
to retire, and tells more about the extent of reorganization required.

setts, and elected the much more partisan Charles Halleck of Indiana. After many conservative Republicans were defeated along with Barry Goldwater in 1964, younger Republicans led another revolt which transferred leadership from Halleck to Gerald Ford of Michigan. And in the aftermath of the 1974 elections, four Democratic committee chairmen were deprived of control of their committees, a major change in the workings of the seniority system.

Leadership contests, of course, also take place on the death or retirement of the incumbent. The most recent hard fought contest was that for the Democratic majority leadership in 1976. Speaker Carl Albert had announced his retirement at the end of the 94th Congress, and Majority Leader Tip O'Neill was expected to succeed Albert without a contest, and did so. Since every Democratic floor leader beginning with John Nance Garner, minority leader during 1929–31, had succeeded to the speakership, most Democrats assumed that in electing the floor leader to succeed O'Neill, they were very likely selecting the next Speaker. There were four candidates, and there was very little ideological distance between them. The most liberal was Phillip Burton of California, who had been elected caucus chairman two years earlier, and used this position as a base to get still more power. Next was Richard Bolling of Missouri. Earlier in his career, he was known as a protege of Harry Truman and Sam Rayburn; at 60 he had become an exponent of institutional reform and a senior member of the Rules Committee. John McFall, who might have expected to move up from the position of whip, had been hurt by the revelation that he had received a cash contribution from a Korean lobbyist, Tongsun Park. The most conservative candidate, though liberal for a Texan, was James C. Wright. Given this structure of competition, the question for Burton was how he was going to keep liberal votes from going to Bolling; for Bolling and McFall, how they were going to put together center coalitions; and for Wright, how he was going to get enough of the center vote to put together a center-conservative coalition.

Burton, Bolling, and McFall had all been campaigning informally since the fall of 1975, and when joined by Wright in the summer of 1976, the support of other Democratic members was actively sought for six months before the December 6 vote. Burton and Wright contacted prospective members at the 1976 Democratic convention; Wright went to 23 House districts to campaign for Democratic candidates; campaign funds were channeled to prospective supporters; "Dear Colleague" letters were written; telephone calls were made; and so forth. Under the rules, the candidate with the fewest votes drops out after each ballot. On that December 6, John McFall was the first to go. The second ballot was Burton, 107; Wright, 95; Bolling, 93. By two votes, Bolling, whom most thought could beat either Burton or Wright one-on-one, was forced out. The final vote was 148 for Wright to 147 for Burton. The organization of the 95th Congress "began," then, with the narrowest possible vote, and after six months of effort at the end of the 94th Congress.

The election of Robert Michel as Republican floor leader at the end of 1980 was simpler. There were two candidates. Robert Michel of Illinois had been Republican whip since 1974, and Guy Vander Jagt was chairman of the Republican congressional campaign committee. Michel was well liked, and was known as a skillful legislative technician; Vander Jagt was a better speaker, and was preferred by some younger Republicans who wanted a more aggressive posture. Unlike the Democrats, Republicans do not have a history of automatically moving one of their leaders from a lesser position into the leadership. And unlike the Democrats, Republicans do more frequently decide these matters by letting them go to a vote of the conference[2] (Peabody, 1976). In this particular case, Robert Michel was highly regarded by more of his peers, and on December 8, 1980, he won over Guy Vander Jagt by a vote of 103 to 87.

Senate Leadership Selection

The Senate is better protected from the vicissitudes of electoral fortune by the constitutional provision that only one-third of its members are up for election at one time. On the other hand, a higher proportion of those senators running are likely to be defeated. The net of both of these tendencies is that a slightly higher proportion of the Senate returns (an average of 86.7 percent), and that the Senate has sometimes had some of its greatest changes in different elections than those affecting the House. Both chambers were affected by 1946, 1948 and 1958. But the Senate experienced less of an impact from the 1964 and 1974 elections, and it shifted perceptibly in 1976, 1978, and 1980 when the House was relatively stable. Because of the six year pattern of its elections, the Senate is often affected when a class with a larger number of weak incumbents comes up for reelection.

In any case, there are no recent instances of a successful revolt against Senate floor leaders.[3] New majority and minority leaders have been elected on the death or retirement of their predecessors. Senate leadership contests are also much more personal. In the House, one can find the semblance of a campaign structure: A number of people

---

[2] House Republicans call their meeting of all members a conference (as do both parties in the Senate), whereas Democrats call their group a caucus.

[3] The leading scholar of congressional leadership elections, Robert Peabody, classifies leadership change as: routine advancement; consensus (or appointment); open competition; challenge to heir apparent; and revolt. These are ordered from least disruptive to most disruptive of the existing equilibrium. There have been two successful revolts against Senate whips: in 1969 when Edward Kennedy defeated Russell Long, and in 1971 when Robert Byrd (to Long's great delight) defeated Kennedy (Peabody, 1976, chaps. 12, 13).

work on behalf of the candidates; attempts are made to estimate voting strength; and so forth. But in the Senate, as one observer put it:

> It's an inside contest. AAs and LAs [that is, administrative assistants and legislative assistants] can do very little. It's different with legislation. There they can help their principals because they can talk substantively to their peers and they can also help the Senator relate to the constituents. But in a struggle for power, an inside contest, it's confined almost entirely to personal efforts by the candidate. (quoted in Peabody, 1976, p. 374)

Both Senate parties changed their leadership in January 1977. In the Democratic party, Robert Byrd advanced from the whip's post without opposition. In the Republican party, it had been expected that Robert Griffin of Michigan, who had been whip for half a dozen years, would also be promoted. But Howard Baker of Tennessee, who had been unsuccessful in two earlier attempts to gain the Republican leadership, had been taking some soundings to find out how much support he had, and entered at the last minute with the support of such senators as Mathias, Domenici, and Packwood. Baker won on a vote of 19 to 18, reportedly because several Republican senators felt that Baker would be a better public spokesman for the party with a Democrat entering the White House.

Committee Assignment

If the fortunes of would be party leaders at times turn on one- or two-vote margins, the careers of new (and some not so new) members usually depend on the committee assignments they receive. This is especially true for members of the more-specialized House. Freshmen (and nonfreshmen wishing to transfer from their present assignments to more desirable committees) seek allies among senior members of their state delegations, and among groups with similar interests. No instances are completely typical, but a couple will suggest the pattern of activity. One Democrat had intended to ask for Ways and Means, but discovered that a senior member of his state's delegation wanted that and shifted his goal to Appropriations. He contacted members of the Steering and Policy Committee (the committee which makes Democratic committee assignments):

> During the orientation, I made the rounds to the offices of a good number of those committee members—so that they would put a face with a name—and made my pitch. As I visited with the steering committee members, several of them would start off with "So What?" "What else is new?" "You want to be on Appropriations." I would tell them that I had been involved in politics for a while and had served as Speaker [in the state legislature] for six years and that I had to make some tough decisions. Clearly that was helpful in the process. . . . I think that in

> December I saw well over a majority of our Steering and Policy Commit-
> tee, and in cases where I didn't see them, I saw key staff people. (quoted
> in Bibby, 1983, pp. 4–5)

A Republican based his appeal on the needs of his state.

> I started, I think, like everybody else did, immediately after the election,
> the morning after as a matter of fact, and called the two top Republicans,
> Mr. Rhodes and Mr. Michel, whom I already knew. I asked for Interior,
> which I got, because it was basically political. It was important to my
> state, and my Democratic predecessor—the man I replaced—had been
> chairman of the subcommittee there and a longtime member of the com-
> mittee. The second committee was the Ethics Committee, and I took
> that, really, at the request of the leadership. I was asked if I would
> serve on that post, and agreed to do so. (quoted in Bibby, 1983, p. 5)

Not all committees are equally desirable, but aside from a few top
committees—such as the tax committees, Appropriations, and Budget—
the attractiveness of a committee depends on the interests of one's
constituency. A spot on Interior that would be prized by a western
congressman would have little interest to an urban representative. Mer-
chant Marine and Fisheries would be avoided by most, but accepted
by someone from a seacoast district. Banking, Finance, and Urban
Affairs, which handles housing and consumer legislation, is a first
choice for many urban representatives.

The task facing the party leaders and the members of the Committees
on Committees[4] is to match the requests they receive with the committee vacancies available to them to distribute. The question is what
strategy they will follow in doing so. One might be to hold back the
most desirable assignments, distributing them to more senior members,
and giving the junior members the leftovers. The system seems to have
worked that way years ago, but more recently, the Committee on Committees has been pursuing a management goal, acting as "an impersonal
preference aggregation device in an effort to keep the requesters happy"
(Rhode & Shepsle, 1973, p. 899). There is also some evidence that they
try to build up their party's majority since freshmen from marginal
districts (who need good assignments to help their chances of reelection) seem to have a little better chance of getting their first choices.
The numbers vary slightly from study to study, but one recent estimate
is that two thirds of the freshmen get committee assignments they
have requested, and by the time they have begun their third terms,
90 percent of the representatives have desired assignments (Gertzog,
1976, p. 704).

---

[4] The exact composition of the Committee on Committees differs by chambers and
by party: House Democrats use their Steering and Policy Committee; Senate Democrats
their Steering Committee. Republicans in both chambers have an entity called Committee
on Committees, but in the House, most of the work is done by an executive committee
consisting of members of the largest Republican delegations.

All of this takes time. The Senate did not approve their committee assignments (the final step in the process) until January 23, 1979, and the House did not approve their committee assignments (and elect subcommittee chairs) until January 29, January 31, and January 28, in 1977, 1979, and 1981, respectively.

Other Opening Business

The selection of party leaders and committee chairs is perhaps the most important opening business, but other things take place during the Organization stage. In an unusual but important vote in early February 1977, the Senate accepted the first major reorganization of their committee structure in 30 years, reducing the number of committees and subcommittees on which senators sat, thus increasing the chances of obtaining quorums and allowing committees to transact business. In early February that year, the Obey Commission brought in recommendations to the House to eliminate "private" office accounts and to limit outside income, which grew out of concern with the ethics of House members.

A more common activity in the Organization stage is the adoption of changes in the rules. In 1977, the House passed a package of rules changes having to do with committee and floor procedures; in 1979, there was debate on what action would be appropriate for House members indicted on felony charges. In 1981, the Republicans unsuccessfully challenged the Democratic supported rule giving the Democrats two-to-one majorities on the Rules, Budget, and Ways and Means committees while the Democrats held only 56 percent of the House seats; in 1983, rules were adopted making it more difficult for the minority to amend appropriations bills. In both 1977 and 1979, the Senate was concerned with dilatory tactics used after cloture had been voted, and Senator Byrd kept the First Legislative Day going until February 22 to take care of this matter.

Even after both houses have attended to their internal organizational business, they must wait for the State of the Union and Budget Messages to find out what the president's legislative program is going to be. Jimmy Carter's Budget Message went to the Hill on January 22, 1979, the day before his State of the Union Message. Ronald Reagan's State of the Union Message was given on January 25, 1983, and his Budget Message was sent to Congress on January 31 that year. When new presidents are entering office, Congress receives the Messages of the outgoing presidents in January, but it is well into February before the new administration gets their budget changes to the Congress. And, of course, with a new incoming administration, the Senate must spend a substantial amount of time on hearings and confirmation of members of the new administration. The net of all this is that representatives and senators are back home giving their Lincoln and Jefferson-Jackson Day speeches before the Congress is ready for much legislative business; and even then, it begins slowly.

LEGISLATIVE PREPARATION

Once Congress does undertake legislative business, the second stage—Legislative Preparation—begins. This lasts roughly from late February or early March until the annual vacation in August. The work is concentrated in committee at this point, but some bills move toward the floor. In the latter part of this stage, some of the more easily agreed upon appropriations bills emerge from committee and are passed. We can get some sense of what happens during this stage by looking at what Congress was doing during July in three recent years.

When Congress returned from the Independence Day recess in 1977, both the House and Senate had acted on 8 of 13 appropriations bills. The House had acted on two more, and another two had been reported by the Senate Appropriations Committee. Conference reports (which, when adopted, are the final stage of congressional action) were ready on four of the eight bills that had passed both chambers, but none had yet been adopted. The Senate had deleted funds for 9 of the 23 water projects that President Carter wanted to modify or eliminate altogether. The House Agriculture Committee reported a major revision of the food stamp program, generally following recommendations of the Carter administration. The House Education and Labor Committee reported a minimum wage adjustment that had the support of both the administration and organized labor. The Ways and Means Committee took up legislation to make the barge industry pay for the cost of the inland waterway system. The House Democratic leadership overcame objections of Republicans and a few liberal Democrats when the House voted to create a permanent Intelligence Committee. The Senate passed a bill dealing with oil drilling on the outer continental shelf. Both the House and the Senate adopted a conference report on a strip mining control bill, clearing it for President Carter's signature. And as we saw in Chapter 1, the House ad hoc committee on energy was moving the energy bill toward floor action.

In mid-July 1979, the Public Assistance Subcommittee of the Ways and Means Committee began a markup of a Carter administration plan for welfare reform. A hospital cost control bill, pushed by the administration as an anti-inflation measure, was tabled by the Senate Finance Committee; but in the House, Ways and Means reported a standby cost control bill. House and Senate committees were both at work on President Carter's 1979 energy bill even before the President announced it in mid-July. (As we saw in the last chapter, this bill had been "prenegotiated" before it was sent to the Hill.) On the Senate side, the Foreign

Relations Committee began hearings on the SALT II treaty that were to last for some time. By the end of the month, it became clear that some prodefense senators were going to demand increased defense spending as a price for supporting the treaty. A gas rationing bill, which the House leadership had expected would sail through because of lines of cars at gas stations, was pulled from the floor when it attracted some unacceptable amendments, but three other pieces of legislation did pass. The Senate passed an omnibus bill extending housing and community development programs for a year. (It had passed the House in June.) The House passed a bill authorizing a separate Department of Education by a narrow 210 to 206 vote, but with some controversial amendments concerning abortion, school prayer, and busing that were absent from the Senate version. The House passed a major trade bill on which a substantial consensus had been achieved, and the Senate passed it (as soon as the administration forwarded some related trade reorganization proposals). The lopsided votes in both chambers reflected the amount of negotiation that had already taken place, and the bill went to the White House for President Carter's signature before the month was out.

In 1981, the Legislative Preparation stage was dominated by the Reagan economic program. The House had passed the Reconciliation Bill just before the Fourth of July recess. The bill covered so much that 208 representatives and 72 senators devoted substantial portions of their July working time to the Conference Committee. The other major piece of legislation was the administration-sponsored tax cut bill which was being marked up by House Ways and Means at the same time it was on the Senate floor. Both chambers had their crucial floor votes on July 29, when the much-amended Finance Committee version was approved 89 to 11, and the administration backed Conable-Hance bill defeated the Ways and Means version 238 to 195. But with all the attention being given to the fiscal measures, not too much other legislation was developing. The House Judiciary Committee spent much of the month on an extension of the 1965 Voting Rights Act; a subcommittee of Senate Judiciary considered some antiabortion language; the House Interior Committee voted to establish a commission to study water policy. Otherwise, a number of appropriations bills were reaching the floor, but this was about it. Congress can handle only so much legislation at any one time.

There is a good deal of information in these paragraphs about what Congress was doing in each of three Julys. The irony is that although (at a rate of one paragraph per month) we can do no more than mention the high points of congressional activity, this is, at the same time, still more information than one can absorb easily. But if you look for the pattern behind the detail, you will find that two things were happening. One was that certain appropriations bills were being acted upon (usually the appropriations upon which consensus was reached most easily). The other was that there was more substantive legislation still in committee than on the floor.

FLOOR ACTION

Obviously, floor action takes place in all five stages. Some especially pressing legislation may be passed during the Organization stage. We have just seen some consequential floor action during the Legislative Preparation stage, and this continues on through the Closing Rush of Business. (What these stages represent are *tendencies*.) But once Congress returns from its August vacation, there is a tendency for a fair amount of legislation to reach the House and Senate floors. Enough time has passed for many committees to have completed their work, and members are not yet quite as conscious of election year considerations. To see what is taking place in this stage, we'll look at November activity in three nonelection years.

In 1977, in fact, there was relatively little floor activity in November because both chambers were waiting to hear from the energy bill conferees. They did not yet realize how long they were going to have to wait, and intended to hold a couple of pro forma sessions per week. Minority Leader John Rhodes joked with his friends on the Conference Committee saying, "I personally will promise every day that wherever I am at 5 o'clock, I will rise, face Washington, and think kindly thoughts about the conferees on the energy bill." But during October, Congress had completed action on a bill increasing the minimum wage. The House passed a bill October 27 to support social security through a major tax increase, and the Senate passed its version on November 4. The House also passed a bill giving local welfare agencies more discretion to make judgments on how recipients could spend funds, avoiding the need for a conference by adopting Senate changes in their own bill. The House passed bills for investor protection, and pesticide control by EPA, and both houses cleared a safe drinking water act to go to the president. The House and Senate were deadlocked over federally funded abortions, and so passed a continuing resolution to provide funding for HEW and the Labor Department for the month of November. The additional month didn't help; at the end of November, neither chamber was willing to back down. Both the House and Senate agreed to a conference report on child nutrition at the beginning of November, and to one aiding rural health clinics at the end of the month.

In November 1979, some of the legislation that we saw in committee during the Legislative Preparation stage was in fact on the floor for votes. On November 1, the House voted to create the Energy Mobiliza-

tion Board. The following week, the Senate authorized a five-year synthetic fuels program, and both chambers adopted a conference report
containing appropriations for synthetic fuel development. By the end
of the month, the Energy Mobilization Board was ready to go to conference. The welfare reform bill narrowly survived a recommittal motion,
200 to 205, and went on to pass 284 to 222 on November 7, although
it still faced significant Senate opposition. On November 15, the House
voted down the administration's hospital cost control plan by a 166
to 234 vote. (The administration had rejected advice from Rules Chairman Richard Bolling to wait because they didn't have the votes.) On
the Senate side, the Foreign Relations Committee, which had been
working on the SALT II treaty since July, reported it by a 9 to 6 vote,
but statements by individuals suggested that the future of the treaty
was in doubt. And there were a number of authorization and appropriations bills approved by one chamber or the other.

The sharply different nature of the 1981 legislative year can be seen
in the paucity of substantive legislation during the Floor Action stage.
The reconciliation and tax cut bills had been center stage for a long
time, and there just wasn't too much else moving. During November
there were only five substantive bills—and some of them were of less-
than-earthshaking importance. On November 2, the Senate approved
a three-year extension of the Older Americans Act dealing with nutrition, legal services, social centers, and so on. On November 19, the
House passed a bill deregulating the intercity bus industry (which the
Senate had yet to act on). The same day, the Senate passed a bill
granting waivers to the Alaska pipeline, allowing the pipeline to charge
customers for construction costs, even if it were not completed on
schedule. (The House Energy and Commerce Committee voted in favor
of this the same day.) The next day, conferees working on a four-
year omnibus farm bill broke off their negotiations. And on November
23, the Senate clarified the Foreign Corrupt Practices Act by limiting
prosecution to corporate officers who "knowingly" offered bribes (but
that measure had not yet been taken up by the House). *Everything*
else was either an authorization or an appropriations bill needed to
continue the routine business of government. And even that was
stopped when President Reagan vetoed a continuing resolution,[5] and
left the government fundless from midnight Friday until Monday. Then,
before they left for their Thanksgiving recess, Congress passed an emergency continuing resolution to provide government funding for three
more weeks.

---

[5] A continuing resolution authorizes spending to continue at the previously stipulated
level for a period of time.

ELECTION AWARENESS

Elections are never far from the minds of congressmen, but election-derived considerations become inescapable during even years. If members face primary opposition, they have to go home to campaign. Relatively few incumbents are defeated in primaries, but awareness of those unlucky few reminds members of their dependence on the voters. And even if they have no primary opposition, members know that their general election opponents are being recruited by the opposition party, and that the prospective opponents will be watching their voting records for any vulnerability. Consequently, the first half of the second year can be thought of as a stage of Election Awareness.

The question, of course, is how this heightened awareness of elections is going to affect congressional behavior. One possibility is that there will be an increase in partisanship as both parties strive to develop issues that will be helpful in the coming election. This was certainly the posture taken by recently elected Republicans in the late 1970s. A minority party has several strategies open to it—partisan opposition, constructive opposition, cooperation—none of which is ultimately satisfactory (Jones, 1968). The Republicans in the 96th Congress (1979–80) were relatively young; 56 of the 157 House members had been elected either in 1976 or 1978. The newly elected Republicans were ambitious. They wanted control of the House. They thought that more experienced Republicans were "old-fashioned" and too prone to cooperate with the majority Democrats. One of the most prominent members of the Class of 1978, Newt Gingrich of Georgia, said that they preferred a high-risk strategy of developing partisan issues, even if that cost some of them election to a second term. If asked about "responsibility," they would reply that they had to win control of the House first.

Republicans, of course, have no monopoly on developing issues from which they hope to derive partisan advantage. House Democrats were doing the same thing as they tried to distinguish themselves from Republicans during the first years of the Reagan administration. One younger Democratic congressman spoke about this just before the 1982 election:

> The strategy is a very clear one, and Tip O'Neill has said all along that the strategy was to win the November elections. . . . Tip has been consistent all along about how this was going to come together in November of 1982 and to have faith, hang in there. . . . That's all the strategy he has, is that "it's not fair; it's Republican." That message is getting through to the folks. In that respect, I would say that you have to give Tip some credit for having beat away at social security and some of these other issues. He's beat that drum pretty consistently for these two years. (quoted in Bibby, 1983, p. 32)

The opposite argument emphasizes possible incompatibility between the central thrust of the party strategy and the interests of the individual member's constituency. It is all very well for a Republican to follow an aggressively conservative strategy when elected from a conservative district, or for a Democrat to harp on the unfairness of social policies when elected by a blue-collar constituency. But what about the Republican who is running in a moderate suburban district, or the Democrat who must campaign where middle class voters prefer lower taxes to any other policy? These instances imply that the leadership ought to turn their troops loose during election years, and allow them to adapt to constituency preferences rather than seeking partisan adherence. What happens?

TABLE 6-1
Mean Party Support Scores, 1954–1981

Party	Nonelection Year	Election Year
House Democrats	77.4	75.9
House Republicans	78.4	77.2
Senate Democrats	76.5	74.9
Senate Republicans	76.7	74.9

Source: Calculated from Ornstein, Mann, Malbin, and Bibby (1982), Table 8-4.

Table 6-1 presents some data that bear on this question. The party support scores are the percentages of party members voting with their own parties on party unity votes. (A party unity vote is one in which a majority of one party votes on one side, and a majority of the other party votes on the opposite side.) Mean figures have been calculated for nonelection years, and for election years. Two things are evident. First, there are no significant differences between these means.[6] Roughly three quarters of the members vote with their colleagues on party unity votes, regardless of chamber, and regardless of whether it is an odd year or even. But once that is said, a second fact is apparent. In every pair, whether Republicans or Democrats, and whether representatives or senators, the election year party support scores are slightly lower than the nonelection year scores. Thus there is a slight tendency to stray from the party line as the election looms closer.

It must be said that the data in Table 6-1 provide only a weak test. While the differences are all in one direction, the differences are not large, and no effort has been made to control for possible confound-

---

[6] The range varies from a high of 85 percent for both House Republicans and House Democrats in 1959 to a low of 70 percent for House Democrats in 1972.

ing factors. But a carefully conducted study, with proper controls for the demographic characteristics of the district, found that "for both parties, but especially for Republicans,[7] deviant voting results in some bonus over the electoral margin expected on the basis of demographic district characteristics" (Sinclair, 1976, p. 478). This lends support to the inference of Table 6-1. If party disloyalty increases one's chances of reelection, there would be greater motivation to deviate from the party when an election is impending.

There is another point implicit in Table 6-1. This hint rests in the three quarters of the members who are voting with their parties. Both strategies are being pursued at the same time. In the *aggregate*, both parties are following the issue development style advocated by Newt Gingrich for the Republicans and Tip O'Neill for the Democrats. At the same time, *individual* Republicans and Democrats are adapting their own campaign positions by voting against their parties on issues that would threaten their chances. There is an undoubted difference in tone during this stage of Election Awareness. Every member knows just how much time remains before the primary, and how many months there are until November. But the behavioral manifestations of this awareness are more difficult to detect because the same cause leads one member to cleave more closely to the party, and another to stand apart.

CLOSING RUSH OF BUSINESS

If Legislative Preparation, Floor Action, and Election Awareness are relatively indistinct temporal stages, there is no mistaking the Closing Rush of Business. Its defining characteristic is that there is no longer time to consider all of the legislation that is now emerging from committees. Bill after bill is now ready to come to the floor; but without time to enact them all, only selected bills are going to find their way into the statute books. This gives the leaders very considerable power. They no longer need worry as much about defeating legislation they oppose. If they move it down on the legislative agenda, that settles the matter. Other members have an incentive to move business along smartly so legislation they favor can be acted upon, or to search for legislation that looks as though it will pass, and attach their proposals thereto as amendments.

While these characteristics are most evident in the last couple of weeks before adjournment, this stage begins in July. Now that Congress takes an annual break every August, and aims typically for an early

---

[7] For an earlier study which found similar results for Republicans, but no relation between roll call voting and electoral margin for Democrats, see Erikson (1971).

October adjournment so members can go back home to campaign, experienced members know that their September session is going to be of limited duration and will have a very crowded calendar. Therefore, there is at least a preliminary attempt to get as much business done as possible before the August break. July isn't nearly as frantic as late September, but members know that Congress is beginning to run out of time.

There has been some variation from one year to another. In 1978, Congress in fact adjourned in mid-October. In both 1980 and 1982, Congress failed to complete their business, and scheduled postelection sessions. In the last week in 1978, in addition to the major energy legislation reviewed in Chapter 1, Congress gave final clearance to many major bills. These included a major civil service reform, an $18.7 billion tax cut bill with a substantial reduction in capital gains taxes, an ethics bill requiring financial disclosure and setting up procedures for the appointment of a special prosecutor, wiretap legislation, a four-year extension of CETA programs, a grazing lands bill, a waterways bill carrying user fees, a rather diluted version of the Humphrey-Hawkins bill that stated goals of 4 percent unemployment and 3 percent inflation by 1983 (but didn't say how these were to be reached), a beef import measure, a modification of the Endangered Species Act, and airline deregulation.

There were a number of reasons advanced for failing to complete business in time for an October adjournment in 1980: the inability of House Democrats to pass a Second Budget Resolution, the desire of the Senate Democratic leadership to let their endangered colleagues stop voting and go home to campaign, the desire of some protagonists to hold off to see if the election didn't produce a more favorable climate. But whatever the reason, the list of legislation cleared before the October recess was meager compared with two years earlier. A bill to deregulate railroads, and another to extend higher education programs through 1985 might have some claim to importance. But beyond that, there was only an increase in benefits for disabled veterans, one banning police searches of newsrooms, a bill altering regulations for household moving companies, one dealing with pre-1949 claims against China, and a bill providing methods short of impeachment to discipline federal judges.

Once again in 1982, Congress was compelled to recess rather than adjourn in early October because the appropriations bills were not ready. In fact, one of the measures cleared on the last day (October 1) was a continuing appropriations resolution to provide governmental funding until December 17. The same day, the House took up a proposed balanced budget constitutional amendment, and rejected it 236 to 187 (42 votes short of the required two-thirds majority). Because of the time spent on this, the House was unable to complete action on a

nuclear waste disposal bill, but the House leadership wanted to act
on the balanced-budget proposal so as to be in a better position to
control the postelection session. Among the bills that Congress did
pass in the last few days before recessing were a bill to aid savings
and loan institutions, an administration-sponsored job training bill to
replace the expiring CETA legislation, a bill to end ship building subsidies, legislation to set rules governing college loans, a water bill to
enlarge the size of farms entitled to receive irrigated water, a bill to
facilitate debt collection by the government, legislation to give extra
highway funds to states taking action against drunk drivers, and several
minor crime bills.

Congress managed to clear more bills during the Closing Rush of
Business in 1978 and 1982 than it did in 1980. But regardless of the
number of bills passed, there is a great deal of legislative work during
this stage. This implies a number of things. As already noted, the leaders
have a good deal more effective influence at this stage because of
their ability to schedule bills. If a piece of legislation is moved up, it
stands a chance of passage. If a bill is moved down the agenda, it is
effectively killed. Another implication is that a consensus must already
have been developed in favor of the legislation. There simply isn't
time to work out a consensus on the floor through amendments. Moreover, a great deal of House business in the Closing Rush of Business
is done under suspension of the rules. This allows for expeditious consideration. The vote comes after only forty minutes of debate, but no
amendments are allowed, and a two-thirds majority is required for
passage. This procedure is being used more frequently as the House
agenda grows longer. During four days in late September 1978, 57 bills
were taken up under suspension of the rules (*Congressional Quarterly*,
1978, p. 2693). Unless a consensus already exists, trying to pass a bill
under suspension of the rules is a high-risk procedure.

For a person in a position of some power, time can be made an
ally. Year after year, Russell Long, chairman of the Finance Committee
when the Democrats have had a Senate majority, managed to have
something to do with what he called "the last train out of the station,"
a last important bill. We saw one example of this in Chapter 1. In
1976, he attached changes in supplemental security income that *he*
favored to a popular bill revising unemployment compensation. In 1974,
Russell Long was in charge of a trade bill that passed the last day of
the session. On the day before adjournment in 1972, Long saw the
Senate pass a bill increasing social security benefits, but without the
family assistance plan that the Nixon administration favored, and Long
opposed (*Congressional Quarterly*, 1978, pp. 2737–2738). And so on.
By arranging to be in charge of a last-minute piece of legislation, Russell
Long was able to get a lot of things settled on his terms.

But what of the member who does not have such personal power?

In this case, the member proposes his idea as an amendment to a bill that looks as though it will pass. Thus Senator Birch Bayh of Indiana (whose own wife died of cancer) wanted to fund medicare payments for pap tests for elderly women. In the last hours of the 1978 session, he announced that he was "looking for a ship leaving port" because he had some cargo that he wanted to put on board. Noticing that Russell Long and Jacob Javits had already attached amendments to a trade adjustment assistance bill, Bayh offered his, and it was accepted by the Senate. When the bill got to the House, however, Ways and Means members removed the Long, Javits, and Bayh amendments, but then decided that this administration-backed bill looked likely to pass, and added health bills as amendments of their own. But this so delayed the bill that it was the second to last to pass the House, and it didn't get back to the Senate until that body was ready to adjourn. So the trade adjustment bill, the Long, Javits, and Bayh amendments, and the House health amendments all died. In this instance, the ship sailed back and forth between House and Senate so often that it never reached port (*Congressional Quarterly*, 1978, p. 3023).

Mention of the House and the Senate brings up a final important characteristic of the Closing Rush of Business: the difference in the power of the House and Senate leaders. The House leaders have very strong rules that can be used to control the flow of business. The Senate leaders, however, operating largely by unanimous consent, are at the mercy of individual senators who use the proximity of adjournment to gain power through personal filibustering. We saw Senators Abourezk and Metzenbaum doing this in Chapter 1; at the close of business in 1982, Senator Metzenbaum was at it again, this time blocking some Alaskan railroad legislation favored by Senator Stevens of Alaska. Sometimes these determined souls filibuster in favor of something, hoping that the Senate will accept the legislation to get on to other bills. Sometimes they act to block legislation. This hardly helps their popularity with other senators, since cooperation is vital to transact business in these closing hours. But the senators who have engaged in last-minute maneuvers of this kind—Metzenbaum of Ohio, Gravel of Alaska, Helms of North Carolina—tend to be outsiders, true believers, who are little concerned with acceptance into friendship groups of senators. Convinced of the rightness of *their* causes, they advance them by whatever means, and in the loosely structured Senate, means are not hard to find.

THE SESSION AND RECESS CYCLE

In. Out. In. Out. In. Out. Something like the deep breathing of a sleeping person, the congressional year alternates between in and out, between session and recess.[8] Take 1981 as an example. After they convened on January 5, they remained in session for 70 potential working days.[9] Spring recess lasted 11 working days from April 13 through April 27. The next session provided 19 working days until a brief Memorial Day recess began on May 23. Congress came back on May 28 for another month, 22 working days, until the Independence Day recess from June 28 through July 8. The next session lasted for 17 working days until the annual summer recess from August 3 through September 9. When Congress came back in September, they stayed in session for 17 working days until they broke for a Columbus Day recess from October 7 through October 13. From mid-October, they worked for 28 days until a fairly lengthy Thanksgiving recess from November 23 through December 7. The last "in" period lasted only seven working days before Congress adjourned on December 16.

The 1981 schedule is quite typical of the first year of congressional sessions. The second year, of course, is an election year. The summer recess is a little shorter in even years, and legislative business stops, usually in early October, to allow incumbents to go home for intensive preelection campaigning. Sometimes there is a postelection session; sometimes not. In presidential election years, summer recesses are timed to coincide with the two nominating conventions.

The division of the congressional year into sessions and recesses has two implications for legislative behavior. One is the limited amount of time to transact business (about which more in a moment). The other is the use of recesses as action-forcing devices by the leadership. Essentially, the last working days before a recess provide in a weak sense what the Closing Rush of Business provides in a strong sense. When Congress is about to adjourn, legislative work must be done if it is ever going to get done. When the House or Senate are about to recess, there is a lesser imperative to get work finished. This imperative arises from commitments the members have already made to be in their constituencies (or elsewhere) as soon as the recess begins. When members are debating on the floor with plane tickets in their pockets, and packed luggage waiting in their offices, they are less anxious to

---

[8] A few years ago, the House began to call recesses "district work sessions." There was a fair amount of journalistic snickering about this, the implication being that everyone "knew" that members of Congress weren't working that hard back home. In fact, as Richard Fenno has shown brilliantly in *Home Style* (1978), representatives are working very hard maintaining contact with their constituents. I use the word *recess* rather than district work session because session-and-recess cycle conveys my meaning better than session-and-session cycle.

[9] I have simply counted the number of working days (Monday through Friday) between recesses to determine how much time was available. This does not mean that a session of the House was held each day, and certainly not that all legislators were in Washington when Congress was in session. The figures are for the House; the dates for the Senate are slightly different.

prolong debate than otherwise would be the case. Therefore important bills are often brought to the floor on the Thursday before an Easter recess, or the Wednesday before a Christmas recess. We saw an example of this in Chapter 1 when Speaker O'Neill instructed the ad hoc energy committee to bring the energy bill to the House floor for action shortly before the long summer recess in 1977.

The average period between recesses has been rather stable. In three odd years (1977, 1979, and 1981), the average session lengths were 24.1, 24.6, and 26 days, respectively. In three even years (1978, 1980, and 1982), the average session lengths were 28.7, 28.3, and 23.1 days, respectively.[10] Thus, over these six years the average "in" period was 25.8 working days. (1981 was typical because the average time between recesses was 26 working days.) It follows that the usual question facing the leadership is how much business they can transact in just over five working weeks.

There are obvious limits to what can be accomplished in five weeks, especially in the Senate, which transacts its business largely by unanimous consent agreements (meaning that any one senator can block business), and where there is always the possibility of a filibuster. What does get scheduled in this limited time? Jack Walker (1977) has suggested that the congressional agenda can be divided into required and discretionary portions. There are three classes of required items. The first is the "periodically recurring" problems that regularly turn up on the legislators' desks. The budget cycle produces a lot of these. Another example would be the periodic increase in the "temporary" debt limit that is required whenever the national debt exceeds the previously stipulated figure. Still more required action comes from expiring legislation. Extension of the Voting Rights Act was hardly a priority of the Reagan administration, but the act was expiring and some action had to be taken.

A second class, according to Walker, consists of "sporadically recurring" problems that do not recur as frequently, but are part of the required agenda. Because of major legislation already passed:

> Small political systems have been established revolving around executive agencies, professional groups, suppliers and clients, all of whom operate according to rules and understandings that have developed as the programs have evolved. . . . Once major disagreements arise within these systems . . . they exercise a compelling claim on the attention of key Senators who control the committee and subcommittees that oversee their activities. (pp. 425–26)

---

[10] In the three non-election years, the House leaders had 75, 76, and 70 percent of the total number of working days available to them. During the election years, the sessions lasted for 66, 66, and 60 percent of the working days. In election years, Congress has a little less total time to complete its work because of the pre-election adjournment (or recess).

The third class of required agenda items arise from crises or pressing problems. These happen in random fashion, but command a high place on the congressional agenda when they do occur. Thus, clarification of the status of the marines in Lebanon under the War Powers Act became a high priority in the fall of 1983. Dealing with a rail strike, a gasoline shortage, or a sharp economic slump have been urgent matters in other congressional sessions.

This required agenda takes a great deal of time, but there is some time left for what Walker calls discretionary items. What discretionary items are important enough for congressional attention? California Congressman Clem Miller wrote his constituents a remarkably lucid series of letters about the Congresses in which he served from 1958 until killed in a plane crash in 1962. In one such, he explained:

> Great legislation is scarce. There are only half a dozen bills of overriding importance in a session. The very process of selection takes an impressive block of time each year. Much of the preliminary jockeying for position and priorities is quite complicated. Is the bill of prime rank? Is it more important than another bill? Should it be considered at all, at least right now?
>
> Through July, August and September [of 1961] such a dispute for priority went on between the Disarmament Agency Bill and the Peace Corps Bill. All were agreed that the Foreign Aid Bill came first. Huge energies were expended on this great bill, of primary rank, and there was no time for the Foreign Affairs Committee to devote to the remaining two until the big one was enacted. Their proponents stood in the wings waiting for clearance through the legislative chutes. . . . It would be fair to say that much of the legislative energies of Congress goes to the assignment of priorities. This is no inconsiderable function. (Polsby, 1971, p. 141)

The required items and the priority discretionary items fill much of the five weeks available to the leadership. They are the blocks around which the legislative calendar is constructed. In the time that remains, Congress does the rest of its business. Much of this minor discretionary business is symbolic or of primary concern to particular constituencies. None of it takes too much time; but of the approximately 700 public and private bills passed by each Congress, a substantial proportion falls into this category. It is fit into the slack time between the required and priority items because the leaders know it is discretionary, but it is of genuine concern to *somebody*, and is therefore acted upon by the Congress of the United States.

THE CONGRESSIONAL BUDGET PROCESS

Another annual sequence—the congressional budget process—is superimposed on the oscillation between sessions and recesses. By the late 1960s, many legislators felt they were losing control over the budget. There were a number of sources of this. Both the Vietnam War and the Great Society programs (especially medicare and medicaid) were very expensive. A large proportion of the budget was dictated either by past commitments or legislation mandating expenditures: 60 percent was uncontrollable in FY (fiscal year) 1967 when these figures were first published, and this has risen to an estimated 75 percent since. And under reform laws requiring open meetings, the tax and appropriations committees holding open hearings were in a weaker position to resist demands than when they met in executive session (Schick, 1981a, pp. 294–95). In an effort to reassert some degree of control, Congress went to a process they had tried briefly in the 1940s, a congressional budget.

Theoretical Deadlines for Congressional Budget Process	
January 18	President's budget submitted.
March 15	Congressional committees advise budget committee of plans.
April 15	Budget Committee Report First Budget Resolution.
May 15	Congress completes action on First Budget Resolution.
Labor Day + 7	Congress completes action on all spending bills.
September 15	Congress completes action on Second Budget Resolution.
October 1	New fiscal year begins.

The Congressional Budget Act of 1974 set forth a very neat process that is summarized in the accompanying box. The president would, as heretofore, present his budget in January. The act specified that this was to be done 15 days after Congress convenes. By March 15, both the Appropriations Committees and authorization committees were to notify the Budget Committee of any plans that would lead to spending. By mid-April, the Budget Committee would prepare a First Budget Resolution which would state the amount of revenue to be expected, and would set spending targets in 19 broad categories. Congress was to act on this by mid-May. The spending targets were to be borne in mind by the Appropriations Committees handling the spending bills, and by the authorizing committees in any actions they took in ensuing months. Action on all spending bills was to be completed

seven days after Labor Day, and by mid-September, Congress was
to complete action on a Second Budget Resolution. This Second Resolution would contain binding revenue and spending figures. With the
budget process complete, the new fiscal year would begin on October 1.[11]

This was all very neat, but the process hasn't worked out quite
this way. The May and September deadlines for the First and Second
Budget Resolutions were met during the first three years of the congressional budget process (1976, 1977, and 1978), but haven't been met
since. The record has been worse on appropriations. 1976 was the
only year (so far) when Congress passed all the appropriations bills
in time for the beginning of the new fiscal year on October 1.

The First Budget Resolution was defeated in the House in 1977,
though a revised Resolution was passed soon thereafter. And while
the First and Second Resolutions passed when they came up in 1978,
a Third Resolution had to be passed in the spring of 1979 for FY 1978
because spending was greater than envisioned. (Fortunately, revenues
were also up that year.) In 1979, Congress passed a First Resolution
by late May which called for a balanced budget by 1981, but House
and Senate Conferees did not agree on a Second Resolution until October 31, and it was late November before this finally cleared the House.
In the Senate debate, Henry Bellmon (the ranking Republican) said
for the Budget Committee, "We are making it clear now that we will
not have a Third Budget Resolution to bail out committees who do
not make the concessions" necessary to bring spending into line.

The 1974 Congressional Budget Act included a process called reconciliation, but this was not used until 1980. While the budget resolutions
made estimates about revenues, and set spending limits, they did not
have the force of law. Reconciliation, however, is a two-stage process
that instructs committees to achieve certain savings (or raise taxes),
and then incorporates these changes into a bill. Until 1980, the Budget
Committees relied on pleas and dire warnings to preserve the budget
process. In 1980, however, Congress was unable to agree to a Conference Report on a First Budget Resolution until June 12 (nearly a month
late), and then it ordered reconciliation to be used. The House adopted
a reconciliation bill in early September, but Senate Democrats blocked
Republican attempts to bring it to the floor in late September, reportedly
because the Democrats did not want to go into a presidential election
with a budget calling for a deficit. On November 20, Congress finally
passed a Second Resolution, and then on December 23, Congress passed
its first reconciliation bill, calling for $4.6 billion in savings and $3.6
billion in tax increases.

---

[11] Congress gave itself three additional months to get all this done. The old fiscal
year began on July 1.

Three important changes took place in the budget process in 1981. These increased the impact of the Reagan budget legislation, but were independent of the administration's desire for budget cutting and could have taken place without it. First, the reconciliation bill was moved back to be associated with the First Budget Resolution. It had become obvious that if reconciliation was to have any effect, the bill would have to be passed early enough in the session to control committee actions for the balance of the year. Second, reconciliation (which had originally been envisioned as a tactical device for adjusting small differences between spending bills and the budget resolution) was used in a major strategic way. Third, for the first time, the 1981 reconciliation bill ordered specific changes in substantive legislation, thus making the budget process superior to the authorizing committees. In addition to all this, the Reagan administration used reconciliation to win their big budget victories of 1981. The First Resolution cleared Congress on May 21, only a few days behind schedule, and the House (where the administration faced their greatest test because of the Democratic majority) passed the reconciliation bill 217 to 211. But none of the FY 1982 appropriation bills were passed by October 1, and a Second Resolution simply reaffirming the First (and in any case less important since reconciliation had been moved to the First Resolution) was passed at the end of the session.

Some six weeks in the spring of 1982 were spent in an effort to find a compromise that both the White House and House Democrats could support. When that failed, the Senate adopted a First Resolution acceptable to the White House and Senate Republicans leaders on May 21. On the House side, no less than eight budget resolutions proposed by different coalitions were voted down on May 21. It was not until June 10 that the House adopted a First Resolution that was very similar to that which had passed the Senate, and it cleared Congress on June 23. Nearly two months later (August 18), Congress passed a reconciliation bill. The First Budget Resolution was readopted later in the year as a pro forma Second Budget Resolution, but once again in 1982, the appropriation bills were not ready by the beginning of the Fiscal Year on October 1. Indeed, only three of the regular appropriation bills had been passed by December 20, and Congress again turned to the temporizing measure of continuing resolutions.

There are four things that should be borne in mind to understand what was happening during the first decade of the congressional budget process. First, the Budget Committees were new, and had to contend for power against the Tax Committees (House Ways and Means and Senate Finance), and the Appropriations Committees. If the Budget Committees had tried to assert strength immediately, the whole process could have failed. Second, the votes on the budget resolutions in the House were highly partisan. With almost all of one party voting against

a budget resolution, it took only a few defections from the other to
defeat it. Consequently, a good deal of consensus building was necessary to get a budget resolution that would pass. Third, while Congress
was getting further and further behind their deadlines, it was including
more in each legislative package. The 1981 Reconciliation Bill had much
more legislative potency that the pleas of the mid-to-late 70s. Finally,
in Allan Schick's words:

> Power is widely dispersed in Congress, there are multiple opportunities
> for access and influence, and important decisions are often made piece-
> meal, in an inconsistent manner. These characteristics are political im-
> peratives for a legislature whose distinctive role is the representation of
> diverse interests. . . . But budgeting's essential purpose is the coordina-
> tion of many decisions and many decision makers to achieve a reasonably
> comprehensive and consistent outcome. (1981a, p. 325)

Budgeting is therefore very difficult for any legislature to accomplish.

In view of the changes from year to year, any prediction about the
ultimate form (or indeed the survival) of congressional budgeting is
hazardous. All that can be said about its temporal impact is that it
dominates that portion of the annual schedule when it is being debated,
and that it has become more prominent. Whether future budgeting will
focus on a strong First Resolution with appropriations bills coming
along later, return to spring and fall periods of concentration on a
First Resolution and then a Second Resolution, or assume some other
form, remains to be seen.

THE TWO-YEAR REPRESENTATIVE AND

THE SIX-YEAR SENATOR

The final temporal pattern in Congress is rooted in the Constitution.
It arises from the two-year terms of representatives and six-year terms
of senators. As business comes to a close during even years, all House
members are necessarily concerned with the immediate needs of their
reelection campaigns. In the other body, only one third of the members
need do so.

The differences in the two-year cycle of the representative, and the
six-year cycle of the senator have been skillfully analyzed by Richard
Fenno (1983). Quantitative evidence about the differences is hard to
come by. If one looks at roll-call voting, the number of trips home, or
the patterns of expenditures, there seems to be something there, but
the pattern is not terribly clear. Part of the problem, as usual, is that
confounding factors prevent any clear picture from emerging. Some
senators are raising money to pay off past campaign debts; some are
raising money in midterm to appear strong; some are raising money

because of an immediately impending election. Some senators spend a lot of time in their home states because they simply like to campaign; some do so because they live so close to the District of Columbia. Hence the data do not organize themselves neatly along a time line. Considering all these things, Fenno concludes "there is weakly supportive evidence for the operation of an electoral cycle and for its systematic impact on campaign activity" (p. 37).

Richard Fenno's own sensitive impressions of the lives of representatives and senators, though, point to some very real differences between them. One is that House members never really stop campaigning whereas senators do. Having traveled with congressmen in their districts both in nonelection years and in the immediate pre-election periods, he notes a fundamental similarity of behavior. Senators, on the other hand, find that a campaign six years earlier is hard to recall distinctly, and even if it could be, there may have been enough of a shift in public opinion that it would not be wise to repeat it. What constituent in 1980 cared about their senator's 1974 views on Watergate? And what difference does it make to a voter in 1984 if their senator favored or opposed Jimmy Carter's 1978 economic policies?

Senators undergo two transition periods in each six-year term. One is during their first year when they're coming off the campaign. This doesn't happen all at once, and the campaign activity tends to shape a senator's noncampaign activity. There are some key staff members from the campaign "who have a first hand sensitivity to electoral forces and electoral problems in the state" (Fenno, 1983, p. 40), and these staff members retain a campaign perspective. Their senator is, after all, at least a potential candidate for reelection. The campaign also affects noncampaign activity because of positions taken and promises made. If a senate candidate promises constituents that he will vote to cut taxes, that candidate as senator is more likely to do so than another who has given speeches about the need to maintain a decent level of government services.

The other transition comes about the fifth year, and is the switch back to campaign behavior. Campaign funds are raised; trips back to the home state are made; there is a heightened sensitivity to state concerns. All this is intended to position the senator as a strong candidate, but there is another concern as well. Potential opponents are making their decisions about running at this time, and if the senator seems to have sufficient resources, potentially strong opponents may back off. If this happens, the activity in this transition period may be the most important thing the senator does to ensure reelection.

The basic characteristic of the six-year Senate term, though, is that it is long enough to allow a period of campaigning and a period of governing. The first-year transition from campaigning to governing does not take place instantly, but it does take place. A senator in the second year of his first term said that his campaign was now "a war story." The details of the campaign were fresh enough to be easily remembered, but campaign concerns were no longer at the center of his consciousness. This gives senators freedom to focus on public policy. They spoke about this. One said, "I wouldn't have voted against food stamps as I did last Saturday if I had to run in a year. The six-year term gives you some insurance. Well, not exactly—It gives you a cushion. It gives you some squirming room" (Fenno, 1983, p. 37). Not all senators are concerned with the opportunity to affect policy, of course. Some are more concerned with power. Some have listened to the importunings of the party, and have run because they were popular enough to hold the seat for their party. But for those who are interested, the period of governing does give them the freedom to affect the course of public affairs.

Summary

The temporal pattern of Congress is complex, but it can be analyzed into four patterns. There are the five stages—Organization, Legislative Preparation, Floor Action, Election Awareness, and Closing Rush of Business—that divide the two-year life of a Congress. The short session-and-recess cycle recurs several times during a year. The congressional budget process lasts roughly a year, although it may get carried over to the following year by continuing resolutions and supplemental appropriations. And the Constitution gives senators some breathing room with their six-year terms.

The temporal pattern of Congress results from the superimposition of each of these cycles on all of the others. Sometimes the juxtaposition is regular. The appropriation bills and Second Budget Resolution needed for the beginning of the next fiscal year come at the same time as the Closing Rush of Business in every even year. At other times, the simultaneous effects are less predictable. But each of these patterns is part of the larger sequence of congressional events, and taken together they afford some understanding of legislative politics.

CHAPTER 7

THE STRUCTURES OF
LEGISLATIVE POLITICS

Each Congress is different. This does not mean we cannot make statements that hold true for several Congresses. The internal and external structures discussed in this chapter can be used to conceptualize any Congress. The units from which the internal structure is constructed are the members themselves. Groups are formed containing sets of members, and coalitions are formed containing sets of groups. Similarly, the external structures we shall consider here (namely, the institutional responsibilities that bear on public policy)—incubation, legislation, and oversight—also apply across a succession of Congresses.

But since the internal structure begins with the members, and since each Congress contains some new members, it follows that the Congresses themselves will be different. As we have seen, some elections result in strikingly different bodies. This happened with the House in 1974 and the Senate in 1980. But even if there are relatively few new members, and even though the House and Senate are amalgams of the new members and a much larger number of returning members, the combinatorial possibilities are different. Some groups will be slightly larger, and some will be slightly smaller. And all groups will view the election mandate through the lenses of their own interests, and want to form coalitions to carry out their views of that mandate. In many cases, coalitions result that are very similar to those formed in the preceding Congress. But in each Congress the effort to move in a slightly different direction begins with the infusion of new members. So, let us begin our analysis with a look at the members. What are their backgrounds? And what do these backgrounds imply about the nature of Congress?

THE INTERNAL STRUCTURES OF CONGRESS

THE MEMBERS

When Henry Kissinger was sworn in as Secretary of State, he made some moving comments:

> Mr. President, you referred to my background, and it is true, there is no country in the world where a man of my background could be standing here next to the President. . . . And if my origin can contribute anything to the formulation of our policy, it is that at an early age I have seen what can happen to a society that is based on hatred and strength and distrust, and that I experienced then what America means to other people, its hope and its idealism.

Driven from his native Germany as a boy, Henry Kissinger fought as an enlisted man in World War II. After the war, he went to Harvard with the help of the GI Bill of Rights, ultimately earning a Ph.D. degree. After establishing a front-rank intellectual reputation, he had come to the White House as President Nixon's national security advisor. Now he was being sworn in as the senior member of the cabinet. It was certainly understandable that he spoke with a full heart. But there is another point as well. Henry Kissinger's great political success came in appointive office in the executive branch. It is almost inconceivable that a Jewish Republican professor—no matter what his personal qualifications—could have been elected to the House of Representatives from Cambridge, Massachusetts, in 1972.

The congressman from the eighth district of Massachusetts was Thomas P. (Tip) O'Neill, Jr. After earning his B.A. degree from Boston College, he went into the insurance business, and was elected to the General Court of Massachusetts (the name of the legislature since colonial times) when he was 24 years old. By 1947, he was minority leader, and after the 1948 election, he became the first Democratic Speaker in the history of Massachusetts. In 1952, a seat in the House opened up when Representative John F. Kennedy ran for the Senate. O'Neill was elected to the House of Representatives when he was 40, and by the time Henry Kissinger was sworn in as secretary of state, he had become majority leader. Speaker O'Neill's career is atypical in certain respects. He did not take a law degree; he was a little too young when elected to the state legislature; he has become too famous in recent years. But otherwise, the elements of a typical (successful) House career were present. O'Neill represents the partisan and ethnic majorities in his district; he had established solid credentials in state politics before he was elected to Congress; he became more influential in the House with the passage of time.

The steps in Tip O'Neill's career may be seen over and over in House biographies. Eligio (Kika) de la Garza obtained his law degree in 1952, took up the practice of law in south Texas, and was elected to the Texas legislature the same year. He got the Democratic nomination for a U.S. House seat in 1964, and after eight terms, became chairman of the Agriculture Committee. Henry Hyde got his law degree at Loyola University in 1949. After 16 years as a practicing attorney, he was elected to the Illinois House of Representatives in 1966, and had one term (1971–72) as majority leader. Elected to the U.S. House in 1974, his name became familiar to the general public as the author of "Hyde amendments" banning the use of federal funds for abortions, but he was better known to his Republican colleagues as an able legislator. Charles Rangel took both his undergraduate and law degrees after a hitch in the army, getting the latter degree from St. John's in 1960. After some appointive positions, he was elected to the New York Assembly in 1966, and then defeated longtime Congressman Adam Clayton Powell in the Democratic primary in 1970. Rangel was a member of the Judiciary Committee at the time of the Nixon impeachment hearings, but then moved to Ways and Means when Hugh Carey was elected governor of New York. Over and over, the steps are repeated: law degree; state (or local) political career; election to Congress.

TABLE 7-1
Educational Backgrounds in Executive and Legislative Politics

Degree	White House Staff	House Members	Senators
None	1%	12%	7%
Bachelor's	24	25	20
Law	31	46	61
Master's	19	11	9
Doctor's	25	5	3

Source: White House staff, interview data; representatives and senators; compiled from *Almanac of American Politics 1984.*

Data comparing the educational backgrounds of the Carter and Reagan staff members with those of members of the 98th Congress (1983–84) are presented in Table 7-1. There are still a few members of Congress without baccalaureate degrees.[1] No substantial difference exists between executive and legislative activists in the proportions having undergraduate degrees, but very substantial differences are to

---

[1] In 1966, 21 percent of the House and 17 percent of the Senate lacked any degree (Ripley, 1983, p. 95). The majority of the nongraduates, in both the 1960s and the 1980s, had begun college somewhere, but had not completed degree requirements.

be found at the postgraduate level. Representatives are much more likely than White House staffers to have law degrees, and senators are still more likely to be lawyers. Conversely, the master's and doctoral degrees connoting mastery of some specialized subject matter, such as international affairs or economics, are much more common in the White House.[2]

In Chapter 4, we saw that Heclo's finding that cabinet members tend to come from the four great estates of academia, corporate business and the law, the government bureaucracy, and elective politics, could be used—with a little adaptation, to describe the backgrounds of White House staff members. The resulting classification (from Table 4-1) is used in Table 7-2 to compare the occupations of White House staff members and legislators. In compiling the data for this chart, I have assumed that anyone who has been in a given occupation for at least 10 years should now be so classified, whatever the former occupation. From 1950 through 1956, for example, Mark Hatfield taught political science and served as dean of students at Willamette University, but since 1957, he has served Oregon as secretary of state, governor, and senator. Therefore, he is counted under government, not academia. (There are also some legislators so classified who have been employed by government for less than a decade, but who began their governmental careers so young that they had no other vocation.) When this is done, government—meaning elective politics for virtually all the legislators—swamps all the other categories. Of the "governmental" legislators, just over half the representatives, and two thirds of the senators have been in Congress for over a decade. For the rest, though, "government" refers to state or local careers. As with Tip O'Neill on Boston's Beacon Hill, or Henry Hyde in Lincoln's Springfield, their views of life are developed closer to their constituents than Washington, D.C. Note also in Table 7-2 the relative absence on Capitol Hill of those coming from journalism, academic life, or think tanks. This means policy analysis on the Hill is going to be more political, and profit less from the insights of academic disciplines.

Since governmental careers so dominate the occupations in Table 7-2, we need to "unpack" it by examining the pregovernmental occupations for those listed under government in that table. When this is done, we discover that the pregovernmental career for 25 percent of the House members and 15 percent of the senators was government. This points to two categories. There are a number of veteran legislators with 10 years or more in Washington who had long political careers before being elected to Congress. Their current career is "federal gov-

---

[2] The gap in Ph.D.s is even more in the White House's favor than it seems from the table. A third of the congressional doctor's degrees are medical (M.D., D.D.S. or D.V.M.) or scientific (D.Sc.).

TABLE 7-2
Occupational Backgrounds in Executive and
Legislative Politics

Occupation	White House Staff	House Members	Senators
Law	25%	14%	10%
Government	19	64	74
Business	8	10	10
Journalism/ advertising	21	3	0
Academia	16	2	1
Consulting/ think tank	11	0	0

Source: White House staff, interview data; representatives and senators; compiled from *Almanac of American Politics 1984*.

ernment," and their preceding career was "state and local government." The other category consists of those who began in politics so young that they had no prepolitical careers. Most of this second grouping are relatively new to Washington, but have spent some time moving up the political ladder at home. Otherwise, 39 percent of the representatives and 59 percent of the senators were lawyers, proportions corresponding to the many law degrees we saw in the members' educational backgrounds. Business remains as the principal alternative to law as a precongressional career route, and there are relatively few journalists, and very few from academic or quasi-academic backgrounds.

This does not exhaust the occupational backgrounds. In the House, one finds a few farmers, a few teachers,[3] some physicians and dentists, four veterans of the labor movement, four who have worked with other interest groups, three former morticians, and a scattering of other vocations. Similarly, the Senate includes an astronaut, a professional basketball player, a retired admiral, and a few other occupations, but there are too few such persons to impart any characteristic to the Senate.

Another marked difference with executive politics is that in the executive branch there are many people who have moved among the great estates. It is not uncommon to find White House staffers with previous experience in more than one of the estates before their present appointments. But it is uncommon to find legislators with prior federal experience. There are only five former members of White House staffs who are now in the House: James Jones of Oklahoma, a member of Johnson's staff; Richard Cheney of Wyoming, Gerald Ford's chief of staff; Tom

---

[3] The definition of academia in Table 7-2 was restricted to higher education to maintain comparability with the White House staff.

Loeffler of Texas, a Ford legislative liaison staffer; Estaban Torres of California, special assistant to President Carter for Hispanic affairs; and Marcy Kaptur of Ohio who was on the Carter Domestic Policy Staff. (We may be seeing something new here. Jones was elected in 1972; the other four in 1978 or later.)

There are a few more who have been assistants to former members, and then have gone back to their boss's district and been elected in their own right. This would seem to be a natural move since congressional staffers would already have contacts with political leaders in the districts, but it is still unusual. Several members who did have prior Washington experience have become leaders: Robert Michel and Trent Lott, the Republican leader and the whip, were both administrative assistants to their predecessors. James Jones has become chairman of the House Budget Committee, and Richard Cheney was elected chairman of the Republican Policy Committee after only a single term. So it would seem that knowledge pays off. Still, those who have gone from Washington back to the districts, and returned as members are only a handful. The single dominant pattern is a law practice in the district,[4] and then a move to Washington.

Now what does the prevalence of law imply about congressional activity? First of all, lawyers are advocates who serve clients. Their goal is not dispassionate analysis, but the best presentation of their client's side of a case. The goal of pleadings before a court, moreover, is to isolate a single point of fact or law on which the parties are in dispute. Therefore, lawyers are characteristically skilled in arguing one side of one issue on behalf of one client. As representatives and senators, they continue to do this.

Senators and representatives are perhaps best understood as solitary political entrepreneurs. They build their own political organizations, and make their own judgments about what risks to take and avoid. When should they hold on to the safe seat in the state senate, and when should they try for a House nomination? How did Henry Hyde sense that he should run for Congress in 1974? 1974 was a terrible year for Republicans, and there was a very strong Democrat running against him. How did Charles Rangel figure out that Adam Clayton Powell, who had been elected regularly since 1944, could be beaten in 1970? Similarly, how did Congressman Charles Mathias decide he had a good chance to defeat Senator Daniel Brewster in Maryland in 1968, and how did Congressman William Cohen figure out that 1978 was a good year for him to run against Senator William Hathaway

---

[4] The district law practice is a particular type. It tends to be a "political" law practice, one that produces enough income to permit the aspiring legislators to pursue their political avocations. The law offices do not have the thick rugs and expensive furniture that suggest wealthy corporate clients, and the lawyers are more apt to gain political visibility than to become eminent leaders of the bar.

in Maine? The political graveyard is filled with the corpses of those who have taken risks at the wrong time, and there are a good many state legislators who stay at that level because they opt for safety rather than ever taking the risk of running for higher office. Congress is composed of those who, with whatever combination of skill and luck, have estimated the risks correctly, and then acted.

ISSUE GROUPS

Knowing that many members are lawyers, and all the members are successful political entrepreneurs tells us something about the tone of the body, but nothing about the policies that are likely to be adopted. One lawyer may be passionately liberal. Another may be a determined conservative. A third may be a moderate who views his role as quasi-judicial, and therefore weighs the claims of competing interest groups. To have any sense of the policy tendencies of the congressional parties, we need to know how many there are of each type, and how they combine into issue groups.

Issue groups may be discovered in legislative politics by using the same methods described in Chapter 4 for executive politics. Agreement scores are first calculated for every pair of members, and are then used as input to a cluster program to find groups of legislators who take common positions. The data that are used to calculate the agreement scores are different, though. For the legislators, we have used data based on roll-call votes.[5] Therefore the inference is reversed. With the White House staffs (and the electoral activists analyzed in Chapter 10), one has attitudinal data and assumes that those with similar attitudes will behave in the same way. With the legislators, we know how they voted, and assume that common behavior implies similar underlying attitudes.

The data come from an analysis of the 95th Congress by Aage R. Clausen.[6] (The 95th Congress is the most recent for which such an analysis is available.) Following procedures he developed in analyses of earlier Congresses (Clausen, 1973), he has produced scales representing policy dimensions. The votes of all the representatives and senators have been scored so their positions on these scales represent their liberal or conservative tendencies. These policy dimensions are very similar to the policy areas used in Chapters 4 and 5.[7] The single policy area of international involvement is decomposed into a national secu-

---

[5] Of course, attitudinal data could be used if they were available.

[6] I should like to thank Professor Clausen for so generously sharing his data.

[7] Indeed, a major reason for using these policy areas is that Professor Clausen and I found such similar phenomena when investigating different data sets from different institutional domains, using different techniques.

rity dimension reflecting feelings about the wisdom of relying on American military power, and the already established international involvement dimension principally concerning foreign aid (Clausen & Van Horn, 1977). Labor votes are included under social benefits instead of economic management, and natural resources is included with economic management instead of being treated as a separate policy. And Clausen has found a new dimension formed by votes on abortion. This splits both parties in very different ways than the previously existing policy dimensions. Otherwise, the policy classification is identical with that already discussed.

The positions of the representatives and senators on the scales have been used to calculate agreement scores. If a pair of legislators have identical scores on every scale, they have an agreement score of 1.0. If their positions are no closer than would be expected by chance, then they have an agreement score of 0. Further information on the agreement scores and the cluster analysis may be found in Appendix A-7.1.

House Republicans

There were five Republican issue groups in the House. The Hard-Line Conservatives were a bit more conservative than other House Republicans on every domestic issue except agriculture, and distinctly more conservative on national security and international involvement. The Pro-Farm Republicans took typical GOP positions in every policy area except agriculture, but were supportive of agricultural assistance programs. The Domestic Conservatives were more liberal than the Hard-Line Conservatives in domestic policy areas (that is, they were moderate conservative as opposed to conservative) and they cast liberal votes on international involvement. The Republican Moderates took moderate positions in most policy areas, but liberal positions on international involvement and abortion. The Republicans Leaders, a very small group that happened to include some leading Republicans, cast typical Republican votes in most policy areas, but showed liberal tendencies in international involvement and abortion.

Figure 7-1 gives an *approximate* idea of the location of the Republican groups in an issue space. The *centers* of the circles indicate how close or distant the groups are from each other. Their locations were derived from the multidimensional scaling technique used to produce the plots of issue agreement structures in Chapter 4. The sizes of the circles, however, have been drawn so the areas of each correspond to the size of each group.[8] The Hard-Line Conservatives were the largest Republican group in the 95th Congress (1977–78), and the Republican

---

[8] For further information about the multidimensional plots of House and Senate issue groups, see Appendix A-7.2.

FIGURE 7-1
House Republican Issue Groups, 95th Congress

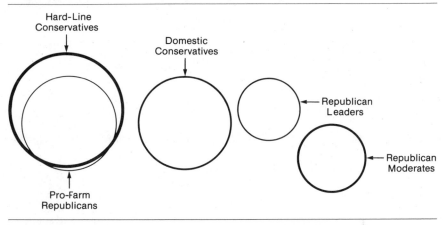

Leaders the smallest. Therefore the circle for the Hard-Line Conservatives is the largest, and that for the Republican Leaders is the smallest.
The horizontal axis is a conservative-liberal dimension for issues other
than defense or agriculture. The Hard-Line Conservatives are therefore
farthest to the left, and the Republican Moderates are farthest to the
right. The vertical axis appears to be the national security dimension.
Since there is little disagreement among Republican groups on defense,
there is little dispersion along the vertical axis, but the Hard-Line Conservatives are located a little higher than the Republican Moderates.

The issue groups can be described more precisely by using their
median scores and their membership. Each group's median scores are
given in Table 7-3. I gathered additional information about the groups
by asking knowledgeable persons what members of the groups had
in common.[9]

The Hard-Line Conservatives were the largest Republican group,
and the most conservative. In policy areas where the party median
was moderate conservative, they were often conservative. Bud Schuster
of Pennsylvania, Robert Bauman of Maryland, Sam Devine of Ohio,
and Marjorie Holt of Maryland were all in this group.[10] A Republican
said they're "all basically conservative, especially on national defense

---

[9] The knowledgeable persons were either observers or participants. The observers
were all political scientists who had Washington jobs permitting them to watch Congress
at very close range. The participants will not be otherwise identified, but whenever a
participant is being quoted, his party affiliation will be given.—The issue groups that
could be most easily identified, incidentally, were those on the party extremes. Issue
groups that were located closer to the center of their party, or which differed on only
one or two issues were harder to recognize.

[10] The members whose names are given as typical of the group are those with very
high agreement scores with other group members. This means that their personal voting
records are, in fact, representative of the issue group tendencies.

TABLE 7-3
Median Scores of House Republican Issue Groups

Issue Group	Position in Policy Area							Number and Percent
	National Security	International Involvement	Economic Management	Social Benefits	Civil Liberties	Abortion	Agriculture	
All House Republicans	Conservative (26.1)	Moderate (20.6)	Moderate Conservative (24.8)	Moderate Conservative (25.0)	Conservative (26.7)	Conservative (29.1)	Moderate Conservative (24.1)	
Hard-Line Conservatives	Conservative (28.5)	Moderate Conservative (25.5)	Conservative (27.5)	Conservative (27.9)	Conservative (28.8)	Conservative (29.7)	Moderate Conservative (24.8)	48 32.9%
Pro-Farm Republicans	Conservative (26.8)	Moderate (21.2)	Moderate Conservative (24.9)	Moderate Conservative (24.9)	Conservative (26.9)	Conservative (29.5)	Moderate Liberal (15.2)	32 15.2%
Domestic Conservatives	Moderate Conservative (22.6)	Liberal (13.6)	Moderate Conservative (22.8)	Moderate Conservative (22.9)	Moderate (24.0)	Conservative (29.6)	Moderate Conservative (24.7)	31 21.2%
Republican Leaders	Moderate Conservative (24.0)	Moderate Liberal (15.5)	Moderate Conservative (24.9)	Conservative (26.6)	Moderate Conservative (25.5)	Liberal (12.6)	Moderate Conservative (23.7)	13 8.9%
Republican Moderates	Moderate (18.7)	Liberal (12.3)	Moderate (20.6)	Moderate (19.0)	Moderate (19.2)	Liberal (11.9)	Moderate Conservative (24.3)	15 10.3%

Note: The figures are median scores on scales that vary between 10 and 30. In general, a low score (10) represents a dove position in national security and international involvement, and a willingness to use government power and resources in the domestic policy areas. A high score (30) represents the opposite.

The convention followed for substantive interpretation of the scale scores was: 10 to 14, liberal; 14.1 to 18, moderate liberal; 18.1 to 21.9, moderate; 22 to 25.9, moderate conservative; 26 to 30, conservative. This classification is arbitrary, and is intended only as an aid to understanding. Notice, for example, that if the boundary of moderate had been raised from 21.9 to 22.9, the Domestic Conservatives would have been classified as moderate in three policy areas where they are now classified as moderate conservative.

Data source: Professor Aage Clausen's study of the 95th Congress, unpublished.

issues." An observer commented, "You're certainly talking about what is now [1981] mainstream, aggressive Republicanism. They're outspoken, and take a hard conservative line."

The Pro-Farm Republicans included Don Young of Alaska, Ron Marlenee of Montana, and William Whitehurst of Virginia. What these members would have in common was a puzzle to both colleagues and observers, but it was one of two groups (the other was Democratic) whose distinctiveness came on agriculture. The Pro-Farm Republicans were much more supportive of agricultural assistance programs than their colleagues.

The Domestic Conservatives had the same relation to their Hard-Line colleagues that the Domestic Conservatives did to the Unalloyed Conservatives in the Reagan White House. Both were slightly more moderate on domestic issues, and quite different on international involvement. Domestic conservatives in the House included Guy Vander Jagt of Michigan, Ralph Regula of Ohio, and Henry Hyde of Illinois. A fellow Republican commented, "All would be classed pretty much as regular Republicans. No flamers on either end of the spectrum."

The Republican Moderates cast liberal votes on international involvement and abortion, moderate conservative votes on agriculture, and moderate votes in every other issue area. They included Ben Gilman of New York, Stuart McKinney of Connecticut, Harold Hollenbeck of New Jersey, and Joel Pritchard of Washington. Observers immediately spotted these as among the most liberal Republicans. "Moderate Republicans, I guess we should call them. They would be referred to by their colleagues as liberals." Indeed, this was the case. A Republican called them "very liberal." One was "a guy the leaders always have trouble with on party-line matters," and another was "a very liberal Republican of the old northeast establishment mode."

The smallest Republican group included a large proportion of leaders. Robert Michel and Barber Conable, the senior Republican on Ways and Means, were both in this group, as were David Stockman, who became OMB director, and Charles Wiggins, who made such a skillful defense of Richard Nixon in the impeachment hearings. Their votes were very close to the party median, except on international involvement and abortion, where they were nearly as liberal as the Republican Moderates. Interestingly, they were seen by a Republican as "fairly conservative, fairly consistent on regular Republican types of issues like economics, and on budget and tax matters." Observers pointed to their pragmatism. They were "old-style, main-street Republicans," as well as "insiders who worked within the institution."

House Democrats

The House Democratic issue structure is much more complex, and based much more on geography. There were eight Democratic issue

groups in the 95th Congress whose size and *approximate* relationship
to each other is suggested by Figure 7-2.[11] The vertical axis is a liberal-
conservative dimension, with the most liberal groups at the top and
the most conservative at the bottom. The horizontal axis concerns national security, with prodefense groups to the left, and more-dovish
Democrats to the right. The left wing of the House Democratic coalition
is made up of Liberals who favor abortion. They are at the top, and
slightly to the right. Immediately below them, is a smaller group of
antiabortion Liberals. The voting records of the two groups were very
similar except on abortion, where they are quite opposed. The Dominant
group is the largest group of Democrats. They also cast liberal votes,
but seemed a little less motivated by ideology. The Democratic Moderates, a group of Northeasterners and Midwesterners, fell just about
at their party's median on most issues. The Neoliberals are recently
elected members whose location in issue space is about the same as
the Democratic Moderates. The Pro-Farm Democrats are southern and
border-state Democrats, whose positions on nonagricultural domestic
issues put them at the same vertical location as the Democratic Moderates, but their greater tendency to vote for defense locates them to
the left of the Democratic Moderates. The last two groups as we move
down Figure 7-2 are both southern. The Traditionalists are the larger.
The Democratic Fundamentalists are the smallest issue group, and constitute their party's right wing.

The Liberals who favor abortion were almost all from the North,
including a dozen from New York. Typical members of this group included Ben Rosenthal of New York, John Seiberling of Ohio, and Pete
Stark of California. One observer commented, "The left wing of the
Democratic party. Sort of automatic liberals. Guaranteed to take the
liberal position on any issue." A Democrat echoed, "Roaring liberal.
All definite full-blown liberal. No question about it. Three of the most
liberal members of the House."

The Liberals who oppose abortion were from the East and Midwest,
and included such members as Edward Boland of Massachusetts, David
Bonior of Michigan, and Bruce Vento of Minnesota. They were a group
that puzzled the Congress watchers. A Democrat said, "Bonior and
Vento are two of the most liberal members. They're younger, vocal,
and both pretty effective." They were indeed liberal, but Boland, Bonior,
and Vento were all Roman Catholic, and it was the single issue of
abortion that separated this group's voting record from the better-
known "automatic liberals."

The Dominant group was the largest issue group in the House, with
68 members, only 7 of whom came from the South. Norman Mineta

---

[11] Since their issue structure was so complex, it was very hard to find an interpretable
multidimensional plot for them. Figure 7-2 is based on two dimensions of a five-dimen-
sional solution.

FIGURE 7-2
House Democratic Issue Groups, 95th Congress

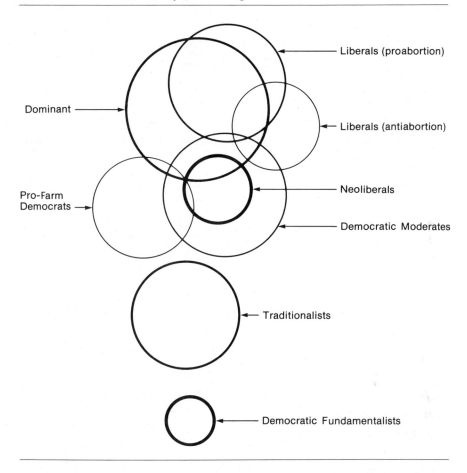

and Henry Waxman of California belonged to this group, as did John Dingell of Michigan and Charles Rangel of New York. Two observers agreed, "They're all mainstream, urban Democrats who differ among themselves on certain types of growth versus environmental concerns, and on some regional issues." A Democrat distinguished this group from the first group of Liberals by saying, "If I had to put Waxman and Rangel together with Stark and Seiberling, and ask the Speaker who he wanted to talk to, I think he'd choose Waxman and Rangel." Indeed. In addition to being the largest group, the Dominant group was the home of the Democratic leadership. Majority Leader Jim Wright, Majority Whip John Brademas, his successor Thomas Foley, and longtime Rules Committee member Richard Bolling were all members of this group.

TABLE 7-4
Median Scores of House Democratic Issue Groups

Issue Group	Position in Policy Area							
	National Security	International Involvement	Economic Management	Social Benefits	Civil Liberties	Abortion	Agri-culture	Number and Percent
All House Democrats	Moderate Liberal (17.0)	Moderate Liberal (14.1)	Liberal (14.0)	Liberal (13.0)	Moderate Liberal (15.1)	Moderate Liberal (15.8)	Liberal (13.2)	
Liberals (proabortion)	Liberal (11.7)	Liberal (12.8)	Liberal (11.8)	Liberal (11.4)	Liberal (11.5)	Moderate Liberal (16.7)	Moderate Liberal (15.5)	44 15.3%
Liberals (antiabortion)	Liberal (12.9)	Liberal (12.5)	Liberal (12.3)	Liberal (11.5)	Liberal (13.2)	Conservative (28.2)	Liberal (13.0)	24 8.4%
Dominant	Liberal (14.0)	Liberal (12.1)	Liberal (12.8)	Liberal (11.8)	Liberal (12.7)	Liberal (10.4)	Liberal (12.1)	68 23.7%
Democratic Moderates	Moderate (18.1)	Liberal (13.4)	Liberal (13.8)	Liberal (12.4)	Moderate Liberal (16.3)	Conservative (29.7)	Liberal (12.9)	50 17.4%
Neoliberals	Moderate (19.0)	Moderate (19.2)	Moderate Liberal (16.0)	Moderate Liberal (16.0)	Moderate Liberal (17.0)	Liberal (12.7)	Moderate (19.4)	14 4.9%
Pro-Farm Democrats	Moderate Conservative (22.1)	Moderate Liberal (17.5)	Moderate Liberal (17.5)	Moderate Liberal (16.7)	Moderate Liberal (19.4)	Liberal (12.4)	Liberal (11.1)	33 11.5%
Traditionalists	Conservative (26.6)	Moderate Conservative (23.6)	Moderate Conservative (22.4)	Moderate (21.6)	Moderate Conservative (24.3)	Conservative (27.9)	Liberal (10.9)	37 12.9%
Democratic Fundamentalists	Conservative (29.3)	Conservative (27.8)	Conservative (27.0)	Conservative (27.2)	Conservative (28.7)	Conservative (27.0)	Moderate (20.0)	7 2.4%

Note: The figures are median scores on scales that vary between 10 and 30. In general, a low score (10) represents a dove position in national security and international involvement, and a willingness to use government power and resources in the domestic policy areas. A high score (30) represents the opposite. For the convention used to categorize the scores, see the note at the bottom of Table 7-3.

Data source: Professor Aage Clausen's study of the 95th Congress, unpublished.

The Democratic Moderates were largely from the Northeast and Midwest with a few from the border states. This group included such congressmen as Joe Gaydos from Pennsylvania, Doug Applegate from Ohio, Leo Zaferetti from New York, and William Natcher from Kentucky. An observer said that these members were "all among the more conservative nonsouthern Democrats." A Democrat (also from the North) said "Gaydos is pretty conservative. Zaferetti's got conservative tendencies. Applegate's so goddamn conservative, he rides on the right wing of the plane going home."[12] Another Democrat added, "Those two guys are people the leaders almost instinctively check with. Even if the whip count comes back and says that Ohio's OK, Pennsylvania's OK, they'd still want someone to check with Applegate and Gaydos."

Unlike the Pro-Farm Republicans, the Pro-Farm Democrats were not distinctive solely because of their support of agriculture. They also favored a strong defense, were one of the groups favoring abortion, and otherwise were just a bit more conservative than the Democratic median. They were largely a southern and border-state group including Bill Hefner and Ike Andrews of North Carolina and Ronnie Flippo of Alabama, who were seen as "dependable" Southerners. One observer stated they were the "moderate Southerners. You might not think that if you'd see their ADA ratings, but they're a little more likely to go along with the leadership than a [Traditionalist] would be." A northern Democrat agreed. "They are people you can talk to, who want to be national Democrats, and are really caught in that crossfire more than most."

The Traditionalists were entirely a southern group, and save for their support of agriculture, were distinctly to the right of center in the Democratic party. Kika de la Garza of Texas belonged to this group, as did Jack Brinkley from Jimmy Carter's home district in Georgia, Glenn English of Oklahoma, and the man regarded as the brains of the conservative southern Democrats, Sonny Montgomery of Mississippi. Aside from the Traditionalists' conservatism, observers said, the one thing that would bind them together was that they were all from agricultural districts, and therefore quite supportive of farm programs.

The Democratic Fundamentalists were still more conservative. They took more conservative positions in every policy area (save the special case of abortion) than any other group in the Democratic party. On economic management, social benefits, and civil liberties, they were indistinguishable from the Republican Hard-Line Conservatives, and on national security and international involvement, they were the most

---

[12] It is interesting how participants, hypersensitive to intraparty differences, exaggerate these differences in making comparisons. A glance at Table 7-4 shows that the Democratic Moderates are a litle more conservative than the preceding three groups, but by no means conservative (except on abortion) in absolute terms.

conservative group in the entire House. This small group included Dan
Daniel of Virginia, Larry McDonald of Georgia, and Bob Stump of Arizona. This group was instantly recognizable. "Right-wing ideologues,"
said one observer. "They're like Republicans," added another. "There's
no southern, rural populism to them. They look like Republicans and
act like Republicans." A Democrat asserted, "Those are three prime
candidates for crossovers, especially McDonald and Stump." And, in
fact, Bob Stump did switch to the Republican party in 1982.

The Neoliberals are listed last because they were the one Democratic
group that was spread across all geographic regions. Rather than having
a region in common, this group was all of a single generation. They
were younger members who had been elected in 1974 or later, often
from formerly Republican districts. "The Class of 1974," a Democrat
reflected, "was almost a new breed type of ideology. Not so much
New Deal or Great Society, but refinement, good government. They
didn't think they were like the previous liberals. They didn't think
they were like the previous Democrats. They felt they were intelligent,
thoughtful, critical." In fact, their rethinking of liberalism led them to
take generally moderate positions, and they ended up squarely in the
center of the Democratic party.

Senate Republicans

James Reichley (1981) has suggested that each party can be divided
into four issue groups. Republicans can be analyzed into Progressives,
Moderates, Stalwarts, and Fundamentalists. The Progressives are those
birthright Republicans who believe in the party of Abraham Lincoln
and Theodore Roosevelt, and think government can be used to promote
economic growth and social progress. The Moderates are less likely
to stimulate change, but are willing to accommodate it. Often acting
as spokesmen for corporate interests, they are fond of talking about
the virtues of efficient government organization. The Stalwarts' great
days came in the turn-of-the century era of Main Street America. They
wish to preserve what they see as a healthy society, and are loyal
to the Republican party as such. The Fundamentalists are the newest
Republican issue group, emerging after World War II. Worried about
communism abroad and what they see as social decay at home, many
of the Fundamentalists are Roman Catholics or Southerners who were
one-time Democrats.

Reichley's Democratic issue groups are Liberals, Regulars, Centrists,
and Traditionalists. The Liberals have rather consistently pushed for
expansion of the federal welfare state, and greater equality in society.
The Regulars often come from city political organizations, and while
they support economic benefits, they are much more cautious on civil
liberties questions such as race or lifestyle. The Centrists tended to

be supportive of New Deal reforms, but to have questions about the further expansion of government under the Great Society programs. Traditionalists come from the South and tend to oppose expansion of the federal government, especially on civil rights matters, but to be supportive of defense.

The Reichley analysis almost fits the Senate issue groups found in the 95th Congress. The issue structure in the Senate is the simplest found in any of the institutions I have examined, and by the time of the 95th Congress, a single liberal-conservative dimension captured a lot of the issue structure in the Senate (Smith, 1981). The issue groups in both parties can be arrayed along a single liberal-conservative dimension *if* one ignores the policy areas of abortion and agriculture, and combines two Republican groups that are split only on the question of abortion. And most, but not all, of the issue groups posited by James Reichley were found in the 95th Senate.[13]

The sizes and *approximate* positions of the five Republican issue groups found in the 95th Senate are indicated in Figure 7-3. The vertical

FIGURE 7-3
Senate Republican Issue Groups, 95th Congress

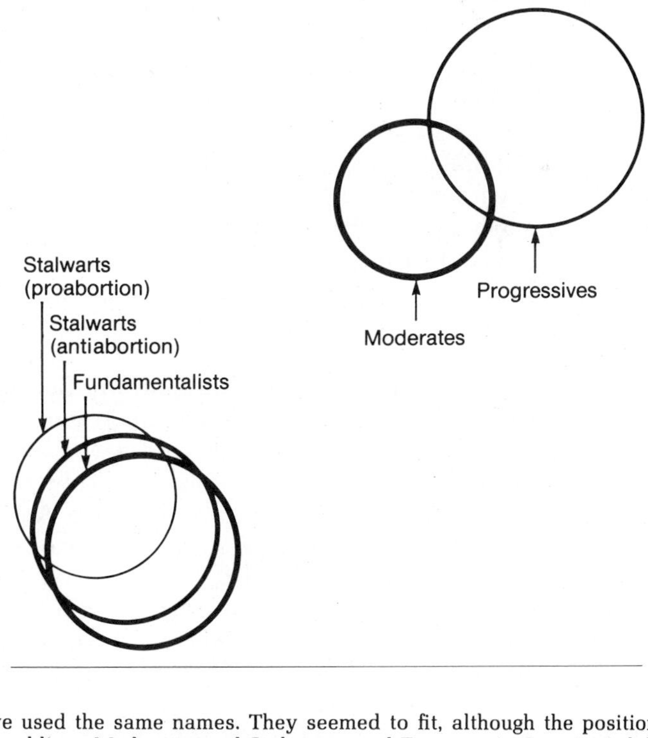

Stalwarts (proabortion)

Stalwarts (antiabortion)

Fundamentalists

Moderates

Progressives

---

[13] I have used the same names. They seemed to fit, although the positions of some groups (Republican Moderates and Stalwarts, and Democratic Centrists) did not correspond to the ideal types described by Reichley.

axis concerns relative positions on international involvement, with a
more internationalist position to the top and a more nationalist position
below. The horizontal axis denotes the groups' positions on social benefit programs, with support for such programs increasing as one moves
from left to right. In these two policy areas, therefore, there is a classic
Republican liberal-conservative split between the Progressives and the
Moderates located in the "northeast" (of the figure) and the Stalwarts
(both proabortion and antiabortion) and Fundamentalists located in
the "southwest." While it is certainly true that the issue structure divided the Senate Republicans into liberal and conservative wings, Figure 7-3 exaggerates this by focusing only on issues that divided the
five groups in this particular way. This plot does not reflect economic
management—which would have separated the Progressives and the
Moderates—and it does not reflect abortion—which would have produced greater distance between the two groups of Stalwarts.

The Progressives were a nine-member group that, except for its opposition to agricultural assistance,[14] took liberal or moderate liberal
stands in every policy area. They included Senators Javits of New
York, Case of New Jersey, Mathias of Maryland, and Percy of Illinois,
the latter two being the only Progressives who were not from the Northeast. They were identified without difficulty. An observer said, "Those
are your eastern moderate-to-liberal Republicans." "All of them," a
Republican pointed out, "are relatively liberal on foreign policy issues.
All of them are relatively liberal on social issues."

The Moderates were a very small group consisting of the two senators from Oregon, Hatfield and Packwood, Senator Danforth of Missouri, and Senator Pearson of Kansas. This small set was a puzzle to
Congress watchers which they resolved by opposing them to other
groups. "All that one could safely say," mused a Republican, "is that
none of them could be considered a member of the hard right." An
observer concluded, "I guess you'd call them liberals, but independent
liberals."

The split between the proabortion and antiabortion Stalwarts produced another one of the puzzles arising from separation on a single
issue. There were five proabortion Stalwarts and seven antiabortion
Stalwarts. The Proabortion group included Senators Tower of Texas,
Schmitt of New Mexico, and Wallop of Wyoming; the Antiabortion
group Senators Dole of Kansas, Domenici of New Mexico, and Lugar
of Indiana. Taken together, they defined the center, or perhaps the
center right, of the Senate Republican coalition. But apart? One observer
said with considerable justification, "I don't distinguish those two
groups." A Republican said that the antiabortion Stalwarts "would

---

[14] Opposition to farm aid programs was also characteristic of the Republican Moderates in the House.

TABLE 7-5
Median Scores of Senate Republican Issue Groups

Issue Group	National Security	International Involvement	Economic Management	Social Benefits	Civil Liberties	Abortion	Agriculture	Number and Percent
					Position in Policy Area			
All Senate Republicans	Moderate Conservative (25.8)	Moderate (20.8)	Moderate Conservative (24.5)	Moderate Conservative (25.0)	Moderate Conservative (22.8)	Liberal (14.0)	Moderate Conservative (23.0)	
Progressives	Liberal (13.0)	Moderate Liberal (15.0)	Moderate Liberal (14.2)	Liberal (13.0)	Liberal (12.0)	Liberal (10.6)	Conservative (29.6)	9 24%
Moderates	Liberal (13.5)	Moderate Liberal (14.7)	Moderate (21.0)	Moderate (18.5)	Moderate Liberal (15.0)	Moderate Liberal (14.5)	Liberal (13.0)	4 11%
Stalwarts (proabortion)	Conservative (27.8)	Moderate Conservative (23.5)	Conservative (27.3)	Conservative (28.2)	Conservative (26.2)	Liberal (13.3)	Moderate Liberal (14.5)	5 14%
Stalwarts (antiabortion)	Conservative (27.7)	Conservative (26.0)	Conservative (26.2)	Conservative (26.0)	Moderate Conservative (24.4)	Conservative (28.5)	Liberal (13.5)	7 19%
Fundamentalists	Conservative (28.6)	Conservative (27.7)	Conservative (28.0)	Conservative (28.0)	Conservative (28.2)	Conservative (27.0)	Moderate Conservative (24.0)	7 19%

Note: The figures are median scores on scales that vary between 10 and 30. In general, a low score (10) represents a dove position in national security and international involvement, and a willingness to use government power and resources in the domestic policy areas. A high score (30) represents the opposite.
For the convention used to categorize the scores, see the note at the bottom of Table 7-3.
Data source: Professor Aage Clausen's study of the 95th Congress, unpublished.

not be a voting bloc (in the 97th Congress)." Taken together, they are
supportive of agriculture programs, but otherwise take moderate conservative, or conservative, positions in all the policy areas. But the
two groups do split on abortion, and as if to demonstrate the multidi-
mensionality of the issue structure, the antiabortion group takes positions that are just a shade more moderate than those of the proabortion
group in every other domestic policy area.

When we reach the Fundamentalists, we find another quite recognizable group. This group, including Senators Goldwater of Arizona, Laxalt
of Nevada, and Helms of North Carolina, takes conservative positions
in every single policy area except agricultural assistance. Here they
moderate their opposition to government sufficiently to merit a moderate conservative classification. A Republican agreed that this "would
be a very conservative group in the Republican party," and an observer
simply commented that this would be a new right group.

Senate Democrats

The sizes and *approximate* locations of the four issue groups found
among Senate Democrats in the 95th Congress—Liberals, City Liberals,
Centrists, and Traditionalists—are shown in Figure 7-4. The vertical
axis is the major one here, and appears to indicate the groups' positions
regarding economic management and civil liberties. The higher a
group's location, the more supportive they were of government activities
to shape the economy and the more zealously they protected personal
liberties. The horizontal axis shows their positions on abortion, with
a position to the left denoting tolerance of abortion, and a position
to the right, opposition. The Liberals were the largest group, and they
did in fact take liberal positions. The City Liberals are located slightly
to the left of the Liberals because of their slightly greater support of
abortion. The City Liberals are contained within the Liberals' circle
in Figure 7-4, not because their positions are identical, but because
the Liberals are such a large group. The Centrists are located midway
between the Liberals and Traditionalists on the vertical axis because
their economic and civil liberties votes locate them half-way between,
but they are off to the right because they are the most conservative
group on abortion. And the Traditionalists oppose federal activity in
general, and in economics and civil rights in particular.

As their positions in Table 7-6 indicate, the Liberals are no challenge
to describe. They are, as one observer put it, "the ADA type," and
as another added, "you're talking about your core support for social
programs there." The Liberals included senators long identified with
the left side of the Democratic party, such as Gary Hart, Edward Kennedy, and George McGovern. What made this group so important in
the 95th Congress, though, was its size. With 26 members, it dominated

FIGURE 7-4
Senate Democratic Issue Groups, 95th Congress

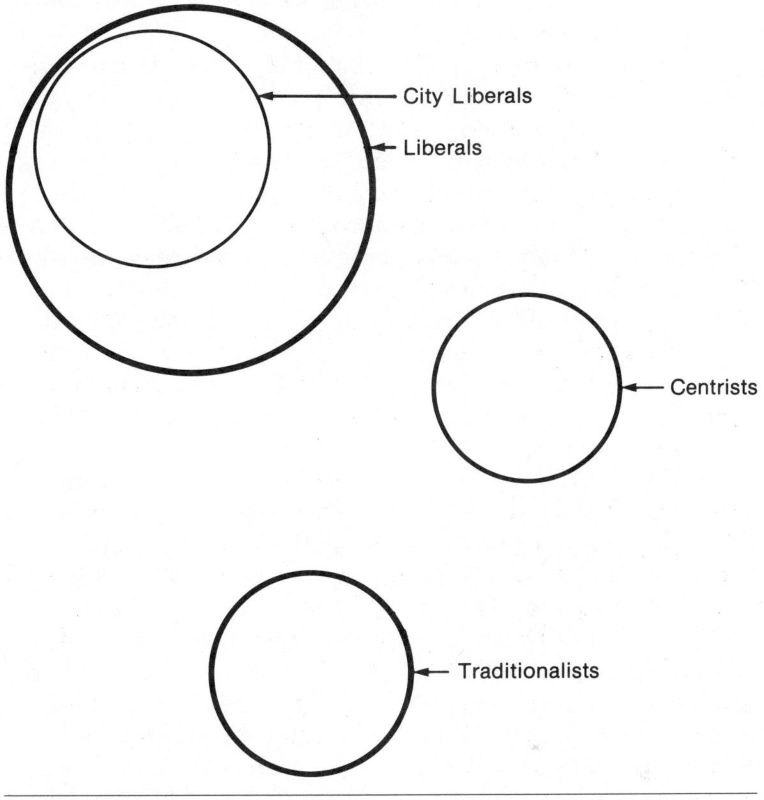

City Liberals

Liberals

Centrists

Traditionalists

the Senate Democratic coalition, and gave a distinctly liberal cast to the entire Senate.[15] And the disappearance of 15 of these Liberals by the 97th Congress had a lot to do with the much more conservative Senate that greeted President Reagan when he took office.

Of the eight issue groups suggested by James Reichley, only Regular Democrats could not be found in the 95th Congress (perhaps because they are distinguished from other liberals as much by style as voting pattern). Instead, there was a group of City Liberals. The members of this group, Robert Byrd of West Virginia, Daniel Patrick Moynihan of New York, John Glenn of Ohio, and others, are frequently distinguished from Liberals by a greater readiness to vote for defense spending. As one observer put it, "Well, I see that group as a little more prodefense, a little more hawkish than the group to their left." But in fact, this group had a voting pattern identical to that of the similarly named group found by Aage Clausen (1973, pp. 107–108) in the 85th

---

[15] Only three Liberals—Sasser of Tennessee, Bumpers of Arkansas, and Sparkman of Alabama—were from the South.

and 86th Congresses. Their voting pattern was almost the same as
the Liberals except on agricultural assistance. Most of the City Liberals
were from urban states, and they were the only group of Democrats
who opposed farm programs.[16]

The Centrists were generally in the middle of the Democratic party.
This group included Senators Ford and Huddleston of Kentucky, Eagleton of Missouri, and DeConcini of Arizona. One observer said that
this was a group that would be called "moderate conservative, centrist
in the Democratic party." Another said it was a "hodge-podge. A kind
of a potpourri of people who are more conservative, somewhat pork-
barrelish, border statish." The description of the group as a mixture
was apt in another sense. While they do tend to be in the middle of
the Democratic party, their votes run the full ideological spectrum.
The Centrists are (barely) liberal on social benefits and agricultural
assistance, moderate liberal on economic management and civil liberties, moderate on national security and international involvement, and
conservative on abortion.

Seven of the eight Traditionalists were from the South, and in five
of the seven policy areas, they cast moderate conservative votes. They
did take a conservative posture on international involvement, and along
with many others from agricultural areas, they cast liberal votes in
favor of farm programs. They were also a recognizable issue group.
One observer said, "They're very traditional conservative Democrats.
Not strong ideologues. A Richard Russell mold, I guess." There was
unintended irony in this comment. In the great days of Richard Russell,
who represented Georgia in the Senate for 38 years and who was
the most influential Southerner of his generation, the Senate was often
said to be a southern club. By the time of the 97th Congress, there
were only three southern Traditionalists[17] left, John Stennis of Mississippi, J. Bennett Johnston of Louisiana, and Sam Nunn of Georgia.

The Senate leadership repeats a pattern we saw earlier in the House.
At least in the 95th Congress, the Democratic leaders tended to come
from the dominant group, while the Republican leaders established
patterns of their own. Democratic Floor Leader Robert Byrd was a
City Liberal, while Democratic Whip Alan Cranston belonged to the
Liberals. Republican Floor Leader Howard Baker, Republican Whip

---

[16] This vote profile, incidentally, was identical with that of the Republican Progressives, most of whom also came from the same part of the country.

[17] The more precise statement would be that there were only three southern senators
left who had been classified as Traditionalists in the 95th Congress. There were three
more southern Democrats, Bentsen, Long, and Chiles, who were isolates (i.e., not members
of any issue group) in this analysis. In general, I have ignored isolates in this chapter
because such a high proportion of the members belonged to the issue groups. Ninety-
six percent of House Republicans, 96 percent of House Democrats, 82 percent of Senate
Republicans, and 88 percent of Senate Democrats could be assigned to one of the issue
groups.

TABLE 7-6
Median Score of Senate Democratic Issue Groups

Issue Group	National Security	International Involvement	Economic Management	Social Benefits	Civil Liberties	Abortion	Agriculture	Number and Percent
			Position in Policy Area					
All Senate Democrats	Liberal (13.6)	Moderate Liberal (16.3)	Moderate Liberal (14.6)	Liberal (13.5)	Liberal (13.8)	Liberal (13.7)	Moderate Liberal (15.1)	
Liberals	Liberal (12.3)	Liberal (13.0)	Liberal (13.2)	Liberal (12.4)	Liberal (12.5)	Liberal (12.2)	Moderate Liberal (14.1)	26 45%
City Liberals	Liberal (12.8)	Moderate Liberal (14.5)	Liberal (13.2)	Liberal (12.1)	Liberal (12.4)	Liberal (12.0)	Conservative (28.2)	11 19%
Centrists	Moderate (21.0)	Moderate (20.0)	Moderate Liberal (17.0)	Liberal (14.0)	Moderate Liberal (17.0)	Conservative (29.0)	Liberal (14.0)	7 12%
Traditionalists	Moderate Conservative (23.0)	Conservative (26.5)	Moderate Conservative (22.0)	Moderate Conservative (23.5)	Moderate Conservative (23.5)	Moderate Conservative (24.5)	Liberal (13.0)	8 14%

Note: The figures are median scores on scales that vary between 10 and 30. In general, a low score (10) represents a dove position in national security and international involvement, and a willingness to use government power and resources in the domestic policy areas. A high score (30) represents the opposite. For the convention used to categorize the scores, see the note at the bottom of Table 7-3.

Data source: Professor Aage Clausen's study of the 95th Congress, unpublished.

Ted Stevens, and Robert Griffin (who had been whip in the 94th Congress) were all isolates. Their own scores on the issue scales would put them close to one group on one set of issues, and a different group on another set of issues. The Republican issue groups were split 3 to 2 on six issues (that is, three groups with relative liberal scores and two with relatively conservative scores or the other way round), and 4 to 1 on the last. In six of the seven policy areas, Baker's own voting record put him on the side occupied by the larger number of Republican groups. In this Congress, it was as if Democrats expected their leaders to be close to the dominant issue group, but Republican leaders had to be somewhat more dexterous in staking out positions that would not alienate any important segment of their following.

Finally, it should be emphasized that this issue structure existed in the 95th Congress, 1977–78, and one should be careful about making inferences to other Congresses. The most recent analysis available at this writing is *National Journal*'s analysis of congressional voting in 1982. This used three scales—economic, social, and foreign policy issues—that were highly correlated with each other. In the House, 151 Democrats and 15 Republicans were classified as very liberal or fairly liberal; 41 Democrats and 35 Republicans as moderate; and 42 Democrats and 137 Republicans as fairly conservative or very conservative. In the Senate, 31 Democrats and 7 Republicans were liberal; 11 Democrats and 9 Republicans were moderate; 4 Democrats and 38 Republicans were conservative (Schneider, 1983, p. 952). This analysis is sufficiently different from that based on policy areas, so that only tenuous comparisons can be made. But it appears that the *within* party issue structure in the House did not change much between the two Congresses. In the Senate, however, the Liberals were much weaker in the Democratic party than they had been four years earlier, and the Stalwarts and Fundamentalists had gained strength in the Republican party. More generally, it seems likely that at least the details of the issue structure change over time (for example, a group that had a moderate position in a policy area shifts to a moderate liberal posture), and the sizes of the issue groups can change quite rapidly as electoral fortunes bless one group and smite another.

OVERLAPPING MEMBERSHIP IN OTHER GROUPS

David Truman, in his classic, *The Governmental Process*, wrote:

> No individual is wholly absorbed in any group to which he belongs. Only a fraction of his attitudes is expressed through any one such affiliation, though in many instances a major fraction. . . . What happens to the individual [who experiences overlapping memberships]? We must start from the fact that the equilibrium of an individual consists in his adjustment to the various institutionalized groups . . . to which he belongs. (1971, pp. 157, 162)

What Truman argues is generally true of groups is certainly true of the issue groups we have been considering. These are abstractions that summarize much of the members' voting behavior, and as such, they are helpful in understanding Congress. But representatives and senators belong to other groups as well, and we can enhance our understanding by looking at three of the most important of these—state delegations, informal caucuses, and committees.[18]

State Delegations

An Oregon congressman was once discussing an insect problem that was causing crop damage in his state: "We were doing everything we could think of to try to get the Department of Agriculture to help our farmers with this, and we just weren't getting anywhere. Then the insect crossed the state line and became a California problem. Boy, did we get results then!" Once the insect crossed the state line, the Oregonians gained the assistance of one of the largest and most active state delegations.

State delegations have been shown to be excellent predictors of how representatives vote.[19] This effect is evident even after taking account of the influence of party and constituency. The influence of the state delegation is not the same across policy areas or across all states. A study of the 85th and 86th Congresses showed that state party was least influential in economic management (where most of the variance was already accounted for by party and constituency), and then was increasingly important in agriculture, international involvement, social benefits, and most important in civil rights (Clausen, 1972, p. 93).

Some states have a good deal more division within their delegations than others. Of the 10 Massachusetts Democrats in the 95th Congress, 4 were proabortion Liberals and 4 were antiabortion Liberals (and the Speaker doesn't vote). There were 6 Traditionalists and 2 Neoliberals among the 10 Georgia Democrats, and of the 29 California Democrats, 20 were in the Dominant group, another 6 were Liberals (proabortion), and 2 new members were Neoliberals. But the 27 New York Democrats were split with 12 Liberals (proabortion), only 4 in the Domi-

---

[18] There are other groups that would have to be included in any complete catalog of congressional groups. For example, class organizations consisting of newly elected members are often important communication vehicles during the early years of a House career. And, especially in the House Republican party, social clubs such as SOS and the Chowder and Marching Society, give members a chance to sound each other out on proposals and share House gossip.

[19] When we speak of state delegations, we are by and large speaking of the House of Representatives. There are states, however, whose senators meet together with their representatives. Senator Edmund Muskie reportedly played a role in beginning periodic meetings of the Maine delegation which he and Senator Margaret Chase Smith attended regularly.

nant group, and 11 Democratic Moderates. The 22 Texas Democrats included 10 Traditionalists, 5 Pro-Farm Democrats who often vote with the leadership, and, of course, James C. Wright, a member of the Dominant group. Given the similarity or dissimilarity between these issue groups, state party ought to be a very good predictor for Massachusetts, Georgia, and California Democrats, and less satisfactory for Texas or New York Democrats.[20]

The state delegations meet together with varying frequency. The Texas Democrats have had a weekly luncheon for many years, and the California Democrats a weekly breakfast. The Wisconsin Republicans and the Illinois Republicans meet at least once a month (Sinclair, 1972) as do the Georgia Democrats. Some delegations hold no formal meetings at all, but see one another on the floor and in the cloakrooms.

One obvious thing that the delegations do in concert is to advance the interests of their state. Obtaining a defense facility, a research installation, or a contract brings dollars and jobs to a state economy. They work together to see, for example, that the Argonne Laboratory is located in Illinois and not at one of the other 200 sites that were considered. We have a hint of a more important function in the last chapter's references to state delegation activity in obtaining committee seats for their new members. This helps the new members, but it also lays the foundation for information sharing among the delegation. A study of the Washington delegation showed that the source most often consulted in deciding how to vote was a fellow partisan on the committee handling the bill. To the extent that members of a state delegation have members sitting on important committees, they have a network that provides accurate information. And since there are more legislative developments than most legislators can keep up with, having reliable information available at low cost to them is vital to their effectiveness.

This point on information sharing can be generalized a bit more. Recall the earlier point about legislators as individual political entrepreneurs who had learned to judge risks correctly. Consider then this statement about Georgia Democrats: "The members watch each other very closely. Those people are extremely cautious, not just conservative. Conservative, yes, but also cautious." They are watching each other to pick up cues about risk assessment. When can they afford to go along with the relatively liberal House leadership, and when ought they cast conservative votes to stay out of trouble back home? All of the members have to make their own judgments, of course, but in making up their minds, they can draw on the experience of colleagues who have been making similar assessments with districts akin to their own.

---

[20] State party is probably a good general predictor for congressional voting because it is an excellent variable to use for some state delegations and not too bad for others.

Informal Caucuses

There are any number of informal caucuses, most of which were founded during the 1970s. These include groups formed to protect the interests of particular industries, such as the steel caucus, the textile caucus, the rail caucus, the coal caucus, and so on; ethnic caucuses, such as the congressional black caucus, the Hispanic caucus, and the friends of Ireland; and regionally based groups, including the Sunbelt caucus, the Northeast-Midwest coalition, and the New England congressional caucus. These groups provide vehicles for sharing information, aggregating member goals, and advancing the interests suggested by their names. The extent of their organization varies widely, but most are bipartisan groups that welcome any member who shares their goals. For our purposes, though, the most important groups are partisan caucuses that, because of common ideology, tend to reinforce the tendencies of certain issue groups.

The oldest caucus, and the prototype after which other groups were modeled, is the Democratic study group (DSG). The DSG was founded in 1959 by some 40 liberal House Democrats who were frustrated by the lack of progress of liberal legislation in spite of a 130 seat Democratic majority (Ferber, 1971). In time, the members agreed to contribute a portion of their clerk hire funds (changed to a dues arrangement in 1981) which allowed the DSG to hire a staff. With a staff of 20 and over 200 members, the DSG has now taken on an institutionalized form. The DSG provides analyses of pending legislation, some broader studies, roll-call analyses, financial support for selected candidates, and perhaps most important, operates a whip system to encourage liberal Democrats to vote on important measures. Since its membership now includes a majority of House Democrats, the DSG is an important force; but as its numbers have increased, its cohesion has been reduced.

The conservative Democratic counterpart of the DSG is a group of Southerners, popularly known as the "Boll Weevils." Their most recent institutional form is the conservative Democratic forum. This group met regularly, and used their 47 votes in the 97th Congress to cooperate at times with the Democratic leadership and at times with the Reagan administration. They argued within the Democratic party for good committee assignments for conservative members, but were the focus of much of the Reagan administration strategy in the budget and tax fights of 1981, and provided the Republicans with their margin of victory. While publicity went to some more vocal members of the forum, Charles Stenholm and Phil Gramm of Texas, E. V. (Sonny) Montgomery of Mississippi was said to be the guiding intelligence behind this group.

There have been two groups of moderate House Republicans. The older, dating from 1963, is the Wednesday group. It slowly grew from a membership of 15 to 36 in the mid-70s. The staff of four produced analyses of legislation, and it was regarded as important by those who joined; but it was viewed with some suspicion by the much more numerous conservative Republicans. A more recent group of "Gypsy Moths" was formed in 1981 by moderate Republicans who felt betrayed when programs they had been promised would be protected (e.g., medicaid, student loans, mass transit) were scheduled for budget cuts. The Gypsy Moths did meet together, but didn't have any dues or staff.

There have also been groups of conservative Republicans. In 1969, Sam Devine of Ohio organized a group called Republican regulars to oppose Nixon administration legislation they regarded as too liberal. In 1973, a Republican study committee came into being, and was said to provide similar services to those provided by the DSG for liberal Democrats. Within a few years, they had a staff of 11, and a membership of around 60, but their output was limited to fact sheets. The most recent conservative Republican group was the "Yellow Jackets," a voting bloc formed during the 97th Congress to insist that the House Republican party become still more conservative.

The insect groups—the Boll Weevils, the Gypsy Moths, and the Yellow Jackets—are relatively new on the legislative scene,[21] and may be transitory, but they were visible enough in the 97th Congress that President Reagan met with their leaders to seek their support, and to make legislative plans. And in terms of broad policy, even less-organized groups can be important in the House of Representatives. For example, in 1982, a "Gang of Four"—Leon Panetta and Norman Mineta of California, Tim Werth of Colorado, and Richard Gephardt of Missouri—worked together to convince colleagues that it was important that the House pass *a* budget. And a group of Democrats led informally by David Obey of Wisconsin felt that for strategic reasons, the Democrats ought to lose in order to keep pressure on the Republicans. Attitudes such as these are important in understanding what coalitions form in the House.

The Senate, of course, is a smaller body with somewhat less need for group structures, but caucuses have spread to that body as well. There was one Democratic caucus, a group of about a dozen relatively conservative senators who began meeting in 1981. Unlike the conservative Democratic forum in the House, they conducted their business in a low-key way, and were not considered to be "off the reservation" by the Democratic leadership. The two Republican groups both met each Wednesday. The Republican steering committee was the conservative group. Senators belonging to the steering committee contributed staff allowance funds to support a staff. The steering committee also

---

[21] Obviously issue groups of conservative Democrats, moderate Republicans, and conservative Republicans have been around for some time. It's just the names and organizational forms that are new.

had some members who were new right leaders rather than senators or staff members. The Wednesday group tended to reflect moderate-to-liberal views, but was also self-consciously informal. The only obligation of senators belonging to the Wednesday group was to host a luncheon for fellow members once a year, and some Republican senators belonged to the Wednesday group because they preferred its informality.[22] There was also a group of six Progressives (Andrews, Chafee, Hatfield, Mathias, Stafford, and Weicker) who began meeting every other week in 1983 to coordinate their strategy.

Committees

The ability of any of the preceding groups—the issue groups, the state delegations, the various caucuses—to affect public policy is shaped by the House and Senate committees. Some of these have great power. A consensus list of the most important (Goodwin, 1970, pp. 114–15; Jewell & Chu, 1974, p. 437; Jones, 1982, p. 206; Ray, 1982, p. 610; Ripley, 1983, p. 174) would include Rules, Ways and Means, Appropriations, Foreign Affairs, and Armed Services in the House, and Foreign Relations, Finance, Appropriations, Judiciary, and Armed Services in the Senate. To this list of prestige committees, Budget should now be added.[23] But whether the committee is one of the giants of its chamber or is conspicuously less attractive, the committees individually and collectively constrain everyone's ability to attain desired ends.

There are three member goals, Richard Fenno (1973) tells us, that are particularly important in understanding Congress and its committee structure. Members want to be re-elected. They want to achieve influence within the House. They want to leave their stamp on public policy. There are other goals, such as a career beyond the House of Representatives, but all members seek these three. Committees vary, however, in the opportunities they offer members to realize these goals. And Fenno found that representatives sought committees which gave them the best chance to realize their most important goal.

The Interior Committee and the Post Office Committee attract representatives who see constituency service as a way of building a political base, and improving their chances of reelection. In the last chapter, we saw a congressman who wanted assignment to the Interior Commit-

---

[22] One sign of Howard Baker's leadership skill was that the Republican steering committee and the Wednesday group began meeting together on the first Wednesday of each month.

[23] This is a slightly complicated question because the House Budget Committee is composed of 5 members from Ways and Means, 5 members from Appropriations, 11 members of other committees, and 1 member each from the majority and minority leadership. It seems clear, however, that the Budget Committees have been playing a vital role in recent sessions.

tee for the strictly political (read reelection) reason that it was important
to his state. Similarly, Post Office Committee members are likely to
point to the number of civil service employees whose support they
may be able to obtain. This does not lead to power in the chamber
(Post Office is the least attractive committee), and the policy questions
aren't very exciting, but if the representative can win reelection, these
other goals can be sought later on.

Ways and Means and Appropriations, however, are prestige committees. They do offer some chance to affect policy because of the range
of programs that come before them, and because tax and spending
constitute the heart of fiscal policy. But that was not what members
spoke about when Richard Fenno asked them why they wanted to
get on these committees. "The process here is one where consent must
be obtained before anything gets done. If you are one of those from
whom consent must be obtained, then you are an important person
in the House," a member of Appropriations said (1973, p. 3). It is possible
to get on these prestige committees a bit earlier now, but they are
still committees where those who aspire to House careers are likely
to be found.

Education and Labor and Foreign Affairs are neither the most important nor the least important House committees, but they are attractive
because they give the members a chance to make a contribution to
public policy. Education and Labor deals with all the questions of education policy, and gives those with close ties to labor or business the
opportunity to write labor relations laws that are helpful to these constituencies. Members of Foreign Affairs are in frequent touch with the
State Department (through a series of consultative subcommittees), and
are likely to talk about having been interested in foreign policy for
as long as they can remember. To repeat, it is not that any of the
committees deny members an opportunity to pursue all three goals.
It is that each type of committee makes it particularly easy to achieve
their primary goal.

Senators, Fenno found, have the same goals, and are therefore led
to join the parallel committees in that chamber. There is, however,
an important difference. Finance and Appropriations are important
committees in the Senate for the same reasons that Ways and Means
and Appropriations are important in the House. But senators "want
to, can, and do sustain a decision-making process that is more individualistic and gives greater influence to the individual legislator than
is the case in the House" (Fenno, 1973, p. 146). Since senators are
already important simply by virtue of being senators, they have less
need to rely on membership on Finance and Appropriations for influence. Individual senators are able to accomplish things that individual
representatives cannot, and therefore committees do not dominate the

decision-making process in the Senate to the extent that committees do in the House.

In 1981, all six committees analyzed by Fenno were as liberal as the House as a whole, and three of them—Foreign Affairs, Education and Labor, and Post Office—were distinctly more liberal.[24] In the Senate, Appropriations and Finance were slightly more conservative than the chamber as a whole, but the two policy committees—Foreign Affairs, and Labor and Human Resources—were again distinctly more liberal. A different policy bias is present on the Agriculture and Armed Services committees, which are distinctly more conservative in both the House and the Senate. Agriculture, which does much of its business through crop subcommittees, fairly clearly fits into the constituency service-reelection pattern (Jones, 1961) although ideology has become more important in recent years (Parker and Parker, 1979). A decade and a half ago, Armed Services tended not to go into "military policy in terms of its meaning for some national or international political objective," but was primarily "a real estate committee" (Dexter, 1969, pp. 176–82). Armed Services is still interested in real estate, but has come to have more of an interest in policy as witness the members' concern with our policy in Lebanon in 1983–84.

Fenno extends his analysis by asking how the goals of the committee members are constrained by other actors in the committee's environment (the parent chamber, the executive branch, clientele groups, and political parties). Strategic premises for each committee are derived from the joint effects of member goals and environmental constraints. (In the language of this book, this asks how attitudes of individual activists are affected by the external structure of the committee in order to form the group's shared attitudes.) On House Ways and Means, for example, the strategic premises are to write a bill that will pass the House, and to prosecute policy partisanship. But for the Senate Finance Committee, the strategic premises are to give remedial assistance to clientele groups who appeal to them for redress from House decisions, and to pursue policy individualism.

"The zenith of committee government," writes Roger Davidson, "occurred between the years 1937 and 1971, when it seemed that Congress was ruled by a relatively small coterie of powerful committee chairmen"

---

[24] This is based on a comparison of the mean committee support score for the conservative coalition with the mean score for the entire chamber. The mean score for the entire House was 61, and the standard deviation of mean committee scores was 9.06. Committees called "distinctly more liberal" are those with scores of 52 or less; those called "distinctly more conservative" had scores of 70 or more. The mean score for the entire Senate was 65, and the standard deviation of mean committee scores was 6.8. Committees called "distinctly more liberal" are those with scores of 58 or less; those called "distinctly more conservative" had scores of 72 or more (Data Source: Ornstein, Mann, Malbin, & Bibby, 1982, Tables 8-7, 8-8).

(1981, p. 103). For example, Carl Vinson, longtime chairman of the Naval Affairs Committee and its successor Armed Services Committee, kept control of the committee in his own hands, tightly circumscribing sub-committees' jurisdiction, and often ignoring junior members of the com-mittee. Several things happened to restrict the power of autocratic chairmen in the House (where committees, in any case, had been more important). There was first a loosening of the seniority system to share the good committee assignments more widely, and to make chairman-ships somewhat contingent. Then the chairmen of the full committees were limited to heading a single subcommittee. Next caucuses of each committee's majority members (in the Democratic party, but this effec-tively meant in the House) were given the right to determine the sub-committees' power. Finally, each committee was required to set up a minimum number of subcommittees.

These changes led to a system of subcommittee government (David-son, 1981). Whereas committee power formerly had been concentrated in the hands of a few committee chairmen, by the 96th Congress, 55 percent of the majority members had committee or subcommittee chair-manships (Jones, 1982, p. 203). Individual legislators also had a large number of committee and subcommittee assignments. The average rep-resentative had 6.1 committee and subcommittee assignments in the 97th Congress, and the average senator had 10.7 assignments (Ornstein et al., 1982, Tables 4-4 and 4-5).[25] The large number of assignments increased the opportunities open to the legislative entrepreneurs, but also tended to transfer power to staff (Malbin, 1980). Speaker O'Neill summed up the changes from committee government to subcommittee government:

> Old Sam Rayburn used to get on the telephone and call committee chair-men and tell them to put things in bills. Now when I call them, they tell me they have to talk to the subcommittee chairman, and then the subcommittee chairman says he has to talk to the staff. (All Things Con-sidered, August 8, 1983)

ISSUE COALITIONS

Just how the issue groups combine to form coalitions is constrained by the other groups to which the members belong as well as other institutional forces. Issue coalitions, however, must be formed if any legislation is to pass. The largest issue group in the House, the Dominant Democratic group, casts only 16 percent of the votes in that chamber, and the Liberals cast just over a quarter of the votes in the 95th Senate. And if these large issue groups need allies to prevail, the case is even stronger with smaller groups.

---

[25] The average number of assignments per senator had reached 17.6 in the 94th Con-gress before the Senate committee structure was reorganized and consolidated in 1977.

The distribution of views in both chambers is such that coalitions do not form automatically. The issue groups themselves are quite cohesive in their voting. Their agreement scores are quite high.[26] But the agreement score for all House members and that for all Senate members is less than would be expected by chance: $-.05$ for the House and $-.04$ for the Senate. The agreement scores for three of the four parties are not terribly high: .16 for House Democrats, .24 for House Republicans, and .21 for Senate Democrats. And the agreement score for Senate Republicans in the 95th Congress was actually negative, $-.05$.[27] The considerable agreement within each of the issue groups, and the disagreement among larger aggregations, implies that some effort would be necessary for winning coalitions to form.

CONSUMER WARNING

The reader should be cautioned about an important point here. The agreement scores based on the policy scales are different for the same "true" agreement than those based on attitudinal data in other sections of the book. This is because the distributions on attitude scales differ from scales constructed from roll-call data. An attitudinal response of "slightly agree" or "not sure" tends to translate into a "moderate" scale position. However, roll-call votes cast consistently in one direction or the other produce "liberal" or "conservative" scale positions. Therefore, there is a greater tendency for attitude scales to have unimodal distributions, and for roll-call scales to have bimodal distributions. Moreover, I do not know how different the two types of scores are for the same "true" level of interpersonal agreement. Consequently, comparisons can be made safely between House or Senate data, but caution should be used in executive-legislative or electoral-legislative comparisons. The policy areas are the same, but the measurement methods are different.

One way to find out what issue coalition will form is to begin with the largest issue group, and ask sequentially what other groups are most likely to coalesce with it in a given policy area. (This assumes that the largest group will have the easiest time attracting allies. But in these instances, the largest groups in both chambers were in the majority party, which has an institutional responsibility for passing

---

[26] The range of agreement scores ran from .50 (the Neoliberals) to .63 (the Dominant group) among House Democrats; from .47 (Republican Moderates) to .59 (Hard-Line Conservatives) among House Republicans; from .45 (Centrists) to .65 (Liberals) among Senate Democrats; and from .51 (Moderates) to .65 (Antiabortion Stalwarts) among Senate Republicans. (Remember that an agreement score of .50 means agreement 50 percent above what would be expected by chance.)

[27] A glance back at Figure 7-3 will suggest why.

legislation, and there were likely allies available.) Take the example of National Security. The median score of the Dominant group (shown in Table 7-4) is 14.0. The group with the closest score is the Liberal (antiabortion) group with a score of 12.9. The group whose median score is closest to the Dominant/Liberal (antiabortion) protocoalition is the Liberal (proabortion) group with 11.7. The next group to be added sequentially is the Democratic Moderate group with a score of 18.1. To this point, the issue groups have all been Democratic, but now a question of issue distance versus partisanship arises. The most proximate group is the Republican Moderate group (18.7), but there is a Democratic group, Neoliberal (19.0) that is nearly as good, so it seemed probable that Democrats would prefer not to cross party lines. The Neoliberal group was therfore added to the protocoalition. The question remained for the next group to be added, though. This time the choice was between the Republican Moderates who had a moderate position, and the Pro-Farm Democrats who had a moderate conservative position (22.1) on national security. Since the protocoalition was moderate liberal, and the issue distance was greater, the Republican Moderates were assigned to the coalition. This made it a winning coalition with a median score of 15.3.

In other policy areas—economic management, social benefits, civil liberties, and agriculture—it is possible for the Dominant group to build to majority size by adding only Democratic issue groups. In economic management, for example, the groups making up a winning coalition are Dominant (median score = 12.8), antiabortion Liberal (12.3), proabortion Liberal (11.8), Democratic Moderates (13.8), Neoliberals (16.0), and Pro-Farm Democrats (17.5). These groups constitute a winning coalition with a liberal median score of 13.3.

Table 7-7 gives the median scores for the Dominant Coalitions (the winning coalitions formed according to the procedure just outlined) and the Losing Coalitions in the 95th House. In every case except abortion, the Dominant Coalition is more liberal than the entire House, and the Losing Coalition is more conservative. Republican Moderates are part of the Dominant Coalition in national security, and Republican Moderates and Republican Leaders are included on international involvement.[28] Otherwise, coalitions composed entirely of Democrats dominate. The same coalitions win on economic management, social benefits, and civil liberties. In agriculture, the Traditionalists and Pro-Farm Democrats supply votes so that neither the Neoliberals nor any Republican groups are needed.

With abortion, the issue that splinters both parties, the winning coalition in the 95th House was made up of the Traditionalists, Democratic Moderates, Democratic Fundamentalists, antiabortion Liberals, Hard-

---

[28] The Neoliberals are not part of the Dominant Coalition on this issue.

TABLE 7-7
Median Scores of House Coalitions, 95th Congress

			Position in Policy Area				
Coalition	National Security	International Involvement	Economic Management	Social Benefits	Civil Liberties	Abortion	Agriculture
Entire House	Moderate (20.2)	Moderate Liberal (15.3)	Moderate Liberal (17.4)	Moderate Liberal (16.1)	Moderate (18.6)	Moderate Conservative (24.6)	Moderate Liberal (15.4)
Dominant Coalition	Moderate Liberal (15.3)	Liberal (12.8)	Liberal (13.3)	Liberal (12.3)	Liberal (13.9)	Conservative (29.6)	Liberal (10.9)
Losing Coalition	Conservative (26.2)	Moderate (21.7)	Moderate Conservative (24.6)	Moderate Conservative (24.5)	Conservative (26.5)	Liberal (11.6)	Moderate Conservative (24.4)

Note: The figures are median scores on scales that vary between 10 and 30. In general, a low score (10) represents a dove position in national security and international involvement, and a willingness to use government power and resources in the domestic policy areas. A high score (30) represents the opposite. For the convention used to categorize the scores, see the note at the bottom of Table 7-3.

Data source: Professor Aage Clausen's study of the 95th Congress, unpublished.

Line Conservatives, Domestic Conservatives, and Pro-Farm Republicans. This was the one case where a right-wing coalition could be composed more swiftly than one including the Dominant group. Neither the Dominant nor the Losing Coalition resembled the coalitions being formed in other policy areas at all.

Table 7-8 presents data about the Dominant and Losing Coalitions in the 95th Senate. In the Senate, the Dominant Coalition was more liberal than the entire chamber in every case, and the Losing Coalition was more conservative in every case. As compared to the House, there was slightly more issue distance between the winners and losers. Furthermore, in every case the Dominant Coalition in the 95th Senate was a bipartisan coalition. This was because of the issue structures within the two Senate parties. Two Senate Democratic groups (Liberals and City Liberals) were large enough together that they needed only a dozen more votes to win, and two Republican groups (Progressives and Moderates) were close enough to them that they often formed the most natural coalition.

On national security, international involvement, and civil liberties, the Progressives and the Moderates were closer to the Liberals and the City Liberals than either of the other two Democratic issue groups. Hence the Dominant Coalitions in these policy areas were composed of two Democratic and two Republican groups. On economics and social benefits, the Progressives were most proximate to the Liberal/ City Liberal protocoalition, so they joined it first, followed by the Centrists. In these two cases, the Dominant Coalition was composed of three Democratic issue groups and the Republican Progressives. The most unusual Dominant Coalition was in agriculture. Neither the City Liberals or Progressives supported agricultural subsidy programs. Without these two groups (which were in every other Dominant Coalition), the Dominant Coalition consisted of the Liberals, Centrists, Traditionalists, Moderates, and both groups of Stalwarts—three Democratic issue groups and the middle of the Republican party.

Abortion issues produced still another Dominant Coalition, though not such an uncommon one as in the House. Here the proabortion Stalwarts joined the same coalition that won on other civil liberties issues (and foreign policy) ahead of the Moderates to produce a slightly larger winning coalition. Abortion did split both parties in the Senate as in the House, and also produced winning and losing coalitions with a great deal of issue distance between them. The difference was that in the Senate, the Dominant Coalition was proabortion while in the House it was antiabortion. With both parties split in both chambers, and with fragile coalitions taking diametrically opposed positions, it is small wonder that it was difficult for Congress to deal with abortion issues.

Three general points should be made about these issue coalitions.

TABLE 7-8
Median Scores of Senate Coalitions, 95th Congress

Coalition	Position in Policy Area						
	National Security	International Involvement	Economic Management	Social Benefits	Civil Liberties	Abortion	Agriculture
Entire Senate	Moderate Liberal (15.3)	Moderate Liberal (17.4)	Moderate Liberal (17.0)	Moderate Liberal (15.3)	Moderate Liberal (15.4)	Moderate Liberal (14.2)	Moderate Liberal (16.2)
Dominant Coalition	Liberal (12.7)	Moderate Liberal (14.1)	Liberal (13.7)	Liberal (12.5)	Liberal (12.6)	Liberal (12.3)	Liberal (13.8)
Losing Coalition	Conservative (26.1)	Moderate Conservative (25.8)	Conservative (26.0)	Moderate Conservative (25.6)	Moderate Conservative (24.4)	Conservative (27.6)	Conservative (28.3)

Note: The figures are median scores on scales that vary between 10 and 30. In general, a low score (10) represents a dove position in national security and international involvement, and a willingness to use government power and resources in the domestic policy areas. A high score (30) represents the opposite. For the convention used to categorize the scores, see the note at the bottom of Table 7-3.

Data source: Professor Aage Clausen's study of the 95th Congress.

The first is that these coalitions, while perhaps the most easily formed, are by no means the only ones that could or did form. In most cases, the Dominant Coalitions described here are minimum winning coalitions. This means that if a single group drops out, the remaining groups could no longer prevail. Assuming the defecting group could not be enticed back, one of two things would happen. Either the defecting group would join the losing coalition and convert them to winners, or another group (or groups) would have to be found to replace them. This would change the character of the winning coalition, and the character of the legislation they could pass. We saw an illustration of this in Chapter 1. When the Carter energy legislation first passed the House in 1977, it was supported by a liberal Democratic coalition. But when the compromise legislation came back from the Senate in 1978, the two groups of Liberals (proabortion and antiabortion) were no longer willing to support it, and so these liberal votes had to be replaced with those from other issue groups. The issue coalitions described here, in other words, are probably those which form most easily in each issue area, and as such are useful to understand the House and the Senate. But they are abstractions from an underlying reality, and in the real world of legislative politics, many different coalitions are likely to form.

Second, the possibility of legislative success varies from one policy area to another. In a study of the legislative proposals submitted by Presidents Eisenhower through Ford, LeLoup and Shull (1979) were able to show several things. Democratic presidents submitted more proposals per year than Republican presidents. Democrats were most likely to submit proposals in social benefits, then economic management, then foreign and defense policy. Republican presidents were most likely to ask Congress to act on foreign and defense policy, then economic management, then social benefits. Presidents of both parties were least likely to submit proposals in natural resources, agriculture, and civil liberties (with civil liberties ranking last). The success rates for the Democratic proposals (with the percentages of initiatives approved in parentheses) were: foreign and defense (63 percent), social benefits (58 percent), agriculture (44 percent), natural resources (41 percent), government management (36 percent), and civil liberties (21 percent). The success rates for Republican initiatives were: agriculture (55 percent), foreign and defense (51 percent), government management (37 percent), social benefits (35 percent), natural resources (27 percent), and civil liberties (21 percent). To be sure, presidential urging and congressional reaction involve *much* more than legislative coalition formation. Still, the striking difference LeLoup and Shull found in success rate from one policy area to another reinforces the importance of specifying the policy area in order to make meaningful statements.

The third general point is that the Dominant Coalitions are able to prevail because of the *sizes* of the issue groups. Usually, some issue groups increase and others decrease in size as a result of elections. All of the issue groups are likely to interpret the election mandate in the light of their own preferences, but those that gain in size are particularly likely to try to organize coalitions to implement their mandate. Therefore Dominant Coalitions may be converted into Losing Coalitions. Just this happened between the 95th and 97th Congresses. To the extent that comparisons can be made between this issue group analysis and the *National Journal* analysis of 1982 voting, the proportion of House members that were very liberal or fairly liberal dropped from 49 to 40 percent, and the proportion of very conservative or fairly conservative House members increased from 38 to 42 percent. In the Senate, the changes were more substantial. The proportion of very liberal or fairly liberal senators dropped from 55 percent to 42 percent, and the proportion of very conservative or fairly conservative senators increased from 32 percent to 42 percent. Therefore the liberal Dominant Coalitions of the 95th Congress were no longer in charge in the 97th Congress. The Losing Coalition on economic management in the House in 1977–78 was composed of the Republican issue groups, the Democratic Fundamentalists, the Traditionalists, and the Pro-Farm Democrats. By 1981, a coalition consisting of the Republican issue groups, the Democratic Fundamentalists, and about half of the Traditionalists was large enough to sustain President Reagan's economic program in the House. And, of course, in 1981 the Senate had a Republican majority.

THE EXTERNAL STRUCTURES

OF CONGRESS

In order to affect public policy, Congress must engage in three activities. First there is *incubation,* introducing a new idea, focusing publicity on it, and developing support for it. Once a consensus exists in favor of the measure, there is *legislation* proper. And after a law is on the books, there is congressional *oversight* of the persons charged with the administration of the program.[29] In each of these stages, Congress

---

[29] There are, of course, other ways of conceptualizing all this. For example, Randall B. Ripley distinguishes between agenda-setting, policy formulation and legitimation, program implementation, and decisions about the future (1983, p. 390). In a closely related scheme, Charles O. Jones points to problem definition, priority setting, program formulation, program approval and appropriation, program implementation, and program evaluation (1982, p. 357). These are both more-inclusive categorizations of the entire policy process, and concern many other actors besides legislators. Some of Ripley's and Jones's interests with program formulation have been touched on in the discussion of the policy areas in the executive branch. Others, such as program implementation, lie beyond the scope of this book. I am using incubation, legislation, and oversight because I want to focus on the policy-oriented activities of legislators.

is looking outward toward the executive agencies concerned with the legislation, interest groups that support or oppose it, and the public whose conduct is affected by it. None of these three activities is exclusively partisan in nature, but each has important partisan implications. We shall look at each in turn.

INCUBATION

When Congress passed the medicare legislation in 1965, the bill signing ceremony took place in Independence, Missouri. The reason was that President Truman had called for federal health insurance legislation in 1945, and President Johnson wanted him to witness the successful outcome of a 20-year legislative struggle. In fact, others had preceded Truman. A 1935 report to President Franklin D. Roosevelt that led to social security had endorsed the principle of national health insurance, and Senators Wagner and Murray and Representative John Dingell (the father of the present congressman from Michigan) introduced legislation in 1943 to broaden social security to this end. In the years between President Truman's efforts and the 1965 legislation, there had been the Forand bill in 1957, the Forand-Kennedy bill in 1960, the Kerr-Mills bill in 1960, the King-Anderson bill in 1961, 1962, and 1963, and a Gore amendment to a social security bill in 1964. The particulars of these proposals varied. The Murray-Wagner-Dingell bill and many successors would have created health insurance for everyone, not just the elderly as medicare ultimately did. But whatever the details, health insurance had been kept in the public eye and on the congressional agenda for decades before the 1965 bill signing ceremony.

Incubation begins with the recognition of an idea by a potential sponsor. In order for the idea to be taken seriously as a legislative proposal, a bill must be drafted and introduced. This requires at least some effort by someone on the member's staff. Next comes a search for cosponsors, and then if enough allies are found for the idea to be viable, speeches, publicity—and repetition of all this, often over a period of several years. This kind of activity is more likely to appeal to activist legislators, as well as those who are attracted to ideas and want to affect public policy. James Sundquist has distinguished between "program leadership and floor leadership," between "trail-blazing and consensus building." He pointed out that of 16 measures cosponsored by Senate Democrats in the late 50s, 14 were sponsored by five activist senators; Hubert Humphrey, Paul Douglas, James Murray, Joseph Clark, and Patrick McNamera (1968, pp. 400–402; see also Panning, 1982). Probably the most important figure here was Hubert Humphrey. As Nelson Polsby has pointed out, he set a new style, one that grew "in popularity among younger senators as the role of the Senate as an appropriate place in the political system for the incubation of new policy" emerged (1969, p. 34).

Jack Walker (1977) has made a careful study of activism in the Senate from 1947 through 1972. He began by constructing an index of activism based on the number of sponsorships and cosponsorships. This showed clearly that each senator established a habit of promoting new ideas or not doing so by the end of two years. Further, Walker reported "an increasing tendency throughout this period for legislative activism to be centered among young, liberal senators from larger, more politically competitive states" (1977, p. 429). This tendency was particularly noticeable after the election of a large number of such senators in 1958. The type of proposal that was most attractive was one having three characteristics: (a) having an impact on a large number of persons (b) being addressed to a serious public problem and (c) containing an easily understood solution to that problem. Walker argued that when a senator is able to discover a proposal with this felicitous combination, a new coalition may be formed in support of it, and this may lead to a spate of similar legislation. As an example of this, he pointed to the Highway Safety Act of 1966 sponsored by Senator Abraham Ribicoff of Connecticut (with the help of a young attorney named Ralph Nader), and series of similar safety bills passed in the late 1960s and early 1970s.

Incubation also takes place in the House. Here too, according to Representative Richard Cheney, this tends

> as much as anything to be the result of individual initiative. That is, the party does not so much decide that we're going to have a project of developing a project in this area and then produce it, as a situation in which an individual member will decide he wants to pursue a particular object, and he is successful in getting his colleagues to support it to the point where it becomes policy. That's much more often the way these things develop than anything else.

One of the most notable recent examples of this was Congressman Jack Kemp's advocacy of a substantial tax cut. He became convinced by a number of supply-side advocates that what America needed was a 10 percent tax cut in each of three years. Kemp developed this in the late 70s into what became known as the Kemp-Roth bill. Tax cutting has always been popular with Republicans, and Kemp quickly gathered party support. A plane called the "Tax Clipper" made stops around the country in the fall of 1978 to publicize the idea, and when Congress passed a tax cut bill that fall, Republicans passed out cigars at a press conference, calling the bill "Son of Kemp-Roth." For a while, it seemed as if Kemp-Roth would not get beyond the popular idea stage, but it was embraced by presidential candidate Ronald Reagan, and in 1981, a version of Kemp-Roth was passed as one of the central elements in President Reagan's economic program. Although Kemp-Roth was the most publicized example of a successful incubation in the Reagan program, there was also the "10-5-3" plan to stimulate more business investment through accelerated depreciation. This was a bipartisan incubation effort on the part of Representatives Barber Conable and James Jones, and it was also enacted in 1981. And, of course, the idea of a constitutional amendment requiring a balanced budget had been advocated by a number of members of the House and Senate, and while this was voted down by the House, it was advocated by President Reagan. Ronald Reagan, as other presidents before him, inherited a number of proposals from representatives and senators who devoted substantial time to breathing legislative life into new-born ideas.

Many of the ideas that are incubated never become law. Take the case of Elliott Levitas and the legislative veto. As an Atlanta attorney and member of the Georgia legislature, Levitas had been concerned with the lack of bureaucratic accountability. Shortly after his election to Congress in 1964, he said,

> Some constituents of mine came in. They had just had a meeting down at the Federal Trade Commission. There was a proposed rule that in their opinion was arbitrary, did not respond to the problem, was very costly, and so forth. What really blew their mind was that after a short period of time, the person at the FTC with whom they were talking said, "Well, I've heard enough, and I don't have to listen to you anyway." And these just happened to be citizens and taxpayers, and this bureaucrat told them this. That really got me convinced that something had to be done, and I turned to the legislative-veto approach.

Working with his staff, he developed and introduced a bill providing for a legislative veto. (There are various forms of this, but esentially one or both branches can disallow agency actions.) It gained support, especially from newly elected members, as an action to control government capriciousness in the immediate post-Watergate atmosphere, and by the end of the year Levitas had lined up 85 cosponsors.

When the idea was first proposed, it wasn't taken too seriously, and there was little opposition. But once the bill moved through the Judiciary Committee with the aid of Walter Flowers, opposition began to focus and the Rules Committee wouldn't allow it to come to the floor. At the end of the year, the Speaker allowed it to come up under suspension of the rules, and it came within two votes of getting the required two-thirds vote to pass. As a result, there were 265 members on record for it. In Levitas's second term, there was more opposition to the general proposal, and Levitas began to offer a legislative veto amendment whenever a bill was offered with regulatory authority. The most important of these was a bill reauthorizing the Federal Trade Commission. This was rejected by the Senate and by the Conference Committee, with the result that the House rejected the Conference

Report. In 1980, the House repeated their action, and this time the Senate accepted it. It was, in Levitas's view, a "major breakthrough with a major agency," and he was optimistic that his omnibus bill would pass soon in spite of the opposition of Speaker O'Neill, Rules Chairman Bolling, and organized labor. But on June 23, 1983, the Supreme Court declared the legislative veto unconstitutional, and Congressman Levitas was forced to consider alternate means of opposing bureaucratic rule making.

LEGISLATION

The first thing to be said about legislation is that there is less of it than there used to be. As Table 7-9 indicates, there has been a decline in the number of bills passed. This has had an effect on the kind of legislation that is being passed. With relatively little being enacted (once private bills and other narrowly focused laws are excluded), much congressional attention is devoted to authorization (or reauthorization) and appropriations bills that must be enacted simply to keep the government in business. Rather than make futile attempts to draft separate bills, members wait until something comes along that must pass (such as an increase in the debt limit) and offer their proposals as amendments to bills whose priority is such that they stand some chance of getting through.

TABLE 7-9
Number of Bills Passed, Selected Years

Session of Congress	Number of Bills Passed	
	House	Senate
84th (1955–56)	2,360	2,550
89th (1965–66)	1,565	1,636
94th (1975–76)	968	1,038
97th (1981 *only*)	270	274

Data source: Ornstein, Mann, Malbin, & Bibby, 1982, Tables 6-1, 6-2.

While the number of enactments has declined, the legislative workload has been increasing. The reason for this paradox is that with resources scarce and power widely distributed, it takes greater effort to pass each bill. Allan Schick explains what has happened:

> In an era of adversary politics, it takes more exertion to clear a bill because more conflicting interests have to be reconciled. Committees must hold more hearings because more divergent parties insist on being heard and because members insist on offering amendments during markup. Much the same happens on the floor. . . . Members and interest group representatives [scan] the legislative calendar to identify "vehicles"

> onto which limiting amendments [can] be added. In this process, propo-
> nents [get] their bills and adversaries [get] their limitations. Often accep-
> tance of limitations [is] the price floor managers [have] to pay for moving
> their legislation through the House or the Senate. (1983, pp. 168–69)

The additional effort to pass each bill, and the smaller number of
bills that do pass, also mean that there is greater likelihood of bills
getting lost in the Closing Rush of Business. A congressional consensus
had developed in favor of an immigration bill by the end of the 97th
Congress, for example, but the bill did not pass simply because time
ran out.

The list of party legislation is also quite abbreviated. With the Democratic party in the House, there are perhaps 10 bills during a year
that have been designated as party bills by the Steering and Policy
Committee, and on which the full weight of party support is provided.
And even if one includes bills that are de facto party bills because
they accord with historic Democratic party principles, and are supported by virtually all party members, the number goes up to only 20
or 25. This is a separate matter from the decline in the total number
of bills. The restrictions on the number of party bills are the lack of
influence the leaders have over individual members, the time and effort
it takes to exercise the limited influence party leaders have, and the
individual members' insistence on their right to make up their own
minds. Given all this, leadership attempts to produce, say, 50 party-
line votes a year would break down because the leaders' efforts would
be spread too thin, and because of the opposition these efforts would
engender on the part of the members.

What items are included on the short list of party legislation? The
first set consists of the presidential "must" items. Republican Richard
Cheney said (in the summer of 1981), "So far our task has been relatively
easy in the 97th Congress, but then the agenda's been pretty much
set by the President. The issues that we're having to deal with are
those issues that he's placed before the Congress." Democrat Thomas
Foley said that their list "has something to do with whether there is
an administration in office initiating legislation and asking party leadership for support on these initiatives."[30] Congressional budget votes
in the House have been rather partisan. House Republicans voted 146
to 2 against the Second Budget Resolution for FY 1981 (the last while
Carter was in office), and 186 to 1 for the First Budget Resolution for
FY 1982 (the first when Reagan was in office). The third set of items
likely to be included would be those on which there is a high degree
of consensus among party members. This would include economic management and national security for Republicans, and social benefits for

---

[30] The role of the president in congressional agenda setting is one reason why legislative politics should be included in a consideration of presidential parties.

Democrats. Abortion is a classic example of something that would not become a party issue. Finally, there are the votes on rules that occur during the Organization stage of a Congress. Party positions are taken on these, and they are regarded almost as an extension of the vote for Speaker.

In both parties in the House, formal action is usually taken if a party position is to be designated on pending legislation. The Democrats use their Steering and Policy Committee for this, and the Republicans their Policy Committee. As noted above, the Democrats circumscribe party issues rather closely. Republicans tend to work with their ranking members. Again, Richard Cheney:

> Usually what we'll do is wait until an issue is getting close to floor consideration. Then at that point, we'll sit down, convene the Policy Committee, and draft a statement about party position, usually with the support and in conjunction with what the senior Republicans on that committee want to do. That's not always the case. Legal services recently came up. The senior Republican on the committee was Tom Railsback. He disagreed with the President. The majority of the Republicans on the committee disagreed with the President, and the Policy Committee overrode them and adopted a position that was consistent with what the President wanted, and what the majority of House Republicans wanted. But that's fairly rare. There's still a strong sentiment around here that you develop an expertise, and the committee or subcommittee has first crack at such issues.

In the more individualistic Senate, leadership is important, but party unity on legislation depends a bit more on the attitudes of individual senators. In the 97th Congress, majority Republicans voted together because that was the only way they were going to win. There had been what amounted to a test vote in March 1981 when Senator Melcher (a Democrat) offered an amendment to a dairy subsidy bill having to do with casein. Majority Leader Howard Baker moved to table the amendment, and when eight Republicans voted with Melcher, Baker's motion lost 53 to 45. Senator Richard Lugar explained what happened at this point:

> Now everything came to a halt for a week. All of us looked eyeball to eyeball, and appreciated that if each one of us opted out as a geographical group, as a group that was moderate as opposed to conservative or ultra-conservative, or people from the west who were interested in the Sage-brush Rebellion, there just wasn't going to be a program at all.

The result was a lot of party-line voting during the balance of the 97th Congress, especially on critical elements of the Reagan program. This cohesion on voting subsided a bit in the 98th Congress as basic disagreements between the Progressives and the Fundamentalists began to reassert themselves (*National Journal*, September 10, 1983, pp. 1824–1829).

However the congressional parties decide on their positions, what means do the leaders have of persuading party members to vote with them? The answer is the same that longtime Senate Majority Leader Mike Mansfield gave when asked what power he exercised: "Not much." One important attitude shared by members of the House and Senate is that any member has the right to make up his or her own mind about voting. Explained Thomas Foley:

> There isn't much a leadership person can do except try to persuade him on the merits that a position is better than another position that the member may be inclined to vote. If he's inclined to vote that way, it's very hard to avoid accepting it. You can ask him to reconsider, ask him to think about it, not to make up his mind prematurely, ask him if it would be all right to talk to him again about it, but it's a very deferential and civilized kind of conversation. And efforts to say, well now, in the future sometime, if you vote this way, something might be remembered— most members would take instant offense at that, and probably it would be enough to break off communication on that issue.

Moreover, the present mode of distributing committee assignments and subcommittee chairmanships is one of rewarding as many party members as possible. A revolt against one's own party has to be egregious before any sanctions are taken. (This poses an obvious morale problem for those who are supporting the party continuously, but receive no more consideration than those who defect continuously.) Consider the cases of three Texas Democrats, James C. Wright, Kent Hance, and Phil Gramm. Majority Leader Wright wrote in his diary on January 9, 1981: "Once again we got everything we asked for from Steering and Policy for our Texas delegation. Kent Hance goes on Ways and Means. Phil Gramm on Budget. . . . It pleases me to think that I'm not forgetting in all of our national priorities to look out after our own. Sam Rayburn always did this" (Broder, 1981). Wright had mixed feelings about Gramm, whom he regarded as a gadfly, but he felt (as did Speaker O'Neill) that conservative Democrats ought to be given good committee assignments. As things turned out, Hance, under considerable district pressure, voted for the Reagan budget and tax bill, but Gramm revealed Democratic budget strategy to David Stockman. In April, Wright wrote that Gramm's "blatant open split with the Democrats has made me look a bit like a fool" (Broder, 1981). Then in 1982, Hance worked to raise money for Democrats while Gramm continued to seek headlines. The result was that Hance was welcomed back into the Democratic caucus while the Democrats denied Gramm reappointment to the Budget Committee at the beginning of the 98th Congress. This was most unusual.[31] In Gramm's case, he resigned, went back to his district, and won reelection as a Republican. Apparently, he was vindicated, but House Democrats who knew of the choice committee assignment he had been given, and the way he had responded, were given a clear signal about behavior that would not be tolerated.

OVERSIGHT

The third of the three ways in which Congress ought to be affecting public policy is through oversight, monitoring the administration of the legislation they have passed. Yet when legislators are asked about oversight, their answers suggest that they rarely engage in much of it themselves. A senator said, "I suspect this often harks back to those who were most interested in the thing to begin with. You still remain intensely interested in how your offspring did, how it is being treated, whether the regulations have been promulgated, and whether the money has happened. Often the interest just sort of follows along." A congressman was more direct. "It's something we all talk about, and very few people ever do anything about."

To be sure, it is difficult to distinguish between legislation and oversight. Many oversight activities—questioning agency heads during hearings, giving agencies directions within committee reports, inserting limiting amendments in appropriations bills—take place within the context of legislation. Still, a thoroughgoing program of oversight would be very difficult. In the words of a careful student of oversight, Morris Ogul:

> The plain but seldom acknowledged fact is that systematic, all-inclusive oversight is simply impossible to perform. No amount of congressional dedication and energy, no conceivable increase in the size of committee staffs, and no boost in committee budgets will enable Congress to oversee policy implementation in a comprehensive and systematic manner. The job is too large for the members and staff to master. (1981, pp. 318–19)

Legislative oversight, for very similar reasons, resembles White House monitoring of executive agencies. As we saw in the analysis of time devoted to various tasks by the White House staff, actually keeping track of what the government was doing was the task to which they devoted the least attention.

---

[31] House Democrats had voted to censure John Bell Williams of Mississippi and Albert W. Watson of South Carolina and had stripped them of seniority after they had supported Republican presidential candidate Barry Goldwater in 1964. (In this case, too, the question was one of open disloyalty to the party.) Watson resigned and was reelected as a Republican, and Williams left the House when he was elected governor of Mississippi.

If oversight is difficult, and if (as we have already seen) members have other goals, it follows that oversight is likely to be selective, and that there must be some special motivation for members to engage in it. What kind of motivation might suffice? Becoming engaged in a personal controversy is one. A clear example of this involved the late Senator John McClellan of Arkansas. In the early 1950s, the senator was in Europe, and wanted to come home on an air force plane. None were available, he was told. The senator thereupon demanded that a plane be flown to Europe to bring him back to the United States. An aircraft was dispatched, but the news media were also notified. When the plane arrived in the United States, waiting newsmen asked Senator McClellan if he had been embarrassed by the incident. "I refuse to be embarrassed," he replied, and walked off. Not too many months later, the assistant secretary who had authorized release of the news was being investigated by Senator McClellan's committee. His wife, it seems, owned some stock in a company that had an air force contract, and the senator accused him of conflict of interest, leading to the assistant secretary's resignation.[32]

If representatives and senators are pleased with the way in which programs are being conducted, they have little incentive to engage in oversight. By and large, this means that congressional Democrats are not going to investigate Democratic administrations, and congressional Republicans are not going to investigate Republican administrations. But when they are of the opposite party, then oversight becomes a euphemism for trying to make a political case against the administration. This is not to say there aren't legitimate policy questions to be raised, or that oversight is not the logical companion of incubation and legislation. For example, the House Interior Committee held hearings to question Interior Secretary James Watt about the Office of Surface Mining. Committee Democrats and their conservationist allies were deeply concerned about Secretary Watt's policies regarding strip mining, and they wanted to hold hearings to alert the public to these dangers. But as a Republican put it, "it's not so much that we want to know what's going on as it's because Mo Udall wants to get Jim Watt up here and beat him about the head and shoulders." Both explanations were true. There were policy questions to be raised, and there were partisan ends to be served. But this was hardly the only time when policy goals and party goals were being simultaneously pursued. Politics is always this way.

---

[32] I have always been curious why the newsmen who went out to meet the senator's plane were unable to see the relation between the release of the news and the subsequent investigation.

Summary

We began our analysis of internal structure with a look at the members themselves. In background, the typical member is a lawyer who has been active in state or local politics; in behavior, the typical member is a successful political entrepreneur. An analysis of the issue groups derived from their voting behavior showed more groups among House Democrats than among House Republicans. There was one more issue group among Senate Republicans than among Senate Democrats if abortion was included, an equal number if it was not. Democratic groups in both bodies were more likely to be geographically based; Republican issue groups were more likely to be ideologically based. These are not the only groups which shape members' activities. State delegations, informal caucuses, and committees also had to be considered. And while there was a high level of agreement within the issue groups, there was little agreement across the entire House or the entire Senate. This implied difficulty in forming winning coalitions. The Dominant Coalitions in the 95th Congress were more liberal (except on abortion in the House) than either the entire House or the entire Senate.

The external structures reviewed were the legislative activities concerned with policy. We first saw the individual effort related to the incubation of legislative ideas. Next we saw that while the legislative workload is increasing, the number of bills passed is declining. Given the limited resources of party leaders, relatively few bills are treated as party bills. Those so designated include presidential "must" bills, many budget resolutions in the House, those with an abnormally high degree of party consensus, and some organizational votes at the beginning of each Congress. Finally, we saw that, as with White House monitoring of agency activity, oversight is a difficult activity to which relatively little time is being devoted.

PART FOUR

NOMINATION POLITICS

CHAPTER 8

NOMINATION POLITICS: EARLY DAYS AND INITIAL CONTESTS

Some Early Activity

On June 25, 1982, some 3,000 Democrats met in Philadelphia for a three-day, midterm party conference. In 1974 and 1978, these miniconventions had met after the fall elections. In 1982, party leaders had scheduled the conference well before the election in the hope of making it a party-uniting election rally rather than a party-dividing debate over policy. The 897 delegates did adopt a number of resolutions on policy, but more attention was devoted to the possible contenders for the 1984 Democratic presidential nomination: Senator Edward M. Kennedy of Massachusetts, former Vice President Walter F. Mondale of Minnesota, Senator John Glenn of Ohio, Senator Alan Cranston of California, Senator Gary Hart of Colorado, Senator Ernest F. Hollings of South Carolina, and former Governor Reubin Askew of Florida.

Kennedy (then still viewed as a probable contender) and Mondale were regarded as the front runners. Senator Kennedy, who enjoyed wide recognition because of the family name and his own extensive public career, was running ahead of all other Democrats in the polls. Walter Mondale, who had the active support of many of the most talented members of the Carter administration, was far and away the best-organized candidate. Mondale's and Kennedy's speeches were being eagerly awaited, and they both gave good ones. Not surprisingly, they told their fellow Democrats that President Reagan was responsible for America's problems. "Whether they are teachers in Birmingham, students in San Diego, woodworkers in Portland, or auto workers in Detroit," declared Mondale, "good, solid, decent Americans are suffering through no fault of their own." And referring to presidential Counselor Edwin Meese's decision not to waken President Reagan to tell him of combat between Libyan and American aircraft, Senator Kennedy joked: "If Ronald Reagan does not know the facts about how this recession began, then Ed Meese ought to wake him up and tell him."

None of the less well known candidates could realistically hope to displace the front-runners at Philadelphia, but each faced the challenge of how he was going to draw attention to himself as the "third" candidate who ought to be taken seriously. Senator Hollings challenged the relatively liberal delegates by reminding them that "on the all-important issue of the economy, people still shy from us." Reubin Askew chose not to make a speech because, as Florida broadcasters told their audiences over and over, he wanted to have a low-key approach. Senator John Glenn, the well-known former astronaut who was running third in the polls after Kennedy and Mondale, adopted a moderate policy mix—a strong defense, but recognition of nuclear arsenals as warning bells, an emphasis on research, and support of social programs. Gary Hart, who wanted to draw attention to himself as an issues candidate, avoided the use of a trailer (where all the other candidates except Hollings met delegates), and led a workshop discussion on the use of issues in campaigns. Senator Cranston hoped that delegates would remember his leadership position (as minority whip in the Senate), and reminded delegates of his long standing as a member of the party's liberal wing by calling for the total abolition of nuclear weapons. When the Democrats left Philadelphia late Sunday, the 1984 nomination contest was much the same as it had been when they arrived. Several of the candidates had made good impressions, but there hadn't been much net movement. Indeed, there was no real movement until early December when Senator Kennedy, citing personal reasons, announced he would not seek the Democratic nomination. This had the effect of establishing Walter Mondale as the undisputed early front-runner.

On the Republican side, the only discernible nomination politics was some speculation on whether President Reagan would run for a second term. The President would not commit himself, but did say he had told his staff that they shouldn't look for other employment. This hint reminded other Republicans that he might be in the Oval Office for some years, and that it would be prudent to support Reagan programs rather than plan to run for the presidency themselves.

The most significant fact about the Philadelphia miniconvention and the concurrent activity in the Republican party was that it was June 1982—nearly two years before the parties' nominating conventions would meet. Some perspective can be gained by asking what was happening at this point in other nomination contests. In June 1978, the news was that the consumer price index had risen .9 percent (an annual rate of 10.8 percent), and California voters had approved Proposition 13, an initiative to cut property taxes by a little more than half. In June 1974, Richard Nixon took two trips, a nine-day visit to the Middle East followed by an eight-day trip to Moscow. The House Judiciary Committee was making preparations for impeachment hearings, but was not to meet until July 24. That same month, Governor Jimmy Carter of Georgia gave a speech on zero-based budgeting to the National Governors Conference. In June 1970, President Nixon gave a televised speech on the problems of avoiding a recession while bringing a major war to an end. The Senate was debating the Cooper-Church amendment which would have forbidden any use of funds to pay U.S. forces in Cambodia. Senator George McGovern attacked the administration's policy in Southeast Asia in a commencement address at Dartmouth College, and en route persuaded Gary Hart to commute between Colorado and Washington, D.C., to begin setting up a campaign organization. There were certainly portents here of the nomination campaigns to come, but that's about all that can be said. No commentators, for example, told us that we should pay attention to a senator named George McGovern or a governor named Jimmy Carter because they were going to emerge as the Democratic nominees for president. It was too early for that.

If there was anything unusual about the Democratic meeting in Philadelphia, it was that there was so much visible activity so early. As late as November 1943, New York Governor Thomas E. Dewey (the 1944 presidential Republican nominee) was writing to a political ally, "You and I know better than most people that this is just plain too early" for any public campaigning (Smith, 1982, p. 389). But Theodore White began chronicling the long preconvention campaigns of aspirants in 1960, and both George McGovern and Jimmy Carter were successful with campaigns that began very early. In recent decades, nomination campaigns have become longer and longer. The early activity in Philadelphia was the most recent indication of the lengthening of nomination politics.

THE STAGES OF NOMINATION POLITICS

Early Days

At least four stages can be distinguished in nomination politics. The first is Early Days, the period prior to the initial selection of delegates. There may well be some organizational work before the midterm election, but campaigning at this stage is still gentle. Early forays help build name recognition for the candidate, and the candidate often helps those seeking other offices in anticipation of potential help from them later. But at this stage, no one can be certain who will survive the election. If a senator or governor wins by a big margin, it may set the stage for a presidential bid two years later. On the other hand, candidates rejected by the voters of their own states may not even be in a position to influence their own state delegations. Without information on the identity of the players, it is difficult to do more than make tentative plans.

What happens during Early Days depends on whether a decision has been made to make an active bid for the White House. (Barry Goldwater, for example, had not made his decision during 1963, nor had Nelson Rockefeller during 1967.) If this decision has not been made, then the candidate spends a lot of time listening to the importunings of persons who would like to see an active candidacy, and a lot more time trying to figure out whether these urgings reflect the interests of the people doing the coaxing or are, in fact, grounded in genuine public support.

If the potential candidate is even thinking seriously about running, then an early step will now be the creation of an exploratory committee that is empowered to receive contributions. This is because of the Federal Election Campaign Act of 1974 (actually, amendments to the 1971 act) that inaugurated federal financing of presidential campaigns. This has had a number of consequences. First, a candidate must raise $5,000 in each of 20 states in contributions of not more than $250. As national campaign expenses go, $100,000 is not a lot of money, but it does require the creation of an organization to raise money over a large area. Second, the federal fund will provide up to 50 percent of $10 million (plus an inflation allowance). Since the federal fund matches money raised by the candidate, this doubles any disparity that may result from fund-raising capacity. In other words, if Candidate A raises the minimum $100,000 and Candidate B raises $1 million, the matching funds will give Candidate B a financial advantage of $2 million to Candidate A's $200,000. Third, this may lead candidates to take stands that will stimulate gifts from donors, and it does stimulate much more organized Early Days activity. Serious contenders are forced into early fund raising if only to keep from entering the race too far behind their competitors.

If the decision to run has been made, then Early Days revolves around planning and organizing. At least the outline of a strategy is needed. Which primaries will be entered? What stands will the candidate take? An initial staff must be recruited. In addition to the aforementioned need for a fund raiser, an absolute minimum requirement is someone to handle the media, and someone to organize the campaign. Once these essentials are in hand, then the candidate begins making forays into those states in which the first delegates are to be chosen.

These activities are intertwined with one another. The staff members are likely to take part in initial strategy discussions, and residents of early primary states who tell a campaigner how impressed they are may find themselves recruited into the candidate's state campaign organization.

Early Days is also marked by a lack of information about the opposition. If a potential candidate has not decided whether to run, others certainly don't know. And even among announced candidates, it is too soon to know how well organized they are, how well financed they will be, or how attractive they are to the voters. Given this lack of solid information, the media have considerable ability to promote or handicap a contender by just writing that Candidate A is being taken seriously or that Candidate B is lightly regarded. Such articles can be of tactical benefit to a favored candidate as they help the candidate acquire more resources. But experienced professionals—both politicians and reporters—know that only preliminary judgments can be made about who the strong contenders will be and who will soon disappear for lack of support.

Initial Contests

The Initial Contests are, of course, the first campaigns for delegates. New Hampshire has traditionally held the first primary election, although a number of other states have scheduled early primaries in recent years. Iowa has also gained attention recently by holding the first party caucuses in which delegates are selected. Considerable attention is paid to Iowa and New Hampshire just because they are first; but the crucial point is whether or not they are being contested, especially by those regarded by the media as strong candidates. As long as New Hampshire is first and contested, it will be an important primary; but if a New Hampshire governor were to run as a favorite son and was strong enough to keep other candidates out, attention would shift elsewhere.

The number of states in which candidates seek delegates depends on their strength and resources. If aspirants have the funds and organizations to make it feasible, they may enter a large number of primaries and seek delegates in several caucus states. With this kind of strategy, the Initial Contests phase is not so critical. Obviously it helps to win, but a defeated candidate who is confident that support can be picked up later in other parts of the country can afford to take a more detached view. For less well supported candidates, however, success in the Initial Contests is imperative. Their hope is that they can generate some enthusiasm among the voters, which in turn will produce the resources that will enable them to enter later primaries. If support from the voters is not there, the only option is to drop out of the race.

The Initial Contests are watched very closely by the media. The three national networks broadcast 100 stories on the New Hampshire primary in 1976 in which 38 delegates were being chosen, compared to 30 stories on New York's April 6 primary in which 428 delegates were being chosen (Robinson, 1976). Whether a candidate has won or lost becomes less important in media interpretation than how the candidate's performance measures up against expectations. Needless to say, candidate organizations go to great effort to establish low expectations so they can be "pleasantly surprised" by the actual results. Reporters, however, are equally interested in establishing more objective standards. Among other things, they refer to historical standards (how well the candidate has done in the same state on previous occasions), preprimary polls, geographical propinquity (whether the candidate comes from a nearby state), and the investment of time and resources made by the candidate (Matthews, 1978; cf. Arterton, 1984). If a candidate does better than expected, it is hailed as a victory, and the candidate gains precious momentum. If a candidate does about as well as expected, not too much attention is paid. If a candidate falls below expectation, then articles are written analyzing the failure of the campaign.

There have been complaints about this measurement of performance against expectation. By this logic, although he won 46.4 percent of the vote to Senator George McGovern's 37.2 percent, Senator Edmund Muskie was said to have lost the 1972 New Hampshire primary because he had been expected to do better. Similarly, Congressman John Anderson got most of the headlines after the 1980 Massachusetts primary because he did so much better than expected, although George Bush got 31.0 percent of the vote to Anderson's 30.7 percent. This cost Bush an opportunity to regain the momentum he had lost to Ronald Reagan the week before in New Hampshire. This seems perverse, but in the absence of "hard" information about the progress of coalition building, the expectations developed by the media probably provide better standards of comparison than the claims of the candidates.

Mist Clearing

The third phase of nomination politics is hardest to pinpoint at a particular point in time, but it usually occurs while the delegates are still being chosen.[1] It is marked by a reduction of the uncertainty which has thus far attended the nomination process, and in this sense is

---

[1] Mist clearing *may* occur very early in 1984 because of the large number of Initial Contests taking place in March. The Democrats scheduled a large number of caucuses and primaries in the weeks immediately following the Iowa caucuses and New Hampshire primary. By St. Patrick's Day, 28.2 percent of the delegates will have been chosen (Cattani, 1983; Shafer, 1983a, 1983b).

akin to the clearing of a mist that allows one to see the pine trees across a woods or cars several hundred yards down the road. Whereas vital pieces of information are missing during Early Days, and subjective impressions of reporters provide the best standards for judgment during Initial Contests, Mist Clearing allows one to know how many serious contenders there are for the nomination, and what their strength is vis-à-vis one another. Some candidates who have failed to gain much support may remain in the race to give voice to a point of view (or to collect federal matching funds to pay off campaign debts), but effective campaigning will be carried on only by the serious contenders for the nomination.

In campaigning, the principal shift from Initial Contests to Mist Clearing is from a desire to create an impression of movement to a prevailing concern with the acquisition of delegates. A shift from the first 20 delegates to, say, 200 delegates implies a change in the method of campaigning as well as a more complex campaign organization. Whereas the earlier appeal had to be on the grounds that the candidate was the most attractive among half a dozen or more declared aspirants, the appeal now can be that while the candidate may not be ideal, he is the one who comes close to the stands the delegates would prefer *and* has a real chance of winning. If a candidate has already attracted 200 delegates, then there is a coalition in being. The groups of delegates who make up the coalition do not all have identical views, and a certain amount of organizational effort is needed to hold the coalition together at the same time that additional groups of delegates are being recruited.

Relationships between the candidates and reporters are also rather different in this phase of nomination politics. Early on, the candidate is anxious to create news and make himself available to the few reporters who take the trouble to cover the campaign. By the Mist Clearing stage, the candidate's success makes him a prime news source, so he has a much larger press entourage. This shift gives the campaign staff a better opportunity to control the news by rationing the candidate's time among the greater number of reporters who want to see him. On the other hand, whatever the candidate says is now subject to much greater scrutiny. When he was one of several candidates during Initial Contests, not much space could be devoted to his issue statements or to those of any one candidate. Now that he is one of two or three who may be a major party nominee, statements on foreign policy or economics or whatever are more carefully analyzed.

There is sometimes a flurry of activity during this phase on the part of a late entrant in the race. Pennsylvania Governor William Scranton did not declare his candidacy until June 1964; New York Governor Nelson Rockefeller did so in May 1968 after having announced earlier that he would not run; Governor Jerry Brown of California and Senator Frank Church of Idaho made their decisions in March 1976, but the first contests they were able to enter did not take place until May. The late entrant is likely to get a fair amount of media attention; the new candidacy enlivens what may be an all-but-decided contest. But the late entrant is likely to be giving voice to different attitudes than those held by the probable winning coalition, or he may be simply attracting publicity with an eye to a future campaign. Unless there are very unusual circumstances, there are just too few delegates remaining to be chosen to give the late entrant any real chance of building a winning coalition.

The Convention

In recent decades, conventions have ratified earlier decisions by nominating the leading presidential candidate on the first ballot. The last multiballot conventions were in 1952 for the Democrats, and in 1948 for the Republicans. The last truly deadlocked conventions were in 1924 for the Democrats, and in 1920 for the Republicans. It is always possible that we might see another multiballot convention, especially if there are two strong coalitions, each powerful enough to keep its rival from winning, but without the leverage necessary to pick up the few additional votes to achieve victory. The dominant pattern, though, is one of first-ballot nominations. The wide publicity now given to primaries and caucuses in which the delegates are selected gives ample indication of the likelihood that one candidate or another will win. The "tests of strength" that took place on early ballots at multiballot conventions are no longer essential to provide clues about this.

Even so, the Convention is a consequential stage in the nominating process. There are a series of decisions made by the conventions before the nomination of the presidential candidate. These are taken by voting to approve (or reject, or amend) reports from several committees. The first is a Committee on Credentials, which makes recommendations on which delegates are to be seated. The second is a Committee on Permanent Organization, which suggests permanent officers to replace the temporary officers who have guided the convention in its opening sessions. Next comes a Committee on Rules, which proposes rules to govern the present convention, authorizes a National Committee to transact party business during the next four years, and (in the Republican party) sets forth the procedure for calling the next convention. Finally, a Committee on Resolutions presents the party platform for adoption. These are important decisions. Credentials, Permanent Organization, and Rules are important in the short term of the convention itself. By seating certain delegates—for example, McGovern delegates rather than Humphrey delegates from Illinois and California in 1972—one can create a majority in favor of one candidate. The rules may favor one side or another. Thus, Kennedy supporters claimed that Rule

F3(c), binding delegates to be faithful to the candidate in whose behalf they had been elected, gave the Carter forces an advantage at the 1980 convention. And the permanent chairperson may enforce the rules so as to give an advantage to one of the contenders. Rules and the platform have long-term consequences as well. Both parties have adopted rules at recent conventions that have mandated reforms in the composition or procedures of future conventions. For instance, the McGovern-Fraser Commission, which recommended a new set of procedures for the selection of delegates to the 1972 Democratic convention, was appointed under the authority of a rule adopted in 1968. And a careful study of party platforms over a 34-year period has shown that 75 percent of the pledges were implemented by the party winning the White House (Pomper & Lederman, 1980, chap. 8).

These Convention votes also play a role in the contest over the presidential nominee. What happens in any particular convention depends on the strength of the contending coalitions. Let's say there is a winning coalition that does not have too many votes to spare, and at least one reasonably strong challenging coalition. This has been a fairly common situation in recent conventions. In these circumstances, the challenging coalition will try for a test vote on an issue that will maximize its strength. It may come on the adoption of a rule that the challenging coalition thinks will be attractive to uncommitted delegates, or it may come on a platform plank that will tend to split the winning coalition. Whatever the topic, the object is to pick an issue that will attract more votes than the challenging coalition can muster on behalf of its candidate. The winning coalition, on the other hand, will be more interested in the presidential roll call to come, and may just accept the proposed change as long as it feels it can live with it. If the winning coalition is in a very strong position, it will have the votes to beat back any challenges. In these circumstances, motions challenging credentials, rules, or platform are likely to be made only by those who feel very strongly about the issue as a matter of principle.

In view of the possibility of contests on a number of issues, the coalition leaders must have some way of communicating with their groups of delegates. When the convention is not in session, the delegates will be lodged in hotels all over the city. Some person will normally be designated as the contact for each coalition's delegates in each state, though communication is awkward when delegates are spread all over a large metropolitan area. On the convention floor, the key coalition leaders will usually be in some central location (often in a trailer parked outside the convention hall), which provides telephone or walkie-talkie communication with the state delegation leaders. This allows rapid dissemination of a decision to try to beat back a challenge, to accept it, or to take no position on it.

Finally, the Convention stage is both the conclusion of nomination politics and the beginning of electoral politics. Nomination and electoral politics differ in fundamental ways. The prime objective of the former is to attract enough delegates to win the nomination; the prime objective of the latter is to convince voters to support the candidate in November. But the conventions are widely reported by press and television, and while the delegates are listening to speeches and casting votes, citizens are making up their minds about the coming general election. Just over a quarter of presidential voting decisions in the elections since 1948 have been made during the conventions. There have been conventions—such as the 1964 Republican convention when Governor Nelson Rockefeller was booed while addressing the delegates, and the 1968 Democratic convention with a bloody confrontation between Chicago police and antiwar demonstrators—which seriously handicapped the parties in the fall campaign. And even without events as dramatic as these, the identity of the nominee, the vice presidential candidate he selects, and the issues that are stressed are important considerations in the citizen's own presidential choice.

Some Effects of this Temporal Pattern

These four phases—Early Days, Initial Contests, Mist Clearing, and Convention—blend into one another. Time is continuous. The campaign forays of Early Days, and the skeleton organizations that are set up in Iowa, New Hampshire, and elsewhere set the stage for the Initial Contests. Victory in the Initial Contests provides pledged delegates, and delegates continue to accumulate until the genuine strength of one or more coalitions becomes apparent in the Mist Clearing phase. And while appointments to the convention committees are not formally made until the convention opens, decisions about who is going to be involved are made well in advance, and preliminary meetings of the Platform Committee (or at least of a drafting subcommittee) take place while the competing coalitions are still seeking delegate support.

Still, it is useful to consider these phases separately. To a greater degree than is true in other forms of politics, both the internal and external structures change as the nomination contest moves from one stage to the next. When planning begins in Early Days, the internal structure may consist of the candidate and a very few close advisors. If successful, by the time of the Convention, the coalition will include hundreds of delegates with a variety of goals and policy preferences. At the outset, the external structure of competition will include a reasonably large number of potential candidates. Some of them may not run, but their possible impact must be considered. The most important external audiences are contributors and national reporters who will provide, or withhold, necessary financial and publicity resources. By the time of the Convention, the structure of competition will be much simpler. All but the strongest challengers will have disappeared. And by Convention time, a successful coalition will be covered by a multitude of media representatives, and the coalition leaders will be working through them to reach voters who are pondering their November choices. Since both internal and external structures change so much, we shall discuss nomination politics by looking at recent nomination contests as they passed through these four stages. Then we shall draw some strands together by making some general statements about internal and external structure.

In this chapter, we shall review the 1976 and 1980 nomination contests as they passed through the four stages. The contests won by Governor Carter in 1976 and Governor Reagan in 1980 are typical of those in which there are several potential nominees during Early Days and the eventual winner gradually pulls away from the field. The 1976 Ford versus Reagan and 1980 Carter versus Kennedy battles were essentially two-candidate struggles that lasted from Early Days on through Convention.[2]

EARLY DAYS

Carter, 1976.   Jimmy Carter announced his candidacy for president early (December 12, 1974), but his planning and organization had begun even earlier. His own decision had been made in the fall of 1972, and his aide, Hamilton Jordan, had written a memorandum setting forth a detailed strategy: "The New Hampshire and Florida primaries provide a unique opportunity for you to demonstrate your abilities and strengths at an early stage of the campaign." The memorandum went on to point out that New Hampshire was a small, rural state that would be receptive to a candidate of Carter's background and campaign style, and that Florida had advantages for a southern candidate. It also urged that Carter use the governorship to establish contacts, begin to read the *New York Times* and *Washington Post* regularly, and travel abroad to be able to claim familiarity with foreign affairs (Schram, 1977, pp. 52–71).

The most important contact Carter made was with Robert Strauss. The Democratic national chairman visited Atlanta in March 1973, and the conversation led to an invitation for Carter to serve as chairman of the 1974 Democratic campaign. Hamilton Jordan moved to Washington in May, and Governor Carter spent much of 1974 traveling around the country in behalf of Democratic candidates, thereby making the

---

[2] These are two of the three modern patterns of nomination. The third pattern is that in which the identity of the probable nominee is known from the outset, as with Lyndon Johnson in 1964 or Richard Nixon in 1972. This hardly requires any analysis.

contacts with Democrats that were to be the basis of his own presidential campaign. (Senator George McGovern had a similar opportunity to become known in party circles in 1969–70 as chairman of the McGovern-Fraser Commission that wrote the rules that were to govern 1972 delegate selection. Party activity is a very important part of the answer to the question, "Where did such an improbable candidate come from?")

By 1975, Jimmy Carter was ready to spend a lot of time in Iowa, New Hampshire, and Florida. Seven aspirants were invited to a celebration of Marie Jahn's 37 years as Plymouth County (Iowa) recorder in 1975. Only Jimmy Carter came. While he was there, he also taped a show on the local radio station and had interviews with the *LeMars Daily Sentinel* and a nearby college newspaper. Within two weeks, all the local Democrats he had met had received personal letters from him. The Plymouth County Democrats, and others whom Carter had met on his 21 trips to Iowa that year, were contacted soon thereafter by Tim Kraft, a New Mexico Democrat who was coordinating Carter's Iowa activities, and in due course there was a 20-person Iowa Carter for President Steering Committee (Lelyveld, 1976c).

Reporters were not paying much attention to Carter's Early Days activities, but this ended with a straw poll taken at a Democratic dinner in Ames, Iowa, on October 25. Acting on a hunch that someone would take a straw poll, Tim Kraft urged Carter Steering Committee members to get as many supporters as possible to come to the dinner, and to persuade others attending to vote for Carter. The *Des Moines Register* did take a poll; Carter got 23 percent; no one else got over 12 percent. On this basis, the *New York Times'* respected R. W. (Johnny) Apple wrote a front-page story headlined, "Carter Appears to Hold a Solid Lead in Iowa" and this led to media attention for the hitherto neglected ex-governor of Georgia.

Jimmy Carter was not the only aspirant to make an early decision to run, but he was the only one who also concentrated on building a base in Iowa, New Hampshire, and Florida. Senator Henry Jackson of Washington formed an exploratory committee, and raised over $1 million in 1974, but his strategy was keyed toward winning a lot of delegates in the New York primary. Arizona Congressman Morris Udall made his decision to run in mid-1974 after being approached by two liberal representatives from Wisconsin, David Obey and Henry Reuss. He announced in November 1974, and began focusing on New Hampshire (Ivins, 1976). Senator Birch Bayh of Indiana waited through much of 1975 before making any decision, and by the time he did announce his candidacy in September, other candidates had spent months planning, organizing, and campaigning in the early states (Witcover, 1977).

Reagan, 1980. If few early observers picked Carter as the one who would pull away from the field in 1976, many thought Ronald

Reagan would be the strongest Republican candidate in 1980. Reagan had harbored presidential ambitions for a long time, and nearly won the nomination in 1976. There was a solid Reagan constituency in existence, and a core group of experienced campaign organizers. Given the level of support, the 1980 nomination was probably Reagan's unless he lost it. Therefore his central strategy question was how to hold on to the support he already had. To answer this, two things had to be determined. First, should Governor Reagan stress conservatism in order to fire up his workers and strengthen his hold on his natural constituency, *or* should he moderate some of his positions in order to broaden his appeal within the Republican party and be better positioned for the general election? Second, should he limit his activities and statements, on the assumption that his constituency would stay with him unless he did something to upset them, *or* should he continue to campaign much as he had in the past?

The posture adopted by the Reagan coalition was that favored by John Sears, who was then in charge of the campaign. Issues were stressed that looked to gaining additional Republican support in the primaries, and Democratic votes in the general election. The importance of strong leadership was stressed—in conscious counterpoint to President Carter's emphasis on malaise—and when he announced, Reagan called for a North American Accord to improve the quality of life in Canada, the United States, and Mexico. Organizationally, Sears built up a network of 18 field offices across the country. Most importantly, he reached for support in the Northeast that had been let go to Ford by default in 1976. To this end, he enlisted such talent as Drew Lewis, who had led the Pennsylvania Ford campaign four years earlier. The Reagan posture was explained by California pollster Mervin Field: "The strategy is to run him as an incumbent—with set speeches, and as few as possible. It's ball control. What he wants is a fast ticking of the clock until the convention." There were tensions within the Reagan core group that were not unrelated to these choices. Over the course of 1979, longtime Reagan aides Franklyn (Lyn) Nofziger, Michael Deaver, and Martin Anderson all departed from the Reagan campaign. Some of these resignations grew out of personal struggles as Sears reached for greater and greater power within the Reagan organization, but Nofziger and Anderson certainly preferred an unabashed conservatism.

Each of the other Republican aspirants hoped to present himself as *the* alternative to Reagan. Three aspirants were competing with Reagan for the votes of conservative Republicans: Congressman Philip Crane of Illinois, Senator Robert Dole of Kansas, and former Governor John Connally of Texas. Crane and Dole both saw themselves as younger alternatives to Reagan, although Dole, the 1976 vice presidential nominee, could claim a good deal more national visibility. John Connally brought two formidable assets to the campaign: a dominant personality and access to great corporate wealth. The former treasury secretary's strong personality was seen as the means of distinguishing him from Reagan. The Connally campaign had two unusual features. First, Connally declined federal matching funds. (This meant more fund raising, but also freed Connally from certain restrictions on how the money could be spent.) Second, rather than going into specific states to build bases for Initial Contests, the Connally campaign hoped that national exposure would build up their candidate.

Two Republicans were contesting for the position of the moderate alternative to Reagan: Howard Baker and George Bush. Senate Republican Leader Baker had the advantages of electability, leadership experience, and a posture as a party unifier. He had been elected to the Senate three times from a competitive state, and was, in the judgment of David Broder, "the most principled and skillful Republican leader in the Senate since Robert Taft." The Senate leadership post was both an advantage and a disadvantage to Baker (much as it had been for Lyndon Johnson when he sought the Democratic nomination in 1960). On the one hand, it guaranteed him a degree of prominence; on the other, Senate responsibilities kept him in Washington and away from the campaign trail. The developing SALT II debate was also a challenge and an opportunity. Republican conservatives, already suspicious because Baker had supported the Panama Canal treaty, were alert to any further hints of liberalism. But if Baker were to oppose a treaty that was in the best interests of the country, he could lose his reputation for responsibility. Baker himself looked to the debate as an opportunity to demonstrate his leadership on a major issue. Unfortunately, the debate never came. Even costlier to Baker's chances was a tendency to put off organizational decisions. By the time he got around to setting up a field organization, he found that many of his natural supporters had already been recruited by others, especially George Bush.

George Bush had held a number of positions, but two of them were particularly important to his presidential bid. As a former chairman of the Republican National Committee, he was well known to Republican activists. And as an unemployed millionaire, he could afford to devote the time needed for a long primary campaign. Bush surrounded himself with a number of experienced organizers, including James Baker, Gerald Ford's 1976 campaign director (after he had gotten a go-ahead from Mr. Ford); Robert Teeter, who had done Ford's polling; and David Keene, who had worked the South for Ronald Reagan in 1976. In December 1978, George Bush and James Baker decided on the classic strategy of concentrating on Iowa and New Hampshire, and hoping for enough momentum from those races to carry them through the other early primaries. They assumed that by the time of the March 18 Illinois primary, the race would be down to two candidates, Bush and Reagan.

The most liberal of the Republican aspirants was Illinois Congressman John Anderson. Anderson's intelligence was well known in Washington, though not to the general public. He was chairman of the House Republican Conference, but had not been a viable candidate for the top Republican leadership position because he was something of a loner and his positions were too liberal for many Republican congressmen. With more limited finances and less of an organization than any other Republican aspirant, Anderson hoped to "stay alive" in the New England primaries, and thought he might do better when the race got to his native Illinois and adjacent Wisconsin.

Ford versus Reagan, 1976.   There had been talk for some time about a Ronald Reagan candidacy in 1976, but Gerald Ford's advisors did not seem to believe it. In common with many organization Republicans, Ford advisors were worried about the harm conservative ideologues could do to the party in a general election, but seemed to think that if enough gestures were made in their direction they would stop acting as ideologues and support moderate candidates in the interest of party unity. Ford's first gesture—coming at about the same time as his summertime announcement of candidacy—was the appointment of former Army Secretary Howard (Bo) Callaway to head the President Ford Committee. Callaway had achieved some success in Georgia politics (a term in Congress, a near miss for the governorship), but he had no national experience, and at once began talking about the possibility that Vice President Nelson Rockefeller would be dropped in 1976. The eventual result was that Rockefeller departed from the ticket, but conservatives kept right on supporting Ronald Reagan.

In other respects, the Ford Early Days posture was a classic strategy for an incumbent: try to demonstrate to any potential opponent that the president has enough support in his party to make opposition impractical. Some moves in the service of this strategy were important. Republican parties in large states—Ohio, New York, Pennsylvania and Michigan—endorsed the President for reelection, as did several prominent California Republicans. Two important personnel appointments were made in the fall. Professional campaign manager Stuart Spencer and newspaperman Peter Kaye, both long active in California Republican politics, were brought in respectively as director of organization and as press secretary of the President Ford Committee. Spencer also lacked national campaign experience, but brought real expertise to the committee, and at once turned to the task of creating a good New Hampshire organization along with Congressman James Cleveland (Witcover, 1977, chaps. 4, 6).

The serious conversations about a Reagan candidacy took place between the governor and several advisors who had been close to him in his California administration: Lyn Nofziger, Michael Deaver, Peter Hannaford, and others. In 1974, they expanded their group by recruiting a campaign director, John P. Sears. Sears, a lawyer who had gained delegate-hunting experience in the successful 1968 Nixon campaign, and who had opened a Washington law office after a brief stint on the White House staff, was an able and resourceful tactician.

With a new Republican president in the White House, Ronald Reagan was not at all sure he wanted to run. His personal decision was not made until the spring of 1975, and even then, he delayed any public announcement. John Sears and Lyn Nofziger started letting conservatives know that Reagan would run, recruited Nevada Senator Paul Laxalt as national chairman, and put together a New Hampshire committee headed by ex-Governor Hugh Gregg. When Reagan was ready to announce in November, his manner of doing so showed the strength of the challenge he was to make. The night before, he answered questions in New Hampshire, then flew to Washington's National Press Club for the announcement itself, then went on for press conferences in Florida, North Carolina, and California. Ronald Reagan was a highly articulate conservative, and three of the early primaries—New Hampshire, Florida, and North Carolina—were to be held in states where a conservative should garner a lot of Republican votes.

Carter versus Kennedy, 1980.   There was never any doubt in Jimmy Carter's mind about running for reelection, and preparations for that began with the creation of a Carter-Mondale Committee early in 1979. Senior White House officials, such as Hamilton Jordan, kept in close touch with the group led by Tim Kraft, who had been put in charge of these early operations. The Carter leaders did not know if they would face primary opposition, but simply went ahead with their plans. "We're not going to make the same mistake Ford made with Reagan in 1976," one of them explained. "They spent the bulk of their time in 1975 worrying about whether Reagan would run instead of raising money and preparing for him if he did run" (Smith, 1979, p. 28).

The Carter coalition did get on with the business of raising money, but they also attended to the equally important business of adjusting the rules so as to favor the President. The vote required before proportional representation went into effect (and each candidate got his proportionate share of the delegates) had been set at 15 percent.[3] This meant that no one but a strong challenger could take delegates away from President Carter. One could not get a few delegates simply by entering and picking up, say, 11 percent of the primary vote.

The Carter coalition also altered a number of primary dates. The

---

[3] These rules had been set by the Winograd Commission, appointed by the Democratic National Committee. Carter supporters (and others) wanted to set a high threshold to keep the vote from being splintered among too many candidates. Those who wanted an open process favored a low threshold. The compromise reached by the commission was that the threshold for caucus states and delegates elected statewide could be set by each state at any point between a minimum of 15 percent and a maximum of 20 percent. The threshold for district delegates was to be found by dividing 100 by the number of delegates in each district. Thus, if a district had four delegates, the threshold for that district would be 25 percent.

Alabama and Georgia primaries were moved ahead to March 11 to coincide with the Florida primary and create a block of delegates Carter could be expected to win. On the other hand, the Maine caucuses were not moved because they were scheduled early, and the Carter leaders reckoned that they would be able to win them.

While this organization work was going on in his behalf, Carter's public support was ebbing rapidly. By June, Carter's Gallup Poll "approval rating" among Democrats fell to 34 percent, the lowest rating in history for a president among his own party members. Inflation and gasoline lines were cutting into the limited support the administration still enjoyed. Pollster Pat Caddell had argued in a memorandum that "This crisis is not your fault as president. It is the natural result of historic forces and events that have been in motion for 20 years." Accepting this thesis, the President's response was the July 15 "malaise" speech. This speech was more than politics; it was an effort at national leadership. But some of the subsequent events were pure politics.

One of the things the President said was that he wanted to get away from the "island" of Washington and make more contact with the people. The following month, the Carters took a vacation cruise on the Delta Queen—which began in Minnesota, an early caucus state, and ended in Iowa, the very first caucus state. Between July and December, he visted 24 states, all but 6 of which were going to hold early primary elections.

The week following the malaise speech came major cabinet changes. Whatever virtues the departed members may have had, their replacements showed a clear White House interest in constituency politics: Patricia Roberts Harris, a black woman, was promoted to Health and Human Services; two Catholics, Benjamin Civiletti and Moon Landrieu, became attorney general and HUD secretary; and two Jews, Philip Klutznick and Neil Goldschmidt, took over the Commerce and Transportation departments. The administration had a good deal of discretionary funding that could be distributed, and much of this money went to cities whose mayors had seen the wisdom of supporting Jimmy Carter. Ultimately the mayors of New York City, Los Angeles, Detroit, San Francisco, Baltimore, Atlanta, Miami, St. Louis, Pittsburgh, Denver, Salt Lake City, and Seattle all endorsed the President.

There were two symbolic gestures that summer that seemed to be inconsistent. One was a story about President Carter defending himself with a boat oar against a rabbit that was said to have attacked him while he was fishing. The other was a presidential boast that, if Senator Kennedy did run against him, he'd "whip his ass." How could a president so weakened that he was vulnerable to attack by rabbits hope to defeat the popular Massachusetts senator? One answer is that a great deal of solid political work had been done even though its effects were not yet visible.

Throughout the spring of 1979, Edward Kennedy answered all questions about 1980 politics with his expect-expect-intend formula: "I expect the President to be renominated and I expect him to be reelected and I intend to support him." These words reflected the senator's real feelings, but even as he spoke them, events were carrying him into opposition. Every time polls appeared that showed Carter to be unpopular and Kennedy the preferred alternative (and Kennedy was leading Carter by 62 to 24 percent in early June), other Democrats would seek out Senator Kennedy, and urge him to run to prevent a Democratic defeat in 1980. Much of this was private, but there were some public signs. For example, five Democratic congressmen—Richard Ottinger of New York, Richard Nolen of Minnesota, John Conyers of Michigan, Fortney Stark of California, and Edward Beard of Rhode Island—announced a campaign to draft Kennedy. "There is tremendous unhappiness with Carter's policies," said Ottinger. "Also, I think the public's perception of Carter's performance is not high, and we'd like to see a Democratic victory next year." But at least some of the pressure was self-generated. Senator Kennedy regarded himself as one of the most consistent supporters of the Carter administration in the Senate, yet he was unsatisfied with the trend of Carter policies in health care, foreign policy, energy, and the economy. President Carter's malaise speech was another crystallizing point in Kennedy's thinking. "That speech," Kennedy later recalled, "was so completely contrary to everything I believe in that it upset me" (White, 1982, pp. 270–71). So the senator returned to Hyannisport. There, sometime during August, he reached his own decision to challenge Jimmy Carter for the 1980 nomination.

What the senator brought to the campaign was a deserved reputation as a better legislator than either of his brothers had been, and a belief that the Kennedy skill in politics would allow him to prevail. But the political skill that brought the 1960 nomination to his brother John had been exercised against rather unsubstantial opposition, and Edward was challenging an incumbent president. Furthermore, at the point when Senator Kennedy's decision to run was made, President Carter's campaigners had been busy planning, fund raising, and organizing in the early states for a good six months. It wasn't going to be enough for Kennedy to be a good campaigner. He had to be better.

All of the planning and organizing that normally occupies Early Days had to be done in a very short time. What issues could Kennedy stress that would both distinguish him from President Carter and make him a viable candidate? Which primaries should be entered? How were organizations going to be created in the states where he did enter that could compete with the already existing Carter organizations? What national staff would coordinate activities across the country? How would funds be raised to pay for all this? That answers to all of these questions could not be found instantly was apparent in the ragged start of the Kennedy campaign. For example, when Roger Mudd asked him on CBS television about reports linking him to other women, he said: "I'm . . . I'm married; I care very deeply about my wife, and my children, and we've . . . we have a rather special set of circumstances which is . . . perhaps somewhat unique. . . ." In a speech in Philadephia, he used the phrases "lead," "leadership," or "led" some 17 times. This just wasn't good enough.

Senator Kennedy did find noble phrases when he announced his candidacy at Boston's Faneuil Hall on November 7.

> For many months, we have been sinking into crisis. Yet we hear no clear summons from the center of power. Aims are not set. The means of realizing them are neglected. . . . Surely the nation that came back from the depression half a century ago can roll back the tide of inflation. . . . The most important task of presidential leadership is to release the native energy of the people. The only thing that paralyzes us today is the myth that we cannot move.

These lines were well written and well spoken, but they were not the lead item on the news that evening. Three days earlier a group of Iranian students had overrun the embassy in Teheran, and American diplomats had been taken hostage.[4]

INITIAL CONTESTS

Carter, 1976. Once the Initial Contests begin, something is known about the structure of competition. The relative strength of the candidates is difficult to determine this early, but the ideological positioning of the candidates can be discerned from the policy statements they make; and surveys soon reveal the types of voters that various candidates are going to be able to attract. Speaking very generally, the initial Democratic structure of competition found former Oklahoma Senator Fred Harris on the far left; Birch Bayh, Morris Udall, and 1972 vice presidential candidate Sargent Shriver on the moderate left; Henry Jackson and Jimmy Carter in the center; and Alabama Governor George Wallace on the right.[5] Bayh, Udall, and (to a lesser extent) Harris and Shriver were competing for the same constituency: young, liberal, college educated, white-collar. Jackson's appeal was supposed to be to

---

[4] This analysis of the 1980 Democratic contest as a two-candidate race ignores the role of California Governor Jerry Brown. The reason is that the essential dynamics of the campaign followed the two-candidate mode. Brown contested only two primaries (New Hampshire and Wisconsin), and ended up with only one delegate.

[5] Other announced candidates were Pennsylvania Governor Milton Shapp, Duke University President Terry Sanford, Texas Senator Lloyd Bentsen, and antiabortion candidate Ellen McCormack. California Governor Jerry Brown and Idaho Senator Frank Church entered later.

union members and blue-collar workers, although it turned out to be to Jewish voters and older persons. Jimmy Carter was positioned so he could attract different voters from state to state, depending on the nature of the opposition. There was considerable difference in the Carter constituencies in the North and South. In the North, his constant supporters were less educated, black, rural, and Protestant; in the South, he attracted a much wider following. The Wallace constituency' was motivated by a mistrust of government. They were conservative, law-and-order types with high school educations, and tended to be middle-aged with average incomes (Orren, 1978).

The general structure of competition is less consequential in the Initial Contests, though, than who is entered in each state. In Iowa, as we have seen, Carter had been campaigning for a year. Fred Harris had also been working for some time, although there was less popular support for the populist positions he was taking. When Birch Bayh made his late decision to run, he chose to make an effort in Iowa, and Morris Udall reversed his decision to have his early focus in New Hampshire and made a last-minute effort in Iowa. Sargent Shriver, the only Catholic candidate, hoped for some support in Catholic areas. This meant that Harris, Bayh, Udall, and Shriver were all competing for the liberal vote, and Jimmy Carter was the only one appealing primarily to the moderate and conservative voters. "Uncommitted" won, receiving 37 percent of the precinct vote to Carter's 28, Bayh's 13, Harris's 10, and Udall's 6. "Uncommitted," however, was unavailable to appear on network television, whereas Jimmy Carter was in New York City, and appeared as the Iowa winner on NBC's "Today," ABC's "Good Morning America," and "CBS Morning News" the following day (Drew, 1977, p. 16).

The field of candidates was identical in New Hampshire. The principal difference was that both Carter and Udall were well organized. The Udall campaign was headed by David Evans, a 1972 McGovern worker, and Maria Currier, the 1972 state coordinator for Muskie. They organized a thorough canvass: that is, contacting voters to ask who they support, thus learning who is likely to vote for your candidate. The Carter campaign had both a door-to-door canvass and a telephone canvass. The Bayh campaign tried using volunteers over the weekend to canvass, but couldn't match Carter and Udall (Witcover, 1977, chap. 16). Fred Harris had been helped by a small band of faithful supporters, and Sargent Shriver hoped to do better because of the Kennedy reputation in New England (he was married to Eunice Kennedy) and because of the larger Roman Catholic population. But the structure of competition was again Udall, Bayh, Harris and Shriver competing for the liberal vote, and Carter appealing to moderates and conservatives. Udall was the best organized of the liberals and therefore did relatively well; but the vote was 30 percent for Carter, 24 percent Udall, 16 percent

Bayh, 11 percent Harris, and 9 percent Shriver. Jimmy Carter again appeared as the victor on television, and now predicted a first-ballot nomination.

The structure of competition was different in Florida. This time the major candidates were Henry Jackson, relatively liberal on everything except foreign policy, Jimmy Carter in the center, and George Wallace on the right. The Wallace vote was assumed to be reasonably fixed because of Wallace campaign efforts in Florida in past years, and because large numbers of Florida immigrants come from Alabama. The question was how the non-Wallace vote would be split between Jackson and Carter. And it happened that there were quite a few Georgians who had moved to Florida (Gatlin, 1973), and Carter had been busy campaigning for a year. In the campaigning just before the election, Jimmy Carter became particularly critical of Henry Jackson because both were fighting for the same vote. It turned out that the non-Wallace vote was larger in 1976 than it had been earlier, and Jimmy Carter got more of it than Henry Jackson. Carter ended up with 34 percent of the vote, Wallace with 31, and Jackson with 24.

The Carter strategy had been an Initial Contests strategy. Virtually all of their resources—campaign time, organization, money—had been committed to the early contests in Iowa, New Hampshire, and Florida. Carter's national finance director Joel McCleary later explained, "We had no structure after Florida; we had no organization. We had planned only for the short haul. After Florida, it was all NBC, CBS, and the *New York Times*" (Arterton, 1984). If this Initial Contests strategy had not worked out, the Carter campaign would have been in serious difficulty; but luck was with them, and at the end of this phase, Jimmy Carter had established himself as a serious contender.

Reagan, 1980. The relative strength of the candidates coming into the Iowa caucuses on January 21 was largely a consequence of the strategies they had been following. John Connally's strategy of campaigning nationally through the mass media had not proven successful. Connally made some last-minute, state-oriented efforts—for example, hiring a bus to campaign for 40 hours across Iowa—but this was inadequate.[6] Senator Howard Baker had waited too long to begin his campaign, and had no real organization in Iowa. The Baker coalition did spend a good deal on media. Given their competition with George Bush for the moderate vote, they felt it was essential to beat Bush; a last-minute media campaign was their only hope of doing so. George Bush had been campaigning for a very long time in Iowa, and a poll of county chairpersons showed that he was running neck and neck

---

[6] The two other conservative candidates, Robert Dole and Philip Crane, were also unable to establish themselves as alternatives to Ronald Reagan in spite of very hard campaigning.

with Reagan. Governor Reagan, in keeping with John Sears' ball control strategy, chose not to take part in a widely publicized debate among Republican candidates,[7] and also limited his own campaigning to a few brief appearances. The precinct caucuses gave Bush 33 percent, Reagan 27 percent, Baker 14 percent, and Connally 10 percent.

The Iowa results brought major changes to the Reagan campaign. The most immediate was that the Governor went back on the road, devoting almost full time to appearances in New Hampshire, Florida, and South Carolina. Ronald Reagan as a campaigner was the best asset the Reagan coalition had, an asset that hadn't been used in Iowa. Another change was the firing of John Sears as campaign director, along with invitations to long-time Reagan aides Michael Deaver, Lyn Nofziger, and Martin Anderson to rejoin the campaign. This was not just because of the Iowa defeat. (It actually took place on the day of the New Hampshire primary.) In part, Sears had provoked Governor Reagan by reaching for more organizational power at the expense of other Reagan associates. In part, the Sears-led campaign, while grandly conceived, had proved to be very expensive. By the time of New Hampshire, three quarters of all available funds had been spent. This left the Reagan campaign quite vulnerable to any strong challenge.

The Iowa results also dramatically changed the attention being paid to George Bush. Among Republican and independent voters, he had been behind Ronald Reagan by a margin of 38 percent to 6 percent as recently as November. After Iowa, he was suddenly ahead 32 percent to 29 percent. Ignored earlier, Bush was now on magazine covers. The difficulty was that, while the Bush leaders had longed for just this kind of attention, they had no strategy to take advantage of it. Mr. Bush talked about "Big Mo," which sounded preppy, rather than being able to give solid reasons why his new supporters should stay with him.

George Bush enjoyed a slight lead in New Hampshire until a Manchester debate in which Ronald Reagan joined the six candidates who had debated in Iowa. Traveling reporters weren't too impressed with this debate, but subsequent polls showed that this gave the lead back to Reagan, and this lead was solidified at a two-candidate debate in Nashua, where Reagan protested the exclusion of four other Republican candidates. Reagan gained 50 percent of the February 2 vote, a long

---

[7] All of the Republican candidates in this debate acquitted themselves well, but John Anderson drew particular attention to himself by his candor. Whereas other candidates could not recall anything they wished they had done differently in their public lives, he said he wished he had voted against the Gulf of Tonkin resolution. When asked how one could balance the budget, reduce taxes, and increase defense spending all at the same time, he responded, "It's very simple. You do it with mirrors!" This performance did not have any impact on the Iowa outcome, but it did catch the eye of voters and journalists elsewhere.

way ahead of Bush's 23 percent, Baker's 13 percent, and Anderson's 10 percent.

The Bush campaign was looking past New Hampshire to the Massachusetts primary the following week. This was foresighted. Bush won the Massachusetts primary, drawing votes from all socioeconomic groups, and making effective use of his claim to experience. Moreover, Senator Howard Baker withdrew the following day, leaving Bush as the candidate of the moderate conservative Republicans. Unfortunately for Bush, what also happened in Massachusetts was the emergence of Congressman John Anderson. Anderson ran barely behind Bush in Massachusetts, barely behind Reagan in the same-day primary in Vermont, and demonstrated great strength with independents and well-educated voters. George Bush had defeated Howard Baker, the man he had to get by in order to take on Ronald Reagan in a head-to-head race, only to see the emergence of another rival for media attention and moderate-to-liberal Republican votes.

John Connally played a very small role in these New England Initial Contests because he was concentrating on the South Carolina primary. Having made a belated decision to try to build state strength, and competing with Reagan for conservative support, he needed to show that he could beat Reagan somewhere. South Carolina was small enough to be affected by Connally's ample resources, and conservative enough to be a good testing ground for him. Governor Connally had the support of Senator Strom Thurmond, but even so, Reagan got 55 percent of the vote to Connally's 30 and Bush's 15. Three days later, Ronald Reagan's southern strength was further demonstrated with votes of 73 percent, 70 percent, and 55 percent, respectively, in Georgia, Alabama, and Florida; but by then, John Connally was no longer in the race.

Ford versus Reagan, 1976.   Most of the doubts about the structure of competition that mark multicandidate races are absent from two-person contests. In this 1976 battle, it was moderate versus conservative, although it wasn't quite a straight ideological contest. Gerald Ford won some support from conservatives because he was president, and Ronald Reagan had some appeal to middle-of-the-road Republicans because of his platform skill. Still, both camps placed great importance on the Initial Contests, and both tried to rob the opponent of credibility. The Ford campaign sought to depict Ronald Reagan as given to irresponsible ideas, and the Reagan campaign tried to convey the idea that President Ford was not an effective leader.

Many early polls in New Hampshire gave Reagan a lead, and the Reagan campaign tried to hold this lead with "citizen's press conferences," in which members of the audience (rather than experienced reporters) asked questions. In his replies, Reagan did not attack Ford directly, but placed himself on the side of "the people" as opposed to "the government." Defense spending? "Well, here again, is where I believe a president must take his case to the people, and the people must be told the facts." Angola? "The government has left the American people in complete ignorance." He stressed that he was an outsider, "not part of the Establishment in Washington, and therefore not part of that buddy system that goes on." Reagan spent 15 days in the state, and the applause lines from the citizen's press conferences were used in television commercials.

That Reagan was unable to hold his lead over Ford was partly due to an improvement in the economy, which helped the incumbent, and partly due to the skill of Ford campaigners, especially Stuart Spencer. In September, Ronald Reagan gave a speech in Chicago that included the claim that "transfer of authority in whole or in part [in welfare, education, housing, food stamps, medicaid, community and regional development, and revenue sharing] would reduce the outlay of the federal government by more than $90 billion." Not much attention was paid at the time, but it caught Stuart Spencer's eye, and he had some research done on its implications. Peter Kaye, the press secretary, made arrangements for the New Hampshire speaker of the house and senate president to hold a press conference denouncing the plan on Reagan's first trip into New Hampshire, and the issue dogged Reagan throughout the campaign. Later, Reagan made a comment about investing social security funds "in the industrial might of the country," and Commerce Secretary Elliot Richardson promptly interpreted that as a suggestion to risk social security funds in the stock market (Witcover, 1977, chap. 25; Arterton, 1984). The improvement in the economy and television ads showing Gerald Ford at work in the Oval Office made the incumbent look a little better; questions raised about Ronald Reagan's proposals made him look a little less responsible. New Hampshire voters gave the President 50.6 percent of their vote.

The Florida primary was another in a conservative state that was won by the moderate Mr. Ford. Three things helped Ford here. First, Stuart Spencer hired the other half of the Spencer-Roberts campaign management firm, William Roberts, and placed him in charge of the Florida campaign. Second, the President, having won New Hampshire by however narrow a margin, seemed stronger; this impression was strengthened by uncontested victories in Vermont and Massachusetts. Third, Ford began to remind people he was the head of the federal government, announcing such things as a missile contract award and the completion of an interstate highway. On election night, the President got 53 percent of the vote, and the next day the *New York Times'* R. W. Apple wrote that Reagan's loss had drastically reduced his chances. "With only two contestants, a consistent loser soon finds himself without the funds and the campaign workers to keep him fighting."

Carter versus Kennedy, 1980.   The political fortunes of President Carter and Senator Kennedy changed almost the moment that Kennedy announced his candidacy. While the Iranian hostage crisis was ultimately to prove costly to the President, at the outset it was a boon to him. The proportion approving Carter's handling of his job jumped from 32 percent in early November to 61 percent a month later. In early January, he withdrew from a scheduled debate with Senator Kennedy, pleading the need to remain in the White House to deal with the hostage crisis. In fact, a good deal of attention was being devoted to Iowa. Rosalynn Carter, Walter Mondale, and other administration luminaries were out campaigning, and President Carter spent hours telephoning Iowa Democrats. One made news by refusing to take the President's call because she was watching television and because he was calling so many people that it was becoming commonplace.

The other change that took place was that the focus of public opinion shifted from President Carter's record to Senator Kennedy's character. For example, a Des Moines lawyer was quoted as saying: "Carter may have done a lot of things that were not as well thought out as they might have been. But he comes across as sincere. That's not true for Senator Kennedy. I'm suspicious of his motives." For his part, Kennedy knew that Carter was far ahead in Iowa, but being aware of the importance of Initial Contests, felt he had to campaign in Iowa in the hope of attracting enough support to get off to a reasonably good start. This didn't happen. The Iranian crisis, very effective constituency politics, and Senator Kennedy's own difficulties resulted in a 2 to 1 margin for the President.

Kennedy's Iowa defeat resulted in two important changes. One was a major financial crisis that was to last throughout the nomination contest. Not only did the senator give up his chartered plane and lay off paid staff, but the finances severely limited the number of primary elections that Kennedy could contest. The other change was to resolve a debate within the Kennedy coalition on whether to take relatively moderate positions to expand Kennedy's appeal or more liberal positions to solidify existing support. The senator gave a speech at Georgetown University, saying:

> The 1980 election should not be a plebiscite on the Ayatollah or Afghanistan. The real question is whether America can afford four more years of uncertain policy and certain crisis, of an administration that tells us to rally around their failures, of an inconsistent nonpolicy that may confront us with a stark choice between retreat and war. These are the policies that must be debated in the campaign.

In the speech, Kennedy also opposed draft registration, and called for a six-month, wage-price freeze. The decision had been made to nail down the liberal constituency.

New Hampshire was seen as critical by many observers. Senator Kennedy was thought to be on stronger ground because he was from neighboring Massachusetts. The Carter coalition tried, with some success, to plant the story that Kennedy had to win in New Hampshire in order to remain as a viable candidate, while they were pouring resources into the Granite State to make sure that he lost. On election day, Kennedy did get the votes of liberals who agreed with him on economics, but only 29 percent of New Hampshire Democrats described themselves as liberals, and Carter beat Kennedy 47 percent to 37 percent.

His home state of Massachusetts provided better news for the senator.[8] He did well among all categories of voters, especially among the wealthy, the elderly, Catholics, and moderates. The proportion that thought he was lying was only half as large as it was nationally, and he gained a lot more support because of his economic positions. Jimmy Carter did relatively well among conservatives, and actually had a majority among Protestants, but lost 65 percent to 29 percent.

In important respects, the Carter primary strategy was built around an understanding of proportional representation. This method of selecting delegates gives each candidate approximately the same ratio of delegates as he receives votes, as long as the candidate gets more than a minimum vote. This minimum level was set at 15 percent in 1980. The Alabama, Georgia, and Florida primaries had all been scheduled for March 11, a week after the Massachusetts primary. The Carter coalition poured resources into these primaries, not because they were in any danger of losing any of them, but because they wanted to keep Senator Kennedy below 15 percent, and thus deprive him of delegates. Edward Kennedy was too strong for the Carter forces to do this in Florida, but in Alabama, he was held to 13 percent, and in Jimmy Carter's native Georgia, to a mere 8 percent.

Of the seven Initial Contests, Edward Kennedy won only in Massachusetts. It was clear that President Carter had shown himself to be much the stronger candidate. What was not clear was whether Senator Kennedy won in Massachusetts only because it was his home state— or whether Massachusetts happened to be the first contest in the urban, industrial East where Senator Kennedy could be expected to do very well.

Summary

In this chapter, we have reviewed the first two stages of the nominating process, Early Days and Initial Contests. Both are necessary pre-

---

[8] Anticipating this, Hamilton Jordan directed that a serious Carter effort be made in the same-day Vermont primary. Ronna Freiberg was put in charge of that effort, and Carter won Vermont by 73 percent to 26 percent. This affected the way newspaper stories were written the following day.

ludes for the activity that is going to take place, but neither provides any certain knowledge about the outcome. For example, by 1982 Walter Mondale had created a Political Action Committee that could raise and spend money. Governor Askew had been in all 50 states, and Senator Cranston traveled widely as chairman of the Leadership Circle, a Democratic Senate fund-raising unit. Senators John Glenn, Ernest Hollings, and Gary Hart maintained extensive speaking schedules. None of this made it certain that these men would emerge as candidates for the Democratic nomination in 1984, but all were clearly positioning themselves for the contest. (In time, all declared their candidacies. In late 1983, they were joined by Jesse Jackson who spoke of the possibility of a "rainbow coalition," and by former Senator George McGovern who seemed to remember the cheers he heard in 1972.)

A similar point can be made about the Initial Contests. There is now more information about the structure of competition. Now you know who has decided to enter the lists and who is remaining on the sidelines. But Initial Contests may be either revealing or deceptive. For example, the Iowa caucuses accurately foretold Jimmy Carter's eventual success in 1976 and 1980, but George Bush did not go on to win the Republican nomination in 1980. There are two kinds of conclusions that one can draw after the Initial Contests. One concerns the weaker candidates in a multicandidate race who are forced out for lack of support. The other is that if there are two strong candidates with support across the country, and both do reasonably well in the Initial Contests, then it is likely (but not yet certain) that there will be a relatively stable two-candidate race which will last through the Convention stage. For more than this, one has to wait for Mist Clearing, and it is to this stage of nomination politics that we now turn.

CHAPTER 9

NOMINATION POLITICS: MIST CLEARING AND THE CONVENTION

MIST CLEARING

Carter, 1976. By the time the Pennsylvania primary approached, the Democratic structure of competition could be clearly perceived. There were fewer competitors, and enough delegates had been won so that one knew something about the relative strength of the candidates, in addition to their ideological positioning. Birch Bayh dropped out after the Massachusetts primary; Pennsylvania Governor Milton Shapp (who was not a major candidate, but who might have played some role in his home state primary if he had shown any strength at all) dropped out after Florida; Sargent Shriver after Illinois; Fred Harris after Wisconsin. George Wallace did not end his campaign, but he was not a serious candidate after Carter beat him in Florida, Illinois, and North Carolina. This left Morris Udall on the left, and Henry Jackson and Jimmy Carter in the center. The Carter coalition had 267 delegates at this point, Jackson 175, and Udall 150. Carter had only 18 percent of the 1,505 delegates needed for the nomination, but that number constituted 28 percent of those chosen thus far. Jackson, his nearest rival, had only 18 percent of those selected.

Senator Jackson had been pursuing a large-state strategy. He won in Massachusetts and again in New York. Since Jimmy Carter and Morris Udall were also on the ballot in Pennsylvania, this race was watched very closely. Carter got 37 percent of the vote to 25 for Jackson and 19 for Udall, and won 64 delegates to 24 for Udall and 14 for Jackson. Jackson had been counting on organized labor, regular Democrats, and a good media campaign. Yet Jimmy Carter actually did better among union voters; the regular Democrats preferred noncandidate Hubert Humphrey; and because of heavy spending in earlier primaries and lack of federal matching funds (due to a Supreme Court decision), money wasn't available for the media campaign. Governor Carter did well everywhere in the state, benefiting especially from Protestants and small-town, rural votes, both of which are numerous in the Keystone State.

Hubert Humphrey now came under considerable pressure to become an active candidate. Two days after the Pennsylvania primary, Senator Humphrey called a press conference to say, "I shall not seek it. I shall not compete for it. I shall not search for it. I shall not scramble for it." Over the weekend, Senator Jackson withdrew. This left Jimmy Carter and Morris Udall, and Carter had twice as many delegates.

There were further developments. Governor Jerry Brown and Senator Frank Church became active candidates, and both won some primaries. But the effect of their entry after Pennsylvania was to create a structure of competition with Jimmy Carter in the center with 331 delegates, and Morris Udall (174 delegates), Jerry Brown (0 delegates), and Frank Church (0 delegates) all on the left. In fact, Carter did much less well in subsequent primaries. He won in Georgia, Arkansas, Kentucky, and Tennessee, but lost 9 of the 13 nonsouthern primaries. With this structure of competition, though, it didn't make any difference in the outcome.

Reagan, 1980.   On the surface, the structure of competition looked very clear as the Illinois primary approached. Ronald Reagan, who was appealing to conservative voters, had 167 delegates; George Bush, whose ideological position was less distinct, but who was appealing to moderate conservatives, had 45; John Anderson, appealing to moderates and liberals, had 13. (Illinois Congressman Philip Crane, a determined conservative who still hadn't withdrawn, didn't have any delegates.) At the same time, none of the three candidates were very secure. The Reagan coalition, having spent most of their money, would be all right as long as they kept on winning, but they were not in a position to defeat any strong challenge. The Bush campaign was still struggling to get into a one-on-one posture against Reagan, but was losing conservative support to Reagan, and moderate-to-liberal support to Anderson. John Anderson's positions were appealing to independents, but made it very difficult for him to attract support from conservative voters in Republican primaries.

Reagan was helped by a debate between the candidates. Bush and Crane were quite direct in their attacks on Anderson; Bush attacked him as a liberal masquerading as a Republican. Reagan showed a much lighter touch, asking "John, would you really prefer Teddy Kennedy to me?" When the Illinois vote came in, Ronald Reagan had a 3 to 1 margin among conservatives. John Anderson had a small lead among moderates, and a 4 to 1 lead among liberals. But there were so many more conservatives voting that this translated into an overall vote of 47 percent for Reagan, 37 percent for Anderson, and 11 percent for Bush.

George Bush managed to get back on his feet the following week in Connecticut. Feeling that their chances of winning in Illinois were rather bleak and that they *had* to win in Connecticut, where Bush's father had been a U.S. senator, the Bush coalition concentrated on the New England state. The short-of-resources Reagan coalition decided that they could afford to lose Connecticut, and didn't put on much of a campaign there. The results gave some pleasure to all the candidates. With 39 percent, Bush could point to his first victory since Massachusetts. With 34 percent, Reagan could claim some support and more delegates (and a lot more the same day in New York) to add to his growing total. With 22 percent, Anderson could point to another "strong showing."

The expectations coming into Wisconsin were much the same as they had been in Illinois. It was assumed that there might be a chance for Bush and Anderson because Wisconsin permitted crossover voting (in which Democrats could vote in the Republican primary and vice versa). It was further assumed that this was a state where John Anderson *had* to win because there was no other primary coming along where conditions would be as favorable. There was a crossover vote, and Anderson did get the largest share of it. The crossover vote, however, was split among all the candidates, and the overall result was 40 percent for Reagan, 30 percent for Bush, and 27 percent for Anderson. Shortly thereafter, John Anderson abandoned his race for the Republican nomination, and began his "National Unity" third-party effort. He had gained a number of "moral victories," but had not won a single primary, and had few delegates to show for his efforts.

The Illinois, Connecticut, and Wisconsin primaries provide good illustrations of the differences between multicandidate and two-candidate nomination contests. Since Reagan was regularly winning most of the conservative vote, Bush and Anderson were competing for the nonconservative vote, and they were splitting it with each other. Now suppose that there had been a single moderate candidate. Given the results of the three-candidate races, it is likely that Reagan would have won in Illinois while "Bush-Anderson" would have won in both Connecticut and Wisconsin. There is also a more subtle distinction. A multicandidate race makes it more difficult for candidates to exceed expectations (Aldrich, 1980a, 1980b). In both Connecticut and Wisconsin, a moderate Republican might have been expected to win. Relatively liberal Republicans have done well in Connecticut, and such candidates can attract independent support in Wisconsin. Measured against an expectation of victory, Anderson did not do well in Connecticut, and neither Bush nor Anderson did well in Wisconsin. Falling below expectations makes it harder to raise funds for further primaries. Since a larger number of candidates means that more of them will fail to meet expectations, this also increases the likelihood that there will be a larger proportion of dropouts in a multicandidate race.

After the Mist Clearing primaries, the capacities of the Bush and Reagan coalitions were evident. Bush could beat Reagan by outspending him in large industrial states, and Reagan could win the nomination. Bush did win in Pennsylvania on April 22, and in Michigan on May 20. He also showed real strength in Texas, holding Reagan to a victory margin of 51 percent to 47 percent. By remaining in the race and demonstrating political strength, Bush was safeguarding his political future, but his continuing efforts had less and less to do with the 1980 Republican nomination; and on May 26, Bush conceded to Reagan.

The Reagan coalition was guided during this phase by a remarkably farsighted memorandum written in late March by pollster Richard Wirthlin.

> With over a third of the 998 delegate votes needed now locked into the Governor's column and with his best states only now starting to come up on the primary calendar, the general election campaign, from our point of view, starts today. . . . We must position the Governor, in these early stages (of the *general election* campaign) so that he is viewed as less dangerous in the foreign affairs area, more competent in the economic area, more compassionate on the domestic issues, and less of a conservative zealot than his opponents and the press now paint him to be.

Wirthlin went on to point out the importance of expanding the Reagan coalition by gathering additional support from less-conservative elements of the Republican party, including supporters of the now-defeated aspirants, and concluded, "Plans should be prepared now to garner the full and active support of George Bush, once he realizes that his candidacy has lost its viability. . . . His support and resources should be absorbed by our campaign fully and enthusiastically." (Drew, 1981b, pp. 351–55)

Ford versus Reagan, 1976.   Ronald Reagan's campaign did not look too strong after his defeat in the Initial Contests, and Ford sympathizers began to urge him to drop out of the race. There was one meeting between John Sears and Rogers Morton, the new President Ford Committee chairman, about conditions under which a withdrawal might take place (Witcover, 1977, p. 413). Three things, however, combined to revive the Reagan campaign. First, Ronald Reagan began to focus on three international issues—detente, the proposed Panama Canal treaty, and Secretary of State Kissinger—on which pollster Richard Wirthlin's surveys had uncovered a fair amount of criticism of the Ford administration among Republican activists (Moore & Fraser, 1977, p. 46). Second, there was a nationally televised speech by Governor Reagan that brought in contributions at a time when the campaign was badly in debt. Third, many of the later primaries were scheduled to take place in states where conservatives were quite strong.

Governor Reagan's campaign began to work in North Carolina where last-minute decision making carried him to victory. This quickly ended calls for him to abandon his candidacy. Mist Clearing really came, though, in early May.[1] In the Texas primary on May 1, Ronald Reagan carried every congressional district and picked up 96 delegates. Even Senator John Tower, running as a Ford delegate, was defeated. In the Alabama, Georgia, and Indiana primaries on May 4, Ronald Reagan got 130 delegates to Gerald Ford's 9. This brought the strength of the Reagan coalition to 313 delegates to 241 for the incumbent President. These figures did not reflect the large New York and Pennsylvania delegations, formally uncommitted though likely to support Ford; but with many remaining primaries in conservative states, it was clear that this was a contest between two strong coalitions. It was not clear which would win.

Carter versus Kennedy, 1980. Illinois was important to Democrats in 1980 for two reasons. First, there was the question about whether Senator Kennedy could win in another big, industrial state besides Massachusetts. Second, the Illinois primary had long been identified as crucial by the Carter coalition in much the same way that they had anticipated the decisiveness of the Pennsylvania primary in 1976. Not only was it "neutral" (that is, neither New England nor southern), but Illinois did not use proportional representation. And just as the Carter leaders had been alert to earlier opportunities to keep the Kennedy delegate total down by working hard in Alabama and Georgia, they were alert to an opportunity to run up the Carter delegate total by making a special effort in Illinois. The Carter campaign emphasized "character" and "trust," not too subtly calling attention to Chappaquiddick and Senator Kennedy's marital problems and thus undercutting his appeal to Chicago's rather conservative Catholic voters. As things turned out, Edward Kennedy lost Chicago, the Catholic vote, the labor vote, and the blue-collar vote. More important, Jimmy Carter won 165 of Illinois's 179 delegates. When added to the delegates won in previous primaries, that meant President Carter already had 38 percent of the votes needed to nominate. Conversely, for Senator Kennedy to get the nomination, he would have to win 61 percent of the delegates re-

---

[1] There were only two primaries during the whole month of April. Ford beat Reagan in Wisconsin, and Reagan was not on the ballot in Pennsylvania.

maining to be chosen. In other words, Jimmy Carter's renomination was a virtual certainty.

The Illinois results also seemed to imply that Kennedy's victory in Massachusetts had been a home state phenomenon. Not so. If Edward Kennedy was not popular in Illinois, Jimmy Carter was even less popular in New York. There were indications of loss of support for the President in preelection polls, and the Carter coalition's worst fears were confirmed on election day. Senator Kennedy beat President Carter by 3 to 1 among Jews, 3 to 2 among Hispanics, and 5 to 4 among blacks and Catholics. Jews had been angered when United Nations Delegate Donald McHenry cast an anti-Israeli vote, and then was repudiated by the White House; but the New York vote was not a specific response to one incident. It was a general protest against the administration, with attitudes about inflation having the greatest impact on the vote. Senator Kennedy received 59 percent of the vote, and carried all six congressional districts in neighboring Connecticut.

The pattern was now set. There were three general circumstances that affected the results of the remaining primaries. One was organization. President Carter was able to contest every single primary. The Kennedy coalition was so short of resources that it could only afford to challenge the Carter forces in selected primaries. The second was geography. Speaking generally, Senator Kennedy won in the industrial Northeast, and President Carter won everywhere else.[2] Finally, there was the question of the dominant issue in the campaign. Whenever the election focused on Senator Kennedy's character, Carter won. Whenever the election focused on President Carter's achievements in office, Kennedy won.

The last consideration—essentially that the ability of either candidate to win depended on the weakness of the other—affected relationships between the two camps. From Senator Kennedy's point of view, there were serious issues that needed to be debated.[3] When the Carter campaign attacked Kennedy, as in Pennsylvania, with television ads with citizens expressing their doubts about Kennedy ("I don't believe him." "I don't trust him." "Between Kennedy and Carter, I would definitely go with Carter myself. I trust him.") this seemed to Kennedy partisans to be a deliberate evasion of a much-needed discussion of issues. But from President Carter's point of view, he deserved to be the Democratic nominee because he had dealt with tough issues in

---

[2] Finally, on "Super Tuesday" (June 3), Kennedy beat Carter in California, New Jersey, Rhode Island, New Mexico, and South Dakota. Carter won in Ohio, Montana, and West Virginia. The Kennedy victories in California, New Mexico, and South Dakota signaled a low point in Carter fortunes.

[3] In May, Senator Kennedy offered to release his delegates if President Carter would agree to a debate. The view of the Kennedy campaign within the Carter core group was so negative at that time that the offer was not seriously explored.

the White House, and given the arithmetic of the delegate count, he was going to be the nominee. Therefore, when Edward Kennedy urged a crowd in Philadelphia to "No more hostages, no more high inflation, no more high interest rates, *no more Jimmy Carter*," Carter partisans saw this as deliberately undercutting the Democratic party's chances of retaining the White House in the fall.

Finally, we should note the effect of proportional representation on a two-candidate contest such as this. President Carter's strength was not simply a result of proportional representation. Organizational strength, a decision to enter every primary, and other factors that we have discussed, all contributed to Carter's lead. But the Carter camp's tactical use of proportional representation, as in their Alabama-Georgia effort to keep Kennedy from getting any delegates and the Illinois work to get more Carter delegates, certainly augmented the number of Carter delegates. On the other hand, since Kennedy was strong enough to get more than the 15 percent cutoff, he was going to pick up delegates in almost every primary. Even if he can't win, a reasonably strong second candidate aided by proportional representation is going to have enough of a delegate base to mount a serious challenge.[4] Thus the Democrats' situation in the spring of 1980. The rules acted to produce two viable coalitions, and relations between the leaders of the two coalitions were very bad.

THE CONVENTION

Carter, 1976. With the Carter coalition in firm control in 1976, there were no real challenges to their leadership. Platform Committee members meeting in Washington in June were supplied with a 37-page statement of Carter's positions; Carter issues specialist Stuart Eizenstat was in attendance to handle the few questions that did come up. The platform, which was adopted by the convention without controversy, did not contain any statements that were unacceptable to Jimmy Carter. The closest thing to a fight came over Rules Committee recommendations on representation at future conventions. A number of women wanted a requirement of equal numbers of male and female delegates, but the National Women's Political Caucus (not part of the convention, but influential with feminist delegates) voted to accept a Carter-proffered compromise that would encourage states to work toward equal numbers of men and women in their delegations.

The only question of any consequence was who would be chosen

---

[4] If the two candidates had been of more equal strength, as Eisenhower and Taft in 1952 or Ford and Reagan in 1976, proportional representation could have produced a very even contest.

as the vice presidential nominee. Governor Carter considered this with
unusual care. In the weeks before the convention opened, information
was gathered about potential running mates, the most promising of
whom were interviewed by Carter associates. Then Carter himself interviewed the "finalists" either in Plains, Georgia, just before the convention, or in New York City after his arrival at the convention site.
The three to whom the most serious consideration was given were
all northern senators: John Glenn of Ohio, Edmund Muskie of Maine,
and Walter Mondale of Minnesota. The choice went to Mondale because he was bright, the personal chemistry between Carter and Mondale was good, and Mondale had links to a number of groups in the
Democratic party where Carter himself was not strong. By attracting
liberal support, Mondale broadened the Carter coalition as it moved
from nomination politics to electoral politics.

   Reagan, 1980.   To an unusual degree, the 1980 Republican National
Convention was part of the general election campaign. There were
two scripts that had been written for it, one approved by the Reagan
strategy group, and the other constructed by the Republican National
Committee which had the formal responsibility for organizing the convention. In late April, Richard Wirthlin, aware that the nomination
was effectively in hand, put political scientist Richard Beal to work
on strategy for the general election. Beal, in concert with others at
Decision/Making/Information (Wirthlin's polling firm) worked throughout May and began writing in early June. Once a draft was ready, it
was reviewed by Edwin Meese, William Casey, Peter Dailey, and William Timmons.[5] By the Fourth of July, 10 days before the convention
began, it had been approved and was in effect. The plan focused on
the larger states whose votes would be needed to put together an Electoral College majority. Therefore, California, Texas, and Florida (considered to be part of Reagan's base) and several target states around
the Great Lakes, were regarded as particularly important. The plan
also assumed that Governor Reagan would move toward the political
center as he sought support of swing voters in those states.

   There was no essential conflict between this plan and the goals of
William Brock. As Republican national chairman, Brock had built up
the organizational muscle of the party. His plans were based on a
November 1979 study conducted by Robert Teeter of Market Opinion
Research. This showed that economic issues were going to be decisive
in 1980, and that there was a large bloc of nonvoters under 40 whom
Brock hoped to attract (Republican National Committee Chairman's

---

   [5] The composition of this strategy group itself marked an expansion of the Reagan
coalition to include other Republicans. Meese and Wirthlin had been associated with
Reagan for some time. Casey, Dailey, and Timmons had worked for other Republicans
before 1980.

Report, 1980). When the identity of the candidate is already known, there are normally three things in a convention that provide opportunities to attract voters: the platform, the selection of the vice presidential candidate, and the acceptance speech. The first two of these were to be affected by things that weren't in either the Reagan or the National Committee script—the attitudes of conservative zealots on the Platform Committee, and the negotiations with Gerald Ford over the vice presidential nomination—but otherwise the convention proceeded according to plan.

The platform struggles were between different shades of conservatism: organized conservatism as reflected in the leadership of the committee, and a more zealous version exhibited by individual committee members. Senator John Tower of Texas was the chairman; Representative Trent Lott of Mississippi was vice chairman.[6] Roger Semerad, the executive director who supervised the committee's operations, and Michael Baroody, the editor who did much of the actual writing, both came from the Republican National Committee. Thanks to Baroody, the platform was organized around a series of themes: the individual, the family, the neighborhood, jobs and the workplace, the nation, and peace and freedom. (Three of these—the family, the neighborhood, the workplace—reflected thinking about mediating institutions through which the individual is associated with the larger society.) The Reagan coalition was represented by Richard Allen and Martin Anderson. Anderson was much in evidence once the nomination was securely Reagan's. In Detroit, these organization conservatives came up against such committee members as Donald E. White of Alaska, a supporter of the Moral Majority; Guy O. Farley, a leader of the New Right in Virginia; and the vocal Glenda Mattoon of Oklahoma. They had come to Detroit to write their views into the platform, and were unmoved by grander goals such as electing a Republican president.

Perhaps the most sensitive issues were the Equal Rights Amendment (ERA) and abortion. The difficulty with ERA was that the Republican party had been the first party to endorse it, and had done so in every platform since 1940, but was about to nominate the only major aspirant in either party who opposed its ratification. The platform drafters therefore wrote straddling language saying that the party "did not renounce" its historic commitment to equal rights and equality for women. Additionally, the National Federation of Republican Women prepared a rather lengthy bill of rights for women, which had been cleared with Reagan. After a good deal of maneuvering in subcommittee and the

---

[6] The conservative nature of the leadership can be better grasped from the identity of the subcommittee chairs. These included Senators Dole and Roth, and Representatives Michel, Stockman, Holt, Rousselot, Edwards, and Kemp. Senator Dole and Representatives Michel and Heckler occasionally had moderate thoughts. All the rest were determined conservatives.

full committee, the platform "acknowledged the legitimate efforts of those who support or oppose ratification" of ERA, "reaffirmed" the historic commitment to equal rights, and contained part of the women's bill of rights. Neither the New Right nor pro-ERA activists were happy with this compromise, but neither side was being read out of the party. Abortion was not compromised. The drafters had tried to straddle this one, too, saying that it was a "difficult and controversial" question on which Republicans could disagree. This was changed into endorsement of a constitutional amendment protecting "the right to life for unborn children," opposition to use of tax funds for abortions, and a call for the appointment of judges who respected "traditional family values and the sanctity of innocent human life." Supporters of ERA and family planning had to accept these changes, since they did not even have enough strength to force a debate on the convention floor (Malbin, 1981).

As is almost always the case, the *bulk* of the platform was endorsed exactly as it had been written. But the debate over these social issues drew the attention of the media.[7] This was hardly what the convention scripts had anticipated. The Reagan strategy wanted to move the candidate toward the center, not draw attention to an area where he was undeniably conservative. And the National Committee plan called for emphasis on vote-producing economic issues, not party-dividing social issues.

Another opportunity to broaden (or narrow) the base of the Reagan coalition came in the selection of the vice presidential nominee. The possibilities were Representative Jack Kemp of New York, Senator Paul Laxalt (Reagan's close friend from Nevada), former Treasury Secretary William Simon, Representative Guy Vander Jagt of Michigan, Senator Richard Lugar of Indiana, former Defense Secretary Donald Rumsfeld, former Ambassador Anne Armstrong of Texas, George Bush, and Senator Howard Baker. By selecting one of those at the beginning of the list, such as Kemp or Laxalt, Reagan would have gladdened the hearts of conservative delegates, but not moved toward the political center. Selecting someone from the end of the list, such as Bush or Baker, would have produced the opposite result. Reagan strategists had been using the preconvention period to study the situation, and Richard Wirthlin had been polling to determine what differences vice presidential candidates would make. These polls showed that only one name would significantly improve Reagan's chances: Gerald R. Ford. Therefore Reagan decided to explore this possibility before making any other choice.

---

[7] Unable to do anything with the platform, ERA supporters had organized a parade outside the convention. Some 17 pro-ERA Republican women also met with Governor Reagan. These events conveyed the idea that some Republicans were not as conservative as the Platform Committee, but they also kept attention on social issues.

The negotiations with Ford lasted from Tuesday morning until late Wednesday evening. The former President was disinclined to run but, under pressure to do so, was willing to explore whether the office of vice president could be enhanced enough to make it worthwhile. Ford aides (among them Henry Kissinger and Alan Greenspan) and Reagan aides (including Edwin Meese and William Casey) attempted to work something out. By midday on Wednesday, their discussions reached the point of augmenting the vice president's role by placing the National Security Council and Office of Management and Budget under his direction, but several things happened to prevent an agreement being reached. First, Reagan leaders got the impression that Kissinger and Greenspan were to be part of a Reagan-Ford administration. Second, Reagan was startled to hear Ford answer, when Walter Cronkite asked him on CBS television about a *co-presidency* (a term that had not been used in the negotiations), "That's something Governor Reagan really ought to consider." Finally, when all the television networks were announcing that Ford was going to be the vice presidential nominee, Reagan sent word that he had to have an answer. As it happened, Ford had nearly made up his mind not to run anyway, and Reagan's request crystallized his refusal. Much has been written about what caused the breakdown in these negotiations. Perhaps the most crucial factor, though, is that even if all other barriers could have been surmounted, there would have remained the very difficult constitutional question of how the powers of the presidency could be shared.

Governor Reagan immediately called George Bush and offered him the nomination, thus expanding his coalition as John Kennedy did in 1960 by offering the vice presidential nomination to Lyndon Johnson, and as Jimmy Carter did in 1976 by picking Walter Mondale. Bush had shown an appeal to suburban voters in Texas and Florida, two of Reagan's base states, and he had carried both Michigan and Pennsylvania, two of the target states in the Reagan strategy. And as Charles O. Jones has pointed out, the negotiations with Ford had the side effect of making the Bush selection a good deal more palatable to conservatives. Bush seemed not to have been Reagan's first choice, and the attention that was devoted to the Ford possibility kept conservatives from putting together a campaign for someone more to their liking (Jones, 1981b, p. 95). The Ford negotiations were not designed to distract, but they did produce this unplanned bonus for Ronald Reagan.

With his acceptance speech on Thursday night, Ronald Reagan could finally go back to what was in the scripts. From the first paragraph that echoed the organizing concepts of the platform:

> I am very proud of our party. We have shown to all America a party united, with positive programs for solving the nation's problems; a party ready to build a new consensus with all those across the land who share

a community of values embodied in these words: family, work, neighbor-hood, peace, and freedom.

to a call for a moment of silent prayer at the end, Governor Reagan was able to say what he wanted to say to the large television audience attracted by the closing hours of the convention.

Ford versus Reagan, 1976.   In the two-person contest four years earlier, neither camp had the luxury of being able to write a script. As the Convention neared, Ford was in the better position. The Reagan forces had mounted the strongest challenge to an incumbent president in over half a century, but when the last delegate was selected, the *Washington Post* delegate count showed Ford with 1,093, Reagan with 1,030, and 136 uncommitted. With 1,130 needed to nominate, Ford stood a much better chance of getting the uncommitted delegates that he needed. Furthermore, almost all of the ideological conservatives were already supporting Reagan. There was no further move open which would please his conservative supporters and impress uncommitted delegates. "What we direly needed," John Sears said later, "was some way to carry the fight, to get maneuverability again. At this particular juncture, the perception was growing that if things stayed as they were, we were going to get counted out of the race" (Moore & Fraser, 1977, p. 48). What John Sears proposed, and Ronald Reagan accepted, was the announcement that if Reagan were nominated, moderate Pennsylvania Senator Richard Schweiker would be tapped as his running mate. As things turned out, this did not gain additional delegates for Reagan; but the unhappiness it caused, specifically in the Mississippi delegation, ultimately led to an advantage for Ford.

John Sears selected a rules proposal as the vehicle for the Reagan coalition's principal tactical challenge. The proposal, known as Rule 16-C, would have required that presidential candidates make their vice presidential choices known before the balloting for president. There were two reasons for this selection. First, the uncommitted delegates were not ideological conservatives, and so might be more easily per-suaded to support a "neutral" procedural point. Second, it was hoped that Ford's choice (if he could be forced to make one) would cause enough unhappiness within his coalition so some Ford delegates could be wooed by Reaganites. This proposal was rejected on a 59 to 44 vote within the Rules Committee itself, but the decisive vote was to come on the convention floor. At the end of that roll call, the vote stood 1,041 in favor of Reagan's 16-C motion and 1,112 against. Neither side had the 1,130 votes for a majority. Then Florida, where Ford had won an early primary, cast 28 votes for and 38 votes against, and Mississippi, the object of intense effort by the Ford leaders ever since the Schweiker ploy, cast 30 votes against. The principal Reagan chal-lenge was turned back.

There were more votes to come. There were some determined conservatives, such as North Carolina Senator Jesse Helms, who were not responsive to the Reagan leadership. They thought it would be better to have the decisive vote on a "red meat" conservative policy issue, and presented a "Morality in Foreign Policy" amendment to the report of the Platform Committee. This was intended to symbolize conservative belief in moral purpose, as opposed to the realpolitik of Secretary of State Henry Kissinger, but the amendment was stated in very general language, and the Ford leaders decided not to oppose it.

Ford received 1,187 votes on the presidential roll call to Reagan's 1,070. The regional nature of their support was quite apparent. President Ford got 73 percent of the votes cast by eastern and midwestern delegates. Governor Reagan got 72 percent of the votes cast by southern and western delegates.

Reagan agreed to a meeting with Ford afterward on condition that he not be offered the vice presidential nomination. Ford mentioned other persons he was considering, and Reagan said he thought Senator Robert Dole would be acceptable. The others who were given the most serious consideration—both before the convention and in an all-night meeting between Ford and his advisors after he was nominated—were former Deputy Attorney General William Ruckelshaus, Senator Howard Baker, and Anne Armstrong, the ambassador to England. None of these three was a flaming liberal, but each would have broadened the ticket. In the end, it came down to Dole. Ford was comfortable with him; he was popular within the party; his nomination could be got through a conservative and unpredictable convention. In a sense, the selection of Dole was comparable to Carter's selection of Mondale, and Reagan's of Schweiker. In each case, the presidential contender was reaching out for a representative of the other wing of the party. The difference was that when Carter, a moderate Democrat, picked a liberal Mondale, or when Reagan, a conservative Republican, said he would choose Schweiker, the tickets' chances in the general election were strengthened. But when Ford, a moderate conservative from the Midwest, chose Dole, a conservative from the Midwest, the appeal of the ticket was narrowed.

Carter versus Kennedy, 1980.   The 1952 and 1976 Republican conventions were the culminations of classic two-candidate contests. Both Eisenhower and Taft in 1952, and Ford and Reagan in 1976, came to the convention with enough delegates to make the nomination of either man entirely plausible. The 1980 Democratic convention was a variant on the classic two-candidate Convention. President Carter had an 8 to 5 advantage in pledged delegates. Therefore Senator Kennedy was in the position of a very strong challenger rather than a likely nominee. Even so, the fates of Kennedy and Carter were bound together by the dynamics of a two-candidate struggle.

What were Senator Kennedy's major goals? The odds were against his nomination, and his hope lay in a rules change that would free Carter delegates of their pledges to vote for the President. If the Kennedy coalition was successful in this first instance, then a debate on issues *might* create a momentum which *might* create a possibility of a Kennedy nomination. Failing that unlikely sequence, Kennedy needed a way of rationalizing support for the President in the fall. If there were a debate on issues, then perhaps Senator Kennedy could claim that "enough" of his views had been accepted for him to support the President he had been opposing for nine months. Given Senator Kennedy's oratorical skills, such a rationalization could best be presented in a prime-time television address. The problem with all this was that the Carter majority controlled the rules, the platform, and access to the podium. The Kennedy coalition's goals could be reached only with the acquiescence of the Carter coalition.

Now, what were the goals of the Carter coalition? As the probable nominee, Jimmy Carter could not take more-liberal positions without risking a vote loss to Ronald Reagan. The Carter coalition did not want a debate in which the Carter administration was subject to additional criticism. And President Carter wanted to emerge from the convention with the support of all Democrats, especially Edward M. Kennedy. These were things the Kennedy coalition could prevent. They could offer platform amendments that were popular enough with Democrats to be approved by the convention, but which President Carter could not accept without the specter of still more deficit spending. They could criticize the Carter administration at length, and, of course, they might choose to "sit out" the fall election. Thus both coalitions, bitter rivals for some months, were dependent on each other to achieve their goals.

Senator Kennedy and President Carter met after the last primary. This meeting was inconclusive, but Richard Moe, Vice President Mondale's top aide, and Paul Kirk, political director of the Kennedy campaign, were designated to keep the lines of communication open between the two coalitions. Further contact developed as a result of a conversation between Tom Donilon, who had become Carter's chief delegate counter while still in his early 20s, and Carl Wagner, Kennedy's director of field operations, after a meeting of the Credentials Committee in July. This led to four meetings in which Hamilton Jordan, Richard Moe, and Tom Donilon represented Carter; and Paul Kirk, Carl Wagner, and two of Wagner's aides, Jack English and Harold Ickes, represented Kennedy. When platform contents were to be discussed, they were joined by Stuart Eizenstat and David Rubenstein of the White House Domestic Policy Staff, and Susan Estridge, Kennedy's issues specialist. In a series of one-for-one trades (the Carter coalition gave up something when the Kennedy coalition gave up something), these negotiators worked out understandings about the conduct of the Convention. The sequence they arrived at—rules votes on Monday night, platform votes and a prime-time Kennedy speech on Tuesday night—was one in which both the Carter and Kennedy coalitions could pursue their central goals. This was confirmed in an agreement signed by Hamilton Jordan, Paul Kirk, and Democratic National Chairman John C. White.

The rule chosen by the Kennedy coalition for their first tactical challenge was F3(c), which stated "All delegates to the national convention shall be bound to vote for the presidential candidate whom they were elected to support." There were strong logical arguments on both sides. The Carter coalition, favoring the rule, declared that the delegates ought to keep faith with the voters who had elected them to support a particular candidate. The Kennedy coalition's explicit argument was that the delegates ought to be free to vote their own consciences. Their implicit argument was that President Carter was no longer as popular as he had been in the early primaries, and that to nominate him was to risk defeat. Behind the logical arguments lay Senator Kennedy's need to free the delegates of this obligation if he was to have any chance of the nomination, and the determination of the Carter coalition to use this vote to demonstrate that they were in control of the convention. When the vote was taken, the rule was supported 1,936.4 to 1,390.6. The Carter coalition had been only 30 votes off in their vote estimate; the Kennedy coalition had been 500 votes off. Shortly thereafter, Senator Kennedy announced that his name would not be put in nomination.

The Kennedy coalition, now fighting over issues, was on much stronger ground during the platform debate on Tuesday night. They were supporting four minority economic planks. One called for wage and price controls; the second prohibited any action that would result in a significant increase in unemployment; number three favored a $12 billion job-creation program endorsed by the AFL-CIO; the fourth said that high interest rates and unemployment should not be used to fight inflation. These were popular with the liberal convention delegates.[8] Moreover, the labor unions were working hard for these planks, and they were able to reach a number of Carter delegates. The Kennedy leaders wanted roll-call votes on all four of the minority planks. The Carter leaders felt they could not accept a roll-call vote on wage and price controls. This would be too much of a handicap in the fall cam-

---

[8] A New York Times/CBS survey in the summer of 1980 found that 17 percent of adult Americans considered themselves liberal, 49 percent moderate, and 28 percent conservative. The Democratic delegates were 46 percent liberal, 42 percent moderate, and 6 percent conservative. The Republican delegates had been 2 percent liberal, 36 percent moderate, and 58 percent conservative. The delegates to both conventions were unrepresentative even of their own parties. The conservative bias at the Republican convention was worse than the liberal bias at the Democratic convention, but both conventions were a long way from the political center.

paign. So agreement was reached on a roll-call vote on the $12 billion jobs program, and voice votes on all the rest.

The roll-call vote became impossible because of Senator Kennedy's speech. It had been written, principally by Robert Shrum and Carey Parker, so it could be used as the Kennedy peroration, whatever that happened to be. Kennedy's delivery made this one of the historic moments in convention speechmaking. When he reached his conclusion:

> For me, a few hours ago, this campaign came to an end. For all those whose cares have been our concern, the work goes on, the cause endures, the hope still lives, and the dream shall never die.

the delegates erupted in a demonstration that House Speaker Tip O'Neill, the permanent chairman of the convention, could not gavel to a close. Finally, he gave up the idea of a roll-call vote, and called for voice votes on all four amendments. On wage and price controls, he announced that the nays had it, and on the three other amendments, he declared that the ayes had it. If O'Neill's judgments did not accord with those of other observers, it was simply because he was enforcing the agreement that Kennedy and Carter leaders had reached earlier.

All else was anticlimax. The minimum goals of both coalitions were realized. Senator Kennedy lost the nomination, but was able to force some changes in the platform, and his speech was the high point of the convention. President Carter was duly renominated. Criticism of the Carter administration was limited, the worst damage in the platform was averted, and the cooperation between the Carter and Kennedy leaders set the stage for Kennedy campaigners to work for the President in the fall.

THE STRUCTURE OF COMPETITION

How did we end up with these two candidates? Can't America do better than Reagan and Carter? Or Nixon and McGovern? Or whomever the major party nominees happen to be in 1984? This question is asked constantly during election years. It reflects dissatisfaction with the quality of the nominees, but it may also reveal a lack of understanding of what the nominees represent. Our president is a symbol for the country. He is treated with respect; we speak of his wife as the First Lady. There is an implication here that he should be the best among all Americans. This isn't necessarily so. The best person, depending on the context, may be a path-breaking scientist, a skillful surgeon, an accomplished musician, or someone who has demonstrated his or her talent in any of dozens of different pursuits. What we need from a president is not talent or virtue measured on some absolute scale, but political leadership. Specifically, he should advocate policies that are acceptable to a majority of citizens, and have the competence to get these policies accepted and implemented. It follows that a presidential nominee should represent policies that are acceptable to a majority of the members of his or her political party, and that the party members think he or she can do the job.

Acceptable policies and personal competence are not unrelated to winning the nomination, but they are not directly tested by the candidate's ability to win delegates. As we have seen, the ability to win delegates is very much affected by the structure of competition. Suppose there had been a moderate midwestern governor in 1976 who split the moderate Democratic vote with Jimmy Carter in Iowa and New Hampshire. This would have meant that Birch Bayh would have gotten the most delegates in Iowa, and that Morris Udall would have won in New Hampshire. Or suppose that John Anderson had not run in 1980, and that George Bush had therefore gotten the moderate votes that went to Anderson. This would have meant Bush victories in Vermont and Wisconsin, and much larger Bush margins in Massachusetts and Connecticut. We can't be sure of these "might-have-beens," but we can be certain that winning or losing a presidential nomination does not depend on the intrinsic merit of an aspirant. *Success in nomination politics depends on both the strategy that is followed and the structure of competition.*

Frank Mankiewicz, Senator George McGovern's 1972 campaign director, compared the success of the McGovern strategy to bidding a grand slam in bridge. "You get to the point where your partner puts his cards down and you see it can be won, but only if the trumps break right, if the queen is where you want it, and all the finesses work" (Lydon, 1972). The 1972 structure of competition had McGovern and New York Mayor John Lindsay on the left, Senators Hubert Humphrey and Edmund Muskie on the center left, Senator Henry Jackson and Congressman Wilbur Mills (longtime chairman of the Ways and Means Committee) on the center right, and Governor George Wallace on the right. McGovern was stronger on the left than Lindsay (who dropped out after Wisconsin), and Wallace was more popular in the South than Mills. The Muskie campaign collapsed midway through the primaries, and Jackson did not prove to be a strong candidate. Consequently, the final structure of competition had McGovern on the left, Humphrey center left, and Wallace on the right. There were votes on the right, but not enough to nominate Wallace, and given the 1972 delegate selection procedures (Lengle & Shafer, 1976), McGovern got more delegates than Humphrey. Did this prove that George McGovern was the best Democrat who could have been nominated in 1972? Not at all. It is simply another illustration that winning the nomination means that the candidate's strategy has been successful in view of the structure of competition in the party that year.

A second major point we have seen in this chapter is that *there is a fundamental difference between a multicandidate structure of competition and a two-candidate structure of competition.* We have seen multicandidate structures of competition in the cases of the 1976 Carter and 1980 Reagan nominations, and two-candidate structures of competition in the cases of the 1976 Ford and 1980 Carter nominations. In the first two instances, it was not at all clear during Early Days who would emerge from the nomination process. Once Carter and Reagan did emerge during Mist Clearing, though, the odds were against anyone being able to mount a successful challenge against them. In the Ford-versus-Reagan and Carter-versus-Kennedy cases, the structure of competition remained about the same from Early Days on through the Convention itself. Ford and Reagan, and Carter and Kennedy, were strong candidates when the races began, and all came to their respective conventions with substantial delegate support.

John Aldrich, who developed a formal model of the nomination process (1980a, 1980b), found that a multicandidate structure of competition tends to be unstable. His reasoning is this. All candidates (and the reporters covering them) develop expectations about how well they should do. If they do better than expectations, they develop positive momentum. If they just meet expectations, then there's a "that's what they were expected to do" reaction. If they do less well, then their campaigns are in trouble. "The larger the number of candidates," Aldrich writes, "the greater the number who cannot possibly meet . . . expectations" (1980b, p. 664). Therefore, early in the race, we should expect the field to be "winnowed down" to a much smaller number of viable candidates. In other words, Fred Harris, Sargent Shriver, Birch Bayh, and Morris Udall could not possibly get the same liberal Democratic votes in 1976, and Howard Baker, George Bush, and John Anderson were all fighting for the same moderate Republican votes in 1980. In a two-candidate contest, on the other hand, both coalitions could have legitimate expectations of getting about half of the delegates over the long run. These expectations have a better chance of being borne out, as they were with Ford and Reagan in 1976, in which case the structure of competition can remain stable from Early Days on through the Convention.

A third conclusion has to do with the impact of the temporal pattern on the structure of competition. *The four stages of nomination politics can be understood in terms of increasing information about the structure of competition.* During Early Days, we do not even know who all the competitors will be. Some plausible candidates may consider making the race, then decide not to do so. When Initial Contests begin, we know who the candidates are, and who is likely to be fighting for liberal, centrist, and conservative votes, but we do not yet know which of the candidates will be successful in attracting this support. By Mist

Clearing, information about the delegate strength of the surviving coalitions can be added to the left-right positioning of the candidates. This gives much more substantial information about the structure of competition than earlier guesses based on the momentum that a candidate is thought to have established. Finally, test votes at a Convention provide nearly complete information about relative coalition strength. Even the absence of a test vote may suggest that a winning coalition is in too strong a position to be challenged.

Knowing the structure of competition leads to a more important general point. Structure is important. What we have seen in these sketches of four nominations is the gradual organization of a winning coalition around the successful candidate. These coalitions have both *internal structure*, which depends on their composition, and *external structure,* which includes those activities the coalition must carry out to reach audiences whose support is necessary and those activities that are shaped by the context in which the coalition finds itself. Both internal structure and external structure change as the coalition moves through the four stages of nomination politics. The internal structure becomes more complex, and the external stucture varies as the context changes. To see this, we shall look at internal structure and external structure in a little more detail.

EXTERNAL STRUCTURE

We have already looked at one very important element of external structure—the structure of competition—in some detail. Clearly it makes a difference whether a candidate is the only one who is appealing to a segment of party support or if the candidate is one of four fighting for the same votes. Now what else is there? For a nomination coalition to succeed, it must be able to gain delegates. To do this the coalition must be able to reach *reporters, voters in the primary election states,* and the *delegates* themselves. Its chances of successfully doing so are affected by the *structure of competition,* the *legal requirements that set the dates and conditions of delegate selection,* and the *convention rules.* In nomination politics, external structure is focused on these elements.

From the time of the Early Days decision to enter until at least through the Initial Contests, perhaps the most important element of external structure is the media. There are two phrases used to refer to the traveling press corps: "surrogate audience" and "alternate audience." The former refers to the reporters' view of themselves; the latter to the politicians' view of the reporters (Arterton, 1984). The view of the reporters as surrogates implies that they are substitutes for citizens who are busy elsewhere, and that the reporters' task is to ask questions on behalf of the general public. The national political reporters who travel with the candidates during Early Days and prior to Initial Contests are quite conscious that they constitute a screening committee that plays an important part in the winnowing process (Broder, 1970, pp. 11–14). They carefully consider problems in reporting past campaigns—such as neglecting long-shot candidates who turn out to do quite well, putting too much attention on the "horse race" aspects of the campaign, not providing enough information about candidates so readers can make judgments about their character, not examining issues in enough detail—and they do their best to cope with these problems (Matthews, 1978). The reporters' goal is to bring the public solid information about the serious candidates.

The campaigners, however, treat the reporters as an alternate audience—that is, one to be treated differently from the voters to whom candidate images and issue positions are being projected. The coalition leaders observe that the media gives greater coverage to "serious" candidates; therefore they spend a great deal of time trying to convince the press that their candidate is "serious." Part of this is done by arranging the schedule of the candidate or campaign spokespersons, or both, so they can spend time with the press. Part of it is done by trying to manipulate press expectations so the candidate will meet them. For example, as part of his standard itinerary in any community, Jimmy Carter met with newspaper editorial boards. Also, in New Hampshire in 1976, the Carter entourage consistently talked of that state's Democratic primary as a race between Carter and Udall, thus drawing attention away from the structure-of-competition advantage Carter had as the only center-conservative candidate in New Hampshire. The most advantageous thing that can be done, of course, is for the candidates to be available at a time when there is hard evidence that they have met the media's expectations of a serious candidate. Thus, instead of leaving to campaign in Massachusetts and Florida, Jimmy Carter stayed in New Hampshire in 1976 to be available to the press when favorable returns came in. The result was that he was on all three television networks, and on the covers of *Time* and *Newsweek*.

When the Mist Clearing stage arrives, the surviving candidates have a changed relation with the press. First, they are now indisputable news sources, and they will receive coverage without having to make special arrangements to be available to reporters. For example, from the week of the Nebraska primary (just after the Texas, Indiana, Georgia, and Alabama primaries when he had done very well) until the end of the 1976 primaries, Ronald Reagan received more coverage in the *Washington Post* than Gerald Ford (Aldrich, Gant, & Simon, 1978). Second, the size of the traveling press corps increases, and there are more requests for information and interviews. This requires additional staff to handle the reporters. These two developments, the greater prominence of the candidate and the increasing number of reporters, give the campaign more control over what is written. At the same time, when an aspirant is viewed as a likely nominee, his or her statements may be scrutinized more closely. For example, Jimmy Carter was long troubled by a charge that he was fuzzy on the issues, and after his 1976 Pennsylvania victory, he began getting questions about where he stood on specific pieces of federal legislation (Matthews, 1978; Arterton, 1984; Witcover, 1977). Similarly, in the spring of 1980, newspaper articles began to appear with headlines such as "Reagan Economic Views Still Show Few Specifics," and containing sentences saying such things as economic "generalities persist, even when unresolved contradictions lurk beneath them." This closer scrutiny after Mist Clearing means that a candidate may have more difficulty with issue positions he or she takes than heretofore in the campaign.

Another change in external structure at the Mist Clearing stage is greater concern with the acquisition of delegates. Obviously, there has been some concern with this all along, but so few delegates are at stake in the early primaries that impressions of probable success are more important. Impressions, however, cannot move a candidate from the 200 or 300 delegate votes that establish him as a formidable contender to the 1,500 needed to nominate.[9] In the 1980 New York primary, for example, Senator Kennedy got 59 percent of the vote to President Carter's 41. The *New York Times* story began, "Senator Edward M. Kennedy decisively defeated President Carter in the New York and Connecticut primaries yesterday." But because of greater attention to the task of delegate acquisition, President Carter got 129 delegates, 46 percent of New York's total, and in defeat moved 8 percent closer to the number of delegates needed for renomination.

Delegate acquisition also means that the coalition must be able to work state (and district) conventions, and put on primary campaigns. In 1980, 13 states selected their delegates through some combination of conventions and caucuses, and another half dozen did so for the delegates for only one party. But three quarters of all 1980 delegates were selected or bound by primary elections, so that the ability to put on a primary campaign that impresses the voters in a state is now more important than the capacity to bargain with state political leaders who are presumably influential in conventions. This, in turn, calls attention to another feature of external structure in nomination politics: the rules that specify how votes are to be cast and how delegates are to be allocated to one candidate or another.

Votes are presently cast under a system in which each voter casts

---

[9] These numbers are simply illustrative. The actual numbers vary from convention to convention. The Democrats had 3,008 delegates in 1976 and 3,331 in 1980. There were 2,259 Republican delegates in 1976 and 1,994 in 1980.

a single ballot for the preferred candidate. This is an important reason
why the structure of competition is so important in multicandidate
contests. In 1976, a liberal Democrat in New Hampshire had to decide
whether to cast that single vote for Udall or Bayh or Shriver or Harris.
In 1980, a moderate Republican in New Hampshire had to decide
whether to cast a single vote for Bush or Baker or Anderson. Among
other things, this requires that voters decide which candidate they
prefer among several who are advocating very similar policies, and
(even more difficult) that they figure out which candidates have the
best chance of surviving so their votes aren't "wasted" on candidates
who are about to be winnowed out. Steven J. Brams has suggested
an alternative called *approval voting* in which the voters are allowed
to cast votes for as many candidates as they choose, but cannot cast
more than a single vote for each candidate.[10] Brams has shown that
approval voting has a number of desirable properties—for instance,
it eases the burden for the voter, and it favors the strongest candidate—
but the most important property for our present concern is that it is
insensitive to the number of candidates in multicandidate races. Voters
can cast ballots for the candidates they favor whether there are two
or seven or any other number running (Brams & Fishburn, 1978, 1983).
In an exit survey at the time of the 1980 New Hampshire primary,
ABC News asked voters whom they would have supported if they
had been able to vote for as many candidates as they chose. Recall
that the election results were Reagan, 50 percent; Bush, 23 percent;
Baker, 13 percent; and Anderson, 10 percent. The "approval voting"
results were Reagan, 58 percent; Bush, 39 percent; Baker, 41 percent;
and Anderson 26 percent. Reagan continued to be the most popular
candidate, but with support from moderate Republicans no longer split,
the votes for the moderate candidates increased dramatically. If
adopted, approval voting would tend to reduce the importance of the
structure of competition and slow down winnowing so that multicandidate races would be more stable.

There are three basic ways in which election results are used to
divide delegates among candidates: a winner-take-all system, in which
the candidate with the largest number of votes gets all of that state's
delegates; a proportional scheme, in which each candidate who gets
more than some threshold share of the vote receives a proportionate
share of the state's delegates; and a district plan, in which delegates
are divided among candidates depending on who gets how many votes
within congressional districts. The rules vary from state to state, but

---

[10] There are other voting schemes such as negative voting, in which one can cast
negative votes for candidates one dislikes, cumulative voting, where one can cast multiple
votes for candidates one particularly likes, and so forth.

each state has some variation of these basic forms. The effect of the actual rules, the melange used in a given year, has been studied by comparing the actual delegate count with what would have resulted if some alternate form had been used. Senator McGovern would have had the largest number of delegates using any of the three pure forms in 1972 (Pomper, 1979), but if winner-take-all rules had been in effect, Senator Hubert Humphrey would have gone into the California primary with substantially more delegates than McGovern (Lengle & Shafer, 1976). Similarly, Gerald Ford and Jimmy Carter would have had the largest number of delegates in their respective parties in 1976 under any of the three pure systems (Pomper, 1979; Gerston, Burstein, & Cohen, 1979). But if pure proportional representation had been in effect in 1976, Carter's rivals would have been in a stronger position; and if winner-take-all rules had been in effect, Carter would have obtained a decisive lead even more quickly. On the Republican side, if pure proportional representation had been in effect, Ford would have led Reagan after the Pennsylvania primary by a ratio of 1.3 to 1. If winner-take-all rules had been in effect, Ford would have led Reagan in delegates by a ratio of 5.4 to 1. Ford actually led at this point (ignoring the New York and Pennsylvania delegations as do the above figures) by a ratio of 3.2 to 1. In other words, the effect of a different set of delegate allocation rules would have been to change the strategic situation at important junctures during the nomination contest. Would Hubert Humphrey have won in California if he, and not George McGovern, had come in as the front-runner? Would Ronald Reagan have dropped out if Gerald Ford had had five times as many delegates as he did? Obviously, we don't know; but the rules on delegate allocation do affect the perceived strength of a candidate. The strength of a coalition, in turn, affects its ability to acquire resources, and this certainly *could* affect the outcome of subsequent primary elections.

The Convention stage has the most elaborate set of rules. A convention organizes itself by receiving a series of committee reports: credentials, permanent organization, rules, and platform. In recent decades, there have been battles waged over three of these: credentials, rules, and platform. The last big credentials fight came in 1972 when the Democrats voted to seat McGovern delegations rather than rival delegations from California and Illinois. Rule 16-C, which would have required prior announcement of the vice presidential nominee, was the major tactical battle at the 1976 Republican convention, and Rule F3(c), which would have released delegates from their obligations to support particular candidates, was contested at the 1980 Democratic convention. Platform fights were features of the 1976 Republican convention and the 1980 Democratic convention. Each of these contests was initiated because a coalition (usually a challenging coalition) thought they would get some tactical advantage if they were able to win. But the contests also say that coalition leaders think credentials, rules, and platform are important in shaping the outcome of the convention.

One group of delegates—members of Congress—is favored because the convention proceeds under the rules of the House of Representatives. The House rules are designed to allow business to be transacted in a large body, and this of course is what a national convention is; but the House rules are different than the more familiar *Robert's Rules of Order,* and representatives who know which motion is proper enjoy a real advantage in a hotly contested floor fight. The platform has less impact on the convention itself than the rules, but has been shown to have real consequences for the actions of the executive and legislative coalitions to come (Pomper & Lederman, 1980, chap. 8).

INTERNAL STRUCTURE

How does the internal structure of a coalition develop in the four stages of nomination politics? Until the candidate decides to seek the nomination during Early Days, there isn't any meaningful distinction between internal and external structure. At most, there are groups of potential supporters. There is likely to be a tiny group of close advisors with whom the candidate takes counsel, and who may perceive a possible candidacy when it is invisible to everyone else. The group of Georgians who began thinking about the possibility of a Carter candidacy is an example of this. There may also be enthusiasts without any close ties, such as liberal Democrats who were anxious for Edward Kennedy to run when Jimmy Carter seemed so weak in mid-1979.

Depending on the skills contained within the candidate's core group, they may constitute all the structure there is for a while, or they may recruit a few key persons, such as a press aide, fund raiser, and so on. The next groups likely to be created are those who will run the campaign in those states where the Initial Contests will take place. If the campaign does not meet expectations, the structure—as the candidacy itself—may collapse at this point. Otherwise, an initial group of delegates is acquired and coalition building begins.

The first groups of delegates are likely to admire the candidate and to be in close agreement with the candidate on policy questions. By the Mist Clearing stage this may not be so. Assuming the candidacy is still viable, two closely related things are likely to have happened. The appeal of the candidate is likely to have changed from "Our governor is the perfect candidate for you" to "Our governor may not be the *perfect* candidate for you, but he's certainly better than any of the other candidates, and he stands a real chance to win." Morris Udall used a version of this argument in the spring of 1976 when he said he was the only horse the liberal Democrats had to ride. The related change in Mist Clearing is that different groups of delegates are going to be attracted—groups whose first choice was some other contender and who are in less than full agreement with the candidate on policy questions. Therefore coalition management becomes more of a priority, because of the greater number of groups in the coalition and the increasing diversity of the groups.

By the time of every recent convention, there has been a winning coalition in being. This means, of course, that the leaders of the winning coalition need to stay in touch with all of their member groups, and keep them on board. Leaders of challenging coalitions want just the opposite. That means that appeals will be focused on those groups thought to be unhappy for one reason or another, and on those issues to which these groups might be responsive. Thus the Ford coalition began to woo Mississippi delegates just as soon as Ronald Reagan announced that he was going to tap Richard Schweiker as his vice presidential nominee. And on the night of the crucial 16-C vote, when a story appeared in the *Birmingham News* headlined "Ford Would Write Off Cotton South?" President Ford himself called Mississippi Chairman Clarke Reed to deny that such a strategy was being considered. Similarly, when the Kennedy coalition wanted to challenge the Carter coalition at the 1980 Democratic convention, they offered platform amendments dealing with potential unemployment and picked up votes from groups of Carter delegates who were also labor union members.

The composition of the coalitions has a great deal to do with the policies endorsed by the convention when the platform is adopted or a candidate is nominated. In 1968, for example, James Clarke and John Soule found that 85 percent of the Democratic delegates and 90 percent of the Republican delegates said that the most important attribute for a presidential candidate was agreement in principle between the candidate and the delegate (Clarke, 1970). In 1972, Jeane Kirkpatrick reported that 90 percent of the Democratic delegates and 81 percent of the Republican delegates said that a chance to influence the party on policy was either an extremely important or a very important reason for their participation in politics (1976, p. 101). The extremely conservative 1980 Republican platform and the liberal 1980 Democratic platform certainly reflected the views of the coalitions at those conventions.

Not only are policies important, but there is some consistency over time in the states that join liberal and conservative coalitions. A study of five contested Democratic conventions between 1952 and 1976 found that the states with the most liberal voting records were Wisconsin, Oregon, Arizona, New Hampshire, Michigan, Massachusetts, Iowa, South Dakota, Vermont, and New York; those with the most conservative voting records were South Carolina, Louisiana, North Carolina,

Texas, Delaware, Arkansas, Florida, Kentucky, Missouri, and Georgia. A parallel study of six Republican conventions between 1940 and 1976 shows that the states with the most moderate voting records were Connecticut, New York, New Hampshire, Oregon, Vermont, Maine, New Jersey, Michigan, Massachusetts, and Maryland. The state delegations with the most conservative voting records were Texas, Mississippi, California, Alabama, North Carolina, Idaho, Louisiana, Ohio, New Mexico, and Oklahoma (Costain, 1978, appendix 2).[11]

The Republican coalitions have been a little more stable over time than the Democratic. There has been a strong tendency for southern Republicans to be conservative, and for the East plus Michigan, Minnesota, and Oregon to end up in moderate coalitions. Still, comparison of these findings with an earlier study (Munger & Blackhurst, 1965) indicates that recent coalitions are less regional in character. The left coalition in the Democratic party includes groups from all regions except the South. The right coalition in the Republican party has included groups from all regions of the country except the East, and in 1980 the Reagan coalition reached into Pennsylvania, New York, and New England for support. Increasingly, Democratic conventions are ending up as contests between left and nonleft coalitions, and Republican conventions as struggles between right and nonright coalitions (Costain, 1978). Hence, the change in internal structure from Early Days to the Convention is apt to be a growth from a single group composed of the candidate and his closest advisors to a coalition whose groups have been drawn from all parts of the country.

Summary

Substantively, this part of the book has covered the two principal patterns of contested presidential nominations: the unstable multicandidate contest, in which one candidate tends to pull away from the field, and the relatively stable two-candidate race, in which two strong contenders struggle from Early Days on through the Convention itself. We have seen two examples of both of these. Carter in 1976 and Reagan in 1980 are examples of races in which one candidate was able to do so well that he was established as the probable nominee by the Mist Clearing stage. Ford versus Reagan in 1976 followed the classic two-candidate pattern, and Carter versus Kennedy in 1980 approxi-

---

[11] It should also be remembered that there is considerable turnover in delegates from convention to convention. From 1944 through 1968, 65 percent of Republican delegates and 64 percent of Democratic delegates were attending their first conventions (Johnson & Hahn, 1973, p. 148). Therefore the same state may have quite different groups of delegates attending conventions at different points in time. For example, the California Republican Assembly whose hero was Governor Earl Warren in 1952 was very different from the California Republican Assembly of 1976 and 1980 whose hero was Governor Ronald Reagan.

mated this. There are, of course, variations from one nomination to another; but if you understand these two basic patterns, you ought to be able to explain future nominations.

Conceptually, this chapter has explicated the ideas of internal structure, external structure, and time in nomination politics. The internal structure of a nomination coalition is the same as that of other coalitions. It is made up of activists who are aggregated into the groups that constitute the coalition. The external structure of a nomination coalition consists of the activities necessary to reach voters, reporters, and delegates; the structure of competition; the rules that state how and when votes will be cast and delegates allocated between candidates; and the rules and procedures of the convention. The four stages of the temporal pattern are Early Days, Initial Contests, Mist Clearing, and the Convention. By using these concepts you ought to be able to understand the strategies employed by those seeking presidential nominations.

PART FIVE

ELECTORAL POLITICS

CHAPTER 10

ELECTORAL POLITICS: TIME AND INTERNAL STRUCTURE

Introduction

There are substantial differences between nomination politics and electoral politics. Nomination coalitions are made up of those groups willing to give their all for a particular candidate, whereas electoral coalitions are usually made up of all groups in the party. Nomination campaigns are aimed at getting delegates; electoral campaigns are aimed at winning votes.

Primary elections begin in late February and last until early June. The general election takes place in every single state on the same day in November. The planning and organization for nomination politics begin at least a couple of years before the convention. All of electoral politics is compressed into the few months between the convention and the general election. In brief, electoral politics is partywide, nationwide, and short.

There are some hints of the nature of electoral politics in the closing hours of the national convention, when the nomination has been captured and electoral politics has begun. After the acceptance speeches, division is put aside, and the assembly is transformed into a victory rally. The presidential candidate is joined by the vice presidential candidate, and both are joined by their families. The cheers continue, and the traditional pictures are taken. Then other party leaders come forward—those who played key roles and others who have sought the nomination themselves. At the 1980 Democratic convention, the demonstration was prolonged by inviting numerous Democratic leaders—National Chairman John White, Health and Human Services Secretary Patricia Roberts Harris, Mayor Thomas Bradley of Los Angeles, Mayor Dianne Feinstein of San Francisco, and so on—until Senator Edward Kennedy finally appeared on the platform. At the Republican National Convention in Detroit a few weeks earlier, Ronald Reagan was flanked by vice presidential nominee George Bush and former President Gerald Ford. The presence of Kennedy before the Democratic convention, and of Bush and Ford at the Republican rostrum, symbolized the partywide backing to be given to the presidential nominees in the fall campaign.

In part, this demonstration of unity is aimed at the millions of voters watching on television across the nation. While coalitions are struggling for the nomination, citizens are making tentative voting decisions. From 1948 through 1980, an average of 38 percent reported they had made their presidential choices before the conventions. Another 25 percent said they had made up their minds during the conventions. The remaining three eighths of the electorate includes many who have only a minimal interest in politics. The faces on the convention stage constitute the image the party will present as they strive to gain the attention and win the support of these voters by November.

It would be a mistake, though, to think of this victory rally as *only* a public show. There is an affective unity—an emotional sense of belonging akin to that felt by a team of athletes—within a political party during an election campaign. The cheers of the delegates help to cement this feeling. Those who have supported the successful candidate get the thrill of seeing him as the party nominee. Those who worked just as hard for an unsuccessful aspirant get the chance for a few personal cheers when he comes to the stage. This common experience helps unify the party and set the stage for the campaign to come. After all, there is a great deal of work to be done by the party activists, and the time is very short.

THE TEMPORAL PATTERN OF
ELECTORAL POLITICS

THE STERN LIMITS OF TIME

The first thing mentioned by McGovern campaign director Gary Hart in his discussion of the differences between nomination politics and a general election campaign is that the latter "is a much briefer, more compact experience" (1973, p. 249). Of the various forms of politics, electoral politics has the most truncated time frame. Depending on when the national convention is scheduled, there may be as much as 3½ months or as little as 2 months between the convention and the general election. There is some plasticity in the limits within which one must work, but even if the party opts for an early July convention, more must be accomplished in less time than in any other political setting.

It might seem that the campaign strategists would look ahead to this situation, and try to prepare for it by making plans for the election campaign. But this overlooks what the candidate and his closest advisors are doing prior to the convention. Winning the nomination itself is the goal to which their actions are directed for a good many months. It may be that there are real questions about winning the nomination. How would the credentials fight turn out in the 1972 Democratic convention? Would McGovern get the disputed California delegates, or would he have to split them with Humphrey, making things much closer? Would Ford be able to withstand the 1976 Reagan challenges on convention rules, and would his very narrow margin in delegate support hold up? And even if the candidate appears to have a large enough nomination coalition to win, obtaining these delegates is the focus of attention of the coalition strategists for a long enough time that they are likely to continue to organize their thinking around the imperatives of nomination politics. Questions about how the nomination is going to be ensured—for example, do you have good communications to the delegates on the floor?—occur to them a good deal more quickly than questions about what is going to be done in an ensuing fall campaign.

There are, of course, some presidents who can look forward to their own renomination. (This is a smaller number than all incumbents. Some cannot seek another nomination because of the 22nd Amendment; others are subject to a serious challenge from within their own party.) In this case, their attention may well be focused on the imperatives of executive politics. If they have a foreign policy crisis on their hands, or if the economy is shaky, they are going to give more attention to the troublesome policy area than to the relatively distant fall campaign.

The implication is that the only candidates who can "expand" the time available for electoral politics are those who can manage to assemble a winning nomination coalition early on, and who are themselves free from the responsibilities of office. In recent years, this would be only Nixon in 1968, Carter in 1976, and Reagan in 1980. The work done in advance of the conventions in the last two cases—the careful selection of Walter Mondale as Jimmy Carter's running mate in 1976, and especially the selection of George Bush and the extensive strategic planning done for Ronald Reagan in 1980—was important to the success of the general election campaigns. Still, such advance planning requires special circumstances. Most modern electoral coalitions are not able to focus on the fall campaigns until after the convention. The normal pattern forces them to work within tight, fixed time limits.

The sense of working within a very short time period is reinforced by polls that repeatedly announce the candidates' standings. These

serve as reminders that only so many weeks remain until the election—
and in the elections from 1964 through 1976, these tidings were particularly ominous for one candidate or the other. In 1964 and 1972, the
challengers began their campaigns far behind incumbent presidents;
and while their campaigns made progress, they could not close gaps
of such magnitude. The first postconvention poll in 1964 gave Goldwater
all of 31 percent. This rose only to 39 percent by election day. In late
August 1972, the Gallup Poll gave McGovern only 30 percent, and he
too ended up with 39 percent in the election. In 1968 and 1976, candidates of the out party had commanding leads at the beginning, but
then watched them dissolve as the campaigns progressed. On Labor
Day weekend in 1968, Richard Nixon had 43 percent of the vote to
31 percent for Hubert Humphrey and 19 percent for George Wallace.
Come election day, Nixon received 43.4 percent of the vote while Humphrey got 42.7 percent. After the 1976 Democratic convention, the Gallup
Poll gave Jimmy Carter a 62 to 29 percent lead over Gerald Ford; but
in the election, Carter received just a shade over 50 percent while
Ford got 48 percent. The 1964 and 1972 challengers, Goldwater and
McGovern, were trapped by time. The election was only a short way
off, and in spite of their best efforts, there seemed to be little they
could do to convince the voters to move in their direction. In the 1968
and 1976 campaigns, supporters of the candidate whose lead was evap-
orating felt that the election was too far away. Still, all they could
do was hope that the front-runner's lead would hold up until election
day. From the Humphrey and Ford viewpoints, of course, the hope
was that they would be able to gain fast enough to pass their rivals.
But regardless of their position, all had their eyes on the calendar,
and all knew that the season of passionate appeal to the electorate
would be short.

One often hears pleas that American election campaigns be further
shortened. The basis of this argument is that, especially after protracted
nomination contests, the candidates are exhausted, campaign debts
have been run up, and the voters are bored. There is something to
this, and such an argument often is made by a weary campaign manager
or a journalist who has gotten up at 6:00 A.M. time and again to cover
another full day of campaigning. What the argument for a shorter electoral period overlooks, I think, is the number of things that must be
done to conduct a presidential campaign on a subcontinental scale.
Just as is true of nomination politics, there are a number of stages to
a typical campaign, and it is hard to see how any of them could be
omitted.

ORGANIZATION AND PLANNING

Organization and planning go on more or less simultaneously in
the weeks following the national convention. The first question is who

is going to fill the top jobs in the campaign organization. Not infrequently, more people feel they ought to be given top jobs than there are top jobs to fill. In 1964, for instance, Barry Goldwater decided that his longtime friend Denison Kitchell would be "head honcho," and that Dean Burch would be chairperson of the Republican National Committee. But F. Clifton White, who played an important part in rounding up delegates, very much wanted to be national chairperson, and something had to be done about him. He was persuaded to accept the chair of Citizens for Goldwater-Miller. In 1972, George McGovern promised three people—Jean Westwood, Lawrence O'Brien, and Pierre Salinger—that each would be chairperson of the Democratic National Committee. It took some time to find assignments that O'Brien and Salinger were willing to accept after Westwood got the job.[1]

Selection of a national chairperson is only the beginning. As we will see in Chapter 11, there are four principal activities that must be carried on by a campaign staff: campaign operations, public relations, research, and finance. Individuals must be recruited who have the skills and contacts to handle each of these responsibilities. And once the national appointments are made, the head of the campaign division must locate regional coordinators, each of whom will handle the campaign in several contiguous states. The regional coordinators, in turn, must tap state coordinators.

The staff needed to run in successive primary campaigns is much smaller than the nationwide organization required for the general election campaign. As Hamilton Jordan recalled the 1976 Carter campaign: "Early on, we had three very talented people that we just rotated in the primary period from Iowa to Massachusetts to Ohio to Florida to Wisconsin to Maryland and then to New Jersey. Of the 45 to 50 state coordinators, only 5 or 6 had been involved in our campaign previously" (Moore & Fraser, 1977, p. 132). Where do the other 40-odd state coordinators come from? Some have been involved in the nomination campaigns of losing aspirants. Some have been identified in the course of spring contests, especially if the nominee entered the primary in that state. Some come from other states. (The Kennedy organization in 1960 and the Carter organization in 1976 picked their state chairpersons from states other than those for which they had responsibility.) Perhaps the most fertile sources of leaders for the state campaigns are the regular party organizations in the state. Wherever the state chairpersons come from, the appointment is cleared with the state party organization unless the circumstances are very unusual.

---

[1] A related problem is that organizations sometimes want to use the talent of a person, and an appropriate position must be found for that purpose. In 1980, for instance, the Reagan coalition wanted to use the very real skills of James Baker, who had been in charge of the 1976 Ford campaign and the 1980 Bush nomination campaign. Baker wanted something that he would be in charge of himself, and was given the task of preparing for the debates with Anderson and Carter.

Finally, the state leaders have to recruit county leaders (or town leaders in New England). As we will see later in this chapter, the heads of the presidential campaigns at the county level are largely Republican or Democratic activists who were involved in previous presidential campaigns.

The organization of the campaign committees from nation to region to state to county has two consequences. The first is that there is a progressively greater overlap between the presidential campaign committees and the regular party organizations as one moves from the national to the county levels. While the staff of the Republican National Committee was located in Washington, D.C., and the national staff of the Reagan Bush Committee had their offices across the Potomac River in Arlington, Virginia, the chairpersons of the Republican party and the Reagan Bush Committee in Franklin County, Ohio, were well known to each other. Second, and more germane to our concern with the temporal pattern of electoral politics, all this organization takes time. The national chairperson has to pick a campaign director; the campaign director has to pick regional coordinators; the regional coordinators have to pick state directors; state directors have to tap county leaders. Assignments have to be made in research, public relations, and finance as well. Since each person selects his or her subordinates in consultation with other party leaders, this process goes on sequentially. Finally, all those who are selected have to get to know one another and establish working relationships. It takes just as much time for a collection of individuals to become a functioning organization in electoral politics as in any other sphere of life. There is no way of rushing the creation of a nationwide campaign organization.

Planning begins as soon as individuals know what responsibilities they are going to have in the campaign. This involves decisions about geographic concentration, positions to be taken on issues, media use, how the candidate is going to be portrayed, how the opposition candidate is to be attacked and by whom, what themes will tie all this together, and so on. Some of these things may not be worked out in detail in advance, but they are going to be decided *somehow*. It may be that a key decision will be made when a reporter asks a question: The candidate answers off the top of his head because he thinks an answer is required, and thus goes on the record with an issue statement or a characterization of his opponent. It may be that a partial plan will be thrown together hurriedly, as Joseph Napolitan did once Hubert Humphrey won the Democratic nomination in 1968. "I'm writing the campaign plan," he told Theodore White. "Do you know there isn't *any* campaign plan? I have to get this ready tomorrow!" (White, 1969, p. 338) Or the plan may be quite comprehensive. The basic Reagan campaign plan in 1980 filled two bulky notebooks, and there were in fact more than 20 plans that were written for specific circumstances as they arose in the course of the campaign. There is considerable variation here. What is improvised in one campaign is systematically planned in another. Over time, systematic planning is becoming more frequent, but in one way or another, decisions will be made.

The Organization and Planning stage is not very visible to the general public. After the 1976 campaign, Hamilton Jordan was asked why the Carter people let so much time go by after the Democratic convention without active campaigning. He replied: "Carter was in Plains most of the time with an occasional trip out, but we were busting our ass to put the fall campaign together. Tim Kraft and Phil Wise assembled a first-rate field organization, and we got control of our budget. Rafshoon was working on the media, and Pat Caddell started doing surveys in critical states. The time was well spent" (Moore & Fraser, 1977, p. 130). He might have added that the Carter coalition had time to do this because the 1976 Democratic convention was held in the first half of July. When a convention is held in late August, the Organization and Planning stage is forced into the early weeks of the campaign proper. Whenever it comes, though, and however thoroughly or hastily it is handled, Organization and Planning is a necessary prelude to the rest of the campaign.

GRAND OPENING

The Grand Opening is the stage of the campaign when the efforts that follow from the plans made during the preceding stage first become visible to the public. This stage includes all those activities that have been designed with an eye to sustaining and increasing the candidate's standing with the voters. Just as the grand opening of a commercial venture is intended to bring customers to the establishment, and just as the opening night of a play is intended to spur lines at the box office, so the Grand Opening of a campaign should maintain a front runner's lead in the polls, or allow an underdog to catch up.

Grand Opening certainly includes the initial major speeches and the first campaign swings. For instance, Democratic candidates have often given their first speeches in Cadillac Square in Detroit on Labor Day, and then have gone on about the country. Jimmy Carter chose to open his 1976 campaign on Labor Day with a speech at Franklin Roosevelt's "Little White House" at Warm Springs, Georgia, and then began a 10-state swing that took him to the Deep South, New York, Connecticut, the Midwest, and Florida. Ronald Reagan made a number of appearances before Labor Day 1980, employing "focused impact" to draw public attention to selected issues such as foreign policy. Incumbent presidents often stay close to the White House during the Grand Opening. Gerald Ford followed this pattern during September 1976, when he made any number of Rose Garden appearances. These were designed to keep the media spotlight on challenger Jimmy Carter and to permit Ford to appear presidential. The Grand Opening also includes any initial advertising. Carter media advisor Gerald Rafshoon found during the primaries that when Carter advertising started before the opposition's, the campaigns could survive later anti-Carter advertising. Hence they began the Carter media campaign during Grand Opening (Moore & Fraser, 1977, p. 128). Reagan strategists wanted to remind voters of his executive experience in order to lay a foundation for later themes. Therefore their Grand Opening included television spots showing Reagan being sworn in as governor of California.

How long the Grand Opening lasts depends on whether the campaign strategy appears to be leading toward the hoped for results. Essentially, this stage of the campaign lasts as long as it is successful. Occasionally, a Grand Opening goes so well that it lasts for most of the campaign. Such was the case with the 1972 Nixon campaign. Even if the hopes of the campaign strategies are not being met, Grand Opening usually lasts for much of September. It takes at least that long to discover that things are not going well, and to devise an acceptable substitute course of action.

CAMPAIGN ADJUSTMENTS

The next stage of a campaign does not occur at a specific point in time, but when the need for an Adjustment becomes obvious. There are two general types of alteration: Tactical Adjustment and Strategic Adjustment. Tactical Adjustment is much the simpler of the two. It is a response to some development. This may be a news bulletin that calls attention to a policy area and therefore suggests the desirability of the candidate's competence to deal with the question. It may be some troubling development within the campaign organization, or an awkward statement by the candidate himself, such as Gerald Ford's reference to no Soviet domination in Eastern Europe in the second debate in 1976. The Tactical Adjustment in this case included a public statement by the President that he knew there were divisions of Russian troops in Poland, a telephone call to Aloysius Mazewski, the president of the Polish-American Congress, and some meetings with ethnic group leaders. A Tactical Adjustment is focused on the original development, contained in time, and does not involve any general changes in campaign strategy.

An *attempted* tactical adjustment involved the "meanness" issue that developed in the 1980 campaign when President Carter was viewed as making unnecessarily vindictive statements about Governor Reagan. Carter made an appearance on a Barbara Walters television interview where he promised to "do the best I can to refrain from any sort of personal relationship with Mr. Reagan so far as criticisms are concerned." The attempt was unsuccessful because two days later President Carter said, "Reagan is not a good man to trust with the affairs of this nation." The suggestion that Governor Reagan was untrustworthy was enough to revive the meanness issue in the press.

A Strategic Adjustment is a somewhat more serious matter. It suggests that the campaign may be in real difficulty. If a projection of poll results shows a probable election loss, then groups in the electoral coalition are going to make their unhappiness known. If there is enough expression of discontent, then the campaign strategists are likely to try some new approach. In part, this is because they can see the same difficulties as the members of the supporting coalition, and in part because they need to do something to convince workers that an effort is being made to extricate the campaign from its difficulties. A 1972 shift on the part of George McGovern from positive presentations of his own ideas to negative attacks on Richard Nixon is an example of a Strategic Adjustment intended to bolster the sagging fortunes of that campaign.

A Strategic Adjustment cannot be devised very quickly. It takes some time for complaints to work their way up through the campaign structure, and it takes more time for the strategy group to realize that the Grand Opening (in which they have some psychological investment since they approved it) is not bringing about the desired results. It requires still more time for the strategy group to agree on the nature of the adjustment. The Grand Opening probably represented the satisficing agreement (that is, one acceptable to all group members) that they could reach most easily, and some time is required to discover an alternative approach that is acceptable to coalition members and has some promise of persuading voters. In fact, enough time is needed to realize that a Strategic Adjustment is called for, and then to figure out what to do, that not more than one or two real Strategic Adjustments can occur in a campaign.

TIME'S UP

The last stage of a campaign is usually referred to by the media as the final drive or the climax of the campaign. It would be more accurate to call it the Time's Up stage. It is one of the ironies of electoral politics that the period just before the election is the time when the candidates have a chance to reach the largest possible audience because of the intense preelection coverage, and it is also the time when the strategists have the least control over what is happening. The meaning of Time's Up is that it is too late to make any more television commercials, too late to buy any more television time, too late to implement any new campaign emphases, too late to do the necessary advance work to prepare for more campaign appearances—too late, in sum, to do much more than carry out the plans that have already been made, and hope that these efforts will be rewarded when the voters reach the polls.

The manifest tone of the campaign in the Time's Up phase depends on the probable outcome of the election. If the candidate is far in front, then his public appearances will have the aura of triumph. Other candidates will jostle for the honor of appearing at his elbow. The candidate may be weary, but the adrenalin stimulated by being at the top of a career in politics is enough to keep him going through the final days. If the candidate is far behind, we are likely to hear some bitter comments about the voters' failure to understand or his coalition's inability to work hard enough. He is tired, knows that he has done what he can, and needs to steel his ego against the bruises of defeat. If the race is close, then extra physical effort is put forth. It is hard to say where the reserves of energy that allow this come from. The extra bit of energy expended on the campaign means that the candidate's voice sometimes fails, and he is bone weary. But in the Time's Up stage, it is too late to make any further plans or implement any new strategies. And since the extra bit of effort may make the difference, he gives it willingly.

Summary

Of all the major forms of politics, electoral politics has the shortest time span. The limits vary from 3½ months to a little more than 2. Organization and Planning, Grand Opening, Adjustments, and Time's Up stages follow one another in rapid succession. The hope that the nominees bring from their convention triumphs leads to electoral glory for one and weary defeat for the other.

INTERNAL STRUCTURE OF

ELECTORAL COALITIONS

Introduction

Who are the activists involved in electoral politics? To which groups do their common attitudes lead them? How do these groups coalesce? Asking these questions calls our attention to a series of important political questions. How long have the activists been involved in politics? Are they more interested in patronage or the direction of public policy? Are their issue preferences representative of the communities where they live, or are they closer to the preferences of fellow party members? Do the activists' shared attitudes make it more appropriate to think of parties being made up of issue groups or of demographic groups? Do the coalitions that are formed by the issue groups tend toward the center or toward the ends of the political spectrum? The answers to these questions lead to very different kinds of political parties. If, for example, the activists are more interested in their own jobs, are simply spokespersons for their own communities, share attitudes with others in the same demographic categories (union members, farmers, and so on), and form coalitions that tend toward the center of the political spectrum, then we have sluggish political parties that offer few choices to citizens. If, on the other hand, we have activists who are interested in issues, combine with others taking similar positions, and tend to form liberal or conservative coalitions (depending on the party), then the citizens are being presented with choices between quite diverse policies.

CORE GROUPS AND STRATEGY GROUPS

The most important strategists are those who belong to the *core group* and the *strategy group*. The core group consists of the candidate's own confidants, persons he has known well or worked closely with for some years. In Jimmy Carter's case, this certainly included Atlanta attorney Charles Kirbo, and both Hamilton Jordan and Jody Powell, who were with Carter since his days as governor of Georgia. In Ronald Reagan's case, some members of the California "Kitchen Cabinet" were core group members, as were longtime associates Edwin Meese, Michael Deaver, and William Clark. If the candidate's wife is interested in politics, she would obviously be a member of this core group. Rosalynn Carter and Nancy Reagan were among the most important of their husbands' political confidants, but Pat Nixon apparently was somewhat less involved.

The strategy group is made up of those persons who are making the basic decisions about the campaign. Its membership is quite restricted, and it should not be confused with a publicly announced "strategy committee," some of whose members are likely to be key decision makers while others are included because their status calls for some kind of recognition. There is likely to be at least a partial overlap between the core group of confidants and the strategy group of decision makers. If the candidate himself is not present when the key decisions are being made (and he may be off campaigning somewhere), there must be persons present who know the candidate well enough to speak for him.

There are also likely to be members who have important operating responsibilities, but who *may* not be as well acquainted with the candidate. These opposite tendencies were nicely illustrated by the two 1976 strategy groups. The Carter strategy was virtually an extension

of the core group. Kirbo, Jordan, and Powell were members, as were
media consultant Gerald Rafshoon, pollster Pat Caddell, attorney Robert Lipshutz, and issues specialist Stuart Eizenstat. This strategy group
was almost completely Georgian and, with the exceptions of Caddell
and Eizenstat, completely lacking in national campaign experience.
The principal members of the Ford strategy group, on the other hand,
consisted of White House Chief of Staff Richard Cheney, President
Ford Committee chairperson James Baker, Ford Committee organization
director Stuart Spencer, media consultant John Deardourff, and pollster
Robert Teeter.[2] Cheney, who as a graduate student had coauthored
an elegant analysis of congressional policy dimensions (Clausen & Cheney, 1970) and who was later elected to Congress himself, and Baker,
a Houston attorney who was in charge of the Ford delegate hunt during
the primaries, had not been through a national campaign before. But
Robert Teeter had considerable experience in political polling with
the Detroit firm of Market Opinion Research, and Stuart Spencer and
John Deardourff were two of the best professional campaign managers
in the country. Between them, they could put together about 50 years
of campaign experience. Where the Carter strategy group was unusual
in being composed almost entirely of persons who knew Carter for
some time, the Ford strategy group was unusual in its professional
orientation.

In 1980, the two major strategy groups were more typical in representing both tendencies. The senior Carter strategists—Jordan, Powell,
Rafshoon, and Caddell—had all been through the 1976 campaign, and
Caddell had 1972 experience as well. On the Republican side, the most
important strategists were Edwin Meese, Richard Wirthlin, William
Timmons, and William Casey. Meese was a veteran of Reagan's governorship; Wirthlin had been doing Reagan's polling for some years; Timmons' first presidential campaign experience was in 1968; Casey played
minor roles in Republican campaigns as far back as 1948.

While core groups and strategy groups are fundamental, they are
no more than the essential beginning of a campaign organization. The

---

[2] Robert Teeter provided a very nice description of the Ford strategy group. "The
week spent at Vail (Ford's vacation home in Colorado) right after the convention was
the key to the development of the fall campaign. . . . We came out of the Vail meeting
a small group of men who got along, who knew and understood each other, who had
a strategy in mind for the campaign. . . . Jim Baker, Dick Cheney, Stu Spencer, John
Deardourff, and I were five people who got along as one unit and had a strategy in
mind for what we were going to try to accomplish in the campaign" (Moore & Fraser,
1977, p. 123). Teeter did not use the formal language of group theory, such as David
Truman's ("These interactions . . . because they have a certain character and frequency,
give the group its moulding and guiding powers. . . . [From] interactions in groups arise
certain common habits of response, which may be called norms, or shared attitudes.
These afford the participants frames of reference for interpreting and evaluating events
and behaviors." [1971, pp. 24, 33]), but his reference to five individuals "who got along
as one unit" is precisely why group theory is a useful way to analyze politics.

strategy groups make decisions about campaign emphases, but they cannot carry them out themselves. And they certainly are not a party-wide coalition capable of reaching a national constituency.

ACTIVISTS

The 1972 Hofstetter Study

The *only* nationwide study we have of campaign activists was conducted by Richard Hofstetter in 1972 as part of a broader investigation of television coverage on the Nixon-McGovern campaign (Hofstetter, 1976). The persons to be interviewed were selected the same way the leaders themselves were chosen: by nomination downward. The names of state campaign directors were obtained from the national offices of the Committee to Re-Elect the President and the McGovern-Shriver Committee. The state leaders were then asked to supply names of the persons in charge in counties that were part of a national sampling frame. One hundred and ninety-seven Democrats and 204 Republican county leaders were contacted and interviewed. One series of questions dealt with the activists' backgrounds, motivations, and activities. Another dealt with their issue positions, their perceptions of the candidates, and their perceptions of the preferences of voters in their counties. (This latter series of questions was identical to questions being put to citizens who lived in the same counties.) The first set provided information about the county leaders' attitudes and activities; the second set told us how representative these leaders were.

Since many of the findings to be discussed in this chapter rely on the Hofstetter study, the reader ought to be warned about the limits of this data set. We have a limited number of interviews, they come from a single election year, they are now a dozen years old.[3] This does not mean that we cannot draw inferences about the electoral parties. As we shall see, there is reason to believe that the 1972 activists were not atypical. But with only a single study, we don't know how representative the 1972 sample was of the Republican and Democratic parties over time.[4] There has undoubtedly been some change between 1972 and 1984. The problem is that we don't know *how much,* and therefore we have to be careful in drawing inferences.

---

[3] That the study has not been replicated is itself a discouraging comment about political scientists' lack of attention to political parties. Apparently some scholars would rather write tracts about how parties are "disappearing" than go to the hard work of gathering data and sifting through the evidence to find out what the parties *are* doing.

[4] My *guess* is that the sample is least representative of the Democratic party in the South.

WHO ARE THE ELECTORAL ACTIVISTS?

Since delegates to national conventions have been extensively studied (McClosky, Hoffman, & O'Hara, 1960; Niemi & Jennings, 1968; Soule & Clarke, 1970; Soule & McGrath, 1975; Johnson & Hahn, 1973; Sullivan, Pressman, Page, & Lyons, 1974; Kirkpatrick, 1976; Farah, 1982; and many others), it is useful to compare the county campaign leaders with convention delegates from the same year. The background characteristics of activists in the two institutional domains are shown in Table 10-1. There were a few differences. Among convention delegates, Democrats were more likely to be young and nonwhite than Republicans. Democratic campaign leaders were more likely to be young and to have lower incomes than any other category. (The largest proportion of Republican campaign activists, 45 percent, fell into the 30–45 age bracket.) Campaign leaders are more likely to have professional or managerial occupations than convention delegates (although this difference is slightly exaggerated in Table 10-1 due to coding variations). But what is most striking about these data is that regardless of the background characteristics and regardless of the category of activist, almost all come from the upper socioeconomic strata.

What one makes of these characteristics is a matter of perspective. On the one hand, politics is a complicated business. If one is to keep track of the various motions being voted on at a national convention, or if one is to run a county campaign, stay in touch with workers, coordinate activities with state and national organizations, and so on,

TABLE 10-1
Comparison of Selected Background Characteristics: 1972 Convention Delegates and Electoral Activists

Background Characteristic*	Convention Delegates		Electoral Activists	
	Republicans	Democrats	Republicans	Democrats
Under 30	8%	22%	8%	48%
Professional or manager	71	73	90	91
Income over $10,000	94	87		
Income over $12,000			86	66
Attended college	87	87	84	91
Caucasian	94	80	97	93
Political generation				
Pre-1945	14	7	10	5
1946–1959	41	32	35	18
1960–1967	36	31	33	28
1968–1972	9	30	22	49

* Cell entries are percentages of persons having characteristic.

Data sources: Convention Delegates, adapted from Tables 3.1, 3.2, 7.7, and 7.8 in *The New Presidential Elite,* by Jeane Kirkpatrick, © 1976 by the Russell Sage Foundation, New York. Electoral Activists, 1972 Hofstetter study.

organizational and communication skills are necessary. These are most often associated with higher education and white-collar jobs. Moreover, college educations and professional status are increasingly common in modern American society. On the other hand, persons who have these advantages are less likely to have been unemployed, or to have faced the problems of feeding one's family on food stamps. Since they lack the personal experience of making ends meet on a very limited income, they *may* be less sensitive to issues affecting poor people.

When we turn to the question of experience, there are pronounced differences between the convention delegates and the electoral activists. To begin with, the data on political generation in Table 10-1 show that much larger proportions of county campaign leaders in both parties had their political initiations in the 1968–72 period. But it is the convention delegates, not the campaign activists, who are less experienced at what they are doing. A high rate of delegate turnover has long been one of the most important facts about national conventions. An examination of delegate rosters showed that from 1944 through 1968, 64 percent of the Democratic delegates and 65 percent of the Republican delegates were attending their first conventions. Another 22 percent of the Democrats and 21 percent of the Republicans had only attended one prior convention (Johnson & Hahn, 1973). The convention delegates tend to be experienced politicians, and are often fairly important figures in their home communities; but at the convention itself, most of them are seeking their footing on unfamiliar terrain.

In contrast, most of the county campaign leaders are experienced in presidential campaigns. Most of them began that way. A majority of both parties—50 percent of the Republicans and 62 percent of the Democrats—reported that their first campaigns were presidential campaigns. Four times as many began in presidential campaigns as in *any* other type. Furthermore, the second most frequent form of political initiation was in gubernatorial politics. Twelve percent of the Republicans and 15 percent of the Democrats started this way. Clearly, these activists are attracted to high-visibility executive politics.

The average experience of the county campaign leaders was 14 years for the Republicans and 10 years for the Democrats. When this is added to origins in presidential politics and their relative youth, the modal activist seems to have been attracted to presidential politics in the late teens or 20s, and to have been active in politics for just over a decade before being given the responsibility of running a county campaign.

Another important fact about the electoral activists is the high proportion who began their political careers in presidential campaign years. Two thirds of the Republicans and 72 percent of the Democrats began in such a year. The years are portrayed in Figure 10-1. The activists who were working in behalf of George McGovern and Sargent

FIGURE 10-1
Presidential Parties as Residues of Past Campaigns: Proportions of Electoral Activists with First Experience in Presidential Campaign Years

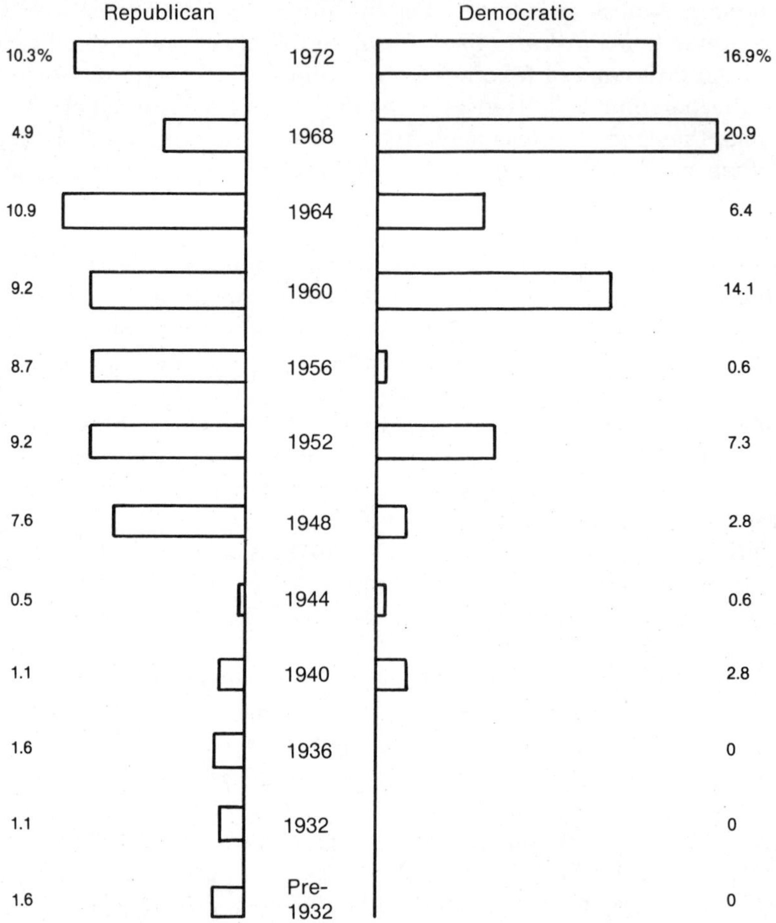

	Republican		Democratic	

Republican	Year	Democratic
10.3%	1972	16.9%
4.9	1968	20.9
10.9	1964	6.4
9.2	1960	14.1
8.7	1956	0.6
9.2	1952	7.3
7.6	1948	2.8
0.5	1944	0.6
1.1	1940	2.8
1.6	1936	0
1.1	1932	0
1.6	Pre-1932	0

Shriver included significant numbers who had been brought into politics during the campaigns of Lyndon Johnson, John Kennedy, Adlai Stevenson, Harry Truman, or Franklin Roosevelt. The committee to reelect Richard Nixon as president included those who had rallied to the banners of Dwight Eisenhower, Thomas Dewey, Wendell Willkie, or even Herbert Hoover. In fact, the activist with the longest campaign experience who turned up in the sample had begun his political career working for Charles Evans Hughes over half a century earlier!

This suggests a conclusion of some significance: *A presidential party at any time is a residue of its past campaigns.* This has consequences for the inferences we can draw from the 1972 data. We can be certain that the activists working for the Committee to Re-Elect the President and the McGovern-Shriver Committee were not wildly atypical of Republicans and Democrats in previous campaigns because 90 percent of the Republicans and 83 percent of the Democrats had begun in earlier campaigns. At the same time, we know that the parties in 1984 will be somehow different from the 1972 parties because of the new cohorts of activists brought into politics by the 1976, 1980, and 1984 campaigns.[5]

ADVOCACY PARTIES

The activists' characteristics hint at the nature of the campaign organizations they might form. The educational and occupational characteristics suggest they might be more sensitive to middle-class issues. Their greater attraction to high-visibility executive politics hints at a greater concern with policies followed by government after the election than with patronage in the county auditor's office. The experience of the activists implies some organizational continuity in spite of the unique policy tendencies of a particular nominee.

Half a dozen questions in the 1972 study dealt directly with the activists' attitudes about engaging in, or avoiding, certain types of party activity. Two of the questions concerned the importance of issues, two tapped the importance of prior party service in candidate selection or patronage, and two dealt with discipline that ought to apply to party leaders or to the activists themselves.

An analysis of the responses to these queries about party norms appears in Table 10-2. The higher the difference score for a given item, the greater the obligation the activists felt to engage in that behavior. There were noticeable differences between the parties. Issues were more important to the Democrats in 1972, both in their belief that they ought to have strong views themselves and in their belief that the nominee ought to be committed on a number of issues. Republicans were more likely to emphasize organization. This is reflected in the higher scores for the consideration of party work in candidate selection and patronage. The activists of both parties were in close agreement on the inappropriateness of party discipline as it applied to themselves.

Important as these party differences are, the similarities between the parties are more consequential. As you read down either party column in Table 10-2, it is clear that much more emphasis in placed

---

[5] This recruitment process spells out limits to the hopes of groups such as the moderate Republicans, who wanted to go back to "normal" pre-Goldwater politics after 1964, and the "Coalition for a Democratic Majority," which wanted to repudiate the "New Politics" of George McGovern after 1972. A party is never completely taken over by the new arrivals who come into politics in a given campaign, but it never goes back to being what it was before that campaign either.

TABLE 10-2
Activists' Feelings of Obligation about Party Work

Activity about Which Attitude Is Held	Difference Score*	
	Democrats	Republicans
Hold strong personal beliefs about a number of different issues	72.3	54.4
Select nominee strongly committed on variety of issue positions	73.0	46.5
Weigh party service very heavily in selecting candidate for nomination	3.2	23.0
See that those who work for party get help in form of job and other things if needed	6.5	23.2
Keep elected officials strictly accountable to party organization	4.4	13.2
Follow decisions of party leaders even when you disagree	−9.4	0

* Higher scores mean greater obligation to engage in activity. For details, see Appendix A-10.1.
Data source: 1972 Hofstetter study.

on issues than on any other activity. The next most important party norms, those concerning party service and patronage, come a long way back of the issue items. Most electoral activists have a strong interest in the policies followed by the government once they are in office. It would be too much to say that an interest in issues draws them to politics in the first place. The activists are likely to speak of their motivations in global terms; they are attracted to politics per se. But it is also clear that an interest in issues is an important component in their attraction to politics, and in the way they participate once they are involved.[6]

Electoral activists agree with their party colleagues to a greater degree than they agree with their constituents. This was rather a surprising finding since parties are often regarded as representative institutions that articulate the preferences of less-involved members of the public. Party activists have been assumed to be persons with distinctive skills in knowing what their constituents want, and in being able to assemble these preferences in packages that win votes at election time. Yet the data indicate that this is *not* what these electoral activists are doing.

One of the advantages of the Hofstetter study was that voters living in the same counties as the party activists were also interviewed, thus presenting the opportunity to address parallel questions to both sets of respondents. There are two ways in which the activists might represent their constituents. One is what Aage Clausen calls "involuntary

[6] Of the many types of local politicos reported in the literature, these electoral activists most closely resemble the citizen politicians in western cities such as Los Angeles and Tucson (Marvick, 1983; Arrington, 1975). Here, too, one finds an emphasis on issue politics, and relative disinterest in patronage.

representation," a process through which the personal attitudes of the party leaders happen to coincide with those of their fellow citizens. The party leaders have the same attitudes, presumably through living in the same community and being exposed to the same influences, but the process is as unconscious as other involuntary processes, such as breathing. The other type of representation does not call for any such coincidence between the leaders' attitudes and those of their fellow citizens, but does assume that the leaders are able to perceive their constituents' attitudes accurately.

It is possible to determine the coincidence of attitudes between activists and constituents, and the extent to which the activists' perceptions coincide with constituents' attitudes, by calculating agreement scores.[7] When this is done, it becomes evident that neither one of these possible modes of representation is working very well. Considering both parties together, involuntary representation is working a little better. The scores reflecting attitudinal agreement are 17 percent better that one would expect by chance, and the scores reflecting perceptual accuracy are only 2 percent better than chance.

When this analysis was done separately for each party, the average agreement score for similarity of attitudes with constituents was .22 for Republicans and .12 for Democrats. (This means 22 percent better than chance for Republicans and 12 percent better than chance for Democrats.) The average agreement scores for perceptual accuracy were 0 for Republicans and .05 for Democrats (Yarnell, 1975). The similarity of attitudes between activists and constituents is not impressive, and the political leaders' presumed competence at knowing what their constituents prefer is nonexistent.

In contrast, the average agreement scores among all Republican activists was .29, and that among all Democratic activists was .30. These figures are almost identical for both parties, and denote agreement among activists about 30 percent beyond what one would expect by chance. Even more important, the scores tell us we can know more about activists' attitudes by learning whether they are Republicans or Democrats than by knowing anything about attitudes in the communities from which they come.[8] The implication is that they are not

---

[7] These are the same agreement scores that were used in the analysis of attitudes of White House staff members in Chapter 4. If both persons give the same answer to every question they are asked, they will have an agreement score of 1.0. If their agreement is no better than chance, the agreement score will be 0. Thus, the agreement score between two political activists (or in this case, between a county leader and the average response of citizens in that county) represents the extent of agreement beyond what would be expected by chance. For further details, see Appendix A-10.2.

[8] Notice, however, that this conclusion depends on lack of agreement between Democrats and residents of their counties in 1972. The agreement score between Republicans and citizens of their communities in 1972 was .22, and the agreement score among all Republicans was .29. This difference is not great, and the results might be different in some future year.

giving voice to their constituents' views. Rather, they are urging policies that their colleagues think wise. American parties are not representative entities, but *advocacy parties.*[9]

GROUPS

REPUBLICAN ISSUE GROUPS

In choosing concepts to analyze the internal structure of coalitions, we have assumed that groups composed of activists with shared attitudes would be important. When we put this assumption together with the finding that issues are central to the thinking of presidential activists, it follows that issue groups composed of persons with shared attitudes on public policy ought to be a useful way to understand electoral parties. The characteristics of such groups should tell us what the party is agreed upon, when questions divide it, and something of the dynamics by which the party determines its positions on issues that cause internal division.

Issue groups of this kind have been isolated by means of the same kind of cluster analysis used to locate issue groups in the White House and Congress. The details of this procedure are set forth in Appendix A-10.3, but the essential point is that each activist is assigned to the issue group with which the activist has the highest average agreement. If any activists do not have the stipulated level of agreement with any group, then they are treated as isolates. Thus we can be sure that we have groups whose members share common outlooks on questions of public policy, and a number of activists who do not belong to any group because their own views are unique.

There were four Republican issue groups in 1972, and seven Democratic groups.[10] The sizes and *approximate* locations of the Republican groups with respect to each other are depicted in Figure 10-2. The word *approximate* is stressed because the issue space is multidimensional. We are using four policy areas: international involvement, economic management, social benefits, and civil liberties. One group might agree with a second on international involvement but disagree on eco-

---

[9] There are choices that county leaders can make about issues, particularly in selecting which issues to emphasize and which to ignore in their local campaign. As we shall presently see, their attitudes about issues do have consequences in the choices they make, and in the strategy which the electoral party implements across the country. However, the full range of their activity is better understood as activity in behalf of a candidate with known issue positions than as full-time espousal of issues. Party activity in the executive and legislative domains, however, is fully consistent with the connotations of "advocacy party."

[10] This analysis of group characteristics is based largely on a memorandum written by Stephen D. Shaffer.

FIGURE 10-2
Republican Issue Groups

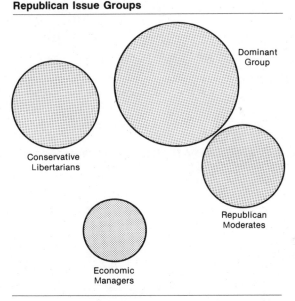

The size of the circles corresponds to the size of each group. The location suggests the *approximate* location of each with respect to the others in issue space. For details, see Appendix A-10.4.

nomic management, and agree with a third on international involvement and economic management but disagree on civil liberties. Therefore, no *two*-dimensional analysis (such as Figure 10-2) is going to be able to depict all of the relationships between the issue groups. The positions of the issue groups in all four policy areas are summarized in Table 10-3.

All four Republican issue groups took moderate positions on public-policy questions. The Dominant group was poised on the boundary between moderate and moderate conservative. Within this group, there was likely to be disagreement on individual questions relating to international involvement and economic management. For example, about a quarter of the members—a larger proportion than any other GOP group—were willing to entertain the idea of bringing some American troops back from overseas. As with other Republican groups, there was some disagreement on social benefits, and considerable consensus on civil liberties. This high rate of agreement on civil liberties, an agreement that tends slightly in a conservative direction, may reflect the large number of southern Republicans in this group. Half of the southern Republican activists belonged to the Dominant group. This was the *only* case in *either* party where a majority of those from *any* region could be found in a single group.

TABLE 10-3
Republican Issue Groups: Varieties of Moderation

Group	Position in Policy Area*				Percent of Activists in Group
	International Involvement	Economic Management	Social Benefits	Civil Liberties	
Dominant Group	Moderate (3.5)	Moderate (3.6)	Moderate (3.5)	Moderate conservative (3.2)	29.8%
Conservative Libertarians	Moderate conservative (3.2)	Moderate conservative (3.3)	Moderate conservative (2.7)	Moderate (3.8)	14.9
Economic Managers	Moderate (3.8)	Moderate liberal (4.9)	Moderate (3.5)	Moderate conservative (3.3)	7.7
Republican Moderates	Moderate (4.1)	Moderate (3.7)	Moderate (4.3)	Moderate conservative (3.3)	11.6
Isolates	Moderate (4.4)	Moderate (4.1)	Moderate (3.6)	Moderate (3.5)	35.9

* The figures in parentheses are median positions on scales that vary between 1 and 7. In general a high score (7) represents a dove position in international involvement, and a willingness to use government power and resources in the domestic policy areas. A low score (1) represents the opposite.

The convention followed for substantive interpretation of the scale scores was: values from 1 to 2.4, conservative; 2.5 to 3.4, moderate conservative; 3.5 to 4.5, moderate; 4.6 to 5.5, moderate liberal; 5.6 to 7, liberal. This classification is nothing more than an aid to understanding, and should not be taken as a precise denotation. Note, for example, that if the upper boundary of moderate conservative had been moved from 3.4 to 3.5, there would have been 10 moderate conservative scores rather than 6.

Data source: 1972 Hofstetter study.

The Conservative Libertarians[11] had slightly more conservative positions on international and economic matters, and much more conservative preferences on social benefits. On civil liberties questions, though, they depart from the other Republican groups in a liberal direction. The Conservative Libertarians were much more skeptical about the wisdom of increasing police authority, and were much more in favor of open housing. It was in this group that one hears the strongest echo of the historic Republican position in favor of civil rights.

The Economic Managers were the smallest Republican group, and departed from the dominant group's issue profile primarily on economic questions. They were slightly less in favor of cutting spending, and

---

[11] The names I have given these issue groups can only suggest their policy tendencies, not serve as complete descriptions. With four different policy areas, a name that stated a group's full set of preferences would be too long to be useful. The problem is the same as with your family name. Your genetic inheritance comes equally from all four grandparents, but for the sake of convenience, your paternal grandfather's name is used as your family name.

were far more willing to use federal instrumentalities to regulate the economy than any other Republican group. Not only did they provide the single example of a Republican group taking a moderate liberal position, but the Economic Managers were less worried about the power of the federal government than any *Democratic* group.

The Republican Moderates were close to the Dominant group's positions on economics and civil liberties, but took more liberal positions with respect to international involvement and social benefits. The Republican Moderates were much more in favor of foreign aid than any other Republican group. It was the only GOP group in which a majority was open to the idea or supportive of increasing welfare payments, and the only one that was united in favor of a social security increase.

The isolates were also essential to an understanding of the internal structure of the Republican party. Consider the information in Table 10-3. There were more Republicans who were isolates than there were in any one of the Republican groups. Furthermore, their policy preferences were moderate in all four policy areas. Since the isolates were more numerous and relatively liberal, it would *seem* that they ought to have been able to move the Republican party somewhat to the left. Yet they weren't. Why not?

One explanation was that the isolates were not members of any group. The workings of the computer program through which these groups were found are such that if an activist had agreed with even one other activist (at a stipulated level), they would have been joined in a two-person group. Therefore we know that these persons tended to be isolated from each other. Since they lacked allies, it was hard for them to move their party in any direction. Here is a reason for the political impotence of the relatively small band of Republican liberals. Not only were they outnumbered, but they disagreed among themselves.

DEMOCRATIC ISSUE GROUPS

The Democratic issue groups are portrayed in Figure 10-3, and their issue preferences are summarized in Table 10-4. The issue space is again multidimensional, but because Democratic disagreements in 1972 were focused on international questions and economic matters, in this figure it is posible to think of the vertical dimension as being related to international questions and the horizontal dimension as being related to domestic matters. This analogy should *not* be pressed very far; some groups are out of place with respect to some other groups in certain policy areas. But the upper left-hand group, the Liberal Pacifists, was the most dovish and the most liberal on domestic questions, and the group farthest to the right, the Coercive Individualists, tended to be hawkish and conservative.

FIGURE 10-3
Democratic Issue Groups

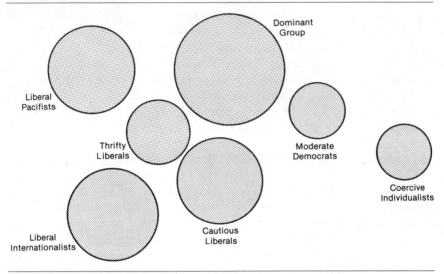

The size of the circles corresponds to the size of each group. The location suggests the *approximate* location of each with respect to the others in issue space. For details, see Appendix A-10.4.

The Dominant group in 1972 took prototypical Democratic positions. It was united in favor of social benefits, and in favor of protecting the civil liberties of minorities. On foreign policy it opposed defense spending, but was divided on questions of foreign aid and keeping American troops overseas. On economic matters it contained some skeptics about continued reliance on the federal government, and showed real division on federal spending.

The Liberal Pacifists and Liberal Internationalists both took even more liberal positions on social benefits, but these two groups departed from the Dominant group in opposite directions on international matters. The Liberal Pacifists wanted to bring American troops back home, did not want to spend for defense, and had doubts about foreign aid.[12] This group represents a tradition in the Democratic party that goes back to Henry Wallace and William Jennings Bryan. The Liberal Internationalists were solidly in favor of defense spending and foreign aid. This group represents those favoring international involvement who

---

[12] In our coding decisions, we called these dovish positions "liberal," and the positions taken by the liberal internationalists were called "moderate." In so doing, we followed the usage of most commentators on the 1972 election. These coding decisions had no bearing on the group structure we found. However we had decided, there would have been one Democratic group departing from the Dominant group in the direction of more overseas participation, and one in favor of withdrawing.

have found spokesmen in John F. Kennedy, Dean Acheson, and Franklin D. Roosevelt.

The other Democratic groups all departed from the Dominant group in a conservative direction in one or more issue areas. The profile of the Cautious Liberals was quite similar to that of the Dominant group, but a shade more conservative on several items. The Cautious Liberals were more willing to spend for military purposes, much more divided on the wisdom of national health care, and perceptibly more favorable to the police. It was this last difference that moved the Cautious Liberals from liberal to moderate liberal on civil liberties.

The Thrifty Liberals took positions similar to the Dominant group except on economic questions. Here their difference was quite pro-

TABLE 10-4
Democratic Issue Groups: Varieties of Liberalism

Group	International Involvement	Economic Management	Social Benefits	Civil Liberties	Percent of Activists in Group
	Position in Policy Area*				
Dominant Group	Moderate liberal (5.1)	Moderate (4.4)	Liberal (5.8)	Liberal (6.5)	22.0%
Liberal Pacifists	Liberal (6.1)	Moderate liberal (5.0)	Liberal (6.4)	Liberal (6.5)	14.3
Liberal Internationalists	Moderate (4.3)	Moderate (4.5)	Liberal (6.2)	Liberal (6.5)	14.8
Cautious Liberals	Moderate liberal (4.8)	Moderate (4.5)	Liberal (5.7)	Moderate liberal (5.2)	14.3
Thrifty Liberals	Moderate liberal (4.6)	Moderate conservative (3.3)	Liberal (5.7)	Liberal (6.3)	7.1
Democratic Moderate	Moderate liberal (5.1)	Moderate conservative (3.4)	Moderate (4.5)	Moderate liberal (5.1)	5.5
Coercive Individualists	Moderate (4.0)	Moderate conservative (3.2)	Moderate liberal (4.6)	Moderate (3.8)	6.0
Isolates	Moderate (4.1)	Moderate (4.3)	Liberal (5.9)	Moderate liberal (5.0)	15.9

* The figures in parentheses are median positions on scales that vary between 1 and 7. In general a high score (7) represents a dove position in international involvement, and a willingness to use government power and resources in the domestic policy areas. A low score (1) represents the opposite. For the convention followed in giving substantive interpretations of these scores, see the explanation at the bottom of Table 10-3.

Data source: 1972 Hofstetter study.

nounced. For example, the Dominant group was split on the question of cutting government spending. All the Thrifty Liberals thought that government spending ought to be reduced.

The Democratic Moderates were the smallest Democratic group, and while they had similar international positions to the dominant group, they took more conservative positions in all the domestic policy areas. Along with the Thrifty Liberals, all the Democratic Moderates favored a reduction in government spending. They were also less enthusiastic about social programs and protecting minority rights than the dominant group. As a matter of fact, a majority of this group opposed any increase in welfare payments.

The Coercive Individualists, so called because they wanted the government to let them alone to conduct their own business affairs but were quite willing to use the police at home and the military abroad to intervene in the lives of others, marked the Democrats' conservative perimeter. The Coercive Individualists were about as hawkish as the Liberal Internationalists, and opposed foreign aid as well. They were almost as opposed to federal spending as the Thrifty Liberals, and more resistant to a strong federal government. Some 55 percent of this group opposed national health care, whereas only 20 percent of the Democratic Moderates did so. And the Coercive Individualists were the only group of Democratic activists who maintained that the police should be given increased authority. In every single policy area, the Coercive Individualists took the most conservative Democratic position.

The Democratic isolates were mirror images of the Republican isolates. Both held minority views within their own parties. The Republican isolates were relatively liberal; the Democratic isolates were relatively conservative. Neither set of isolates was very influential because of lack of agreement among themselves or with any of the issue groups. The major contrast was that the Democratic isolates were less important to an understanding of the Democratic structure because they were so much less numerous.

A NEW VIEW OF ELECTORAL PARTIES

The character of these issue groups is clear. They may be understood in terms of their size, the generally moderate positions taken by the Republican party, and the generally liberal positions taken by the Democratic groups. This is a different view of party groups than is usually offered. The standard interpretation, especially of the Democratic party, is that the party is made up of demographic groupings. For example, Robert Axelrod (1972) names the Democratic groups as the poor, blacks, union members, Catholics, southerners, and central-city residents. Andrew Greeley writes that the political party "is comprised of voluntary associations (such as trade unions), interest groups (civil rights organizations), strictly political groups (Cook County Democratic party), and major portions of population groups (blacks, Catholics, or Jews)" (1974, pp. 172–73). I (1968, 1974) have said that the normal Democratic coalition was made up of Southerners, Westerners, urbanites, union members, and blacks.[13] In other words, the Democratic party is usually seen as a coalition of minorities. Why shouldn't we follow this line of analysis instead of seeking groups with distinctive attitudes in policy areas?

The most direct answer is that activists who fall into the traditional categories do not have shared attitudes from which we can infer probable behavior. Therefore it is much less useful to attempt to interpret parties this way. Two tests were used to try to find attitude groups that corresponded to the traditional classifications. In the first, a mean agreement score was calculated for all activists who fit into one of the categories. (These agreement scores, you will recall, represent the extent of agreement beyond that to be expected by chance.) The data are presented in Table 10-5. The extent of agreement among activists in the categoric groupings is much less than in the issue groups. The average scores for the groupings in Table 10-5 (grand means) are .29 for the Republicans and .29 for the Democrats. The average agreement scores for the electoral issue groups are .48 for the Republicans and .50 for the Democrats. The average agreement scores among all electoral activists are .29 for Republicans and .30 for Democrats. In other words, the categoric groupings do not provide any information beyond what we already have by just knowing whether the activists are Democrats or Republicans. The issue groups are much more distinctive.

The second test—a cluster analysis of all those who fell into the traditional categories—attempted to see whether each set of activists, black Democrats, eastern Republicans, or whatever, would form groups. The data resulting from this test also appear in Table 10-5. In most cases, either multiple groups were formed—which means that the members of each group had different attitudes—or no groups were formed—which means that the activists were isolates who didn't agree with anyone.

Three fifths of the time, multiple groups were formed. The most extreme cases were the urban Democrats, the southern Democrats, and the liberal Democrats. These categories all contained large numbers of Democratic activists. Their potential influence was limited, however, as they would have the Democratic party move in three or four *different*

---

[13] I did classify Republican groups on the basis of their attitudes on issues. Warren Miller and Teresa Levitin's (1976) classification of voters as "Silent Minority," "Center," and "New Liberals" is also a move in this direction. For other analyses of the Democratic party on the basis of demographic groupings, see Ladd & Hadley (1978), Nie, Verba, & Petrocik (1976, chaps. 13–14), and Rubin (1976). These are but examples. Many scholars have used demographic classifications of one kind or another.

TABLE 10-5
Agreement and Clusters Formed within Categoric Groupings

Category	Mean Agreement* Score	Number of Clusters	Percent Unclustered
Republicans			
Blacks†	—	—	—
Roman Catholics	.25	2	42.2%
Urban	.27	2	47.2
East................................	.25	1	53.9
Midwest	.26	1	50.8
South...............................	.34	2	31.4
Deep South	.45	1	33.3
Self-identified liberals	.14	0	100.0
Self-identified conservatives	.32	2	32.9
Democrats			
Blacks	.31	0	100.0
Roman Catholics	.24	1	69.0
Urban	.27	3	26.7
East................................	.25	2	45.2
Midwest	.37	2	31.5
South...............................	.24	3	34.5
Deep South†	—	—	—
Self-identified liberals	.34	4	23.1
Self-identified conservatives†	—	—	—

* The higher the agreement score, the greater the agreement between members of the category.
† Too few cases for analysis.
Data source: 1972 Hofstetter study.

directions. In a couple of instances, liberal Republicans and black Democrats, no groups were formed. These groups were made up entirely of isolates. In three of the four cases in which a single group was formed, a majority of the members of the category remained outside the group. In only one instance, Republicans from the Deep South, is there a high agreement score and a group that includes a majority of the activists in the category. As we have already seen, southern Republicans also provide the *only* case in which a majority of the activists from a single region belong to one attitudinal group.[14] There was a time when a demographic classification of party groups was reasonably exact. Not too long ago, Arthur Holcombe could write:

> The Democratic party, since the great realignment of parties in the course of the struggle over slavery, has consisted of three principal factions:

---

[14] This was the Dominant group in the Republican party. Even in this case, it is not very useful to think of the issue group in regional terms. Fifty-four percent of the members of the Dominant Republican group came from outside the South, and 80 percent came from outside the Deep South.

the cotton and tobacco planters and associated interests in the South, a substantial part of the grain growers and cattlemen and associated interests in the North and West, and a diversified group of urban interests in the same sections, in which since the Al Smith campaign of 1928 labor interests have been growing more important. (1950, p. 122)

Any such classification rested, of course, on an assumption of regional (or occupational, or ethnic, or whatever) homogeneity. Southerners, for example, were assumed to have sufficiently similar attitudes so a group of Southerners would act coherently within a political party. V. O. Key, prescient on this as on so many matters, pointed out that "for 50 years changes in both the North and South have been undermining southern solidarity" (1964, p. 239). These changes have continued apace. National media, mobility from one section of the country to another, and many other forces have eroded sectional and ethnic homogeneity. For some years, we have had a national culture. Southerners and Westerners, Irish-Americans and Polish-Americans, and all the other once distinctive categories are best understood as having subcultures that incorporate most of the features of the national culture.

In a similar way, our national political culture may be thought of as having a moderate political tone. Democrats tend toward the liberal side; Republicans to the conservative side. Democrats and Republicans are best analyzed by finding groups in which these liberal or conservative tendencies vary across particular policy areas. In this way, we achieve more precision than when we use demographic categories of fading utility.

This does not mean that we can afford to abandon all references to southern Democrats or eastern Republicans. While an analysis that uses issue groups is more powerful, the data that allow us to do this in electoral politics come (so far) from a single year. Therefore we have no choice but to use the more general ideological or demographic references in other circumstances.

ORGANIZATIONAL GROUPS

The members of an issue group do share common attitudes. Since they are active members of the same national campaign organization, they are also tied together in a common communication network. But the members of these groups are spread out across the country. The Republicans in Boston and Birmingham and Boise who are all Economic Managers do not talk with each other and then act collectively as a unit. Their political actions are taken in their own communities along with other members of their local campaign organizations. The same is true of Democratic Liberal Internationalists in Trenton and Toledo and Tacoma. Consequently, if we want to understand the positions the parties take on various policies, we need to see how the issue groups combine into issue coalitions (and we shall do so presently). But a full understanding of campaign activities also requires that we look at *organizational groups* such as those of the formal party committees.

There are distinctions between the presidential parties and the formal party committees that are important to keep in mind. Most of the presidential activists are also members of state or local committees. Five eighths of the Republican campaign activists and half of the Democratic campaign activists held some party office in 1972, and 76 percent of the Republicans and 69 percent of the Democrats had held some party position prior to 1972. These figures probably underestimate the extent of involvement of presidential activists in formal party activities, since one can be active without being elected to party office.

While most presidential activists have been involved in the formal party organization, the reverse is *not* true. There are quite a few party committee members who have not been active in presidential campaigns. As we saw in the discussion of the Organization and Planning phase, a presidential campaign is organized downward. Regional chairs pick the state chairs who in turn pick the county chairs. And most people who have organized states in presidential campaigns can think of at least *one or two* county chairs they have been cautioned to stay away from, either because these county chairs' reputations would harm the presidential campaign, or because their activity level was so close to zero that there was no hope of getting them to do any work. Of course, there are also county leaders who do excellent jobs. Ray Bliss and John Bailey, for example, both built strong local organizations in Akron, Ohio, and Hartford, Connecticut, respectively, before either one became state chairman, and then national chairman of his own party. Considering all this, it is important to know something about state and county committees in order to understand activities carried on at that level, but we should not think of the presidential parties and the formal party organizations as identical.

Until very recently, we knew everything and nothing about state and local party organizations. We knew a great deal because there has been a long tradition of careful studies of party organizations. Harold Gosnell's classic *Machine Politics: Chicago Model,* and David H. Kurtzman's richly detailed *Methods of Controlling Votes in Philadelphia* both date from the mid-1930s, and there are many analyses from still earlier periods. At the same time, we knew rather little because it has been almost impossible to generalize from individual studies. What was found in Los Angeles was not found in Detroit. The motive patterns discovered in Massachusetts and North Carolina conflicted with motive patterns found in Oklahoma and Illinois, and neither set of findings seemed to apply in St. Louis. As long as we were dependent on studies in particular localities, we could not tell whether there was a national pattern with some local exceptions, or regional patterns, or one pattern for the majority party and another for the minority party, or just what. All we knew was that things differed from one locality to another. Fortunately, a good nationwide study of state and local party organizations was recently conducted by Cornelius P. Cotter, John F. Bibby, James L. Gibson, and Robert J. Huckshorn.[15] They gave us some carefully researched answers to these questions about general patterns, and I am relying on their study in the discussion that follows.

County Committees

Almost everywhere in America, the local units of political parties are county committees. There are some exceptions in areas where counties are less important political units, such as the town committees in New England, but county committees are by far the most common. The county committees are stable volunteer organizations led by long-time community residents. There are few paid staff members on the local level, but the vast majority of the committees (90 percent for the Democrats, 80 percent for the Republicans) do have full sets of officers. Chairing a county organization is a part-time job; the median number of hours worked each week during a campaign is 12. The average chairperson has lived in the community for about 30 years and is 49 years old, 10 years older than the average county leader in a presidential campaign. Both age and length of residence reflect the stable nature of these committees (Gibson, Cotter, Bibby, & Huckshorn, 1982, pp. 15–16).

The county committees have essentially three clusters of activities. The first has a campaign focus and involves staying in touch with the candidate organizations (such as those supporting the presidential candidates), and carrying on their own campaign activities. More than three quarters of the county committees distribute campaign literature. Roughly two thirds raise funds and distribute money to candidates, organize campaign rallies, conduct telephone campaigns, and publicize candidates through newspapers, posters, and yard signs. About half send press releases to the media and mailings to voters, and conduct registration drives and door-to-door canvassing. A third of the committees buy radio or television time, and relatively few use opinion surveys or buy billboard space. Democratic committees are more likely to conduct registration drives; Republicans are more likely to give money

---

[15] Three of these principal investigators—Bibby, Cotter, and Huckshorn—were National Committee Fellows during the 1960s under a program sponsored by the National Center for Education in Politics, and they maintained an active interest in politics thereafter. Because of their first-hand knowledge, they had reason to be suspicious of claims made by other academics that parties were disappearing.

to candidates, send out mailings, and use opinion surveys. Otherwise the activity levels of the two parties are virtually identical. The other activity clusters of county committees are both organizational. One is a fairly common set of election period behaviors such as bimonthly meetings and having a formal budget. The other is a much less common activity cluster involving organizational maintenance between election periods through such means as a year-round headquarters and having a telephone listing (Gibson and others, 1982, pp. 20–21, tables 3, 5).

Neither the Democratic nor the Republican party had stronger county committees. In fact, both the Democratic and Republican county committees were strongest in the East, next strongest in the West, next in the Midwest, and weakest in the South. Since both parties had the same regional pattern of strength and weakness, this seemed to reflect traditional local ways of doing things rather than party organizational efforts. Both parties had much stronger county committees in the most populous counties (Gibson and others, 1982, pp. 24–28).

Finally, the investigators found no evidence that county committees were declining in strength. To the extent that there was change, it was in the direction of stronger local parties. Fifty percent of Democratic chairs and 58 percent of Republican chairs said that their county organizations were stronger than had been the case 5 to 10 years earlier. When the records of specific party activities in the same counties were compared with Paul Beck's analysis of 1964 data (1974), by far the most common pattern was no change. In other words, the county committees that were conducting registration drives, or distributing literature, or whatever, in 1964 were still doing so in 1979–80. Where there was change, it was in the direction of increased activity (Gibson and others, 1982, tables 10, 12).

State Committees

Whereas the county committees are almost all part-time volunteer organizations that become dormant between campaigns, this is no longer true of state committees. As recently as the early 1960s, four fifths of the state committees curtailed their staff operations between campaigns. Now only half of them do so, and 90 percent have a permanent headquarters location. The role of the state party chair depends on which party controls the governorship. The out party (that is, the party that does not control the governorship) is always led by what Huckshorn calls an Out-Party Independent. In the case of an in party, the chair may be either a Political Agent—a designee of the governor who normally follows the governor's lead—or an In-Party Independent whose own power base is independent of the governor (Huckshorn, 1976, chap. 4). Regardless of the chair's relationship with the governor, over 90 percent of the state parties have either a full-time chair or

TABLE 10-6
Organizational Strength of State Parties, 1975–1980

Organizational Strength	Number of State Parties		
	Republican	Democratic	Total
Strong	8	2	10
Moderately strong	27	11	38
Moderately weak	9	26	35
Weak	1	6	7
Total	45	45	90*

* Data were available for 90 of the 100 state parties.
Source: Bibby, Cotter, Gibson, & Huckshorn, 1982.

an executive director. The average state party has a staff of just over seven employees, and a budget of $340,000.

State committee activities may be divided into institutional support, those that benefit the entire party, and candidate support. Institutional support involves such things as voter identification, registration, and get-out-the-vote drives, as well as polling. More than two thirds of the state parties are engaged in voter mobilization activities, and more than half do polling. Both of these figures have been stable since the early 70s. About half of the state parties are also involved in issue development. Voter mobilization and polling are, of course, also of benefit to candidates running for office. In addition, nearly 90 percent of the state committees conduct seminars in campaign methods, many offer research assistance, and about half of the state parties make contributions to candidates. The proportion of state committees making candidate contributions has dropped a bit in recent years (Gibson, Cotter, Bibby, & Huckshorn, 1981, pp. 22–28).

There are important variations in the strength of the two parties at the state level. To begin with, the Republicans have a decided advantage in organizational strength. Table 10-6 shows the results obtained when a robust index of party institutionalization[16] was used to categorize the strength of the state parties. Seventy-eight percent of the Republican state committees fell into the moderately strong or strong categories; 71 percent of the Democratic state committees fell into the moderately weak or weak categories. Both parties had their strongest organizations—by far—in the Midwest, but thereafter the regional patterns were different. The next strongest Democratic parties were in the West, then in the East, and the weakest Democratic parties were in the South. The second strongest Republican party organizations were

---

[16] The success of the research team in devising indexes in a substantive area that has long resisted quantitative analysis is likely due to the happy combination of long familiarity with political parties (Bibby, Cotter, and Huckshorn) and technical skill (Gibson).

in the South, the third strongest in the West, and the weakest Republican parties were in the East (Gibson and others, 1982, pp. 24–25). The research team also had state data from five time periods since 1960, and this allowed them to investigate directly whether state parties were declining as some writers allege. The mean index of institutionalization did not show any dramatic change in either direction, and Gibson, Cotter, Bibby, and Huckshorn concluded that "direct attention to party organization produces results which fail to support the party demise thesis. In the last twenty years . . . state party organizations have become more, not less institutionalized, despite some slippage in the very late 1970s" (1981, p. 53).

National Committees

We shall look at the campaign activities of national campaign organizations in some detail in the next chapter. For the moment, though, there are a few points that should be made to facilitate comparison between local, state, and national committees. To begin with, when one moves from the state to the national level, there is a continuation in the shift from part time to full time, and from volunteer to paid staff that we saw between the local and state levels. The national committees have been organized for a longer time, have larger staffs, and differ from state committees in the same ways that state committees differ from local committees.

A major difference between the state and national committees is that an in-party state chair may be either a Political Agent of the governor or an In-Party Independent, but the national chairperson of the in party is always the designee of the president. This practice had a strong test when President Nixon wanted to replace Republican National Chairman Ray C. Bliss. Bliss had been given widespread credit for rebuilding the party after 1964, and members of the Republican National Committee made it abundantly clear that they wanted him to keep the chairmanship. Nonetheless, when Nixon sent an emissary to Bliss to ask for his resignation, Bliss obliged.

In partial consequence of this presidential dominance, the major organizational developments in both national committees have taken place when the party was out of office. In theory, a president could pay attention to party organization. In practice, presidents have been so busy with affairs of state that they have had little time to concern themselves with party organization. (The recent president who was most interested in his party was Gerald Ford. The Republican National Committee did make some progress under Mary Louise Smith when he was in office.) Consequently, national Democratic party building took place under Paul Butler in the late 50s, under Robert Strauss between 1973 and 1977. Some has been taking place under Charles Manatt since the Democrats left office in 1981. The Republicans benefited from major developmental periods under Ray Bliss from 1965 to 1969, and under William Brock from 1977 to 1981.

The net of these party-building efforts has left the Republican National Committee in a far stronger position than the Democratic National Committee. Part of this is due to the considerable skill of the two most recent Republican out-party chairmen, Ray Bliss and William Brock. Part of it is also due to the greater neglect of their National Committee staffs by the two most recent Democratic presidents, Lyndon Johnson and Jimmy Carter. Both were from the South where, as we have seen, the Democrats have their weakest state and local parties. Whether lack of experience with strong party organizations contributed to their neglect of the Democratic National Committee, we cannot know. What is clear is that the Republican National Committee began the 1980s with a substantial organizational and financial advantage.

COALITIONS

REPUBLICAN ISSUE COALITIONS

In our discussion of activists and issue groups, we saw that issues were important to electoral activists, and that the Republican and Democratic activists could be regarded as belonging to issue groups with different sets of policy preferences. Now, what kinds of coalitions can be formed by these groups? The fundamental answer is that in electoral politics, the Dominant group ends up in a key position in the Dominant Coalition formed in each policy area. This hardly sounds surprising, but the reason is that we have been calling these groups "Dominant." So far we haven't said why they should be so regarded.

Take the Dominant Republican group. It is the largest Republican group, and this makes it easier for other groups joining with it to form a majority coalition. But one could construct a case to show why other groups would form coalitions among themselves rather than with the Dominant group. The Dominant group is the largest, but it includes fewer than 3 out of 10 Republican activists. Moreover, the median positions of the Dominant group are more conservative than the median positions taken by all Republicans in each policy area. Why shouldn't the Republican activists who prefer more liberal postures form coalitions to move the party toward the center?

The reason for the strength of the Dominant group lies in its ability to recruit allies whose policy preferences are closer to its own than to moderate opponents. The issue coalitions differ from one policy area to another, but the Dominant group ends up as a member of each winning coalition. The Republican Moderates take a more liberal position in international involvement, but the Dominant group can form a coalition with the Conservative Libertarians and the Economic Managers. The Economic Managers prefer a more liberal posture with respect to the federal government's role in fiscal affairs, but the Dominant group can coalesce with the Republican Moderates and the Conservative Libertarians. The situation with regard to social benefits is the same as for international involvement. In civil liberties, the Conservative Libertarians would prefer a more moderate posture, but the Dominant group can form a coalition with the Republican Moderates and the Economic Managers. Thus, there are three different coalitions in the four policy areas, and each one tends in a conservative direction.

The strength of the Dominant group thus lies both in its relative size and in its ability to find partners. The weakness of the Republican Moderates, conversely, lies not only in their minority status but also in their difficulty in finding groups with whom they can combine.

DEMOCRATIC ISSUE COALITIONS

The internal issue structure of the Democrats is somewhat more complex than that of the Republicans, but the process of coalition formation is essentially a mirror image of the Republican process. There are more issue groups in the Democratic party; there is greater issue distance between the most liberal and the most conservative Democratic groups, and the Coercive Individualists take relatively conservative positions in every policy area. But the Dominant Democratic group, as the Dominant Republican group, is the largest and has the easiest time finding policy partners.

In international involvement, the Dominant group faces opposition in one direction from the Liberal Pacifists, and in the other direction from the Liberal Internationalists and the Coercive Individualists. But they can form a moderate-liberal coalition in company with the Democratic Moderates, the Cautious Liberals, and the Thrifty Liberals. There is pronounced division among Democrats on economic matters; but a majority coalition can be formed by the Dominant group, the Cautious Liberals, the Liberal Internationalists, and the Liberal Pacifists. In social benefits, a winning coalition can be formed by the Dominant group, the Cautious Liberals, the Thrifty Liberals, and the Liberal Internationalists. On civil liberties, the views of the Dominant group, the Liberal Pacifists, the Liberal Internationalists, and the Thrifty Liberals are so similar that the process of coalition formation is almost automatic.

There are differences between the parties in the degree of exclusion. In the Republican party, the Conservative Libertarians and the Economic Managers are members of the Dominant Coalition in three of the four policy areas, and the Republican Moderates are twice. In the Democratic party, the Democratic Moderates are part of a winning coalition only on international questions, and the Coercive Individualists are never part of a winning coalition. In the Republican party, the more conservative groups are always members of the Dominant Coalition. In the Democratic party, the most liberal group (the Liberal Pacifists) is included only twice. But in both electoral parties, the Dominant group is a member of the Dominant Coalition in all four policy areas.

There are two ways these predictions about coalitions can be checked. One is to take the between-group agreement scores (which may be found in Appendix A-10.5) that are calculated across all the policy areas, and assume that the two groups with the highest agreement scores will form an initial protocoalition. At that point, agreement scores are recalculated between that protocoalition and the remaining groups, and the process is repeated until a winning coalition is formed. The second way to check the process of coalition formation is to use the cluster procedure by which the issue groups were isolated, and gradually lower the criteria for admission until the equivalent of a multigroup coalition is found. There are variations in detail in what one observes, but essentially these procedures verify the existence of the issue coalitions that we have just discussed.

ISSUE COALITION DIFFERENCES
BETWEEN THE PARTIES

The processes of coalition formation have consequences. Some of the most important can be seen in Table 10-7. In every policy area, the median policy preferences of the dominant Republican coalitions are more conservative than those of all Republican activists. In every policy area, the median policy preferences of the dominant Democratic coalitions are more liberal than those of all Democratic activists. Thus, the process of coalition formation in electoral politics[17] has a tendency to polarize the alternatives presented to the voters rather than move them toward the center of the political spectrum.

The polarization is more pronounced in the dominant Republican coalition for a couple of reasons. For one thing, the more conservative Republican groups are always members of the dominant Republican coalitions, while the most liberal Democratic group is not part of the dominant Democratic coalition in international involvement or social

---

[17] Something of the same thing takes place in legislative politics. Except on abortion, the Dominant Coalition in the 95th House was more liberal than the entire House and the entire Democratic party. The Losing Coalition was more conservative than the entire House (except on abortion), and more conservative than the entire Republican party in four of seven policy areas. In the 95th Senate, the Dominant Coalition was more liberal than the entire Senate and the entire Democratic party, and the Losing Coalition was more conservative than the entire Senate and the entire Republican party.

TABLE 10-7
Comparison of Issue Coalitions with All Party Activists

	Position in Policy Area*			
Group	International Involvement	Economic Management	Social Benefits	Civil Liberties
Dominant Republican coalition	Moderate conservative (3.4)	Moderate (3.5)	Moderate conservative (3.2)	Moderate conservative (3.2)
All Republican activists	Moderate (4.0)	Moderate (3.8)	Moderate (3.6)	Moderate (3.5)
Dominant Democratic coalition	Moderate liberal (5.0)	Moderate liberal (4.6)	Liberal (6.0)	Liberal (6.5)
All Democratic activists	Moderate liberal (4.9)	Moderate (4.4)	Liberal (5.9)	Liberal (6.0)

* The figures in parentheses are median positions on scales that vary between 1 and 7. In general a high score (7) represents a dove position in international involvement, and a willingness to use government power and resources in the domestic policy areas. A low score (1) represents the opposite. For the convention followed in giving substantive interpretations to these scores, see the explanation at the bottom of Table 10-3.

Data source: 1972 Hofstetter study.

benefits. For another, the policy preferences of the dominant Republican group are all more conservative than the median preference of all Republican activists, whereas only in civil liberties are the policy preferences of the dominant Democratic group distinctly more liberal than the Democratic median. Hence the dominant Republican coalitions are noticeably more conservative in every instance, while the dominant Democratic coalition is equally far away only in civil liberties.

The data in Table 10-7 also suggest the nature of the choice the electoral parties presented to the citizen in 1972. The choice was most pronounced with respect to social benefits and civil liberties. In these areas, Democratic policies were liberal, and Republican policies were moderate conservative. In international involvement, the citizen's choice was between moderate liberal and moderate conservative policies. A tendency toward the center was most notable in economic management, where Democratic policies were moderate liberal and Republican policies were moderate.

To understand party differences, one should also consider intraparty consensus. The consensus scores for all Republican activists and all Democratic activists, respectively, in the four policy areas are: international involvement, .57, .31; economic management, .62, .48; social benefits, .44, .66; civil liberties, .61, .73. The consensus scores have a value of 1.0 when everyone takes the same position, and a value of 0 when agreement is no greater than would be expected with an equal distribution, so these consensus scores tell us where we can expect strains and disagreements to show up within the parties.[18] The Republicans were least agreed about social benefit programs, but the similar sizes of the four consensus scores imply that Republican disagreements were spread rather equally across the four policy areas. In the Democratic case, however, disagreements were concentrated on foreign policy and economics. Democrats were united in favor of liberal positions on social benefits and civil liberties.

CAMPAIGN IMPLICATIONS OF ISSUE COALITIONS

Earlier in this chapter, we said that the activists' interest in issues made it appropriate to think of the parties as advocacy parties, but that in electoral politics, "advocacy" had to be understood in the light of what the activists were free to do. In the midst of a presidential campaign, groups of activists are not free to devise campaign strategies of their own. If the presidential candidate is giving speech after speech promising to cut spending, for example, activists in the party are hardly free to claim that he will increase spending once he is in the White House. But they can choose which issues they are going to emphasize in their own localities. In some cases, the choice is forced on them. If they are printing their own campaign pamphlets, they must decide which material about the presidential candidate they are going to include. If they are embarking on a doorbelling campaign, they must decide what they are going to tell voters about the candidate. The other way they "advocate" policies is to report their own attitudes upwards to coalition leaders. The policy preferences of leaders in a single county are hardly going to determine national strategy, but as these reports are aggregated, they indicate the policy preferences of the coalition to the strategy group. These aggregated preferences are taken into account.

Data are available that make it possible to verify these campaign implications of group and coalition preferences. In the case of the issue groups, there are data on the intensity of their feelings (whether they feel strongly or not), the extent of consensus (whether the members agree with each other on the issue), and whether or not the issue was emphasized. As you might expect, the intensity of group feelings was significantly related to the emphasis placed on the issue. That is, the more strongly they felt for or against a question, the more likely they were to stress that issue in their local campaigning. The Pearsonian correlation, r, was .32. (If you have not encountered bivariate correla-

---

[18] See Appendix A-10.6 for an explanation of how these consensus scores are calculated.

tion before, you might want to consult the box on that topic in Chapter 14.) But in addition, consensus is related to issue emphasis ($r = .17$). This can be understood because of the group dynamics of reinforcement and sharing. Consensus is a vital property of a group, and therefore related to group behavior.

There also appears to be a strong relationship between coalition emphases and candidate emphases. The coalition emphases can be determined from the data set we have been using, and we know the candidate emphases from a content analysis of their speeches (Kessel, 1977). The correlation (r) between Senator McGovern's emphases and those of the Democratic coalition is .36.[19] That between President Nixon and the Republican coalition is .57; and if one excludes natural resources, which Nixon barely mentioned, the correlation goes up to .84. Data on the candidate's policy preferences are not available for Senator McGovern, but good estimates of Nixon's preferences are available from members of the Nixon Domestic Council staff who could observe the President at close range. Here again there was a strong relationship ($r = .56$) between the mean policy preferences of the coalition and those of the candidate.

The linkage between coalition and candidate flows in both directions. The candidate learns of coalition preferences through reports that are aggregated by the campaign organization. The coalition members learn of the candidate's positions from his many public statements as well as from communications that come through party channels. The coalition cannot prevent a candidate from taking a position about which he feels strongly. Nor can the candidate force the coalition to emphasize issues on which they think he is taking an unwise stand. But there are forces that work toward mutual accommodation. The candidate doesn't want to get too far away from his supporters, and the coalition members can work most effectively for their candidate through a faithful representation of his positions.

Summary

The electoral parties consist of activists who have been recruited through one or another of the presidential campaigns through which the party has passed. The activists are middle class, interested in issues, and are more likely to agree with their fellow partisans than with residents of their own communities. Their attitudes on issues allow them to be combined into groups. In 1972, there were four generally

---

[19] One must be cautious in interpreting this relationship. The relevant data from the content analysis are the frequencies of reference to the six policy areas (the four used in this chapter plus natural resources and agriculture). A correlation resting on six data points is hardly reliable.

moderate groups in the Republican party, and seven generally liberal groups in the Democratic party. These nationwide issue groups tell us more about the parties than the traditional demographic categories. When these particular groups are aggregated, the resulting issue coalitions are more conservative in the Republican party, and more liberal in the Democratic party. The policy preferences of the groups correspond to the issues they emphasize, and the issues emphasized by the coalitions correspond to the issues stressed by the presidential candidates. Thus the internal structure of the electoral parties does affect their campaign strategies.

The more general argument, of course, is that the reasons *why* a coalition behaves as it does will depend, in electoral politics as elsewhere, on its internal structure and its external structure, and the reasons for taking action *when* it does are to be found in the temporal pattern. In this chapter, we have focused on the temporal pattern and the internal structure of electoral politics. We saw a hint of external structure in our discussion of the organizational groups on the local, state, and national levels. Now it is time to turn directly to those outward-looking activities that arise from the need of the electoral coalitions to reach the voters.

CHAPTER 11

ELECTORAL POLITICS: EXTERNAL STRUCTURE

To a greater degree than is true of any other kind of politics, electoral politics is aimed at one primary audience: the voters.[1] Hundreds of persons are engaged in the four types of activities necessary to reach this audience—*campaign operations, research, public relations,* and *finance.* In this chapter, we shall want to review these activities in

---

[1] A useful distinction can be drawn between primary and secondary audiences. Primary audiences are those whose support is essential for success in a given institutional domain. Secondary audiences are those whose political reactions are consequential, but come (often later) in another institutional domain. Thus, voters whose ballots will not be cast until the general election are a secondary audience for nomination politics, but become a primary audience for electoral politics.

There are some secondary audiences for electoral politics. If a candidate (or someone in his core group) is unusually reflective, or if he is running so far ahead as to be regarded as almost certain of election, there may be concerns for how his positions on issues are going to be viewed by the bureaucracy and Congress, and how this is going to affect the candidate's ability to accomplish things in executive or legislative politics if he is elected. Thus in 1960, Senator John Kennedy asked Clark Clifford and Richard Neustadt to draft reports on what should be done. In 1972, Clark Clifford, Theodore Sorenson, and Harry MacPherson were asked to contribute ideas for a possible McGovern administration. In 1976, Jimmy Carter set up a staff headed by Atlanta attorney Jack Watson that worked separately from the campaign staff to make plans for a possible transition.

Plans for the Reagan transition began to be laid in November 1979. Transition planners' preparations were relatively detailed, but they worked on a low-key basis to avoid distracting anyone from the campaign. The transition planners were also separate from the campaign staff, but they reported through campaign Chief of Staff Edwin Meese, thereby avoiding some staff rivalries. (*continued*)

some detail. Before doing so, though, we ought to review two general points about campaign organizations: their growth and development, and the division of authority.

DEVELOPMENT OF CAMPAIGN STAFFS

The staffs that carry on the functions of electoral parties are 20th-century developments, as is the staff that serves the institutionalized presidency. Until the 1920s, national parties largely disappeared between elections. The national chairperson of the incumbent party was frequently appointed postmaster general, a post from which he could conduct party affairs.[2] For example, Will Hayes was appointed Postmaster General during the Harding administration. One looked in vain, though, for any substantial party headquarters. Party activity was so sporadic that most of it could be taken care of from the personal office of whoever happened to be the party chairman at the time.

For both parties, the beginnings of professional staffing came in the wake of major defeats. After the election of 1928, in which Herbert Hoover received 444 electoral votes to Al Smith's 87, Democratic National Chairman John Raskob hired talented phrasemaker Charles Michelson.[3] Michelson's publicity helped to ensure that Hoover's popularity was short lived; and in the happier year of 1932, he was joined by (among others) Emil Hurja, a mining engineer who introduced Democrats to systematic analysis of voting data (Herring, 1940, pp. 208, 265; Michelson, 1944).

The beginnings of modern Republican organization came after the election of 1936, in which Franklin Roosevelt carried 46 states while Kansas Governor Alf Landon carried only Maine and Vermont. John D. M. Hamilton, Republican National Chairman during the ensuing four

---

A related situation concerns an incumbent president who is also a candidate for reelection. In this case, a president is simultaneously engaged in electoral politics and executive politics. The primary audiences for executive politics are likely to pay attention to the president's campaign statements to see if they signal any switch in administration policy. The president is aware of both executive and electoral audiences, and has, of course, extensive structures to link him to both.

[2] The movement of party leaders from the postmaster generalship—Will Hayes, James Farley, Robert Hannegan—to the attorney generalship—Howard McGrath, Herbert Brownell, Robert Kennedy, John Mitchell—was a sign that patronage involving U. S. attorneys and federal judgeships was becoming more important in running national campaigns than the appointment of postmasters and rural mail carriers. This change took place during the Truman administration.

[3] Charles Michelson was, incidentally, the brother of Nobel prize-winning physicist Albert A. Michelson.

years, appears to have been the first full-time salaried national chairman. He gave the GOP some staff to work with, and envisioned a corps of party civil servants with lifetime careers and a pension plan. Hamilton also took steps toward regular party financing with a system of state quotas and sustaining memberships (Cotter & Hennessy, 1964; Lamb, 1966).

From these beginnings, party headquarters grew from "two ladies occupying one room in a Washington office building," as Franklin Roosevelt described Democratic headquarters in the 1920s (Key, 1964, p. 322), to institutions that employ scores of persons during noncampaign years, and even more during the campaign proper (Bone, 1971, p. 170). Parallel growth has taken place on the state level, although the development of staff is even more recent. Huckshorn reports that during 1962–63, when he visited some 18 Republican state parties, 7 still did not have a permanent headquarters (1976, pp. 254–55). As we saw in the last chapter, 90 percent of the state parties now have a permanent headquarters.

Another surge of Republican organizational activity took place after 1976. National Chairman Bill Brock was concerned about the future of the party, which, at the state level, was about as weak as it had been following the defeats of 1936 and 1964. Brock supplied organizational directors for all state parties at a cost of $1 million, and put together a staff of 15 regional political directors to provide liaison between the national committee and the state committees. A local-election campaign division, with 15 staff members working directly in local election campaigns, especially those for state legislatures, was particularly important. In the judgment of John Bibby (1981), the Brock program of assistance to party organizations has been unprecedented in the history of American political parties.

In 1981, the Democratic National Committee began to do some of the things the Republican National Committee had been doing: fund raising through mass mailings, candidate recruitment, publicity efforts, and so forth. They had a long way to go. For example, their contributors list rose from 20,000 in 1981 to 150,000 in mid-1982, while the Republican contributors list was increasing from 1.3 million to 1.5 million. Eugene Eidenberg, DNC executive director during 1981 and 1982, said that he thought the critical four-year period in the Democratic building effort would be from 1985 to 1989.

> From 1981 to 1985, we'll be starting to build the foundation. If we win in 1984, the tendency will be to turn the DNC back into the personal political arm of the president. The vital thing will be for the next chairman and the next staff to continue, not every detail, but to continue the basic direction of building an effective national political organization.

DIVISION OF AUTHORITY

Division of authority in political organizations is hardly a recent development. History tells us of many struggles for the ears of monarchs, and there are various bases of power in all forms of politics. Similarly, there are organizational features that tend to fragment authority in electoral politics, and we need to know what these are. As we have just seen, in recent decades the national committees have developed staffs capable of conducting national campaigns. Many candidates, however, have chosen to work through their own organizations, such as the Reagan Bush Committee and the Carter/Mondale Re-Election Committee in 1980. A candidate organization does the same things as a national committee staff, speech writing, media contact, and the like. But the existence of a candidate organization separate from the national committee staff means that there are at least two campaign chairpersons and two rival sets of division heads. Furthermore, the candidate is not part of either organization. Most of the time, he is off campaigning, and therefore physically separated from both headquarters. And the candidate has some staff, often including some of the core group, traveling with him. This creates a third headquarters, or at the very least a third point at which many executive decisions about the campaign are made.

All of the arguments for responsibility, efficiency, and economy would seem to go against multiple centers of authority and duplicate senior staffs. Why do they exist? The most important reason is that the national committee is, by tradition, neutral in nomination politics. There are good reasons for this. The national committee is charged with making the arrangements for the national convention. Given at least two candidates, if the national committee were to facilitate the chances of Candidate A, Candidate B would have every reason to be angry. So the national committee is neutral. It doesn't take any action to harm Candidate A or Candidate B, but neither does it promote the candidacy of either at the expense of other aspirants.

As we have already seen, the staff needed for nomination politics is much smaller than the staff needed for a general election campaign. Still, to be nominated, a candidate must have speeches written, press releases distributed, polls taken, funds raised, and so on. In the course of a quest for the nomination, close working relations develop between the senior members of this staff and the candidate. Many become members of the candidate's core group. At a minimum, the candidate knows what senior members of this staff can do, and how well they can do it.

Once the nomination is in hand, there are two prospective campaign staffs in being: the candidate's own staff that has taken him through the convention, and the national committee staff. Rivalries separate these staffs. The national committee staff includes persons who have had experience in previous presidential campaigns, experience that is often in short supply on the candidate's own staff. They have been in touch with the state party organizations. They know, for example, if there is a split in the state party in Montana and just who is on which side. They know which state organizations can get things done on their own, and which state organizations are going to need close supervision to accomplish essential campaign tasks. The candidate's staff members, of course, think that they have the more essential knowledge. They know how to do what the candidate wants done. The national committee staff, which has been occupied with routine activities while the candidate's staff has been out winning primary elections, seems stuffy and slow to react. And while others were skeptical early on, the campaign staff has seen their leader triumph in nomination politics. They feel they have earned the right to conduct the fall campaign. In short, after the convention, there are two rival staffs, and—especially if the convention has been held in late summer—there is little time to deal with this dilemma.

Multiple Headquarters

While there have been a good many variations, there are two basic organizational patterns in electoral politics. The first is to merge the two staffs and conduct a unified campaign through the national committee staff. The second is to allow the existing candidate organization to conduct the campaign and have the national committee staff take care of "other party business." The advantage of the former is that you can utilize an experienced staff, and you have established lines of communication into every state, whether the candidate was involved there in the springtime or not. The advantage of the separate approach is that there is a working organization in being, and separateness allows the candidate to stress his independence from other politicians. Thus, when Adlai Stevenson wanted to underscore his independence from an unpopular Truman administration, he had his headquarters in Springfield, Illinois; and when Jimmy Carter wanted to emphasize that he was not part of the Washington scene in 1976, Carter headquarters was kept in Atlanta.

Many proponents of a unified campaign point to that of Franklin Roosevelt in 1932 as an example of how a campaign should be run. Dwight Eisenhower in 1956, Adlai Stevenson the same year, John Kennedy in 1960, Barry Goldwater in 1964, Lyndon Johnson the same year, and Hubert Humphrey all conducted their campaigns from national committee headquarters. Adlai Stevenson in 1952, Richard Nixon in 1960, 1968, and 1972, George McGovern in 1972, Gerald Ford in 1976, Jimmy Carter in 1976 and 1980, and Ronald Reagan in 1980 all maintained separate campaign headquarters (Ogden & Peterson, 1968, chap. 5; Cotter & Hennessy, 1964, pp. 122–27). A minimum requirement for a unified campaign is someone who can exercise unquestioned control over the merged staffs and who has the complete trust of the candidate. Robert Kennedy played this role at the Democratic National Committee in 1960. Even so, it was difficult to overcome some of the rivalries among other staff members.

The tendency to have the campaign conducted by a separate candidate organization was given a powerful push by the Federal Election Campaign Act of 1974. The act stipulates that federal funds will go to a separate candidate organization during the primaries. There is an option under which the candidate may designate the national committee as the agent to spend federal funds in the general election campaign; but by the time this choice is made, all the accounting and reporting procedures have been set up in the candidate organization. No candidate exercised this option in 1976 or 1980. Gerald Ford wrote in his memoirs that he wanted to run his 1976 campaign through the Republican National Committee, but apparently was told (erroneously) that he could not do so (Ford, 1979, p. 295).

Regardless of where the headquarters offices are located or how many of them there are, there is another campaign headquarters, and that is wherever the candidate happens to be. This used to be "the train;" now it is "the plane." Not only does the physical presence of the candidate signify the location of "the campaign" as far as most media representatives are concerned, but there are certain things that can be done from "the plane" (or sometimes from a motorcade en route to a campaign event) and nowhere else. The candidate is moved on jet aircraft, not only to respond to as many requests for candidate appearances as possible, but also to appear in as many media markets as can be done between sunrise and sunset and thus generate broader coverage in the local press. Speeches must be ready for each stop. And there are likely to be over a hundred reporters flying along, most of them in a press plane, whose needs must be borne in mind and whose questions require answers.

A reasonably large staff must accompany the candidate. Senior speechwriters need to be close at hand to alter speeches to take account of late-breaking events, and to work with the candidate during in-flight time. A press secretary needs to be along to handle the traveling press and those encountered along the way. Often persons close to the candidate travel along so there will be a few familiar faces among the blur he sees moving from airport to airport, and to help provide background for reporters. Usually there is a very senior staff person who goes along to organize all this. Governor Sherman Adams of New Hampshire rode Eisenhower's campaign train in 1952 to provide liaison between the train and other campaign leaders. H. R. Haldeman was in charge of Nixon's campaign plane in 1968. Both, of course, ended up as chiefs of staff once the candidate was in the White House.

In theory, basic decisions are made when the candidate is available to meet with his strategy group, or the candidate delegates authority to others to act in his name. In practice, there are unexpected developments—a foreign crisis, a charge by the opposition—that require instant response from "the plane." This is frustrating to those in the headquarters. Although they are supposed to be in instant radio communication with "the plane," sometimes they must wait until the plane is on the ground and a telephone line is available, or until the traveling party returns from a campaign event somewhere. Gary Hart recalled the situation in the 1972 McGovern campaign:

> Generally, the communications between the traveling party and the headquarters were good. . . . But occasionally, some momentous decision would be made by the Senator which we would find out about only third-hand, hours after the fact. That sprang from a feeling which one gets traveling on the plane with the candidate, traveling staff, and reporters, that the entire campaign is there and that everything else is at best secondary and will follow along, like the camel's body following its nose wherever it is led. (1973, p. 300)

Frustrating though it is, this situation is likely to continue.

Multiple Chairpersons

Since a campaign is being led from at least three sources—the national committee, the candidate's personal staff, and "the plane"—there is considerable fragmentation of authority. Nor is this all. It is not uncommon for more than one person to believe that they have been promised the leadership position in a campaign. In the 1960 Nixon campaign, former Republican National Chairman Leonard Hall was given the title of campaign chairman, and Robert Finch, a close friend of the candidate from Los Angeles, was called campaign director. In the 1972 McGovern campaign, Gary Hart, Frank Mankiewicz, and Lawrence O'Brien, who had been recruited in that order, all had titles suggesting they were in charge of that campaign. (Of course, there were also Thruston B. Morton and Jean Westwood, who were the Republican and Democratic National Committee chairpersons during these campaigns.) Each of these persons was, in fact, playing an important role in these campaigns, and that role varied according to the background and skills of the particular individual. Who was in charge? That question was deliberately left unresolved by the candidate, who wanted to use all these people in the campaign.

Multiple Groups and Multiple Bases of Authority

On top of all this, there are different points of view that arise as one person or another acts as a spokesperson for one of the groups in the candidate's supporting coalition. As we have seen, each issue group has a different set of policy preferences, and its members attempt to persuade the candidate to move closer to their position. Finally, as we are about to see, different types of expertise are needed in a campaign—speech writing, fund raising, and so on—and these give rise to a functional division of authority. The regional directors in campaign operations feel that the speechwriters don't have a feel for how the campaign is moving out in the country; the speechwriters think that the regional directors don't understand the issues; the finance people think that the other groups are spending money altogether too fast. Since each of these actors is expert in his or her own area, each has a basis on which to speak. The division of responsibility between the few at the apex of the campaign and those with specific responsibilities is not unlike that in Congress between the floor leaders and committee chairmen. Nonetheless, this is a source of tension within a campaign organization. Thus, one of the reasons given by F. Clifton White for Barry Goldwater's defeat in 1964 was not that the Senator was a candidate of a minority party who took policy positions at some remove from the majority of the American people. Rather:

> The really important decisions of the campaign were . . . hammered out in the so-called "Think Tank" on the third floor of an office building at 1625 I Street in downtown Washington. There Denison Kitchel, Bill Baroody and their stable of speech writers and research experts held court. It was a court that was notably unreceptive to ideas from outside its own circle. (1967, pp. 415–16)

Clif White happened to be the director of Citizens for Goldwater-Miller, and in this quote, he was expressing his unhappiness with the research division. But the quote could just as easily have come from an ad agency person whose favorite slogan had been rejected, or from a regional coordinator who felt that others just didn't understand New England.

Multiple headquarters. Multiple chairpersons. Multiple groups. Multiple bases of expertise. How seriously do these affect the progress of the campaign? Many things determine the answer to this, but one of the most important is the candidate's standing with the voters. If the candidate is popular, and running well ahead of his opponent, then organizational problems are not too serious. Staff members' morale is high, and visions of White House offices dance in their heads. If the contestants are in a tight race, there is anxiety; but along with the anxiety, there is some extra effort put forth because it might make a difference in the election. But if the candidate is running behind, then organizational tensions are felt. Reluctant to believe that the candidate is unpopular or saying the wrong things about issues, staff members tend to think that improper tactics are being used, or that there is some organizational defect. It is easy to think that it is *someone else's* fault that the party is running behind, and with responsibility so divided, there are many scapegoats close at hand.[4]

CAMPAIGN OPERATIONS

Whatever else it may be, a campaign staff is not a tidy structure. It does not retain the same institutional form from one campaign to another. Divison titles change from campaign to campaign. Activities found in one organizational unit in a given campaign may have been assigned to another unit four years earlier. Fortunately, we are not interested in who has which title, or what an organization chart would look like. We are interested in what the campaign organization *does*. In this regard, it is safe to assume that there are four sets of activities: campaign operations, research, public relations, and finance. Each of these is needed to reach the voters, and each will be carried out by persons located somewhere within any campaign organization.

Where to Campaign?

Of all the decisions made in a campaign, those which concern geographic concentration have the most extensive implications for what the campaign organization does. Many things that will affect the outcome of an election—the attitudes the voters have at the outset of a campaign, the positions set forth by the opposition candidate—are beyond the control of the campaign managers. They can make decisions, though, about how they will use the resources they control. Essentially this refers to where the candidate will campaign, where money will be spent, and what organizational efforts will be made. Given finite time and finite resources, which cannot be expended everywhere, there are obvious incentives to use them where there will be the greatest return in votes.

As long as we continue to elect our presidents through the Electoral College, and as long as the states cast all of their electoral votes for

---

[4] One could argue that a losing campaign is the best to study. There are likely to be just as many organizational problems in a winning campaign organization, but the euphoria that goes with victory tends to hide these problems from participants and observers.

the candidate receiving a plurality in the state,[5] this decision is going
to be geographic. There are 538 electoral votes in all, and since the
number of votes cast is roughly proportional to the state's population,
there is a premium on carrying large states. If they all voted for the
same candidate, the 12 largest states—after the 1980 census, California,
New York, Texas, Pennsylvania, Illinois, Ohio, Florida, Michigan, New
Jersey, Massachusetts, North Carolina, and either Indiana *or* Georgia
or Virginia—could elect a president regardless of what the other 38
did. If the Electoral College were to be abolished, then the emphasis
would shift to ways and means of getting the largest majorities of
popular votes. It is conceivable that such a decision might be made
on a nongeographic basis, such as a campaign aimed at middle-class
voters; but for the present, the decisions rest on the traditional criteria.

The decision is likely to be made at the highest levels of the campaign
organization. The way it is made depends on the quality of information
available to the decision makers, and how systematic their analysis
is. As long ago as 1932, James A. Farley was making decisions based
on analyses of probable Democratic majorities in each state.

> Acting on the principle that success can do its own succeeding without
> help from anyone, the Democratic National Committee merely adapted
> its campaign expenditures to Mr. Hurja's method. A campaign chairman,
> with the evenhanded justice of a blinded divinity, would spill his funds
> equitably and inefficiently over an entire map. Armed with the Hurja
> prognostication Mr. Farley . . . tempered the wind to the shorn lamb,
> turned the hose on the dry ground, and made his nickels last. (*Fortune*,
> April 1935, p. 136, quoted in Herring, 1940)

In 1976 and 1980, both parties made their decisions about geographic
concentration quite systematically. In 1976, Hamilton Jordan wrote a
long memorandum for Jimmy Carter and Walter Mondale in which
31 pages were devoted to formulas to determine the amount of effort
to be devoted to each state. These formulas reflected three criteria:
size, Democratic potential, and need. Size reflected the number of electoral votes cast. There were four categories of Democratic potential
which reflected the state's likelihood of voting Democratic if worked
effectively. The estimates of need were based on four pieces of information: strategic premises, survey information, whether Carter had campaigned in a primary election in the state, and the results of that primary. Finally, the entire percent-of-effort computation (based on size,
Democratic potential, and need) was matched against a "value of a

---

[5] Seemingly forgotten in the recurring discussion about possible elimination of the
Electoral College is the state's power to cast its electoral votes in some other way
than by giving all of them to the candidate winning a plurality. Michigan cast its electoral
votes by congressional district in 1892, and its right to do so was upheld by the Supreme
Court in *Shoemaker* v. *United States* (Corwin, 1948, pp. 50, 418).

day's campaigning" estimate, in which Jimmy Carter, for example, was assigned 7 points and Chip Carter only 2 points to determine how often spokespersons for the ticket ought to go into a state (Schram, 1977, pp. 239–50, 386–91).

The 1976 Republican plan was quite different. It was a long document that took into account the position in which Ford found himself (far behind Carter) and the voters' perceptions of the candidates, and then set forth a strategy to change those perceptions so they would be more favorable to Ford. A threefold classification of states—"our base," "swing states," and "his base"—was included in this strategy plan. In general, the classification of states by the Republican strategy group was similar to Jordan's, except that the Republican group had a much longer list of swing states, and they saw Ford's base as being much smaller than the Carter base envisioned by Jordan.

In 1980, the allocation of resources to states in the Democratic campaign was governed by a document known as the "Orange Book." A regression analysis of the Democratic presidential vote from 1956 through 1976 yielded estimates of turnout, average Democratic vote, and "persuadability." Three states were classified as "safe," 4 as "marginal plus," 24 as "marginal," 3 as "marginal minus," and 17 as "lost." This classification was based essentially on the mean Democratic vote from 1956 through 1976, although 11 states had their classifications shifted because of special considerations. For example, Massachusetts was shifted from safe to marginal plus because of the attractiveness of John Anderson to Bay State voters, and Georgia was shifted from marginal to safe because it was Carter's home state. No resources were to be devoted to the safe states or the lost states, and twice as many resources were to be devoted to the marginal states as to the marginal-plus or the marginal-minus states. For example, 10.8 percent of all effort was to be devoted to New York because the Empire State was on the marginal list, and because it cast 41 electoral votes. Thus, Democratic targeting was a function of the likelihood of a state's voting Democratic, and of the number of its electoral votes.[6]

The 1980 Reagan strategy had a regional character, but it wasn't based on regional assumptions. The strategists' first assumption, based on survey data, was that whatever electoral base Jimmy Carter had assembled in 1976 no longer existed by 1980. They further assumed that Ronald Reagan could not be presumed to have an electoral base because he had never been a candidate in a general election. Their third assumption was that, since Governor Reagan was a conservative candidate who would move toward the center in the course of the campaign, the election was likely to turn on states where there were

---

[6] Further calculations extended this reasoning down to the county and media market level.

large numbers of independent and moderate voters, specifically a few Great Lakes states. Not surprisingly, when Richard Wirthlin, Richard Beal, and their colleagues began to count electoral votes most likely to be cast for Reagan, they came from the West, the Pacific Coast to the plains states, plus Indiana and Virginia. This initial Reagan base added up to 162 electoral votes, which was important because it meant that there were several different ways they could get from there to the needed 270. When Texas, Florida, Iowa, and Kentucky were added, the Reagan base was increased to 213. This meant that the election could be won by carrying any two of the four Great Lakes target states: Illinois, Michigan, Ohio, and Pennsylvania. (New Jersey, Connecticut, and Mississippi were alternate targets in case three Great Lakes states eluded them.) Therefore, advertising and organizational efforts were fairly soft in the West, a little heavier in the Pacific Northwest, still heavier in Texas, Florida, Missouri, Kentucky, and Virginia, and concentrated as much as possible in the four Great Lakes target states.

While the tendency toward the systematic use of campaign resources has become much more pronounced in recent years, campaigners do not always make rational decisions. In 1960, Richard Nixon pledged to visit all 50 states; in order to do so, he devoted most of the Sunday before the election to a long flight to Alaska, a state that cast barely 1 percent of the electoral votes needed. During the final week of the 1964 campaign, Barry Goldwater visited four great metropolitan centers, but he also devoted time to the voters in Dover, Delaware; Cedar Rapids, Iowa; Cheyenne, Wyoming; and Las Vegas, Nevada. These were not locations where the election was going to be won or lost. But even if the campaign managers do nothing more than acquiesce to local pressures—schedule the candidate where state leaders want him to come, and keep him away from areas where he is unpopular—this acquiescence is a decision that controls much of what the campaign does.

The Plane

Wherever it is decided that the candidate will go, there must be some way of moving him around, and this means "the plane."[7] The shift to aircraft as the primary means of moving the candidate around has been a gradual consequence of technological developments. The advent of jet aircraft meant that it was no longer possible to reject the plea of a West Coast politico for a presidential candidate's appearance on the grounds that he was campaigning in, say, Pennsylvania

---

[7] "The plane" appears in quotation marks because the phrase has a variety of meanings in conversations at campaign headquarters. It may refer to a "rival" headquarters, or the traveling party, or the present geographic location of the aircraft.

that day. Now it is possible to get him to the West Coast if the reason is sufficiently compelling. A second crucial step was the development of the Boeing 727; this made it possible to stay on the same aircraft and still get into smaller airports with shorter runways. Finally, the development of communications equipment (and having enough money to install it in the aircraft) meant reasonably constant communications between "the plane" and other campaign headquarters.

Campaign trains are still used, but as a way of evoking nostalgia for "traditional" politics, giving the television cameramen something different to shoot, and reaching groups of small- and medium-size cities that might affect important electoral votes. Thus, in 1976 Jimmy Carter took a whistlestop tour from Newark across New Jersey and Pennsylvania toward Chicago, hoping to evoke the spirit of Harry Truman's 1948 effort, and Gerald Ford campaigned across Illinois. And, of course, there is the motorcade that is used to move the candidate through suburban areas and back and forth from an airport to a rally site.

As is obvious, more is involved here than just moving the candidate himself. A considerable retinue accompanies him, and this sometimes complicates logistics. A plane, such as Peanut One that carried Jimmy Carter in 1976, or Yai Bi Kin (Navajo for House in the Sky) used by Barry Goldwater in 1964, usually carries senior advisors and friends, speechwriters, press secretary and aides, state dignitaries, Secret Service personnel, pool reporters, and the secretaries to help these people get their work done. The configuration of the plane must provide some privacy for the candidate, working space, an area for typewriters, mimeograph, photocopier, and communications equipment. Since there isn't enough space aboard the candidate's plane for the traveling press, there is also a press plane that follows along.

Scheduling

Responsibility for planning campaign trips is divided among four sets of persons: the strategy committee (or some ranking decision maker), regional and state coordinators and state party leaders, the tour committee, and advance men. The basic decisions about time allocations are made at the highest levels of the campaign in the manner already discussed. Questions about where the candidate will go within the state have been talked out between regional and state coordinators, and party leaders within the state. (This decision is beginning to move to national strategists as they have more refined ideas about the target audience *within* the state they want to reach. There was noticeable movement in this direction in the Reagan campaign in 1980. Needless to say, state leaders are not happy about losing control of a decison they have been accustomed to making.) The candidate's general schedule (3:00 P.M., press plane arrives Metropolitan Airport; 3:30 P.M., candidate plane arrives Metropolitan Airport; 3:45 P.M., candidate departs for Metro City Hotel; and so on) is worked out by a person on the tour committee.[8] Since the candidate will be making appearances in several cities in a single day, all of these details have to be combined into a master schedule. Finally, responsibility for arrangements in the community where the candidate is to appear is in the hands of an advance man.

The Advance Man

The person who advances a candidate's appearance usually gets to the city about five days to a week before the appearance. Any number of things must be done. The route between the airport and the rally site must be checked out and timed exactly in traffic conditions similar to those the candidate's motorcade will encounter. The rally site, whether an auditorium, shopping center, or whatever, must be checked out so it will accord with the candidate's preferences, and so that locations for the photographers and press traveling with the candidate will be available but not interfere with the voters who ought to be present. There may be problems with the prospective audience. For example, large numbers of local politicos will want to be close to the candidate, or too small an audience may be in prospect. In these cases, the advance man must cut the number of politicos down to a manageable size, and do what he can to increase the size of the crowd. If the candidate is staying overnight, hotel reservations must be made. Arrangements must be made with the local police to ensure the candidate's safety. If available, the Secret Service can be of great help with all this. They are familiar with the things that need to be done, and there is enough overlap between logistical needs and safety needs that many of the necessary arrangements fall into their province.

The advance man normally has the final say about all of the details of the appearance. There are certain to be things that will be disputed— who will have an opportunity to shake the candidate's hand, whose car will be how close to the candidate's in the motorcade, and so on—and it is up to the advance man to settle these matters.[9] Once

---

[8] The tour committee will typically have one person working on the presidential candidate's schedule; one on the vice presidential candidate's schedule; one handling party notables, such as ex-presidents; one handling celebrities, such as movie stars; and one or more coordinating the appearances of others working on behalf of the ticket.

[9] There are good reasons for this. The local party leaders have to work with each other after the rally, and the object of the whole campaign is to make the candidate more popular rather than less so. Consequently, if the local leaders are going to be angry with anyone, it is better that they be upset with the advance man rather than being angry with each other or with the candidate. Sometimes the advance man can avoid this altogther. If he has any experience, he can assure local leaders that his decisions are exactly in line with procedures followed in all the other campaign events being staged for the candidate.

the candidate shows up, the advance man is at his side and in charge of things as long as the candidate is in the city. When the candidate's plane leaves for the next city, where another advance man will have been setting things up, the advance man says good-bye and leaves for another city to make arrangements for another appearance some days hence (Hoagland, 1960; Ogden & Peterson, 1968, chap. 9).

Demographic Groups

The rest of the persons involved in campaign operations are usually organized along interest group or regional lines. The nature of a demographic group operation is suggested by the names of units that have been organized in one campaign or another: Youth for Reagan, Viva Kennedy, Scientists and Engineers for Johnson-Humphrey, Mothers for a Moral America, Pilots for Goldwater-Miller, Nationalities Division, Civil Rights Division, Citizens—Farm and Food, Funeral Directors Committee for the Reelection of the President, Motorcyclists Committee for the Reelection of the President, Heritage groups, Veteran Voter groups, and National McGovern-Shriver Labor Committee. Each of these campaign units is set up to reach a certain segment of the population. One must know something more than the name of the unit, of course, to be certain that it is a functioning part of the campaign organization. It may be only a paper committee that was set up to sponsor a campaign event, as was Mothers for a Moral America, or it may be essentially a fund-raising operation, in which one receives a membership card in return for the payment of dues.

Assuming that the campaign unit is more than a letterhead committee, it is likely to have certain characteristics. First, the target population must be large enough and have enough political importance for their support to be worth the expenditure of resources. Often attention will be devoted to areas where the party is weak. For example, the Republicans usually have a labor unit whereas the Democrats, who already have a lot of support from organized labor, will often omit a labor unit in their structure. Second, the person in charge of the effort has some knowledge of the population in question. Thus, an Arts and Sciences Division once organized by the Republican National Committee was headed by an academic on leave of absence, and the executive director of the Senior Citizens for Johnson and Humphrey was on leave from the United Automobile Workers' Department of Older and Retired Workers. Third, there needs to be some means of communicating with the target population. A not unusual pattern includes a mailing list and a newsletter. The essential job of the staff members heading these units is to explain the candidate and the positions being taken in language that their groups understand. If they are sufficiently persuasive, they may also convey the wishes of the population segment back to the campaign leaders.

Regional Groups

The alternate form of campaign organization follows geographic lines. In this form, the head of the campaign division will be assisted by regional directors. The regions used vary a little from one campaign to another, but generally adhere to familiar areas, such as the Middle Atlantic states, the Middle West, or the West Coast. If resources permit, a pair of regional directors is used for each area. This allows one to remain at campaign headquarters while the other travels in the region. When this arrangement is used, the codirectors change place every 10 days or so. This means that there is a familiar voice on the headquarters telephone when the state directors call in, and someone out in the field giving encouragement to campaign workers and gathering fresh information.

Establishing lines of communication through regional directors to state directors has the advantage of following the lines of the Electoral College, and the things that the regional directors do are directly related to producing electoral votes in their areas. As already noted, once the strategy group has decided that the candidate or other spokespersons will spend time in the state, then the regional director and the state chairperson are likely to be involved in the decision as to where the appearance should take place. Which areas of the state are most likely to produce votes for the ticket without any effort? Which areas may do so, but require some campaigning? What demographic groupings (located in what part of the state) are targets of state or national campaign strategies? These are factors that would be assessed in making a decision that the candidate ought to appear in, say, Rochester and Syracuse, but not in Buffalo.

Regional directors make similar judgments about states in their areas. This allows decisions to be made about allocations of resources. In 1960, for example, National Campaign Manager Robert Kennedy was told that Democratic prospects did not look good in Iowa, but there was a chance for his brother to carry Illinois. His response was simple: "We'll spend our money in Illinois."

A third activity of regional directors is coordination of straightforward registration and get-out-the-vote drives. Since registration is a major factor holding down election day turnout (Rosenstone & Wolfinger, 1978; Kelley, Ayers, & Bowen, 1967), and since Democrats are less likely to register than Republicans, Democratic campaigns are somewhat more prone to emphasize registration drives than are Republicans.[10] Both parties are interested in maximizing their turnout. The election day efforts to do this were simple in the small towns of

---

[10] The greater tendency for Democratic voters to remain unregistered accounts for the greater Democratic interest in schemes of automatic or permanent registration.

the 19th century. Each party had a poll watcher who knew the town's inhabitants. If supporters of his party did not show up by midafternoon, someone would be sent round to remind them to come and vote. The technique is still essentially the same, though its application has been made more complex by changes in the population, and more efficient through the use of telephones and computers.

For election day activity to be effective, it must be preceded by planning and by identifying one's supporters. One begins with an estimate of the total vote needed to carry a state. A new figure is necessary for each election because, with population growth, the vote that carried the state in the preceding election is likely to be inadequate. The total vote for the state is then decomposed into county quotas, these likewise based on knowledge of party strength and the county populations. If each county meets its quota, then the state goal will be reached.

Next, the county leaders must locate the voters who will enable them to meet their quota. If there is registration by party, they will have a pretty good idea where to start, but even where registration lists are available, additional work needs to be done. Population mobility brings any number of new residents to the community, and the greater incidence of independent voting makes it necessary to ascertain whether each "loyal Democrat" in fact intends to vote for the Democratic candidate. This has been done traditionally by precinct workers calling on voters in their areas. If funds are available to set up phone banks, however, voters can be contacted much more speedily by bringing volunteers together in a "boiler shop" from which telephone calls are placed. The calls usually include a gentle sales pitch; but the crucial elements are to determine whether persons living in the household intend to vote, whether they need any aid in doing so (such as transportation or a baby-sitter), and whether they intend to support the party's candidate, are undecided, or intend to vote for the opposition.

The immediate results of the telephone work provide information on how well the candidate is running. They are aggregated and forwarded up the line to state headquarters and national headquarters. But much of this information is fed into computers in order to provide useful lists and sets of address labels. Those undecided about which candidate to support are sent literature. Depending on the quality of the information elicited and the sophistication of the computer operation, voters may receive personal letters presenting arguments about the issues of concern to them. Those undecided about whether to vote receive extra calls just before the election encouraging them to do so. Names of persons who need transportation to the polls appear on special lists so this can be provided. And the names of all those likely to vote appear on lists that allow traditional election day contact to go forward.

This telephone and computer operation is simple enough to describe, but enormous amounts of effort are necessary to carry it out. During the 1972 Nixon campaign, nearly 16 million households were contacted in this way. More people were reached through this contact operation than had voted for Nixon in 1968. This undoubtedly represented the high point of this kind of campaigning. Some $12 million was poured into this contact operation (White, 1973, pp. 322–28), and money that would allow citizen contact on this lavish a scale is not available under the campaign laws that went into effect in 1974.

RESEARCH

The "research" that is needed in the middle of a campaign has very little to do with academic research. The aim of campaign research is not the discovery of information that may be regarded as a contribution to knowledge. There is an element of discovery in polls taken to determine voters' perceptions, but much more campaign research involves processing already available information so it can be used for electoral purposes. When one speaks of research in campaign headquarters, the usual reference is to the activities of the people who work in a research division. They are the speechwriters, "issue persons," pollsters, and some individuals whose tasks are similar to those of reference librarians.

The Art of Producing Campaign Speeches

The speech that is given most often during a campaign is not written at all. It evolves. The speech is a pastiche of applause lines the candidate has discovered in previous months of campaigning. It is a "theme song" made up of phrases the candidate likes, and which have demonstrated their ability to spark crowd reaction. It includes such lines as John Kennedy's "It's time to get America moving again," George Wallace's references to "pointy-headed bureaucrats who send us guidelines telling us when we can go to sleep at night and when we can get up in the morning," Richard Nixon's 1968 declaration that "It's time for new leadership," and Jimmy Carter's 1976 promise, "I'll never lie to you." Such a speech is used during the numerous brief stops when "remarks" are called for. There are too many of these for anything approaching an original statement to be developed for each, and neither a tired candidate nor a weary speechwriter has any desire to depart from the familiar. The repetition is tedious to the candidate and to reporters who have heard the lines dozens of times, but repetition helps develop a candidate's image in the same way that endless exposure to Alka-Seltzer or Pepto-Bismol commercials fix the names of these products in the minds of television viewers.

Major addresses on foreign policy, economics, welfare, civil rights, or whatever, are quite different. When a candidate is making a major speech to, say, the Detroit Council on Foreign Relations, or giving an address on nationwide television, he is expected to state a position with some precision. Speeches for these occasions are carefully considered, and often pass through several drafts. Just how the candidate and the speechwriters work together in such circumstances varies considerably. Theodore Sorenson drafted most of John Kennedy's speeches in 1960; and those he did not write, he at least reviewed. Most speech topics Sorenson "discussed with the Senator only, and they were decided by him, in his plane or hotel and without reference to other materials, a day or two before the speech was given" (Sorenson, 1965, p. 208). In 1968, Richard Nixon worked with a number of speechwriters, and set forth what he wanted in memoranda or oral instructions. For example, in late September he distributed a memorandum asking for excerpts running a page to a page and a half. The excerpts, he said, should be

> meaty and quotable and . . . zero in primarily on the four major themes. If we scatter-gun too much we are not going to have an impact. . . . We must have at least two excerpts a week which hit some aspect of the law and order theme and one or two a week which hit some aspect of the spending theme and two or three a week which hit the foreign policy-respect for America theme. (Safire, 1975, pp. 71–72)

In a third pattern, members of the strategy group agree that certain material is called for, and set a speechwriter to work on it. For example, late in the 1976 campaign, Jody Powell and Greg Schneiders agreed with speechwriter Patrick Anderson that material was needed for a Pittsburgh dinner that would show Carter knew about the difficulties caused by poor leadership but was optimistic about the future. Anderson wrote a speech including a number of "I see" lines—"I see a new spirit in America. I see a national pride restored. I see a revival of patriotism" (Schram, 1977, p. 344). A similar series of "I see" lines were used in Carter's acceptance speech. For that matter, such lines had been written by William Safire for Richard Nixon in 1968, used by Barry Goldwater in 1964, written by Samuel Rosenman and Robert E. Sherwood for Franklin Roosevelt, and used by Robert Ingersoll when he nominated James G. Blaine for president in 1876 (Safire, 1975, p. 54).

In the case of any major address, drafts flow back and forth between the candidate and the speechwriters. This allows the candidate to continue making changes until he gets what he wants. For example, Patrick Anderson wrote for Jimmy Carter, "When I started to run for president, there were those who said that I would fail, because there was another governor who spoke for the South, a man who once stood in a schoolhouse door and cried out, segregation forever!" Carter, not wishing to insult George Wallace unnecessarily, changed the reason to "there were those who said I would fail because I was from the South" (Schram, 1977, p. 180). Toward the end of the 1968 campaign, Richard Nixon wanted to make a statement concerning then President Lyndon Johnson. As drafted by Bryce Harlow, it began, "Throughout this campaign the President has been evenhanded and straightforward with the major presidential contenders about Vietnam. I know he has been under intense pressure to contrive a fake peace." Nixon altered this to read, "Throughout this campaign I have found the President impartial and candid with the major presidential contenders about Vietnam. I know he has been subjected—for many months, beginning long before the national convention—to intense pressure to contrive what he has appropriately described as a fake peace." (Safire, 1975, p. 85). While the circumstances of a campaign hardly allow a candidate to write every word that he speaks or is released in his name, the speech-writing process certainly allows him to place his personal tone on important texts.

Insofar as the term *speechwriter* suggests that a writer is in control of the process, and the candidate simply reads the words, it distorts what goes on as a candidate presents his ideas to the electorate. Raymond Moley, who wrote speeches for Governor Franklin Roosevelt in 1932, described the process much more clearly. He distinguished between "the principal" who gives the addresses, "the collaborator" who has continuous access to the principal and provides him with drafts, and "the feeders" who route their ideas to the collaborator (1960). The collaborator needs to have a facility with words and some political experience; but more important, the collaborator should have the confidence of the principal, a knowledge of the phrasing the principal likes to use, and a willingness to set forth the ideas the principal wants to use whether the collaborator thinks the ideas are wise or not.

The feeders may be "issues persons" in the campaign organization proper, or they may be interested citizens who simply want to pass ideas along. Their existence does not imply that either the candidate or the speechwriters are barren of ideas themselves, but rather that many ideas are needed in the course of a campaign and a rather large number of people think they have ideas that are going to win the election for the candidate. The combination of a need for good ideas, and a need for enough working time to develop substantive proposals so they will be helpful to the candidate, leads to a unique organizational imperative. There must be some kind of screen to protect the issues staff and the speechwriters from the large number of people who want to help but don't quite know how; yet at the same time, there must be some provision so that good ideas do get through.

New Ideas and the Triple Test

While there are likely to be many good ideas, the number of usable ideas tends to be limited. This may come as a surprise to persons who have not been through a presidential campaign, but there are a number of tests any idea must pass before it is politically useful. If a candidate takes a position that gives offense to any group in the supporting coalition, they may not work for him with continued fervor. If the candidate takes a position that is unappealing to a target constituency, this will reduce the number of votes he might otherwise receive. Furthermore, once a proposal is made, it is certain to be scrutinized by both the opposition and the media. If the program is inconsistent with some previously taken position, the candidate will be asked which of the policies he intends to pursue seriously. If he chooses the earlier policy, the just-announced program will be called frivolous. If he chooses the just-announced policy, he will be accused of inconsistency. If he says he will implement both policies, opponents and reporters will say that he has not thought through the consequences of what he says. Finally, the proposal should be one that can be accomplished with the resources available to the government. It is this triple test—the proposal must be acceptable to coalition members and voters who are potential supporters, consistent with previously announced positions, and something that can be done with existing resources—that limits the number of ideas that are usable in a campaign.

In consequence, the chief qualification of a good issues person is the ability to sense which ideas pass this triple test and should therefore be brought to the attention of the candidate and the speechwriters. This is likely to be someone motivated by an interest in the substance of politics, and with enough previous campaign experience not to be a dogmatic advocate of any particular approach. Persons who have these skills—for example, Bryce Harlow or Bill Prendergast in the Republican party and Ted Van Dyk or John Stewart in the Democratic party—are apt to be well known in the upper echelons of presidential politics and almost invisible to the general public. Because of their reputations with words and issues, they have been involved in the issues end of several campaigns.

In any particular campaign, there is likely to be a small in-house issues staff, and a larger number of outside consultants. The head of the in-house issues staff will be one who has worked with the candidate for some time. Outside consultants are active in many areas, but there are usually special groups dealing with the imperative policy areas of international involvement and economic management. Thus, Jimmy Carter's 1976 issues staff was headed by Stuart Eizenstat, a Harvard Law School graduate who had written speeches in the Johnson White House and had been involved in Humphrey's 1968 issues staff. Zbigniew

Brzezinski, who had taught at Harvard and Columbia, served as a principal advisor on international affairs, and Laurence R. Klein, who taught at the Wharton School and was then president-elect of the American Econometric Association, headed a team of economic consultants. In 1980, Richard Allen, a Washington-based foreign policy consultant, was designated as "senior foreign policy advisor," and Hoover Institution economist Martin Anderson was designated as "senior domestic policy advisor" on the Reagan staff. Both had been members of the 1968 Nixon and the 1976 Reagan campaign staffs.

Polling's Changing Role

The importance of polling has been increasing for some time. This is evident both in the location of the principal pollster within the campaign staff and in the sophistication of the information about the voters that is provided. Private polls for candidates, of course, are not new, but as recently as the 1960s, they were used in a rather rudimentary manner. Older politicians regarded surveys with some skepticism, and even proponents seemed fascinated by any similarity between survey results and election results. The usual pattern was to hire an outside polling firm whose head would come in occasionally during the campaign to present findings. Otherwise, liaison with the polling firm was maintained by a relatively low-ranking staff member. The reliability of the data was kept high through large numbers of interviews, and the presentation of results was restricted to marginals (that is, 57 percent for Candidate A and 43 percent for Candidate B) and very simple cross-tabulations. In the 1964 Goldwater campaign, for example, three national surveys of this kind were taken. The reports were kept by an intelligent young graduate of Stanford Law School (who had no training in survey analysis), and the last scheduled survey was cancelled because the surveys were bringing bad news.

This situation changed, not because of arguments about the importance of surveys, but because successful politicians put great reliance on them. Ray Bliss was known to study his polls very closely, and knowledgeable analysts (especially Louis Harris among the Democrats and Walter deVries among the Republicans) spread the word about what could be done. By 1976, pollsters were principal members of the strategy groups in both parties. Robert Teeter of Market Opinion Research provided continuous information for the Republicans, and Pat Caddell did the same for the Democrats. In 1980, Richard Wirthlin of Decision/Making/Information was one of four senior decision makers on the Republican side, and Pat Caddell continued to play a similar role for the Democrats.

Not only were pollsters located where they could be much more active in charting campaign strategy, but the kind of information they provided was much more detailed. In 1968, David Derge based his analysis for the Nixon campaign on a panel study of voters in 13 states and small daily cross-sections. The state-level data gave information on where campaign resources should be concentrated, and the daily information allowed him to pick up trends as they began to develop. Pat Caddell similarly had daily information that he could provide to the Carter campaign in 1976 and 1980. In 1976, he was able to tell them early on that Carter's support was soft; and as it eroded during the campaign, he was able to point to particular segments of the electorate as contributing disproportionately to Democratic difficulties. Caddell's daily information was accurate enough in 1980 to give him the sad task of telling Carter on election eve, "Mr. President, I'm afraid it's gone."

Robert Teeter added a number of useful analyses for the Republicans in 1976. Telephone polls allowed quick answers of interest to strategists; picked audiences watched the debates, indicating their agreement with the candidates by adjusting rheostats; spatial analyses summarized information on where candidates stood with respect to each other and the voters (Schram, 1977; Parry, 1977). By 1980, Richard Wirthlin and Richard Beal had put together a Political Information System (PINS) that incorporated a great deal of polling data from various sources, and allowed Reagan leaders to simulate the probable consequences of various campaign strategies. The movement from simple cross-tabulations to multidimensional scaling (the type of spatial analysis used to produce Figures 4-1 and 4-2)[11] and simulation, in little more than a decade's time, is a measure of the progress made in using survey information; but having knowledgeable pollsters sitting in on strategy discussions is more important in making effective use of these data.

Information Retrieval in a Campaign

While pollsters and other professionals are making use of survey data at the top levels of campaigns, the "reference librarians" of politics busy themselves storing information so it can be made available when needed and can be distributed throughout the campaign organization. Files are kept of statements made by one's own candidates, and by opposition candidates. The purpose of this is to allow a quick check of what has actually been said when an opponent makes a charge during the campaign. If, for example, an opponent says, "Speaking in Houston last October, the president promised to reduce unemployment to 5 percent," and it is possible for the campaign committee to reply, "The president said that he hoped to reduce unemployment as quickly

---

[11] One wonders what the reaction of the politicos would be if they had any idea of the assumptions necessary to sustain multidimensional scaling.

as possible, but did not mention any specific target," and to release the exact quotation, this can be very helpful in rebutting the charge.

Another standard activity is the production of speaker's manuals and issue books. Stock speeches are written on various issues, and booklets summarize the stands being taken by both parties. These will be broken down by topic and will have facts and quotations showing the virtues of the party's stand juxtaposed with the limitations of what the opposition is doing. These are arranged so that a speaker will be able to find an effective reply even as he or she listens to opposition statements.

A third headquarters project is an "answer desk" with a well-advertised telephone number. The persons who take the incoming calls are likely to be political veterans whose qualifications are similar to those working on the issues staff, and who provide quick replies to what the party's stand is on energy or agriculture or whatever the caller is concerned about. All of these activities are routine. A fair amount of work is necessary, though, to prepare for these tasks, and to keep the files up to date as the campaign develops.

PUBLIC RELATIONS

Gerald Rafshoon. Peter Dailey. John Deardourff. Douglas Bailey. These men are typical of the publicists who carry senior responsibility in political campaigns. Rafshoon and Dailey came from advertising. Gerald Rafshoon Advertising, Inc., is a general advertising firm (that is, the bulk of its income comes from nonpolitical accounts) in Atlanta. Peter Dailey formed Dailey and Associates in Los Angeles in 1968 after gaining experience in some very large advertising firms. Rafshoon, whose ties with Jimmy Carter went back to the first Carter gubernatorial campaign in 1966, was in charge of public relations in both Carter presidential campaigns. Peter Dailey was in charge of the media campaign in 1972, worked on space acquisition during the 1976 Ford campaign, and was again in charge of the Reagan advertising in 1980. Deardourff and Bailey, on the other hand, have a firm that specializes in politics. Both came from a background in Republican politics, Deardourff in New York and Bailey in Massachusetts, and both learned enough about media campaigns that they set up their own campaign management firm.

Being at the center of a campaign organization is not new for publicists. Of all the things done by an electoral coalition to reach their primary audience, public relations is one of the most crucial and has been so recognized for a very long time. Public relations emerged as a distinct occupation in the early decades of the 20th century, and political applications were not too long in coming. Charles Michelson was a member of the Democratic strategy group in 1932; and in 1936, a Chicago advertising man, Hill Blackett, became the Republican's first public relations director (Kelley, 1956, chap. 1).

In developments since that time, the direction of public relations has most commonly been handled by a combination of an in-house public relations division and either a public relations or a campaign management firm. As television has become more important, so have the media specialists. This is *not* to say that public relations men have taken control of campaigns. Public relations is only one segment of a campaign, and the influence of a public relations firm ranges from a maximum, when one of their chiefs sits on the strategy group with the other principals, to a minimum when the agency is restricted to the technical functions of space and time acquisition. Still, the great days of party public relations directors probably came in the 1950s, with Jack Redding and Sam Brightman in the Democratic party, and Robert Humphreys and Lou Guylay in the Republican party. With television so prominent in the 1980s, it was all but inevitable that influence would flow to the Rafshoons, Daileys, Deardourffs, and Baileys who know how to work with that medium.

To keep these things in perspective, it may help to remember that everything but the television material usually comes from the public relations division within the campaign organization. Even in Charles Michelson's time, this was not inconsiderable. Working in an era before electronic media began to rival newspapers, Michelson concentrated on getting stories and phrases into print. He sent statements to prominent Democrats whose names would draw public attention. He sent news items and editorial suggestions directly to newspapers. His basic assumption was that he wanted to create anti-Hoover news, a task that became much easier once the depression began (Kelley, 1956, p. 31).

Newspaper Contact

Michelson's one-man operation evolved into what amounted to a small public relations firm within the national committee staff. This public relations division had a number of responsibilities. First of all, it worked directly with the Washington-based press. This meant the distribution of press releases. These included speeches and statements of the presidential candidate, which were made available in Washington at the same time that they were released on the campaign plane, but also statements by other party leaders as well. (If one wished to attack the opposition candidate directly, such a statement might come from a recognized partisan figure, such as the national chairman. In this way, the presidential candidate could maintain a more statesman-like manner.) Dealing with the press also meant answering media queries. This is less time-consuming now that most of the major media have their political reporters traveling with the candidate, but it still involves some effort.

An activity growing directly out of Michelson's distribution of materials is the press service. This is directed at the weekly newspapers published around the country. Most of them operate with much tighter resources than the dailies, and have no Washington contacts. They are quite willing to run material if it can be provided. Consequently, canned news articles, features, editorials, and photographs are sent out, often in mat format to make reproduction as simple as possible.

Brochures, Bumper Stickers, and Other Campaign Material

A third group of public relations personnel is concerned with art and production. Having an artist available means that pamphlets and brochures can be designed to say exactly what party leaders want them to say. Once the pamphlets are ready to go, they are turned over to a commercial printer in the Washington area. Samples are sent around the country, and anyone wanting them for distribution orders them directly from the printer. The production department also has a small offset press. Photoreproduction makes it possible to make copies of newspaper articles that appear. Obviously, it is an advantage to have favorable comments coming from neutral reporters since their source credibility is so much higher.

The production department is also involved with party publications and campaign newsletters. These, of course, are frankly partisan since they are directed to an audience of committed activists. They vary all the way from one-page, mimeographed newsletters to slickly produced small magazines. With the rise of sustaining memberships, these party publications fit into a useful dual relation. Supporters receive "subscriptions" when they make contributions. Hence, these publications bring in money at the same time that they provide a channel for the distribution of party propaganda.

Campaign materials—bumper stickers, campaign buttons, balloons, hats, inflatable elephants and donkeys, and all the rest—are produced commercially. The public relations division may, to be sure, suggest the wording for a bumper sticker to a friendly supplier, but for the most part, these initiatives come from those who want to make money from the campaign. The task for the public relations division is simply to catalog all these materials and send copies of the catalog out through party channels to persons who might buy them. From that point on, the transactions take place between the buyer and the manufacturer (Guylay, 1960; Cotter & Hennessy, 1964, pp. 129–33).

If any materials are prepared for the electronic media by the public relations staff at campaign headquarters, they are likely to be for radio. There are two reasons for this. Radio spots do not require the elaborate technical facilities needed for television. And since radio time is so much less expensive than television time, it is more feasible for local committees to sponsor radio spots. When that is done, the local sponsors can obtain tapes through the campaign headquarters.

Television

Television materials come from the advertising agency or campaign management firm that has been hired.[12] If there is an advertising section in the headquarters public relations staff, the chances are that its chief activity is liaison with the outside agency. The core of the agency responsibility—that is, the task it handles even if it does nothing else— is the purchase of advertising space (if print media are being used) and television time. This is a technical task that a campaign headquarters is not equipped to undertake. A good advertising agency can immediately translate, by computer, a desired geographic concentration to a number of spots that must be purchased in given market areas. It also knows which programs to buy in order to attract either a large audience or one that has certain characteristics. In 1976, for example, large numbers of Jimmy Carter commercials appeared on "Hee-Haw" and the "Lawrence Welk Show" because large numbers of potential Carter voters watched these programs (Lelyveld, 1976a). The television time itself is sold by station representatives to time buyers in the ad agencies. Given that much political time is purchased late, and that other advertisers are competing for the same time spots (General Motors, General Foods, and all the rest don't suspend their sales campaigns just because there is an election in the offing.), it is in the interests of politicos to have the time buying done by professionals who have been dealing with the sales representatives for a long time. In other words, tell the agency what kind of audience is sought, and leave the decision about how the audience will be reached in its hands.

If there is a heavy concentration on a media campaign—and in 1980, the Carter campaign spent $20.5 million and the Reagan campaign $16.8 million of the federally supplied $29.4 million on mass media advertising—the agency is going to do more than just buy time. The central charge of the media campaign is to devise some way of communicating the candidate's strengths to the voters. There is no single way of doing

---

[12] There is another possibility besides an advertising agency or a campaign management firm. This is the creation of an ad hoc "firm" composed of professional advertising personnel who take leaves of absence from their own firms. This arrangement was used in the 1960 and 1972 Nixon campaigns and the 1980 Reagan campaign. In 1960, the "firm" was called Campaign Associates; in 1972, the November Group; and in 1980, Campaign '80.

this. There are as many variations as there are advertising personnel and candidates. In 1968, Harry Treleaven built a campaign for Nixon around two things. He used commercials made from montages of still photographs, with Nixon's voice on an accompanying sound track. This took advantage of Nixon's greater attractiveness on radio, where only his voice was heard. He also set up a series of studio question-and-answer sessions that allowed Nixon to answer relatively easy questions and thus exhibit his knowledge and experience (McGinniss, 1969). In 1972, the central theme of the campaign was "Reelect the President," not a bad idea since "the President" was undoubtedly more popular than "Richard M. Nixon" (Greenstein, 1974, p. 137).

In the case of Jimmy Carter in 1976, Jerry Rafshoon departed from the general belief that a short commercial was better because of a limited viewer tolerance for politics. He produced five minute and two-minute advertisements on the assumption that Carter was still credible after one had listened to him for a while, and that more time was needed to let that credibility come across to the viewer (Lelyveld, 1976a). In 1980, when the Democratic strategy called for drawing as sharp a distinction between Carter and Reagan as possible, Rafshoon's cameras focused on an empty Oval Office while an announcer asked the audience: "What kind of person should occupy the Oval Office? Should it be . . . Ronald Reagan . . . who attacks the minimum wage and calls unemployment insurance a prepaid vacation? Or should another kind of man sit here, an experienced man who knows how to be responsive to all Americans?"

Since one of the points that the Republican strategists wanted to establish was that Reagan *was* qualified, a frequently used Peter Dailey commercial showed film clips of Reagan as governor while an announcer boasted: "In 1966 he was elected governor of the state of California, next to the president the biggest job in the nation. What he inherited was a state of crisis. . . . Governor Reagan got things back on track." Many Reagan commercials also featured Ronald Reagan speaking as he looked directly into the camera to take advantage of his professional fluency with words and his ability to present a simple and convincing argument.

The themes that are selected to reach the voter are, of course, subject to change. October 25, 1968, and October 19, 1976, both found candidates in New York City. The importance of New York in the Electoral College makes attention to the area almost standard in the closing days of campaigns, but in these instances, candidate Nixon and candidate Carter were both recording new commercials for use in the closing days of the campaigns. Both had started far ahead of their rivals, and both had seen their margins grow smaller and smaller with the passage of time. So now they were trying for themes that would keep them ahead. The aim of the Carter spots was to reassure women voters and to shore up support in the South, two audiences whose judgments about Carter had been trending downward in 1976 (Witcover, 1977, pp. 622–23; Schram, 1977, pp. 330–32; McGinniss, 1969, chap. 1).

While the media specialists are important, it would be well to conclude this discussion with two caveats. First, they cannot erase a candidate's weaknesses. They can remind voters of a candidate's strengths, but advertising could not make Richard Nixon come across as a warm and open human being, or portray Ronald Reagan as having a first-class mind, or convince reporters that Jimmy Carter was being precise on the issues. Second, advertising does not create an entire campaign. As is evident from the other parts of this chapter, public relations is only one part of a campaign. The basic decisions are made by the candidates and the strategy groups on which they rely. The media specialists may be represented in the strategy groups, and if they are skillful, they may be persuasive. But theirs are not the only voices.

RAISING THE MONEY

All the activity we have been discussing increases the ability of the electoral coalition to reach the voters. If a candidate can be moved at jet speed across the country, he will be able to reach more widely dispersed voters than a candidate could when campaigns moved along the rails from one town to another. If pollsters have daily telephone surveys, they can estimate public reaction with vastly more precision than when campaign managers had to rely on such cues as crowd size and how loudly they cheered. If the candidates can reach an audience of 100 million people on television, they are in simultaneous contact with more people than lived in the entire country when Woodrow Wilson was president.[13] So a good case can be made that these developments help make the democratic process more effective. At the same time, many of the same developments have made campaigning much more expensive. Therefore, new methods of fund raising have been necessary.

The Increasing Cost of Campaigning

For some time, the costs of presidential campaigns were relatively stable, at least when compared with changes elsewhere in American society. In 1884, the campaigns of both Blaine and Cleveland cost some $2.7 million. Costs went up and down in ensuing years. The campaigns

---

[13] This is a very high figure. It is the estimated size of the audiences for the first Ford-Carter debate in 1976, and the Carter-Reagan debate in 1980. These were the largest audiences for any political events up to that time.

of 1920, 1928, and 1936 were more expensive than the contests just preceding or just following. But as late as 1948, the costs of the Dewey and Truman campaigns together were estimated at $4.9 million. The costs of campaigning increased some 80 percent, but over 64 years. By 1972, however, the costs of the Nixon and McGovern campaigns had reached $91.4 million. The institution of public funding in 1976 began a different system of finance, but the cost of presidential campaigns had gone up an astronomic 1,879 percent in the 24 years between 1948 and 1972 (Alexander, 1980, p. 5).

What had led to this near 19-fold increase? Part of the cause was specific to 1972: the orgy of spending by the Nixon reelection campaign. They raised and spent some $61.4 million, roughly the amount used by *all* parties for *all* candidates four years earlier. But a more fundamental reason is the cost of the items we have been discussing. The campaign train used by Democrat James Cox in 1920 cost that campaign $20,000; it cost the Republicans $3.9 million to transport their candidates and battalions of surrogates and advance men in 1972. Polling was nonexistent in an earlier day. The 1968 Nixon campaign spent some $384,000 on surveys, and the Humphrey campaign put out $262,000 for theirs. The biggest factor in the constantly increasing costs, though, has been television. In 1948, the last year of principal reliance on radio, the Republicans spent about $500,000 and the Democrats over $600,000 on that medium. In 1952, however, the parties spent about $6.1 million, split about equally between radio and television. From there the media costs went to $9.8 million, $14.2 million, $24.6 million, and $40.4 million in 1956, 1960, 1964, and 1968, respectively, with about twice as much being spent on television as on radio each year. Media costs actually dropped a bit in 1972, primarily because the Republicans put so much effort into the voter contact effort described earlier (Alexander, 1972, 1976).

Professional Fund Raising

While the amount of money needed for political campaigns is modest when compared to commercial advertising, campaign organizations need persons who know how to raise substantial amounts of cash. Professional fund raising came to national politics in 1937 in the person of Carlton G. Ketchum, a professional fund raiser from Pittsburgh. He convinced the Republicans to undertake systematic fund raising based on a number of principles that he had found effective in raising money for private causes. First, there was to be a single fund drive each year so donors would not be subject to repeated appeals. Second, national needs were to be divided into state quotas based on such factors as population and wealth. (The needs of the states and counties where the money was being raised would be added to their national quotas at the time of their annual fund drive.) Third, the money was to be raised by a separate finance committee. This reduced the problem of contributors who wanted to be political strategists, and placed a "fire wall" between the party and any persons who might expect an explicit quid pro quo for making a contribution. Fourth, the fund drives were to be in the hands of professionals, often hired from Ketchum, Inc., for the duration of the fund-raising effort. Many of these principles were neglected in practice. There were emergency drives for individual candidates; many states failed to meet the quotas assigned to them. Still, the basic structure was adopted, and still exists within the Republican party. The system places the Republican National Finance Committee in the same posture as a United Fund. The finance committee must negotiate with the candidates and organizations about the amount of money they need, and they must negotiate with the states about the amount of money they are willing to raise (Heard, 1960, pp. 212–19; Ogden & Peterson, 1968, pp. 284–85).

In spite of this fundamental restructuring, a good deal of improvisation marked fund raising in both parties during the following decades. Both parties raised money any way they could think of—fund-raising dinners, private meetings with leading party figures, personal appeals by candidates to their wealthy friends, and so on. Until the 1960s, a number of things held true. Other things being equal, Republicans were able to raise more money than Democrats, in part because of better access to possible donors, in part because of the Ketchum system just described. One of the things that was not equal was control of the White House. The party in power could raise money with relative ease, while the party out of power had great difficulty in doing so. Neither party began a campaign with enough cash on hand. This prevented budgeting, meant that cash was often required to acquire needed services, and also meant that campaign organizations often had to pay a premium to acquire things (e.g., television time) at the last moment. The net of all this is that both parties ran up debts to finance presidential campaigns, and both hoped they would win in order to be able to pay off the debt with the help of an incumbent president. For example, by the end of the 1960 campaign, the Democrats had a debt of $3.5 million, and the Republicans had a debt of $750,000. With the help of John Kennedy in the White House, though, the Democrats retired all but $500,000 of their debt by early 1963; the Republicans only got their originally much smaller debt down to $225,000 by early 1964 (Cotter & Hennessy, 1964, p. 174). Two developments of the 60s and 70s changed this situation: mass fund appeals and federal financing.

Mass Fund Appeals

Mass fund appeals had been discussed for a long time. There were some obvious advantages to the idea. If the parties could develop a mass base, they would reduce their dependence on large givers and identify a cadre of party supporters. Solicitations for small contributions had been tried on several occasions—for example, by the Republicans in the late 30s and in a Dollars for Democrats drive in the late 50s— but without producing enough revenue to effect any real change in party financing. There were problems. One was the administrative cost of processing a small contribution. After proper records had been made, the donor thanked, and so on, the parties often lost money. Another element was time. It took less time to ask one large donor than a host of small donors, and, in a campaign, money was often needed in a hurry.

The first successful mass fund drive was sponsored by the Republicans in the early 60s under the stimulus of a real financial shortage. The Republican National Committee did not have enough money for its staff operation, since the Democrats were in the White House, and most Republican money was going to the congressional committees in anticipation of the upcoming election. After some discussion, the national committee decided to solicit sustaining memberships at $10 by sending appeals to names that appeared on various commercially available mailing lists. The program was first tried experimentally in three states which were not contributing anything, so as not to upset any ongoing fund-raising operation. When the program proved successful in the test states, appeals were sent nationwide. The program brought in $700,000 in 1962, and slightly over $1 million in 1963, about two thirds of the national committee's operating funds that year. The contributors were sent a party newsletter, thus giving the party an additional publicity opportunity, and many of them provided the names of additional potential donors. Over time, the Republican direct-mail campaign was built up to the point that it was regularly bringing in between $7 million and $8 million, and between 75 and 80 percent of all Republican contributions by the late 1970s. The origin of this successful mass fund drive is usually attributed to the appeal of Barry Goldwater to conservative Republicans in 1964, but credit should be given to William S. Warner, then the executive director of the Republican National Committee, who started the program two years before the Goldwater nomination.

The first real Democratic success with a mass fund appeal was part of the 1972 McGovern campaign. George McGovern had accumulated several lists, some from South Dakota, some from his activity in opposition to the war in Vietnam, and some from various liberal appeals with which he had been associated. When the Senator decided to run, he consulted with an Alabama direct-mail expert, Morris Dees, and Dees brought in Thomas Collins from a New York City direct mail firm. Collins wrote a seven-page letter setting forth McGovern's positions and appealing for funds. (For some reason, contributors to direct mail campaigns are said to prefer long, detailed letters.) This was sent out at the time that McGovern announced his candidacy. The returns were quite good, and a number of subsequent appeals followed. Previous donors were contacted repeatedly; Democratic National Committee lists were used once McGovern was the party nominee; television appeals were combined with direct-mail appeals. The response to this was so substantial that special nighttime mail-opening sessions had to be used just to get the money into the bank. In consequence of these efforts, the McGovern campaign raised $3 million before he was nominated and $12 million during the general election campaign, at a total cost of $4.5 million (Alexander, 1976, pp. 299–304; Hart, 1973, pp. 42–44, 309–10).

The Democratic party was not able to build on the McGovern program during the ensuing decade. Morris Dees was recruited into the 1976 Carter campaign, but reportedly was unable to match his 1972 success. And, as we saw much earlier in this chapter, the Democratic National Committee was far behind its Republican counterpart at the beginning of the 1980s. The Democratic leadership recognized the importance of institutionalized fund raising, but the Republicans had a two-decade head start.

Federal Financing

Beginning in 1976, an entirely new system of financing presidential campaigns was in place. The Federal Election Campaign Act of 1971 was amended in 1974 to provide for public financing of presidential (but not congressional) campaigns. Federal financing had been advocated for some time, in part to reduce the dependence of officeholders on financial supporters, and in part because of the rising cost of campaigning. In the aftermath of the Watergate revelations, it was possible to get such legislation through Congress. The law allowed $20 million plus an inflation allowance for the major presidential candidates. The national committees could also spend two cents per voting-age population ($4.6 million in 1980) on behalf of their candidates. The candidates were not required to accept these funds; but if they did so, they had to promise not to accept other contributions.

This was a major change in the constraints affecting external activities. We have already seen the consequences of this, as they concerned much more organized fund raising in the Early Days of nomination politics and the centralization of authority in a national campaign organization. Now, how did it affect the funds available for the general election campaign and the way they were spent? To begin with, the federal funds were not a great deal of money as national media campaigns go. One way of putting this into perspective is to compare it with the advertising budgets of commercial firms. The largest advertising budget in 1976 was $357.1 million, spent by Procter & Gamble.

The firms with the next largest budgets in 1976 were General Foods ($219.3 million), Bristol-Myers ($146.9 million), and General Motors ($145.1 million). Altogether, 76 American firms had 1976 advertising budgets larger that the $21.8 million allowed each major campaign that year (*Advertising Age*, May 16, 1977 p. 52).[14]

The amounts available were, in effect, expanded in 1979 by further changes in the law. Responding to criticism that the law restricted local activity, one 1979 amendment permitted state and local parties to buy buttons, bumper stickers, pamphlets, yard signs, and so forth. Another allowed state and local parties to conduct registration and get-out-the-vote drives. There were no financial limits placed on what the state and local parties could spend on these activities. The Republicans spent $15 million and the Democrats $4 million on these "local" activities in 1980[15] (Alexander, 1980, 1982).

Even with the additional state and local spending, the constraints imposed by public funding are quite real. In 1976, the Ford strategy group foresaw the consequences of the spending limits a good deal better than the Carter strategists. The latter spent a lot of money during September moving the candidate and his entourage around the country. The Ford strategists held money back for a media effort in the closing days of the campaign, and the Carter forces found they were without money to counter it. By 1980, effects of the spending limits were apparent on both sides. Reflecting on the campaign, Democratic Campaign Manager Les Francis said: "I was meeting every morning with an accountant and a lawyer. Many of our decisions were not based on what we *ought* to do to be politically effective, but on what we *could* do within the law." And on the Republican side, strategist Richard Beal said, "We've got to target (that is, concentrate resources). There just isn't enough money to do anything else."

Prior to federal funding, campaign treasurers had three prime functions: to raise money, to have resources available when needed to undertake critical activities, and to see to it that the laws were adhered to and that records could be produced on the required dates to demonstrate fidelity to the laws. With public financing, they have been relieved of the first obligation, but will have to pay a lot more attention to the others.

If candidates continue to accept federal funds, and the spending limits remain the same, the long-run effect will probably be to force some decisions about which activities are cost effective. The 1972 Nixon voter-contact operation alone cost some $12 million. The 1968 electronic

---

[14] In making this comparison, remember that campaign advertising is concentrated in the couple of months before the election while commercial firms advertise throughout the year, and the federal funds provided for campaigns must cover *all* campaign expenses, not just advertising.

[15] The Republican advantage in this spending was offset by labor spending on similar activities. Organized labor spent $16.5 million, $15 million on behalf of Democrats.

media campaign conducted in Nixon's behalf cost $12.6 million. In other words, these two programs alone would exceed the present spending limits, and this without allowing anything for a campaign tour, polling, print advertising, headquarters salaries, or anything else. In the past, the strong tendency has been to carry on all possible campaign activities on an *implicit* assumption that whatever was done was going to increase a candidate's chances of winning. But is it really true, for example, that a candidate wins votes by campaigning in a community? Could he do better by staying home and, together with his issues staff, working out just what he wants to say? Such questions have not been closely examined, but a fixed limit on spending may provide an impetus in this direction.

Summary

In this chapter, we have covered the four major types of activities that go into a presidential campaign: campaign operations, research, public relations, and finance. Much of this organizational effort goes unreported in media accounts of campaigns; but there must be some way of moving the presidential and vice presidential candidates around the country, figuring out what they are going to say and what the citizens will think of it, getting the campaign story out through the media, and obtaining funds to do all this.

While the internal structure covered in the last chapter was largely ideological, the external activities that we have examined in this chapter can be said to be largely logistical. In other words, a structure of regional and state coordination, survey research to determine voter attitudes, buying television time and producing spots, and raising money are not intrinsically liberal, moderate, or conservative. A campaign organization that can provide these services ought to be able to work for any candidate, regardless of his ideological bent.

While it is certainly true that a conservative or liberal ideologue who lacks organizational, research, communications, or fund-raising skills is next to useless around campaign headquarters, this distinction between ideological positioning and logistical services should not be pressed too far. The personal contacts through which one sets up a campaign organization are different in the two parties. The phrases that ring true in a conservative speech would not fit into a liberal appeal; the sources of funds tend to be different; and so on. But the factor that brings issues most sharply into focus in these external activities is that their intent is to win the support of a particular set of voters. Therefore the appeals that are directed to them must be consistent with their issue preferences. This points up the dual set of constraints that shape any campaign strategy. It must be consistent with the issue preferences of the supporting coalition, and at the same time win the votes of the citizens to whom the campaign appeals are directed.

PART SIX

CAMPAIGN STRATEGIES

CHAPTER 12

TWO-CANDIDATE CAMPAIGNS

"The president defended his economic policy in a speech in New York." Whether this was broadcast as part of a news summary, or was the lead sentence in a newspaper story, or was found in the middle of a paragraph in a history book, it is typical of the events that make up a campaign. By itself, it tells us very little. The sentence is much more interesting for the questions it calls to mind. Was the president running ahead of his opponent or was he behind? If ahead, was he maintaining his lead, or was his opponent catching up? Why was the president talking about economic management instead of international involvement or civil liberties? Was he addressing a business or labor audience? Why was the president giving this speech in New York instead of Chicago or Cheyenne? With answers to these and some related questions in hand, we could give some meaning to the report. Without them, the fact that the president has given a speech on economics tells us no more than any other unexamined event.

Speeches, statements, television spots, and all the rest can be understood as part of a campaign strategy; but in order to do so, we need contextual information. First of all we need to know about the *structural context*. What is the composition of the candidate's supporting coalition? What voters is the candidate trying to reach? What kinds of things can the candidate do and say that are going to win the approbation of the supporting coalition and win votes at the same time? There is also a larger sense in which structural context can be understood. This is the structure formed by the interplay of the major strategies. Are both coalitions intent on winning the swing votes in the large industrial states, as was the case in 1976? Does the strategy of one involve a vigorous exposition of what is a minority view nationwide?

This happened in 1972, and gave the other party a lot of maneuvering room in the middle ground of American politics. Are there a large number of voters unrepresented by the major parties, and is there a candidate who will try to speak to their concerns? This gave rise to important third parties in 1968 and 1980, and the presence of the third party made for much more complex politics.

Another important set of questions concerns the *temporal context*. In a narrow sense, these questions arise from the temporal pattern that we reviewed at the beginning of Chapter 10. Is the speech a trial balloon that is given during the Planning stage of the campaign? Is it a considered statement that is part of the Grand Opening? Is it a Strategic Adjustment that tries to respond to some particular problem? Or is it part of a last attempt that comes during the Time's Up stage?

What might be called a longer-term temporal concern also leads to questions about the *historic context*. What did citizens regard as the leading problems in a given election year? How widely were looming problems, such as those implicit in baby booms or energy shortages, understood in the society? Was America involved in a war, or was there a real threat of war? Was the economy prosperous, or were inflation or unemployment, or both, problems? All these considerations are important in understanding the opportunities open to campaign strategists, and you will want to keep them in mind when reading about specific campaigns.

THE 1972 CAMPAIGN

The 1972 campaign is often interpreted as a mirror image of 1964, when Lyndon Johnson decisively defeated Barry Goldwater. In important ways, this is true. In 1964, a Democratic incumbent faced a Republican challenge from the right; in 1972, a Republican incumbent faced a Democratic challenge from the left. Both challengers proposed fairly drastic policy reorientations, and both had difficulty obtaining electoral support. Both incumbents had considerable freedom of action in selecting their strategies, and both won victories of historic proportions. But there were also features of the 1972 campaign quite unlike anything seen eight years earlier.

The issues were different in 1972. The nation was not confronted with serious international or economic problems in the mid-60s, but these were the major points of contention in 1972. In spite of four years of negotiations, and (by 1972) a total withdrawal of American ground troops, the Vietnam War was not over. Early in the year, President Nixon traveled to China, with which diplomatic contacts had begun, and in late spring, he went to Moscow to sign the first Strategic Arms Limitations Treaty. In domestic affairs, the inflation that began as a consequence of the Vietnam War was proving difficult to check, and wage and price controls were instituted in 1971. With controls in place, the rise in the consumer price index was held to 3.3 percent in 1972.

There were two events unique to 1972: the replacement of Democratic vice presidential candidate Thomas Eagleton, and the break-in at the Democratic National Committee headquarters by five men working for the Committee to Re-elect the President. In early August, Senator Eagleton revealed that he had been hospitalized for nervous exhaustion and had received shock treatment. Senator McGovern immediately stated that he was "1,000 percent for Tom Eagleton" and had no intention of dropping him from the ticket, but within two weeks he accepted his resignation. It never became clear what the five men were looking for at the Democratic National Committee, but we do know that they were working for the Committee to Re-elect the President, and that committee officials, White House staff members, and President Nixon himself took action to prevent legal authorities from finding out what had happened. The departure of Senator Eagleton had more serious political consequences in 1972. What became known as the Watergate affair had fewer consequences that year. The cover-up kept the public in the dark until after the election, and those who distrusted Richard Nixon enough to believe that he was personally involved were likely to vote for George McGovern in any case. Ultimately, of course, the Watergate affair was to force Nixon from office.

GEORGE McGOVERN'S MORAL CHALLENGE

George McGovern's bid for the presidency was reminiscent of William Jennings Bryan's campaign in 1900. Both men came from the plains, and both spoke in tones of moral certainty. McGovern's views about the influence of business in the Nixon administration could be seen as a latter-day instance of Bryan's "Democracy against Plutocracy," and his attacks on Nixon's Vietnam policies showed the same fervor as Bryan's complaints about American imperialism. This analogy is only suggestive. America in the 1970s was very different from the turn-of-the-century country just emerging as a world power. Still, the Bryan comparison sheds some light on the questions McGovern was trying to raise, and on his political difficulties in doing so.

McGovern's Left-Center Plan and Organizational Difficulties

The organizational stage of the McGovern campaign would have been difficult in the best of circumstances. His nomination coalition was built around the most liberal groups in the Democratic party: the antiwar movement and those favoring much expanded social programs and further busing. The idea behind this was a left-centrist strategy: to co-opt the left as a base for a nomination drive, but to keep the organization open to centrist politicians so that McGovern could appeal to a normal Democratic spectrum in the general election. The Democratic left was co-opted all right, but many of their views and personnel were unacceptable to veterans of past Democratic campaigns. One standard way of handling this situation is to work through those with good ties to both the successful nomination coalition and party groups that are not part of this winning coalition. Lawrence O'Brien and Senator Thomas Eagleton might have been very effective in this task. O'Brien had reassumed the chairmanship of the Democratic National Committee a couple of years earlier because he was the one person acceptable to all the leading Democrats, and Eagleton was a Roman Catholic with good ties to urban politicians and organized labor. But their organizational talents were not to be used. O'Brien was unhappy about the way the campaign was structured, and Eagleton was forced to resign as the vice presidential candidate.

The Eagleton affair was costly to Senator McGovern's standing with the public. McGovern's swift move from "1,000 percent support" for Eagleton to willingness to accept his resignation raised troublesome questions about his competence. But to appreciate the temporal impact of the affair, one must remember that it came smack in the middle of what should have been the Organization phase of the campaign. In place of contributions and appointments, there were statements from Democratic leaders and the mass media, many to the effect that Senator Eagleton should leave the ticket. Contributors who had pledged large amounts to get the campaign started let McGovern leaders know the money might not be forthcoming. Regional directors and state leaders reported no activity going on in the field. The reaction of the McGovern core group to all this was that Eagleton must go. There might be costs to dropping him from the ticket, but the campaign could not get under way with him.

August, the extra month normally available to the out party because of the earlier convention, was largely devoted to repair efforts of one kind and another. First came the selection of Sargent Shriver to replace Senator Eagleton. Some prominent Democrats were not interested in running with McGovern, but Shriver accepted eagerly, and his selection was ratified at a meeting of the Democratic National Committee. Organizational difficulties continued, notably over the management and budget for an urgent get-out-the-vote drive, but a campaign staff (regional and state coordinators) came into being, and some activity began throughout the country.

Senator McGovern did make two or three campaign trips during August to keep his name in the headlines. Perhaps the most important of these was a speech to the New York Society of Security Analysts on August 29. During the primaries, the Senator had proposed giving $1,000 a month to every American, and had rather casually attached a cost figure of $21 in additional taxation for persons earning $20,000 or more. Now, after some weeks of staff analysis, McGovern was ready to present a more carefully thought out proposal (White, 1973, pp. 126–28; Hart, 1973, p. 279). In his New York speech, he called for a $10 billion cut in defense spending over each of the next three years, and a "fair-share tax reform" that would bring in an additional $22 billion by various changes in the tax laws. These funds would be used for two programs: $15 billion to local school systems, and a "National Income Insurance Program," consisting of public service jobs, expansion of social security, and "approximately $4,000 in cash and food stamps for a family of four with no other income who are unable to work."

Multiple Plans and External Troubles

There did not appear to be an agreed-upon plan for the McGovern coalition by the time of the Grand Opening. Rather, there were a number of plans. None of these lasted long, and portions of each appeared to conflict with other plans that were presumably in effect. For example, George McGovern told Theodore White he thought he would carry California and New York, and the geographic concentration of the campaign would be on Illinois, Michigan, Ohio, Pennsylvania, and New Jersey (White, 1973, p. 168). But the McGovern coalition was responsible for expelling Chicago's Mayor Richard Daley from the Democratic convention, and in spite of a personal appeal, Mayor Daley stated that each member of his organization was free to make his own judgment about supporting the McGovern-Shriver ticket. Labor would also be important in winning this band of states, but McGovern had only about half the labor support assembled for most Democrats, and AFL-CIO President George Meany announced that he was neutral between Nixon and McGovern.

Then there was the matter of the positions McGovern was taking. In international involvement, George McGovern wanted an immediate cessation of Vietnam hostilities, as well as a rather deep cut in defense spending. His New York economic speech called for higher taxes and further spending. Social benefits programs included income maintenance, more school aid, and national health insurance. On civil liberties, the Senator supported busing, favored control of hand guns, and said that crime was related to economic and racial discrimination. These liberal positions were quite consistent with the internal structure of the McGovern coalition, but they caused external trouble with the voters George McGovern was trying to reach. Pennsylvania steelworkers, for example, saw McGovern's position on the Vietnam War as the equivalent of surrender, and felt that he wanted to give welfare recipients more than they were making in take-home pay (Sperling, 1972). It might be said that the lack of an overall campaign plan was the least of McGovern's difficulties. The McGovern coalition was short on many of the essentials of a successful campaign: a smoothly working organization, external support, and positions that would attract large numbers of voters.

In part because of a lack of resources, in part to take advantage of the speed of jet travel, and in part because of a hope that the Senator could arouse American voters, the McGovern campaign scheduled appearances in two to four different media markets each day. On September 6, for example, he was in San Diego, Dallas, and Houston. On September 12, he campaigned in Chicago, Cleveland, and Detroit. The idea was to generate local stories in addition to those filed by the traveling press for the national media. The underlying theme of these stories, regardless of the policy area being discussed, was one of opposition to the Nixon administration. In fact, a controversy over how this opposition should be conveyed was taking place within the McGovern coalition leadership. Frank Mankiewicz, Larry O'Brien, and Ted Van Dyk favored a negative accent on Nixon and the Republicans. Charles Guggenheim, Liz Stevens, and Gary Hart wanted more positive material used. A key factor in this dispute was the Senator's own sense of moral fervor. He didn't need a plan to tell him that Richard Nixon and all of his works were evil, and as September wore on, he became more and more negative.[1] Speaking in the inner-city Hill district of Pittsburgh, for example, he explicitly blamed poverty conditions on the war in Vietnam:

> As much as any village bombed into rubble, the Hill district is a victim of the war in Vietnam—the longest, the cruelest, and the stupidest war in American history. Why aren't there any better schools here? Because your money has been used to blow up schools in Vietnam. Why aren't there more clinics to protect your health? Because your money has been used to bomb the life out of innocent civilians in Indochina. Every bomb that is dropped and every bullet that is fired in Southeast Asia has an echo that is heard in the Hill district. We have paid for the devastation of another land with the devastation, not just of our conscience, but of our own country.

Such language portrayed the depth of Senator McGovern's feelings, but it was not adding much support to his coalition. Nor were the efforts of the campaigners who were working in McGovern's behalf.

---

[1] This conclusion about McGovern's negativism, and those to follow about a positive or negative tone to the 1972 campaign or policy areas being emphasized, are based on a content analysis of the McGovern and Nixon speeches.

The polls, public and private, continued to show President Nixon far in the lead. This disheartening situation produced anxiety among the coalition leaders. As campaign director Gary Hart put it:

> There was nothing tangible, nothing concrete, nothing to show movement and progress. At the headquarters, the staff and volunteers grasped at straws for encouragement, cheering each appearance of one of the candidates on the evening news, savoring each favorable editorial or report of new administrative malfeasance, longing for some proof that victory lay ahead. (Hart, 1973, pp. 299-300)

A Strategic Turn to a More Positive Approach

The manifest lack of progress dictated a Strategic Adjustment. Senator McGovern decided to make a series of nationally televised addresses during October, and reduced the number of negative references in his own public statements. The first televised speech on October 10 dealt with McGovern's plan to end the Vietnam War by withdrawing all American forces within 90 days.

> When all is said and done, our purpose in Vietman now comes down to this—our policymakers want to save face and they want to save the Saigon regime of General Thieu. Now that is a fundamental difference between President Nixon and me. . . . It is a choice between four more years of war; or four years of peace. . . . On the night when the last American soldier from Vietnam has landed in San Francisco, there will be a new birth of confidence and hope for all of us.

The Senator's second speech on October 20 dealt with economic management, the policy area to which he devoted the most attention during the fall campaign. McGovern criticized Nixon administration policies concerning interest, employment, wage and price controls, and taxes, linking all of these to the administration's economic philosophy.

> Every single time this administration has faced an important economic choice, they have picked a policy that was right for the few and wrong for you. . . . This election is more than a contest between George McGovern and Richard Nixon. It is a fundamental struggle between the little people of America and the big rich of America, between the average working man or woman and a powerful elite. . . . I want to be the kind of president who will see to it that America is good to every one of her people. I want us to claim that promise of Isaiah, "The people shall be righteous and they shall inherit the land."

These October efforts did produce some financial results. An appeal for funds at the end of the Vietnam speech brought in more than a million dollars, and by the end of the month, so much money was coming in that there was difficulty in opening the mail. This was a happy contrast to the desperate lack of financial resources in August, but there was still no evidence that American voters were changing their minds.

A Final Bitterness

By the time of the third speech, on October 25, a good deal of negativism was creeping back into Senator McGovern's rhetoric. The theme for this speech was corruption in the Nixon administration. Favors extended to campaign contributors, Watergate, and extensions of executive power were all discussed.

> The men who have collected millions in secret money, who have passed out special favors, who have ordered political sabotage, who have invaded our offices in the dead of night—all these men work for Mr. Nixon. Most of them he hired himself. And their power comes from him alone. They act on his behalf, and they accept his orders.

This speech, a direct attack on Nixon's integrity, was symptomatic of McGovern's mood as the campaign moved into the Time's Up stage. It was now clear that he was not going to win, and the Senator became increasingly bitter in his public comments. In late October, statements from both Hanoi and Washington indicated the probability of success in peace negotiations. Senator McGovern's reaction was to say that "when Dr. Kissinger came out and said peace is at hand, he was misleading the American people. He knew what he said was false." McGovern told questioners in Los Angeles that Nixon had "conducted an evil administration. . . . I think exploiting of racial fears is an evil practice. . . . I think the aerial bombardment of Southeast Asia by Richard Nixon is the most evil thing ever done by any American president." And in Chicago, on the Saturday night before the election, George McGovern said:

> It's all right for the people to be fooled once as they were in 1968. If they do it again, if they let this man lead them down the false hope of peace once again in 1972, then the people have nobody to blame but themselves. . . . I'm going to give you one more warning. If Mr. Nixon is reelected on Tuesday, we may very well have four more years of war in Southeast Asia. Our prisoners will sit in their cells for another four years. Don't let this man trick you into believing that he stands for peace, when he's a man who makes war.

It was almost as though Senator McGovern was angry with the voters for refusing to listen to him. Whether or no, he was in the same position as Senator Goldwater on election eve in 1964. He had tried to raise some fundamental questions, and he knew that this would not lead to electoral success.

REELECT THE PRESIDENT: NIXON 1972

A Positive, Ethnic, Centrist Approach

"I ask everyone listening to me tonight—Democrats, Republicans, and independents—to join our new majority; not on the basis of the party label you wear on your lapel but what you believe in you hearts." This appeal for a new majority was an important part of Richard Nixon's acceptance speech in 1972. Internally, the Nixon coalition was composed of groups supporting American involvement overseas and a strong defense posture, conservative economics, few new social programs, increased police authority, and opposition to busing. The new majority Nixon sought referred to his coalition's need for additional external support. Many moves had been made by his administration to win support from three traditional Democratic groupings: Catholics, labor, and Southerners. The nomination of a Democrat unpopular with these constituencies gave Nixon a chance to capitalize on the moves he had already made. This was the major focus of the 1972 Republican campaign.

Perhaps the most important move to gain Catholic support was Nixon's consistent championship of aid to parochial schools. He urged this on a number of occasions, such as in a 1971 speech to the Knights of Columbus. Nixon also made known his opposition to abortion in a letter to Terence Cardinal Cooke of New York. During the election campaign, an unusual amount of effort went into Heritage (that is, white ethnic) groups, and three of the ethnic groups selected for inclusion in a massive mailing campaign conducted that year were Irish, Polish, and Italian. Among other things, the President visited an immigration museum at the Statue of Liberty; stopped his motorcade in Wilkes-Barre, Pennsylvania, in order to pose with members of an Italian wedding party that happened to be emerging from a church as he drove by; turned up at an Italian-American celebration in Maryland, explaining that his daughter Julie couldn't make it and he was substituting for her; and spoke at a Columbus Day dinner. In this speech, he said;

> When we honor [labor leader] Peter Fosco, we see [an important attribute] quite clearly, and that is, putting it quite bluntly, hard work. Italian-Americans came to this country by the hundreds of thousands, and then by the millions. They came here not asking for something, only asking for the opportunity to work. They have worked and they have built. There is a second feature which is represented by this head table tonight. Those of Italian background bring with them a very deep religious faith.

This prose was typical of the 1972 Nixon campaign in two respects. First, Nixon spoke positively of the virtues of whatever group he was addressing. Second, his constant references to the importance of hard work were an integral part of his appeal to blue-collar voters.

Relations between organized labor and the Nixon administration had been cool, and were to become so again, but in 1972 there was a tactical truce that presented an unusual opportunity for the Republicans to get labor votes. Labor was by no means pro-Nixon. Rather, McGovern positions reduced the amount of labor support that would normally flow to a Democratic candidate.[2] As one labor leader put it, "Most of our members get the creeps when they think about Nixon, but McGovern worries them." The AFL-CIO was neutral, and the Nixon administration worked hard to take advantage of this posture. A well-advertised golf game was played by Richard Nixon and AFL-CIO president George Meany, and a plank supporting Section 14-B of the Taft-Hartley Act (permitting state right-to-work laws that were anathema to organized labor) was dropped from the Republican platform. Secretary of Labor James Hodgson addressed the Steelworkers, who did not endorse either candidate, but canceled a speech before the Machinists, who endorsed McGovern.

In his Labor Day speech, which had been reviewed with AFL-CIO leaders before delivery (Safire, 1975, p. 595), President Nixon drew a contrast betwen the work ethic and the welfare ethic. "Above all," he argued, "the work ethic puts responsibility in the hands of the individual, in the belief that self-reliance and the willingness to work makes a person a better human being . . . [whereas] the welfare ethic destroys character and leads to a vicious cycle of dependency." Richard Nixon cited hard work over and over again during the campaign. He believed that it was responsible for his own success, and it was a natural link with the labor vote he hoped to win.

Southern support for a Republican presidential candidate was not unusual. Herbert Hoover carried five states in the "Solid South" as long ago as 1928, and Republicans had been making real efforts to increase their strength there since the 1950s. Still, southern voters were another large group of Democrats who disliked George McGovern and to whom the center-right policies of the Nixon administration were acceptable. Some seven former Democratic governors, and scores of lesser Democratic officials in the South, endorsed Richard Nixon rather than George McGovern. When President Nixon visited John Connally's Texas ranch in September, he was welcomed by some 200 Democrats, mostly southern, whom Connally had recruited to the Democrats for Nixon organization he headed. And when Nixon campaigned in Atlanta, he argued that Southerners were not racist, any more than Michiganders were racist, because they opposed busing. "It simply means . . . parents

---

[2] Twenty individual unions endorsed McGovern; only the Teamsters endorsed Nixon.

in Georgia and parents all over the country want better education for their children, and that better education is going to come in the schools that are close to home and not clear across town." He went on to assert that issues that were important in the South—peace, jobs, safety, local control—were the same issues that were important all over the country.

A Triumphal March for the Incumbent

There were few temporal effects in the 1972 Nixon campaign. All the appeals to give added external support to his coalition—those to Catholics, labor, and the South—were in place by the Grand Opening, and the campaign went well enough that there was no need for either Strategic or Tactical Adjustments. Nixon used the traditional techniques of the incumbent: the ability to schedule headline-making events when his opponent was trying to make news, conferences with foreign leaders, a fiscal policy designed to stimulate the economy at election time, and visibly being president while surrogates spoke around the country in his name.

Nixon resurrected one technique he had begun in his 1968 campaign: using radio for more thoughtful addresses. Several of these were delivered. One devoted to his philosophy picked up the theme of a new majority, and contained a good exposition of moderate conservative beliefs:

> The new American majority believes that each person should have more of the say in how he lives his own life . . . in taking care of those persons who cannot take care of themselves . . . in taking whatever action is needed to hold down the cost of living . . . and in a national defense second to none. . . . These are not the beliefs of a selfish people. On the contrary, they are the beliefs of a generous and self-reliant people, a people of intellect and character, whose values deserve respect in every segment of our population.

Richard Nixon's greatest asset in 1972, of course, was not a capacity to give an articulate presentation of his political philosophy, but the success of his foreign policy. He had made trips to Beijing and Moscow earlier in the year; and the announcement of a breakthrough in the Vietnam peace negotiations, being conducted in France between Henry Kissinger and Le Duc Tho, more or less coincided with the Time's Up phase when the President began campaigning full time. He devoted much more attention to international involvement than to any other policy area throughout the campaign, and concluded his campaign in Ontario, California, on election eve with further references to his foreign policy record and his hopes for a "Generation of Peace":

Finally we have had a breakthrough in the [Vietnam peace] negotiations
and I can tell you today that the significant point of that breakthrough
is the three principles that I laid down on May 8 . . . have been agreed
to. . . . The trip to Beijing . . . has great meaning . . . to [the] younger
generation. . . . Imagine how dangerous the world would be if one-fourth
of all the people in the world who live in the People's Republic of China,
10, 15 years from now had gathered enormous nuclear capability and
had no communication with the United States. . . . We cannot allow
that danger. . . . The trip to Moscow had a similar purpose. Imagine
what we would leave to the younger generation had we . . . gone down
the road to an inevitable confrontation and a nuclear explosion that
would have destroyed civilization as we know it.

In common with many winning campaigns, the 1972 Nixon campaign
went too smoothly. There was electoral success based on appeals to
Democrats alienated by the McGovern candidacy, and a foreign policy
record that was appreciated by many voters. But as all too soon became
apparent, there was also political sabotage, vast overspending, and a
cover-up involving the President himself. This was tragic for Nixon
and his hopes for future accomplishment. In 1960, he showed a high
order of statesmanship on at least two occasions: in forbidding any
discussion of his opponent's religion, and in refusing to bring on a
constitutional crisis by challenging the very close election results. Had
a hint of these values been reflected in the actions of Richard Nixon
and his appointees, he would have been able to govern on the basis
of the record majority he won, and to lead the nation in its bicentennial
in 1976.

THE 1976 CAMPAIGN

The 1976 campaign was normal, and it was anything but normal.
For the first time since 1960, most Democrats were in the Democratic
coalition, and most Republicans were in the Republican coalition. But
the Democratic coalition was organized in support of a one-term governor from the Deep South, and the Republican coalition was led by a
former congressman from Grand Rapids who was the first unelected
president in American history. Neither candidate could count on full
support from *all* his nominal partisans, and therein lay the interesting
strategic challenges of the 1976 campaign.

Gerald Ford began his short administration with the reassuring statement that "our long national nightmare is over." But his initial popularity dropped sharply after he pardoned Richard Nixon, and by fall 1974,
America was in a deep recession. The unemployment rate was 8.4
percent in 1975, and inflation (led by sharp increases in the costs of

food, fuel, housing, and medical care) was worse than ever. By 1976, a 1972 dollar was worth only 73 cents![3] Against this background of Watergate and economic problems, questions of which candidate could be trusted and who could manage the economy loomed large in 1976.

AN OUTSIDER LEADS THE MAJORITY PARTY

In midsummer, there were certainly some favorable omens for the Carter coalition. Internally, the coalition was expanded in the classic manner by the selection of a vice presidential candidate, Walter Mondale, who was highly respected by liberals. Externally, the Gallup Poll showed Jimmy Carter running ahead of Gerald Ford by a remarkable 62 to 29 percent margin.

But to those who looked a bit more closely, there were signs of possible trouble. The campaign organization made minimal use of the Democratic talent now available to Carter. Walter Mondale and his ranking aide, Richard Moe, were admitted to the strategy group, but that was the only expansion. Campaign headquarters were kept in Atlanta, and staff responsibilities remained essentially what they had been. Following a 1960 Kennedy pattern, Carter designees from out of state were put in charge of each state's presidential campaign. And while the external support available for Carter was widespread, it was very soft. Jimmy Carter might be the majority party's nominee, but many Democrats and independents were unenthusiastic about him.

A Southern-Based Strategy

Planning for the campaign, summarized in two memoranda written by campaign director Hamilton Jordan in June and August, did not assume that the early support would hold up. Quite the opposite. "We will probably not know until mid-October if the election is going to be close or if there is potential for a big victory." Therefore, Jordan asserted, the Carter coalition must "always maintain a high degree of flexibility in the allocation of our resources and the objectives of strategy." But the main key to the Carter strategy was an assumption that had not been possible to make since 1944: a sweep of the southern and border states. The South is the largest of the four sections of the country, and when Jordan added the District of Columbia, Massachusetts, Minnesota, and Wisconsin to this base, there was a total of 199 electoral votes. This would not be enough to win; additional electoral votes would have to come from eight large industrial states, such as New York and Pennsylvania, and these critical states were sched-

---

[3] As of 1976, this was the worst four-year record on inflation since World War II. The 1976–80 record was to be even worse. A 1976 dollar was worth only 69 cents in 1980, but 1976 voters had no way of knowing that.

uled for more intensive campaign efforts. If the 199-vote base held, though, the additional necessary votes could be obtained by winning any of several combinations of states. Therefore, Jordan claimed, "the only way we can lose in November is to have this base fragmented" (Schram, 1977, pp. 239–50; Witcover, 1977, chap. 35).

The Jordan plan was quite specific about where the campaign was to be waged, but not about how it was to be done. The plan was silent about the issues that were to be used to appeal to voters in large industrial states while retaining support in the essential southern base. Indeed, it was not until nearly time for the Grand Opening that Carter himself asked his strategy group, "What are our themes going to be?" The absence of a clear answer to this question was to hobble the Carter campaign throughout the fall.

A Downhill Slide

The implicit statement made by the Grand Opening was that the Roosevelt coalition had been reassembled. The formal opening took place at FDR's "Little White House" in Warm Springs, Georgia, with two Roosevelt sons present, and the late President's favorite black accordionist playing "Happy Days Are Here Again." This was followed by a couple of other regional stops, presumably sufficient to reinforce regional pride, and then the Carter entourage moved north, where the additional electoral votes had to be won. In the following days, Governor Carter met voters at a New York subway stop and at a suburban rally in Columbus, Ohio; put on a "Polish Hill" T-shirt in Pittsburgh; addressed the AFL-CIO convention in Dearborn, Michigan; took part in a torchlight parade in Chicago; and rode across Pennsylvania on a campaign train in emulation of Harry Truman's whistle-stop campaign of 1948.

A lot of little things seemed to go wrong as Carter sought support from blue-collar, ethnic voters. There was difficulty in dealing with questions about abortion, a fluff in which he said that he would shift the tax burden to those over the median income, and publicity about an interview in *Playboy* in which he admitted lust in his heart and made some adverse comments about Lyndon Johnson. The difficulty with Carter's Grand Opening, though, was not little things going wrong. It was a lack of big things going right. On the one hand, he identified with liberal Democratic predecessors, and invoked their names whenever possible. But he was also making conservative statements, such as "Whenever there's a choice between government performing a function and the private sector performing a function, I believe in the private sector," and undecided voters did not know what to make of the contrast.

On September 23, the campaign was punctuated by the first of a series of televised debates. If any advantage was to be gained, it would likely come in the first debate "because of the large audience, and the mild 'openness' encouraged in the uncommitted by the debate format." The advantage went to President Ford, in part because of the candidates' performances, but much more because of the postdebate media focus on the question of who won (Sears, 1977; Sears & Chaffee, 1979). By this point, the race between Carter and Ford was even outside the South.

Tactical Adjustments

At this juncture, there was a Tactical Adjustment. Jimmy Carter became much more negative in his comments about Gerald Ford. A number of explanations were given for this: that Carter was frustrated by the difficulty of running against an incumbent, that Carter hoped to go for the kill, and so on. Whatever the reason, President Ford was now likened to a car with four flat tires. His vetoes were said to be designed to keep people out of work. "Gerald Ford," Carter charged in Cleveland, "has hidden himself from the public even more than Richard Nixon at the depths of Watergate." After the President's second debate gaffe, denying Soviet domination of Eastern Europe, Carter continued this attack, calling Ford's comment "a disgrace to the country." This gambit did not work. By mid-October, Harris showed Carter with a 4 percent lead nationwide, Gallup showed a 6 percent lead, and Pat Caddell's state-by-state polls for Carter showed a decline "in the West, in the border states, and even in the South" (Schram, 1977, p. 329).

Bad news, of course, increases tension among campaign leaders. When Elizabeth Drew was interviewing at this time, she found that the Carter leaders, "for all their confident talk, seemed tense and skittish. . . . It is clear that a decision has been made among Carter's top aides in Atlanta that he must cut out the strident tone that his campaign has taken on recently" (1977, p. 471). Another Tactical Adjustment was in order. This time a decision was made to spend money on media in the South to protect the essential base, and to prepare new television ads for voters elsewhere, especially women, who preferred Carter on issues but thought Ford a lesser risk in the White House. An announcer on a commercial for the South claimed that "the South is being readmitted to the Union on November 2"; and in a commercial aimed at wavering Northerners, Carter stated that mismanagement affected the quality of lives. These ads were taped on October 19. Efforts were also made to present a reassuring Carter during the third debate (in place of the aggressive Carter of the second debate), but essentially the last Tactical Adjustment of the campaign was made (Schram, 1977, pp. 329–36; Witcover, 1977, pp. 622–23).

Hang On and Hope

The principal activity of the Time's Up phase could be described as "hang on and hope." Hope that the southern base would hold. Hope that enough wavering voters would eventually come down on Carter's side. Because a large proportion of the available federal funds had been spent earlier in the campaign, there were no more resources to be committed. The Carter strategy could operate only at the margins. The candidate's time was devoted to crucial states: New York, New Jersey, Pennsylvania, Ohio, Illinois, Texas (to protect the southern base), and California. Appeals were made to Democrats to turn out on election day. The local Democratic parties could provide some help here (although spending limits meant that the presidential campaign could not encourage them by providing "walking-around money"), and the AFL-CIO could provide more substantial assistance. Political director Al Barkan pledged to have 100,000 workers on telephones and in the streets to turn out the labor vote. And finally, Governor Carter seemed to be reaching for the moderate vote when he modified liberal pledges already made by stating that a tax cut was a possibility in a Carter administration. Still, the principal ingredient of the Time's Up stage was hope. The final polls showed a virtual tie.

THE 1976 FORD REELECTION FIGHT

A Bold Plan to Obtain External Support

Three plans had been written for the Ford campaign. There was a long basic document (120 pages plus appendices) written by several planners under the direction of White House Chief of Staff Richard Cheney. There were plans emerging from the polls conducted by Robert Teeter. And there was a media plan developed by Doug Bailey and John Deardourff. What was unusual about these plans was the extent to which they coincided, the directness with which they dealt with Gerald Ford's weaknesses, and the degree to which they dealt with the external need to reach the voters rather than the internal need to hold the supporting coalition together. These unusual aspects could be traced to the professional backgrounds (political science, polling, campaigning) of the planners.

The one major violation of the plans was the selection of Robert Dole as the vice presidential nominee. The campaign plan had called for a nominee "who is perceived as an independent, or at least as a moderate Republican, without strong party identification [and with] . . . a strong image of freshness and non-Washington establishment." These were not Robert Dole's characteristics. His selection served an internal need to satisfy conservative groups that had supported Ronald Reagan's drive for the nomination.

The campaign plans dealt with the voters' perception of the candidates as individuals, their perception of issue stands, geographic concentration, timing, and the use of available funds. Discussion of the candidates as individuals stressed differences between their actual strengths and weaknesses and public perceptions of them. Ford was perceived as an honest and decent person, but there were questions as to whether he was intelligent enough to be president and decisive enough as a leader. Carter had the advantage of supporting traditional American values and being a member of the majority party, but he lacked a record of accomplishment and was vague on issues. The implication of this was a campaign that would lay to rest questions about President Ford's intelligence and leadership capacity, and attack Governor Carter's inexperience and wavering stand on issues.

The plans dealing with issues grew out of the first use in a presidential campaign of multidimensional scaling (the type of spatial analysis used to produce Figures 4-1 and 4-2). A two-dimensional solution was used, in which the horizontal dimension represented partisanship and economic management, and the vertical dimension reflected a social issue (that is, defense spending, and civil liberties questions about lifestyle). Not surprisingly, Carter was slightly to the left and Ford slightly to the right on the partisan-economic dimension. But to Robert Teeter's considerable astonishment, Jimmy Carter was seen as relatively conservative and Gerald Ford as relatively liberal on the social question. This implied an attack on Governor Carter's positions to try to alter the advantageous posture he enjoyed, and a campaign that would stress Gerald Ford's support of traditional positions on the social issue.

The audience to whom the campaign should be directed was described in some detail. The Electoral College was divided into "our base" (83 votes principally from the plains states and the mountain states), "his base" (87 votes principally from the South), and the balance of 368 votes designated as "swing states," including most of the large industrial states. How did the Ford strategists hope to carry these states, considering that Carter was far ahead in the polls in midsummer when these were drawn? The report pointed to a specific swing constituency:

> The target constituency in the suburbs for the president is the upper blue-collar and white-collar workers, often from a family that has risen in mobility in the last generation. . . . The upwardly mobile Catholics are a group becoming more independent and conservative, and they represent the key to victory in the northern industrial states where they are from 25% to 48% of the voters. (Schram, 1977, p. 263)

So far as timing was concerned, the President was told to hold off campaigning as long as possible. He should stay in the White House, appear "presidential," and husband resources for a final blitz. The financial recommendations carried the same message. Of the $21.8 million, only $500,000 was allocated for presidential travel, compared to $800,000 for polling. The largest allocation was $10 million for a media campaign. The plan said that perceptions of both Ford and Carter had to be altered. "In order to win, we must persuade over 15 percent (or about 10 million people) to change their opinions. *This will require very aggressive—media oriented efforts.*" Finally, another $2.8 million was to be set aside as a reserve to be used as necessary in the final days of the campaign.

This was a bold, intelligent plan that gave President Ford some chance of catching up with his rival.[4] As already noted, it was unusual in the amount of attention it paid to the external needs of the Ford coalition, and in the bluntness with which it addressed Ford's own liabilities. Gerald Ford had spent a decade as Republican leader in Congress, as vice president, and as president; the report told him that he was not seen as an effective leader. Ford had spent as many as 200 days a year on the road and loved to campaign; the document stated flatly that he was a terrible campaigner. The President's reaction was that it was pretty strong stuff; but after thinking about it overnight, he told his strategy group to go ahead (Schram, 1977, pp. 251–71; Witcover, 1977, chap. 36; Naughton, 1976; Parry, 1977).

A Quiet Opening

Since the plans developed by the strategists were in effect during the Grand Opening, there was little visible campaigning on the President's part. During September, he held cabinet meetings, signed bills passed by Congress, talked about tax reform while strolling around the Rose Garden, and said that he was dismayed about Hanoi's failure to do more about American servicemen missing in action in the Vietnam War. Not forgetting who his primary audience was, Ford also met with six Roman Catholic bishops to discuss abortion, and posed for pictures with Polish Americans. When he did go to the University of Michigan for a campaign speech, and newsmen asked press secretary Ron Nessen if this was the formal beginning of the campaign, Nessen replied that this was the first campaign speech since the last one. All this made Ford look presidential, husbanded resources, and kept the focus of attention on Jimmy Carter, about whom many voters were undecided. Combined with Ford's success in the first debate, this strategy turned a wide Carter margin into a very tight race by the end of September.

Gerald Ford took one brief campaign swing through the Deep South

---

[4] The one bit of bad advice contained in the plan was that Carter, a native of the Deep South (which had *never* seen one of its citizens elected to the White House), would be vulnerable in the South.

after the first debate, then headed back to Washington to prepare for the second. Since this was to deal with foreign affairs, the Ford strategy group was optimistic and arranged a campaign trip through southern California, Texas, and Oklahoma to capitalize on what it expected to be Ford's continued success. It was in the course of the second debate, though, that Ford made a gaffe about the autonomy of Eastern European governments.[5] Further, it took some time for Ford to concede that he had made a mistake. The beginning of a Tactical Adjustment came the following afternoon in a hastily called news conference. But it was not until five days later, after a meeting with ethnic leaders, that Ford said unequivocally, "I made a mistake." The original statement was not all that unusual a form of verbal reversal, but it was given considerable coverage by the media after the debate, and it concerned precisely the constituency that was the focus of the Ford strategy. "The Poles hadn't made up their minds," said Andrew Greeley, "but they have now and there's nothing Ford can do to change it" (Apple, 1976). This judgment was later confirmed in a study of ethnic voters. Eighty percent heard of this comment, and those who did were very likely to cite it as a reason for their vote (Sears & Chaffee, 1979).

A Final Media Blitz

Mid-October was not the best of times for the Ford campaign. Agriculture Secretary Earl Butz was forced to resign because of a widely reported racial slur, and there were some charges about Ford's personal and political finances. But soon it was late October, and the resources that had been carefully set aside for the Time's Up phase could be used. A new series of commercials were prepared by the Deardourff-Bailey firm, and these were widely used during the closing days of the campaign. One raised questions about Governor Carter's ability, through the use of films of Atlanta residents saying they did not want Carter to become president. Others portrayed Ford as a man who inspired confidence. In one, an announcer praised Ford's quiet style of leadership, and the President pointed out that, "We've certainly created in the Ford administration a nonimperial presidency." Still another sketched warm relationships within the Ford family. Michael Ford, a divinity student, spoke of his father as very devout; Susan and Jack Ford had kind things to say about their father; Susan Ford was shown hugging her father from the back. "Sometimes," the announcer said, "a man's family can say a lot about a man." Together, the Deardourff-Bailey commercials presented Ford rather than Carter as the man to be trusted by wavering voters (Lelyveld, 1976b).

---

[5] In answering a question about relations with the Soviet Union, President Ford said, "There is no Soviet domination of Eastern Europe, and there never will be under a Ford administration."

Another element of the television strategy was a series of conversations between President Ford, Edith Green (an Oregon Democrat Ford had known when both were in the House of Representatives) and sportscaster Joe Garagiola, whose political preferences were unknown, but whose sports background was in keeping with the Jocks-for-Jerry tone of the campaign, and whose visible Italian-Americanism was perfect. Garagiola proved to be an effective interlocutor for the President. For example, he asked about the difference between the Nixon and Ford administrations, allowing Ford to reply, "Joe, there's one very, very fundamental difference. Under President Ford, there's not an imperial White House, which means there's no pomp, there's no ceremony, there's no dictatorial authority."

A final element to the Time's Up drive was intensive personal campaigning by the President himself, quite unlike the September seclusion. Much was said that was not memorable. For instance, in Columbus, Ohio, Ford told a crowd, "Let's make it a home run and a touchdown for the winning team of Jerry Ford and Bob Dole." (Even in his favorite field, sports, Ford managed to mix his metaphors.) More generally, though, he spoke for a strong policy in international involvement and moderate conservatism in economic management. "Give me your mandate," he implored. "I stand on your side, for limited government, for fiscal responsibility, for rising prosperity, for lower taxes, for military strength, and for peace in the world."

What Mr. Ford said was perhaps less important than where he said it, and to whom he said it. His trip included some stops in middle-size states thought to be close (Virginia, the Carolinas, Missouri, Oregon, and Washington), but the bulk of his time was devoted to California, Illinois, Ohio, Pennsylvania, New Jersey, and New York. In Columbus, Ohio, and Syracuse, New York, he appeared with football coaches Woody Hayes and Ben Schwartzwalder, but also with Frank Lausche (a former five-time governor of Ohio who had come out of the "nationality" politics of Cleveland), with Cardinal Krol in Philadelphia, and with Cardinal Cooke in New York. Ford was reaching as best he could for those last few needed votes, and he poured all his energy into it. By the time he reached Grand Rapids on election eve, his voice was gone, and his wife, Betty, had to read his concession statement the day after the election. The Carter coalition prevailed, but Gerald Ford and his strategy group had the satisfaction of knowing that their plan almost led to a come-from-far-behind victory.

Summary

The 1972 and 1976 campaigns both involved a Republican incumbent who followed moderate-conservative policies and a Democratic challenger, but once that was said, there were enormous differences between the two races. In 1972, the challenge came from the left side of the Democratic party. Senator McGovern proposed policies that were very different than those being followed by the Nixon administration. Since McGovern's positions made it difficult for him to compete for the moderate vote, President Nixon had a good deal of freedom in deciding on his strategy. The President was far ahead of his challenger at the beginning of the campaign, and remained so throughout. The passage of time, therefore, brought a sense of triumph to the incumbent, and a sense of bitter hopelessness to the challenger.

In 1976, on the other hand, both parties were fighting for the political center. The incumbent emphasized restraint in spending, but held out the possibility of social programs in some areas. The challenger emphasized social justice, but held out the possibility of a tax cut. In other words, center-right versus center-left. Jimmy Carter had a substantial lead over Gerald Ford after the two conventions, but saw the lead fade away as the election drew closer. President Ford had a well-planned campaign, and came from far behind to near victory. Both had well-grounded hopes for victory as the votes were being counted.

In addition to these specific differences between the two campaigns, there are some more general points that can be made about internal constraints, external constraints, and temporal constraints. But before dealing with these, let us look at the more complex maneuvering that takes place when there are three candidates instead of two.

CHAPTER 13

THREE-CANDIDATE CAMPAIGNS

The presence of a relatively strong third candidate alters the opportunities open to campaign strategists. It introduces into general election politics a little of the structure-of-competition problem that is part of multiple-candidate nomination politics. The third candidate has an importance in campaign strategy that is greater than the number of votes he ultimately receives. In two-candidate campaigns, a strategist for Candidate A must think of things that will attract voters to Candidate A rather than Candidate B without offending members of Candidate A's supporting coalition. In three-candidate campaigns, a strategist for Candidate A must think of things that will attract voters to Candidate A rather than Candidate B without offending members of Candidate A's supporting coalition, *and* without losing voters to Candidate C. Thus the strategic opportunities for Candidate A are reduced.

In the most recent three-candidate campaigns, George Wallace and John Anderson had the potential of taking votes from both major party candidates. Wallace could have taken votes from Hubert Humphrey because many of his supporters were southern Democrats, and could have taken votes from Richard Nixon because he provided an alternative for conservative voters. Anderson could have taken votes from Ronald Reagan because many of his supporters were independent Republicans, and could have taken votes from Jimmy Carter because he provided a moderate-liberal alternative. Just whose strategy *was* affected by the presence of the third candidate depends on the interplay between the three strategies, and it is to this that we now turn.

THE 1968 CAMPAIGN

There was much the Johnson administration could point to with justified pride. Under Lyndon Johnson's driving leadership, the 89th Congress had passed most of the legislation that had been on the Democratic party's agenda for two decades. By 1968, however, this historic accomplishment was obscured by more dramatic developments. The President who spoke in 1964 of the need to handle foreign tests "with care, coolness, and courage" had dispatched 500,000 troops to Vietnam, and 35,000 of them had been killed. A virulent inflation (which was to become more of a political issue in the 1970s) began with Lyndon Johnson's decision not to ask for a tax increase to finance the war. The hope of peaceful progress in civil rights was lost in urban riots, which brought flames to cities across the country; and the most beloved black leader, Martin Luther King, Jr., was slain in early April.

These events undercut President Johnson's political base, and he withdrew from the contest for the Democratic nomination. The contenders were Senator Eugene McCarthy of Minnesota and Senator Robert F. Kennedy of New York, both of whom entered primaries, and Vice President Hubert Humphrey, who did not. But death was to be a participant in this contest, too. Moments after he won the California primary in early June, Robert Kennedy was assassinated. As things turned out, Vice President Humphrey had the strength to get the nomination, but not before a brutal confrontation between Chicago police and antiwar protestors. But even with the Democratic nomination, Humphrey did not have the support of the Democratic party. He faced opposition on the left from those opposed to the war (many of whom had been working in the Kennedy or McCarthy nomination campaigns), and on the right from many southern Democrats who were backing Alabama Governor George Wallace's third-party candidacy.

The Republicans selected former Vice President Richard Nixon to face Humphrey and Wallace. Nixon began his quest of the nomination early, and beat New York Governor Nelson Rockefeller (who did not enter the race until after the King assassination) and California Governor Ronald Reagan, who made his national political debut with a last-minute effort at the Republican National Convention.

GEORGE WALLACE'S THIRD PARTY

George C. Wallace was an Alabama governor who came to national attention by calling for "segregation forever" in his 1963 inaugural address, and by "standing in the schoolhouse door" later that spring as a symbol of resistance to federal desegregation of the University of Alabama. He had entered Democratic presidential primaries in 1964 and had done well in view of Lyndon Johnson's high popularity in his first year in office. In 1968, Wallace opted for a third-party effort. His hope was that, in a three-way race, no candidate would be able to get the required majority of Electoral College votes and the election would therefore have to be decided in the House of Representatives.

There was precious little internal structure to the Wallace coalition. The core group was made up of men who had been close to Wallace in Alabama politics—Seymour Trammell, Bill Jones, and Cecil Jackson—and the members of the coalition were the state and local chairpersons who had been identified through mailings and other contacts from Montgomery. Every presidential coalition is held together by loyalty to the candidate, but with the Wallace coalition, this was almost the only unifying characteristic. The American Independent party was created to put Governor Wallace on the ballot, but the identifiable structure and familiar activities of a political party were absent. Party conventions were held only where required by state law; and the party platform, issued in mid-October, was significant only as a statement of Wallace's personal views.

Wallace's Plan to Go National

The first order of business in the Planning phase was a need to master the arcane details of each state's electoral law in order to get on the ballot. This required considerable effort, since most of the laws benefit the major parties by making it difficult for any new party to qualify. It was eventually necessary to go to the U.S. Supreme Court to get on the ballot in Ohio, but when this was done, the Governor was duly qualified in all 50 states.

A more general strategic problem was how the Wallace forces were going to attract nonsouthern support *without* alienating the Southerners already supporting Wallace. The central answer was a class-based strategy outside the South, to aim for blue-collar votes by stressing law and order and promising to stop government interference in the lives of the people. In this way, his opposition to segregation became a special case of a more general opposition to any governmental activity beyond traditional police powers.

The question of geographic concentration did not have such a neat answer. As Cecil Jackson explained the thinking of the core group:

> At first the basic idea was to sweep from Maryland to Texas, including Oklahoma, Kentucky, and Delaware. Then, obviously, we would have to carry six or eight additional states. We planned to concentrate on key areas and big electoral votes. But we had so much trouble culling them down that we decided we're gonna hit the country. (Jenkins, 1968)

In other words, no decision had been made.

Grand Opening Third-Party Style

When Governor Wallace began speaking in the Grand Opening phase, his class-based strategy was revealed. His appeal was to blue-collar workers with high school educations and moderate incomes, and to small-town and rural residents with strong beliefs in traditional values. This came across in both positive and negative references. The positive references were to "the barber, beautician, cab driver, and steelworker."

> You'd better be thankful for the police and firemen, 'cause if it wasn't for them you couldn't walk the streets. The wife of a working man couldn't go to the supermarket without the fear of being assaulted.

The nice things being said about cab drivers, steelworkers, policemen, and their wives pointed to the votes Wallace hoped to get, but the negative references were just as telling. George Wallace was opposed to the elite, and not just any elite, but to rule makers and symbol manipulators. The opponents he chose were judges, bureaucrats, editors, intellectuals, and foundation officials.[1] These were the persons responsible for America's troubles, but all this would change once he took office. Over and over again, he promised to summon all the bureaucrats to Washington and have them throw their briefcases in the Potomac River. As policy, this was ridiculous; but as symbolism—the vanquished official being forced to part with one of the signs of his authority—it was brilliant. And reminding his listeners of an overbearing government, Wallace told his listeners, "We've had so much stuff jammed down our throats, there's nothing left to jam. Everybody's going to get a chance for a good throat clearing on November 5."

Governor Wallace did not neglect his southern base. In fact, he used the same "they're looking down their noses at us" to appeal to Dixie audiences. When Richard Nixon said that George Wallace wasn't fit to be president, the Governor replied: "Do you know what he was saying? He was saying no Southerner is fit to be president." And he attacked newspapers with the words: "Every one of the large newspapers are making fun of our movement. They're making fun of Southerners, that's what they're doing."

A Strategic Adjustment

The Wallace campaign went well as long as he stayed on the racial issue, which helped him in the South, and the law-and-order issue, which aided him throughout the country. But in October, what

---

[1] He also attacked hippies, militant revolutionary anarchists, and communists, none of whom vote in very great numbers.

amounted to a Strategic Adjustment was forced on him by the requirement that he have a vice presidential candidate. A number of possibilities were considered, but none who were approached were interested.
Finally, Wallace chose General Curtis E. LeMay, a bomber commander
who had led the Strategic Air Command, and then had been Air Force
chief of staff. At a Pittsburgh news conference announcing LeMay's
selection, this exchange took place:

Question: *If you found it necessary to end the* [Vietnam] *War, you would use
nuclear weapons, wouldn't you?*

LeMay: If I found it necessary, I would use anything we could dream up—anything we could dream up—including nuclear weapons, if it was necessary.

Governor Wallace fairly sped to the microphone.

> All General LeMay has said—and I know you fellows better than he
> does because I've had to deal with you—he said that if the security of
> the United States depended on the use of any weapon in the future, he
> would use it. But he said he prefers not to use any sort of weapon. He
> prefers to negotiate. I believe we must defend our country, but I've always
> said we can win and defend in Vietnam without the use of nuclear weap-
> ons. But General LeMay hasn't said anything about the use of nuclear
> weapons.

Of course, General LeMay had talked about nuclear weapons, and
what he said produced a good many headlines. The General was
promptly sent to Vietnam on an inspection tour, but the damage had
been done.

A Fading Close

Wallace strength faded perceptibly after this point in early October,
and might have done so even without the LeMay remark. Richard Nixon,
anxious to contain Wallace to the Deep South so he could pick up
electoral votes in the Peripheral South, began to attack Wallace sharply.
Labor union leaders, who saw Wallace's blue-collar appeal as a threat
to their ability to lead their own members, organized a massive anti-
Wallace, pro-Humphrey campaign. They gave wide circulation, for
example, to a letter from an Alabama worker detailing unpleasant
working conditions in Wallace's home state. Themes from other policy
areas—international involvement and economic management—were
used to counteract the Governor's appeal on civil liberties. Wallace
support was also reduced through the traditional warning: Don't waste
your vote on a third-party candidate.
    When the Gallup Poll showed Wallace strength ebbing in late Octo-
ber, the Governor attacked the poll, linking it to his opponents. "They
lie when they poll. They are trying to rig an election. Eastern money
runs everything. They are going to be pointed out as the liars they

are." All in all, the Time's Up phase was not pleasant for George Wallace. He was tired, and he knew that his hope of gaining electoral votes outside the South was forlorn. The day before the election, he was campaigning in front of the Georgia State House in the company of Georgia's segregationist Governor, Lester Maddox. As is often the case with third-party candidates, at the end he was reduced to the core of his support.

HUBERT HUMPHREY, THE HAPPY WARRIOR OF 1968

Hubert H. Humphrey brought boundless enthusiasm, optimism, and energy to politics. It must have taken all of these qualities to sustain him in the opening stages of the 1968 campaign. He was finally at the helm of the party whose leadership he had sought repeatedly, but the coalition he hoped to lead was badly divided. On top of the defection to Wallace of many southern Democrats, those who opposed the Vietnam War were quite unwilling to work for Humphrey. They had suffered a double wound: defeat in a major platform battle, and seeing many of their fellows suffer from the tear gas and billy clubs of the Chicago police. Compounding this problem was the relation of Vice President Humphrey to President Johnson and his supporters. Any serious move to bring the Democratic doves back into the Humphrey coalition risked instant repudiation from the administration that was simultaneously fighting a war and trying to get peace talks started in Paris.

A Rushed Beginning

As if the problems with internal structure weren't bad enough, there was no time to organize a campaign or plan how to handle this very difficult situation. The late-August convention, natural for a party in power on the assumption that the incumbent president would run, deprived the Humphrey core group of any time for the normal early stages of a campaign. Larry O'Brien was prevailed upon to stay as Democratic national chairman, and he had his fellow Springfield (Massachusetts) native, Joseph Napolitan, draw up a campaign plan. Humphrey could also rely on such talented Minnesotans as Orville Freeman and Walter Mondale. Even so, there was only time for some hasty conferences at Humphrey's home in Waverly, Minnesota, to worry about how to deal with lack of money, lack of support, lack of time, and lack of good ideas about how to heal the ruptures in the Democratic party.

The Grand Opening was a mixture of improvisation and hope. The Vice President inaugurated his campaign on September 9 with appearances in Philadelphia, Denver, and Los Angeles, and continued on the following days with appearances elsewhere. He spoke on pacific international programs—Food for Peace, the Peace Corps, and disarmament and arms control—in an effort to reach antiwar Democrats.[2] Humphrey called attention to other policy areas on which Democrats were united. These included administration accomplishments in social benefits— medicare, the Department of Housing and Urban Development, the Job Corps, education, and housing—and real progress in civil rights. He attacked Richard Nixon, whom many Democrats detested. But none of these appeals seemed to help. When Humphrey appeared on the hustings, he was confronted by demonstrators who chanted, "Dump the Hump," "Chicago, Chicago," "Seig Heil!" and the like. When he made a suggestion that some American troops could soon be brought back from Vietnam, it was repudiated by both the President and the Secretary of State. By the end of September, Humphrey was still trailing Nixon 44 percent to 29 percent in the Gallup Poll. The possibility of some event that would shift momentum—a Nixon mistake, a North Vietnamese decision to begin serious negotiations to end the war, or something equally helpful—seemed more and more remote. The internal problems of the Humphrey coalition were going to have to be dealt with before any external strategy aimed at voters would be worthwhile. This meant that the nettle of Vietnam must be grasped by Humphrey himself.

The Salt Lake City Adjustment

Mr. Humphrey made this Strategic Adjustment in a nationally televised speech from the Mormon Tabernacle in Salt Lake City on September 30. In several ways—by removing the vice presidential seal from the rostrum, by notifying President Johnson only after copies of the speech were given to newsmen, and by explicit references in the speech itself—Hubert Humphrey emphasized that he was speaking for himself and not as a member of the Johnson administration. His words were:

> As president, I would be willing to stop the bombing of North Vietnam as an acceptable risk for peace, because I believe that it could lead to success in negotiations and a shorter war. . . . In weighing the risk— and before taking action—I would place key importance on evidence, direct and indirect, by deed or word, of Communist willingness to restore the Demilitarized Zone between North and South Vietnam. If the govern-

---

[2] Just like other vice presidents who were nominated to run for president, Humphrey found himself identified willy-nilly with both the successes and the failures of the incumbent administration. It was ironic that Humphrey, whose own record of policy initiatives was matched by few in American political history, was so handicapped in 1968 by the Johnson Vietnam policy. He had almost nothing to do with policy decisions in this area. He did work out a compromise that antiwar leaders would have been willing to accept at the Democratic convention, but this compromise was rejected by President Johnson.

ment of North Vietnam were to show bad faith, I would reserve the right to resume the bombing.

Lyndon Johnson was not pleased with this speech, but there were more positive reactions. A plea for funds was added at the end, and the speech was no sooner over than pledges began to be phoned in. The demonstrators disappeared from Humphrey crowds and were replaced by friendlier faces. It was now possible to get about the business of appealing to voters, but time was very short.

A More Optimistic October

The outline of a viable strategy began to emerge on the basis of some private polls. While conceding that Humphrey was still far behind in the national polls, state polls showed something different. Humphrey leaders claimed that it might be possible for the Vice President to win by carrying some larger states—such as New York, New Jersey, Pennsylvania, Michigan, Minnesota, Missouri, and Texas—by quite small margins even though he lost other states by very large margins. They also claimed that their own polls showed Humphrey ahead, however narrowly, in these states. This claim rested on a very weak foundation. Some of the "polls" were conducted by Joseph Napolitan himself. The results were aimed at journalists, potential donors, and political workers, all of whom Humphrey leaders wanted to convince of the plausibility of a Humphrey victory. Their plan worked (Chester, Hodgson, & Page, 1969, pp. 711–14; Frankel, 1968). The money and effort that was forthcoming certainly improved Humphrey's chances in fact. Even more important, the geographic concentration implied by these poll results was the one way that the Vice President might get the electoral votes he needed.

In his campaigning, Humphrey continued to emphasize the issues that had served the Democrats well. In economic management, he did not emphasize the level of government spending, but rather Democratic support for employment. He favored making the federal government the employer of last resort, and while he stopped short of calling for income maintenance, he did favor increases in income supports. Fears of unemployment were summoned: "Imagine what it'll be like if the unemployment rate is up to 7 percent. Who's to be unemployed? Which worker is to be laid off? Which family is to be without a check?"

Memories of the 1930s depression were further stirred by a Democratic pamphlet that urged younger voters to ask their fathers what things were like during the depression if they couldn't remember themselves. On social benefits, Vice President Humphrey called for a full 50 percent increase in social security benefits, sweeping aid to education coming directly from the federal government, comprehensive prenatal care for all low-income women and medical care for all poor children during the first year of life. On civil liberties questions, Humphrey reiterated his support for the civil rights acts that had been passed, and generally endorsed Supreme Court decisions favoring rights of the accused.[3] The Vice President did temper his outspoken enthusiasm for civil rights, matching the decrease in civil rights support among the electorate. He put civil rights in an employment context.

> I know what the opposition puts out to the blue-collar worker. He says, "Watch out for that Humphrey. He is going to get a black man a job, and that means your job." I said, "Now listen here. I am for jobs. I am for an expanded economy in this country. I am for decent jobs and I don't care whether the worker is black, white, green, or purple; fat, thin, tall, or short. I am for jobs."

He further argued that he was in the best position to assure racial harmony after the election as he was the only one of the three candidates who was trusted by both blacks and whites.[4]

All this almost worked. Between early October and late October, the Nixon-Humphrey margin in the national Gallup Poll closed from 43–31 percent to 44–36 percent, and the margin was even closer in the East. The Time's Up phase was a good deal more pleasant than the Grand Opening had been for the Democratic coalition. The candidate campaigned across big states he hoped to carry, while the media campaign emphasized issues known to produce Democratic votes. One spot featured a man laughing for nearly a full minute, and closed with the message: "Agnew for vice president? This would be funny if it weren't so serious. . . ." On October 29, Senator Eugene McCarthy finally endorsed Humphrey; and on October 31, President Johnson announced an immediate suspension to bombing North Vietnam, and said that serious peace talks would begin in Paris the following week. The McCarthy endorsement and the imminence of peace negotiations with North Vietnam did not convert foreign policy into a Democratic

---

[3] Richard Nixon took positions "opposite" to those of Humphrey's on all the topics mentioned in this paragraph. For instance, whereas Humphrey called for a 50 percent increase in social security benefits, Nixon endorsed a number of expansions in benefits that he said would be less costly. Benjamin Page (1978, chaps. 3, 4) has done an extensive analysis of the positions taken by the two major party candidates. The most frequent case was that Humphrey and Nixon took essentially the same stand. This happened on two thirds of all foreign issues and on many domestic issues. Where the candidates differed, they reflected traditional party divisions. When party differences were low, as they were on 89 percent of foreign issues and 56 percent of domestic issues, candidate differences were low 66 percent of the time. On those topics where party divisions were high, candidate differences were high 66 percent of the time. For obvious reasons, most attention is paid to the points on which candidates differ. It is worth remembering, though, that parties and candidates take essentially similar postures most of the time.

[4] Joe Napolitan took stronger measures to deemphasize civil rights in the Humphrey media campaign. He issued instructions that no black persons were to appear in any television spots.

advantage, but they were sufficient to allow pro-Democratic issues, such as social benefits and jobs, to have greater impact. The Gallup and Harris polls on the Sunday before the election showed Nixon with only a 42 to 40 percent lead over Humphrey. In the month since his Salt Lake City speech, Hubert Humphrey had almost led his coalition to victory.

THE POSSIBILITY OF A REPUBLICAN VICTORY

Just as Woodrow Wilson was given an opportunity in 1912 by the split of the then majority Republican party, Richard Nixon was given an opportunity in 1968 by the fragmentation of the Democratic party. Ever since the 1930s, Republican candidates have had to take most of the independent vote and pick up at least a few Democratic votes to win. But with George Wallace attracting many Democratic and independent votes, and the antiwar Democratic activists sitting on their hands, Richard Nixon had an unusual chance to win with the normal Republican vote.

External Threats and Nixon's Plan from the Center

In spite of this happy augury, the Nixon coalition faced a difficult political problem because of the three-candidate situation. Hubert Humphrey was taking more liberal positions and George Wallace was taking more conservative positions. This didn't pose too much of an internal problem; Republican activists were unlikely to support Humphrey or Wallace. It did, however, pose quite an external problem. If Nixon took relatively liberal positions in order to woo voters away from Humphrey, he risked losing support to Wallace. If he took relatively conservative positions to woo voters away from Wallace, he risked losing support to Humphrey.

The problem can be seen in the geographic concentration planned for the campaign. The list of states was selected by Nixon himself for extensive personal campaigning and for concentrated media efforts. The 14 states seemed to reflect a concern for Electoral College arithmetic (297 votes), and a determination to get even for his 1960 defeat. Nine of the states had gone for John F. Kennedy in 1960. Nixon's list included California in the West; South Carolina in the Deep South; Texas, Florida, North Carolina, and Virginia in the Peripheral South; Ohio, Illinois, Michigan, Wisconsin, and Missouri (all urban midwestern states); and Pennsylvania, New Jersey, and New York in the East (Chester, Hodgson, & Page, 1969, p. 621). To the extent that Nixon took positions that would win support away from Wallace in the southern states on the list, he would be vulnerable to Humphrey in the East and the

Midwest. To the extent that he took positions that would win support away from Humphrey in the East and the Midwest, he risked losing states in the South to Wallace. If Richard Nixon was going to win the required majority of Electoral College votes, he needed to maintain a precarious balance between his two opponents. This meant that he had to sketch out his generally moderate-conservative position, to create the impression of movement, to make statements, but to do all this without saying anything so definite that it would cause the majority of voters then leaning to Nixon to reevaluate their positions.

A Symbolic Chicago Opening

The Grand Opening of the Nixon campaign began in Chicago on September 4. A parade through the downtown area was seen by hundreds of thousands of persons, seemingly relieved by the contrast between Nixon's peaceful arrival and the violence that had marked the Democratic convention a few weeks earlier. The centerpiece of the Chicago visit, though, was a telecast during which Nixon was interviewed by a panel of representative citizens. The panel members had been screened, and this gave Nixon the chance to make statements without being pressed, as he might have been during a debate or if confronted by a determined newsman. In the opening exchange, for example, he was asked:

> Would you care to comment on the accusation which was made from time to time that your views have shifted and that they are based on expediencies?

Nixon replied:

> I suppose what you are referring to is: Is there a new Nixon or an old Nixon? . . . My answer is, yes, there is a new Nixon, if you are talking in terms of new ideas for a new world and the America we live in. In terms of what I believe in the American view and the American dream, I think I am just where I was eight years ago.

Later a black panel member asked, "What do law and order mean to you?" This time the reply was:

> I am quite aware that the black community, when they hear it, think of power as being used in a way that is destructive to them; and yet I think we have to also remember that the black community as well as the white community has an interest in law and order, providing that law is with justice. To me law and order must be combined with justice. Now that's what I want for America. I want the kind of law and order which deserves respect. (McGinniss, 1969, pp. 70–71)

This opportunity to appear responsive, and to associate himself with such popular symbols as the American dream and justice, was ideal for a candidate who had to maintain a delicate political balance. The television format was sharpened a bit, but was not basically altered, and was used in 10 cities in the course of the campaign.

From Chicago, the campaign moved on to rallies on succeeding days in San Francisco, Houston, Pittsburgh, and White Plains (New York). Richard Nixon drew middle-class audiences, and made his appeal to those he termed *forgotten Americans:*

> those who did not indulge in violence, those who did not break the law, those who pay taxes and go to work, people who send their children to school, who go to their churches, people who are not haters, people who love this country.

These were inclusive categories; most people do obey the law, pay their taxes, go to work, and so on. Certainly there was nothing in this language to disturb either moderate or conservative supporters.

As the campaign developed, Mr. Nixon sent two types of messages. One was "the speech." This had a standard content. The tested applause lines were the same whether they came at a giant rally, after music and cascading balloons, or whether they were uttered at a brief stop at a community airport.

> We need new leadership that will not only end the war in Vietnam but keep the nation out of other wars for eight years.
>
> I say that when crime has been going up nine times as fast as the population, when 43 percent of the people living in American cities are afraid to go out after dark, I say we need a complete housecleaning.
>
> The American flag is not going to be used as a doormat for anybody when we get in.
>
> Well, my friends, I say this, that when you are on the wrong road and you reach a dead end, the thing you do is get off that road and onto a new road.

These statements were not unusual campaign oratory. Almost every candidate develops a standard speech, and certainly every out-party candidate tells his audience that a new administration is needed.

Nixon's other type of message was more innovative. He used radio, a low-cost, low-salience medium for longer discussions directed to the more limited audience he thought might be interested in issues. In the course of the campaign, he gave speeches on the presidency, order and justice, black capitalism, a new political coalition, training programs for the urban poor, revenue sharing, social security, NATO, the Alliance for Progress, the problems of youth, and defense policy. The combination of the set stump speech and the more thoughtful radio address afforded a contrast in style (Semple, 1968). One type of message was directed to a mass audience that wasn't sufficiently interested to think past slogans; the other to an attentive elite that was interested in public policy. And the two types of messages seemed to be directed to separate audiences whose policy preferences might differ. Consider these passages from two of his radio addresses. When calling for an open presidency, Mr. Nixon said:

> A president has to hear not only the clamorous voices of the organized, but also the quiet voices, the inner voices—the voices that speak from the heart and conscience. . . . A president must tell the people what cannot be done immediately, as well as what can. Hope is fragile, and too easily shattered by the disappointment that follows inevitably on promises unkept and unkeepable.

In another address entitled "Order and Justice under Law," he explained:

> It is true that law enforcement is primarily a local responsibility—but the public climate with respect to law is a function of national leadership. . . . A National Academy of Law Enforcement . . . would enable our law enforcement agencies to be equipped for the complex tasks they face in our modern world.

Nothing in these words disavowed positions taken in the stump speeches, but the tone was certainly different. Where "the speech" declared that the American flag wouldn't be used as a doormat, and suggested that a complete housecleaning would solve the problems of crime, the radio addresses spoke of fragile hope and complex tasks. It was as though the applause lines were delivered to conservatives who thought that problems could be solved if the government were just tough enough, and the radio speeches were addressed to moderates. Whether there was an explicit strategy of dual messages or not, we don't know. We do know that both sets of voters had to be reached, and that Nixon continued to use both types of speeches throughout the campaign.

Tactical Adjustments

The Nixon campaign was well enough planned that no Strategic Adjustments were necessary. There were some Tactical Adjustments from time to time. The first was a move to counter George Wallace as his strength peaked in late September and early October. In Atlanta on October 3, Nixon said that he and Wallace were both opposed to foreign policy failings and the rise in crime at home. But he challenged Wallace because of the latter's statement that if any demonstrator laid down in front of his car it would be the last such occasion.

> We need politics at home that will go beyond simply saying that if somebody lies down in front of my presidential limousine it will be the last one he lies down in front of. Now look here. No president of the United

States is going to do that, and anybody who says so shouldn't be president of the United States.

Campaigning later in Florida, he asked his audience: "Does Florida want to go off onto a third-party kick? Or does it want to play a role in the great decision of 1968?" It would be unwise to claim too much for the effects of these speeches; other anti-Wallace forces were active at the same time. Still, Wallace strength did subside during October, and this left Nixon in a much stronger position in the Peripheral South.

A more serious challenge to Nixon was coming from the other direction. By mid-October, the Nixon coalition was aware of growing Humphrey strength. Consequently, the core group met with the candidate at his Key Biscayne home on the weekend of October 13. Some previously taken decisions were reaffirmed. Nixon would continue to avoid debates with Humphrey, and continue to rely on radio speeches to delineate his positions. But there were some Tactical Adjustments as well. In order to counter Democratic success on social benefits questions, Nixon would stress his own support for social security, and he would begin to attack Vice President Humphrey more directly (White, 1969, pp. 370–71).

The Key Biscayne meeting was followed by stronger phrases. Vice President Humphrey became "the most expensive senator in American history," and "a man who gives no indication he believes there's any bottom to the well of the U.S. Treasury." Nixon seemed particularly fond of the phrase "sock it to 'em" from a then-popular TV show, "Laugh In." In Columbus, Ohio, for example, he said Ohio State played "rock 'em, sock 'em football, and that's just what we're going to do for the rest of the campaign. From now on we're going to sock it to 'em with everything we've got." In fact, though, Mr. Nixon continued to pursue very cautious, centrist politics. The number of appearances he made in any day was limited. He continued to take positions close to the known preferences of voters.[5]

No Room Left for Maneuver

Reporters traveling with Richard Nixon in late October noticed any number of fluffs and misstatements. The Time's Up stage of the campaign had arrived, and the candidate was doubtless tired; but there was more to it than that. He was caught in the middle in three-candidate politics. Having decided to position himself to take southern states from Wallace, he had given up the opportunity to prevent a resurgence of normal Democratic support for Humphrey in the East. Nixon's only

---

[5] Page's study (1978, chap. 3) shows that Nixon took positions close to those of a plurality of the electorate on 79 percent of the issues, compared to 69 percent for Humphrey.

new policy position was a call for clear-cut military superiority over the Soviet Union. Beyond this, he urged Humphrey to join him in a pledge to support the candidate who got the largest number of popular votes if no one won a majority in the Electoral College. Vice President Humphrey was no more likely to accept this proposal than Nixon had been to accept Humphrey's earlier challenge to debate. But as things turned out, luck was with Nixon. By three o'clock of the morning after the election, it was apparent that Richard Nixon had carried Ohio, Illinois, and California, and had narrowly won the office that had eluded him eight years earlier.

THE 1980 CAMPAIGN

The economic issues that troubled Americans during the 1970s continued to dominate their thinking in 1980. The inflation rate got worse in every year of the Carter administration. The consumer price index rose 6.5 percent in 1977, 7.6 percent in 1978, 11.5 percent in 1979, and 13.5 percent in 1980. Other worries about loss of jobs showed up in an increasing number of people who, even in the face of uncontrolled inflation, thought unemployment was more important. On the foreign scene, no war loomed on the horizon; but the continuing plight of the diplomats held hostage in Tehran seemed to symbolize American incapacity overseas. All of these together contributed to a public perception of Jimmy Carter as a good man, but an incompetent president.

Many voters were no more taken with Ronald Reagan. On Friday, April 18, an article appeared on the front page of the *New York Times*. "To half the American public," the lead sentence said, "President Carter and Ronald Reagan . . . represent an unsatisfactory choice for president, [according to] the latest New York Times/CBS News Poll." Even more opposition was to be found in certain groups of voters. Sixty percent of eastern liberals, western liberals, and college graduates wanted a choice other than Carter and Reagan, as did 56 percent of the 18- to 29-year-olds, and 54 percent of independent voters.

Obviously, there were voters who regarded Ronald Reagan and Jimmy Carter as eminently satisfactory candidates. Governor Reagan was passionately supported by the conservative Republicans he had led for over a decade, and President Carter had the respectful support of Democrats who thought he had done his best with difficult problems. As time passed, and Reagan and Carter became their parties' nominees, the number of their supporters grew, and 92 percent of the voters ended up casting ballots for one of the major party candidates. Even so, the extent of dissatisfaction with Reagan and Carter said something about the strategic opportunities that were open to the major contenders in 1980. This discontent also indicated an unusual opportunity for a third-party candidate; on April 24, John Anderson, having concluded that he could not win the Republican nomination and that he had something he wanted to say, announced his "National Unity" campaign.

JOHN ANDERSON'S SOLITARY QUEST

Both George Wallace and John Anderson discovered constituencies that were at least temporarily neglected by the major parties, but there were differences in the Wallace and Anderson constituencies. Both had an appeal to young voters, and to independents, as is typical of third-party candidates. But George Wallace's 1968 supporters tended to have high school educations, blue-collar occupations, and middle-level incomes. John Anderson's constituency was disproportionately affluent, well educated, and professional. George Wallace's supporters were worried about changes they found threatening. John Anderson's backers represented a growing segment of American society, but one that was far too small to elect a president by itself.

A second important difference was that George Wallace's support was much more concentrated geographically than John Anderson's. This had consequences for Electoral College possibilities. With the electoral votes of the Deep South likely to be his, Wallace could have forced the presidential selection into the House of Representatives if there had been a fairly even split of the rest between Nixon and Humphrey. With Anderson support spread across campuses and suburbs in several parts of the country, he could affect outcomes in individual states by taking votes from Carter or Reagan, but was less likely to get electoral votes unless his national standing rose impressively.

Finally, Governor Wallace was more conservative than either Richard Nixon or Hubert Humphrey. As things turned out, he was more of a threat to Nixon's freedom of action than to Humphrey's. Once Nixon had positioned himself to contain Wallace, he could not move back to the center to hold off Humphrey's late threat. John Anderson, however, was positioned between Jimmy Carter and Ronald Reagan on most issues. This meant that Anderson was going to have to fight both candidates for the votes of the political center.

The Problem of Remaining Visible

A third-party candidate has a few advantages and a lot of disadvantages. Not bound by past positions, he has tactical mobility and an ability to present new ideas. But without support from an existing party, he lacks an experienced campaign organization, the capacity to locate voters and get them to the polls, and the financial support the federal government makes available to the major party candidates. Moreover, the record of history is that third-party candidates lose votes to major party candidates as the election approaches.

This last consideration was perhaps Anderson's most important challenge. A Louis Harris poll taken in May showed candidate standings of Reagan, 39 percent; Carter, 33 percent; and Anderson, 23 percent. But when respondents were asked who they would vote for if Anderson had a real chance to win, the trial heat changed to Reagan, 35 percent; Carter 31 percent; and Anderson, 29 percent. If Anderson remained a credible candidate, he could challenge both Reagan and Carter. If voters became skeptical, then he faced an erosion of support.

As John Anderson undertook his independent candidacy, there were four small groups and one large "group" in his nascent coalition. First of all, there were members of his congressional staff such as Robert Walker, Michael MacLeod, and Kirk Walder. Second, there were persons who had been active in the Ripon Society, a liberal Republican organization. Michael MacLeod had been executive director, and he recruited others including Clifford Brown, who was to become research director. After Anderson's strong showing in the Massachusetts primary, a third group became involved, veterans of Congressman Morris Udall's 1976 presidential campaign including Edward Coyle, Francis Sheehan, and Michael Fernandez. This group was important because they provided contacts with Democratic politicians. Fourth, when Anderson launched his National Unity campaign, they were joined by some experienced campaigners, of whom the most important were David Garth and Tom Matthews. Garth was a well-known campaign consultant whose ties with the New York-based media community enabled him to give credibility to the thought that Anderson could win, and Matthews was a direct-mail expert who had worked for a number of liberal causes. The large "group" was made up of inexperienced, but enthusiastic, volunteers.[6] Their only common element was that they were attracted to John Anderson. Some of them came to play prominent roles as they gradually gained political experience.

During the summer of 1980, the candidate himself was kept in the news while serious organization and planning work went forward. During the Republican National Convention, Congressman Anderson went off to visit Israel, Egypt, Germany, France, and Britain. His meetings with foreign leaders were not very substantive, and in his efforts to court Jewish support, he came close to endorsement of many Israeli foreign policy goals. At the end of July, Edward Coyle arranged a meeting between Congressman Anderson and Senator Kennedy. Not much happened in the meeting. Speaking to the press later, Kennedy said that his nomination could "eliminate the need" for a third-party candidacy, and Anderson said he *might* not run if the Democrats did not nominate Carter. These events generated some publicity, but they could hardly be called political triumphs.

---

[6] There were two important exceptions to this. Both Barbara Andrews and Char Sadalak had political experience which they used to good effect in creating a field organization for John Anderson.

Throughout the summer, the principal organizational effort was to get Anderson's name on the ballot. The regional and state organizations were heavily involved in this because many states required large numbers of signatures (e.g., over 100,000 in California) to qualify a candidate for a ballot position. The ballot effort also required substantial litigation. In addition to the suits necessary to get on the ballot in some states, the Democratic National Committee set aside $225,000 for litigation to keep Anderson *off* the ballot in states such as Massachusetts where they thought that Anderson would be popular enough to draw votes away from Carter. Milton Ragovin's legal work on Anderson's behalf was remarkably successful, although quite expensive. He won every suit he filed, getting the laws of five states declared unconstitutional, and persuading a federal district judge to overrule the Georgia Supreme Court. John Anderson's name appeared on the ballot in all 50 states, but at a cost of $2 million for organization and legal services, a substantial drain on the lean Anderson treasury.[7]

The other major requirement for legitimacy was finding a vice presidential candidate. The ideal vice presidential candidate was easy to describe: a well-known Democrat from a major state such as New York or California with a reputation for independence, a lot of voter appeal, and policy views similar to Congressman Anderson's. Such qualifications would have added votes to the National Unity ticket. The problem, of course, was that most prominent Democrats who had even some of these ideal qualifications were not anxious to risk their political careers by running on a minor ticket. But with the help of Udall veteran Edward Coyle, Patrick J. Lucey was persuaded to accept the vice presidential designation. If Lucey was not the strongest possible candidate, he was at least plausible. He was active in the John F. Kennedy campaign in 1960 as Wisconsin Democratic state chairman, was elected to two terms as governor of Wisconsin, served briefly as ambassador to Mexico, and then worked for the nomination of Edward Kennedy after a falling out with President Carter. So, with the announcement on August 25 that Lucey would run, the Anderson coalition could feel that they had made reasonable progress in remaining in the public eye while getting on the ballot.

A Third-Party Strategy

There were several elements to the Anderson strategy: the relative strength of the major candidates, geographic concentration, demographic concentration, and issues. A common consideration linking all of these was the Anderson coalition's lack of resources. Without strength themselves, they had to rely on the jujitsu method of anticipating an opponent's moves so that the opponent's weight and motion

---

[7] The total expenditures of the Anderson general election campaign were $14.4 million.

can be turned against him. This, of course, was risky business. The assumptions about Reagan's and Carter's strategies had to be correct, Anderson's feints had to be made at just the right time, and there had to be *at least some* resources just to make the needed moves in this underdog strategy.

John Anderson's ultimate goal was to become the second candidate so that voters would think of Reagan versus Anderson, or Carter versus Anderson, rather than Reagan versus Carter with Anderson being considered only in case the first two were unsatisfactory. (Theodore Roosevelt, who ran second to Woodrow Wilson as the Bull Moose candidate in 1912, was the only third-party candidate able to accomplish this in this century.) In thinking about this, Anderson strategists reckoned that Reagan had a solid conservative base that guaranteed him about 30 percent, no matter what. Carter, they felt, had no solid support except from blacks. This meant that Reagan was going to be the strongest man in a three-candidate race. Therefore, they had little hope of getting ahead of Reagan in the polls by taking moderate-conservative positions, but they could perhaps get ahead of Carter by taking moderate-liberal positions. They recognized that they had to fight Carter first in order to get the voters to eventually think of Reagan and Anderson as alternatives. Carter was the immediate tactical opponent. If all went well, Reagan would be the ultimate strategic opponent.

It was assumed that Carter would try to build on a southern base by adding frequently Democratic industrial states in the Northeast. Reagan, however, was seen as stronger than Carter in the South. The Anderson strategists felt that President Carter could carry Georgia and Arkansas, but that Governor Reagan could take the rest. Therefore the most rational Reagan strategy was to concentrate on the South, to win by adding Indiana, Kentucky, Tennessee, and several southern states to his western base, to pay attention to Ohio and Illinois as insurance states, and not bother with the upper Midwest or the Northeast.

The Anderson geographic targets were based on these assumptions about what Carter and Reagan were likely to do, and survey results. A Louis Harris poll, again asking respondents how they would vote if they thought Anderson could win, found Anderson leads in Massachusetts, New York, New Jersey, Pennsylvania, Ohio, Illinois, and California. These states, which cast 216 electoral votes, were Anderson's prime targets.[8] This implied Carter as the principal opponent in New York, New Jersey, and Pennsylvania; Reagan as the principal opponent

---

[8] Anderson's secondary targets were Connecticut, Rhode Island, Vermont, and Maine in New England; Delaware and Maryland; Wisconsin, Minnesota, Iowa, and South Dakota in the upper Midwest; Colorado; Hawaii; and Oregon and Washington in the Pacific Northwest. These secondary target states cast an additional 91 electoral votes in 1980, giving Anderson 307 electoral votes if he won *all* the primary and secondary target states.

only in California (where they thought Carter was too weak to make much of a race); and a three-candidate contest only in Ohio and Illinois. This was a second reason why Carter was seen as Anderson's tactical opponent. There were simply more states where they thought they would be in a contest with Carter.[9]

Strategically, John Anderson faced much the same challenge that confronted George Wallace in 1968. He had a firm base, but the base was too small to win. The most likely Anderson voters were upper middle-class professionals. The problem was how to expand the Anderson coalition by extending it beyond the "brie and chablis" set to include more of Middle America. If Anderson was to become a genuine contender, he needed to gain the support of blue-collar voters, of blacks, and of Hispanics, but *without* losing the support that was coming from suburbs and campuses.

The National Unity issue positions were chosen with an eye to attracting these additional voters. There were very strong urban and civil rights emphases. An urban reinvestment trust fund was to be established to rebuild streets, bridges, sidewalks, sewers, and other deteriorating facilities, and neighborhood development was to be emphasized. John Anderson had a strong civil rights record, including support for open housing, and this was also stressed. The repair of infrastructure and emphasis on civil liberties were both compatible with fiscal conservatism, and in this way, the Anderson coalition hoped to attract Middle American support without losing votes from the suburbs. For this to work, of course, Middle America had to be paying attention.

A Month of Auspicious Developments

Electoral campaigns usually do not open with a crisis, but third-party activities often depart from the customary. The immediate cause of the crisis was financial. The ballot access campaign, while successful, had been very costly. Money was flowing from national headquarters to the field. Now, short of funds, the Anderson campaign had to decide between continuing to sustain the field operation and putting on a media campaign. The August 28 decision was to ask the state organizations to raise money, to spend no more than absolutely necessary on travel, and to concentrate whatever funds were available on media. At the same time, media advisor David Garth was put in full control of the campaign. (His first decision was to cancel a $225,000 whistle-stop tour from Illinois to Pennsylvania.) Garth's appointment led to

---

[9] Another implication of this strategy was that the Anderson tacticians recognized there were whole regions of the country—the South and the intermountain West—where there was nothing they could do to affect the outcome.

the departure of the senior Udall veterans who had been building bridges to the Democratic party—Edward Coyle, Francis Sheehan, and Michael Fernandez—and Char Sadalak who had been an important leader of the field organization. This shake-up did not resolve the central problem of a general shortage of resources, but it settled how the scarce resources were to be used.

On Labor Day weekend, the Anderson-Lucey campaign released their platform. The positions were reflections of the stands that Congressman Anderson had been taking for some time, and were useful in reaching the voters they hoped to attract. The contents could be summarized as liberal in international involvement (reflecting what had been bipartisan foreign policy in former years), conservative in economic management, moderate in social benefits, liberal in civil liberties, and liberal in natural resources. The natural resources provisions, designed to attract environmentalists, represented the only real shift from recent Anderson positions. The platform was touted as longer and more meaningful than "normal" party platforms. These claims were exaggerated. It was, however, more coherent, having been spared the bargaining that is part of a convention. It had been written by the research division under John Anderson's active, personal direction, and also reflected a number of suggestions made by Patrick Lucey. Another unusual feature was the promise to release a detailed budget analysis of the cost of the platform if implemented.[10] *Washington Post* reporter David S. Broder wrote that the Anderson platform "may be the most valuable collection of innovative policy ideas so far assembled for the 1980s."

The month of September was hopeful for the Anderson campaign. The first auspicious development was an innovative ruling from the Federal Election Commission that the National Unity campaign would be eligible for federal funds providing that Anderson received at least 5 percent of the total vote. The basis for this was the conclusion that the Anderson effort was the functional equivalent of a political party. This ruling brought hope of an end to the financial drought; Anderson leaders planned to approach banks to seek $10 million in bank loans. Such loans could be used for a media campaign, and could be repaid when federal moneys became available.

The following weekend, the policy committee of the Liberal party in New York State recommended that the party endorse John Anderson. This was important for both symbolic and practical reasons. Symbolically, it gave Anderson an endorsement that had gone to Democratic candidates during the party's 36-year history, thus strengthening Anderson's claim to nonpartisan support. Practically, the endorsement guaranteed Anderson a party line (and thus a number of votes) in New

---

[10] This was released on October 13.

York, and thus strengthened his hand against Jimmy Carter in the Empire State.

Still another happy development came with the League of Women Voters' decision that John Anderson—slightly above the league's 15 percent criterion in some polls and slightly below in others—should be invited to take part in the presidential debates the league was sponsoring. This brought different reactions from the two major parties. Reagan strategists were willing to take part in a debate that included Anderson, but Carter strategists were not. Carter leaders, simultaneously trying to convince banks they should *not* give Anderson any loans, reasoned that they just could not afford to give the Anderson candidacy the credibility that would come with an appearance against the President. Therefore a Reagan-Anderson debate was scheduled in Baltimore for Sunday, September 21.

Congressman Anderson, by now aiming more and more of his salvos at President Carter, broke off his campaigning on the preceding Wednesday morning, and returned to Washington to rest and prepare for the debate. For a person as intelligent and as familiar with issues as Anderson, it wasn't necessary to spend a lot of time in preparation. It was more a matter of organizing his thoughts around topics that were likely to come up than of augmenting his already broad understanding. The debate showed two able candidates who differed on almost every single issue. Both showed their strengths very well. Anderson was the more impressive intellectually, and perhaps better able to state facts. Reagan was more relaxed. Viewers could see him as a plausible president, one who did not seem likely to start a nuclear war as soon as he was sworn in. The difference was in the stakes of the debate for the two. For Reagan, a major party nominee with ample resources, the debate was one of a series of campaign events. For Anderson, as the *New York Times* headline put it, the future was a single hour. And after the debate was over, the spotlight of attention began to dim.

Fading Hopes

The immediate postdebate polls suggested that both Anderson and Reagan did about equally well. The Harris results showed that Anderson did a little better; the Gallup results showed Reagan with an edge. But John Anderson was not able to capitalize on his hour in the sun to improve his standing against the two major party candidates, and more serious difficulties became apparent in the postdebate campaigning. Gambling as they had to that their candidate would do well in the debate, Anderson leaders organized major appearances for the day after the debate, and an augmented press corps went along to see how he would do. Things went well at a noon-hour rally in Chicago, where Anderson enjoyed attacking Carter for his refusal to debate, but not that evening in Philadelphia. Appearing in a 3,500-seat auditorium, he faced a painfully small crowd of about 500. The headline in the *Philadelphia Inquirer* was "Empty Hall Swallows Anderson Momentum," and David Broder pointed out that Anderson lacked just the kind of support that a political party can provide for its candidate.

By the end of the week, a number of political observers had concluded that the Anderson campaign was likely to meet the fate of most third-party efforts. Writing in the *Washington Star,* Jack Germond and Jules Witcover asserted: "With some exceptions, Anderson's leading supporters and advisors . . . now see the rest of the campaign as a case of playing out their hand against essentially hopeless odds." This was challenged in a letter to the *Star* signed by Anderson's 10 senior advisors, but while the political judgment of the media experts could be controverted, the effects of their editorial judgment could not. John Anderson was all but invisible on the television network newscasts on Tuesday, Wednesday, Thursday, and Friday of the week after the Baltimore debate. And on September 30, a *Washington Post* story on Anderson was relegated to page 6.

The news judgment that cost John Anderson television time and removed him from front pages was the more harmful because the Anderson forces still lacked the resources to afford a media campaign. Anderson leaders were not able to borrow money from the banks. In part, the problem was White House opposition, but it was also the risky nature of the loans from the banks' perspective. Anderson's problem was that his collateral was to be found in public opinion polls. His standing was well above the required 5 percent at the time the loans were being sought, but the Anderson coalition could not *guarantee* the banks that Anderson's standing would not drop below 5 percent by election day.[11] Consequently, the Anderson forces tried another tactic. On September 29, they mailed letters to previous Anderson donors, asking that they make small loans to the Anderson campaign to be paid back when federal funds became available. Almost $1 million was raised this way by mid-October. This was far short of the $10 million that was originally sought from banks, but enough to permit a *very* modest media campaign.

These adverse developments did not spell the end of the campaign. Anderson support was declining, but it did not disappear. Anderson voters continued to be found among young people, among the better educated, among professionals, on campuses, and in suburbs. If the Anderson coalition was not able to expand to include blue-collar workers, there were also supporters who were staying with him. And the

---

[11] The effort to obtain bank loans was not given up until October 15.

candidate himself continued his own efforts. When he was good, as
he often was in campus appearances, he could engender excitement
about himself and the ideas about which he spoke. But on other occasions, he sounded strident, stubborn, and had a tendency to preach
to his audiences. These not-so-good appearances happened too frequently. The truth was that John Anderson was by now very tired.
Lacking resources for a media campaign that would amplify his own
voice, he had been carrying much of the campaign himself for a long
time, and weariness often reduced his effectiveness as a campaigner.

The Anderson strategy was in many ways the most interesting of
those adopted by the three candidates. Even if the resources to implement it were not available, it was recognized from the outset as a
long shot. And to the extent that resources were available, the plan
remained in effect from the Grand Opening throughout much of the
campaign. Decisions about Congressman Anderson's schedule and the
limited media campaign were made in accordance with it. This meant
that for much of the campaign, the Anderson coalition *was* trying to
win. It was not until Time's Up that the strategy was altered. In the
last week of the campaign, Anderson's schedule was changed. A final
swing through the Midwest was canceled, and John Anderson went
instead to New England and California, his two strongest areas. In
this Time's Up effort, it was thought that it would look better on television to have the larger crowds more likely to turn out in friendly terri-
tory. When he did return to his own alma mater on the night before
the election, John Anderson could say:

> Whatever the outcome, our goal has been to wake up America and to
> bring a new sense of hope in the future of our country. You give me
> heart to believe that in the hearts of young Americans we have succeeded.

But for most of the campaign, he was trying to win the election as
well.

KEEPING THE WOLF FROM THE DOOR:
CARTER 1980

Organization and Planning

By 1980, the political novices who had managed the 1976 campaign
had the advantage of four years of experience. This could be seen in
some of their plans. But they also bore the scars of a number of political
defeats. Their precarious situation was summarized in pollster Pat Caddell's reflections: "Simply stated . . . our strategy was . . . trying to
keep the wolf from the door. . . . I often had the terrible feeling we

were like the German army being sent to Moscow to take it without winter uniforms."

The leadership of the 1980 coalition consisted of a core group that was augmented from time to time. The four central decision makers were Hamilton Jordan, who came from the White House to take charge of the campaign in June, presidential press secretary Jody Powell, media specialist Gerald Rafshoon, and Pat Caddell. Jordan, Powell, and Rafshoon had worked with each other since the days of Carter's gubernatorial campaigns; Caddell had worked with them since 1976. Robert Strauss, who bore the title of chairman, provided liaison with the media, potential donors, and Democrats outside the Carter coalition. Others were brought into campaign decision making from time to time, depending on the question that arose. These included Stuart Eizenstat, head of the White House Domestic Policy Staff, Richard Moe of Vice President Mondale's staff, Tim Kraft, Les Francis, and Tom Donilon of the field staff, Tim Finchem, the staff director, and Tim Smith, the legal counsel.[12] Jack English and Carl Wagner, ranking Kennedy aides, were hired right after the Democratic National Convention, and provided a link to Kennedy groups that were working on behalf of the President.

There were three layers to the Carter strategy in 1980. The most fundamental layer was a strategy memorandum written for President Carter by Hamilton Jordan as soon as he moved from the White House to the campaign staff. The second layer was the "Orange Book," a geographic analysis that indicated where the electoral votes would have to be sought. This was compiled by Chris Brown, director of the Targeting Division of the Democratic National Committee. The Orange Book was used, especially early in the campaign, to guide decisions about field budget, travel, and phone banks. The third layer was a series of memoranda written by Pat Caddell on the basis of surveys. The first of these went to President Carter on June 25, the same day as the Jordan memorandum. The poll information kept the strategy current during the campaign, and was used to make decisions about scheduling, and whether or not to take part in presidential debates.[13]

---

[12] Finchem and Smith were important because they were close to Hamilton Jordan.

[13] A number of these documents were published after the campaign was over, as was the case in 1976. Their availability gives the analyst a chance to see what recommendations are being made during the campaign. A short portion of the Jordan memorandum appears in his book, *Crisis*, on pp. 305–9. Two memoranda written by Pat Caddell and five memoranda written by Richard Wirthlin for Governor Reagan appear in the appendix of *Portrait of an Election*, by Elizabeth Drew. A very informative discussion between Pat Caddell and Richard Wirthlin appears in the December 1980/January 1981 issue of *Public Opinion*, published by the American Enterprise Institute. And an article by Richard Wirthlin, Vincent Breglio, and Richard Beal in the February/March 1981 issue of *Public Opinion* presents the strategy that the Reagan coalition was following during the last month of the campaign.

None of these three analyses suggested that it would be easy to reelect Jimmy Carter.

The Jordan memorandum began by placing the blame for the difficult political situation not on any failures of the preceding four years, but rather on "Kennedy's sustained and exaggerated attacks on your record." The central strategic message of Jordan's analysis was:

> You will not be elected President unless we succeed partially in dispelling the notion that it doesn't matter who the President is, unless we convince the American people that this is a critical election in the life of our country and that there are real and substantial differences between you and Ronald Reagan. (Jordan, 1982, p. 308)

Unless voters were convinced that it made a real difference whether Carter or Reagan was elected, Jordan predicted a number of untoward consequences: the Democratic coalition would not come together, minority voters would not turn out, liberals would defect, and the Anderson candidacy would flourish. All of these were the opposite of what Jordan wanted. Hence, drawing a sharp distinction between Carter and Reagan became the cornerstone supporting the entire Carter strategy.

The Orange Book was based on an analysis of election data from 1956 through 1976. These elections were chosen because they included three Republican and three Democratic victories, and because going back to 1956 would begin the time series with a normal-turnout election rather than the high-turnout election of 1960. The analysis proper was focused on three political concerns: turnout, performance, and persuadability. The measure of probable 1980 turnout was a projection of the regression line for each state from 1956 through 1976. Democratic performance was measured by the mean Democratic vote over this time period, and persuadability was measured by the standard deviation of this mean. In practice, Democratic performance was the basic consideration in determining targeting. After inspecting the mean Democratic vote, and making certain "commonsense" adjustments, all states were classified as safe, marginal, or lost. The marginal states were subclassified into marginal plus, marginal, and marginal minus. Considerations of turnout and persuadability, converted into estimates of the amount of effort required to produce electoral votes, were raised only after the basic decision about the likelihood of a state voting Democratic had been made.

The grim prospect facing a Democratic candidate[14] can be seen from

---

[14] Remember that this calculation was based on the average Democratic vote, and did not reflect any additional liabilities Jimmy Carter might have because of his personal unpopularity in 1980. Taking this series of elections, however, did produce a slight Republican bias. There were three close elections (1960, 1968, and 1976), one Democratic landslide (1964), and two Republican landslides (1956 and 1972). Consequently a typical Democratic candidate should have done slightly better than these estimates.

adding up the electoral votes that could be regarded as safe, marginal, and lost. Only two states, Georgia and West Virginia, and the District of Columbia were regarded as safe. Four more states—Massachusetts, Rhode Island, Minnesota, and Hawaii—were classified as marginal plus. Twenty-four more states—including all the rest of the South, the Middle Atlantic states, and the Great Lakes states except Indiana—were seen as marginal. The safe states cast 21 electoral votes, and the marginal-plus states cast 32 more. This meant that for the Democrats to win, they would have to get 217 (65 percent) of the 335 electoral votes being cast by the marginal states. Consequently, the targeting committee recommended concentrating all resources on the marginal states, spending proportionately to the size of each state's electoral vote, and spending half as much on the 5 marginal-plus states and the 3 marginal-minus states as on the 24 marginal states. So the Democrats began their campaign devoting the greatest amount of their resources to New York, Pennsylvania, Texas, Illinois, and Ohio (in that order)—the marginal states casting the largest electoral votes—and intending to spend nothing on the 3 safe states or the 17 lost states.

If the Carter coalition was to carry enough of the southern states, and the northern industrial states that the Orange Book identified as essential to a Democratic electoral victory, the first order of business had to be assembling a strong Democratic coalition. This meant Catholics, labor union members, Jews, and blacks—all members of the normal Democratic coalition. Running against Ronald Reagan, it also meant women. They also planned to appeal to suburban voters. When Carter ran against Ford in 1976, Ford had more appeal in the suburbs, but Jimmy Carter was able to compensate for that by an unusual appeal (for a Democrat) to small-town residents in some areas such as central Pennsylvania and southern Ohio. Facing someone with Ronald Reagan's small-town appeal, Jimmy Carter could not duplicate his 1976 feat, but his strategists hoped that he could compensate by getting votes in the suburbs where Reagan might be less attractive. The problem with this strategy, of course, was that John Anderson also was attractive to suburban voters.

In past campaigns, as Pat Caddell pointed out in his first memorandum on election strategy, Jimmy Carter had been positioned in the political center with an ability to move right or left as the situation required. In 1980, he saw two problems with this:

> First, Carter is in jeopardy of losing the center to Reagan. Surveys already indicate that Reagan is placed by the electorate as closer to them on general issues than Carter. Second, in a general election sense Anderson is assaulting much of Carter's liberal base whose normal certainty would allow Carter to move right toward Reagan. These factors are further complicated by the fact that Carter, to win, must hold the more conservative South and the more liberal blue collar Northeast. An all out move

to secure one area could lead to the alienation of the other. (Drew, 1981b, p. 402)

All of this led to a general strategy of emphasizing the differences between President Carter and Governor Reagan, especially on foreign policy, as much as possible, together with specific appeals to the groups they hoped to entice to the Carter coalition. The general contrast the Democrats wanted to stress was a choice between two different visions of the American future.[15] The central Democratic themes were set forth in the convention speeches of Senator Kennedy and Vice President Mondale. When Kennedy pointed out that the Republican nominee, no friend of labor, had said: "Unemployment insurance is a prepaid vacation plan for freeloaders," and when Mondale said that Ronald Reagan had advocated sending troops to Angola, Rhodesia, Panama, Ecuador, North Korea, Pakistan, Cyprus, and the Middle East, but the American people want a president "who's demonstrated he knows how to keep the peace," they were emphasizing the choice Carter strategists wanted the voters to think about.

There were no distinctive issues emphasized to attract Catholic voters. "With Catholics," as a campaign leader put it, "it's a matter of working the community. Going out and campaigning through their areas." However, there were issues that were stressed for each of the other groups. Close ties had existed between labor leaders and Democratic leaders for some time, and there was cooperation in 1980. In appealing to labor, Carter supporters underscored the Reagan and Anderson records. Old Reagan quotes were resurrected. In commenting in May 1976 on Carter's support for the Humphrey-Hawkins bill, Governor Reagan said, "If ever there was a design for fascism, that's it. Fascism was really the basis for the New Deal." In John Anderson's case, the Carterites went back to his voting record. They pointed to an AFL-CIO COPE statement that Anderson voted "right" only 52 times during his career, and "wrong" 136 times. Anderson's antilabor votes included Section 14b of the Taft-Hartley Act, common situs picketing, minimum wage, and the Davis-Bacon Act, all issues of great concern to labor leaders. Blacks were reminded of Jimmy Carter's judicial appointments, and of the budget commitments the Carter administration had made to support civil rights activities. An ad was run in black newspapers reading: "Jimmy Carter has named 37 black judges. Cracked down on job bias. And created 1 million jobs. That's why

---

[15] The Carter core group wanted above all to avoid making the election a referendum on the Carter administration. There were some Carter aides, especially those involved in policy formation, who wanted to explain the accomplishments of the Carter administration. Surveys, however, suggested that if the election turned on what the Carter administration had done, Carter would lose. Carter strategists felt that the two-month election campaign was too short a time to alter perceptions that had taken four years to form.

the Republicans are out to beat him." To appeal to Jews, considerable emphasis was given to the peace issue. Jewish fears about weakening the separation between church and state were appealed to by pointing to Ronald Reagan's support of school prayer and John Anderson's Christianity amendment.[16] And women were reminded of Ronald Reagan's opposition to abortion, to the Equal Rights Amendment, and to equal opportunity in general. None of these specific appeals conflicted with the general theme that Carter and Reagan had different visions of the future of America, but the emphasis given them was intended to facilitate coalition building.

A Double Offensive

When Jimmy Carter began his public campaigning, he was faced with the need for a double offensive. He had to draw the distinction between himself and Ronald Reagan to portray the different futures the Democrats wanted voters to contemplate, and he had to show that he was the *real* liberal in order to prevent John Anderson from taking Carter votes in industrial states. The Carter offensive against Reagan had to be highly visible, but the anti-Anderson effort had to be less visible so Anderson's candidacy would not be given credibility.

The television ads that began running the first week of September were subtle rather than strident. The emphasis was on the complexity of the presidency. The pictures showed President Carter working in the Oval Office, conferring with foreign leaders, or taking part in the "town meetings" that he had held in various communities. The announcer read messages such as "Today, the chief of state is an international figure," "The office has a powerful effect on the United States and upon the whole world," and "The responsibility never ends." There were positive references about Jimmy Carter, not negative references to Ronald Reagan. It was left to the viewer to make a comparison between the two men, and wonder which would be better suited for the presidency.

President Carter began his own campaigning on Labor Day in Tuscumbia, Alabama, to shore up his southern support. The President did make reference to the two-futures theme, but was joined on the platform by southern Democratic leaders, and told the crowd: "You people here have the same background, the same families, the same upbringing that I have. . . . I've come back to the part of this nation that will always be my home to ask you to join me once again." His schedule thereafter paid attention to states classified as marginal in the Orange

---

[16] Early in his congressional career, Anderson had proposed adding "This Nation devoutly recognized the authority and law of Jesus Christ, Savior and Ruler of nations, through whom are bestowed the blessings of Almighty God" to the Constitution.

Book. The next day, he went to Harry Truman's hometown, Independence, Missouri, and on Wednesday, he campaigned through ethnic neighborhoods in Philadelphia. The next week, Carter went to Perth Amboy, New Jersey, for the opening of a new steel plant, and the third week of September, he took a two-day swing through Texas, Georgia, South Carolina, and Ohio.

Some of the things that the President said on the hustings, however, went beyond the campaign plans. In his basic campaign memorandum, Hamilton Jordan reminded Mr. Carter:

> You were at times strident and personal in your attacks on President Ford. Because Ford was widely perceived as being a "good man" rhetoric directed at Ford that seemed personal and harsh hurt us. I believe that we will find ourselves in a similar posture in the fall campaign when anything that smacks of a personal attack on Reagan will be counterproductive. (Jordan, 1982, p. 309)

But in a town meeting in Independence, Missouri, President Carter charged that Governor Reagan would break off a tradition of arms control negotiations that went back to President Eisenhower. "I consider this," the President continued, "one of the most serious threats to the safety and the peace of our nation and of the world that is being dramatized in this 1980 election." And speaking in Martin Luther King, Sr.'s, church in Atlanta, Jimmy Carter told the audience, "You've seen in this campaign the stirrings of hate and the rebirth of code words like 'state's rights' in a speech in Mississippi, in a campaign reference to the Ku Klux Klan relating to the South." Charges that Governor Reagan was a threat to world peace, and that Reagan had introduced hatred and racism into the campaign were hardly in keeping with the advice to avoid personal attacks on the Governor. Jimmy Carter was not completely responsible for this. The Democratic plan called for Vice President Mondale to carry the brunt of the attack on Governor Reagan. The media, however, failed to carry Mondale's attacks. But Carter, attacking Reagan's position on nuclear arms negotiations on September 2, did not wait to see what would happen before making charges himself. And in an editorial entitled "Running Mean," the *Washington Post* said that the racial attack "fits into Jimmy Carter's miserable record of personally savaging political opponents (Hubert Humphrey, Edward Kennedy) whenever the going got rough."

The Carter coalition's offensive against John Anderson wasn't attracting nearly as much attention, but it was being pursued seriously because of the Anderson threat to the Carter strategy. They didn't think that John Anderson could win, but they did think that he was a threat in nine key industrial states. Carter leaders also discovered, to their horror, that the Anderson strategy of trying to add to his campus-suburban base was making some headway. There was an Anderson vote among young working people; there was an Anderson vote among young blacks; there was an Anderson vote among Jews. Therefore, while public statements were made about falling Anderson support, specific appeals were made to each of these audiences.

The anti-Anderson appeal to young labor was essentially that already referred to: Anderson had voted against many labor positions while a member of the Republican leadership in Congress. Therefore labor voters should not be taken in by his 1980 rhetoric. The anti-Anderson argument to blacks took two forms. The more prominent argument was that, while Anderson had an "adequate civil rights record,"[17] the real issues in 1980 were economic; Anderson was an economic conservative; and Anderson would end up electing the even worse Ronald Reagan by drawing votes away from Jimmy Carter. The sub rosa anti-Anderson move was a distortion of Anderson's civil rights record that was played on local radio stations. When Anderson supporters complained in Detroit, the tape was pulled—and moved to Chicago. From Chicago, it was moved to Seattle. A centerpiece in the appeal to Jewish voters, and to liberal voters more generally, was a pamphlet entitled "Will the Real John Anderson Please Stand Up?" This asked whether John Anderson should be judged by his progressive campaign rhetoric of 1980 or by his 19 years in the Republican congressional mainstream. The answer, with references to issues particularly important to groups sought for the Carter coalition, was that Anderson was fundamentally a conservative.

Perhaps the most salient Anderson question in September was whether President Carter should take part in a debate after the League of Women Voters invited both Governor Reagan and Congressman Anderson. Campaign Director Les Francis described this decision:

> It occupied a good deal of discussion at several meetings. . . . Essentially it came down to the fact that a large number of people were moving in the direction of Anderson at the time, at least more potential Carter voters than potential Reagan voters. So we felt that being involved in the debate would enhance Mr. Anderson's credibility as a candidate and make it harder to get those people back. (Moore, 1981, pp. 201–2)

Francis went on to say that this was the toughest political call he'd seen anyone have to make, but once the decision was made, they all felt comfortable with it.

From Debate to Debate

Since President Carter did not participate in the Baltimore debate, there was nothing the Carter camp could do to control the outcome.

---

[17] In fact, Congressman John Anderson had voted consistently for civil rights legislation in the early 1960s while State Senator Jimmy Carter had been very silent on this issue.

All they had was hope that Anderson and Reagan would not do well. This turned out to be a reasonable bet about Anderson. As we have seen, Anderson did well in the debate itself, but the media stopped taking him seriously shortly thereafter. The Carter coalition added to Anderson's troubles by making a small Strategic Adjustment. They began to emphasize the "Anderson is a spoiler" argument. Until this time, the Anderson candidacy had been publicly ignored by the Carter field organization. Now they were instructed to argue that a vote for John Anderson was a vote for Ronald Reagan.

The Carter forces were not so lucky with Ronald Reagan. The former California governor emerged from the Baltimore debate as a plausible presidential candidate. This was costly because of temporal assumptions that had been built into the Democratic strategy. Since late summer polls showed that President Carter was behind Governor Reagan, September was intended to be a catch-up month. The Carter strategists wanted to get to a situation by early October where the two candidates were about even, and where doubts had been raised about Reagan's competence which they hoped would be decisive in the end. Pat Caddell's polls showed that they were successful in moving in this direction until the debate, but then Reagan pulled ahead again. By staying out of the Baltimore debate, the Carter coalition avoided giving credibility to the Anderson candidacy, but that cost them time in their strategy against Reagan.

At this point, some Strategic and Tactical Adjustments were made. The Strategic Adjustment was to give greater emphasis to the war-and-peace issue. This was an issue where polls showed that Carter was making some progress at Reagan's expense, and it was an issue that was persuading women to vote for Carter rather than Reagan. Some new television commercials emphasized this. One, an imitation of a very successful Ford ad of 1976 in which Georgia residents said they did not intend to vote for Governor Carter, had California residents expressing their concerns about whether Governor Reagan would shoot from the hip if he were elected president.

Second, President Carter continued to make harsh public criticisms of Governor Reagan. Why was this a Tactical Adjustment if Carter had already been doing so? The difference was that Carter strategists had now decided that questions *must* be raised about Reagan to catch up in the polls, and that the only way they could get coverage was to have the President make the charges himself. In California the night after the debate, Jimmy Carter said that American voters faced a choice between peace and war in November. At a fund raiser in Washington, he suggested that a Reagan victory would mean "the alienation of black from white, Christian from Jew, rich from poor, and North from South." In Chicago on October 6, the President said, "If . . . you just want to push people around and show the macho of the United States, that is an excellent way to lead our country toward war."

The President was paying a price for this stridency in many media comments about the "meanness" issue. According to the evidence of the Caddell polls, the meanness issue was not having much impact on the general public. Nonetheless, Hamilton Jordan decided on another Tactical Adjustment: Jimmy Carter would apologize. On an already scheduled interview with Barbara Walters, the President said: "Some of the issues are just burning with fervor in my mind and in my heart and I have to sometimes speak extemporaneously and I have gotten carried away on a couple of occasions. . . . I'll try . . . to be sure that we do not have a lowering of the tone of the campaign." The following day, attacks on Reagan came not from the President, but from Secretary of Defense Harold Brown, and Labor Secretary Ray Marshall. All this was as intended, but two days later Carter said in Florida that Reagan "would not be a good president or a good man to trust with the affairs of this nation," and the meanness issue was revived.

A more hopeful change took place in mid-October when Senator Kennedy began to make appearances for President Carter. Carter had an urgent need of Kennedy's support to bring liberal Democrats back to the fold, and Kennedy had an interest in demonstrating his support of the Democratic candidate. In postconvention negotiations, Carter leaders agreed to help Kennedy retire his primary campaign debt, and Kennedy aide Jack English became a deputy campaign manager to handle liaison with Senator Kennedy. Kennedy taped some television commercials endorsing Carter, although he insisted that these be made by a media specialist with whom he often worked rather than by Gerald Rafshoon. During the week of October 13, Kennedy and Carter appeared together in Massachusetts (where Anderson was still showing a lot of strength), New Jersey, and Washington, D.C. The Senator made trips by himself to other areas where he was popular: Detroit, Wisconsin, and the Chicano area of Texas.

Poll information was also becoming a little more encouraging in mid-October. In the second wave of a panel study directed by Pat Caddell, interviewers discovered that 95 percent of the respondents who supported either Reagan or Carter prior to the Baltimore debate were still in favor of the same candidate. President Carter apparently had begun to catch up again after Governor Reagan's postdebate surge. In the public polls, Gallup, Harris, and NBC/Associated Press all continued to show Reagan leads, but in their October 16–20 survey, CBS News/New York Times found a very small Carter lead. This did not lead to wild optimism, but it did hold open the possibility that a Carter victory was still possible.

The Cleveland Debate and the End

On October 17, the equilibrium in the campaign was upset by a Reagan decision. Governor Reagan agreed to meet President Carter in a one-on-one debate. Although Reagan had been insisting that John Anderson be included in any debate, Reagan leaders had taken care not to close the door absolutely, and the positions taken by the Carter coalition left them with no alternative but to accept. Within the Carter core group, having a debate was strongly opposed by Pat Caddell. Richard Wirthlin took a similar position in the Reagan core group. Both pollsters saw debates as high-risk events, and since this debate was scheduled for October 28, a bare week before the election,[18] there would be almost no time to recover from any major error. Caddell was more worried than Wirthlin because Carter was running behind.

Pat Caddell wrote a 29-page memorandum placing the coming debate in a strategic context. It contained a great deal of information, too much to be easily summarized, but it did make three vital points. First, he pointed out the risk to Jimmy Carter. "We can think of our debate as a football game with each team having only one chance to move the ball and score. However, we get the ball on our five yard line. Reagan starts with the ball on *our* 40 yard line" (Drew, 1981b, p. 412). Therefore, Caddell went on, only "excellent precision, bold strategies, and high-risk plays" were likely to lead to real Carter success. Second, there were two target groups: college-educated voters and women. College-educated voters were more likely than others to support Anderson, and they were less likely to support Reagan than previous Republican candidates. Women were supporting Carter in much greater numbers than men. Third, issues were classified from those that showed a large Carter edge, and should therefore be emphasized, to those that showed a large Reagan edge and were therefore likely to be dangerous. Among the issues helping Carter were war and peace, the Equal Rights Amendment, and social issues. Issues where the polls showed a Reagan edge[19] included inflation and unemployment (Drew, 1981b, pp. 431–32).

The debate drew an enormous audience. According to the Nielson organization, 58.9 percent of all television homes watched the debate. President Carter did many of the things that were vital to his strategy. He suggested several times that issues were more complex than Governor Reagan seemed to think (an important point in appealing to the college-educated target group), and discussed their differences on the Equal Rights Amendment and social issues. But in discussing arms control, he referred to a discussion with his 13-year-old daughter Amy

---

[18] This was much closer to the election than previously. The last of four 1960 debates took place on October 21, and the final Ford-Carter debate was on October 22, 1976.

[19] Discussing advantage alone simplifies what Caddell said. He considered both saliency and partisan advantage.

in which "she said she thought nuclear weaponry and control of nuclear arms (were) the most important issues," thus trivializing the war-and-peace issue that had been one of his few real advantages. And in his closing statement, Governor Reagan suggested a series of questions for voters to think about: "Are you better off than you were four years ago? Is it easier for you to go and buy things in the stores than it was four years ago? Is there more or less unemployment in the country than there was four years ago?" By asking these questions, Ronald Reagan put the focus of attention on inflation and unemployment, two issues of enormous benefit to him.[20]

The postdebate surveys were mixed, but CBS reported that 44 percent thought that Reagan won the debate compared to 36 percent who thought that Carter won. The Associated Press found that both candidates gained 6 percent additional support, but they had been showing Mr. Reagan ahead, and an equal gain implied victory for the Republican. Louis Harris said that the election was now Reagan's to lose, and Gerald Rafshoon said, "The wolf was no longer at the door. He was inside, running through the house" (White, 1982, p. 405).

For the balance of the week, President Carter campaigned through critical states. The day after the debate, he went to Pittsburgh, Rochester, Newark, and Philadelphia. On Thursday, he began in Philadelphia, went to New York City for a big noontime garment district rally, and then ended up in South Carolina. The next two days were devoted to more southern and border states: Mississippi, Florida, Texas, Tennessee, and Missouri. He continued to stress issues that were strategically important, often using statements made during the debate. "Every American," the President told a Pittsburgh town meeting, "ought to stop and think what will happen to this world if we have no control over nuclear weapons between ourselves and the Soviet Union." "Governor Reagan may not have known" the country had a racial problem when he was young, Carter told a black congregation in Newark, "but to millions and millions of Americans . . . it was not simply a problem, but a lifelong disaster." And in Texas on Saturday, he repeated once again, "In four years as president, I've learned a great deal."

The President's campaigning was broken off early Sunday morning to return to the White House. The Iranian Parliament had stated four conditions for the release of the diplomats being held hostage in Tehran,

---

[20] This description of the Carter-Reagan debate was written long before there was any public knowledge that Reagan campaigners had obtained debate materials from the Carter camp, but there does not seem to be any need to modify it. While those who offered, accepted, or used any confidential papers violated moral standards, it seems unlikely that Carter papers played any vital role in the outcome of the debate. On the two most important points in the debate, Jimmy Carter's reference to his daughter Amy was his own doing, and Reagan's emphasis on economics at the end followed a strategy that had been developed months earlier.

and Mr. Carter had to see the exact translation, as well as confer with his foreign policy advisors, to know how to reply. A statement was agreed on and released, and the President departed on Monday morning for one last, long day of campaigning.[21] It was after midnight in Seattle when the phone call from Washington brought the bad news to the President. "Mr. President," said Pat Caddell, "I'm afraid that it's gone." Caddell had now seen the final day's survey data. The conclusion that he shared with fellow senior strategists Jordan, Rafshoon, and Powell—and now the President—was that Jimmy Carter was going to lose by 8 to 10 percentage points (Jordan, 1982, pp. 367–68).

RONALD REAGAN'S CONSERVATIVE CRUSADE

An Early Comprehensive Plan

In one sense, the 1980 Reagan strategy was set forth earlier than in any preceding campaign. In another, it was not. The reason for this seeming contradiction was the nature of the campaign plan. The campaign plan—written, approved, and adopted before the Fourth of July—filled two large loose leaf notebooks. This document, however, was more of a statement of how strategists Richard Wirthlin and Richard Beal conceptualized the electorate than a series of operational steps. The basic plan, for example, contained a list called "Conditions of Victory." It did not, however, state how these conditions were to be achieved. The specific steps to do this were provided in a series of memoranda written throughout the campaign on the basis of the latest survey information. The campaign plan in effect at any time was the June document as updated by the latest memoranda.[22]

There were originally some 21 Conditions of Victory. The number was gradually reduced as succeeding memoranda were written. Two things were happening to shorten the list. One was that some of the conditions were coming to be seen as more important. Keeping them on a shorter list was a way of accenting them. The other was that certain conditions had been satisfied and could therefore be removed. By early October, there were seven Conditions of Victory being focused upon, and by the end of the campaign, there were only five.

The list of target states was also being updated constantly. The

---

[21] The fatigue of the Time's Up phase was particularly evident to those who had been involved since the beginning of nomination politics. During the last week, Campaign Director Les Francis said: "Of course, we had a vigorous contest for the nomination. But then there's the length of the contest itself. There's a lot of wear and tear on the campaign staff. There are a lot of people around here who are just goddamned tired. They are just holding on now. There is similar wear and tear on the candidate." In the face of such exhaustion, it is not surprising that there are occasional fluffs and mistakes. The surprise is that they do not occur more often.

[22] Several of these memoranda have been published. The basic document, kept locked in a safe at campaign headquarters, has not.

original Reagan base consisted of the West plus Indiana and Virginia. If Texas, Florida, Kentucky, and Iowa were added, the number of electoral votes rose to 213. The original battleground states were therefore seen as four industrialized states around the Great Lakes: Illinois, Ohio, Pennsylvania, and Michigan. Allocations of the candidate's time, media placement, and organizational effort were all heaviest in the battleground states. As time went on, it appeared that this list of states that Governor Reagan might hope to carry was too modest. In September, Wisconsin, Connecticut, New Jersey, and Louisiana became possible Reagan targets. The greatest change took place in October, by which time substantial cracks were appearing in Carter's southern base. Tennessee, North Carolina, Mississippi, Alabama, South Carolina, and Arkansas all were added as battleground states. (There were resource considerations in these southern additions. The Reagan strategists believed that they could hold their western base by spending 15 percent of their resources, principally on the Pacific Coast states. If they could force the Carter coalition to spend as much as 30 percent of its resources defending its southern base, the Reagan coalition would have more of a competitive advantage in the large industrial states that both were contesting.) Finally, at the end of October, it even seemed possible to carry New York. As this list of target states was expanding, the dimensions of the Reagan Electoral College victory were increasing. The number of electoral votes for Reagan if they held their base and carried *all* of their target states increased from 302 at the end of June to 367 by the end of September to 472 at the end of October.

A closely related objective had to do with target populations. In general, Governor Reagan had to pick up support from moderates. The Wirthlin polls showed that he had a majority of conservative votes in June, but only a quarter of the moderates intended to cast Reagan ballots. While it was heartening to know that Reagan was supported by his fellow conservatives, there just weren't enough of them to elect him, so gains with moderates were essential. There were three demographic targets: Catholics, labor, and senior citizens. Each of these was a group where Richard Wirthlin felt Reagan had shown some special appeal. More importantly, each of these groups was large enough to affect the outcome in some target states. The labor vote was concentrated in Pennsylvania, Ohio, Illinois, and Michigan. The Catholic vote was less concentrated. Substantial numbers were to be found in New England and New York, which weren't geographic targets, but also in New Jersey, Pennsylvania, Ohio, Illinois, Louisiana, and Texas, which were. The senior citizen efforts were carried on primarily in Florida, with some attention to southern California. Thus the demographic and geographic strategies were coordinated with one another.

The section of the campaign plan dealing with issues began with a review of a summer 1979 survey of the values and aspirations of the American people. Decision/Making/Information (the name of the

Wirthlin firm) found that the public was fundamentally optimistic. Turning more directly to issues, they reported that the issue agenda had been quite stable for the preceding two years. Inflation was the most important issue, then the need for improvement in the economy, and either national security or unemployment showed up as the third issue. Selection of an issue as important, however, was not related to vote intent. The link to vote intent came through the question of leadership. Since the public tended to have a "can do" point of view, it followed that the country could accomplish more with better leaders. Leadership, therefore, had to be stressed along with economics. It was not enough to talk about inflation; the message had to be that Ronald Reagan could do something about inflation because he was an effective leader.[23]

Still another section of the campaign plan laid out the expected Carter attack strategy. The attack could be expected to say that the Governor was dumb, dangerous, and deceitful. Dumb in that he was over his head in government, dangerous because he was a right-wing, knee-jerk reactionary, and deceitful on the grounds that he was exaggerating his claims of accomplishment as governor of California. Having anticipated this Carter attack strategy, the Reagan campaign plan then made some suggestions for dealing with it. The Republican National Convention, for example, should be used to inoculate the public against these anticipated charges by having other speakers portray Reagan as conservative, but reasonable, and as one who *had* accomplished some things as governor of California.

Perhaps most important for an understanding of the Reagan strategy, the campaign plan divided the campaign into three periods, each of which was to have a different objective. The first phase, from the end of the Democratic convention until shortly after Labor Day, was called "Deal to Strength." It was to be used to solidify the geographic and ideological base that Reagan had established. The Reagan coalition did not want to spend many resources on this base, but they wanted to make sure that it was solid (especially California's 45 electoral votes) so they could proceed. The second temporal period, from about the second week of September until October 20, was to be used to deepen public perceptions of Governor Reagan, and to broaden his political base. However much he was respected by conservative Republicans, there weren't enough of them to elect him president. Therefore, a number of things had to be done to establish the Governor as strong, competent, and caring, and to go after the independent vote. The third period, from October 20 until November 4, was seen as the period in which the election would be won. Resources—money, candidate time, and

---

[23] See Edwards (1983) for a similar finding that the public's perception of the skill of the president in managing the economy, not the economic record per se, is related to the president's approval rating.

professional time—should be husbanded so that they could be used in a way that would have the highest impact. How these resources should be used could not be anticipated far in advance, but they should be kept ready to motivate the Reagan vote to turn out on election day. In brief, first solidify the Reagan vote, then broaden it, then turn it out.

The Four Blunders and the Death of Focused Impact

One of the problems of a challenger is how to get his stories carried by the news media. An incumbent president can make news in a number of ways: by signing a piece of legislation, by appointing a government official, by conferring with a foreign leader, and so on. He can be sure that each of these things will be duly recorded by the news media. The idea of focused impact was to give a challenger a similar capacity. By selecting a chosen theme, and by speaking only about that topic for a given period of time, the challenger could ensure that the media would report *something* about this subject. Further, if several stories succeeded one another, the person who was paying casual attention (i.e., the average voter) would get an impression that the candidate was dealing with the subject.

The subject selected for the first focused impact was foreign affairs, and Ambassador Bush's trip to China was to be part of it. Foreign affairs was selected because the strategists saw this as Carter's issue rather than Reagan's. The Camp David agreement between Israel and Egypt had been the high point of the Carter administration, and one that the President could be expected to stress. The economy was Reagan's issue. Therefore, the strategists wanted to do something with foreign affairs, but to do it early. Then they could come back to it later in the campaign if they chose. Since George Bush had been permanent representative in China, he could go there on a fact-finding mission. The posture would not be one of announcing plans for a Reagan administration, but to talk with the Chinese leaders to gain their views, and then return and report to Governor Reagan.

The planned sequence was to begin with a press conference at the time of Ambassador Bush's departure. While Bush was in China, Reagan would give two defense speeches to conservative audiences. The speech to the Veterans of Foreign Wars was to emphasize peace, and the address to the American Legion would focus on strength. When George Bush returned for the debriefing, there would be another press conference at which he would do most of the talking. This would build up Bush a bit, and demonstrate the competence of a Reagan-Bush administration to handle foreign affairs.

What did happen was this. At the departure press conference, Gover-

nor Reagan said that he would favor an "official government relationship" with Taiwan. This would be illegal according to the Taiwan
Relations Act, and the Governor's statement produced headlines and
ensured a chilly reception for Ambassador Bush in Beijing. In his "Peace
through Strength" speech to the VFW in Chicago two days later, Governor Reagan brought up the subject of Vietnam, adding "It is time that
we recognized that ours, in truth, was a noble cause." There were
many who did not consider Vietnam to have been a noble cause, of
course, and this reference produced more headlines and cartoons. Nothing unplanned took place at the American Legion speech on Wednesday; but on Friday, August 22, in Dallas to speak to fundamentalist
Christians, Reagan was asked at a press conference for his views on
creationism. "I think that recent discoveries down through the years
have pointed [to] great flaws in" the theory of evolution, he replied,
suggesting that creationism might be taught as an alternative. At the
press conference after Ambassador Bush's return, a nine-page statement was issued stating that Reagan would continue the unofficial
relationship with Taiwan. This was consistent with existing American
law and what Bush had been saying in China, but produced headlines
such as "Reagan Abandons Taiwan Office Plan." This succession of
stories certainly produced a focused impact, but hardly the one the
Reagan strategists had in mind.

The second focused impact was to deal with the pocketbook. Pocketbook issues, inflation and unemployment, were seen as highly salient
and favorable to Reagan. The first event was to be a short speech to
the Ohio Teamsters' Conference in Cleveland on August 27. When
Governor Reagan arrived in Ohio, he was urged by Governor James
A. Rhodes to use strong and specific language in speaking about jobs.
In response, a reference in Reagan's speech to a U.S. "recession" was
changed to a "severe depression." Alan Greenspan, who was not consulted about this change although he was traveling with Reagan as
an economic advisor, said this was not the word he would have
chosen.[24] Reagan countered by adding some lines to his Labor Day
speech, "A recession is when a neighbor loses his job. A depression
is when you lose yours. Recovery is when Jimmy Carter loses his."
But the same papers that carried this Reagan speech added that he
had departed from his economics text at the Michigan State Fair later
the same day to say, "I'm happy to be here where you're dealing at
first hand with [economics] . . . and [President Carter's] opening his
campaign down in the city that gave birth to and is the parent body

---

[24] The common distinction between recessions and depressions is that depressions
are of much longer duration, and have much more widespread unemployment. During
the recession of 1957–58, the unemployment rate was 7.5 percent; in the recession of
1973–75, it reached 9.0 percent. In the depression year of 1932, in contrast, the unemployment rate was 25 percent. In July 1980, unemployment stood at 7.8 percent.

of the Ku Klux Klan." In fact, Tuscumbia, Alabama, was not the city where the Klan was founded, and President Carter had been sharply critical of the organization.[25]

At campaign headquarters, these Reagan comments—that Vietnam was a noble cause, that creationism should be taught as an alternative to evolution, that the country was in a depression rather than a recession, and the reference to the Ku Klux Klan—were known as the Four Blunders. None was very helpful to the campaign, to put it most gently, but it was the sequence of events in connection with George Bush's China trip that had the most pronounced strategic consequences. The idea of focused impact had been to have a high concentration on a single topic, but what was in fact being communicated was the wreckage resulting from the gaffes. With nothing else scheduled, there was nothing to which the campaigners could shift to divert attention from the embarrassing statements. Consequently, by the middle of September, there was a Strategic Adjustment in which the whole idea of focused impact was dropped.

The coalition leadership had evolved into two groups: the headquarters group in Arlington, Virginia, and the tour group that traveled with Reagan on the plane, LeaderShip '80. The key players in the headquarters group varied depending on the question. The essential participants in decisions on how to handle an issue included chief of staff Ed Meese, William Casey, who bore the title of national campaign director, Richard Wirthlin, and William Timmons, who was in charge of campaign operations. One of the ideas behind appealing to groups already in Reagan's political base during the first period of the campaign was that Timmons would be simultaneously recruiting a field organization, and appeals familiar to conservative ears might facilitate this. Whether the campaigning helped or not is difficult to say, but Bill Timmons did put together a strong field organization.

The most important members of the tour group—aside from Ronald and Nancy Reagan—included Michael Deaver (the tour chief of staff), press secretary Lyn Nofziger, James Brady (who had come from the Connally campaign and handled a mix of press and substantive matters), policy advisors Martin Anderson and Richard Allen, and speechwriter Ken Khachigian. During the period of the Four Blunders, it became painfully evident that what was missing from the tour group was someone with a good sense of the political impact of issues, and who was close enough to Governor Reagan to speak with authority. The person recruited to play this role was Stuart Spencer, the California campaign consultant who managed Ronald Reagan's gubernatorial

---

[25] Mr. Carter departed from his text, saying: "As the first man from the Deep South in 140 years to be president of this nation, I say these people in white sheets do not understand our region and what it's been through. They do not understand what our country stands for."

campaigns, and played such an important role in the 1976 Ford campaign. Three days after the Ku Klux Klan blunder, Stuart Spencer was on the plane.

The addition of Spencer began to remove some of the rough edges from the tour. While other members of the tour group had been close to Reagan for some time, none had been through a national campaign before, and they had a hard time distinguishing between tactics appropriate for primary campaigns (where they had a lot of experience) and tactics appropriate to a general election campaign. Eventually, the tour leaders settled into a pattern of two planning meetings every evening. The first dealt with logistics for the following day: the timing of events, the motorcade routes, and so on. Mike Deaver presided over this meeting. Then came a strategy meeting whose agenda varied all the way from major questions such as whether the Governor should take part in debates to smaller questions such as how a particular statement ought to be phrased. This meeting was jointly run by Deaver and Spencer. As would be expected, there were misunderstandings between the headquarters group and the tour group, but one important link between the two existed between Stu Spencer and Richard Wirthlin. Spencer, a believer in data, was in daily contact with Wirthlin, and this helped the two groups to coordinate their efforts.

Broadening the Reagan Appeal

The Reagan campaign plan called for a shift in mid-September. There were two things that needed to be done. Public perceptions of the Governor needed to be given greater depth, and he needed much greater appeal to voters in the middle of the political spectrum. The Wirthlin survey data showed that, while Governor Reagan had widespread name recognition, most Americans knew only three things about him: his name, that he had been a movie star, and that he was a conservative. This information level was too low for citizens to feel comfortable in voting for him, and insufficient to establish the Governor as a credible spokesman. The strategists had found out very early that Reagan's record as governor of California was a useful vehicle to establish him as a credible public figure.

Peter Dailey prepared a series of commercials of varying length presenting Reagan as governor of California. In one, the announcer boasted:

> In 1966 he was elected governor of the state of California, next to president the biggest job in the nation. What he inherited was a state of crisis. . . . Working with teams of volunteers from all sectors, Governor Reagan got things back on track. His commonsense style and strong, creative leadership won him a second term in 1970. Governor Reagan was the greatest tax reformer in the state's history.

These commercials began running quite early, and their use peaked during this second phase of the campaign. Political buffs who already knew Reagan had been governor wondered why they had to watch him being sworn in over and over and over, but the idea was to get the less attentive, average citizen to begin to think of Reagan as a man with executive experience and a good record in California.

Another opportunity to present Ronald Reagan as a credible political leader came with the Reagan-Anderson debate on September 21. Richard Wirthlin was a key player in setting the strategy for the debate, but the preparations for the debate were put in the hands of a separate group headed by James A. Baker, who managed the Ford campaign in 1976 and the Bush primary campaign in 1980.[26] The essential goal was to reassure the country that Reagan was a man who was competent, and who knew what he was talking about. Consequently, much of the preparation consisted of putting questions to Reagan, who would give his answer, after which Stockman would give the Anderson answer. Reagan intentionally went into the debate without any notes to demonstrate that he could think on his feet. The other major point to the debate strategy was that the Reagan leaders did not want Anderson to disappear as a factor in the election.[27] They wanted to make sure that they "won" the debate, but had no interest in harming Anderson too much in the process. So Reagan was following a "pass through" strategy: go through Anderson to get at Carter. And even when allusions were being made to Carter, the references should not be too strident—in part because Carter wasn't there, and in part because the campaign had been so negative that the Reagan strategists wanted to offer some

[26] The Reagan leadership was anxious to use Baker's talents, and Baker wanted something that could be segmented off and would be his responsibility. When the decision to give Baker authority over the debate was made, Baker recruited the people he wanted to work on it. David Gergen was in charge of putting together briefing books, and Bill Carruthers was in charge of some of the television aspects. Gergen thought that David Stockman, a Michigan congressman who had once been an assistant to John Anderson, would be a good impersonator for Anderson in the debate preparation. Three of the four—Baker, Gergen, and Stockman—ended up in senior positions in the Reagan White House. Presumably Reagan's satisfaction with the debate preparation had something to do with this.

[27] There were some interesting arguments about who was being hurt more by Anderson's candidacy. The core of the Anderson vote was made up of independent Republicans. Therefore, if the Anderson vote was reduced to this core, most of the votes would come from Reagan. But the argument is complicated by the location of the Anderson vote. All three camps thought that Anderson was taking more votes from Carter in the East, but was competing with both Reagan and Carter in the Great Lakes states of Illinois and Ohio. Given Reagan's strategy, if he hoped for only a minimum Electoral College victory, he should have tried to eliminate Anderson to ensure a Reagan victory in Illinois and Ohio. On the other hand, if Reagan was optimistic about his electoral vote count, he should have tried to keep Anderson alive in order to carry some of the "bonus" states in the East. Whatever the arguments, the Carter strategists were desperately anxious to eliminate Anderson, and the Reagan strategists wanted to keep him as a factor in the election.

reassurance. Governor Reagan did appear to be relaxed and sufficiently competent, and the postdebate polls showed small increases in the proportions of voters intending to vote for him. Even more important, the debate aided in the major objective of this phase of the campaign: to deepen the voters' understanding of Ronald Reagan.

In order to give Governor Reagan more appeal to voters in the middle of the political spectrum, steps were taken to erase any image he might have as a doctrinaire conservative. The "move toward the middle" was not accomplished by changing any of the Governor's basic public policy, but by making some changes on a few specific issues which, in turn, suggested that Reagan was willing to change his mind on occasion. Social security is a case in point. In 1964, Reagan endorsed making social security voluntary, and in 1976, he suggested investing social security funds "in the industrial might of America." But in 1980, surveys implied that if there was any hint that social security would be eliminated, then the whole senior citizen vote was gone. Hence Reagan began talking about reform of social security rather than any attack on the system itself. Campaigning in St. Petersburg, Florida, for example, he said that the provision under which benefits are reduced by earnings over $5,000 should be eliminated, and thus came out on the positive side of social security. Similar shifts on other matters led to press comments such as "the Republican candidate appears to have modified his views on such potentially costly issues as federal aid to New York City, bailouts like Chrysler's, occupational health policy, and labor policy." President Carter also attacked some of the Reagan proposals; but the more the media pointed to policy changes and the more Carter attacked, the better the Reagan strategists liked it. Inconsistency in policy suggested flexibility, and their goal was to present Governor Reagan as a flexible leader rather than a rigid conservative.

While this middle phase of the campaign was accomplishing its objectives of increasing the information level about Reagan, and modifying his positions on enough issues to make him more attractive to moderate voters, there was pressure within the Reagan coalition for a Strategic Adjustment. There were three reasons for this. First of all, the campaigning was rather boring. After focused impact was abandoned, the campaign went first to stump speeches and then podium speeches with "local inserts." The podium speeches were short speeches, about four or five pages, that were standard Reagan prose. The local inserts were references to topics of special interest to the areas where Governor Reagan was campaigning that might provide a news line. In Miami, Florida, for example, Reagan attacked Fidel Castro; in El Paso, Texas, he said that Carter had "broken a solemn promise" to the governors of Louisiana, Oklahoma, and Texas to work for deregulation of natural gas prices; in Catholic areas of Pennsylvania and New Jersey, he endorsed the idea of tuition tax credits. All this was rather pedestrian. It reduced the danger of gaffes,[28] but it also meant that the candidate's voice was muted. It seemed as though little was happening in the campaign.

A second problem was that the strategy of moderating Reagan stands on selected issues was directed to the external need of communicating with independent voters rather than the internal need of keeping conservative groups already in the Reagan coalition happy. Media specialist Peter Dailey reflected about this:

> There were tremendous pressures for change, and it was because of a fundamental difference in dimension of the '76 and the '80 campaigns, versus 1972. It was interesting to me to have been in both campaigns to see that change. In 1972, in going after the 10–15 percent of the undecided independents and Democrats, the strategy and the tactics to reach them happened to be the same strategy and tactics to reinforce your own core vote. So every time you ran an ad that was directed at them, your own people said, "That's terrific." In 1980 the strategy to reach the undecided 10 or 12 percent—which we absolutely had to have or we would have had a marvelous Goldwater campaign and all gone home losers—did not necessarily reinforce your core old-line Reagan votes. So, the campaign moved along; the core group, particularly the old-line people and the workers, became more and more incensed. (Moore, 1981, pp. 211–12)

True believers, unaware of the campaign plan that was being followed, suspected that the relatively moderate statements reflected the influence of Stuart Spencer, Bill Timmons, and James Baker, all of whom had worked for Ford in 1976.

Perhaps the most worrisome factor was the information arriving in the Wirthlin polls during early October. The Reagan vote was remaining fairly constant in the 39–42 percent range. But the Carter vote was climbing from 33 to 35 to 37 to 39 percent. Then on October 11, the data showed a narrow Carter lead. Within the Reagan campaign, the survey data showing a Reagan lead had been trusted all along. But some campaigners feared the same thing that the Democrats were counting upon: that as the election drew close, many of the undecided would make up their minds to vote for the President simply because he was the trusted incumbent. The gain in the Carter vote made it look as though this was about to happen.

In spite of a good deal of pressure, including some from Governor Reagan who was becoming anxious to go after President Carter more aggressively, the campaign plan was not abandoned. For one thing,

---

[28] It did not eliminate them. In Steubenville, Ohio, he said that the eruption of Mount St. Helens had released more sulphur dioxide than 10 years of automobile driving, and defended a previous statement about trees being a source of air pollution. When he arrived on a college campus a couple of days later, someone had put a sign on a tree saying "Chop Me Down Before I Kill Again."

the plan called for a shift on October 20 anyway. For another, Richard
Wirthlin and Richard Beal were quite confident that Reagan would
win the electoral vote. In one of the true innovations of 1980, they
created an elaborate political information system (for which the acronym was PINS). PINS contained two ways to estimate the probable
electoral vote. The simpler was an "electoral scoreboard" that calculated the electoral vote as a function of selected variables—for example,
that a candidate had x percent of the Catholic vote or y percent of
the rural vote. The more elaborate was a simulation that first eliminated
the undecided vote, and then provided a series of questions so that the
analyst could state the assumptions he wished to make, such as the
proportion of the vote Anderson was expected to keep. The simulation also took into consideration the analyst's expectations about trend.
The simulation would then calculate the changes that would take place
between that date and the election, and produced electoral counts
for each assumption the analyst made. On the basis of their PINS
analyses, Wirthlin and Beal never thought that Carter was close in
the electoral vote, however well he might be doing in nationwide trial
heats.

The mounting criticism did, however, lead to two decisions important
enough to be taken as Strategic Adjustments. The polls, both public
and private, were showing what has come to be called a gender gap.
Women were about 10 percent less likely to vote for Reagan than
men. Fear that Reagan might lead the nation into war was related to
this, as well as the fact that the Governor was the only major candidate
to oppose the Equal Rights Amendment in 1980. So, at a news conference on October 14, Governor Reagan declared, "It is time for a woman
to sit among our highest jurists," and pledged to name a woman to
"one of the first Supreme Court vacancies in my administration."

The more important decision was to accept a two-person debate
with President Carter. This decision was one that found important
members of the tour group—Stuart Spencer, Mike Deaver, and Lyn
Nofziger—opposing two key headquarters decision makers, Bill Timmons and Richard Wirthlin. While everybody agreed that Reagan
would do well in a debate against Carter (especially after seeing the
two of them together at the Alfred E. Smith Memorial Dinner in New
York), the leaders of the tour group had a stronger sense of the campaign
having gone flat and being in need of something to give it additional
movement. Timmons' opposition was based on his knowledge that the
campaign plan had set aside abundant resources for use in the closing
days of the campaign, and his belief in the relative strength of the
field organization he had built. Wirthlin, while he also thought a debate
unnecessary, was most concerned about the timing. Another person
close to this discussion explained the timing consideration speaking
privately on October 1:

> Everyone agrees that he's got to debate by the 20th or so. He can't debate much later than that because you need those last 14 days to go around and touch your significant bases. Also, it's much higher risk. If you make a mistake, it's too late. If you make a mistake and you've still got 14 days or so, you've got a chance to turn it around.

Governor Reagan made the debate decision himself. After listening to the arguments on both sides, he concluded that if he wanted to succeed Jimmy Carter in the White House, he ought to be willing to debate him face to face.

One final point on the debate decision. On October 17, the pollsters began their daily tracking. They used a three-day moving average with a total of 1,500 respondents, adding 500 new ones each day, and dropping 500 after they had been contacted for three days. When the debate decision was made, the Wirthlin data showed Reagan leading Carter 43 percent to 37 percent, and the most likely outcome from their PINS electoral projections was 310 votes for Reagan, 40 more than necessary. The Reagan coalition was heading into the final phase of the campaign in a strong position and with resources set aside.

Motivating a Reagan Vote

The third phase of the Reagan campaign was the least completely described in the campaign plan. The plan said that resources—money, professional time, candidate time—should be allocated so that they would have the highest impact. It also said that the election would be won between October 20 and November 4. But it did not say how these resources should be allocated, or how the election would be won.

When the last phase of the campaign began, most of the Reagan base looked safe, but most of the Carter base was being contested. The final list of battleground states *excluded* Virginia, Indiana, and all of the West except the three Pacific Coast states. The campaign focused upon the seven largest states, the Middle Atlantic region, and all of the South except Georgia. And at least $7 million had been set aside for media directed to these battleground states.

While the goals of the long middle phase had been to give depth to Governor Reagan and to make him more appealing to moderate voters, the goal of this phase was to motivate voters to turn out on election day. This could be done best, the strategists felt, by attacking President Carter. The television mix had heretofore been about 80 percent positive ads about Ronald Reagan and 20 percent negative ads about Jimmy Carter. In the attack phase, this was shifted to 60 percent positive and 40 percent negative, and then to a 50–50 mix as election day neared. The negative ads were not too harsh. One showed Ronald Reagan standing in a meat market behind two shopping carts. One was filled with the quantity of meat, milk, and bread that $60 would buy in 1976; the other contained the smaller amount that $60 would buy in 1980. Governor Reagan concluded his statement by saying: "If you are better off today than you were four years ago, vote for Jimmy Carter." Another spot used graphics to make the point that food prices had increased 35 percent while Carter had been in office, automobile prices 31 percent, and clothing prices 20 percent. Simply reminding viewers of the record was sufficient when inflation was the dominant issue, and the voters were already conscious of President Carter's record in office.

The ads were only one part of the television campaign. Another was programs that were designed for use in parts of battleground states where votes were urgently being sought. Sometimes these were "citizen's press conferences" where residents were given a chance to ask questions. Another was called "TV Wrap-Up," 15-minute programs in which the candidate said, in essence, "I've been campaigning in this area, and here are my views on some of the issues people have asked me about." A third element was a series of nationally broadcast speeches by Mr. Reagan. The first, on October 19, dealt with foreign policy. In this, Reagan called for "a realistic and balanced policy toward the Soviet Union," and said that "as president, I will make immediate preparations for negotiations on a SALT III treaty." On October 24, he repeated an eight-point economic plan offered early in September, and also continued his attack on President Carter's economic record: "He promised to bring inflation down to 4 percent. It's now running at double-digit rates, and hit 18.2 percent earlier this year. . . . In fact, between January 1977 and August 1980, consumer prices have risen 42.3 percent." On October 31, the best portions of a longer speech given at Southern Methodist University in Dallas two days earlier were nationally televised. And on election eve, a final speech dealt with Governor Reagan's vision of America: "still strong, still compassionate, still clinging fast to the dream of peace and freedom." There was little new to these speeches, and certainly no concrete information about just what Reagan would do as president, but together they adhered to the 50–50 mix of projecting a combination of compassion, care, and strength about himself while attacking President Carter.

In the strategists' view, the campaign was now at the stage where the candidate was the only useful asset. In was not that the television campaign was not having an effect, or that the field organization would not be conducting a get-out-the-vote drive on election day. Rather it was sufficiently late in the campaign so that everything had to be in place—the media time purchased, the phone banks active, and so on— or there wouldn't be time to get it in place. Therefore, the candidate's time and words were the only maneuverable resource left to implement strategy.

The most important event in Ronald Reagan's last week was the debate with Jimmy Carter in Cleveland. The preparations for the debate were in the hands of the same group headed by James Baker which had worked with Governor Reagan prior to the debate with John Anderson, and they seem to have been equally effective. There were two points made by Mr. Reagan during the debate that were particularly compelling. When President Carter attacked his record on medicare, Governor Reagan shook his head and said, "There you go again."[29] This reminded those who had been following the campaign of the many Carter attacks on Reagan, and drew an effective contrast between the humorless President and his challenger. And in his peroration, Ronald Reagan drew attention to the central economic issue by asking the series of questions beginning "Are you better off than you were four years ago?" Some knowledgeable observers claimed that Governor Reagan won the election by asking that question. It certainly helped, but as we know from the Reagan strategy, the conclusion of the debate was just the most visible occasion on which Governor Reagan made this point. He was repeating it again and again during this attack phase of the campaign.

The favorable survey results after the debate brought a Time's Up feeling of impending triumph to the Reagan entourage. But the locations visited by Governor Reagan pointed out areas of continuing concern to the strategists. These were chosen through the use of the PINS simulations, and in consultation with Bill Timmons' field organization. The day after the debate, Reagan was in Dallas, Fort Worth, and Houston, Texas. On Thursday, he went to Texarkana, New Orleans, and on to New Jersey and Pennsylvania. Friday and Saturday were spent in Illinois, Wisconsin, and Michigan. Sunday morning, Governor Reagan went to church in Columbus, Ohio, then went to Marietta and took a swing through the southern part of the Buckeye State, ending up in Dayton. The Monday before the election, he appeared in Peoria, Illinois, flew on to Portland, Oregon, and ended up in San Diego. The Reagans were returning to California to vote, of course, but the political meaning of the travel schedule was that the strategists wanted to make sure of Texas, thought they had chances to carry Arkansas, Louisiana, Wisconsin, Michigan, and Oregon, and were worried about softness in the Reagan vote around Philadelphia, and in southwestern Ohio and central Illinois.

The Reagan speeches were in keeping with the attack theme. In New Orleans, he said that "in place of competence, (Carter) has given

---

[29] There are two versions of the origin of this statement. President Reagan told Theodore White, "That was certainly unpremeditated and off the top of my head" (White, 1982, p. 404). But Lou Cannon wrote that Reagan, in reviewing answers after one of the rehearsals, said: "I was about ready to say, 'There you go again.' I may save it for the debate" (1982, p. 297).

us ineptitude." In Des Plaines, Illinois, Reagan said Carter was "like the guy who can name you 50 parts of a car—he just can't drive it or fix it." In Dayton, he accused President Carter of mismanagement of the economy, and on his last day of campaigning, he continued to ask, "Are you happier today than when Mr. Carter became president of the United States?"

The mood aboard LeaderShip '80 as the plane headed west on the last campaign swing was variously described as "exhilarated," and "exhausted but happy." It certainly must have been pleasant for Ronald Reagan to know that the conservative crusade he had been leading for years was going to culminate in his own election as president. But the feeling of intellectual elation belonged to the strategists who had written the campaign plan six months earlier. When their final simulation was run at Reagan headquarters on October 31, the vote estimation was: Reagan 50.0 percent, Carter 40.5 percent, and Anderson 9.3 percent. The actual election result on November 4 was: Reagan 50.8 percent, Carter 41.0 percent, and Anderson 6.6 percent.

CONSTRAINTS

As we have seen, the selection of a campaign strategy is subject to very real constraints. Candidates are not free to express all of their inner yearnings. A strategy group is not free to come up with any approach it thinks might win votes. Instead, there are *internal constraints*, *external constraints*, and *temporal constraints*.

INTERNAL CONSTRAINTS

The internal constraints arise from the attitudes of the groups that are members of the coalition. As we saw in Chapter 10, there was a substantial correlation between the attitudes of the Nixon and McGovern coalitions and the positions emphasized by these candidates. In a similar way, one could argue that all of the strategies surveyed in this section of the book were acceptable to members of the supporting coalitions. Thus we saw Richard Nixon carefully charting a course in 1968 between the moderate and conservative wings of the Republican party, Hubert Humphrey relying on traditional New Deal/Fair Deal appeals, Gerald Ford favoring moderately conservative economic policies, Jimmy Carter supporting a number of social programs favored by Democratic groups, John Anderson proposing only those programs that could be fit into the federal budget, and Ronald Reagan calling for a reduction in government spending and activities.

But what is more important—at least to understand internal constraints—is what was *not* done. George McGovern could have moderated his springtime appeals, and Ronald Reagan could have done more than just suggest an open mind on such issues as social security and federal aid to New York City. This would have made it easier to reach middle-of-the-road voters, but would have disappointed the young militants supporting McGovern and would have cost Reagan the support of conservative ideologues. Or Senator McGovern could have proposed more radical redistributions of wealth, and Governor Reagan could have confined his campaign to the more conservative parts of the country. Either strategy would have made it more difficult for them to retain support from moderate members of their own coalitions. In 1968, Richard Nixon could have told the electorate that better relations with China were needed, and Hubert Humphrey could have said that the glut of social legislation passed by the 89th Congress meant that there were few resources available for any more social programs. Neutral observers were making both points. But many conservatives were dismayed when Richard Nixon did go to Beijing, and frank talk about the fiscal consequences of Great Society programs was not what the urban/labor/black wing of the Democratic party wanted to hear. Elizabeth Drew pointed out that both President Ford and Governor Carter were committed to expensive programs in 1976. Shortly after the Republican convention, Ford called for further progress in housing, health, recreation, and education; Carter was pledged to support job programs, health insurance, child care, federalization of welfare, housing, aid to cities, and aid to education (Drew, 1977, p. 438). Both Ford and Carter could have consistently argued that, to accomplish the goals to which their parties were pledged, some increase in taxes would be necessary. But to assert this would offend economic conservatives who were to be found in both the Ford and Carter coalitions. President Ford could certainly have found a vice presidential candidate who would have had greater appeal to independent voters in large industrial states than Robert Dole, but selection of a more moderate running mate would have put off Reagan supporters. And Ronald Reagan logically could have said either that we need to rebuild our defenses and we need taxes to do it, *or* that the American economy needs the stimulus of a tax cut, and therefore we must defer a substantial increase in military expenditures. But many conservatives (including Reagan himself) wanted both a big tax cut and a big arms build up. Doubtless you can think of other plausible campaign strategies consistent with some campaign goal or with a fair reading of public policy. The central point, though, is that none of the strategies mentioned in this list was used. Each was avoided because it would have given offense to some group in the candidate's supporting coalition.

EXTERNAL CONSTRAINTS

External constraints result from some inadequacy in the structure needed to obtain citizen support, from the need to reach some particular set of voters, or from lack of freedom to maneuver because of the positions taken by an opposing coalition. The most common defects with respect to campaign operations, research, or public relations result from inexperience. Unless an incumbent president has been renominated, an electoral coalition is based on the preceding nomination coalition. Especially in the out party, key decision makers may be taking part in their first general election campaign for the presidency. This was true, for example, of John Mitchell in the 1968 Nixon campaign, Gary Hart in the 1972 McGovern campaign, Hamilton Jordan and Jody Powell in the 1976 Carter effort, and Edwin Meese and Michael Deaver in the 1980 Reagan campaign. There are usually some persons around with experience, but there have been campaigns—Carter in 1976, for example—run almost entirely by novices. Newspaper articles are written about the "political geniuses" who are managing the campaign, but the simple fact is that they are in a situation they do not understand. Frequently, they will try to repeat tactics to which they attribute their success in nomination politics, and these tactics are often inappropriate.

Financial inadequacies have hobbled campaigns in two ways. Prior to federal funding, it was a simple lack of cash for candidates thought to be running behind. Among the campaigns we've reviewed, this constraint was probably most serious for the Humphrey campaign in 1968. It was also a very serious problem for the Anderson campaign in 1980, even though this was a special case of a third party for which federal funds were not made available *during* the campaign. Since federal funds have been made available to the major parties, the funding limit has brought the need for much more careful planning for the use of available, but finite, resources. Such planning gave the Ford coalition a real strategic advantage in the closing days of the 1976 campaign.

The need—real or perceived—to reach certain sets of voters often excludes certain campaign gambits. For example, in 1972, President Nixon could have attacked the Democratic party quite directly by telling voters: "For years, we've been telling you that the Democrats were controlled by radicals and you wouldn't listen. Now you have proof! They've nominated George McGovern!" Such an attack could have had a long-term payoff by weakening identification with the Democratic party, but it would also have hampered Nixon's 1972 efforts to get Democrats to cast Nixon votes. Hence this plausible strategy was not used.

The activities of the rival coalition (or coalitions) create an external constraint similar to that resulting from the structure of competition in nomination politics. A candidate frequently lacks maneuvering room because of positions already taken by a rival, or because of positions the candidate has already taken in response to a rival's gambit. For example, when Jimmy Carter spoke about a tax cut in a last-minute appeal to voters who were worried about the cost of living, he was moving into a position that Gerald Ford had already occupied with a highly advertised tax cut plan. In 1968, when Richard Nixon took relatively conservative positions to counter George Wallace's attractiveness to the Peripheral South, he was ill-positioned to respond to Hubert Humphrey when the Vice President began to make headway in the East with more liberal appeals. And in 1980, when Ronald Reagan had (for a Republican) relatively less appeal to well-educated suburban voters, and Jimmy Carter hoped to pick up some of this support, he found that he had to contend with the suburban appeal of John Anderson.

A further difficulty, of course, is that internal and external constraints often have different consequences. Few of the groups with the 1972 Nixon coalition would have been offended by an attack on Democrats, but this was not done because of external constraints. The 1976 Ford coalition would certainly have been strengthened externally by the selection of a moderate vice presidential candidate, but this was not done because of internal constraints. In recent campaigns, professional campaign managers have tended to pay less attention to internal constraints in order to design a strategy that is better suited to the external need to attract certain sets of voters. There was an unusual external emphasis to the Ford strategy in 1976 and to the Reagan strategy in 1980. In time, this tendency may be strengthened. But it is still preferable to find a strategy that is acceptable in view of both internal and external constraints.

TEMPORAL CONSTRAINTS

The temporal constraints have already been discussed rather explicitly, so there is little need to do more than summarize them here. An electoral coalition has relatively little time for organization and planning. Plans adopted and launched during the Grand Opening are difficult to modify. It takes time to learn that a strategy is inappropriate, and still more time to hit on a politically viable alternative. Hence one seldom sees more than one or two Strategic Adjustments, even though it may be apparent to outside observers that a strategy is unsuccessful. Temporal constraints are more apparent, of course, during the Time's Up stage. Both candidates are likely to be bone-tired by this point; but both know that one will soon begin the slow transition from titular leader of the party to the "where are they now" category, while the other will soon experience the exhilarations and the frustrations of the White House.

PART SEVEN

THE CITIZEN IN PRESIDENTIAL ELECTIONS

CHAPTER 14

THE STRUCTURE OF CITIZEN KNOWLEDGE

The difference is dramatic. Throughout the campaign, thousands of persons are engaged in the joint enterprise of trying to persuade the electorate to support one party or the other. On election day, the solitary citizen is alone in the voting booth. To be sure, the outcome of the election is the result of decisions made by millions of voters across the country, but each choice is made by an individual citizen.

To this point, the principal acting unit has been the coalition-in-institution. In order to analyze these acting units, we considered the individuals aggregated into groups that made up the internal structure of the coalition, the institutionally patterned activities that constituted the external structure, and observed these as they moved through the stages of the temporal pattern. Now our acting unit becomes the individual.

The link between campaign strategy and citizen response is information. Broadly speaking, the aim of the entire campaign is to transmit information to the electorate. The citizen's response is similarly based on knowledge. If very little is known, the citizen may not bother to vote. If the bulk of what is known favors one party, the citizen is likely to vote for that party's candidate. If the citizen is aware of information favoring both sides, there must be some means of resolving this conflict. It follows that to analyze this individual activity, ***the internal structure is the citizen's cognitive structure,*** specifically what the citizen knows about politics.[1]

As we saw at the end of Chapter 2, there are several elements of cognitive structure that will be of concern to us. Perhaps the most

---

[1] There are, of course, other internal structures that could be used for individual-level analysis. *Personality* is often used, as is *motivation*. In common with cognitive structure, these cannot be directly observed, but must be inferred from other evidence. Cognitive structure is the concept that is more appropriate for analysis of this subject matter.

basic is *information level,* how much the citizen knows. However much information a citizen possesses, it is organized into *attitudes,* valenced cognitions about political objects. Since attitudes may be positive, negative, or neutral, one is led to theories of *cognitive consistency.* And since attitude objects are not all of equal importance, we need to pay attention to the variations in the relative prominence of attitude objects, known as *salience* and *centrality.*

On the individual level, the ***external structure consists of the informational environment and the citizen's opportunities for political participation.*** The notion of an informational environment is that an individual is surrounded at all times by a number of information sources. In Chapter 2, we saw how laws concerning registration affected the likelihood that an individual would cast a ballot. In this chapter, we shall see how citizens' knowledge about politics is affected by the information available in the media and by the extent to which the media are used.

There are also temporal patterns on the individual level. A citizen's attitudes, or behavior, or both, may remain stable or fluctuate. The resulting ***temporal patterns may be observed within a campaign, between elections, or over one's lifetime.*** In general, a person who is concerned about politics and who strongly identifies with one political party is more likely to exhibit stable attitudes and stable behavior. A person with little political information and little interest may show quite irregular behavior—not bothering to vote in many instances and swinging unpredictably between the parties when casting a ballot. Also speaking generally, the longer the time period, the greater the likelihood of a change in attitudes or a variation in behavior. In this section of the book, we shall be concerned with all these matters as they affect a citizen's response to campaign strategies.

In this chapter, we shall first ask how much citizens know—what the distribution of information is across the electorate. Then we shall turn to the content of political information in the mass media—the relationship between the information in the media and the citizen's political knowledge, and the degree to which that knowledge depends on the citizen's involvement with the informational environment. We shall conclude with a look at the temporal patterns that can be discerned within a campaign. Chapter 15 will deal with the relationships between citizen attitudes and presidential choice. Chapter 16 will look at party identification, cognitive consistency, and the stability of attitudes between elections.

HOW MUCH DO CITIZENS KNOW ABOUT
PRESIDENTIAL POLITICS?

At 6:25 P.M. on Monday, September 27, 1976, an interviewer from the Center for Political Studies at the University of Michigan began questioning a 34-year-old airline ramp attendant who lived on Long Island. After some initial items, the interviewer came to a series of questions that the Center of Political Studies has used in every election survey since 1952.

Interviewer: *Now, back to national politics, I'd like to ask what you think are the good and bad points about both parties. Is there anything in particular that you like about the Democratic party?*

Respondent: They will spend more domestically than out of the country.

Interviewer: *Is there anything in particular that you don't like about the Democratic party?*

Respondent: No.

Interviewer: *Is there anything in particular that you like about the Republican party?*

Respondent: Ford's firm stand in Korea, and getting people out of Lebanon.

Interviewer: *Is there anything in particular that you don't like about the Republican party?*

Respondent: Lack of Domestic spending.

Interviewer: *Now I'd like to ask you about the good and bad points of the two major candidates for president. Is there anything in particular about Mr. Carter that might make you want to vote for him?*

Respondent: Just a change.

Interviewer: *Is there anything in particular about Mr. Carter that might make you want to vote against him?*

Respondent: No.

Interviewer: *Is there anything in particular about Mr. Ford that might make you want to vote for him?*

Respondent: I like his foreign policy.

Interviewer: *Is there anything in particular about Mr. Ford that might make you want to vote against him?*

Respondent: Cutting domestic spending.

This voter was close to the middle of several social and political spectra. He was in his mid-30s, a high school graduate, regarded himself as average middle class, and was an independent. He liked Republican foreign policy and Democratic domestic spending. As a Catholic who lived in New York, he was also the type of voter regarded as crucial in both the Ford and Carter campaign strategies. Balanced between the attractions of Republican foreign policy and Democratic domestic policy, he resolved his own dilemma with the belief that it was time for a change. He decided to vote for Jimmy Carter during the Democratic convention, and did so in November. What is most important to our present purpose, though, is the amount of information the airline ramp attendant showed in his responses. He was as close to the average level of information as it was possible to be.

However typical this airline employee may have been, it is hazardous to rest an analysis on any single case. We can develop a better sense of information levels by seeing how several citizens answered this series of questions. Let's begin with a woman from Philadelphia. She was 30 years old, single, and a free-lance photographer who was working as an artist. Politically, she was an independent; and she had a good deal to say about the parties and candidates.[2]

Interviewer: *Like about the Democratic party?*

Respondent: I think in general that the Democrats have more interest in the average person. The social reform and work with the underprivileged is stronger.

Interviewer: *Anything else?*

Respondent: Their economic policies are usually different than the Republicans; there is usually larger government spending and more concern about unemployment.

Interviewer: *Dislike about the Democratic party?*

Respondent: I don't like the close identification with the labor movement—an inordinate amount of influence.

Interviewer: *Anything else?*

Respondent: There is corruption in all the parties, especially at the local level.

Interviewer: *Like about the Republican party?*

Respondent: To me financially, the usual tax shelters and financial policies are better due to my income.

Interviewer: *Anything else?*

Respondent: At times there is not a great deal of difference. The liberal part of the Republican party is much more applicable to me. I don't like to see the two-party system die.

Interviewer: *Dislike about the Republican party?*

Respondent: I don't like the increased military spending. The ultraconservative factions. The often large influence by the very powerful large companies.

Interviewer: *Anything else?*

Respondent: That's all.

Interviewer: *Like about Carter?*

Respondent: He seems very sincere; that's possibly cosmetically done. I prefer his stands on abortion and I admire him for standing up for that—not being snowed under by the Catholic Church.

Interviewer: *Dislike about Carter?*

Respondent: The main thing is not knowing enough about him. I think he's naive in international affairs.

Interviewer: *Anything else?*

Respondent: At times the whole southern Mafia type of feeling upsets me. I'm also concerned about how his tax changes would affect my bracket.

Interviewer: *Like about Ford?*

---

[2] Since the full wording of the basic question sequence was given for the ramp attendant, an abbreviated form will be used for the photographer and subsequent examples.

Respondent: "Old Jer's too dumb to be crooked." That's facetious. I think he's very honest.

Interviewer: *Anything else?*

Respondent: He's certainly had enough practice so the country won't have to sit around and wait another one-and-a-half years to figure out what's going on the way Carter will I'm afraid.

Interviewer: *Dislike about Ford?*

Respondent: His increased military spending. His stand on abortion.

Interviewer: *Anything else?*

Respondent: That's all I can think of right now. Lackluster. Neither of them are terribly attractive.

In comparison with other respondents, this photographer was quite articulate—enough so that it would be risky to assert which of her many attitudes was most important in her voting decision. She delayed making her choice until mid-October, and then concluded that she would vote for "Old Jer."

An interviewer in St. Louis talked with a 67-year-old woman who was born in central Europe and lived there until World War I. Her husband had been a tool and die maker until his retirement. She impressed the interviewer with her warmth and expansiveness.

Interviewer: *Like about the Democratic party?*

Respondent: They are more progressive; do more for the workers. They believe in the unions. Of course, the Teamsters are overdoing it. They are for socialized medicine to curb doctors' abuses; they charge too much.

Interviewer: *Anything else?*

Respondent: More for the people. I'd like to see Mondale for president and Carter v.p. It's not true they're warmongers. It's not true they're big spenders. The Republicans are big spenders too. The Democrats gave us social security and medicare. It's not like we paid for it.

Interviewer: *Dislike about the Democratic party?*

Respondent: A few old fogies I don't care for: Hays, Wilbur Mills. I wish they would vote some old fogies out and vote some new, young ones in.

Interviewer: *Like about the Republican party?*

Respondent: There are some good progressive ones: Javits, Brooke, Percy.

Interviewer: *Dislike about the Republican party?*

Respondent: Too conservative. They should help the cities, not give money to foreign countries. That nutty Kissinger; they depend too much on him.

Interviewer: *Anything else?*

Respondent: Why do we have to have a foreign-born secretary of state? Of course, I'm foreign born.

Interviewer: *Like about Carter?*

Respondent: He promises to do something about unemployment and inflation. Government should do something about unemployment—teach a trade rather than pass out food stamps and welfare. He promises to pass socialized medicine; cut out bureaucrats, expensive do-nothing bureaucrats in Washington. He says he never told a lie. He shouldn't have interviewed *Playboy*. Carter's and Ford's stands are the same on abortion. He's not connected with the Washington Establishment. He'll work with Congress.

Interviewer: *Dislike about Carter?*

Respondent: No.

Interviewer: *Like about Ford?*

Respondent: No.

Interviewer: *Dislike about Ford?*

Respondent: I don't like his vetoes, his pardon of Nixon, so many things. He's a do-nothing president. He's for unemployment to curb the inflation. Always against progressiveness.

Interviewer: *Anything else?*

Respondent: He was the biggest hawk in Congress. Now he's talking about peace. He's picking on Carter on the Yugoslav issue; that means he would send troops to Yugoslavia. We're from Yugoslavia. Why should we support one communist regime against another? That makes no sense! We were there five years ago. No freedom. Americans are good politicians, but bad statesmen. Europeans outwit us all the time.

In contrast with the balanced comments of the airline ramp attendant and the photographer, almost everything this woman said favored the Democrats. Not surprisingly, she had decided to vote for Jimmy Carter during the primaries.

Our next example is a 40-year-old housewife who lived in a frame house in Bellingham, Washington. A staunch Lutheran, she had been in the middle of a conversation about church affairs when the interviewer arrived.

Interviewer: *Like about the Democratic party?*

Respondent: One thing that has been good: tax loopholes are going to have to be checked a lot more, they are saying.

Interviewer: *Dislike about the Democratic party?*

Respondent: I feel that their platform at the convention just wanted to do too much and it worries me. Too expensive.

Interviewer: *Like about the Republican party?*

Respondent: The fact that they didn't want to do quite as much. They didn't want to get quite as many new projects going.

Interviewer: *Anything else?*

Respondent: They feel that private enterprise should be encouraged more to solve the problems of inflation. It's a matter of degree with the two parties. They are not as much for price control either. Things would have to be pretty bad before I'd go for price controls. Republicans wouldn't be as hasty as Democrats on this.

Interviewer: *Dislike about the Republican party?*

Respondent: No.

Interviewer: *Like about Carter?*

Respondent: Certainly a personable guy. He seems so very human. The fact that he's a Christian—not that Ford isn't. He seems to be very honest.

Interviewer: *Dislike about Carter?*

Respondent: I think he hasn't had anywhere near the experience that President Ford has had. And he seems to want to start a lot of programs that would cost a lot of money.

Interviewer: *Like about Ford?*

Respondent: I think his experience above all. He was in Congress before. He has had to deal with national and international issues, and his record has been good.

Interviewer: *Dislike about Ford?*

Respondent: I wasn't happy about his having Dole. That's about all.

Things that she liked about the Republicans came as easily to the mind of this middle-class Westerner as attractive aspects of the Democratic party came to the St. Louis immigrant. Both could list things they liked about the opposition, but both made their own voting decisions very early. The St. Louis resident voted for Carter; the Washingtonian voted for Ford.

A 32-year-old Arkansan had grown up in a family of 10 children. She now had two of her own, and juggled a busy schedule so as to care for them and work as a counselor in a Little Rock high school.

Interviewer: *Like about the Democratic party?*

Respondent: As a party, concern with the small person. The average person tends to see them as a party with strength.

Interviewer: *Anything else?*

Respondent: No. I'm not much for following politicians.

Interviewer: *Dislike about the Democratic party?*

Respondent: Even though it seems they're working for the poor excluded urban groups and ethnic groups, I still think they have a lot of work to be done on involvement on the part of women.

Interviewer: *Like about the Republican party?*

Respondent: No.

Interviewer: *Dislike about the Republican party?*

Respondent: Favoritism toward big business. It shows up in the way they like to run government.

Interviewer: *Anything else?*

Respondent: Just their feeling that money is power.

Interviewer: *Like about Carter?*

Respondent: He hasn't been president before. Therefore he hasn't had a chance to make errors. I'll give him a chance.

Interviewer: *Anything else?*

Respondent: Basic cut of honesty.

Interviewer: *Dislike about Carter?*

Respondent: I'm skeptical as most blacks about his being a southern white. I know that's prejudiced, but I just can't help it.

Interviewer: *Like about Ford?*

Respondent: I think his experience gives him the potential to do . . . a good job if he'd use his experience.

Interviewer: *Anything else?*

Respondent: That's his only asset.

Interviewer: *Dislike about Ford?*

Respondent: He's a Richard Nixon appointee.

Interviewer: *Anything else?*

Respondent: I could go on and scream about failure to act on positive social legislation and his general unconcern for the working class.

In spite of her generally pro-Democratic attitudes, her skepticism about Carter and positive view of President Ford's experience were enough to delay her decision until election day. Then she voted for Carter.

Then there was a high school graduate in Findlay, Ohio. He spent his working hours making pull tabs for the tops of beer cans.

Interviewer: *Like about the Democratic party?*

Respondent: No.

Interviewer: *Dislike about the Democratic party?*

Respondent: Just somewhat of the talk I've heard about Carter's opinions.

Interviewer: *What did you hear?*

Respondent: How he won't let the money get back to the people.

Interviewer: *What money?*

Respondent: The government money.

Interviewer: *Anything else?*

Respondent: No.

Interviewer: *Like about the Republican party?*

Respondent: I like what Ford has already done in office. Nothing in particular.

Interviewer: *Dislike about the Republican party?*

Respondent: No.

Interviewer: *Like about Carter?*

Respondent: When I first saw him on TV and such, he gave me the impression of a real go-getter—one who wanted to do everything.

Interviewer: *Dislike about Carter?*

Respondent: Just the talk I've heard.

Interviewer: *What?*

Respondent: All about taking money from people, the programs, cutting the budget.

Interviewer: *Like about Ford?*

Respondent: His past experience. And I think he shows his power more than Carter.

Interviewer: *Dislike about Ford?*

Respondent: No.

There is no way to know from the interview what this Findlay worker had heard about Jimmy Carter's spending plans, but he was disturbed about it. In any case, he was pro-Ford because of his positive, if amorphous, attitude about Ford's experience. He had decided to vote for President Ford before either convention.

Finally, there was a white-haired, 72-year-old lady who lived with her daughter's family in a small frame house outside Richmond, Virginia. Her education had stopped with the 10th grade, and her knowledge of politics was meager.

Interviewer: *Like about the Democratic party?*

Respondent: No.

Interviewer: *Dislike about the Democratic party?*

Respondent: They're different from the Republicans.

Interviewer: *Like about the Republican party?*

Respondent: No.

Interviewer: *Dislike about the Republican party?*

Respondent: No.

Interviewer: *Like about Carter?*

Respondent: No.

Interviewer: *Dislike about Carter?*

Respondent: No.

Interviewer: *Like about Ford?*

Respondent: No.

Interviewer: *Dislike about Ford?*

Respondent: No.

How this woman might have decided between the candidates, knowing only that there was some kind of difference between the parties makes for interesting speculation, but no more. Along with many other uninformed persons, she didn't vote.

With seven examples, we are in a little better position to understand citizens' perceptions than when we had only one.[3] We have the views of two Easterners, two Midwesterners, two Southerners, and one Westerner. In a very close election, three respondents reported voting for

---

[3] This subsample of seven respondents also illustrates why it is risky to generalize on the basis of a small number of cases. For instance, our seven respondents included no one in their 20s or their 50s, no one from any of the Sunbelt states, and only two men.

FIGURE 14-1
Distribution of Information Levels, 1976

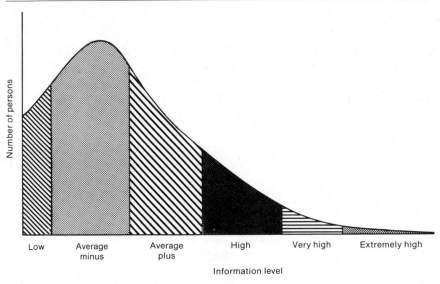

Carter, three for Ford, and one did not vote. We certainly saw some common attitudes: that the Democratic party takes more interest in the underprivileged, that Republican fiscal policies are more advantageous for the middle class, admiration for Jimmy Carter's sincerity, and trust of Gerald Ford's experience. But what these seven interviews best illustrate are the various information levels among the electorate. The Long Island airline ramp attendant had an average level of information, and the succeeding half-dozen examples illustrated—in decreasing order—the various levels of knowledge about politics.

Figure 14-1 portrays the distribution of the information levels these examples typify. (The distribution of information across the electorate appears to be relatively stable over time. Figure 17-1 shows very similar curves for 1976 and 1980. Hence we are not being misled by using 1976 examples.) The free-lance photographer from Philadelphia is in the *extremely-high* category.[4] The Yugoslav immigrant living in St. Louis comes from the *very-high* category. The housewife from Bellingham, Washington, displayed *high* knowledge. The school counselor in Little Rock was closer to typical, and is in the middle of the *average-*

---

[4] While the language that follows will be varied to avoid six identically worded sentences, each of the examples comes from the middle of the range that it typifies. For a discussion of how the information-level categories were constructed, see Appendix A-14.1.

TABLE 14-1
Distribution of Information Levels
within Electorate

Information Level	Percent of Electorate
Low	17.5%
Average minus	41.2
Average plus	25.5
High	11.7
Very high	3.2
Extremely high	0.9

Data source: 1976 Election Study, Center for Political Studies.

plus category. The ramp attendant from Long Island falls right between the *average-plus* and the *average-minus* ranges. The worker from the Findlay, Ohio, beer-can factory knows a little less than most American citizens, and thus represents the *average-minus* category. The elderly lady living outside Richmond, Virginia, showed a *low* level of information.[5]

The proportions of citizens falling into each of the information categories are shown in Table 14-1. Fully two thirds of all citizens are in either the average-minus or average-plus categories. The low and high categories account for another 29 percent. The very-high and extremely-high categories are quite rare; together they account for only 4 percent of all the responses. Put another way, there were four times as many persons as uninformed as the elderly Virginia woman as there were persons as knowledgeable as the St. Louis immigrant *and* the Philadelphia photographer. If you want a sense of Americans' political knowledge, think of the Ohio beer-can worker, the Long Island airline ramp attendant, and the Little Rock high school counselor. Two out of three Americans know this much about politics.

SOURCES OF INFORMATION

ABOUT POLITICS

CONTACT WITH ELECTRONIC AND PRINT SOURCES

Why do citizens have the amount of information that they do? Why are there more persons in the average-minus category than any other?

---

[5] There are three high categories and only one low category because the names were chosen to indicate how far away from the mean the category is. Since the mean information level itself is close to zero, there is room for only the average-minus and low categories between the mean and zero points.

What allows a few persons to know much more about politics than most of their fellow citizens? There are two basic answers to questions such as these. One deals with the amount of information that is available, the other with the extent to which each citizen seeks knowledge from the informational environment. We shall look at both of these considerations.

Most citizens acquire their information about politics through the mass media. Table 14-2 presents information about the extent of use of the mass media, and about each medium's impact on information level. Television is the most widely used, as has been the case for some time. Eighty-nine percent report using television as a news source, in contrast to 72 percent who say they read newspapers and slightly less than half who report reading magazines. When one looks at the association between use of a news source and information level, however, the ordering is reversed. Television, which is readily available even to those in the low-information category, has the least impact on information level. Newspapers and especially magazines, used by fewer persons and requiring more effort, have a much stronger association with a respondent's level of information.

Why should print media have greater impact than television on what people know about politics? One possible explanation is that people are making different uses of the media. It might be that people are being entertained by watching soap operas, sports, and miniseries on television, while they are reading articles about politics in newspapers and magazines. This is a plausible explanation, but it can be rejected. When the comparison is limited to the prime information sources in

TABLE 14-2
Information Level by Medium Used

Medium Used	Low	Average Minus	Average Plus	High	Very High	Extremely High	Total
				Information Level			
Magazines							
Not used	78.6%	59.5%	42.3%	23.8%	17.3%	13.3%	51.8%
Used	21.4	40.5	57.7	76.2	82.7	86.7	48.2
Kendall's Tau–c = .39							
Newspapers							
Not used	44.3	33.0	21.8	10.3	14.5	11.1	28.3
Used	55.7	67.0	78.2	89.7	85.5	88.9	71.7
Kendall's Tau–c = .23							
Television							
Not used	27.4	11.7	4.8	4.3	2.9	0	11.2
Used	72.6	88.3	95.2	95.7	97.1	100.0	88.8
Kendall's Tau–c = .16							

Data source: 1976 Election Study, Center for Political Studies.

Bivariate Correlation = Association between Two Things

Bivariate correlation may be understood simply as an association between two things that take on different values. The prefix *bi* means two, and a variable is any mathematical term other than a constant. The fundamental idea in correlation is association as opposed to independence. Hence, bivariate correlation just means association between two variables.

The underlying ideas go back some time. The central notion of constant conjunction came from the 18th-century Scotch philosopher, David Hume. John Stuart Mill, the 19th-century British philosopher, extended this idea in his Method of Concomitant Variation. Essentially, if an increase in Variable A tends to produce an increase in Variable B, it may be taken as evidence that the two are associated.

		Information Level					
	Low	Average Minus	Average Plus	High	Very High	Extremely High	Total
Newspapers read?							
No	44.3%	33.0%	21.8%	10.3%	14.5%	11.1%	28.3%
Yes	57.7	67.0	78.2	89.7	85.5	88.9	71.7
Kendall's Tau–c = .23							
Hypothetical variable							
Present	56.1	59.9	59.1	58.0	62.1	60.9	58.9
Absent	43.9	40.1	40.9	42.0	37.9	39.1	41.1
Kendall's Tau–c = 0							

In the accompanying table, information is associated with reading newspapers, but information level is independent of the hypothetical variable. There are two ways to see this. The first is to inspect the pattern of the cell entries (which in this case are column percentages), and compare these to the characteristics of the total sample. Let's take the newspaper example first. Of those in the low-information column, only 55.7 percent read newspapers as compared to 71.7 percent in the total sample. This percentage increases to 67.0 in the average-minus column. By the time we get to the average-plus column, more people are reading newspapers (78.2 percent) than is the case in the total sample. In the high column, 89.7 percent read newspapers as compared to 71.7 percent overall. The percentage drops back just slightly in the very-high column, but then comes back up in the extremely-high column. As you move across all six magnitudes in the information-level scale, the percentage of those reading newspapers increases from 55.7 to 88.9, as compared to 71.7 for the total sample. The opposite is true for those who do not read newspapers. Therefore, you conclude that there is an association between reading newspapers and having a higher information level.

If you read across the rows for the hypothetical variable, and compare the entries with the figures for the total sample, you see that the percentages in both rows are virtually the same as those for the total sample. Since it doesn't make any difference which column a given case falls into, we say that information level is independent of the hypothetical variable.

The second way to tell whether there is an association is to look at the summary measure of association (in this case Kendall's Tau-c) which is printed at the bottom of the tables. It is called a summary measure because it summarizes the strength of the correlation—you can see at a glance that .23 is greater than 0 in the example—but it doesn't tell you anything else. If it has a value of 0, it means that the two variables are totally independent of each other. If it has a value of 1.0 (almost never seen with real-world political data), it means there is complete association between the variables. Generally, you judge the strength of the association by seeing how far away it is from 0. You show that two variables are associated by showing that they are *not* independent of each other.

Different measures of correlation are used depending on the nature of the data. For instance, Kendall's Tau-c was used in this example, but Pearson's r was used in Chapter 10. There are differences between various measures, but the fundamental idea is covariation.

Measures of correlation are often used to infer cause and effect. Before one concludes that there is causation, though, one must show both a statistical association and a logical reason for the relationship between the variables. There may be accidental statistical association. For example, the divorce rate in Manhattan might increase at the same time as wheat production in Kansas. Clearly, Kansas wheat does not cause Manhattan divorces. In the instance of newspaper reading, however, it is plausible to assume that one picks up information from reading newspapers, and since there is also a statistical association, we may say that we have shown cause and effect in this particular sense.

---

both print and electronic media, the print advantage emerges even more strongly. Table 14-3 presents data on the relation between information level and the frequency with which persons read newspaper articles about national politics and watch the evening news shows on television. Again, nearly twice as many persons say they frequently watch network news as report frequently reading about national politics. But watching television news has relatively little impact on one's political knowledge, while reading about national politics has a substantial impact. Why so?

TELEVISION

The first reason why television conveys relatively little information is that there is simply less news on television. The evening network news shows last half an hour, but the average time actually devoted

TABLE 14-3
Information Level by Use of Specific Sources

Frequency of Use	Low	Average Minus	Average Plus	High	Very High	Extremely High	Total
Newspapers to read about national politics							
Never	35.4%	16.8%	6.7%	2.7%	0%	0%	14.8%
Rarely	32.9	24.9	12.6	7.7%	6.9	0	20.0
Sometimes	27.4	42.1	40.0	28.6	36.4	33.3	37.2
Frequently	4.3	16.1	40.7	60.9	56.6	66.7	28.0
Kendall's Tau–*c* = .40							
Television to watch evening network news							
Never	15.2	9.6	6.7	4.8	10.4	11.1	9.2
Rarely	19.1	12.9	12.0	13.7	9.2	8.9	13.6
Sometimes	28.4	24.3	22.1	18.8	18.5	28.9	23.6
Frequently	37.2	53.2	59.2	62.7	61.8	51.1	53.6
Kendall's Tau–*c* = .12							

Data source: 1976 Election Study, Center for Political Studies.

to news in one week was 21 minutes, 17 seconds.[6] Between 15 and 25 stories were carried on each show, with between 4 and 10 on all three networks, and another half dozen on two of them. Lead stories typically lasted a little over two minutes, and quick references later in the show might be as brief as 10 seconds. Only 10 stories in the week lasted longer than three minutes, and only 1 of these (on CBS) was a lead news story. The rest of the longer stories were features or analyses late in the newscasts. CBS, with the smallest number of stories and the most news time, had the longest average story. ABC, with a combination of longer analyses and brief references, and the least total news time, had the shortest average story. These differences, however, were small variations within a similar news format. During the week, CBS presented 90 stories averaging 1 minute, 16 seconds; NBC, 94 stories averaging 1 minute, 10 seconds; ABC, 98 stories averaging 1 minute, 1 second.[7] With little more than a minute to devote to

---

[6] The data in this paragraph come from an analysis of the evening news shows from Monday, September 14, 1981, through Friday, September 18, 1981. No week is "typical," but there is no reason to think this September week was atypical. For similar findings from an analysis of network news coverage during the week of March 7–11, 1977, see Levin (1977). I should like to thank James Barnes for the 1981 data.

[7] There are certainly other possible uses of time. PBS's "MacNeil-Lehrer NewsHour" employs a flexible format to adapt to the news developments of the day, but typically has three stories in addition to a brief recapitulation of the day's major events. The

each story, the standard network format of the early 1980s is essentially a headline service. It scarcely goes beyond the topics on the front page of a newspaper, and even these front-page items are covered in very abbreviated form.

Another consideration is the kind of news on which television chooses to focus. In an exhaustive study of all network newscasts between July 10 and election day 1972, Richard Hofstetter (1976) distinguished between "political bias" (a tendency to favor one candidate or the other) and "structural bias" (a tendency to use a particular kind of story thought to be more appropriate for television). There was very little political bias, but a lot of structural bias. The producers of television news had a preference for pictures over explanation. The consequences of this were pointed out by two other students of television news, Thomas Patterson and Robert McClure:

> "One dimension of the election fits perfectly the networks' demand for good pictures. It is the "horse race" aspect of the run for the White House. For a presidential election is surely a super contest with all of the elements that are associated with spectacular sports events: huge crowds, rabid followers, dramatic do-or-die battles, winners and losers. It is this part of the election that the networks emphasize. (1976, pp. 40–41)

Their analyses showed that horse-race topics dominated political television in both 1972 and 1976. In 1976, 60 percent of television coverage was devoted to horse-race topics, 28 percent to substantive topics, and 12 percent fell into a miscellaneous category (T. E. Patterson, 1978, p. 184).

A Comparison of Television and Newspaper Coverage

Doris Graber (1976, 1980) has been studying television and newspaper coverage of presidential campaigns. During the last 30 days of each campaign, she has obtained and analyzed 20 newspapers published in various parts of the country. For 1972, a similar content analysis was done of videotapes of the network newscasts; for 1968 and 1976, story logs (which contain the same information in more abbreviated form) were analyzed.

The first cut in her coding procedure separated issue coverage from discussion of the qualities of the presidential candidates. For the press,

---

lead story is devoted to interviews with experts together with some background information; the second story is a minidocumentary; the third is along the lines of an essay. NPR's "All Things Considered" has headlines at the beginning of each half hour, and then follows with extended coverage of just a few stories. Both shows are remarkably effective and interesting.

in 1968, the ratio of issues to personal qualities was 44 to 56, devoting greater attention to the candidates, but still more or less in balance. In 1972, however, she found that press attention to issues had slipped, and was about the same as that for television. The ratio of issues to qualities was 39 to 61. Both newspapers and television were carrying about three issue stories for every five dealing with the candidates.

The issue coverage was further analyzed into five categories. The first dealt essentially with international involvement; the second with economic management; the third combined social benefits and civil liberties. The fourth dealt with what might be called general politics: the institutions of government, the incumbent's and the challenger's policies, ethics, opinion polls, and so on. The last dealt with campaign stories. The proportions of television and newspaper coverage in each of these five categories are shown in Table 14-4.

Professor Graber's research supports several generalizations. First, relatively little journalistic attention is being paid to the policy areas. Since 36 percent and 37 percent of all 1972 press and television coverage, respectively, went to issues, the figures in Table 14-4 mean that only 7.5 percent of all press coverage and only 4.9 percent of all television coverage was devoted to international involvement in 1972. Second, the bulk of television coverage has gone to campaign topics. (Graber's estimate of 57 percent of 1976 coverage going to campaign topics appears similar to the McClure-Patterson estimate of 60 percent devoted to horse-race coverage that year.) Third, perhaps most surprising in view of the different needs and capacities of the two media, newspapers have devoted less and less attention to the questions of policy. In a study of *New York Times* coverage of the 1980 campaign, Doris Graber

TABLE 14-4
Issue Coverage in Television and Newspaper

Issue	1968	1972	1976
		Television	
International involvement	11.5%	13.1%	15.8%
Economic management	3.2	6.1	8.8
Social benefits and civil liberties	4.6	4.6	5.9
General politics	23.9	17.0	12.2
Campaign	56.9	59.2	57.2
		Newspapers	
International involvement	26.3%	20.9%	16.9%
Economic management	16.4	12.4	11.9
Social benefits and civil liberties	13.9	7.5	6.4
General politics	23.7	23.7	20.0
Campaign	19.6	35.4	44.9

Source: Doris Graber, *The Mass Media and Politics* (Washington, D.C.: Congressional Quarterly Press, 1980).

found that the proportion of their space devoted to campaign stories stayed about the same as in 1976, but the proportion devoted to general politics increased, and the space given to foreign policy and economics declined from 1976. The amount of space devoted to policy by the *New York Times* was less than a third of the space being devoted to them by newspapers a dozen years earlier (1982b, p. 4).

The televised debates between Gerald Ford and Jimmy Carter in 1976 (and presumably the Reagan-Anderson and the Reagan-Carter debates in 1980) provided an important exception to the media tendency to avoid issues. The first 1976 debate stressed economics, the second foreign policy, and the third a mix of issues. The postdebate coverage did not maintain this focus. Instead, more attention was paid to the familiar questions of personality, performance, and who the media felt had "won" the debate.[8] Even so, issue coverage was estimated at 37 percent for both television and newspapers, a figure substantially higher than that for normal campaign content (Sears & Chaffee, 1979).

PRINT MEDIA

If television has the advantage of vivid pictures, writers have the advantage of being able to discuss topics at sufficient length to convey detailed information. Many of them—and especially the best—worry about what to write. Thus, David Broder, the *Washington Post*'s thoughtful political analyst:

> Where do the candidates come from? What motivates them to want to be president? . . . When they have a decision to make, do they pull in a big group of people or go with whatever seems to be the consensus or do they go off by themselves and meditate on what they should do? . . . Are they really open for questioning, or do they go into a debate or a press conference to defend their own views? (Barber, 1978, p. 134)

Theodore White, author of "The Making of the President" series, has been called by James David Barber "our age's most influential artist of pointillistic journalism: microscopic fact-dots blended by the mind's eye to compose a meaningful conglomerate." One example of this is White's description of the Rockefeller estate at Pocantico Hills:

> Behind a low fieldstone wall stretches some of the loveliest land any- where in America . . . From the terrace on the far side one looks out over the Hudson River . . . As one gazes down in enchantment on the broad-flowing river, it is difficult to imagine sorrow or anger or any other

---

[8] The media concentration on the identity of the "winners" had a decided effect on citizens' judgments about who did better in the debate. The longer the time between the debate itself and a survey about the "winner," the greater the proportion of respondents who named the media-identified "winner" as the candidate who did better.

> ordinary human concern penetrating this paradise. (Barber, 1978, pp. 126–27)

All wordsmiths do not compose their phrases with the skill of a Theodore White, but newspapers, magazines, and books do provide more "microscopic fact-dots" than the electronic media. This is reflected in the stronger relationship between the use of print media and information level.

Another reason for the greater impact of print is the degree of attention it requires. Television is regularly reported to be the most used medium, but what does "watching television" mean? In one careful study of network newscasts, viewers filled out diaries indicating whether they gave the program full attention or partial attention, or whether they were out of the room. During the two-week period of the study, 59 percent of adult Americans did not give full attention to a single evening network program, and only 14 percent gave full attention to more than four newscasts.[9] In contrast, 73 percent reported reading two or more newspapers over any two *days* in the same two-week period (Stevenson, 1978, p. 12; tables 1-3).

Robert Stevenson related this difference between wide apparent use of television and rather casual actual use to the contrasting skills required by television and print media:

> Television, of course, is ideally suited for . . . passive surveillance. It requires (or allows) no personal selection of content like a newspaper does, no active cognitive processing of content as reading does, and no imagination to create in the mind a picture of the event. For people who lack the mental skills to read a newspaper or magazine efficiently or the physical acuity to read easily or the interest to profit from selective reading, television is a psychologically gratifying experience. (Stevenson, 1978, p. 21)

Doris Graber echoes this, as a result of her comparison of newspapers and television. "The reader who finds press coverage confusing as well as depressing can . . . turn to television for a simpler, clearer, and more encouraging image of the unfolding electoral scene" (1976, p. 302).

Thus the content of newspapers and televison, and the cognitive processes engaged by the print and electronic media, provide explanations for the greater impact of print media. The print sources contain somewhat more stories about complex topics, and have sufficient space to develop more in the way of analysis. Therefore, readers must make use of higher cognitive processes to comprehend information from the print media.

---

[9] Those who most frequently watched the network newscasts tended to be over 60 and to have grade school educations. (There *is* a reason for all those false teeth, laxative, and sedative commercials you see while watching network newscasts.)

COGNITIVE INTERACTION WITH THE

INFORMATIONAL ENVIRONMENT

If the content of the informational environment provides one reason why individuals know as much as they do, a second is to be found in the extent of cognitive interaction with that environment. A person's cognitive structure is intimately related to the informational environment in at least two ways. First, an individual continuously monitors the environment to pick up cues. Each person's attention is directed to particular parts of the environment by a perceptual schema. This is the aspect of cognitive structure that guides one's perception, and makes it more likely (but not certain) that some things will be noticed and others neglected. The information that is picked up as a result of this scanning in turn has the capacity to modify the perceptual schema that will guide further monitoring of the environment (Neisser, 1976). Because of this continual monitoring, the informational environment provides a medium that supports a cognitive structure as a person interacts with it, much as the air supports an aircraft as it moves through that medium. If the environment is rich in information, the person has the opportunity to acquire as many facts as can be absorbed.

The ability to absorb information is the second way in which cognitive structure and informational environment are interrelated. The more developed one's cognitive structure, the easier it is to understand new information as it is acquired. An incoming cue takes on meaning to an individual only as it is related to an existing cognitive category with contextual information that allows the person to interpret the cue. As a consequence, the relationship between informational environment and cognitive structure is not additive, but multiplicative. Not only will a person with a well-developed cognitive structure be more likely to pick up information, but that person will be better able to understand the meaning of the newly acquired information.

Table 14-5 shows the relation between information level and three measures of the extent to which one is engaged in the informational environment. The more education a person has, the more likely it is that cognitive skills will exist to allow one to pick up cues from the environment. The more frequently a person is accustomed to following public affairs, the more likely it is that campaign information will be monitored. And the more interested a person is in a specific campaign, the more likely it is that this citizen can follow it. We can see from Table 14-5 that the two factors that directly measure a tendency to be involved with the informational environment, following public affairs and interest in the presidential campaign, have stronger relationships with information level than does education. Therefore, we can infer that each of these three factors serves as an indicator of a generalized

TABLE 14-5
Information Level by Involvement with Informational Environment

				Information Level				
	Low	Average Minus	Average Plus	High	Very High	Extremely High	Total
Education							
Grade school	27.6%	19.6%	11.9%	6.7%	7.6%	5.9%	17.0%
Some high school	20.4	17.5	12.2	7.3	0	5.9	14.8
High school graduate	41.5	39.0	34.8	28.6	13.5	9.8	36.1
Some college	6.0	15.1	20.4	22.1	28.1	37.3	16.3
College graduate	4.5	8.9	20.6	35.3	50.8	41.2	15.8
Kendall's Tau–c = .28							
Frequency with which respondent follows public affairs							
Hardly at all	32.3	13.3	4.0	1.2	2.3	4.4	12.0
Only now and then	30.8	23.2	11.1	6.8	5.2	0	18.4
Some of the time	27.2	34.6	33.9	24.7	28.3	17.8	31.6
Most of the time	9.7	28.9	50.9	67.3	64.2	77.8	38.0
Kendall's Tau–c = .37							
Respondent's interest in political campaign							
Not much interested	52.6	21.5	8.5	6.4	7.7	0	21.2
Somewhat interested	39.1	49.7	40.4	29.6	30.1	23.5	42.3
Very much interested	8.3	28.8	51.1	64.0	62.3	76.5	36.5
Kendall's Tau–c = .40							

Data source: 1976 Election Study, Center for Political Studies.

tendency to monitor the informational environment, and that the more closely a citizen follows politics, the more likely it is that this person will be among the better informed.

Now we have two explanations of why some citizens are well informed and some citizens are poorly informed. The first has to do with how much information a given news source contains and the types of cognitive processes that are activated by use of that news source. The second has to do with how intensively the citizen monitors whatever news sources are available. Which of these is the stronger explanation? This is hard to answer. To some degree, the processes operate jointly. One's knowledge is increased both by an information-rich environment, *and* by more closely monitoring whatever information is available. A further complication is that at least one news source, television, seems to transmit information best to those least able to pay attention. Still, there are a couple of clues. For one thing, the relationships between information level and being engaged in the informational environment are generally stronger than those for use of specific news sources. For another, when one controls the relationship between reliance on a good news source and whether or not the respondent is paying attention, the relation drops sharply.[10] The opposite does not occur. Therefore, how closely a citizen monitors the informational environment appears to be more important than how rich a given information source is.

TIME AND POLITICAL KNOWLEDGE

Internal structure—at least the amount of information arrayed within a cognitive pattern—is dependent on external structure. Are citizens' cognitions also subject to temporal effects? The answer is yes, but under some special circumstances. The first of these is some dramatic event in the campaign itself. For example, when Senator Thomas Eagleton was dropped as the Democratic vice presidential candidate in 1972, this made some difference in how presidential candidate George McGovern was perceived. The special circumstances in this case were obvious. Not only was the resignation of a vice presidential candidate unprecedented, but the event took place so early in the campaign that there were still a good many persons who did not know much about

---

[10] For example, the relation for the total sample between information level and reading about politics in newspapers (Tau-c) is .40. For those who said they were not much interested in the campaign, this relation drops to .19; and for those who said they hardly ever followed public affairs, this same relation drops to .10. No matter how good the news source, if people don't pay attention, they aren't going to pick up that much information.

Senator McGovern. For these reasons, Eagleton's resignation and the context in which it occurred created a vivid first impression.

Another instance of dramatic events that altered cognitive content comes from 1964. During October of that contest between Johnson and Goldwater, certain domestic isues (law and order, alleged corruption, social security, unemployment) were gaining in salience while references to war and peace were declining. The increasingly salient domestic issues were being discussed by the candidates, and there hadn't been much consequential foreign news for a while. Then, within 48 hours, Nikita Khrushchev was deposed as premier of the Soviet Union, the Labour party won an unexpected election victory in Great Britain, and China exploded an atomic device. This caused foreign affairs to gain in salience at the expense of domestic campaign topics. The dramatic events led to an explosion of information on a topic (foreign developments bearing on the chances of war and peace) that was important to voters and about which they knew relatively little. Ordinarily, citizens would have a fair amount of information about topics important to them, and would not care about other matters. Both these circumstances tend to inhibit communication. In this instance, new information about a consequential matter suddenly became available. Therefore international affairs became more salient to many voters.

Perhaps the most important temporal effect takes place over the course of the campaign. For the electorate as a whole, there is no relationship between citizens' information level and time. Well-informed citizens are likely to be as knowledgeable in early September as they are on the day before election, and uninformed persons are not likely to be knowledgeable at any particular time. There is one category of citizens, however, whose information level does tend to increase as the campaign progresses. These are persons who have attended high school, who say they are somewhat interested in the campaign, and who follow public affairs some of the time—persons, in other words, who fall into the *middle* of the scales related to monitoring the informational environment. If one looks at those who have attended college, who say they are very much interested in the campaign, and who follow public affairs most of the time, there is no relation between time and information level. This grouping is constantly monitoring the informational environment, is likely to have picked up a good many cues before the campaign began, and hence is unlikely to learn much new information during the campaign. Nor is there any relation between time and information level for those who didn't go beyond grade school, who say they are not much interested in the campaign, and who follow public affairs only now and then if they do so at all. Politics is so remote from the lives of these people that the campaigners face insurmountable communication thresholds in trying to reach them. But a temporal effect can be found for those who are "average" in their receptivity to political communications, who are neither avid followers of politics, nor among those who ignore public affairs altogether. For those who fall into the middle of all three scales, there is at least a moderate relationship ($r = .19$) between the passage of time in the campaign and information level.[11]

It would be a mistake to regard this temporal effect as either strong or negligible. Essentially what is happening is that as the campaign progresses, there are fewer persons with a "low" information level, and more with an "average plus" information level. This does not mean that a great deal of information is being communicated, but it does mean that the campaign is more than a hollow ritual. When we reviewed the stages of a campaign in Chapter 10, we saw that proposals to shorten presidential campaigns did not take account of the planning and organization necessary to conduct a campaign on a subcontinental scale. To this we can now add that if campaigns were to end a month earlier, there would be a larger number of uninformed citizens, and they would likely be less at ease with the electoral choice they are asked to make.

Summary

In this chapter, we have seen that internal cognitive structure is dependent on external informational environment. Most citizens know relatively little about politics, but there are some who are quite well informed. The well informed are more likely to use print sources. The print sources contain more information to begin with, and require more involved cognitive processes for comprehension. The well informed are also likely to be those who monitor the informational environment most closely because of their education or their interest in politics. The degree to which one is engaged in the informational environment is a stronger explanation of information level than the use of print sources. Finally, time does matter. Neither the very interested, nor the quite uninterested, learn much as a campaign progresses; but citizens with middling involvement tend to increase their understanding as the campaign progresses.

---

[11] It is necessary to isolate those in the middle of all three scales in order to find this relationship. The correlations between time and information level for those in the middle categories of the individual scales are all significant, but lower. For those who attended high school, but did not go on to college, $r = .05$. For those who said they were somewhat interested in the campaign, $r = .06$. For those who said they followed public affairs some of the time, $r = .10$. There were no significant correlations for those on the high or low ends of any of the three scales.

CHAPTER 15

PRESIDENTIAL CHOICE

In this chapter, we shall deal directly with the citizen's use of knowledge to choose between presidential candidates. Whereas the last chapter dealt with how much the citizen knew about politics, now our concern shifts to how this information is organized into attitudes about various political objects, and the relation of these attitudes to voting choice. There are many areas of life in which attitudes are weak predictors of action, but voting is not one of them. Especially when there are well-developed attitudes, one can predict how citizens will vote with considerable confidence. Consequently, if you understand attitudes, you will be able to understand the citizen response to campaign strategies.

SALIENCE, PARTISAN VALENCE, AND IMPORTANCE

There are three attitudinal properties that are especially helpful in understanding voting. The first of these is *salience*, the prominence of an attitudinal object. The more publicized a topic, the more likely that it will be salient for the citizen. The more salient it is, the more likely the citizen is to have an attitude about it. For example, an American would have been much more likely to have an attitude about Southeast Asia during the Vietnam War, when the media were filled with information about it, than in the 1980s, when the topic is much less salient.

The second relevant attitudinal property is *valence*. One's feelings about an attitudinal object may be positive, neutral, or negative. For example, a citizen may have a very positive attitude about one candidate and a slightly negative attitude about another, or a positive attitude about a candidate's trustworthiness and a negative attitude about the

same candidate's intelligence. The citizen reacts positively or negatively to a candidate according to the valence of his or her attitudes
about that candidate. (Remember that chemical ions combine depending on the valence of each ion. When used with attitudes, valence
also suggests a tendency to react positively or negatively.) In the case
of vote choice, we are not concerned with positive or negative attitudes
per se, but with how these attitudes about specific political objects
sum to form a *partisan valence*. If one person had positive attitudes
about the Republican candidate and negative attitudes about the Democratic candidate, we would say that this person's attitudes were pro-
Republican. If another had negative attitudes about the Republican
candidate's views on international involvement and positive attitudes
about the Democratic candidate's views on economic management,
we would say that these attitudes were pro-Democratic. If a third person
had positive attitudes about the Republican candidate's personality
and positive attitudes about the Democratic candidate's stands on issues, we would say that this partisan valence was mixed.

Finally, we are interested in *importance*. Strictly speaking, this is
not an attitudinal property, but the link between the citizen's attitude
and the vote that is cast. An attitude that is salient and quite favorable
to one party is usually important, although that is not always the case.
Voters may base their decisions on other attitudes, or they may believe
that a given issue is not one over which a president will have much
influence. In either situation, the attitude would not be important in
vote choice.

We want to separate these three properties because salience and
partisan valence and importance may vary independently of each other.
As we shall see, attitudes about economic management were salient
in 1980, as were general attitudes about candidates and issues in 1976,
but neither party enjoyed anything more than the barest advantage
in these categories. Attitudes about persons in the parties (other than
the candidates) were decidedly pro-Republican in 1972 and decidedly
pro-Democratic in 1976, but were not salient in either campaign. Attitudes about the public records of the candidates were important in
1976 and 1980, although they were not too salient, and only slightly
favored Gerald Ford and Ronald Reagan. Attitudes about agricultural
policy have never been salient in modern times, have strongly favored
the Democrats in every election save 1968 and 1980, and have been
important only to the small proportion of voters engaged in farming.
So when someone says that a given attitude is consequential in an
election, one must ask whether it is consequential because it is salient,
because it favors one party rather than the other, because it is related
to the voting decision, or some combination of the three.[1]

---

[1] There are a number of well-known explanations of voting that are based on summary
measures of the effects of attitude components. Frequently, these summary measures
are obtained by multiplying a measure of partisan valence by a measure of importance

The same responses that we used to analyze information level in Chapter 14 provide data to analyze these attitudinal properties. The responses are classified by the category of attitude object—at first the broad categories of candidates, parties, and issues, then more detailed categories that allow more specific analysis. The *salience* of a category of attitude objects is measured by the proportion of all comments falling into the category. The larger the proportion of comments, the more salient the category. *Partisan valence* is measured by the proportion of comments in the category favorable to the Democrats. The proportion of comments in the category favoring the Republicans is, of course, the complement of the pro-Democratic percentage, so the single figure tells us which party has how much of an advantage. The higher the figure, the better things are for the Democrats; the lower the figure, the better things are for the Republicans. The *importance* of the category in the voting decision is measured by maximum likelihood estimates obtained through probit analysis. (See box entitled Maximum Likelihood Estimate = Best Guess.) The probit model gives us a very powerful explanation of presidential choice. Between 85 and 90 percent of the individual cases are correctly predicted in the solution for each election year.

Maximum Likelihood Estimate = Best Guess

A literal reduction of the phrase "maximum likelihood estimate" is "best guess." For our purposes in this chapter, it is the best guess about the importance of an attitude in determining a citizen's vote.

The details of the maximum likelihood estimate (MLE) are a little technical, but three ideas are all that are necessary to understand the meaning. First, in common with all statistics derived from surveys, it is an *estimate*. When you read of a survey that finds, for instance, that 40 percent intend to vote for Ronald Reagan if Walter Mondale is his opponent, this 40 percent figure rests on a "confidence limit," say ±3 percent, and a "level of significance," usually 19 chances out of 20. Therefore, the full meaning of "40 percent" is "we estimate that in 19 chances out of 20, the proportion of all population members intending to vote for Reagan will fall between 37 percent and 43 percent." In a similar way, the figure given for the MLE is the best statistical guess about the relative importance of the attitude in determining the vote. The higher the MLE, the more important the attitude.

The second basic idea is that this is a *multivariate* procedure. The bivariate correlation explained in the box in the preceding chapter was an association between two variables, presumably one cause and one effect. A multivariate study permits analysis of multiple variables at the same time. Controls are

---

(Stokes, Campbell, & Miller, 1958; Comparative State Election Project, 1973). These provide good explanations, but, as all summary measures, they contain less information. One cannot tell whether partisan valence or importance is causing the summary measure to go up or down.

exercised over other possible causes. For example, we shall be looking at the effects of attitudes about candidates, parties, and issues on vote. The multivariate analysis allows us to isolate the effect of candidate attitudes while controlling for the effects of party and issue attitudes, to isolate the effect of party attitudes while controlling for the effects of candidate and issue attitudes, and to isolate the effect of issue attitudes while controlling for the effects of candidate and party attitudes.

The third basic idea is that probit analysis, from which the MLEs are derived, is a *curvilinear* rather than a linear procedure. This just means that the data points are assumed to fit a curve rather than a straight line. Linear regression, the form of multivariate analysis most commonly used in political science, assumes that the data points will lie on a straight line. Identical solutions were calculated with 1976 and 1980 data using linear regression and probit analysis. With 1976 data, the linear regression explained 47 percent of the variance in vote; the probit analysis explained 73 percent of the variance in vote. With 1980 data, the linear regression explained 51 percent of the variance; the probit analysis explained 80 percent of the variance. Since the probit predictions were half again more powerful than those obtained from the linear regressions, the curvilinear assumption is clearly more appropriate for voting data.

The MLEs reported in this chapter are standardized. (This is why the MLE columns are headed MLE*.) For additional discussion, and the method used to standardize the probit estimates, see Appendix A-15.1.

CANDIDATES, PARTIES, AND ISSUES

As a first broad approximation, let's look at the pattern formed by the mean figures for attitudes about candidates, parties, and issues. These data are presented in Figure 15-1. The ordering of the three categories is the same for both salience and importance. Issues come first, then candidates, and then—a long way back—come parties. Partisan valence is rather different. The strongest partisan advantage over time goes to the Republicans because of the relative attractiveness of their candidates. Issues, on the other hand, tend to help the Democrats; and the Democrats derive a slight advantage from the less important attitudes about parties.

Figure 15-2 presents the data for these three broad categories over time. There is, to be sure, election-to-election variation. The most pronounced variation is to be found in partisan valence. Democrats had advantages in all three attitude categories in 1964, and the Republicans did in 1968 (when analysis is confined to Nixon and Humphrey voters) and in 1972. (It would be remarkable if we did not find something of this kind, since there was a Democratic landslide in 1964 and a Republican landslide in 1972.) There is also some variation in the salience and importance of the attitude categories. For example, attitudes about

FIGURE 15-1
Broad Attitudes and Presidential Choice, Mean Figures 1952–1980

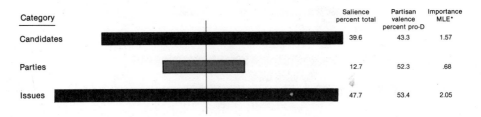

Category		Salience percent total	Partisan valence percent pro-D	Importance MLE*
Candidates		39.6	43.3	1.57
Parties		12.7	52.3	.68
Issues		47.7	53.4	2.05

Explanation of figure: *Salience* is measured by the proportion of the total comments dealing with the attitude object. It is indicated by the total length of the bar. The longer the bar, the more salient the category. *Partisan valence* is measured by the proportion of comments favorable to the Democrats. The farther the bar is to the left, the more favorable to the Democrats. The farther to the right, the more favorable to the Republicans. *Importance,* the relation of the attitude category to vote choice, is measured by a standardized maximum likelihood estimate. (See box on p. 491.) This is indicated in the figure by shade. If a bar is black, the attitude category is very important. If a bar is dark gray, the attitude category is important. If a bar is light gray, the attitude category is somewhat important. If a bar is hollow, the attitude category is not significantly related to vote choice.

Data source: 1952 through 1980 SRC/CPS Election Studies.

candidates were least important in 1952[2] and most important in 1976. But the general pattern is sufficiently stable that individual elections can be explained on the basis of how they depart from the normal pattern, rather than discovering a new pattern in each election. It appears that the interests of the electorate set some bounds to election-to-election variation, and fluctuation takes place between these bounds.

The one clear case of change since the 1950s is a decline in both salience and importance of attitudes about the parties. These attitudes have never been as salient as those about candidates and issues. But they have declined from even this low plateau. They were less consequential in recent elections than they were when General Eisenhower defeated Governor Stevenson.

By far the most noteworthy finding in this analysis is the relative importance of issues.[3] This is remarkable on several grounds. First of

---

[2] This finding is itself worth noting. The 1952 election is usually dismissed as a deviating election, resulting in large part from General Eisenhower's considerable personal popularity. The probit analysis indicates that attitudes about issues and parties were both more important that year.

[3] The salience of issues reflects some coding decisions. References to liberal or conservative policies are regarded as issue comments. Similarly, a person who mentions business or labor is assumed to be talking about economic management; when blacks are mentioned, it is assumed that the reference is to civil liberties; when farmers are mentioned, agriculture. The six-component solution devised by Donald E. Stokes assigns references to liberal or conservative postures to "parties as managers of government," and all references to groups to a separate "group-related" component. When choosing between candidates, parties, and issues, and in view of the vocabulary a respondent might be expected to use, I think it is appropriate to code these as issue references.

FIGURE 15-2
Broad Attitudes and Presidential Choice

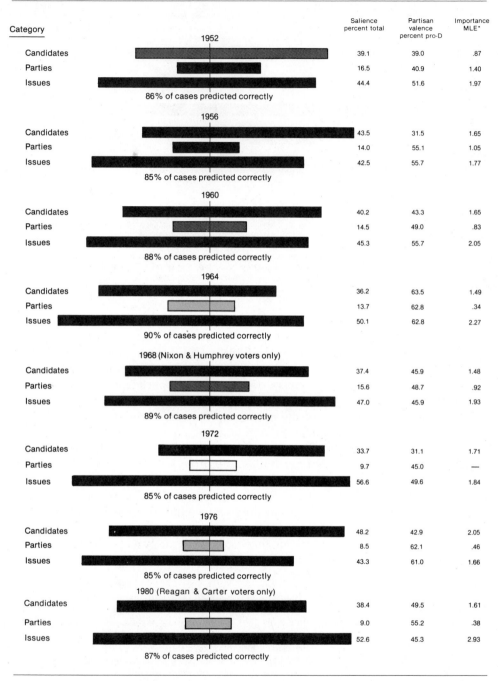

Category		Salience percent total	Partisan valence percent pro-D	Importance MLE*
1952				
Candidates		39.1	39.0	.87
Parties		16.5	40.9	1.40
Issues		44.4	51.6	1.97
86% of cases predicted correctly				
1956				
Candidates		43.5	31.5	1.65
Parties		14.0	55.1	1.05
Issues		42.5	55.7	1.77
85% of cases predicted correctly				
1960				
Candidates		40.2	43.3	1.65
Parties		14.5	49.0	.83
Issues		45.3	55.7	2.05
88% of cases predicted correctly				
1964				
Candidates		36.2	63.5	1.49
Parties		13.7	62.8	.34
Issues		50.1	62.8	2.27
90% of cases predicted correctly				
1968 (Nixon & Humphrey voters only)				
Candidates		37.4	45.9	1.48
Parties		15.6	48.7	.92
Issues		47.0	45.9	1.93
89% of cases predicted correctly				
1972				
Candidates		33.7	31.1	1.71
Parties		9.7	45.0	—
Issues		56.6	49.6	1.84
85% of cases predicted correctly				
1976				
Candidates		48.2	42.9	2.05
Parties		8.5	62.1	.46
Issues		43.3	61.0	1.66
85% of cases predicted correctly				
1980 (Reagan & Carter voters only)				
Candidates		38.4	49.5	1.61
Parties		9.0	55.2	.38
Issues		52.6	45.3	2.93
87% of cases predicted correctly				

—denotes insignificant figure.

Explanation of figure: *Salience* is measured by the proportion of the total comments dealing with the attitude object. It is indicated by the total length of the bar. The longer the bar, the more salient the category. *Partisan valence* is measured by the proportion of comments favorable to the Democrats. The farther the bar is to the left, the more favorable to the Democrats. The farther to the right, the more favorable to the Republicans. *Importance*, the relation of the attitude category to vote choice is measured by a standardized maximum likelihood estimate. (See box on p. 491.) This is indicated in the figure by shade. If a bar is black, the attitude category is very important. If a bar is dark gray, the attitude category is important. If a bar is light gray, the attitude category is somewhat important. If a bar is hollow, the attitude category is not significantly related to vote choice.

Data source: 1952 through 1980 SRC/CPS Election Studies.

all, the questions (quoted early in Chapter 14) do not ask about issues. They ask for the respondents' views about parties and candidates, but the largest part of the answers concern issues. Second, the mass media give less attention to issues than they do to "horse-race" topics. Therefore, issues are much more important within the citizens' cognitive structures than they are in the informational environment from which citizens pick up their cues. Third, many political scientists argue that the 50s were relatively placid. For example, one notable analysis states:

> By the fifties [New Deal] issues had faded. The times were prosperous and the candidates in 1952 and 1956 were not perceived as polarized on the issues. Nor were there other issues to take their place. The result was that citizens did not take coherent issue positions, nor did they vote on the basis of issues. (Nie, Verba, & Petrocik, 1976, p. 192)

Proponents of this position argue that issues did not become important until 1964, when President Johnson and Senator Goldwater offered the voters a clear choice, and again in 1972, when President Nixon and Senator McGovern took distinctive issue stands. There is no support in the data in Figure 15-2 for the argument that voters were unconcerned with issues in the 1950s. Issues were more salient in 1972, 1964, and 1980 than in other years, but the change is on the order of a few percentage points on an already substantial base. This does not represent any sea change in the nature of American politics. Issues were more important in vote choice in 1980 and 1964 than they were in any other years in this time series, but issues were more important in 1960, 1952, and 1968 than they were in 1972. The evidence here points to the continuing consequence of issues in presidential choice, not to their emergence in special circumstances.

Of the three broad categories, candidate attitudes have been salient, usually favorable to the Republicans, and very important in voting choices. Party attitudes have been much less salient, have sometimes favored the Democrats and sometimes favored the Republicans, and have been much less important in recent elections than they were in the 1950s. Issue attitudes have been salient, favorable to the Democrats in five of the eight elections, and very important in voting choices.

REACTION AND CHOICE IN
SPECIFIC ELECTIONS

Useful as these generalizations are, they do not take us very far toward the understanding of any specific election. The categories are too broad to allow us to trace much of the linkage between coalition strategies and citizen response. What is needed for this purpose are categories that are specific enough to permit concrete statements, yet inclusive enough so that statements falling into each will occur over a series of elections. Therefore, we will decompose the 3 broad categories into 16 more specific categories.

Candidate references will be divided into seven classes. Two deal with attitudes about the candidates' experience. *Record and incumbency* concerns perceptions about the candidates' records in public offices they have held previously and—much more frequently—comments about an incumbent when he is running for reelection. *Experience* is a shortened name for nonpublic office experience; military experience, diplomatic background, campaign ability, and so forth would all be included here. Two more categories are also office related. *Management* deals with executive capacity and how the candidate would be likely to run the government if elected. *Intelligence* is given a broad enough definition to include comments about the candidate's education and practical capacity as well as wisdom as such. The other specific categories do not deal with potential executive ability. *Trust* touches upon confidence, honesty, and any specific comments bearing on the candidate's integrity. *Personality* includes any comments about image and mannerisms, such as warmth, aloofness, dignity, and so forth. The *general* category is composed principally of comments that are too general to be assigned to one of the specific categories ("He's a good man" or "I like him"), but also includes some statements on such topics as the candidate's age or wealth or family that did not occur frequently enough to justify the creation of separate, specific categories.

The relatively infrequent party comments were divided into two classes. Attitudes about *people in the party* concern all other party members besides the presidential candidates: incumbent presidents not running for reelection, prominent senators and governors, party workers, and so on. All other party comments were categorized as *party affect.* These included trust of one party or the other, references to party factions, and the importance of achieving or preventing a party victory.

There were seven categories of issue attitudes. Six of these concerned policy areas we have been using throughout this book: *international involvement, economic management, social benefits, civil berties, natural resources*, and *agriculture.* As with the candidate comments, there was a *general* issue category composed of comments too broad to fit into any specific class. These included such items as the policy stands of the parties, liberalism or conservatism, and comments about "domestic policy" without any indication which domestic policy was meant.[4]

Decomposition of the 3 broad categories into 16 relatively specific categories permits a number of things. The essential difference is that

---

[4] For further information on coding decisions, see Appendix A-15.2.

we are trading the simple generalizations derived from the three-compo-
nent solution for a more detailed understanding that can be obtained
by inspecting the more specific categories. The detailed solution will
not support statements that candidate attitudes usually favor Republicans or that issue attitudes favor the Democrats more often than not.
Instead, we see that some candidate attributes favor the Democrats
in some elections while others favor the Republicans, and that certain
issues have usually favored the Democrats while others have usually
favored the Republicans.

The average pattern formed by these 16 categories over the series
of elections from 1952 through 1980 is shown in Figure 15-3. Looking
first at the candidate attitudes, the general attitudes are most salient
and most important of all, perhaps reflecting the generally low level
of information among the voters.[5] Views about the candidates' personalities are next most salient, but rank third in importance. Trust in
the candidates is somewhat less salient than personality but slightly
more important in voting choice. Attitudes concerning record and experience are just a little less important. Of the two, nonoffice experience
is generally more salient, but record in office is both more visible and
more important when an incumbent president is running for reelection.
Management capacity, likewise related to performance in office, is also
more salient when a president is seeking reelection. The least-salient
and least-important candidate attribute is intelligence. This finding—
that intelligence is the last thing Americans consider in voting for the
most demanding office in the Western world—is one of the most dis-
maying in all of political science.

The display in Figure 15-3 has the candidate attitudes at the far
left side, reflecting only salience and importance. There is simply too
much variation from one election to the next for mean partisan valence
figures to have any meaning. The Reagan-Carter comparison in 1980,
for example, engendered quite different attitudes than the preceding
Ford-Carter or Nixon-McGovern comparisons. It is, however, meaningful to speak of an average partisan advantage with regard to the specific
party and issue attitudes.

While the salience and importance of party affect have been declining over time, the average figures still show it to have been more visible
than all but the general candidate comments, and more important than
any of the candidate categories. Attitudes about other party leaders
have not been nearly as salient, and are much less important. The
Democrats have had a slight advantage in party affect, and Republican
party leaders have been slightly more attractive.

---

[5] There is a strong association between salience and importance if one looks at the
mean figures for the whole series of elections. The association is much weaker in particular elections. In individual elections, there appears to be much more chance for an
issue to be salient but not important, and vice versa.

FIGURE 15-3
Specific Attitudes and Presidential Choice, Mean Figures 1952–1980

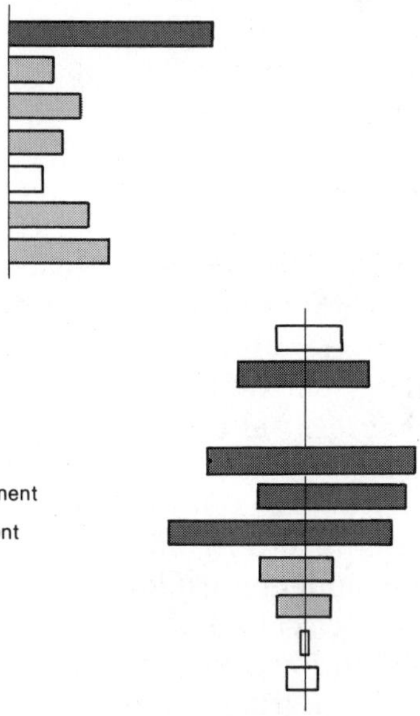

Category	Salience percent total	Partisan valence percent pro-D	Importance MLE*
Candidates			
General	13.6		.70
Record-incumbency	3.0		.41
Experience	4.8		.36
Management	3.6		.27
Intelligence	2.3		.17
Trust	5.3		.48
Personality	6.9		.45
Parties			
People in party	4.2	48.0	.22
Party affect	8.5	53.8	.75
Issues			
General	13.5	47.1	.98
International involvement	9.7	32.0	.66
Economic management	14.7	63.2	.83
Social benefits	4.9	69.2	.32
Civil liberties	3.8	51.3	.37
National resources	0.3	73.6	.06
Agriculture	1.6	65.1	.17

—denotes insignificant figure.

Explanation of figure: *Salience* is measured by the proportion of the total comments dealing with the attitude object. It is indicated by the total length of the bar. The longer the bar, the more salient the category. *Partisan valence* is measured by the proportion of comments favorable to the Democrats. The farther the bar is to the left, the more favorable to the Democrats. The farther to the right, the more favorable to the Republicans. *No partisan valence is reported for the candidate categories. There is so much variation between candidate pairs that mean figures have no significance.* *Importance,* the relation of the attitude category to vote choice, is measured by a standardized maximum likelihood estimate. (See box on p. 491.) It is indicated by the shade of the bar. The darker the bar, the more important the category. The bar is hollow to denote nonsignificance if the category was not significant in the majority of elections.

Data source: 1952 through 1980 SRC/CPS Election Studies.

Among the policy attitudes, economics and general attitudes take turns as the most salient and important. In elections such as 1980 and 1976, when economic circumstances loomed large, general issue comments are both less frequent and less important in vote determination. If inflation or unemployment or similar problems are less serious, then there are many more general comments. The mean figures—with economics the most salient and second in importance, and general comments second in visibility but the most important—result from this oscillation. Economic attitudes have typically given a strong edge to the Democrats, but the general issue attitudes have been favorable to the winning party in every one of the eight elections. It is as though there were groups of persons with stable interests in each of the specific policy areas, so that the subtraction of the specific comments from all issue references results in a general issue category that is a very sensitive indicator of partisan advantage in any particular election.

Of the attitudes regarding the other policy areas, international involvement has been quite salient and usually rather important. It is also the one policy attitude that normally gives the Republicans a substantial advantage. Attitudes about social benefits and civil liberties come next, and are about half as salient as international involvement. Social benefits has usually been of some importance, and has provided a substantial advantage to the Democrats. Civil liberties has been of importance in certain elections, sometimes benefiting the Democrats and sometimes the Republicans. Agriculture and natural resources normally have a strong Democratic valence, but neither policy area has been salient or important.

These mean figures, especially the measures of importance, do not have any particular statistical standing, but they do provide a baseline against which specific elections can be compared. They enable us to see something of the citizens' reactions to campaign strategies, and to know what attitudes determine their choices.[6] Since we know about the campaign strategies from Chapters 12 and 13, we can look for departures from the normal pattern that correspond to the campaign emphases. More specifically, we shall look for citizen *reaction* in *departures from the normal pattern in salience and partisan valence* (and in the absolute pattern of partisan valence in candidate attitudes where no baseline exists). Then we shall explain *choice* in terms of the *absolute pattern of importance and partisan valence in the election in question.* We shall begin with the election of 1968.[7]

A STRUGGLE BETWEEN PARTY REGULARS, 1968

Reaction. George Wallace's campaign was the most formidable third-party challenge since 1924. The Alabama governor definitely had an appeal to certain voters, especially those in the South. But when one restricts the analysis to those voting for Nixon or Humphrey, as

---

[6] I say that we can only see *something* of the citizens' reactions because of the limits of what can be discerned from a single cross-sectional survey of the national electorate. To understand the impact of the campaign in detail, one would need longitudinal data to see what changes took place in voters' attitudes as the campaign progressed, and studies that focus on the particular sets of voters (southern independents, Catholics from industrial states, and so forth) to whom the campaign was being directed.

[7] The detailed solutions for the elections from 1952 through 1964 are given in an endnote at the close of this chapter.

in Figure 15-4, the result is a rather typical party pattern.[8] This should not be too surprising. Both Nixon and Humphrey had been prominent party leaders for about two decades. Both had been vice presidents, and therefore were associated willy-nilly with records made by administrations over which they had little influence. And Page (1978, chaps. 3, 4) has shown that Nixon and Humphrey took similar positions on the majority of issues. Consequently, we should expect to find a typical partisan reaction to a contest between them.

The one category that was sharply more salient and somewhat more Republican than usual was general attitudes on issues. This probably reflected Richard Nixon's purposefully vague statements on issues. Nixon, after all, identified himself with "new ideas" and "the American dream," and called for "new leadership," "a new road," and "a complete housecleaning." These phrases hardly committed Mr. Nixon to any specific course of action, but they sounded positive and seemed to produce a Republican advantage in this attitude category.

Economic management was less salient than usual, and also less helpful to the Democrats than is ordinarily the case. What happened here was that, while Hubert Humphrey stressed traditional Democratic economic themes (for example, reminding his audiences of the specter of unemployment under Republicans), the incumbent Democratic administration was vulnerable because of an inflation that had been started by Vietnam War expenditures. It was this nerve that Nixon touched when he attacked Humphrey as "the most expensive senator in U.S. history." The net of pro-Democratic attitudes on jobs and pro-Republican attitudes on inflation was a less-than-customary Democratic advantage in this policy area. International attitudes were about as salient as usual, and gave the Republicans slightly more than their normal advantage, doubtless a reflection of the Vietnam War.

Confronted with an essentially partisan choice between Humphrey and Nixon, attitudes about parties were a little more visible than usual. The people-in-the-party category was more pro-Republican than usual, due to the unpopularity (by 1968) of Lyndon Johnson.

There was nothing unusual about the salience of the candidate attitudes. Humphrey's record in office was favorably perceived, as was Nixon's nonoffice experience and management capacity. Nixon derived more benefit from the general attitudes about candidates (which again could be seen as reaction to his nonspecific campaigning) because this category, as usual, was the most salient of those concerning candidates.

Choice.   The narrow electoral decision in 1968 was a consequence

---

[8] Restricting the analysis to Nixon and Humphrey voters retains comparability between the 1968 solution and those for other elections. And while the Wallace effort elicited unusual support, 86 percent of the voters still chose one of the major party candidates. For a full analysis of the Wallace vote, as well as the Nixon and Humphrey votes, see Comparative State Election Project, 1973.

FIGURE 15-4
Specific Attitudes and 1968 Presidential Choice
(Nixon and Humphrey voters only)

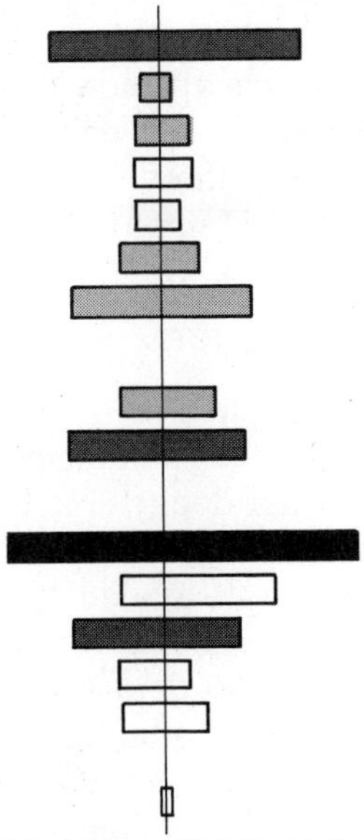

Category	Salience percent total	Partisan valence percent pro-D	Importance MLE*
Candidates			
General	13.8	43.3	.64
Record-incumbency	1.7	61.6	.49
Experience	3.0	39.8	.33
Management	2.6	34.0	—
Intelligence	2.2	50.0	—
Trust	4.3	52.1	.39
Personality	9.9	48.2	.44
Parties			
People in party	5.4	40.9	.44
Party affect	10.2	52.8	.76
Issues			
General	19.7	44.4	1.23
International involvement	8.4	27.2	—
Economic management	9.4	55.0	.61
Social benefits	4.0	67.6	—
Civil liberties	5.1	50.1	—
National resources	—	—	—
Agriculture	0.5	35.7	—

88% of cases predicted correctly

—denotes insignificant figure.

Explanation of figure: *Salience* is measured by the proportion of the total comments dealing with the attitude object. It is indicated by the total length of the bar. The longer the bar, the more salient the category. *Partisan valence* is measured by the proportion of comments favorable to the Democrats. The farther the bar is to the left, the more favorable to the Democrats. The farther to the right, the more favorable to the Republicans. *Importance,* the relation of the attitude category to vote choice, is measured by a standardized maximum likelihood estimate. (See box on p. 491.) This is indicated in the figure by shade. If a bar is black, the attitude category is very important. If a bar is dark gray, the attitude category is important. If a bar is light gray, the attitude category is somewhat important. If a bar is hollow, the attitude category is not significantly related to vote choice.

Data source: 1968 SRC Election Study.

of the offsetting character of a number of pro-Republican attitudes balanced by an almost equal number of pro-Democratic attitudes. Four attitudes had the most effect on vote choice.[9] The general attitudes

---

[9] In view of the attention paid to Vietnam in 1968, it is noteworthy that international attitudes were *not* significantly related to vote. One reason is that Nixon and Humphrey were perceived to be taking very similar stands, and this gave the voters little choice (Page & Brody, 1972). But if the analysis is restricted to those making up their minds late in the campaign, or if the dependent variable is shifted from vote choice to political activity, then attitudes on Vietnam become significant (Comparative State Election Project, 1973).

on issues were very important, and the general attitudes on candidates were important; both of these favored Nixon. Party affect and attitudes about economic management were both important, and these two categories favored Humphrey. Attitudes about experience, personality, and people in the party were all somewhat important, and all favored Nixon. Attitudes about the administration's record and about trust were also somewhat important, and favored Humphrey. In sum, there was a slight Republican advantage in favorable attitudes (5 to 4), and a slight Republican edge in importance. There was an echo of these slight attitudinal advantages in the 43.4 percent of the vote cast for Richard Nixon and the 42.7 percent cast for Hubert Humphrey.

UNUSUAL CANDIDATE POSTURES, 1972

Reaction.   1972 was a year when an incumbent following policies at variance with those he had long espoused was challenged by an opponent calling for even sharper departures from established policies. Richard Nixon, long known as an opponent of communism and government regulation of the economy, traveled to Beijing and Moscow in pursuit of his hope for a "Generation of Peace," and instituted wage and price controls in an attempt to deal with an intractable inflation. George McGovern was calling for a reduction of American involvement overseas, especially in Vietnam, and another quantum increase in the level of government spending and social benefit programs. This confrontation produced a high level of comments on issues, particularly in the three policy areas concerned: international involvement, economic management, and social benefits. If one adds civil liberties, on which there was also substantial disagreement between the candidates and which was a little more salient than usual, there were as many comments on these four policy areas as there were in all the candidate and party categories put together.

Economics might well have been salient because of unarrested inflation even if the candidates had ignored it. Senator McGovern did not. He spoke more about economics than any other policy area, calling for more spending and portraying himself as being on the side of the average person in contrast to powerful, elite interests that had the ear of Richard Nixon. President Nixon took a conservative posture, campaigning against big spenders in the Democratic Congress. The consequence of all this was that economic management was 10 percent more favorable to the Democrats than it usually was.

Both candidates also devoted a good deal of attention to international questions. Richard Nixon constantly referred to his international travels; the SALT treaty was signed in White House ceremonies during October; the "peace is at hand" announcement came shortly before the election. George McGovern stressed his public plan for peace in

Vietnam. The result was that international involvement was more salient than in any other election, and had its normal (pro-Republican) partisan valence.

The most decided shift away from normal partisan valence was in social benefits. Senator McGovern announced his intention to increase school funding, expand social security, provide public service jobs, and give a person unable to work approximately $1,000 a month in cash and food stamps. Mr. Nixon contrasted a work ethic built on self-reliance with a welfare ethic that he claimed destroyed character. As you can see by comparing Figures 15-3 and 15-5, attitudes on social

FIGURE 15-5
Specific Attitudes and 1972 Vote

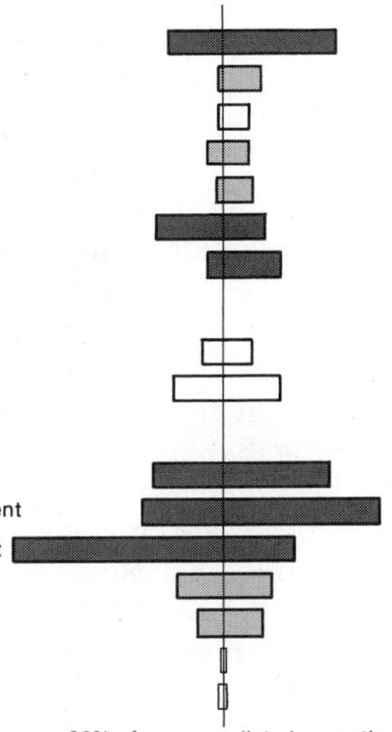

Category		Salience percent total	Partisan valence percent pro-D	Importance MLE*
Candidates				
General		10.9	32.4	.75
Record-incumbency		2.7	5.5	.58
Experience		1.9	22.0	—
Management		4.5	22.1	.28
Intelligence		2.0	11.1	.37
Trust		6.9	60.6	.85
Personality		4.6	20.2	.62
Parties				
People in party		2.9	39.0	—
Party affect		7.1	47.2	—
Issues				
General		12.3	36.2	.94
International involvement		15.2	32.8	.61
Economic management		18.4	75.0	.80
Social benefits		6.2	47.7	.35
Civil liberties		4.2	38.8	.44
National resources		.1	—	—
Agriculture		.3	66.7	—

86% of cases predicted correctly

—denotes insignificant figure.

Explanation of figure: *Salience* is measured by the proportion of the total comments dealing with the attitude object. It is indicated by the total length of the bar. The longer the bar, the more salient the category. *Partisan valence* is measured by the proportion of comments favorable to the Democrats. The farther the bar is to the left, the more favorable to the Democrats. The farther to the right, the more favorable to the Republicans. *Importance,* the relation of the attitude category to vote choice, is measured by a standardized maximum likelihood estimate. (See box on p. 491.) This is indicated in the figure by shade. If a bar is black, the attitude category is very important. If a bar is dark gray, the attitude category is important. If a bar is light gray, the attitude category is somewhat important. If a bar is hollow, the attitude category is not significantly related to vote choice.

Data source: 1972 Election Study, Center for Political Studies.

benefits shifted 22 percent away from normal, and actually produced a slight Republican advantage.

The most prominent civil liberties question in 1972 concerned the use of busing to achieve school integration. Senator McGovern said that he had fought all his political life for integration, and would not change regardless of political cost. Nixon opposed busing on the ground that parents wanted better education for their children, and this meant neighborhood schools. In this policy area, too, there was a marked shift in partisan valence, producing another Republican advantage. At the same time, a parallel shift was taking place with respect to general issue attitudes. These were a little less salient than usual, but also favored the GOP.

Candidate attitudes were less salient with two exceptions. One was management that reflected a public belief that Richard Nixon was better able to cope with the presidency than George McGovern. The other was trust—and while all the other candidate attitudes favored Richard Nixon by rather substantial margins, the voters trusted George Mc-Govern.[10] All the time that the Senator spent reminding the electorate that the "men who . . . have passed out special favors, who have ordered political sabotage . . . work for Mr. Nixon" yielded a real Democratic advantage.

Choice.   Senator McGovern was twice as well off in the attitude-vote relationship as Senator Goldwater had been eight years earlier. Whereas the Arizona senator had only the single attitude of trust (which was only somewhat important), the South Dakota senator enjoyed a partisan advantage on two attitudes, economic management and trust, both of which were important in the voting decisions of 1972. The trouble with that, of course, was that being twice as well off as Senator Goldwater still spelled political defeat.

All the other attitudes predisposed the voters to support the incumbent President. General attitudes on issues, general attitudes about the candidates, attitudes about the candidates' personalities, Nixon's record in office, and international involvement were all important, and all had Republican valence. Attitudes about the candidates' intelligence, management capacity, social benefits, and civil liberties were all somewhat important, and all of these also favored Richard Nixon. President Nixon's 60.7 percent of the vote came close to President Johnson's 61.0 percent eight years earlier. The fortunes of politics allowed both these veteran politicians to return to the White House with substantial margins.

---

[10] The same thing was true of Lyndon Johnson and Barry Goldwater in 1964. Johnson did better in every candidate category besides trust, but Goldwater was trusted. That Johnson was distrusted in 1964 and Nixon was distrusted in 1972 were probably important preludes to the later public reaction to Watergate.

AN OUTSIDER BARELY WINS, 1976

Reaction. A principal assumption of the Carter strategy was that 1976 would be a year when candidates were more important than issues. "There aren't many people, including me, who really understand all the issues," claimed campaign manager Hamilton Jordan. "They're so damned complex that the average fellow out there is looking beyond them to what sort of person the candidate is" (Wooten, 1976). The reaction to the campaign strategies shows this assumption was only partly correct. Comparison of Figures 15-3 and 15-6 indicates that some candidate attitudes were unusually salient in 1976. But Carter's quick rise to prominence would have been followed by an even speedier decline if it had not been for economic issues.

The data in Figure 15-6 suggest that the Ford strategy was much more successful. There were three candidate attitudes that were unusually salient—management capacity, record in office, and trust—and there were Ford advantages in all these areas. Recall that Ford spent most of September in the White House looking presidential, that Carter responded with a personal attack on Ford, that Ford commercials at the end of the campaign featured Georgians questioning the quality of Carter's gubernatorial record, and that other commercials praised Ford's quiet style of leadership. It is therefore significant that there was a decided Republican edge in management, a reasonably strong edge for Ford in trust, and at least a slight Ford advantage when record in office was mentioned. (Nearly a quarter of all comments about Ford's record in office concerned his pardon of former President Nixon. If it had not been for this, the public perception of Ford's record would have been very favorable.) And while the other candidate attitudes were no more salient than usual, they *all* favored Gerald Ford. 1976 was the only election year when this has happened. Since the campaign lasted only two months and Ford had been in the White House for two years, it is likely that the campaign effect was primarily one of reinforcement, but it should not be regarded as less successful for that reason.

The issue attitudes were clearly dominated by economic concerns. In common with most Democratic candidates, Governor Carter pledged to continue a number of expensive programs, although he did admit the possibility of a tax cut in the last week of the campaign. In common with most Republican candidates, President Ford was critical of government spending. He made a tax cut a central feature of his campaign. But more important than the stands being taken by either candidate, the nation had just passed through a relatively short, but rather deep, recession. Evaluations of President Ford were very much affected by whether the respondent had suffered any personal hardship because of the recession, and by the respondent's evaluation of government

FIGURE 15-6
Specific Attitudes and 1976 Vote

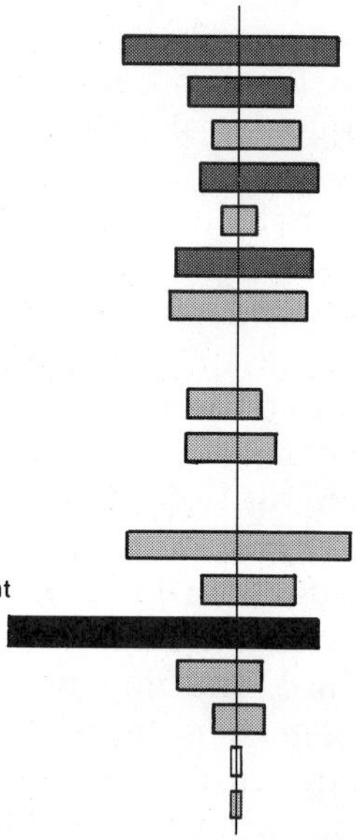

Category	Salience percent total	Partisan valence percent pro-D	Importance MLE*
Candidates			
General	13.1	49.8	.68
Record-incumbency	5.7	48.1	.73
Experience	4.7	28.9	.44
Management	6.7	29.6	.64
Intelligence	2.0	48.4	.27
Trust	8.3	40.8	.80
Personality	7.6	48.0	.47
Parties			
People in party	3.8	69.6	.25
Party affect	4.7	56.0	.39
Issues			
General	12.8	50.3	.48
International involvement	5.0	38.4	.31
Economic management	17.2	74.9	1.10
Social benefits	4.4	69.1	.23
Civil liberties	2.8	45.3	.28
National resources	.5	83.5	—
Agriculture	.5	81.4	.25

85% of cases predicted correctly

—denotes insignificant figure.

Explanation of figure: *Salience* is measured by the proportion of the total comments dealing with the attitude object. It is indicated by the total length of the bar. The longer the bar, the more salient the category. *Partisan valence* is measured by the proportion of comments favorable to the Democrats. The farther the bar is to the left, the more favorable to the Democrats. The farther to the right, the more favorable to the Republicans. *Importance,* the relation of the attitude category to vote choice, is measured by a standardized maximum likelihood estimate. (See box on p. 491.) This is indicated in the figure by shade. If a bar is black, the attitude category is very important. If a bar is dark gray, the attitude category is important. If a bar is light gray, the attitude category is somewhat important. If a bar is hollow, the attitude category is not significantly related to vote choice.

Data source: 1976 Election Study, Center for Political Studies.

economic performance (Miller & Miller, 1977). The voter reaction to all this was that economic management was even more salient than usual, and even more pro-Democratic than usual.

All the attention paid to Gerald Ford's misstatement about Poland in the second debate may have hurt him a bit. The partisan valence in international involvement was not quite as Republican as usual. It is more likely, though, that Ford was handicapped by the relative international tranquillity. Even though Ford's edge was less than that enjoyed by Eisenhower or Nixon, there was a decided Republican advantage in this policy area. But with no visible threat to peace in 1976, international involvement was much less salient.

Choice. The reasons for presidential votes were spread in 1976 as never before. Virtually every attitude category was significantly related to presidential choice. Only natural resources missed, and that by the barest of margins.[11] With so many attitudes involved, one cannot say that any single attitude provided the key to the election. What can be said is that economic management was the only very important attitude category, and the lopsided Democratic margin in this policy area probably sustained Jimmy Carter in the face of a well-executed Republican strategy.

There were four important attitudes. All these dealt with the candidates—trust, record in office, management capacity, and general attitudes—and by varying margins, all favored Gerald Ford. The remaining 10 attitudes were only somewhat important, and they were split 5 to 5. Ford was helped by views on personality, experience, and intelligence, and by the policy areas of international involvement and civil liberties. Carter was aided by both party categories, general issue attitudes, social benefits, and agriculture.

The dominant impression is that Carter was elected because of economic circumstances, and in spite of his being less favorably perceived as a person. If so, this might also explain the collapse of President Carter's popularity in office. No other president had been elected without some personal characteristics that were favorably perceived by the electorate. When the Carter administration was unable to cope with inflation, the major problem in the policy area responsible for his election, there was nothing else to sustain the President's reputation.

"ARE YOU BETTER OFF THAN YOU WERE FOUR YEARS AGO?", 1980

Reaction. Voters' attitudes in the fall of 1980 seem to have been affected by four considerations: the economic havoc caused by the rampant inflation of the preceding four years, the wide difference between the policies being advocated by the major party candidates, the unpopularity of both of these candidates, and the Democratic and Republican campaigns. These are listed in descending order of importance. Consequently, the campaign effects that are easiest to detect are those that took advantage of the more important considerations.[12]

Some traces of the Carter effort to draw a sharp distinction between

---

[11] To be considered statistically significant, a maximum likelihood estimate must be twice its standard error. The MLE for natural resources was 1.98 times its standard error.

[12] As with the 1968 analysis, this is restricted to the two major party candidates. A separate analysis of the Anderson vote will be presented shortly.

the two candidates as individuals can be seen in the comments about the candidates. When all candidate comments are considered, there were in fact more negative comments than positive comments about Governor Reagan. The ratio was 46 percent positive to 54 percent negative. (President Carter had just a few more positive than negative comments, 51 percent to 49 percent, himself. By way of comparison, President Ford enjoyed a 62–38 percent ratio four years earlier.) But when these comments are considered in any detail, the Carter campaign seems less successful. The four candidate categories in Figure 15-7 which show a Carter advantage—general comments, experience, intelligence, and trust—were all less salient than usual. Furthermore, the largest proportion of negative comments about Governor Reagan (22 percent) dealt with his age, and the next largest (another 12 percent) concerned Reagan's own campaign speeches. To be sure, the Carter campaign called attention to what Ronald Reagan was saying, but these liabilities were not anything that the Carter campaign created.

The candidate categories that were more salient than usual were record in office and management capacity. Comments about the candidates' records just barely favored Reagan because there were fewer negative references to the governor's record. There was a decisive Republican advantage in comments about management capacity because of the many negative comments about the job that President Carter had done and the quality of his staff. The public perceptions of Carter as a manager resulted more from his four years in office than from the campaign, but a goal of the Reagan campaign had been to reinforce the image of "Carter as an ineffective and error-prone leader."

There was a larger proportion of comments about issues in 1980 than in any other year except 1972. Furthermore, there were more references in the specific policy areas[13] (except agriculture) and relatively few comments in the vague general category. The one policy area that was both more salient than usual, and more Democratic than usual was civil liberties. The reason for this was the number of negative references to Governor Reagan's stand on the Equal Rights Amendment.[14] Since the Democratic campaign was making special efforts to reach women, they could claim some credit here.

The major impact of the Reagan strategy (and of four years of infla-

---

[13] The glacial speed of the increase in public interest in natural resources is interesting. After the OPEC oil embargo of 1973–74, and major congressional interest in rival energy plans, comments about this policy area increased to the "height" of ½ of 1 percent of all comments in 1976. After the passage of two Carter energy bills, a rapid increase in gasoline costs, and lines at gas stations, public concern reached a new "peak" of $\frac{8}{10}$ of 1 percent in 1980.

[14] There were also a number of references to Reagan's stand on abortion, but this didn't produce any partisan advantage as there were virtually the same number of positive and negative references.

tion) can be seen in economic management. This policy area continued the very high salience of 1972 and 1976, and for the first time in the entire time series, economic attitudes gave an advantage to the Republicans. A Reagan strategy document had said, "We must not break any new ground. . . . The thrust of our speeches must be directed toward: inflation, jobs, economic growth." The success of this can be seen in a 14.5 percent shift in a Republican direction. Inflation was the great cause of this, although the voters also had an adverse impression of Jimmy Carter's ability to manage the economy.

International involvement was about as Republican as usual, but much more salient so that the normal Republican advantage weighed more heavily in the electoral scale. This was not due to the Reagan campaign, but to the American diplomats being held hostage in Iran. More than 40 percent of the comments about President Carter and foreign affairs dealt with the hostages. If it had not been for this, the Carter efforts to raise the war-and-peace issue would have produced an 11 percent shift in a Democratic direction. Social benefits was slightly more salient than usual, and slightly less Democratic than usual, but still a Democratic advantage.

Choice.   To a greater degree than any other modern election, 1980 was determined by issues. As Figure 15-2 shows, the maximum likelihood estimate of the importance of issues was substantially higher than it had been in any other election. Among issues, the two imperative policy areas—economic management and international involvement—were both very important in voting decisions, and both had a Republican valence. Since we know that inflation and Iran were causing the greatest concern in these policy areas, it would not be too much to say that the election turned on dismay over the performance of the Carter administration in these two areas.[15]

Figure 15-7 shows that the important attitudes were more evenly split. There were three that had a Republican valence: the weathervane general issues category, management capacity (where Reagan had an enormous advantage), and personality. The public records of the two candidates were important, but so slightly Republican as to be essentially a standoff. The Democratic advantages came in general comments on the candidates, and in the issue areas of social benefits and civil liberties.

Only two attitudes were somewhat important. These were party affect and trust. Jimmy Carter had worked hard to whip up the former, and had earned the latter, but neither was very consequential in vote choice.

Of all of the attitudes that were significantly related to vote choice

---

[15] This would appear to be another demonstration of the power of retrospective voting. For a general analysis of this important topic, see Morris Fiorina (1981).

FIGURE 15-7
Specific Attitudes and 1980 Vote (Carter and Reagan voters only)

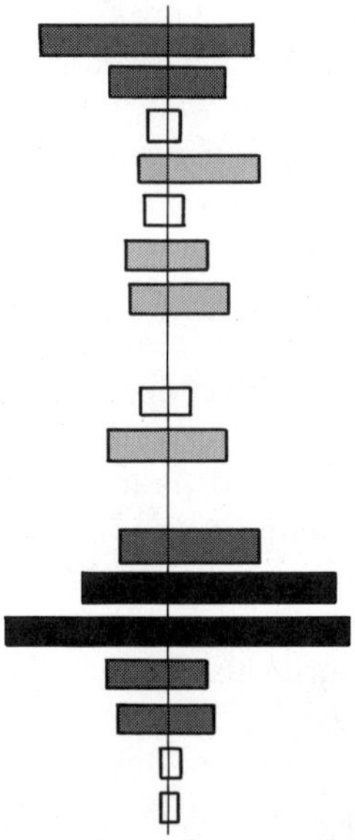

Category	Salience percent total	Partisan valence percent pro-D	Importance MLE*
Candidates			
General	11.9	60.2	.65
Record-incumbency	6.4	49.5	.71
Experience	1.4	63.3	—
Management	6.8	25.7	.57
Intelligence	2.2	62.0	—
Trust	4.4	57.8	.31
Personality	5.4	40.2	.57
Parties			
People in party	2.4	56.8	—
Party affect	6.6	54.6	.39
Issues			
General	7.7	35.9	.75
International involvement	14.0	34.2	1.30
Economic management	19.0	48.7	1.33
Social benefits	5.5	63.0	.63
Civil liberties	5.2	57.4	.81
National resources	.8	47.6	—
Agriculture	.2	40.9	—

87% of cases predicted correctly

—denotes insignificant figure.

Explanation of figure: *Salience* is measured by the proportion of the total comments dealing with the attitude object. It is indicated by the total length of the bar. The longer the bar, the more salient the category. *Partisan valence* is measured by the proportion of comments favorable to the Democrats. The farther the bar is to the left, the more favorable to the Democrats. The farther to the right, the more favorable to the Republicans. *Importance,* the relation of the attitude category to vote choice, is measured by a standardized maximum likelihood estimate. (See box on p. 491.) This is indicated in the figure by shade. If a bar is black, the attitude category is very important. If a bar is dark gray, the attitude category is important. If a bar is light gray, the attitude category is somewhat important. If a bar is hollow, the attitude category is not significantly related to vote choice.

Data source: 1980 Election Study, Center for Political Studies.

in 1980, five were pro-Republican, five were pro-Democratic, and one fundamentally a tie. This does not seem to suggest a landslide, but the 1980 vote was only half a landslide. In view of the negative comments about Reagan himself, the loss of votes to the Democrats on social benefits and civil liberties, and the 51 percent of the vote Reagan received, one could not say that there was a positive landslide for Ronald Reagan or for conservative ideology. But in view of the strength of the adverse judgments about the Carter administration's handling of economics and foreign policy, and the 59 percent of the vote that went to Carter's opponents, one could say that there was a negative landslide against the Carter administration.

THE SPECIAL PROBLEMS OF A THIRD CANDIDATE, ANDERSON 1980

Reaction.   Lacking the resources to carry on a campaign of the same magnitude as the major party candidates, John Anderson had to make just the right moves at just the right time. But to carry out even this long-shot strategy, Anderson needed *some* resources and *some* attention from the media, and these vital ingredients were lacking. It is therefore not surprising that Anderson was less visible during the election than either of his major rivals. While almost all respondents knew something about President Carter and Governor Reagan by April, only half claimed to know about Congressman Anderson by June, and only three quarters did so during the fall (Markus, 1982).

Figure 15-8 presents a probit solution for John Anderson that is parallel to the Reagan-Carter solution.[16] It is somewhat difficult to read implications directly from this solution. Since the choices are "Anderson" or "another candidate," the data are comments about Anderson, Reagan, and Carter. This means, for example, that a "pro-Anderson" comment may be a positive comment about Anderson or a negative comment about either Reagan or Carter. Furthermore, since most of the comments (e.g., 71 percent of all candidate comments) concerned the major party candidates, it is hard to discern any unique Anderson effects.

The first thing worth noting is the change in salience in the broad categories. With only Carter and Reagan, 38 percent, 9 percent, and 53 percent of the comments dealt with candidates, parties, and issues, respectively. When the Anderson comments are added, the proportions change to 55 percent, 4 percent, and 41 percent. In an election when issues were unusually salient, and when he went to considerable effort to stake out positions distinguishable from those of Carter and Reagan, the Anderson issue positions were not very visible.

Congressman Anderson himself was favorably perceived by those who knew about him. When analysis is restricted to the Anderson

---

[16] It is parallel to the Reagan-Carter solution, but not identical to it. In this case, the Anderson voters were added to the Reagan and Carter voters, and vote choice was dichotomized to "Anderson" and "Another Candidate," i.e., either Reagan or Carter. Salience has the same meaning as in the previous analyses, but it does not seem appropriate to point out deviations from the mean figures for the major party races in this series of elections. We have an "Anderson valence" instead of a "partisan valence." The measure is the proportion of the total comments favorable to Anderson, or critical of one of the other candidates. The importance of an attitude is the probit estimate of the likelihood that the attitude is related to casting a vote for Anderson or for another candidate.

FIGURE 15-8
Specific Attitudes and 1980 Anderson Vote

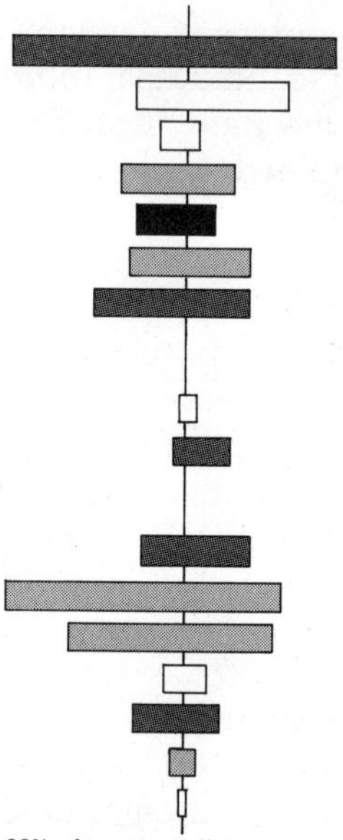

Category	Salience percent total	Anderson valence percent pro-Anderson	Importance MLE*
Candidates			
General	17.8	54.2	.92
Record-incumbency	8.5	34.5	—
Experience	2.1	71.5	—
Management	6.4	59.3	—
Intelligence	4.4	66.9	1.10
Trust	6.7	49.8	.47
Personality	8.7	60.0	.77
Parties			
People in party	0.9	29.3	—
Party affect	3.1	26.9	.83
Issues			
General	6.0	42.5	.93
International involvement	15.3	65.9	—
Economic management	11.3	57.6	—
Social benefits	2.4	50.9	—
Civil liberties	4.8	61.9	.67
National resources	1.3	70.6	—
Agriculture	0.3	72.2	—

92% of cases predicted correctly.

—denotes insignificant figure.

Explanation of figure: *Salience* is measured by the proportion of the total comments dealing with the attitude object. It is indicated by the total length of the bar. The longer the bar, the more salient the category. Anderson *valence* is measured by the proportion of comments favorable to Anderson. The farther the bar is to the left, the more favorable to Anderson. The farther to the right, the more favorable to another candidate. *Importance,* the relation of the attitude category to vote choice, is measured by a standardized maximum likelihood estimate. (See box on p. 491.) This is indicated in the figure by shade. If a bar is black, the attitude category is very important. If a bar is dark gray, the attitude category is important. If a bar is light gray, the attitude category is somewhat important. If a bar is hollow, the attitude category is not significantly related to vote choice.

Data source: 1980 Election Study, Center for Political Studies.

comments alone, views of his record were slightly negative, general comments were slightly positive, and all the other categories were very positive. Very few comments were made about his office-related capacities—record, experience, and management capacity—but substantial proportions of the general comments, and those dealing with intelligence, trust, and personality, were about John Anderson rather than the major party candidates. Mr. Anderson did come across as someone who was smart and trustworthy. These categories were more salient than usual, and fully three quarters of the Anderson comments were favorable.

Congressman Anderson was hobbled by the negative valence of the partisan attitudes, but the valence of the issue categories should have been helpful to him. His positions were favored in all the specific policy areas; only the general comments on issues favored a major party candidate. Anderson's problem, again, was lack of visibility. Only international involvement was slightly more salient in the Anderson solution than in the Reagan-Carter solution. All the other policy areas were less salient.

Choice.   Another limit of a third-party candidacy becomes apparent when the number of important attitudes is compared with the number of attitudes important in the Reagan-Carter choice. There were 11 maximum likelihood estimates that were significant in the Reagan-Carter solution compared to only 7 that were significant in the Anderson solution. With less well developed cognitive images of Anderson, attitudes about him were less likely to motivate citizens to cast Anderson votes.

The only very important attitude, that concerning intelligence, was also the least salient. Those citizens who were concerned about intelligence were likely to cast Anderson votes, but there weren't very many of them. The five important attitudes were split. General comments about candidates, specific comments about personality, and civil liberties (where Anderson had taken a more traditional Republican stand than Reagan) all tended to produce Anderson votes. General comments about issues and party affect, however, both tended to produce votes for the major party candidates. The only somewhat important attitude, trust, had little effect. The voters trusted John Anderson, but they also trusted Jimmy Carter; so this attitude had less impact on vote choice.

Now, if there were only seven attitudes that were significant in determining votes, and four of these favored Congressman Anderson, why did he receive so few votes in the election? One answer is that attitudes that were insignificant in an Anderson choice were significantly related to a choice between Reagan and Carter. Attitudes about economics, international involvement, and management capacity were all producing Reagan votes; attitudes about social benefits were producing Carter votes. Another answer can be obtained from different questions that enable us to ascertain which candidate's position each voter preferred on specific issues.[17] Ninety-six percent of the voters who preferred Reagan's position on whether inflation or unemployment was more important voted for him; 76 percent of those in closest agreement with Carter voted for him; only 43 percent of those who preferred Anderson's position on this issue voted for him. Across four such issues—inflation versus unemployment, defense spending, cutting social services, and whether women should play an equal role in society—Ronald Reagan

---

[17] These questions ask the respondents to state their preferred position on a seven-point scale concerning, say, defense spending, and also to state where they would locate the candidates along the same scale. These data permit us to say which candidate is located closest to each respondent and, therefore, whose position is preferred.

received an average of 86.5 percent of the votes, Jimmy Carter an average of 69.4 percent, and John Anderson an average of only 35.6 percent of the votes of citizens *preferring* the candidate's positions. Since these measure the effect of single issues, the difference between Reagan and Carter shows the effect of other attitudes being more favorable to Reagan. But the difference between the major party candidates and Anderson shows the weakness of a third-party candidacy in the United States.

Summary

By asking how the citizen's political knowledge was organized into attitudes, we have been able to see the relation between what was known and the citizen's choice of presidential candidates. As between the broad categories of candidates, parties, and issues, issues and candidates are much more important. Issues have typically helped the Democrats and candidates have helped the Republicans. Attitudes about parties have not been as consequential, and have become even less so in recent elections.

By decomposing the three broad categories into 16 specific categories, we could see more, but lost the easy generalizations about issues and candidates helping one party or the other. Many citizens are able to discriminate among various facets of politics. For example, even in the face of the victorious campaigns that led to the Johnson and Nixon landslides in 1964 and 1972, voters continued to distrust these presidents while regarding them as qualified in all other respects. A consequence of this ability to discriminate is that it is rare for all of the candidate or issue attitudes to be on one side or the other. Only in 1964 were all the issue attitudes on the Democratic side, and only in 1976 were all the candidate attitudes on the Republican side.

The salience of all candidate attitudes has fluctuated between 34 and 43 percent (of the total), and the salience of all issue attitudes has fluctuated between 43 and 57 percent.[18] Since the attention devoted to both seems to be bounded, it follows that the number of general (usually vague) comments goes down when citizens have specific things to say, and up when they do not.

The principal covariation has been between general issue attitudes and attitudes about economics. When economic management was salient, as it was during the 50s, and again from 1972 through 1980, there were fewer general comments. During the prosperous 60s, there were

---

[18] All of these statements about normal ranges and departures from the mean need to be treated with some caution. Remember that these average figures rest on only eight data points spread over a quarter of a century. We have a baseline against which comparison can be made, but a rather fragile one. The same caveat applies to the interpretation of *reaction* as departures from the mean.

more general comments. It is as though economics reaches enough lives so that, in times of adversity, those suffering from inflation or unemployment have something concrete to talk about. During better times, at least some of these people retreat to more diffuse impressions. The partisan valence of economic attitudes has also varied over a 26-point range. Seventy-four percent of the comments were pro-Democratic in 1956, 56 percent were in 1960, 55 percent in 1968, 75 percent in 1972, 75 percent in 1976, and only 49 percent were pro-Democratic in 1980. In five out of six cases, the variation (from the 63 percent mean) went against an administration that did not seem to be coping well with economic problems.

The salience of the other major policy area, international involvement, was quite stable from 1952 through 1968. In each of these elections, 8 or 9 percent of all comments dealt with this policy area. But in 1972 and 1980, it was more salient, and in 1976, less so.

Among candidate attitudes, the most noteworthy variation in salience was found in trust. It was salient in 1952, then dropped through 1960, became more visible from 1964 through 1976, and dropped again in 1980. Trust disappeared from the forefront of our national consciousness during the Eisenhower years, returned as a more urgent concern with Johnson and Nixon, and then declined in concern after Ford and Carter had been in the White House. Management capacity has also become more salient in the last three elections, an encouraging development as it means that more attention is being paid to a candidate's ability to serve as chief executive.

While we can say just which attitudes are related to vote in any particular election, it's very difficult to make any general statements about importance over time. Indeed only three attitude categories—general attitudes about candidates, general attitudes about issues, and economic management—have been significantly related to vote in each of the eight elections, and only one attitudinal category—natural resources—has not been significantly related to vote in at least one election. There does appear to be a modest relation between the number of important issue categories and an incumbent president running for reelection. In four of the five elections with an incumbent candidate, five issue categories (usually general, international, economics, social benefits, and civil liberties) have been significantly related to vote; in 1976 six issue categories were significant. Without an incumbent candidate, an average of only three categories have been associated with vote choice. This supports the view that when citizens have the opportunity to acquire further information by watching what a president does during his term of office, they will be able to make use of that knowledge.

As is usually the case, there are further questions that grow out of these findings. If citizens can discriminate between different facets

of politics so that some attitudes favor Republicans and other attitudes
favor Democrats, how do they resolve the attitude conflicts that result?
And if attitudes are related to vote choice in a given election, but
are not as important in the following election, what does this imply
about the stability of attitudes from one election to the next? These
are among the questions we shall explore in the following chapter.

ENDNOTE

The table on the opposite page gives detailed solutions for 1952,
1956, 1960, and 1964 elections.

Detailed Solutions for 1952, 1956, 1960, and 1964 Elections

Category	1952 Salience Percent Total	1952 Partisan Valence Percent Pro-D	1952 Importance MLE*	1956 Salience Percent Total	1956 Partisan Valence Percent Pro-D	1956 Importance MLE*	1960 Salience Percent Total	1960 Partisan Valence Percent Pro-D	1960 Importance MLE*	1964 Salience Percent Total	1964 Partisan Valence Percent Pro-D	1964 Importance MLE*
Candidates												
General	11.1%	35.3%	0.26	19.6%	33.2%	0.44	17.3%	41.7%	0.82	10.6	66.5	.86
Record-incumbency	1.0	86.3	—	3.5	13.1	0.38	0.9	35.3	0.22	2.3	93.1	—
Experience	9.1	61.1	0.29	3.7	36.6	0.40	9.1	30.9	1.02	6.3	76.4	—
Management	2.2	21.3	0.29	2.1	41.5	0.44	1.8	34.6	0.24	2.7	64.7	—
Intelligence	1.9	58.5	—	2.6	65.9	—	3.6	63.0	0.26	1.6	75.5	—
Trust	8.7	21.8	0.63	5.9	18.8	—	1.4	46.5	—	2.1	18.2	.38
Personality	5.1	26.7	0.26	6.2	28.3	0.51	6.0	58.2	—	10.4	52.9	.53
Parties												
People in party	5.9	33.6	—	5.2	55.6	0.29	4.9	39.4	—	3.0	49.0	—
Party affect	10.7	45.0	1.36	8.8	54.8	1.10	9.6	53.9	0.76	10.7	66.7	1.12
Issues												
General	8.3	45.8	0.77	10.0	45.7	0.71	19.2	64.3	1.38	17.6	54.5	1.59
International involvement	8.8	20.1	0.76	8.8	16.9	0.58	9.4	32.3	0.80	8.0	54.4	.65
Economic management	22.8	62.5	1.25	13.1	74.1	0.71	10.9	56.1	0.32	7.5	59.5	.55
Social benefits	1.8	80.9	—	5.0	83.5	0.51	1.5	53.4	—	10.5	88.7	.38
Civil liberties	1.4	40.7	—	2.0	46.2	—	2.2	64.6	—	5.5	67.3	.64
National resources	0.2	82.1	—	0.4	67.4	—	0.2	76.2	—	.2	77.3	—
Agriculture	1.1	80.1	0.34	3.1	79.7	0.47	1.9	70.8	—	.7	64.9	—
	87% predicted right			86% predicted right			88% predicted right			90% predicted right		

—denotes insignificant figure.

Data source: 1952 through 1964 Election Studies, Survey Research Center.

CHAPTER 16

PARTY IDENTIFICATION

Another series of questions put to thousands of respondents by interviewers from the Center for Political Studies begins: "Generally speaking, do you think of yourself as a Republican, a Democrat, an independent, or what?" If the respondent says Republican, the next question is: "Would you call yourself a strong Republican or a not very strong Republican?" If, in answer to the first question, the respondent says Democrat, the same follow-up question is asked with respect to the Democratic party. If the answer to the first question is independent, then the respondent is asked: "Do you think of yourself as closer to the Republican or Democratic party?"

Party identification, the concept measured by these questions, is thought of as having a *strength component* and a *direction component.* Each individual is categorized on the strength component according to the answers to the follow-up questions. The respondent who says strong to the partisan follow-up question is treated as a Strong Partisan. With an answer of not very strong, the respondent is called a Weak Partisan. Anyone who answers the independent follow-up question by saying that they are closer to one party rather than the other, is regarded as an Independent Partisan, or Leaner. Only after asserting independence twice is the respondent called an Independent. The direction component is simply Republican versus Democrat. When the strength component and the direction component are combined, the result is a seven-magnitude scale: Strong Democrat, Weak Democrat, Independent Democrat, Independent, Independent Republican, Weak Republican, Strong Republican. An eighth category, Apolitical, is often added, not as a magnitude that belongs at any point on the party identification scale, but as a category to include those few persons who are so uninformed and uninterested in politics that the questions are meaningless.

The basic idea is that each individual has an attachment to, or repulsion from, a political party. Persons attracted to the Republican party are not supposed to be attracted to the Democratic party, and vice versa. As the formal statement in *The American Voter* put it, party identification is "the individual's affective orientation to an important group-object in the environment. . . . The political party serves as the group toward which the individual may develop an identification, positive or negative, of some degree of intensity" (Campbell, Converse, Miller, & Stokes, 1960, pp. 121–22). Party identification is the individual's standing decision to support one party or another.

It is important to note that the party identification question invokes two types of attitude objects. The first is the self in the part of the question that asks "Do you think of yourself . . .?" The second set of attitude objects is comprised of Republicans, Democrats, and independents in the subsequent phrases of the questions. What this implies is that the respondent is in fact being asked: What is your self-perception? What are your perceptions of Republicans, Democrats, and independents? And given your self-perception and your perception of each of these political groups, how do you relate to them? Since an individual's self-image is likely to be both relatively stable and relatively central in the individual's cognitive structure, and since an individual will be on the receiving end of a constant stream of cues about Republicans, Democrats, and independents, this more complex understanding of the question has important implications for the measurement of party identification. This is a point to which we shall want to return.

AGGREGATE STABILITY OF PARTY IDENTIFICATION

Until 1964, the distribution of party identification was remarkably stable. As you can see from the data in Table 16-1, the proportion of Democrats varied between 44 and 47 percent, and the proportion of Republicans varied between 27 and 29 percent. This much variation can be accounted for by sampling error alone. The Democratic advantage of roughly 7 to 4 seemed relatively fixed. A similar point could be made about the strength component alone. The proportions of Strong Partisans (disregarding whether they were Democrats or Republicans) were 35 percent, 36 percent, and 35 percent in 1952, 1956, and 1960, respectively.

But then the proportion of Strong Republicans dropped in 1964, and the proportion of Strong Democrats dropped soon thereafter. In recent elections, the Strong Partisans have been a smaller component of the electorate. The proportions of Strong Partisans in 1972, 1976, and 1980 were 25, 24, and 27, percent, respectively.

Another way of looking at this change is the increase in the number

TABLE 16-1
Distribution of Party Identification by Year

Category	1952	1956	1960	1964	1968	1972	1976	1980
Strong Democrat	22%	21%	21%	26%	20%	15%	15%	18%
Weak Democrat	25	23	25	25	25	25	25	23
Independent Democrat	10	7	8	9	10	11	12	11
Independent	5	9	8	8	11	13	14	13
Independent Republican	7	8	7	6	9	11	10	10
Weak Republican	14	14	13	13	14	13	14	14
Strong Republican . . .	13	15	14	11	10	10	9	9
Apolitical	4	3	4	2	1	2	1	2

Data Source: 1952 through 1980 SRC/CPS Election Studies.

of Independents. If one looks only at the Independents (those in the middle category), the proportion of citizens not identifying with either political party has risen from 5 percent in 1952 to 13 percent in 1980. If the Leaners are included along with the Independents, then the increase is from 22 percent of the electorate in 1952 to 34 percent in 1980. Either way, the greater number of Independents and the smaller number of Strong Partisans open the possibility of much wider swings from one election to the next.

A good deal has been written to the effect that the smaller number of persons identifying with the parties spells party weakness, if not the demise of the party system itself. Consequently, it is worth paying some attention to the evidence of stability in Table 16-1. For one thing, while there are fewer Strong Partisans than once was the case, nothing has happened to the Democrats' advantage over the Republicans. This has varied a bit from one election to the next. Republicans were best off in 1956, and Democrats were in 1964. But if one calculates the ratio of all Strong, Weak, and Independent Democrats to all Strong, Weak, and Independent Republicans, the figures are 1.67, 1.37, 1.58, 2.0, 1.61, 1.50, 1.57, and 1.57 for the presidential election years from 1952 through 1980. The ratios for 1956 (1.37) and 1964 (2.0) stand out from the others in this series, but otherwise the balance has been remarkably stable.

It is also significant that most of the change in the distribution of party identification took place between 1962 and 1972. There was very little change in the first decade in which party identification was measured. Between 1962 and 1972, there was a rapid erosion in the proportion of Strong Partisans. Since 1972, however, the distribution has been nearly as stable as it was in the first decade. There is no way of knowing how long this will last, but so far, we have seen one decade of stability, one decade of change, and another decade of stability.

ASSOCIATION BETWEEN PARTY IDENTIFICATION
AND PRESIDENTIAL CHOICE

Another striking fact about party identification has been the strong association between that attitude and presidential choice. The authors of *The Voter Decides* and *The American Voter* were very careful to avoid saying that party identification caused citizens to vote one way or the other; there were other attitudes involved. (Other authors were not always as meticulous about this point.) It was clear, however, that there was a strong bivariate correlation between party identification and vote choice. If you could know only one thing about each voter, and had to predict the voter's presidential choice on the basis of this fact, party identification would be the best information to have.

Table 16-2 presents the bivariate associations between party identification and vote choice for each presidential election. Several things are evident from these data. For example, except for 1964, Strong Republicans have been more likely to support their candidates than Strong Democrats. The dominant finding, though, is the close association between party identification and presidential vote. The relationship was a little weaker in 1964 when a fair number of Republicans voted for Lyndon Johnson, and in 1972, when a larger number of Democrats voted for Richard Nixon. But a "weaker" association in this case means that Kendall's Tau-*c* correlation drops to "only" .62 in 1964 and .54 in 1972. Even including these figures, the series of correlations is .72, .75, .77, .62, .77, .54, .70, and .72 for the presidential elections from 1972 through 1980. The association has been quite strong and uncommonly stable in view of the variety of candidates and circumstances that have characterized these elections.

Some Questions about Party Identification

Satisfying as these data are in demonstrating the importance of party identification, they also raise some questions. As you run your eye across the percentages in the party identification categories and compare them to the row totals, you can see the patterns of vote by identification category that lead to the very high measures of association. But notice the votes cast by the Weak Partisans. In 1956, 1960, 1964, 1972, and 1976, more Weak Democrats defected to the Republican candidate than did Independent Democrats. And in 1960, 1964, 1968, and 1976, more Weak Republicans defected than did Independent Republicans. Remember that the Weak Partisans identify with a party rather than with independents when answering the first party identification question. What is going on here? In particular, **what are the party identification questions measuring** that would account for this behavior?

A second paradox arises out of the strong bivariate correlations

TABLE 16-2
Association between Party Identification and Presidential Choice

				Party Identification				
Candidate	Strong Dem-ocrat	Weak Dem-ocrat	Inde-pen-dent Dem-ocrat	Inde-pen-dent	Inde-pen-dent Repub-lican	Weak Repub-lican	Strong Repub-lican	Total
1952								
Stevenson	84%	62%	61%	20%	7%	7%	2%	42%
Eisenhower	16	38	39	80	93	93	98	58
Tau–c = .72								
1956								
Stevenson	85	63	67	17	7	7	1	40
Eisenhower	15	37	33	83	93	93	99	60
Tau–c = .75								
1960								
Kennedy	89	72	89	47	13	18	1	50
Nixon	11	28	11	53	87	82	99	50
Tau–c = .77								
1964								
Johnson	95	82	90	77	25	43	10	68
Goldwater	5	18	10	23	75	57	90	32
Tau–c = .62								
1968								
Humphrey	92	68	64	30	5	11	3	46
Nixon	8	32	36	70	95	89	97	54
Tau–c = .77								
1972								
McGovern	73	49	61	30	13	9	3	36
Nixon	27	51	39	70	87	91	97	64
Tau–c = .54								
1976								
Carter	92	75	76	43	14	22	3	51
Ford	8	25	24	57	86	78	97	49
Tau–c = .70								
1980								
Carter	89	65	60	26	13	5	5	44
Reagan	11	35	40	74	87	95	95	56
Tau–c = .72								

Data source: 1952 through 1980 SRC/CPS Election Studies.

between party identification and vote. It is nice to know that the correlation has dropped below .7 only twice in three decades, and even then has shown a very substantial relationship. Standing alone, this doesn't raise any question. But remember what we learned about party attitudes in Chapter 15. The data in Figure 15-2 (and elsewhere) showed that attitudes about parties were steadily declining in their importance

in the vote decision. How can party identification be of continuing importance while attitudes about parties are becoming less consequential?
Specifically, *how does party identification interact with other attitudes
in vote choice?* And how can this interaction explain this paradox?

Third, we saw in Table 16-1 that the 1950s and the decade since
1972 have been periods of stability in the aggregate distribution of
party identification. Aggregate stability, however, may result *either*
from individual stability *or* from an equilibrium condition. Let's assume
that there is a population of 500 made up of 300 Democrats and 200
Republicans. If no Democrats switch to the Republican party, and if
no Republicans switch to the Democratic party, the party balance remains 300 Democrats and 200 Republicans. Here aggregate-level stability results from individual-level stability. Alternatively, if 25 Democrats
switch to the Republican party, and if 25 Republicans switch to the
Democratic party, the party balance still remains the same. In this
case, aggregate-level stability results from an equilibrium condition
in which movements in opposite directions cancel each other out.

Now let's say that over a given time period, 35 Republicans switch
to the Democratic party and only 25 Democrats switch to the Republican
party. There is a considerable difference in the rate of change among
those switching parties: 58 percent moving in the Democratic direction
and only 42 percent moving in a Republican direction. This would
result in a population of 310 Democrats and 190 Republicans. In terms
of overall balance between the parties, this would be only a 2 percent
shift. The nature of equilibrium processes is such that it takes a very
great difference in the rate of change at the individual level before
you notice anything at the aggregate level. Consequently, aggregate-
level stability (especially when it is as approximate as that in Table
16-1) tells you very little about individual-level stability. To say anything more, we must ask: *How stable is party identification at the individual level?*

We shall address these three questions—What is party identification
measuring? How does party identification interact with other attitudes
in vote choice? How stable is party identification?—in the balance of
this chapter.

MEASUREMENT PROBLEMS WITH PARTY

IDENTIFICATION

When the concept of party identification was first introduced in
1954, emphasis was placed on the idea of psychological attachment
to a party. The idea that groups exercised influence over their members
was familiar enough to social psychologists; but at that time, most

political scientists thought of belonging to a political party either in terms of voting for that party or as being registered as a Republican or a Democrat. Consequently, the originators of the concept, Angus Campbell, Gerald Gurin, and Warren Miller, went out of their way to point to parties as groups that were sources of influence:

> The sense of personal attachment which the individual feels toward the group of his choice is referred to . . . as identification, and, with respect to parties as groups, as *party identification.* Strong identification is equated with high significance of the group as an influential standard. . . . [It is assumed] that most Americans identify themselves with one or the other of the two major parties, and that this sense of attachment and belonging is predictably associated with their political behavior. (1954, pp. 88-89, 111)

The theory was no more developed than this quote would suggest. It was accompanied by empirical material showing that most Americans did identify with a party, and that citizens' party identifications were associated with their political behavior.

While the concept of party identification led to some elegant theories in other areas, the question of how members of specific party identification categories should be expected to behave was treated largely as an empirical question. The original investigators were well aware, for example, that Weak Partisans were sometimes more likely to defect than Independent Partisans. They published data showing this, and they made their data available so other scholars could conduct independent investigations. They did not, however, offer any explanations of why this should or should not occur. By the 1970s, with literally hundreds of scholars sifting through the party identification data, a number of persons became uncomfortable with the accumulating findings, and a lively exchange took place in the literature (Petrocik, 1974; Brody, 1977; Wolfinger & others, 1977; Miller & Miller, 1977; Fiorina, 1977; Shively, 1977, 1979; Van Wingen & Valentine, 1978; Weisberg, 1980; Dennis, 1981; Miller & Wattenberg, 1983). The principal questions concerning the categories of party identification were: Why do Weak Partisans sometimes defect at rates greater than Independent Partisans? What does being an Independent mean? Are the Independent Partisans more like the Weak Partisans or the Independents?

One of the most interesting suggestions was that party identification could not be properly conceived as a single dimension (Van Wingen & Valentine, 1978; Weisberg, 1980). The traditional view placed Strong Democrats and Strong Republicans at the opposite end of the scale. This implied that if you were a Strong Democrat, you were attracted toward the Democratic party *and* repelled from the Republican party, with the opposite implication if you were a Strong Republican. If you were an Independent, you were midway between these positions, and not atttracted to either party. But the basic question, "Generally speaking, do you think of yourself as a Republican, a Democrat, an independent, or what?" invokes the respondent's self-image and perceptions of Republicans, Democrats, and independents. The traditional conception was that *one* of these political groups would serve as a reference group (that is, a positively valued source of cues). But if you admit the possibility of *multiple* reference groups, or the possibility that *none* of the political reference groups was positively evaluated, then how respondents see themselves with respect to Republicans, Democrats, and independents becomes a much more complex matter.

The 1980 Election Study contained some evidence supporting the more complex view. Two of the questions asked separately about support for parties and independence. The party item asked: "Do you think of yourself as a supporter of one of the political parties or not?" The independence item asked: "Do you ever think of yourself as a political independent or not?" Table 16-3A shows a cross-tabulation of the answers to these questions. If the traditional interpretation is correct that being an Independent is the opposite of being a Strong Partisan, then all the cases ought to be in either the upper right-hand cell (as party supporters who are not independents) or the lower left-hand cell (as independents who are not party supporters). The data suggest that this traditional interpretation applies to a majority of citizens, but there is a substantial minority to whom it does not. Nearly 15 percent (the upper left-hand cell) have had both parties and independents as reference groups, and double that proportion (the lower right-hand cell) are not accepting cues from either parties or independents.

Those who regard themselves as both partisans and independents do not pose much of a problem to party identification except as they require conceiving of multiple reference groups. These citizens are getting some of their cues from at least one party, and other information from candidate and issue cues as do independents. But those who reject both partisanship and independence are more difficult to handle. They appear to resemble the "no-preference nonpartisans" recently identified by Arthur Miller and Martin Wattenberg.[1] Miller and Wattenberg argue that the no-preference nonpartisans are increasing as parties become less salient in America.

> To these respondents parties are not perceived as relevant to the political process; therefore many of these citizens may not consider themselves to be Independents simply because in their minds there are no meaningful partisan objects to be independent from. (1983, p. 117)

---

[1] The one difference is that the no-preference nonpartisans studied by Miller and Wattenberg are those classified (they argue incorrectly) as either Independent Partisans or Independents. The largest proportion of those who reject both partisanship and independence in the 1980 sample (58 percent) are Weak Partisans.

TABLE 16-3
The Complexity of Party Identification

A. Party Support by Independence

Party Supporter?	Independent?	
	Yes	*No*
Yes	14.8%*	26.2%
No	28.9	30.0

B. What Is Traditional Identification Question Measuring?

Party Supporter or Independent	Traditional Strength Component				
	Strong Partisan	*Weak Partisan*	*Independent Partisan*	*Independent*	*Total*
Party supporter .... (upper right-hand cell)	62.1%†	23.9%	4.1%	0.5%	26.2%
Supports party and independent .... (upper left-hand cell)	18.2	14.8	16.8	6.2	14.8
Neither .... (lower right-hand cell)	15.5	44.0	15.6	33.5	30.0
Only independent .... (lower left-hand cell)	4.2	17.3	63.4	59.3	28.9
Tau–b = .32					

* The cell entries are percentages of the total.
† The cell entries are column percentages.
Source: 1980 Election Study, Center for Political Studies.

In the face of these difficulties, what is the traditional party identification series measuring? Data on this question are shown in Table
16-3B, where the traditional strength component is cross-tabulated
against the four categories from Table 16-3A. Most of the Strong Partisans are, in fact, party supporters. Most of the Independent Partisans
and Independents do, in fact, think of themselves as independents.
They are more similar to each other than either is to the Weak Partisans—although the Independent Partisan category has a larger proportion who think of themselves as both partisans and independents. The
measurement problem comes primarily in the Weak Partisan category.
This category contains a little bit of everything. Moreover, the largest
number of the Weak Partisans are those who reject both parties and
independence and are (from the standpoint of the underlying reference-
group theory) unpredictable in their behavior.

Another series of questions on party identification was added in
the 1980 Election Study. Each respondent was asked "Do any of these
statements come close to what you mean when you say you think of
yourself as an Independent (or whatever the party identification category was)?" Then each was asked to agree or disagree with each of

a series of 6 to 11 statements. The statements (such as "I dislike both parties," or "I don't know enough to make a choice," for Independents) were all plausible interpretations of someone's view of what that party identification category meant. Unfortunately for the cause of certainty, majorities of the respondents *disagreed* with most of the statements.

Strong Partisans agreed with three statements: 65 percent said they "almost always support the Democratic (or Republican) candidates;" 60 percent agreed they were "enthusiastic about what the Democratic (or Republican) party stands for;" and 63 percent said "Ever since I can remember, I've been a Democrat (or Republican)." Habitual voting seemed to be more of a Democratic than a Republican tendency. Seventy-one percent of the Strong Democrats agreed they'd been Democrats "ever since I can remember" compared to 56 percent of the Strong Republicans; and a majority of the Strong Democrats (55 percent) agreed with "My parents were Democrats and I am too," whereas only a minority of Republicans (44 percent) agreed to the comparable statement.

Only one statement was agreed to by Weak Partisans: 66 percent said they would "vote for the person, not the party." (A majority of Weak Republicans—56 percent—said they "usually prefer Republican candidates, but sometimes I support Democrats," but only 44 percent of Weak Democrats assented to the comparable statement.) None of the statements read to Independent Partisans was agreed to by a majority.[2] Independents agreed with two statements: 70 percent said "I decide on the person not the party," and 56 percent assented to "I decide on the issues not the party label."

The rejected alternatives were significant in setting aside some plausible interpretations. Substantial majorities of partisans said that they did not dislike the opposite party, and almost all Independents rejected statements that they disliked both parties. This undercuts a single-dimension interpretation. Being attracted to one political group does not mean being repelled by others. Majorities also said that their party identification did not depend on their views of Jimmy Carter or Gerald Ford. Thinking of oneself as "a Republican, a Democrat, an independent, or what" does not depend on short-term candidate cues.

The only substantive meaning that can be extracted from these responses comes from the Strong Partisans' agreement that they usually vote for the party, the Weak Partisans' statements that they usually vote for the person, and the Independents' agreement that they decide on the basis of the person or the issues. This is consistent with reference-group theory that implies Strong Partisans are accepting cues from their parties, Weak Partisans are accepting voting cues from candidate

---

[2] For whatever reason, only 6 statements were read to the Independent Partisans compared to 8 to both Strong and Weak Partisans, and 11 to Independents.

sources, and Independents are accepting cues from candidate or issue sources, but leaves open the question of what, if anything, is motivating voters who did not agree with these statements.

Finally, note the moderate association (Tau-b = .32) between the traditional party identification classification and that based on separate partisanship and independence questions. This means that the traditional classification is picking up some, but not all, of a more complex reality. This is quite consistent with data that suggest that many, but not all, persons are correctly classified by the traditional scheme. It appears that some citizens have multiple (partisan and independent) reference groups, some citizens have only one such reference group, and some citizens have no such reference group. No one-dimensional taxonomy is going to capture all of this, but the traditional classification is a good first approximation.

INTERACTION BETWEEN PARTY

IDENTIFICATION AND OTHER ATTITUDES

THE EXTENT OF COGNITIVE CONSISTENCY

The extent to which citizens' political cognitions are consistent with one another has been a matter of considerable controversy among political scientists. This is not the place to review all the positions taken by various protagonists (for some of the leading arguments, see Lane, 1973; Nie & Andersen, 1974; Converse, 1975; Bennett, 1977; Sullivan, Piereson, & Marcus, 1978; and Bishop, Tuchfarber, & Oldendick, 1978), but one of the problems concerns how cognitive consistency should be measured.

Any measure of cognitive consistency has two aspects. One is the criterion by which consistency is judged. This criterion may be liberalism-conservatism, partisanship, rules of logic that imply a necessary connection between elements, or something else. If the criterion is, say, liberalism-conservatism, and if all of a person's attitudes are what we have agreed to call liberal, then we would say that, by this criterion, the person has consistent attitudes. If some of the person's attitudes are liberal and others are conservative, then we would say that the person's attitudes are inconsistent.

It is important to know just what criterion is being used. Attitudes that are consistent by one criterion may be inconsistent by another. For example, if Republicans take a more liberal position than Democrats on foreign policy, and a more conservative position on economics, then an individual Republican who held these attitudes would be judged consistent by a partisan criterion, but inconsistent by a liberal-conser-

vative criterion. The criterion for consistency must be explicit so we
know how to judge each case.

The second aspect of measurement is whether the data concern a
population of individuals, or whether there is sufficient information
about each individual to know if each person's own attitudes are consistent. This is essentially a levels-of-analysis problem comparable to
our movement in this book between the coalition and the individual,
except that here the two levels are individual and within-individual.
The data you have determine what inferences can be properly drawn.

If the data concern a population of individuals, then the proper meaning of consistency is that attitudes are consistent across individuals.
For example, if attitudes on civil rights and attitudes on jobs are correlated, then Person A, who favors government action to protect civil
rights, is also likely to favor government action to provide jobs. Person
B, who opposes government activity in the civil rights area, is also
likely to think that people should find their own jobs without government help. The essential variation here is between A and B (and other
members of the population being studied). These data do not demonstrate (although they do not rule out) any necessary relationship between civil rights and jobs in the thinking of either A or B.

On the other hand, if one can "get inside" each person's cognitive
structure, one can make inferences about consistency within the individual. If, for example, one has depth interviews with a person, and
the person has explained the relationship he sees between civil rights
and jobs, then the investigator can assert that these attitudes are consistent for that person. Or if one has survey data that include some criterion that can be applied to each individual, a similar conclusion can
be reached. If a person claims to be a conservative and gives a conservative answer to questions on civil rights and jobs, then that person's
attitudes may be said to be consistent. Since the concept of consistency
is that there are links between elements of an individual's thought,
within-individual data are the proper ones to use.

Table 16-4 gives the distributions for two measures of cognitive consistency that have been constructed using partisan criteria and within-
individual data. The index of partisan issue consistency is based on
proximity measures of issues. To measure proximity, one question asks
where a respondent stands on an issue. A second asks what the respondent's perception is of the candidate's stand on the same issue. With
this information, one can determine the distance (proximity) between
the respondent's preference and perception of the candidate's position.
The index of partisan attitude consistency is based on the same series
of questions we used in Chapter 14 to measure information level and
in Chapter 15 for the probit model of presidential vote choice. Partisan
criteria were used for assessing consistency with both indexes. If the

TABLE 16-4
Distribution of Cognitive Consistency by Two Indexes*

Cognitive Consistency Score†	Percent of Electorate Falling within Range	
	Partisan Issue Consistency, 1972	Partisan Attitude Consistency, 1972
1.0	16.3%	5.8%
.81–.90	13.4	4.1
.71–.80	13.2	10.7
.61–.70	11.4	17.2
.51–.60	7.3	17.4
.5	15.3	18.3
.40–.49	4.1	12.9
.30–.39	3.4	8.5
.20–.29	8.1	2.8
.10–.19	1.8	0.8
0	5.7	1.5

* For details on the construction of these indexes, see Appendix A-16.1.
† A higher consistency score indicates more consistent attitudes.

Data sources: Partisan Issue Consistency Index; 1972 Hofstetter Survey of General Public. Partisan Attitude Consistency Index; 1972 Election Study, Center for Political Studies.

respondents were Republicans, they were regarded as consistent if they perceived the Republican candidate's position to be closer to their own when answering the proximity questions, or if they expressed pro-Republican or anti-Democratic attitudes when answering the series of questions quoted at the outset of Chapter 14. If they were Democrats, they were regarded as consistent if they perceived the Democratic candidate's position to be closer to their own when answering the proximity questions, or if they expressed pro-Democratic or anti-Republican attitudes when answering the longer series of questions. Details about the construction of the two indexes may be found in Appendix A-16.1, but the essential point to bear in mind when examining Table 16-4 is that a high score on either index means greater cognitive consistency.

The cognitive consistency indexes show that most people experienced a moderate degree of partisan inconsistency.[3] The distributions on the two indexes are not identical (nor would they be expected to be since the two indexes were differently constructed), but they are in agreement on three basic points. First, only a relatively small proportion of the total population has completely consistent attitudes. Second, both of the distributions have bulges at the .5 mark, meaning that there are citizens whose attitudes are equally balanced between the two

---

[3] See Figure 17-2 for the distributions of the partisan attitude consistency index for two other years.

major parties.[4] Third, and by far the most important, the largest proportion of citizens (45 percent on the partisan issue consistency index
and 49 percent on the partisan attitude consistency index) have scores
between .6 and .9. This means that the majority of their attitudes favor
their own party, but they can see some favorable aspects about the
opposing party.

Think back to the St. Louis immigrant and the woman living in Bellingham, Washington, whose interviews you read at the beginning of
Chapter 14. These two respondents were high and very high, respectively, in terms of the information levels, but reasonably typical so
far as cognitive consistency was concerned. The St. Louis woman certainly favored the Democrats, but did say that there were some good
progressive Republicans. The Washington housewife leaned toward
the Republicans, but liked Democratic plans to check tax loopholes
and approved of Jimmy Carter's Christianity. To understand how such
persons make their vote choices, we need a theory that will explain
decisions made in the face of a moderate amount of inconsistent information.

PARTY IDENTIFICATION AS ARBITER

Attitude conflict is one of the most familiar findings in the voting
field. Paul Lazarsfeld and his colleagues (Lazarsfeld, Berelson, & Gaudet, 1944) devised a theory of cross-pressures to deal with such conflict
after analyzing data gathered in the first major voting study. Cross-
pressures simply refers to the extent of forces (the citizen's own attitudes, peer influences, or whatever) pulling a person in opposite directions in an election situation. The more cross-pressured a person is,
the more likely that person is to delay their voting decision, or to try
in some similar way to avoid the cross-pressures. More recently, Peter
Sperlich has introduced some qualifications to this straightforward theory:

> First . . . attitudinal conflicts which are not at least of a certain minimum
> importance to the person are not likely to produce cross-pressure effects.
> Second . . . the more important the conflict, the stronger will be the
> behavioral effect. (1971, p. 90)

When he speaks of "importance," Sperlich is referring to centrality
(about which more shortly), but his propositions hold if we understand
importance to refer to the extent of partisan inconsistency, and the
behavioral effect resulting from this inconsistency to be defection to
the opposite party in voting.

---

[4] This is of interest because all Independents were excluded from these indexes.
(A partisan criterion of consistency could not be applied to them.) Hence some Strong
Partisans, Weak Partisans, or Leaners must be equally divided in their attitudes.

FIGURE 16-1
Partisan Defection by Issue Consistency, 1972

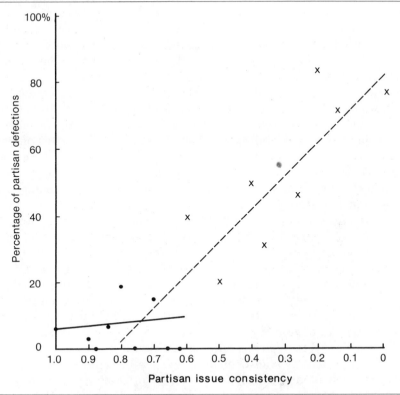

The dots represent defection rates for partisan consistency scores of .6 or higher. The x's represent defection rates for consistency scores of .6 or lower. The regression lines, the lines that represent the prediction one makes about the dependent variable (partisan defection) from knowledge of the independent variable (cognitive consistency), have been calculated by weighting the data points in this figure for the number of cases they represent. For consistency scores higher than .6, represented by the solid line, there is little relation between consistency scores and defection rate: $r = .17$. For consistency scores of .6 or lower, represented by the dashed line, there is a very strong relation: $r = .83$.

Figure 16-1 shows a plot of voting defection by partisan issue consistency. Both of the effects predicted by Sperlich's cross-pressure theory are present. The data points for consistency above .6 are depicted by dots, and the relationship between these consistency scores and the likelihood of defection by the solid line. Both the dots and the solid line appear in the lower left hand of the figure. The consistency scores from .6 down to 0 are depicted by x's, and the relationship between these scores and the likelihood of defection by the dashed line. The x's and the dashed line begin in the lower part, somewhat to the left of center, and proceed to the upper right of the figure.

Now notice that the solid line is nearly parallel to the bottom of the figure. This means that as one increases inconsistency (that is, as the consistency scores decrease), there is very little effect on the probability of defection. Voters, only two thirds of whose attitudes favor their party, are just as likely to support their party as voters whose attitudes are completely consistent. In Sperlich's words, "attitudinal conflicts which are not at least of a certain minimum importance to the person are not likely to produce cross-pressure effects." In 1972, the magnitude of inconsistency necessary before much defection took place was a score of about .6. In contrast, the dashed line representing the relation between inconsistency and defection for low-consistency scores moves upward and to the right. This means that after one has reached a certain threshold (the .6 score in this instance), the more a voter agrees with the opposition, the greater the likelihood the voter will defect. After the threshold is reached, there is a strong relationship between inconsistency and defection.

This relationship appears to be quite robust. That is, one can vary the strength of party identification, interest in the campaign, concern with the outcome of the election, education, newspaper usage, and national television usage—all variables that affect information level and political activity—and obtain roughly the same relationships. Until one reaches a given threshold, there is little relation between partisan inconsistency and vote defection. After that threshold is reached, there is a strong relationship.[5]

All this implies that party identification interacts with other attitudes to affect presidential vote choice in two ways.[6] First, as we saw in the proportion of high-consistency scores in Table 16-4, most of an identifier's perceptions favor his or her party. Second, as we saw in Figure 16-1, party identification appears to act as if it were an arbiter in the face of the moderate cognitive inconsistency that most people experience. Attitude conflicts tend to be resolved in favor of one's own party. Therefore most identifiers vote for their own party's candidate.

PARTY IDENTIFICATION AS CENTRAL

Party identification, acting through the more specific attitudes, appears to exercise a strong effect on presidential vote choice. It continues to do so at a time when attitudes about parties are less consequential. In 1972, the year from which the data for this analysis of cognitive consistency came, party attitudes made up less than 10 percent of the total and were not significantly related to vote choice. How can

---

[5] For a demonstration of similar results, with 1968 data, see Norman Fogel (1974).

[6] Party identification has a different effect on votes for other offices. Among other reasons for this, once you shift from the presidency to subpresidential offices, the voters know much less about the candidates and so are less likely to need an arbiter to resolve attitude conflicts (see Hinckley, Hofstetter, & Kessel, 1974, pp. 143–45).

this paradox of inconsequential party attitudes and very consequential party identification be resolved?

One answer is that party identification is much more likely to be a central attitude. Attitude objects are said to possess centrality when they are of enduring concern to the individual, and such attitudes are more important than others in the individual's cognitive structure. Whatever the degree of a person's interest in politics, the attitude objects in the party identification question are more likely to be of enduring concern (and hence central) than other political objects. If the individual was very interested in politics, and regarded more than one of the political groups (that is, Republicans, Democrats, or independents) as reference groups, then the question would focus both on the self and on multiple reference groups. This would produce a complex attitude, but certainly a central one. If only one political group was a positive reference group for the person, then the likelihood would be that there would be a strong affective tie between the person and the party with which that person identified. For persons relatively unconcerned with politics, at least the self-image would be important, though whether they would say that they thought of themselves as Republicans or Democrats would depend more on chance. In all three cases, though, of a person's political attitudes, party identification would be most likely to be central, and so exercise some influence over other attitudes.

Questions that simply ask about political parties, on the other hand, do not have any special standing. They tap attitudes about objects that are wholly external to the individual. Even if you assume that political parties are important to a person, it follows that the link between the self and the party (or parties) is going to be more important. Hence party identification, rather than an attitude about some aspect of parties, will occupy a central position in the person's cognitive structure. The centrality of party identification thus resolves our paradox of the declining importance of party attitudes and the continued importance of party identification. Even if attitudes about parties as such were to disappear entirely, party identification could continue to act as an arbiter in the face of conflicting attitudes about candidates and issues.

INDIVIDUAL-LEVEL STABILITY OF
PARTY IDENTIFICATION

HOW STABLE IS PARTY IDENTIFICATION?

If party identification is a central attitude, it ought to be a stable attitude. The argument from centrality is that, since other attitudes are arrayed around the central attitude, there are greater psychological

TABLE 16-5
Stability of Political Attitudes, 1972–1976

Attitude	Tau–b Correlation	Percent of Respondents Changing Position*	Mean Change*
Party identification	.69	50.2%	−.10
Neoisolationism	.31		
Foreign aid	.27		
Cut military spending	.36		
Govt. handling of economy	.27		
Tax rate	.26	67.8	.14
Federal power	.28		
Standard of living	.36	67.5	.17
Health insurance	.42	66.2	.15
Civil rights too fast?	.44		
Aid minority groups	.38	67.3	.23
School integration	.41		
Busing	.42	35.4	−.15

* The percent of respondents changing positions and the extent of the mean change is reported only for those attitudes measured on seven-category scales, because a respondent is more likely to select a different answer when given more to choose among. The mean percent of persons reporting changes on seven-category scales is 60.4; on three-category scales, 40.7; on two-category scales, 30.4. The seven-category scales provide the appropriate comparison for party identification.

Data source: 1972–1976 Panel Study, Center for Political Studies. (No 1974 data were used. This analysis was based on only the two time points.)

costs to changing a central attitude (with consequences for a whole cluster of associated attitudes) than to altering one of the peripheral attitudes. We have already seen that party identifcation has been relatively stable on the aggregate level, especially in the 1950s and again in the 1970s. Now how stable is party identification on the individual level? In what has been recognized as a classic analysis, Philip Converse (1964) demonstrated that party identification was more stable on the individual level than were other attitudes. Table 16-5 presents data on this same point from 1972 respondents who were reinterviewed in 1976. Three measures of stability are given: Kendall's Tau-*b* correlations for 1972 and 1976, the proportion of respondents who changed positions between the two time points, and the mean extent of change along the underlying scale.

Table 16-5 compares the stability of party identification with specific attitudes from four policy areas. From top to bottom, they are international involvement, economic management, social benefits, and civil liberties. The attitudes about civil liberties appear to be the most stable of the policy attitudes, but the correlation for party identification between the two time points is far higher.

Both of the other measures confirm this impression of stability. In all but one case, busing,[7] fewer respondents shifted position on party identification than did so on other attitudes. The average extent of change on party identification was also less than it was for any of the specific attitudes.

When changes did take place on party identification, two thirds of the changers moved only one category along the party identification scale. The largest number of changers consisted of 1972 Weak Democrats who said they were Strong Democrats in 1976; the second largest number was made up of 1972 Strong Republicans who said they were Weak Republicans in 1976. Given what we know (from Table 16-3B) about the jumbled nature of the Weak Partisan category, this does not represent much of a change.

INFORMATION LEVEL, COGNITIVE CONSISTENCY, AND PARTY IDENTIFICATION

While party identification as a central attitude exercises some influence on the more specific attitudes, the specific attitudes are also able to alter party identification (Jackson, 1975; Fiorina, 1981, chap. 5). The specific attitudes can influence the stability of party identification in two ways. First, the specific attitudes provide informational support. The more citizens know about politics, the more likely they are to know why they are Republicans or Democrats. Because of this, their party identifications are better anchored in a bed of specific attitudes. Second, the other attitudes support party identification if they are consistent with it. We have already seen that one can tolerate a certain amount of cognitive inconsistency without defecting in voting. It is probable that the same thing applies in party identification. The specific attitudes change rather easily. As long as only a few of the attitudes in the cluster associated with party identification are inconsistent, this can be tolerated. When a substantial number of other attitudes become inconsistent with one's party identification, then the probability of changing party identification becomes much greater.

In Table 16-6, we see what happens to the stability of party identification when we vary the properties of information level and cognitive consistency. In general, the data support the argument in the preceding paragraph. When either information level or cognitive consistency is low, then the correlations (.49 and .56, respectively) are also relatively low. This tells us that party identification is less stable when information or partisan consistency is low. As we move into the average-minus

---

[7] Busing was unusual because both the 1972 and 1976 distributions were skewed due to the strong opposition to busing. Of the 64.6 percent with stable attitudes on this topic, 90 percent were persons who were strongly opposed to busing in both 1972 and 1976.

TABLE 16-6
Stability of Party Identification by Cognitive Properties*

Cognitive Property in 1972	Level			
	Low	Average Minus	Average Plus	High
Information level	.49	.67	.70	.59
Partisan attitude consistency	.56	.60	.73	.63

* Entries are Kendall's Tau-*b* correlations between party identification in 1972 and 1976 for respondents in the category. The correlation for all respondents was .69.

Data source: 1972–1976 Election Study, Center for Political Studies.

and the average-plus categories, the correlations rise. This tells us that party identification becomes more stable as information increases and as other attitudes become more consistent. So far, so good. But notice what happens as we move from the average-plus category to the high category. The correlations decline, meaning that in the high categories, party identification is less stable. Why should this be so?

The reason why party identification becomes less stable when either information level or cognitive consistency is high is to be found in the lack of association between information level and partisan consistency.[8] The best-informed citizens are likely to have attitudes that are inconsistent with their party identifications. Recall the free-lance photographer from Philadelphia. She was the best informed of the seven respondents, and she could certainly see good points about the Republicans and the Democrats. Persons who know this much are open to change because of conflicting attitudes. Citizens with the most consistent attitudes, on the other hand, are not likely to know very much. Recall the beer-can worker from Findlay, Ohio. His attitudes were almost completely pro-Republican, but he was not very well informed. Persons of this kind are open to persuasion of the opposite party—if anyone can get their attention—because they don't have enough information for their attitudes to be very well anchored.

The apparently anomalous results can be reconciled with the general argument about the stabilizing effects of greater information and attitudinal consistency. When examined closely, the expected effects of more information and more consistency can be found. It is just that there are very few people who are both well informed and completely consistent in their attitudes.

---

[8] The relation varies a bit depending on the year and the measure of partisan consistency used. I have plotted information level against partisan attitude consistency for 1952, 1972, and 1976. I have also plotted information level against partisan issue consistency for 1972. In every case, the slope was very close to 0, meaning that information level and partisan consistency were independent of each other.

Summary

In this chapter, we have seen something of the complexity of party identification, its relation to presidential vote choice, and its stability. As to complexity, there is evidence that some citizens have multiple partisan reference groups, some citizens have one, and some citizens have none. The traditional measure of party identification can properly categorize those who get their cues from a single source, but not those with multiple reference groups or no partisan reference group at all. As to presidential vote choice, we saw a strong association at the bivariate level, and later examined this in light of the centrality of party identification when it interacts with more specific attitudes. On stability, party identification was relatively stable on the aggregate level during the 1950s and again since 1972, much more stable at the individual level than other attitudes, and its stability could be increased with enhanced information and greater cognitive consistency.

In this part of the book, we covered the concepts of internal structure, external structure, and time as they applied to citizen activity in presidential elections. Internal cognitive structure was analyzed with respect to information level, and the salience, partisan valence, consistency, and centrality of attitudes. Internal structure was very much dependent on external structure because of the content of the informational environment as affected by media characteristics and campaign strategies, and because of the citizen's involvement with the informational environment. The citizen's activity in the political environment, specifically presidential vote choice, was shown to be highly predictable from the nature of the citizen's attitudes. Temporal effects were shown, both in the modest increase in the "average" citizen's information level in the course of a campaign, and in the variation of both specific attitudes and party identification from one campaign to another.

As we saw in earlier parts of the book, campaign strategists are not free to choose just any strategy. They are limited by the internal composition of their supporting coalition and by the external support they are trying to obtain. Similarly, citizens are unlikely to respond in just any way. They are limited by the matrix of attitudes that exists at the beginning of the campaign. But, just as we have seen a variety of strategies followed by different coalitions with different goals, the response of the electorate also varies from one campaign to the next. For if the matrix of attitudes is relatively inflexible in the very short term, it is rather more flexible in the longer term. And the reaction of the electorate in the next election will be determined by the modification of those attitudes as a result of what the administration does in office over the next four years, by the strategy its opposition chooses to use to challenge it, and by the strategy with which it chooses to defend its record.

PART EIGHT

CONCLUSION

CHAPTER 17

CONCLUSION

THE DISTINCTIVENESS OF INSTITUTIONS

If one wishes to explain the behavior of political parties, it is fruitless to speak of them as collectivities of "all Democrats" or "all Republicans." Both the Democratic party and the Republican party have collective *histories*. Democrats can trace their party back to 1796, and recall such great leaders as Thomas Jefferson, Andrew Jackson, Woodrow Wilson, and Franklin Roosevelt. Republicans can trace their party to 1854, and recall such distinguished leaders as Abraham Lincoln, Theodore Roosevelt, and Dwight Eisenhower. Because of positions taken by the parties over the decades, both "the Democratic party" and "the Republican party" are *symbols*. For the past half century, Democrats have generally favored greater government regulation of the economy, and Republicans have generally favored greater freedom for private enterprise. It is therefore meaningful to speak of a "Democratic" tendency or a "Republican" position. But the *actions* of party members are all taken in specific institutional domains, and if we wish to understand what the Democrats and Republicans are *doing*, then we must understand each of the institutions in which important party activity takes place.

The important party activities are nomination politics, electoral politics, executive politics, and legislative politics. The implication is that a behavioral definition of "the party" includes what is being done in all four institutions. We have sought to explain the behavior in each setting by asking what internal structure, what external structure, and what temporal pattern were characteristic of each institution. Therefore, to describe "the party," we ought to compare the internal structures, external structures, and temporal patterns we have found.

543

INTERNAL STRUCTURES

In nomination politics, the internal structure evolves as the candidate moves from the first tentative exploration to the national convention. At the beginning, there is a very small group made up of the candidate and a few close friends and advisors. If the candidacy commands a lot of support, the coalition may grow rather rapidly.[1] Once the Initial Contests begin, the stronger coalitions begin to add groups of delegates, and the coalitions who fail to meet expectations disappear. By the Convention, the winning coalition consists of groups of delegates from across the country, as do the viable challenging coalitions. In the Republican party, conservative groups supporting one candidate have often been opposed by a nonconservative coalition supporting another. In the Democratic party, liberal groups supporting one candidate have often been opposed by a nonliberal coalition supporting another. Thus nomination coalitions at a convention are apt to be nationwide in scope and ideological in tone.

Our view of the internal structure in electoral politics, executive politics, and legislative politics rests on agreement scores. Recall that an agreement score of 1.0 means that two activists gave identical answers to questions about their policy preferences, or that two legislators cast identical roll-call votes. An agreement score of 0 means that the pair of activists had no greater agreement than one would expect by chance. Therefore an agreement score of .25 would mean interpersonal agreement 25 percent above what one would expect by chance, and an agreement score of .5 would mean interpersonal agreement half way between what one would expect by chance and total agreement.

We have good data on the internal structure of electoral coalitions from one year, 1972. The mean agreement score among all Republican activists was .29. The mean agreement score among all Democratic activists was a virtually identical .30. There were four issue groups[2] found among Republicans, with a grand mean agreement score of .48. There were seven issue groups formed on the Democratic side, but again the level of within-group agreement was nearly identical between the two parties. The grand mean agreement score for the Democrats was .50.

Most of the 1972 Republican issue groups took moderate positions, and most of the Democratic groups took liberal positions. In both parties, the issue groups were spread across the country rather than being concentrated in certain regions. Moreover, when the familiar geographic and demographic categories (eastern Republicans, black Democrats,

---

[1] In early 1984—before a single delegate was chosen—the Mondale coalition was reported to have 75 paid staff members in Washington and another 150 field organizers.

[2] There were also a significant number of isolates among 1972 Republican activists. Their mean agreement score was much lower, .12.

and so forth) were checked, their levels of issue agreement were too low to provide much explanatory power. When the issue groups were combined into coalitions, there was a tendency to polarize. The Dominant Republican Coalition took more conservative positions than the median of all Republican activists, and the Dominant Democratic Coalition took more liberal positions than the median of all Democratic activists. Because of the characteristics of the component issue groups, this tendency to polarize was more pronounced in the Republican party.

In executive politics, the internal structure consists of the president and groups of White House staff members. If the president has a policy preference himself, that decides the matter. Groups of staff members are consequential because there is too much for the president to deal with on his own. We have good information on the issue preferences of the Carter and Reagan staffs, and for one major unit (the Domestic Council staff) from the Nixon White House. There was a considerable difference in the level of agreement among the three administrations. On the Carter White House staff, the mean agreement score was at the same level that we saw for the entire electoral parties, .31. The Nixon Domestic Council staff was notably higher, .40. And the Reagan White House staff had a mean agreement score for the entire staff, .53, that was higher than the electoral issue groups. Moreover, when issue groups were sought using the same criteria as in the other institutional domains, every single member of the Carter White House staff turned out to be an isolate. A similar analysis with the Nixon Domestic Council staff yielded a single group including 56 percent of the staff members. And there was a single group in the Reagan White House that included 82 percent of the staff, and most of the major players.

In order to find issue groups on the Carter staff, it was necessary to lower the interpersonal agreement criteria. When this was done, three issue groups were found. One of the groups, however, took a relatively conservative position on economic management; a second did so on social benefits; and the third did so on civil liberties. This meant that it was exceedingly difficult to form a Dominant Coalition in any of these areas. With the Reagan White House, on the other hand, it was necessary to raise the criteria to decompose the one large group into distinguishable issue groups. All three of them stood for some variety of conservatism, and their issue preferences were so similar that coalition formation was really unnecessary.

Good data on legislative politics are available through roll-call analysis. We looked at the 95th Congress, the most recent for which Aage Clausen's issue dimensions have been computed. One must be *exceedingly* cautious in making any comparisons between the internal structures in legislative politics and other institutional domains, because different data have been used to calculate the agreement scores. It *appears*, however, that the agreement level in both chambers is lower than in the other domains. The mean agreement scores in both the 95th House and the 95th Senate were -.05, meaning 5 percent less than would be expected by chance. The mean agreement scores for all party members in each chamber were also rather low, suggesting that each of the four parties was representing a wider range of opinion than the executive parties. The mean agreement score for the House Democrats was .16, and for the House Republicans, .24. The mean agreement level for the Senate Democrats was .21, and that for the Republicans in the 95th Senate was at the same level as that for the entire Senate— 5 percent below chance agreement.

There were eight issue groups among House Democrats, the largest of which took liberal positions in most issue areas. Unlike the electoral issue groups, all but one were geographically concentrated. Five issue groups were found among House Republicans. The GOP division was a bit more ideological. Senate Democrats were divided into only four issue groups. The Liberals were by far the largest. There were five issue groups among Senate Republicans. The pronounced ideological division among them—from Progressives to Fundamentalists—reflected their very low overall agreement.

While the agreement scores for all representatives and all senators are rather low, the agreement levels within the legislative issue groups are quite high. The grand mean agreement score for House Democratic issue groups is .57; that for the House Republicans is .54. The grand mean agreement score for Senate Democratic issue groups is .55; that for the Senate Republicans is .60. These are higher agreement levels than seen anywhere else except for the Reagan White House. Since the within-group agreement level is quite high, and the overall level of agreement is rather low, this implies that the between-group agreement scores will also be low. Indeed, this is the case. The grand mean between-group agreement score for House Democrats was −.029. The House Republicans were the only ones to have a positive score, .143. The grand mean between-group agreement score for Senate Democrats was −.047, and the score for Senate Republicans, −.185, again reflected their ideological division.[3]

When we turned to legislative coalition formation, we found polarizing tendencies similar to those in electoral politics. In every policy area, the Dominant Coalition in the House was more liberal than the median position of the entire House, and more liberal than the median position of the Democratic party.[4] In every policy area, the Losing Coalition was more conservative than the median position of the entire House, and about the same as the Republican party. In three policy

[3] The full matrices of within-group and between-group agreement scores may be found in Appendix A-7.1.

[4] None of these generalizations about the House apply to abortion, where the Dominant Coalition was more conservative.

areas, the Losing Coalition was slightly more conservative than the median position of Republicans. In three others, the Losing Coalition was slightly less so. The polarizing tendencies were clearer in the Senate. In every policy area, the Dominant Coalition was more liberal than the median position of the entire Senate, and more liberal than the median position of the entire Democratic party. And in every policy area, the Losing Coalition was more conservative than the median position of the entire Senate, and more conservative than the median position of the entire Republican party.

In short, the internal structures are different in each institutional domain. In nomination politics, the structure is quite rudimentary at the beginning, and evolves into a coalition as time passes. In executive politics, the structure consists of the president and groups of his aides. There is a full coalition in electoral politics, but the members are geographically dispersed. And there are full coalitions in legislative politics which are, of course, concentrated on Capitol Hill.

Further generalizations should be regarded as *very* tentative since they rest on so few cases. In these instances, though, it appears that there is the lowest overall level of policy agreement in Congress. There is somewhat more consensus in the electoral parties, with agreement at the same level in both the Republican and Democratic parties. The greatest issue cohesion is found in executive politics, with the Carter White House having the same agreement as the whole electoral party, the Nixon Domestic Council staff somewhat more, and the Reagan White House staff the highest level of issue agreement. The issue groups in Congress also exhibit quite a high level of agreement.

In both electoral politics and legislative politics, there are polarizing tendencies. In these two institutional domains, issue groups can be found that make it possible to determine which coalitions can be formed most easily. And in all four cases—the Democratic and Republican electoral parties, the House, and the Senate—the coalitions tend to take either a more liberal or more conservative position (depending on the party in electoral politics, and on whether the coalition is Dominant or Losing in Congress) than the party or chamber as a whole.

Finally, in every case save one,[5] the Republican structure is simpler and based more on ideological considerations than the Democratic structure. That is, there are fewer Republican issue groups than Democratic issue groups, and the division somehow reflects the Progressive-versus-Fundamentalist distinction. In the Democratic party, on the other hand, there are more issue groups, and the divisions are more apt to have a geographic basis. With so few cases, it is possible that these findings are accidental, reflecting transitory circumstances that hap-

---

[5] The exception is the Senate Republican party that was so badly divided in the 95th Congress.

pened to obtain when the data were collected, but if either—the tendency to polarize in coalition formation, or the simplicity and ideological nature of Republican structure versus the complexity and geographic basis of Democratic structure—is sustained in future investigations, they would be important new understandings of our political parties.

EXTERNAL STRUCTURES

By definition, the external structures in the four institutional domains vary from one another. Since the audiences whose support is needed differ from institution to institution, and since different rules obtain in each one, it follows that the external structures will vary as one moves from nomination politics to electoral politics to executive politics to legislative politics.

Just as with internal structure, the external structure in nomination politics varies as time passes. One element is the structure of competition. This changes as some candidates drop out, and as greater information becomes available about the candidates who remain. There is a changed relationship with the press. At first, their attention is avidly sought as the developing coalition tries to convince others that it should be taken seriously. If time substantiates that claim, then the coalition deals with the press from a position of strength rather than weakness. Another element is some mechanism to seek delegates. This, too, changes as the candidate moves from being one of several possible nominees to becoming the probable nominee. Rules both constrain coalitions and give them opportunities. Among the most important are those setting the dates of primaries, those determining how delegates are to be selected and allocated among the contenders, and those of the convention itself. One set of rules will favor an incumbent or a strong front-runner; another will give greater opportunity to long-shot contenders.

Whereas a nomination contest is aimed at assembling the elements of power within one party, electoral politics is directed at a single audience, the voters. The various external activities are therefore those necessary to sustain an organized effort to reach millions on election day. There is first the operational need to decide where to campaign, and then to move the candidates and their retinues to those parts of the country. The most important research activities do not involve a search for new understanding, but rather speech writing and polling. Television is by now the main public relations vehicle, but it is by no means the only one. And if federal financing has relieved presidential campaigns of the obligation of worrying about fund raising, it has given them new obligations of staying within the law, and using limited resources so as to have the greatest impact on voters.

In executive politics, the president must first of all have some means of coordinating programs in half a dozen policy areas: international involvement, economic management, social benefits, civil liberties, natural resources, and agriculture. For international involvement, this means primarily the National Security Council. In economics, the task of coordination is shared by the Treasury, the Office of Management and Budget, the Council of Economic Advisors, with some help by the independent Federal Reserve. The nonimperative policy areas—social benefits, civil liberties, natural resources, and agriculture—have been handled in recent administrations by a domestic staff which has had a variety of names. These staffs coordinate policy, and link the president to the executive branch, but there are other Washington audiences whose support is also needed. The most important of these are Congress, the media, and interest groups. Liaison with these audiences is provided by the legislative liaison office, the press office, and the Office of Public Liaison.

Congress, of course, deals with the same policy areas as the president, a point that was noted when we saw that the Dominant Coalitions vary from one policy area to the next. There are three types of legislative policy actions, though, that tend to follow one another sequentially. First comes incubation: discovering an idea that addresses some serious public problem, generating publicity to bring public backing, and gathering legislative cosponsors. The legislation itself comes next. The amount of legislation passed has been declining in recent years; and in view of the limited influence of party leaders, and the limited number of topics on which most party members agree, relatively few bills are designated formally as party bills. In theory, Congress ought to exercise oversight concerning the legislation it has passed. In fact, a thorough program of oversight is quite beyond the resources Congress has at its disposal, so relatively little attention is devoted to this. While the foregoing activities link Congress to the world of policy, there is another set of external relationships (unfortunately not dealt with in this book) linking the individual representatives and senators to their constituents. These links sustain the representative function of legislative politics.

In brief, the external structures in nomination and electoral politics have more to do with the acquisition of legitimate power. The outward-looking activities in executive and legislative politics concern the exercise of that power in a governmental context. Nomination and electoral politics involve more passionate appeals to the public; executive and legislative politics are more largely devoted to policy development.[6]

---

[6] As Pomper has shown, however, the platforms adopted in nomination politics are serious policy documents. They are good predictors of what an administration will do if elected (Pomper & Lederman, 1980, chap. 8).

TEMPORAL PATTERNS

Nomination politics has been beginning sooner and sooner. Early Days—the period during which the candidate makes the decision to run, recruits initial staff members, and begins fund raising—is no longer marked by the solitary travels of the candidate and a couple of close aides. In a well-organized campaign, dozens of staff members may be involved, and millions of dollars are raised. The Initial Contests reveal whether all this effort has been worthwhile, as the candidates without adequate support begin to drop by the wayside. By the time of Mist Clearing, there is reasonably certain knowledge about which coalitions will be strong enough to survive. In recent decades, the Convention has confirmed the choice made in the springtime contests. Some other important decisions—the platform, the vice presidential candidate—are made, and the transition to electoral politics begins.

Electoral politics is the most compact experience of any of the four institutional patterns, lasting only from the Convention until the November election. Organization and Planning, largely invisible to the general public, comes first. Once an organization is in place, whatever strategy has been decided upon is undertaken during the Grand Opening. Campaign leaders hope that their work has been done well enough so the strategy can be carried out until November. If things do not go well, the coalition may be forced to adopt one or two Strategic Adjustments. Tactical Adjustments, reactions to particular developments, are even more likely. Soon it is Time's Up. All of the media buys have been made; the candidate's final travel plans are set; and the coalitions can do no more than wait for the electorate's verdict.

In executive politics, Transition begins the day after the election. This is a long period of recruitment and learning, lasting at least until the new administration has experienced one full annual cycle. Then comes Midterm Election when both incumbents and opposition hope to improve their strength on Capitol Hill. The new Congress finds a Maturing Administration, now with enough experience to deal seriously with policy during the third year. The fourth year, of course, is devoted to Reelection. If successful, the now Mature Administration has another opportunity to concentrate on policy, drawing on a renewed mandate and accumulated experience. Soon enough, the final stage of Retirement is marked by attention to likely successors rather than to the incumbents. The temporal pattern of executive politics is made more complex by the simultaneous occurrence of the annual policy cycle, and the temporal patterns that are characteristic of each of the policy areas.

In legislative politics, the Organization stage begins with each election. How long it lasts depends on how disruptive the election has been. When Organization has been completed, Legislative Preparation slowly begins as committees start to consider pending bills. By fall, a fair amount of Floor Action is ready. By the time the new year begins, Congress moves into a period of Election Awareness. Even if incumbents don't face primary challenges, representatives and a third of the senators know that their opponents are being chosen. Finally, there is the Closing Rush of Business just before the election, when the leadership has a chance to pass the legislation it wants because of its control of the calendar. The temporal pattern in legislative politics is made more complex by superimposition of the session and recess cycle, the congressional budget process, and the difference between the two-year election mandate of a representative and the six-year election mandate of a senator onto the five stages of a Congress.

In both nomination politics and electoral politics, the temporal pattern culminates in a decision about the exercise of power, either a convention or an election. In both executive and legislative politics, the temporal pattern begins with an election, and continues until the mandate to act has been exhausted. And the temporal patterns of the two governing institutions are made more complex by the superimposition of a budget cycle, and other patterns. But the time consumed by nomination politics is quite lengthy, while electoral politics is forced into the short period between convention and election. Similarly, an administration lasts for four (sometimes eight) years, while a Congress must complete its business in two.

Differences between the Institutional Domains

As the foregoing recapitulation of our argument makes clear, each institutional domain is different. The internal structures are all aggregated from activists and groups, but they are composed differently in each institutional setting, and there appear to be differences in the extent of issue agreement, and between the Republican and Democratic structures as well. The external structures and temporal patterns of the power-seeking institutions have more in common with each other, as do the external structures and temporal patterns of the power-exercising institutions. But it is easy to distinguish between nomination and electoral politics, and between executive and legislative politics.

The uniqueness of each institution is a point of some importance in understanding political parties. It is all too common for analysts to study some aspect of party activity—for example, the effect of rules governing the selection of convention delegates, or the distribution of power among House Democrats—then present the finding as applicable to "the political party." This is wrong. Since the unit being observed is "coalition-in-institution," what the investigator has found in the first example is limited to nomination politics, and in the second example is limited to legislative (actually House) politics. Most scholars have been careful to recognize that ***findings are time-specific.*** (In other words, one does not assume that attitudes that were important in 1980 voting decisions are also important in 1984 voting decisions until one has a chance to test this by looking at 1984 data.) What needs equal emphasis is that *findings are also institution-specific.*

CONTINUITY AND CHANGE

It has been frequently alleged that political parties have been declining in strength, if not disappearing as a force in American politics. Walter Dean Burnham asserts that:

> The American electorate is now deep into the most sweeping transformation it has experienced since the Civil War. . . . This critical realignment . . . is cutting across older partisan linkages between the rulers and the ruled. The consequence is an astonishingly rapid dissolution of the political party as an effective intervenor between the voter and the objects of his vote at the polls. (1975, p. 308)

Everett Carll Ladd claims that the "series of strange electoral performances [in the 1960s and 1970s] is chiefly the result of the pronounced weakening of American political parties that has taken place in recent decades—a process that has by now brought them to the point of virtual death as organizations" (1982, p. 51). One does not have to look far to find visions of crape; current writings about political parties are filled with "decomposition," "dealignment," "disarray," "decay," and other mournful nouns.

The preceding argument that statements about parties are institution-specific has an important bearing here. Most of those who claim that parties are weaker have something in mind, but as Austin Ranney has pointed out "the commentators do not seem to be talking about quite the same things" (1978, p. 215). The premise of one person's argument is that there are fewer strong partisans in the electorate than there were in the early 1960s. The premise of another person's argument is that delegates chosen under recently revised rules are unrepresentative of the party rank and file. The premise of still another argument is that a given president has been unable to obtain congressional support for elements of his legislative program. The conclusion that all reach from these different premises is: Therefore, parties are becoming weaker. Each of these arguments takes a premise from a single institutional domain, and asserts a conclusion that applies to all. This cannot be done.

Whether parties have changed or remained stable, and whether changes have strengthened or weakened parties are, in fact, very complex questions. In some respects, parties have changed. In others, they have remained stable. In some respects, parties are stronger. In others, they are weaker. But a serious answer to these questions requires that we ask what has taken place in each institutional domain, and what has happened to the electorate. In making this assessment, we will be concerned with events since 1952.

EXECUTIVE POLITICS

Staff Growth

One way of conceptualizing the presidency is that as the actors seek to advance their policy preferences there is a flow of influence and a flow of communication within a well-defined organizational matrix. When Dwight Eisenhower was sworn in as president in 1952, that organizational matrix had begun to emerge, but was far from complete. The Bureau of the Budget (the principal domestic staff unit in the last years of the Roosevelt administration and throughout the Truman administration) was well established and the press secretary's office also dated from FDR's time. The National Security Council (NSC) and the Council of Economic Advisers had been created during the Truman administration. The development of these and subsequently created staff units is the principal change in the presidency in recent decades.

The first major addition was Eisenhower's creation of a legislative liaison staff. In the Kennedy administration, McGeorge Bundy added some foreign policy professionals to the NSC staff to give it the capacity for independent evaluation, and the growth of NSC as an independent entity was emphasized when Henry Kissinger served as Richard Nixon's national security advisor. The big jump in the number of domestic program aides took place in the Johnson administration, and was confirmed in the Nixon administration with the creation of a Domestic Council. At the same time, the Bureau of the Budget was renamed as the Office of Management and Budget to underline its role as the president's management arm. Most of the staff units have gained in size and, of course, there have been a good many alterations in name or precise function of the individual units, but the organizational matrix has remained about the same since 1970.

The existence of this expanded staff has meant another important change. Many more decisions are now being made by presidential staff members rather than by executive agencies. White House aides are fond of saying that they bring a presidential perspective that is presumably lacking in the agencies. Bringing decisions to the White House, or touching base with presidential aides to make sure that no objections are being raised, does give the White House a capacity for coordination, but this change has not been without criticism. Recall that Robert Merriam and Theodore Sorenson, domestic advisors in the Eisenhower and Kennedy administrations, said that they tried to keep decisions out of the White House. Another well-informed critic is Robert C. Wood, who served as Housing and Urban Development secretary at the very end of the Johnson administration.

> The longer one examines the awesome burdens and limited resources of those who help the president from within his immediate circle, the more skeptical one becomes of a strategy of overseeing government by "running" it from 1600 Pennsylvania Avenue. . . . By exhausting the available time, the operational proclivities of the Budget Bureau and the Congressional interest group politicking of White House aides tend to immobilize their overview and directional functions. Too many items handled too quickly under too much pressure multiply the range and detail of the decisions reaching the president himself. There is control in the superficial sense that, somewhere, an Executive Office staff member has grappled with an operational problem. But on matters that require genuine policy attention, control is lacking because time is too short. (1970, pp. 45, 43–44)

The Intrusion of Nomination Concerns

The most important change in the temporal pattern of executive politics has been a consequence of changes in nomination politics. The changes in nomination politics will be discussed presently, but two of them intrude quite directly on executive politics. One is the lengthening of nomination politics; the other is the frequency with which incumbent presidents have been challenged. In the past, incumbent presidents were able to count on renomination if they wanted it. But since 1952, only Dwight Eisenhower in 1956 and Ronald Reagan in 1984 were free from such challenges. If presidents must devote time and energy during their third year to getting themselves renominated and reelected, they have that much less time to deal with the major issues of public policy. What the "Town Meetings" addressed by Jimmy Carter in 1979, and the Hispanic groups wooed by Ronald Reagan in 1983 mean is that the Reelection phase of the presidency is being extended, and the Maturing Administration is being curtailed. And since the Maturing Administration period is one of the best chances for a president to give serious attention to public policy, this change bodes ill.

Some Constant Elements

The principal foci of presidential attention have not changed since the 1950s. Among other things, we expect that presidents will be able to conduct foreign policy, coordinate economic policy, have a domestic program, persuade Congress to adopt some of their recommendations, and maintain popular support by working with the media. Foreign policy and economic policy can be found all the way back to the administration of George Washington; and social programs, leadership of Congress, and use of the media to build popular support are certainly marks of the 20th-century presidency. So, even though modern presidents have much more staff support than their predecessors, the major areas in which they are active are hardly new.

Paradoxically, another constant element in the presidency is change. Change, that is, from one administration to the next. Each new president brings a new staff with him, so there is not the institutional memory embodied in continuing members that is to be found on Capitol Hill. Each new president is determined to avoid the alleged mistakes of his immediate predecessor, and is likely to use slightly different organizational arrangements in an effort to avoid them. And each president has different skills. Dwight Eisenhower and Richard Nixon were particularly good at foreign policy, Lyndon Johnson and Gerald Ford had a well-developed understanding of Congress, and so on. Each administration tends to reflect the skills of the incumbent.

In consequence of all this, President Ronald Reagan was served by a much larger staff than President Dwight Eisenhower. Many more decisions were made in the White House, or were at least reviewed by staff members. President Reagan logged a good deal of campaign time in 1983, whereas in 1955 President Eisenhower had not even decided whether to seek reelection. But both Presidents Reagan and Eisenhower (and all the others in between) had to concern themselves with the same policy areas, and with the maintenance of legislative and public support for their policies. And each administration exhibited unique characteristics because of the distinctive skills of the presidents and the talents of the staff members who supported them.

THE POLICY AREAS

In executive politics, the policy areas have been rather stable. Each administration has, of course, had policies relating to international involvement, economic management, social benefits, civil liberties, natural resources, and agriculture; and the behavioral characteristics (e.g., social benefits tending to be allocative politics focusing on single groups) have remained quite similar for the Truman through the Carter administrations.[7] The principal change has been some blending together of economic management and social benefits. They are not as distinct as they were in the 1950s. There may also have been a shift in the positions taken by issue groups over time. The relative conservatism

---

[7] No analyses of the behavioral characteristics have been done for the Ford or Reagan administrations.

of the Reagan staff when compared to the Nixon staff suggests a possibility of a growing conservatism as one moves from the Eisenhower to the Nixon to the Reagan administrations; but with data limited to the Nixon, Carter, and Reagan staffs, we can only speculate about Republicans, and we can't make any comparisons among Democrats.

Barbara Sinclair, who has made a careful study of changes in congressional policy areas since the 1920s, makes a useful distinction between "agenda change" and "alignment change." Agenda change takes place when new problems are perceived—that is, when new policy areas emerge (for example, the emergence of civil liberties and international involvement in the 1930s). Alignment change "refers to systematic changes in voting response of groups of House members relative to one another" (1982, p. 4).[8] There have been three agenda changes since the 1950s that resulted in new policy areas emerging in Congress. The first two came in the late 1960s. One was a national security commitment reorientation that was related to questions raised by the antiwar movement about American troop commitments overseas and the level of defense spending. The second was a new agriculture dimension that dealt with the amount of money that could be paid to an individual producer (Clausen & Van Horn, 1977; Sinclair, 1982, chap. 7).[9] The third new policy area was abortion, which claimed a place on the congressional agenda during the 1970s. As we saw, abortion votes divided both parties in both chambers in ways quite unrelated to other policies.

The major alignment change was in the Republican party and was related to a shift in the nature of civil rights votes in the latter 1960s. The Republican party had been united in favor of civil rights, and remained so during the passage of the 1964 civil rights bill and the 1965 voting rights bill. But then open housing and busing turned up. As Barbara Sinclair explains, "Given the opposition of their white constituents and the lack of any black constituents, given the increasing loyalty of blacks to the Democratic party and their own dislike of federal legislation which intruded into the private life of the individual, Republican members saw little reason to support further civil rights measures" (1982, p. 96). Republican opposition was also increased by the election of GOP members from the hitherto solid Democratic South. There was also some noticeable alignment change in the Democratic party at about the same time. Southern members were becoming more conservative on economic management and social benefits, and this increased the sectional division with the Democratic coalition on these issues.

---

[8] Sinclair also distinguishes "policy change," change in policy outputs.

[9] The agricultural subsidy limit was not treated as a separate policy area in Chapter 7 because the positions taken by the issue groups were highly correlated to their positions on the other agricultural dimension.

Edward Carmines and James Stimson have traced a parallel change in the electorate. They have suggested a theory of "normal partisan change" which "results from the evolution of new issues coupled with the process of generational replacement. . . . New issues create the opportunity for political change; new citizens are its most likely agents" (1981, p. 108). According to this theory, rapid changes such as were associated with the partisan realignment of the 1930s may be seen as special cases of the normal pace of replacement. The only issue with the required characteristics—deeply felt, visibly different positions, and long on the public agenda—is desegregation. Carmines and Stimson show that the Republican identifiers recruited in 1964 when Senator Goldwater ran were more conservative than previous Republican identifiers, and that there has been an increasing difference between Republican and Democratic identifiers in subsequent elections.

LEGISLATIVE POLITICS

Congress is characterized by a different paradox than the executive branch. It has both continuity and constant change. There is continuity from one Congress to the next because such a high proportion of the members return. But Congress as an institution is constantly reforming itself in response to changing pressures from the political environment, the simultaneous needs to represent and to make policy, and the conflicting desires to share power among the members and to concentrate power in order to act (S.C. Patterson, 1978; Jones, 1982, chap. 15). "Congressional changes," as Samuel Patterson puts it, "are most appropriately viewed as the adaptations through which a very stable institution maintains itself" in the face of these conflicting demands (1978, p. 133). Since it would be a surprise to find that Congress had not changed over any 30-year period, we need to ask simply what reforms have taken place, and to avoid the temptation to single out any one reform and claim that it has fundamentally transformed Congress.

Voting Patterns

As we just saw, a couple of new policy areas have emerged, but the previously existing policy areas can still be found. Counterparts of some of the issue groups found by Clausen in the 85th and 86th Houses (1973, p. 107) still existed in the 95th House. Among Republicans, the Hard-Line Conservatives, Internationalist Conservatives, and the Eastern Moderates of the 85th and 86th had similar policy profiles (in the corresponding policy areas) as the Hard-Line Conservatives, the Domestic Conservatives, and the Republican Moderates, respectively, in the 95th. The Liberals of the 85th and 86th took postures similar to the two groups of Liberals and the Dominant group among the 95th House Democrats, and the Dixie Welfare Populists of the 85th and 86th took positions parallel to the Pro-Farm Democrats of the 95th. Given two more Republican groups in the 95th House, and still more differences among the Democrats, one could not say that the House issue structure remained identical 20 years later, but it could still be recognized.

The decline of the Democratic party in the South and the rise of the Republicans has had important consequences for the legislative parties. In 1949, 53 percent of the House Democrats were from the South or border states. By 1981, that proportion had dropped to 38 percent. During the same time, the proportion of Republican representatives from those regions rose from 4 to 26 percent. In 1949, there were 30 Democratic senators from the South or border states. By 1981, there were only 19. Over the same 32 years, the number of Republican senators from those regions rose from 2 to 13 (Ornstein, Mann, Malbin, & Bibby, 1982, tables 1-3, 1-5). In view of the greater conservatism that developed in the South during the 1960s (Sinclair, 1982, chap. 6), this meant that the Democratic legislative parties became more liberal, but with greater issue distance between their liberal majorities and their southern minorities. The addition of southern Republicans, of course, increased the conservative proclivities of their legislative parties.

The changes in the level of party voting are a bit more complex. The mean proportions of party unity votes (on which a majority of one party votes against a majority of the other) are just over 42 percent for both the House and the Senate.[10] Party unity has dropped in the House, but has been quite stable in the Senate. When the proportion of party unity votes is plotted against time, the slope is $-.46$ for the House, but .01 for the Senate. When the comparison is limited to 1970 through 1981, however, party unity has been increasing in both chambers. The 1970–1981 slope is .81 for the House and .92 for the Senate. As we saw in Table 6-1, the proportion of members voting with their parties on party unity votes was about three quarters for all four parties. Over the longer time period, this proportion has been decreasing for House Democrats, House Republicans, Senate Democrats, and Senate Republicans. But when the proportions of party support are plotted against time for 1970 through 1981, the levels of party support have been increasing for all four parties. Hence one's conclusion about changes in the level of party voting depends on the time period selected for comparison.

---

[10] The time period is from 1953 through 1981 for party unity votes in the House, from 1954 through 1981 for party unity votes in the Senate, and 1954 through 1981 for all comparisons of proportions voting with their parties on unity votes (Ornstein and others, 1982, tables 8-3, 8-4).

Organization

In the internal organization of the House,[11] committees remain central, but committee chairs have become much less powerful. In the 1950s, committee chairs had an effective monopoly of resources. This is no longer the case. Formerly, representatives became chairs through the automatic workings of the seniority system, and could count on automatic reelection as long as they stayed in the House. Committee chairs could control subcommittees, and determine which bills would be referred to them. The (then small) staff reported to the chair, which gave the chair a near monopoly of expertise. When crucial markup sessions came, they were usually closed to outsiders. Committee chairs could often persuade the Rules Committee to grant a closed rule that would prohibit amendments on the floor. Unrecorded votes, often teller votes, made it very difficult to learn how members were voting *unless* one knew what commitments had been made (as the committee chairs usually did), and could therefore watch certain members to see if these commitments were being carried out. *All* of these practices have changed. Instead of an effective monopoly of resources, committee chairs share influence with a large number of other actors (Ornstein, 1983).

The geographic basis of legislative influence is not new. David Truman (1956) showed that state delegations appeared "to have an important influence" in the 81st House of Representatives. There was variation in the nature of this influence between, for example, the Illinois Democrats, Wisconsin Republicans, Texas Democrats, and California Democrats, but similar voting patterns among all or part of state delegations could be detected. Informal groups were much less common in the early 1950s. There were a few—the Chowder and Marching Society, for instance. But such groups, especially those with explicit policy interests, have proliferated in recent years.

The increasing number of recorded votes—from 181 in the first Eisenhower Congress to 1,276 in the last Carter Congress—has diminished the ability of the House leadership to control voting outcomes. In the past, the chair could declare the result on close voice votes, and the leaders could hold back reserves of votes to be used if needed on teller votes. This is much harder to do when everybody casts a publicly recorded vote. The Speaker, however, gained considerable power over the Rules Committee, and over the appointments process generally, in Democratic party reforms of the 1970s. The norms of the Democratic party have been such that this new leadership power over committee appointments has been exercised only in cases of extreme provocation

---

[11] There have been parallel changes in the Senate, but committee structure was more important in the House than it was in the more individualistic Senate.

(i.e., a Phil Gramm), but the power is still there if leaders decide to use it.

Policy Activities

So far as the policy-related activities of Congress are concerned, there is ample evidence of an increased workload: more time spent in session, more committee meetings, more subcommittee meetings, and so forth. But as we saw, less legislation has resulted. In view of the greater difficulty of passing any bill, members are increasingly attaching their proposals as amendments to other bills. The amount of incubation and oversight have both increased. More members have discovered that they can make public reputations by advocating ideas, as activist senators were doing in the 1950s. Jack Kemp and Elliot Levitas spent a good deal of time working for their pet ideas. And Elliot Levitas's interest in the legislative veto is a good example of post-Watergate attention to what executive agencies were doing.

Perhaps the major policy change—and certainly the change that had the greatest impact on the temporal pattern of legislative politics— was the mid-70s adoption of the legislative budget process. This has focused attention on spending patterns at least once or twice a year, and limited the amount of time previously available for consideration of substantive legislation. And by moving the beginning of the fiscal year to October 1, the new process has put budget considerations in the middle of Closing Rush of Business, and made it more difficult to give proper attention to either the appropriation bills or the important substantive legislation.

Legislative politics in the 1980s, then, is quite different from legislative politics in the 1950s. The basis of representation remains geographic, which means that constituency interests and state delegations are still central. But changes in the constituencies—especially the growth of some Republican strength in the South—have meant that the Democratic party has become more liberal, and the Republican party has become more conservative. There have been offsetting trends in the level of party voting. Over a 30-year time period, party voting has been declining; but in the last 10 years, it has been increasing. Presidential leadership of Congress is a slightly different matter, but the two most notable examples of this—Lyndon Johnson in 1965 and Ronald Reagan in 1981—came midway in the time period and at the end.[12] Committee chairs have lost their monopoly of resources to other

---

[12] Reagan's concern with spending cuts, of course, was much more narrowly focused than Johnson's Great Society program. Johnson had the highest proportion of victories in 1965, 93.1 percent. Reagan's 81.9 percent in 1981 ranked behind Johnson (1964 and 1965), Eisenhower (1953 and 1954), and Kennedy (1962 and 1963), but these presidents all had congressional majorities of their own parties whereas Reagan faced a Democratic House (Ornstein and others, 1982, table 8-1).

congressional actors, and many members, whether acting as individuals or as members of informal caucuses, have become active in policy advocacy. The 1980s leadership presides over a more diffuse, less predictable, system, and because of more democratic norms, has not chosen to exercise the appointive power it has been given to instill more party discipline. A couple of new policy areas have emerged (though the five policy areas of the 1950s all remain), and in spite of an increased workload, Congress has been passing less legislation. Finally, in an attempt to do something about fiscal problems, Congress undertook a congressional budget process in the mid-70s that had major consequences.

NOMINATION POLITICS

The Convention Delegates

There has been a limited change in the identity of the actors involved in nomination politics. Calls for party reform go back a long way (Ranney, 1975), but the Democrats' McGovern-Fraser Commission took unusually aggressive action in this direction. They called for quotas for the 1972 convention for hitherto underrepresented population categories: women, blacks, and young persons. More recent Democratic commissions have softened these requirements, and have moved to increase the role of party leaders. The Milkulski Commission opted for an affirmative action program for the 1976 convention. The Winograd Commission recommended that each state's delegation to the 1980 convention be increased by 10 percent and that these seats be filled by party leaders and elected state officials. The Hunt Commission created a bloc of 550 delegate seats to the 1984 Democratic convention to be filled by party officials uncommitted to any candidate. Republican committees (the Delegate and Organization [DO] Committee, the Rule 29 Committee, and the Rules Review Committee) have limited themselves to encouraging state parties to send more female, black, and youthful delegates. The net of all this has been an increase in female delegates, particularly on the Democratic side. Women have increased from 13 percent of the Democratic delegates in 1968 to 42 percent in 1972 to 53 percent in 1980; women were 16 percent of the Republican delegates in 1968, and have been just under one third of the delegates in 1972, 1976, and 1980. Blacks and "under 30s" were 24 percent and 16 percent of the 1972 Democratic delegates, but fell to 14 percent and 7 percent, respectively, in 1980. Blacks and young delegates have remained very small proportions of the Republican delegates (Ranney, 1978, p. 232; Farah, Jennings, & Miller, 1982; Mitofsky & Plissner, 1980).

The delegates also continue to come from the upper socioeconomic strata. Thirty-nine percent of the Republican delegates and 45 percent of the Democratic delegates had postgraduate degrees in 1980; the median income of Republican delegates was $47,000 and that for Democrats was $37,000; virtually all came from white-collar occupations. "Domination of the presidential elite by a skill-based middle class was even more complete in 1972 than it was in 1948–52," concluded Jeane Kirkpatrick (1976, p. 65) after a study of those delegates. Her conclusion remains true today.

The views of Democratic delegates in 1972, 1976, and 1980 were more liberal than citizens who thought of themselves as Democrats; and 1980 GOP delegates were much more conservative than citizen Republicans (Kirkpatrick, 1976, chap. 10; Ladd, 1982, p. 65; Mitofsky & Plissner, 1980). These attitudes, of course, have consequences in the type of platform adopted and the type of candidates nominated by the convention. But differences between activists and citizens are not new. In 1956 and 1964, Republican activists had attitudes that were unrepresentative of Republican citizens (McClosky, Hoffman, & O'Hara, 1960; Jennings, 1966). The only variation here is that it was the Democrats who were unrepresentative in 1972 and 1976, and both parties managed to be simultaneously unrepresentative in 1980.

A Continuing Interest in Issues

What about the delegates' interest in issues? We saw in Chapter 9 that members of nomination coalitions had a strong interest in issues. But is this new? In the absence of hard evidence, this question cannot be answered with complete certainty. What we do know is that as soon as political scientists began asking delegates if they were interested in issues, the answer was yes. The question was not asked directly in the first survey of convention delegates in 1956, but Democratic delegates agreed at levels that "suggested unanimity within the sample" on taxes on small and middle income, slum clearance, social security, and minimum wages, as did Republicans on government regulation of business, business taxes, regulation of trade unions, and minimum wages. Members of both parties' coalitions agreed on issues important to their constituents (McClosky and others, 1960, pp. 424–25). There is no evidence they were uninterested in issues at any point in the time period under consideration, and many instances can be cited of earlier issue-oriented behavior—for example, the positions on civil rights taken by then Minneapolis Mayor Hubert Humphrey and the Dixiecrats at the 1948 Democratic convention.

As between the two parties' nomination coalitions, there appear to have been two reversals of characteristic attitudes. There had been an historic split in the Republican party between internationalist and isolationist wings. Democrats were consequently more willing to favor military alliances and defense spending in 1956 (McClosky and others, 1960, p. 415). By the 70s, Republicans were more likely than Democrats to favor reliance on military means where necessary (Kirkpatrick, 1976, pp. 181–85). The other is the alignment shift already noted in the discussion of policy areas. The Democratic party had been split between northern and southern wings on questions of civil rights, and the Republican party had taken pro-civil liberties positions. The split in the Democratic party has not been eliminated, but the center of gravity has shifted in a liberal direction while Republicans have become more conservative. Otherwise, the parties' relative postures have remained the same.

Costain reports an increase in ideological voting in contests between winning and losing coalitions at Democratic conventions. The "balance of left factional and nonleft factional voting noted in the Humphrey, McGovern, and Carter votes is less likely to indicate the emergence of a new consensus . . . than a continuing struggle between a vital left bloc in the convention and all the other groups which must join together in order to defeat the left" (1978, p. 110). This would be parallel to Republican contests throughout this period, in which all nonright groups have had to coalesce to defeat an increasingly active right coalition.

Continuing Nationalization

There is some evidence that both nomination and electoral coalitions are more national in character. The most liberal groups in earlier Democratic nomination coalitions were all from the West and Midwest. The most conservative groups in earlier Republican nomination coalitions were all southern, with the exceptions of Ohio (which was simply being loyal to Senator Taft) and Illinois (Munger & Blackhurst, 1965). By 1976, the liberal Democratic coalition included groups from every region except the South, and the conservative Republican coalition included groups from every region except the East (Costain, 1978). In 1980, the liberal Kennedy coalition was unable to wrest much southern strength from a southern-based Carter coalition, but the conservative Reagan coalition attracted a number of groups from the East.

In short, coalition building goes on apace. More women are involved; the majority of actors comes from the skill-based middle class. Because of the activists' interest in issues, the coalitions are formed around groups that take similar issue positions, with the principal ideological thrust coming from conservatives in the Republican party and liberals in the Democratic party. These coalitions are increasingly nationwide in scope.

A Longer Nomination Process

The pattern of first-ballot nominations was well established by the 1950s. There have been only three conventions since 1936[13] that did not have first-ballot nominations. The Republicans picked Wendell Willkie on the sixth ballot in 1940 and Thomas E. Dewey on the third ballot in 1948; and the Democrats nominated Adlai Stevenson on the third ballot in 1952. The typical pattern since 1936, though, has been that of a first-ballot ratification of a decision made in preconvention activity.

The nomination process lasts longer now than it did in the 1950s. Among the factors contributing to this were the victories of George McGovern in 1972 and Jimmy Carter in 1976. Unlike earlier aspirants who were well known before the primaries (such as Eisenhower, Kennedy, or Goldwater), both McGovern and Carter had been discounted as serious contenders. But both began very early, both captured the nomination, and together they solidified a pattern of earlier activity that others have followed.

There have been other considerations that have worked in the same direction. The Federal Election Campaign Act of 1974 made it necessary to set up a committee to raise early money in order to qualify for federal matching funds. Party reforms stipulating that more delegates are to be elected at the district (rather than the state) level have also led to more organization. And the heavy press coverage of the first glimmerings of strength—polls reflecting strength in New Hampshire, surveys of delegates likely to attend Iowa caucuses, and straw polls now taken in state conventions more than a year before the first delegate is selected—has placed a premium on a good initial showing. This, of course, requires a lot of effort in the states where these events are being held. For all of these reasons, the nomination process has been pushed back well into the third year of the incumbent president's term.

The Consequences of an Increasing Number of Primaries

The proportion of delegates chosen in primaries increased very sharply in the 1970s. In 1952, 39 percent of both Republican and Demo-

---

[13] Until 1936, the Democrats had a rule that a two-thirds majority was necessary for nomination. Woodrow Wilson was nominated on the 46th ballot in 1912, James M. Cox on the 44th ballot in 1920, John W. Davis on the 104th ballot in 1924, and Franklin D. Roosevelt on the 6th ballot in 1932. Other factors besides the two-thirds rule were involved in these long contests. The relative strength of urban and rural groups in the Democratic party was changing, and poor preconvention communication made multiple ballots valuable as signals of the probable success of various coalitions.

cratic delegates were so selected,[14] and the proportion remained fairly stable through 1968. But the Democratic percentage jumped to 61 percent in 1972, 73 percent in 1976, and 75 percent in 1980, while the Republican proportion rose to 53 percent in 1972, 68 percent in 1976, and 74 percent in 1980 (Arterton, 1978, p. 7; Ranney, 1981, p. 369). This has had some major consequences.

The first clear implication of a high proportion of primaries rather than conventions was to further handicap late entrants. With many delegates chosen before their entrances into the race, their hope of building a winning coalition depended on groups of uncommitted delegates being picked. An uninstructed delegation is more likely to come from a state convention. Political activists attending a convention are more likely than citizens to think of the strategic advantages of joining a coalition at the opportune moment, while citizens voting in primaries tend to opt for the most attractive candidate in preference to "none of the above."

A second consequence of more primaries is to strengthen aspirants— as long as they are equipped to come into a state and run an effective primary campaign—at the expense of state party leaders. This is not new. In California in 1952, for example, "many Democrats, dissatisfied with [the state party] leadership, rallied behind [Senator Estes] Kefauver, whose slate of delegates soundly trounced the so-called 'uninstructed' slate to the national convention" that was made up of party officials (Shields, 1954, p. 674). Increasing the number of primaries simply increases the number of opportunities for coalition leaders to act independently of party leaders. This, in turn, increases the likelihood that an outsider can capture the party's nomination. But this is not new either. The authors of a comprehensive review of the nomination process from the 1830s through 1956 concluded: "It is in the nature of presidential nominating contests that new men are always under consideration and must sometimes be nominated. The Republican choice in 1940, for example, lay mainly between three men whose fame had not yet matured: Dewey, a defeated first-time candidate for governor; Taft, a junior senator of two years' standing; and Willkie, a public utility magnate who had never held public office" (David, Goldman, & Bain, 1960, p. 161). So, presidential aspirants—some of whom are outsiders—gain power at the expense of state and local party leaders. And since one of these aspirants is ultimately elected president, the process tends to produce presidents who are less beholden to these party leaders.

---

[14] Fifty-nine percent of Republican delegates, and 54 percent of Democratic delegates were elected by primaries in 1916. From that point on, the popularity of primaries declined until only 36 percent of both parties' delegates were so chosen in 1948.

A third concomitant of the growing number of primaries has been the establishment of party rules as clearly superior to state law. The McGovern-Fraser guidelines gave states a choice between conventions that adhered to certain criteria or primaries, and many states opted for primaries. These rules were tested in a case growing out of the seating of a reform delegation from Illinois in place of an elected delegation led by Chicago Mayor Richard J. Daley at the 1972 Democratic National Convention. When the case reached the U.S. Supreme Court, Justice Brennan held for the Court: "The convention serves the pervasive national interest in the selection of candidates for national office, and this national interest is greater than any interest of an individual state." This led the leading scholar of party reform to conclude that "the national party organs' power to make rules governing presidential nominating processes is, both in political reality and legal principle, at its highest peak by far since the early 1820s" (Ranney, 1978, p. 230).

Challenging Incumbent Presidents

Yet another change in nomination politics has been the increasing number of challenges to incumbent presidents. Perhaps the most significant were George Wallace's 1964 campaign in the primaries, and the 1972 challenges of liberal Republican Representative Pete McClosky of California and conservative Republican Representative John Ashbrook of Ohio. They were significant because incumbents Lyndon Johnson and Richard Nixon were both certain of renomination, yet both sitting presidents were challenged from within their own parties. And politically vulnerable presidents—Johnson in 1968, Ford in 1976, and Carter in 1980—faced much more serious challenges. Lively nomination politics is no longer confined to the party out of power.

To sum up, the basic pattern of nomination politics was established by the beginning of our time period. What we have seen is an expansion of this pattern. There are now many more primaries; nomination politics lasts quite a bit longer; real contests often take place within the in party. The national parties and the leaders of nomination coalitions have been strengthened at the expense of state political leaders by the spread of this modern pattern.

ELECTORAL POLITICS

Professionalization of Campaigns

As we saw in Chapter 11, the origins of professional campaign staffs came a generation earlier than the 1950s. Expertise was brought to the Democratic National Committee when National Chairman John Raskob hired Charles Michelson to handle publicity in the late 1920s, and

Republican National Chairman John D. M. Hamilton began a tradition of party civil service in the 1936–40 period. One could argue that professionalization has continued since 1952, but the case should not be pressed too far. There are certain slots on a campaign staff that are usually filled by those with appropriate professional backgrounds. "Professionalism," Arterton reminds us, "has succeeded to a greater degree in precisely those areas of campaign behavior that demand a level of expertise: management, polling, computer services, media production, media purchasing, and financial reporting" (1984). Even more important in their impact on campaign strategy has been the incorporation of professionals in the strategy groups that make basic campaign decisions. John Deardourff, Stuart Spencer, and Robert Teeter were making many of the basic Republican decisions in 1976; Stuart Spencer and Richard Wirthlin were doing so four years later; and Jerry Rafshoon and Pat Caddell were ranking strategists on the Democratic side in both of these campaigns.

The reason for not wanting to make too much of the spreading professionalism is that its antecedents are so clear. Campaign management firms were organized well before the 1950s, especially in California. In the 1952 Eisenhower campaign, persons coming from public relations or newspaper backgrounds included Robert Humphreys, James C. Hargerty, Murray Chotnier, and Robert Mullen. Batten, Barton, Durstein, and Osborn as well as the Kudner, Ted Bates, and Whitaker and Baxter firms were all working on the campaign (Kelley, 1956, chaps. 5, 6). The 1952 Republican campaign plan "outlined basic strategy, organization, appeals, types of speeches, literature, advertising, television and radio programs, the relative weight to be given to various media, the kinds, places, and times of campaign trips and rallies, and the areas in which efforts were to be concentrated" (Kelley, 1956, p. 1). This makes it hard to argue that expertise and experience were lacking at the beginning of our three-decade time period.

The National Committees

The Republican National Committee has taken on a number of new activities. Credit for this belongs to Mary Louise Smith, national chairperson during the Ford administration, and particularly to William Brock, who guided the committee from 1977 until 1981. One important Brock innovation was national committee agreement during 1977–78 to pay the salary for an organizational director for each state party. This was subject to some conditions; for instance, the person chosen had to be acceptable to the national committee. But the program meant that every state committee had a trained staff director. In addition, there were 15 field directors, who maintained liaison with state party organizations in two- to six-state areas, such as Michigan and Pennsylvania; Indiana, Kansas, Kentucky, and Missouri; or Arkansas, Louisiana, Mississippi, and Texas. A local election campaign division of equal size focused on state legislative elections across the country in 1978. Their efforts included some 75 campaign seminars, $1 million in direct cash grants to GOP candidates, and help with surveys, radio and TV spots, and scheduling. A computer services division conducted analyses for state parties that installed terminals and paid telephone line charges. In 1978, all this cost some $3 million in direct contributions and the salaries of organizers and consultants, and was in addition to the normal operations of the national committee that were carried forward at the same time (Republican National Committee Chairman's Report, 1979).

The Democratic National Committee made occasional efforts to develop similar strength, most recently in the early 1980s. But it must be said that they were much weaker than the Republicans. One reason was the much stronger financial base established by the GOP. An even more important reason was a lack of concern with the national committees during the presidencies of Lyndon Johnson and Jimmy Carter.

John Bibby (1981) argues that there has been a difference between the parties in the ways they have moved toward nationalization. The Democrats have stressed rule changes through the activities of the McGovern-Fraser, Mikulski, Winograd, and Hunt commissions. The Republicans have stressed organization. While it could be said that the GOP activity strengthens both state and national parties, the ability of the national party to provide cash and campaign services to the states certainly gives the national committee more leverage in state affairs than hitherto.

There has been a move away from a "unified" campaign structure in which presidential campaigns are conducted through the national committee. At least one of the campaigns was run by the national committee staff from 1952 through 1968, and both were organized this way in 1956 and 1964. From 1972 through 1980, though, the campaign headquarters were located in separate presidential campaign committees, and the Federal Election Campaign Act of 1974 makes it likely that this will continue to be the case. Gerald Ford had given a speech as vice president saying that campaigns should be run through the national committee. Ford wanted to run his 1976 campaign that way, but was told that the new campaign finance law required a separate committee (Ford, 1979, p. 275). (President Ford was misinformed about this. There is a provision that allows a candidate to designate the national committee as the agent to spend public funds.) Whatever the rules, the effective location of power to make decisions about national campaign strategy will reside with the persons authorized to act by the presidential candidate. The effect of the 1974 statute is to reduce the candidate's opportunity to concentrate that authority in the national committee if he wishes to do so.

Increasing Technology and Escalating Costs

There have been several changes in campaign technology. One was the move from the campaign train to the campaign plane. The train is now used for nostalgia, and the special circumstance of several medium-size cities that are more conveniently accessible by rail. Otherwise the campaign moves by jet in order to appear in a number of different media markets the same day. This moves the candidate about more rapidly, of course, but it hasn't affected the relative power of national and state parties very much.

Changes have taken place in the communication methods used to reach the voters and to find out what they are thinking. The first year in which extensive use was made of television was 1952. At that time, it was one of several media that were employed, but it soon moved to a position of dominance in the media campaign. Polling was employed in the 1950s, but it was intermittent and focused on high reliability estimates of candidate standing. Two decades later, the information flow was continuous, and there were some instances of very sophisticated analysis. These shifts have moved influence from the state to the national level. Heretofore, state leaders could claim special knowledge of the situations in their states. Now national leaders armed with computer printouts may have better data both on the views of citizens in a given state and on the media outlets that should be used to reach them.[15]

The changes in communication techniques have also shifted power on the national level away from generalists and into the hands of specialists. It is sometimes said that these technological changes have diminished the influence of politicians. A better interpretation would be that power has shifted to different types of politicians—those who have mastered the use of media and polling.[16]

The use of jets, polls, and particularly television has made presidential campaigning much more expensive. Even ignoring the orgy of spending in the 1972 Nixon campaign, the cost of major party general election

[15] Remember our finding in Chapter 10 that the county campaign leaders' perception of views in their community was no better than one would expect by chance. This means that the use of polls is improving politicians' understanding of citizens' thinking.

[16] If we go back to the 1950s, we find Joseph Napolitan active in Springfield, Massachusetts, politics, and we find John Deardourff on the staff of Representative Jessica McC. Weis of New York. Napolitan came into national politics when his Springfield friend, Lawrence O'Brien, was a leader in the Kennedy campaign; Deardourff was on Nelson Rockefeller's staff. Napolitan became a leading Democratic campaign consultant, and Deardourff a leading Republican consultant.

campaigns rose 335 percent from 1952 through 1968. In cost per vote cast, expenditures rose from 19 cents to 60 cents over the same time period (Alexander, 1972, pp. 6–7).

There were also two important developments in campaign funding during this time period. One was the Republican sustaining membership campaign begun in 1962. In 1964, the program brought in some $2 million in average contributions of $10 each. By 1979, there were over 600,000 contributors, and the average Republican contribution was approximately $26. After the 1980 Reagan campaign, the Republicans had 1.5 million contributors.

The second development was federal funding at a level of $20 million in 1974 dollars, $29.4 million in 1980. This direct funding will have at least three effects. First, it will allow campaigns to escape destitution, such as the Humphrey campaign experienced in September 1968. Second, the act guarantees the national committees a minor role (they were authorized to spend $4.6 million in 1980), but it makes it less likely that the campaigns will be run through them. Third, the tight limits—in constant dollars, about 70 percent of the amount spent in 1968—will compel some hard decisions about the best use of the available funds.

Taken together, the conflicting effects of the several developments in electoral politics are not easy to summarize. They certainly tend to favor national party leaders rather than state leaders because they point to centralized decision making. One of the national committees, the Republican, is providing a range of services throughout the country and has developed a mass financial base, but the authority of both national committees has been reduced by provisions of the Federal Election Campaign Act of 1974. Modern modes of transportation and communication have made presidential campaigns much more expensive, and have shifted influence toward politicians who understand these techniques. But in spite of the shifts brought on by technology, the presidential candidate and his advisors still face the central problem of deciding which voters they wish to appeal to, and how they are going to do so successfully.

CITIZEN ATTITUDES AND ACTION

Levels of Information

There is no evidence that American citizens know substantially more or substantially less about politics than they did three decades ago. The information levels for 1952, 1976, and 1980 are shown in Figure 17-1. By comparing the curves, it can be seen that the distributions of the information levels for 1976 and 1980 were virtually identical, and that these information levels were somewhat lower than that ob-

FIGURE 17-1
Distributions of Information Levels, 1952, 1976, and 1980

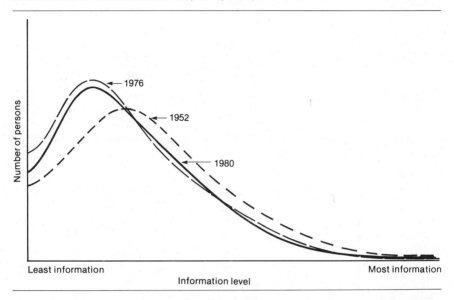

served in 1952. That is, there were a few more people falling into the higher information categories in 1952, and a few more people falling into the lower information categories in 1976 and 1980. But the difference between the means (between 1952 on the one hand, and 1976 or 1980 on the other) is not significant, and the shapes of the curves are similar.

Using the Media

There have been a few changes in the composition of the media since 1952. In 1952, television sets were in 34 percent of U.S. homes, but by 1976, television was available in 97 percent of the homes. The average time per day spent watching TV also increased from 4:51 hours in 1955 to 6:26 in 1975. Total circulation of magazines and newspapers increased, but when adjusted for population growth, magazine circulation went up and newspaper circulation dropped. Daily newspaper circulation moved from 48.2 per 100 adults to 38.2 per 100 adults during our time period, while magazine circulation rose from 142.2 per 100 adults to 157.3 over the same years (Sterling & Haight, 1979).

When asked to identify their sources of information about the campaign, the respondents' answers showed parallel changes. Only half said they learned about politics through television in 1952, but this figure rose to 89 percent in 1976. Newspapers dropped slightly from 79 percent to 72 percent, while magazines rose from 41 percent to 48 percent. The pattern that had become established was one of nearly universal television use, wide newspaper reading, and use of magazines by the more literate half of the population.

Media and Information Levels

When we turn from the use of various media to their impact on citizens' information levels, we see something different. Table 17-1 gives measures of association between use of a given medium and the level of information that a respondent has. In 1952 (when there was a mixed pattern of media use), magazines, newspapers, and television all had the same effect on how much a respondent knew. By 1976, however, we have the pattern that we already saw in Table 14-2. The higher measure of association between magazines and information level, and the lower measure of association between television and information level, means that use of the more demanding print medium was producing more information, whereas television was transmitting less information.

While the effects of obtaining information from one medium or another seem to have changed, the effect of simply being involved with the informational environment has not changed at all. Two of the three questions related to citizens' seeking out information (which were reported in Table 14-5) were also asked in 1952. As you can see from Table 17-1, the association between seeking out information and knowing about politics was exactly the same in 1976 as it was in the early 1950s.

Issues and Candidates

As we saw in Chapter 15, there were very few long-term changes in citizens' attitudes about issues and candidates. In spite of repeated

TABLE 17-1
Association between Information Level and Informational Environment, 1952 and 1976

	Measure of Association (Kendall's Tau-c)	
	1952	1976
Medium used		
Magazines	.28	.39
Newspapers	.27	.23
Television	.30	.16
Involvement with informational environment		
Education	.28	.28
Political interest	.43	.40

Data source: 1952 and 1976 SRC/CPS Election Studies.

assertions in the literature that the 1950s were relatively issueless, and that issues did not emerge until the Goldwater challenge to the status quo in 1964, attitudes about issues were quite salient in every single election. They were somewhat more prominent in 1972, 1980, and 1964, but this change was an increase on an already substantial base. Attitudes about political parties have been less salient since 1972, but parties were considerably less visible than issues or candidates throughout the whole period.[17]

The partisan valence of attitudes, of course, varied from election to election. When considering only the three broad categories, attitudes about candidates usually favored the Republicans, and attitudes about issues more often than not favored the Democrats. There are many exceptions to this when the more detailed set of attitudes is considered, but overall the Republicans had the more attractive candidate every year except 1964, and Democrats profited more from issues save for 1968, 1972, and 1980.

When citizens' attitudes are related to their voting decisions, there has been a decline in the importance of parties, but no long-term change in the importance of attitudes about candidates and issues. Attitudes about parties were very important in the 1950s, but have not been so since and played no role in the 1972 election. Candidate attitudes were very important in every election save 1952, and attitudes about issues were the *most* important category in every election except 1976. The probit analysis relating all the attitudes to presidential choice predicted 86 percent of the cases in 1952 and 87 percent of the cases in 1980.

Party Identification

There have been two related changes in party identification. The first was a sharp decline in the mid-60s in the proportion of persons who thought of themselves as Strong Partisans: 38 percent were either Strong Democrats or Strong Republicans in 1952; 27 percent so regarded themselves in 1980. The second has been a gradual growth in the proportion of Independents who do not see themselves as closer to either party. Only 5 percent fell into this category in 1952; 13 percent did so in 1980.

It is important that the effect of these changes be neither overestimated nor underestimated. The decline in the number of Strong Partisans and the increase in the number of Independents open the possibility of wider fluctuation from one election to the next. Hence, the 1980 election results are not as reliable a guide to the 1984 election outcome

---

[17] Whether there ever was a time when attitudes about parties were as salient as attitudes about candidates or issues cannot be determined with these data. Without pre-1952 evidence, we don't know one way or the other.

as the 1952 results were to the 1956 outcome. At the same time, citizens have not been departing from the political parties in very massive proportions. Ninety-one percent of citizens could be classified as Strong, Weak, or Independent Partisans in 1952; 85 percent could be so classified in 1980. The advantage enjoyed by the Democrats over the Republicans as a consequence of party identification was 57 percent to 34 percent in 1952, and 52 percent to 33 percent in 1980. So if we can expect wider fluctuations, we can also expect those fluctuations to be on either side of the same center of political gravity.

It is also important that this relative stability on the aggregate level not be confused with stability on the individual level. The relative stability of party identification types in the population results from an equilibrium condition in which individual changes in one direction are canceled out by individual changes in the opposite direction. When we move to the individual level, it turns out that attitudes are neither more nor less stable in the 1970s than they were in the 1950s. There have been two panel studies that provide data on individual-level stability and change. One was from 1956 through 1960. The second, which provides the data reviewed in Chapter 16, was from 1972 through 1976. When results of the two studies were compared, party identification was just as stable in the 1970s as it was in the 1950s. And "where more specific issues can be directly matched, continuity values seem amazingly stationary across the two panels" (Converse & Markus, 1979, p. 43).

Cognitive Consistency

The extent of cognitive consistency does not seem to have changed over our time period, at least when consistency is measured against a partisan criterion on the individual level. Figure 17-2 shows the distributions for partisan attitude consistency for 1952 and 1976. Partisan attitude consistency does show some variation from election to election. In 1972, probably because George McGovern was perceived to be taking stands that were inconsistent with the preferences of many Democrats, the proportion of completely consistent attitudes was much lower. But as a comparison of the dashed line for 1952 and the solid line for 1976 shows, the proportions of consistent and inconsistent attitudes over the longer time period are virtually the same.

In sum, there are changes in the available media and in the use that is made of them. There has been a decline in the salience and importance of attitudes about political parties, and in the proportion of citizens who think of themselves as Strong Partisans. However, there have not been any changes in citizens' information levels, in the relation between information level and involvement with the informational environment, in the temporal stability of attitudes, in cognitive consis-

FIGURE 17-2
Distribution of Cognitive Consistency, 1952 and 1976

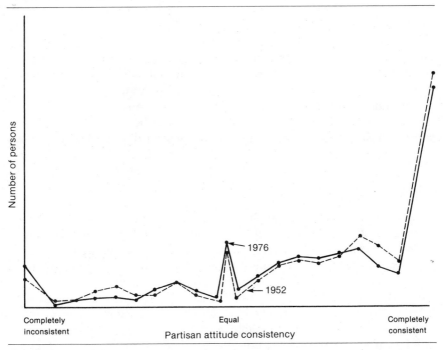

tency, in the partisan advantage resulting from the distribution of party identification, in the salience or importance of attitudes about candidates or issues, or—most important of all—in the relation between these attitudes and the presidential choice made by citizens.

Summary

Enduring Characteristics and Novel Attributes. There is, as always, an amalgam of continuity and change. Let's take the elements of continuity first. Each president has had to address himself to the imperative policy areas, international involvement and economic management, and to the other policy areas as time permitted; each has worked to maintain congressional and public support. The time-use data from the Nixon, Carter, and Reagan administrations suggest that each White House staff is allocating its effort in the same way. Each administration has made a serious effort to avoid the mistakes of its predecessor, and has usually ended up creating new difficulties of its own. Each president has spoken for a national constituency, and has therefore had difficulties persuading representatives and senators that they ought to abandon district and state interests to embrace his vision of the national interest. The level of party voting in Congress has varied in a complex way. The presidents who have been most successful in getting legislative support were those who could work with majorities of their own parties.

The actors who are recruited to nomination and electoral politics continue to be, in Kirkpatrick's nice phrase, the "skill-based middle class." As far back as we have reliable data, activists have been interested in issues. The underlying purposes of coalition building persist. A coalition must recruit delegates to win the nomination, and must persuade voters to win an election. This means there must be a national campaign organization, some means of moving the candidate and his entourage around the country, speeches that explain the candidate's positions, material released in a form that the media can use, funds raised, and so forth. Many of these activities are carried on by professionals, and have been during the period under review.

Most of the cognitive elements underlying citizen response have been quite stable. The amount of information known by the electorate, the partisan consistency of their attitudes, the salience and importance of attitudes about both candidates and issues, and the relation of these attitudes to presidential choice have shown little variation.

What elements have changed? The staff units that served the president in 1950 have been augmented, and new units have been created. More decisions are being brought to the White House to be given "a political twist." Nomination politics has been constricting presidents' opportunities for policy accomplishment because the nomination season is beginning so much earlier, and because incumbents are being challenged more frequently in their own parties. Staffs have also grown considerably on Capitol Hill, but power is now much less concentrated. It is much more difficult for committee chairs to lead their committees, and the House and Senate are more diffuse and less predictable. And with so many more members presenting their own amendments to almost any piece of legislation that comes along, Congress is enacting larger packages of legislation, but fewer of them.

There are now more women among convention delegates. The nomination coalitions are now more apt to be drawn from all parts of the country. Nomination politics now lasts much longer; national party rules are now recognized as superior to state law, and there has been a considerable increase in the proportion of delegates selected in primaries. There have been a number of essentially technological innovations in the conduct of election campaigns. Jet aircraft, television, continual opinion surveys, and computers have become part of campaigns just as they have become part of much of American life in the late 20th century. Professionals who know how to unite this technology with politics now play a larger role in strategy decisions. All this is expensive, and campaigns now cost many times what they did. The Republican party has developed a very successful mass finance drive, and federal funding for presidential campaigns has been available since 1976. At the same time that there has been this increased organizational activity, fewer citizens think of themselves as Strong Partisans, and attitudes about the parties have become even less salient and have declined as factors in determining presidential choice.

Have National Coalitions Become Weaker or Stronger?

Whether any organizational entity has become weaker or stronger depends, of course, on one's point of view. What strengthens one entity may weaken another. Since our concern in this book is with presidential politics, we want to know whether the national coalitions—and the institutions in which they transact their business—have been weakened or strengthened.

To answer this question, we want to focus on the changes just listed. The nonchanges neither weaken nor strengthen. The same thing can be said about short-term changes such as variations in the skill level between one White House staff and its immediate successor, and about offsetting trends in the level of party voting on Capitol Hill. The continuities in organization and citizens' cognitions do mean that parties are *not* disappearing, but that is a slightly different point. So, which changes have weakened and which have strengthened?

I think there are three changes that have weakened national political parties. The first is the frequency with which presidents are challenged for their own party's nomination, and the length of nomination politics. When a president and his immediate assistants have to divert time and resources from executive leadership to protect the president's political base, it becomes more difficult for an administration to make the kind of record on which it should be judged.

Second, I do not think that the Federal Election Campaign Act of 1974 has helped national parties. It does lessen the parties' dependence on interest groups, and it means that the national parties do not have to wait for state parties to meet their quotas in national fund drives. But the act largely removes the national committees from financial decisions about presidential campaigns, and inhibits presidential candidates who might want to conduct their campaigns through the national committees from doing so.

Third, there is the decline in importance of attitudes about parties in citizens' presidential choices and, more particularly, the reduced number of Strong Partisans in the electorate. To be sure, how one sees this depends on whether it is viewed from the perspective of the majority or minority party. From a minority perspective, the increased independence could be seen as giving the minority party a more frequent chance to appeal successfully to enough majority party voters to win. But from the perspective of either party, the smaller number of Strong Partisans means that there is a smaller deliverable vote.

One has to make more contingent judgments, I think, about the organizational changes in the White House and on Capitol Hill. The effect of the increased staff depends very much on the mesh between a given president's needs and his staff's abilities, and on whether a president has the executive capacity to work effectively through a staff. Since presidents are now surrounded by a bureaucracy of several hundred people, it is possible that the staff could become a barrier between the president and other actors whose support he needs. On the other hand, when the staff can give a president information he can use effectively—as the legislative liaison staff's feeding Ronald Reagan accurate information about which members of Congress he ought to contact before an important vote—the staff can genuinely enhance the president's capacity.

The committee chairs have lost power to other members of their committees, but this has not necessarily weakened parties. To the extent that a strong chair supported the party, the party becomes weaker when the chair cannot lead the committee. But Hinckley has shown that 47 percent of Senate Democratic chairs from 1955 through 1966 had party support scores under 60 percent (1971, p. 66). And since party leaders now have greater appointive power (if they choose to exercise it), the leaders are in a stronger position vis-à-vis committee chairs. Speaker O'Neill may look back fondly to the days of Speaker Rayburn, but Speaker O'Neill had much more influence over the Rules Committee chaired by Richard Bolling than Speaker Rayburn ever did over the Rules Committee led by Howard W. Smith.

In general, it could be said that the diffusion of power presents the legislative leadership with a different and probably much more difficult task, but not an impossible one. Party votes have been produced on important occasions. For example, there was a good deal of comment about President Reagan's 217 to 210 victory in the House on a procedural vote that made it possible for the 1981 Gramm-Latta reconciliation bill to pass. But it should be noted that 99 percent of the Republicans voted on one side, and 86 percent of the Democrats voted on the other. These are very high levels of party support, and they hardly sustain any conclusions about weak legislative parties.

And there have been a number of changes that have strengthened *national* parties. The increased number of primaries means that an effectively organized nomination coalition can go into states and win delegates without being beholden to state leaders. The coalitions that are being formed in both nomination and electoral contexts are moving steadily from a regional to a national character. National party rules have been held superior to state law. The Republican party has achieved an independent base of small contributors and now offers a wide range of services. Professionals now have better information about citizens' views and are taking part more frequently in basic strategy decisions. All these changes have tended to produce more nationalized, more professionalized parties.

PRESIDENTIAL PARTIES

In one of the great footnotes in American political science, James Sterling Young commented:

> No nation has been so dependent on statecraft for the effective management of its conflicts and produced so little literature on the subject. (1966, p. 160)

Statecraft, the exercise of political skill, was of particular concern to Young because he was writing about presidential leadership in the Jeffersonian era. The constitution had placed a special responsibility on the president to provide governmental leadership, but it was silent about how that leadership was to be provided. It is likely, Young wrote, that delegates to the constitutional convention

> never comprehended the risks of government by "separate and rival interests," never foresaw a Congress unable to control conflict within itself, and never foresaw that the presidency would have to supply the unifying influence needed to secure the Congress and the fragments of the nation it represented against disintegration. For it would tax the imagination to believe that the framers intended so much to depend on the chance of having a skilled politician for a president. (1966, pp. 159–160)

Political skill is urgently required by the American Constitution. As Richard Neustadt has pointed out, we do not have a separation of powers. Rather we have separate institutions with shared powers. The president submits legislation and vetoes bills he does not like. Congress takes part in the appointive process, and sets the budget. When powers are thus shared, political skill is required on the part of all the actors, but particularly so on the part of the president.

Surveying the long and successful experiment that is American constitutional history, Arthur Holcombe concluded that there have been periods of party government under presidential leadership, party government under congressional leadership, and periods without any effective party leadership (1950, p. 262). His clear preference was for presidential leadership:

> A president who, in dealing with nonpartisan issues, can function effectively as a constitutional chief executive according to the original plan

> can add much to the power and glory of his office, whether he is or is
> not an influential party leader. If he is also an influential party leader,
> he can still further improve his position by a judicious mixture of partisan-
> ship and bipartisanship or nonpartisanship. The superiority of Franklin
> D. Roosevelt's technique of leadership over that of Woodrow Wilson
> is on this point conclusive. (1950, p. 279)

But whatever the form of political leadership, the Constitution made
it inevitable that any American political parties would be presidential
parties. "The heart of national politics," Holcombe wrote, "is the presidential campaign. The only common point about which the leadership
of a durable major party can be organized is the presidency" (1950,
p. 237).

To say that political skill is required, that leadership is important,
and that the presidency is the grand prize in American politics points
to the nature of our constitutional system, but all this does not say
how the leadership is to be supplied. Perhaps the organizing concepts
in this book—internal structure, external structure, and time—permit
some small steps toward an answer.

It is relatively easy to lead within any of the institutional domains
if one is only concerned with internal structure. In nomination politics,
think of the loyalty shown by George Wallace's followers in 1972, by
those who agreed with Ellen McCormack's opposition to abortion in
1976, or by John Anderson's campus supporters in 1980. In electoral
politics, conservative Republicans worked their hearts out for Barry
Goldwater in 1964, just as liberal Democrats did for George McGovern
in 1972. The domestic program submitted to the 81st Congress by President Harry Truman had a good deal of support among Democrats and
in executive agencies. And Minority Leader Charles Halleck was able
to hold House Republicans together in 1962 and 1963 (an average of
82 percent on party unity votes) by emphasizing simple opposition to
President Kennedy's legislative proposals. All of these leaders took
positions popular with members of their coalitions, and all were able
to achieve internal cohesion. But Wallace, McCormack, and Anderson
were unable to attract enough external support for their nomination
bids to become serious. Goldwater and McGovern suffered landslide
defeats. President Truman's domestic program failed to obtain congressional support. And the negative impressions conveyed to the voters
by the Halleck strategy were such that (together with the negative
coattails of the Goldwater campaign) more incumbent Republican representatives were defeated than in any other election since 1950.

The American political system requires the more difficult achievement of maintaining internal support *and* external support. It is even
better if a leader in one institutional domain is able to anticipate the
requirements of another where support for the policies will ultimately
be needed. For example, in March 1980, Richard Wirthlin was already

writing of the need for Governor Reagan to take stands that would better position him for the coming general election campaign, and urging that plans be made to absorb the support of persons then campaigning for George Bush. In 1964, Lyndon Johnson advocated policies in his reelection campaign that he intended to push after the election, and had task forces drawing up specific proposals so he would be in a position to move swiftly to exercise executive leadership. And we saw that, in 1979, Stuart Eizenstat was holding a long series of early evening meetings on energy legislation, and that he was simultaneously consulting with congressional leaders to ascertain the acceptability of the proposals on Capitol Hill. This foresightedness and ability to act on the dual requirements of separate institutional domains brought success to each of these enterprises. Obviously, it is easier to devote attention to external requirements if one is in a strong internal position, but the ability to do so is highly desirable in American statecraft.[18]

Temporal considerations also bear on American political success. In a narrow sense, it is helpful to understand the temporal patterns in one's own institution (and other affected institutions) in order to make time an ally. We saw an example of this in the initial actions plan drawn up by the Reagan aides to take advantage of their early months. With only 51 percent of the 1980 vote, the Reagan administration had a very weak mandate, but their plans allowed them to go far with very modest electoral backing. Senator Russell Long's skillful use of time during the Closing Rush of Business provides another example of the translation of knowledge into political success. In a much broader sense, the proper use of time requires wisdom. The wisdom of being prescient enough to choose an economic policy or energy policy or to launch an international initiative that will pay dividends in unglimpsed years to come. And the wisdom to which Pendleton Herring referred when he wrote, "Leadership under democracy must decide when the times call for consolidation and when they call for renovation to the end that we may advance together to the good life" (1940, p. 86).

In sum, America does not have party government, but constitutional government, and a form of constitutional government that is far more supple, and allows a far wider variety of response, than party government. Leadership in this system does require an understanding of several institutional domains. But given such leadership, our constitutional government should continue to serve us for generations to come.

---

[18] One could generalize this argument to foreign policy as well. The most successful American foreign policy initiatives, such as the Marshall Plan, have been those that were supported by other governments and were drawn with an understanding of the internal situations in the countries to which they were directed.

APPENDIX

INDEXES AND MEASURES

A-4.1 ISSUE SCALES

The basic data for the issue scales were gathered during interviews through a card sorting procedure. Each White House staff member was given a deck of cards with statements such as "America should spend whatever necessary for a strong military force," "Government spending should be cut," and "Busing should not be used to achieve a racial balance in schools." The staff member was asked to indicate his or her position on the issue by placing each card in one of seven squares ranging from "strongly agree" through "not sure" to "strongly disagree."

The items were selected from six policy areas: three items from international involvement, three from economic management, three from social benefits, four from civil liberties,[1] two from natural resources, and one from agriculture. Nine of the items were worded so that agreement would mean taking a conservative position. Agreement with the other seven denoted a liberal position. Eleven of the items corresponded (although the format was different) to questions included in the 1980 fall survey of the electorate conducted by the Center for Political Studies, and eight of the items were repeated from a 1972 study of the Nixon Domestic Council staff.

A few of the respondents took exception to the questions. The essential problem was that they knew too much to respond easily to a simple stimulus. For example, "Government spending should be cut" is imprecise when one has been making decisions about new obligational authority on scores of budget items, and "Welfare payments ought to

---

[1] The "federal power" item, which had been more closely related to economic management in 1972 data, had a higher correlation with the civil liberties cluster in 1980.

be increased" does not correspond to a preference for indexing certain classes of entitlements.[2] But if the card-sort stimuli were too simple to tap everything these elite respondents knew about policy, the items did refer to dimensions that previous investigations had shown were central to presidential policy, and because of its speed the card sort was a useful method to use with exceedingly busy respondents. In short, the card-sort items caused difficulties during a few of the interviews, but nevertheless produced valid measures of the respondents' policy preferences.

The data for members of the Nixon Domestic Council staff were gathered in interviews in November 1972. The data for members of the Carter staff were gathered between October 1980 and March 1981, with the largest number of interviews taking place in December 1980. Collection of the Reagan data was spread over a longer period of time. One respondent was interviewed in December 1980, 3 in January 1981, 21 in March 1981, 4 in July 1981, and 10 in June or July of 1982.[3]

The items and policy areas into which they were grouped to form the issue scales were:

International involvement.
    The government should help countries all over the world. (72)
    America should spend whatever necessary to have a strong military force. (R 72 CPS)
    The United States should try very hard to get along with Russia. (CPS)

Economic management.
    Government spending should be cut. (R 72)
    Inflation must be reduced, even if that means a big increase in unemployment. (R CPS)
    Federal income taxes should be cut. (R CPS)

Social benefits.
    The government ought to help pay everyone's medical bills. (72)
    Welfare payments ought to be increased. (72)
    Government should provide fewer services, even in areas such as health and education. (R CPS)

Civil liberties.
    The federal government is getting too powerful. (R 72 CPS)
    Busing should not be used to achieve a racial balance in schools. (R 72 CPS)

---

[2] The items to which exception was taken were often politically sensitive matters.

[3] For the Reagan staff interviews, the number of respondents and interview dates are for these issue items only. Most other Reagan data were gathered in the summer of 1982, and the number of respondents varied slightly from topic to topic.

> Women should be given preferential treatment in jobs and college
> admission. (CPS)
> Civil rights people have been trying to push too fast. (R CPS)
> Natural resources.
>> Government should relax environmental protection regulations to
>> produce more energy. (R CPS)
> All nuclear power plants should be closed down. (CPS)
> Agriculture.
>> Farmers should be guaranteed a good income. (72)

If agreement would constitute a conservative answer, the item is
followed by an R. Items that were also asked of Nixon staff members
in 1972 are followed by 72. CPS follows items that were on a similar
topic (although worded differently because of the single-stimulus, card-
sort format) to questions asked in the 1980 election study of the Center
for Political Studies.

In scoring the seven items for which agreement was taken to be a
liberal response, strong agreement was given a score of 7 (that is,
most liberal) and strong disagreement was given a score of 1 (that
is, most conservative). With the other nine items, all indicated by an
R, the scoring was reversed, so that strong agreement was given a
score of 1 and strong disagreement a score of 7. Each respondent's
score in each policy area was the mean of the scores for the items
in that policy area.

In order to include comparable Nixon data in Table 4-2, the policy
area scores were calculated using only those items that had been used
both in 1972 and in 1980–82. This did not appreciably change the central
tendencies of the Carter or Reagan staffs, and did permit comparison
of three administrations.

A-4.2 AGREEMENT SCORES

Agreement scores between each pair of White House aides were
calculated on the basis of their answers to the 16 issue items just
discussed in Appendix A-4.1. First, each person's scores were written
as a 16-component vector. As an example, let's take a 10-component
vector, (7,7,7,4,4,4,4,1,1,1). The first three components would correspond
to the most liberal answers; the next four components would correspond
to neutral answers; the last three components would correspond to
the most conservative answers.

Vector subtraction (taking absolute differences) was used to begin
to calculate an observed attitude distance between each pair of persons.
If a person had neutral responses (that is, scores of 4) to every item,
the attitude distance between this person and the example given in
the preceding paragraph would be:

$$(7,7,7,4,4,4,4,1,1,1)$$
$$\underline{(4,4,4,4,4,4,4,4,4,4)}$$
$$(3,3,3,0,0,0,0,3,3,3)$$

One then takes the sum of the components in the vector of absolute differences to obtain an observed attitude distance. In this example, the observed attitude distance would be 18. This procedure assumes that the measurement is accurate enough to permit subtraction (a very strong assumption in view of the measurement method used) and that each attitude is of equal importance, but avoids any other assumption about the spatial location of the components with respect to each other. This is equivalent to what is known as the "city block" method of measuring issue distance. It avoids what I regard as a less-plausible assumption that the issues are related to one another orthogonally, so that euclidean measurement is justified.

The formula for a raw agreement score is:

$$\text{Agreement score} = \left(1 - \frac{\text{Observed attitude distance}}{\text{Maximum attitude distance}}\right)$$

Since the maximum attitude distance in this case is 60 (6 units along each of 10 scales), the raw agreement score in the example would be $(1 - 18/60)$ or .7. The raw agreement scores have the property of varying between a value of 1.0 when both persons give identical responses to every item, and a value of 0 when both persons are located at the opposite ends of every single scale. The agreement scores reported in Chapter 4 (and throughout the book) have been corrected so the 0 point is set at the level that would be obtained with a regular distribution. This follows a suggestion by Weisberg (1978) that a measure should represent percentage agreement over chance. Since a regular distribution has an equal number of responses in each magnitude, this corresponds to the value the agreement score would have by chance when any answer was equally likely to be given. A positive corrected agreement score therefore denotes the extent to which the pair has moved beyond nonconsensus toward complete agreement. A value of 1.0 represents complete agreement with both the raw agreement scores and the corrected agreement scores.

A-4.3 USE OF CLUSTER PROGRAM TO ISOLATE ISSUE GROUPS

The matrix of agreement scores obtained by the procedure just discussed in Appendix A-4.2 was used as input to a modified OSIRIS

CLUSTER program. The OSIRIS CLUSTER program accepts similarities data (for example, correlations or, in this case, agreement scores), and groups the cases with the closest relations to each other in the same cluster. There are three parameters that must be set in the program: STARTMIN, ENDMIN, and STAYMIN. All three stipulate minimum cutoff values that stop the clustering procedure. STARTMIN denotes a minimum score to start a cluster. The clustering procedure begins with the pair of cases having the highest value with respect to each other. As long as there is a pair of cases whose score is higher than STARTMIN when the previous cluster has been assembled, another cluster is begun with the two unclustered cases having the highest score with respect to each other. If there is no pair with a score higher than the stipulated STARTMIN, the clustering procedure terminates. (This is the operational meaning of being an isolate with respect to the issue groups. In addition to being excluded from other groups by the ENDMIN and STAYMIN parameters, there exists no other activist for whom the isolate has an agreement score above the stipulated STARTMIN.)

Once a cluster is begun, the case with the highest average score with respect to the two clustered cases is added to form a three-case cluster. Then the case with the highest average score with respect to the three clustered cases is added to form a four-case cluster. This process continues until there is no unclustered case whose average score with the cases already in the cluster is above ENDMIN. The STAYMIN parameter causes deletion of any case whose average score has fallen below the STAYMIN level (because of the addition of other cases after it was already in the cluster).

Since the procedure considers only unclustered cases when forming new clusters, it has a tendency to inflate earlier clusters at the expense of those formed later. (A later cluster might provide a better fit for a case than the cluster to which it was already assigned, but the case would not be considered for the second cluster.) Therefore, the standard OSIRIS CLUSTER program was modified to check the average score of each case with every existing cluster after all the clusters were formed. Each case with a higher score with another cluster would be moved to it. These moves would, of course, change all the average scores somewhat, so another check would be made, and cases would again be reassigned. The modified program will go through as many iterations of this kind as the user chooses. This is controlled by selecting an ITER parameter. By selecting an appropriately high number, the user can ensure that each case ends up in the cluster with which it has the highest average score.

To this point, the procedure is entirely blind. We do not make any assumptions about the probable character of the groups beyond the definitional stipulation that members of the same group should have common attitudes, and beyond the operational assumption that the clustering procedure would lead to groups with common attitudes. (We avoid any assumption that all lawyers, or all OMB staff members, or all Southerners, or all of any category would belong to the same group.) Once group membership (or the lack of it in the case of isolates) is determined, a new variable is created, denoting the issue group to which each activist belongs, and is added to the data set. The addition of this information as an attribute of each activist made it possible to determine the group characteristics reported in the book.

In the initial analysis runs, the STARTMIN, ENDMIN, and STAYMIN parameters were set at .9, .7, and .7, respectively, for raw agreement scores. The ITER parameter was set at 30. These were the parameters used to isolate issue groups in the House, Senate, and among electoral activists (which are discussed in Chapters 7 and 10). But when these parameters were used with the Carter staff, every staff member turned out to be an isolate, and when they were used with the Reagan staff, a single issue group emerged to which 32 of 39 members belong. In order to find issue groups on the Carter staff, therefore, the STARTMIN, ENDMIN, and STAYMIN parameters were changed from .9, .7, .7 to .85, .7, .7, and to find issue groups on the Reagan staff, the three parameters were changed from .9, .7, .7 to .9, .8, .8. By lowering the STARTMIN parameter for the Carter staff, and raising the ENDMIN and STAYMIN parameters for the Reagan staff, three issue groups were found on both staffs.

The integrity of the issue groups was tested in two ways. First, random scores were generated (and tested for sequential dependency), and were used as data for a hypothetical population. Agreement scores were calculated on the basis of these "attitudes," and the matrix of agreement scores thus derived was used as input to the CLUSTER program. The STARTMIN, ENDMIN, and STAYMIN parameters were again set at .9, .7, .7. No clusters were formed. This meant three things. The level of agreement within our issue groups was above random chance; the procedure used to correct the agreement scores so they would reflect percentage improvement beyond chance was valid; and the issue groups were not just artifacts created by use of the software.

Second, we looked at the within-group and between-group agreement scores of the issue groups. The corrected within-group and between-group agreement scores for the Carter and Reagan staffs are given in Table A-1.

A-4.4 MULTIDIMENSIONAL SCALING

Multidimensional scaling is an analytical technique that accepts similarities data (such as correlations or agreement scores) and provides a geometric plot of the data points, such that the most similar cases

TABLE A-1

	Carter Issue Groups			
	Social Moderates	*Social Liberals*	*Thrifty Libertarians*	*Isolates*
Social Moderates	.44	.25	.31	.24
Social Liberals		.52	.37	.26
Thrifty Libertarians			.49	.24
Isolates				.17

	Reagan Issue Groups			
	Unalloyed Conservatives	*Domestic Conservatives*	*Altruistic Conservatives*	*Isolates*
Unalloyed Conservatives	.69	.59	.51	.40
Domestic Conservatives		.67	.54	.47
Altruistic Conservatives			.66	.37
Isolates				.32

are located closest together and the most dissimilar cases are located farthest apart. Imagine three data points, a, b, and c. Assume that the ab correlation is .9, that the bc correlation is .1, and that the ac correlation is also .1 If these data points were analyzed by multidimensional scaling, a and b should be located quite close together in the resulting plot (because of the high correlation between them), while c should be located equidistant from a and b (because c has the same correlation with both) and much farther away (because the correlation between c and a or b is so low). Achieving such a plot becomes more difficult as the number of data points goes up; but the goal remains that the more closely associated the data, the closer the data points should be to each other. The degree to which this goal is achieved is determined by a measure of the goodness of fit called stress. A stress value of 0 means that the goal has been achieved with every pair of data points; a stress value of 1 means that the configuration is the worst possible.

Multidimensional scaling is a data reduction technique similar to factor analysis or cluster analysis in that it assumes that there is some simpler underlying pattern to the multiple relationships in a large data matrix. If this assumption is correct in a given case, then one should be able to achieve a solution with low stress and low dimensionality. In such a case, the resulting geometric plot can be studied, and the observer's knowledge of the cases may permit an intuitive interpretation of the meaning of the dimensions. For example, if there were a two-dimensional solution in which liberal Democrats appeared in the upper left quadrant, liberal Republicans in the upper right quadrant, conservative Democrats in the lower left quadrant, and conservative Republicans in the lower right quadrant, then the horizontal axis could be interpreted as a Democrat-Republican dimension, and the vertical axis could be interpreted as a liberal-conservative dimension. (For further discussion of the technique itself, see Kruskal & Wish, 1978; and Rabinowitz, 1975.)

The same matrices of agreement scores that were used in the cluster analyses were used as input to the OSIRIS MDSCAL program (the Shepard-Kruskal Multidimensional Scaling Program). With the Carter data, the solution with the lowest stress, .18, had seven dimensions. The stress value meant that this was a good solution, but the seven dimensions meant that there was no simple underlying structure. (The large number of dimensions reflected the extent of disagreement among Carter staff members.) The horizontal axis in Figure 4-1 is the first dimension of the seven-dimension solution. The vertical axis is the second dimension of this seven-dimension solution. With the Reagan staff data, an interpretable plot was found in a four-dimension solution. The stress value, .22, meant this was only a fair solution, but the interpretability and limited number of dimensions were attractive. (There was a five-dimension solution with a lower stress, .18.) The horizontal axis in Figure 4-2 is the first dimension of the four; the vertical axis is the third dimension.

In Figures 4-1 and 4-2, the data points have been denoted by letters corresponding to the issue groups to which the persons belong. In addition to giving some additional understanding of the issue groups through the spatial presentation, it should also suggest the spread in the individual data that underlie our group-level discussion. Members of the same groups appear in the same parts of the issue space, but peripheral members of each group are contiguous to peripheral members of other groups. This form of presentation should also convey some idea of the slightly different results that one obtains by doing a cluster analysis or multidimensional scaling with the same data.

Figures 4-1 and 4-2 should not be compared to each other. The issue space in each results from the relations between the individual data points, and we know that the level of agreement on the Carter staff was much lower than on the Reagan staff.

A-4.5 REDUCED COMMUNICATION MATRICES

The data concerning the communication structures, influence structures, and organizational structures were gathered between October 1980 and March 1981 for the Carter staff, and during the summer of 1982 for the Reagan staff.

Tables 4-5 and 4-6 are second-stage reduced communication matrices. With the Carter staff, the individual data were first arrayed in a 30 × 30 matrix. This matrix was then squared. The resulting second-stage matrix therefore contained information on individuals' abilities to send and receive messages in two stages. Since the principal findings of the communication analysis concerned within-unit and between-unit communication, the 30 × 30 matrix was reduced to focus on the organizational units.

Two things were done in this "reduction." First the 30 × 30 matrix was partitioned so that each row or column contained all the rows (or columns) for persons belonging to a single organizational unit. For example, I had interviewed four members of the National Security Council (NSC) staff, and five economists (four members of the Office of Management and Budget (OMB) staff plus Charles Schultze, the Council of Economic Advisors (CEA) chairman). Therefore the 30 × 30 matrix contained 4 × 4, and 4 × 5, submatrices in the upper left corner corresponding to contacts between these persons. The 4 × 4 submatrix described communications among the NSC staff members, and the 4 × 5 submatrix described communications between the four NSC staff members and the five economists. These submatrices were combined into single cells in Table 4-5. They are the first two cells in the top row. Second, since the sums in the new cells tended to be larger when I had interviewed more persons in a unit, I divided the new cell entry by the mean number of respondents. Since I had interviewed four NSC staff members and five economists, the sum in the leftmost cell in the top row was divided by 4, and the cell next to it was divided by 4.5. Thus the entries that appear in Table 4-5 represent a per capita tendency to send or receive messages.

A similar reduction was carried out with the Reagan data, except that I began with a 32 × 32 matrix because I had communication data on two more staff members. (For further information on the use of communication matrices, see Kemeny, Snell, & Thompson, 1957, pp. 315–19.)

A-4.6 INFLUENCE MATRICES

An influence matrix, as a communication matrix, is a square matrix that contains information on relations between members of the entity being analyzed. The only difference is that the cells in the communication matrix contain 1s or 0s denoting the presence or absence of a communication link, whereas the cells of an influence matrix contain information about the number of influence links. If a person respects another person, regards the person as expert, is concerned about opposition potential, and is subject to the other person's legitimate authority, then the cell entry would be 4. If only three of these bases of influence were available, the entry would be 3; with two bases available, the entry would be 2; and so on down to 0. These cell entries are placed

in the row of the person who is subject to the influence, and in the
column of the person able to exercise the influence. Therefore the row
totals give the total number of influence links to which each individual
is subject. The column totals give the total number of influence links
each person is able to bring to bear. The column totals therefore provide
a measure of each staff member's influence. These are the first-stage
influence scores reported in Tables 4-7 and 4-8.

Arraying the data in this way also allows one to ascertain second-
stage influence relationships by squaring the original matrix. The row
totals are then the number of second-stage influence relationships to
which a person is subject, and the column totals are the number of
second-stage influence relationships a person can bring to bear. The
column totals are the second-stage influence scores reported in Tables
4-7 and 4-8. If one wishes, one can ascertain third-stage influence relationships by taking the cube of the first-stage matrix, fourth-stage relationships by taking it to the fourth power, and so forth. (For further
information on influence matrices, see Kemeny and others, 1957, pp.
307–12.)

Influence data were available for 30 members of the Carter staff,
and 29 members of the Reagan staff, so the analysis began with 30 ×
30, and 29 × 29 matrices, respectively.

Since this method of assessing influence analyzes links between
pairs of individuals, there was a problem with the relative influence
of those who were not interviewed. This was particularly acute with
important persons: Hamilton Jordan and Frank Moore on the Carter
staff, and William Clark, Richard Darman, and David Stockman on
the Reagan staff. In these instances, I inserted a blank row for these
individuals, and a column in which entries were placed when they
were mentioned by persons who were interviewed. This procedure
maintained an equal number of rows and columns, so the matrix could
still be squared to obtain second-stage influence scores. It was in this
way that the estimates were obtained that were reported in Tables
4-7, 4-8, and 4-10. Since the uninterviewed persons were mentioned
by others, and they did not have an opportunity to mention those they
found influential, it is likely that their relative influence was inflated
slightly, particularly in comparison to those they would have mentioned. Obviously, this estimation procedure is not ideal, but it provided
some basis for judgment where the prominence of certain individuals
made this important.

A-4.7 ORGANIZATIONAL IMPORTANCE SCORES

The organizational importance scores were based on responses as
to how much importance one would assign to a recommendation, knowing only the unit from which it had come. The choices were "extremely

important," "very important," "moderately important," "of minor importance," and "of no importance." Interval-level equivalents for these adverbs had been established by psychophysical work in the Laboratory for Political Research at the State University of New York at Stony Brook. The values were: extremely, 79; very, 44; moderate, 10; minor, 5; and of no importance, 1.

The scores reported in Tables 4-9 and 5-3 were grand means (that is, mean scores computed from other means) based on the mean scores of other organizational units. The reason for using this, rather than a mean score of all respondents, can be seen from an example from Carter staff data. The mean importance score for the NSC as estimated by members of Domestic Policy Staff was 44.3; the mean NSC score estimated by members of the NSC staff was 70.3. The mean importance score for the Domestic Policy staff as estimated by members of the NSC staff was 25.8; the mean Domestic Policy Staff score estimated by members of that staff was 58. This illustrates two points. Estimates of the importance of one's own staff tended to be higher. And estimates tended to be higher for other staffs with which one had a lot of contact. (One reason for the discrepancy between the NSC and Domestic Policy Staff estimates was that they didn't have much joint business.) It also happened that I had interviewed seven members of the Domestic Policy Staff, but only four members of the NSC staff. If I had used mean estimates of all respondents, I would have been giving greater weight to the views of staffs where I happened to interview more persons. By excluding estimates of one's own staff, one source of score inflation was removed. And by using a grand mean, greater weight was not given to the views of staffs where I happened to have a larger number of interviews.

As it happens, there was only·one instance on either staff where use of the grand means produced a different ordering of importance. The Carter OMB had a mean rating of 46.4, and a grand mean rating of only 42.3. This small difference was enough to have OMB rank just below the legislative liaison and domestic staffs with the grand mean ratings, instead of just above them as it had with the mean ratings.

A-7.1 CONGRESSIONAL ISSUE GROUPS

The procedure used to isolate issue groups in the House and Senate was the same used to find issue groups on the White House staff, and was discussed in Appendices A-4.2 and A-4.3 above. That is, agreement scores were computed for each pair of representatives, and for each pair of senators. Then the four matrices of agreement scores— one for House Republicans, one for House Democrats, one for Senate Republicans, and one for Senate Democrats—were used as input for the modified OSIRIS CLUSTER programs to find the issue groups. With the White House staff members, however, the agreement scores were computed from their attitudes on individual issues. With the representatives and senators, on the other hand, agreement scores were computed from scale positions based on their roll-call votes.

The scales that were used to compute the agreement scores were the policy dimensions developed by Aage R. Clausen (1973; Clausen and Van Horn, 1977). Professor Clausen had compiled these data, and kindly made his data for the 95th Congress available. Ten policy dimension scales were used to compute the agreement scores for members of the House. They were a national security scale, an international involvement scale, two economic management scales, two social benefit scales, an omnibus civil liberties scale, a civil liberties scale composed of abortion votes, an agricultural subsidy limit scale, and an agricultural assistance scale. The smaller economic management scale, the smaller social benefit scale, and the agricultural subsidy limit scale were not reported in Chapter 7. The smaller economic management and social benefit scales did not contain as many votes, and the median scores of the issue groups on the agricultural subsidy limit scale were quite similar to the median scores on the agricultural assistance scale. But while median scores are only reported on 7 of the scales, all 10 scales were used in the computation of the representatives' agreement scores.

In the Senate, only seven policy scales were used to compute the agreement scores. These seven scales—national security, international involvement, economic management, social benefits, civil liberties, abortion, and agriculture—are all reported in Chapter 7.

The attitude items used to compute the White House agreement scores (and those of the electoral activists) were scales with minimum scores of 1 and maximum scores of 7. The Clausen policy dimension scales had minimum scores of 10 and maximum scores of 30. The attitude distributions were also more likely to be unimodal, while the roll-call distributions were more likely to be bimodal. It was because of these differences in the input data that the "consumer warning" was inserted in Chapter 7. The agreement scores were computed in identical fashion, and the same parameters were used in the CLUSTER program, but I simply do not know whether the same agreement scores represent identical "true" levels of agreement.

The mean corrected within-group and between-group agreement scores for the House and Senate issue groups are shown in Table A-2. Scores for isolates are not included, because such large proportions—96 percent of House Republicans, 96 percent of House Democrats, 82 percent of Senate Republicans, and 88 percent of Senate Democrats—belonged to one of the issue groups.

TABLE A-2

House Democrats

	Pro-abortion Liberals	Anti-abortion Liberals	Dominant Group	Democratic Moderates	Neo-liberals	Pro-Farm Democrats	Tradition-alists	Fundamen-talists
Proabortion Liberals	.61	.36	.45	.09	.25	.02	−.57	−.98
Antiabortion Liberals		.57	.31	.40	.16	−.03	−.29	−.68
Dominant Group			.63	.29	.21	.29	−.28	−.86
Democratic Moderates				.59	.17	.25	.07	−.40
Neoliberals					.50	.28	−.12	−.42
Pro-Farm Democrats						.56	.25	−.32
Traditionalists							.58	.27
Fundamentalists								.51

House Republicans

	Hard-Line Conservatives	Pro-Farm Republicans	Domestic Conservatives	Republican Leaders	Republican Moderates
Hard-Line Conservatives	.59	.40	.23	.21	−.31
Pro-Farm Republicans		.57	.24	.19	−.23
Domestic Conservatives			.56	.28	.21
Republican Leaders				.52	.23
Republican Moderates					.47

Senate Democrats

	Liberals	City Liberals	Centrists	Traditionalists
Liberals	.65	.39	.07	-.30
City Liberals		.60	-.02	-.49
Centrists			.45	.12
Traditionalists				.49

Senate Republicans

	Progressives	Moderates	Proabortion Stalwarts	Antiabortion Stalwarts	Fundamentalists
Progressives	.58	.06	-.63	-.84	-.80
Moderates		.51	-.18	-.11	-.48
Proabortion Stalwarts			.65	.38	.29
Antiabortion Stalwarts				.65	.44
Fundamentalists					.61

A-7.2 MULTIDIMENSIONAL SCALING FOR
CONGRESSIONAL ISSUE GROUPS

Figures 7-1 through 7-4, the two-dimensional portrayals of the legislative issue groups, are based in part on multidimensional scaling. The locations for the centers of the circles representing each of the issue groups were determined through multidimensional scaling. The size of the circles, however, corresponds to the relative size of the groups.

Rather than using the full matrices of agreement scores among all members of the congressional parties as input, the matrices of within- and between-group agreement scores in Table A-2 were used. Since these scores are the mean agreement scores of all members of the group, they correspond in a spatial sense to the centers of the groups. Further, these mean scores yield single data points for each group, and thus suggest group characteristics that would be harder to discern by using individual data, especially with the House of Representatives.

The mean scores were used as input to the OSIRIS MDSCAL program discussed in Appendix A-4.4. Figure 4-1 for House Republicans is based on a three-dimension solution. The horizontal axis is the first dimension, and the vertical axis is the third dimension. Figure 4-2 for House Democrats is based on a five-dimension solution. The horizontal axis is the first dimension, and the vertical axis the second. The figure for the Senate Republicans, 4-3, is based on a two-dimension solution, in which the horizontal axis is the first dimension, and the vertical axis is the second. And Figure 4-4 for the Senate Democrats is based on a three-dimension solution. The horizontal axis is the first dimension, and the vertical axis is the third dimension. The stress values for all of these solutions are virtually 0 (the highest is .005), but with so few data points to plot, it is easy to obtain a perfect solution.

Once the locations for the centers were determined through multidimensional scaling, circles were drawn whose areas were proportional to the sizes of the groups. This has nothing to do with multidimensional scaling at all. The resulting figures should convey two impressions of the issue groups. The relative locations of the groups in issue space can be seen from the *centers* of the circles. And the sizes of the groups should be suggested by the areas of the circles.

A-10.1 DIFFERENCE SCORES

The statement in the interview schedule preceding the six party norms was: "Now let's consider party work. Would you say you feel a *strong* obligation or *some* obligation to do *each of the* following— or to *avoid* doing each of the following—in the conduct of political affairs?" Then each respondent was read statements, such as "Hold strong personal beliefs about a number of different issues" and "Weigh prior service to the party very heavily in selecting candidates for nomination." The answers to these items formed a five-magnitude scale: Strong Obligation to Do, Some Obligation to Do, No Obligation to Do or Avoid, Some Obligation to Avoid, Strong Obligation to Avoid. With Republican activists, for example, the distributions of responses to the two quoted items were:

	Obligation to Do		No Obligation	Obligation to Avoid	
	Strong	Some		Some	Strong
Have personal beliefs	56.5	28.8	12.0	0.5	2.1
Weigh party service	28.8	33.2	30.5	3.7	5.8

The difference scores are simply the difference between the proportion who report a strong obligation to do whatever action is mentioned and the proportion who say they have a strong obligation to avoid that action. This provides a summary measure that can be used in place of the full distribution. In the example, the difference score for Republican activists was 54.4 for holding strong personal issue beliefs, and 23.0 for weighing party service in selecting nominees. Having single numbers facilitates comparisons between parties and between norms. Difference scores of this kind were used by Arthur Miller (1974).

A-10.2 AGREEMENT SCORES FOR ELECTORAL ACTIVISTS

Agreement scores were used for three purposes in the analysis of electoral activists. Agreement scores between activists and citizens were used as measures of attitudinal similarity. Agreement scores using activists' perceptual responses were used with data on citizens' attitudes to measure perceptual accuracy. And agreement scores were computed between each pair of activists to determine their agreement with each other.

For the agreement scores denoting attitudinal similarity, the responses of each activist were matched against the mean responses of citizens interviewed in the activist's county.

In the case of agreement scores for perceptual accuracy, the stimulus items given the activists were adapted to begin with the phrase, "Voters in this area favor . . ." (for example, "Voters in this area favor cutting government spending."). The agreement scores were then calculated between each activist's responses to these perceptual items and the mean responses for the citizens interviewed in the activist's county.

The issue items on which both of the electoral activists' agreement scores with citizens were based were:

International involvement.
   We must bring all American troops back from foreign countries.
   We must have peace in Vietnam.
Economic management.
   Wages and prices should be controlled by the government.
   Government spending should be cut.
Social benefits.
   Welfare payments ought to be increased.
   Social security benefits ought to be increased.
Civil liberties.
   Busing should not be used to desegregate schools.
   The police ought to be given more authority.
Natural resources.
   The government should act to stop pollution.
Agriculture.
   Farmers should be guaranteed a good income.

The agreement scores between the activists themselves were based on the same 10 items, plus 5 more:

International involvement.
   The government should help countries all over the world.
   America should spend whatever is necessary to have a strong
      military force.
Economic management.
   The federal government is getting too powerful.
Social benefits.
   The government ought to help pay everyone's medical bills.
Civil liberties.
   I favor letting Negroes move into white neighborhoods.

All of the agreement scores, whether between activists themselves or between activists and citizens, were computed using the procedure explained in Appendix A-4.2.

A-10.3 ELECTORAL ISSUE GROUPS

Once agreement scores were computed between all Republican activists, and all Democratic activists, the matrices of agreement scores were used as input to the modified OSIRIS CLUSTER program discussed in Appendix A-4.3. After deleting those activists with missing data, we had a 181 × 181 matrix of agreement scores for the Republicans, and a 182 × 182 matrix of agreement scores for the Democrats. In the analysis runs that isolated the issue groups, the STARTMIN, ENDMIN, and STAYMIN parameters were set at .9, .7, .7 for raw agreement scores. The ITER parameter was set at 30. This produced the four Republican issue groups and 65 isolates, and the seven Democratic issue groups and 22 isolates.

Once group membership (or the lack of it in the case of isolates) was determined through this blind procedure, a new variable (denoting the issue group to which each activist belonged) was created and added to the data set. The addition of this information as an attribute of each activist made possible the determination of the attitudinal and demographic characteristic of the groups. The median scores, the discussion of group attitudes on individual issues, the demographic characteristics, and other findings about the electoral issue groups are based on this procedure.

The within- and between-group agreement scores are shown in Appendix A-10.5. The average corrected within-group score was .49 for Republican groups and .51 for Democratic groups. The average corrected between-group score was .35 for Republican groups and .30 for Democratic groups. The average corrected agreement scores were .29 for all Republican activists and .30 for all Democratic activists.

While the CLUSTER program was used in this instance to isolate issue groups from the larger populations of activists, it can also be used to observe how the groups combine into coalitions. This can be done by gradually lowering the parameters, thus determining which cases (and, by inference, which groups) move together. If done in small steps, one can see the stages of coalition formation in something of the same manner that time-lapse photography allows one to observe the opening of a flower. Although no more than a brief reference was made to this in the text, the processes of coalition formation among Republican and Democratic electoral activists were studied in this way. Essentially, the results substantiated the analysis presented in the text.

A-10.4 MULTIDIMENSIONAL SCALING FOR ELECTORAL ISSUE GROUPS

Again, the figures were developed with the aid of multidimensional scaling rather than relying exclusively on that technique. But still another method was used for locating the centers of the circles representing the issue groups. For the electoral activists, five cases were chosen from each of the seven Democratic issue groups, and six cases were chosen from each of the four Republican issue groups. The cases selected from each group were those with the highest average agreement scores with other members of their groups. After this selection, a 35 × 35 matrix of agreement scores was constructed for the Democrats, and a 24 × 24 matrix was constructed for the Republicans. These were used as input to the OSIRIS MDSCAL Program.

Two analysis runs were made with the data for each party. The first began with three dimensions, the second with six. The stress values associated with given numbers of dimensions in each solution are shown in Table A-3. The results suggested several things. The similarity of pattern between the parties (leaving aside the single instance of very high stress for the Democrats) strongly substantiated the argument in the book that the internal structures of the two electoral parties are quite similar. The number of dimensions and high stress values meant that the structures in both parties were multidimensional, and the best MDSCAL solution would have five dimensions. And the lack of a two-dimension solution with a low stress value meant that no two-dimensional plot would provide more than an approximate guide to the location of the groups with respect to each other in an issue space.

The plot that provided the basis for Figure 10-2 came from the four-dimensional Republican solution with dimension 2 as the horizontal axis and dimension 3 as the vertical axis. The plot that provided the basis for Figure 10-3 came from the two-dimensional Democratic solution (in the three-dimension analysis run). Dimension 1 is the horizontal axis, and dimension 2 is the vertical axis. The circles in Figures 10-2 and 10-3 have nothing to do with multidimensional scaling. The MDSCAL plot gave locations for individual group members. I simply assumed that the center of the space defined by the five Democratic or six Republican cases could be taken as the central location of the group in an issue space, and then drew circles proportionate to the size of the groups. The cases belonging to different groups did plot separately in all but one instance. The Dominant Democratic group was located more or less on top of the Thrifty Liberals. I moved the Thrifty Liberals a short distance to an unoccupied area that was consistent with the Thrifty Liberals' proximity to the other Democratic groups.

TABLE A-3

Number of Dimensions	Stress	
	Republicans	Democrats
1	.63	.65
2	.50	.49
3	.41	.38
1	.63	.85
2	.52	.55
3	.38	.36
4	.31	.26
5	.24	.20
6	.25	.21

The *approximate* utility of Figures 10-2 and 10-3 should be emphasized for two reasons. First, the stress values tell us that the Republican
plot gives us only part of a fair solution, and the Democratic plot part
of a poor solution (even before I moved the Thrifty Liberals). Second,
the size of the circles is a useful device to convey an impression of
the relative size of the groups, but some of the individual members
would be located outside the area suggested by the circles. Tables
10-3 and 10-4 contain more accurate information. Figures 10-2 and 10-
3 are visual devices that convey some of this information.

A-10.5 WITHIN- AND BETWEEN-GROUP AGREEMENT SCORES FOR ELECTORAL ISSUE GROUPS

The agreement scores in Table A-4 have been corrected so that 0
corresponds to the degree of agreement expected by chance, and 1.0
corresponds to complete agreement. The figures may therefore be interpreted as the percentage improvement over chance.

A-10.6 CONSENSUS SCORES

The consensus score is another measure of agreement. Whereas
the agreement score is derived from a comparison of individual responses, the consensus score is based on an analysis of the distribution
of responses for the group in question. It rests on two assumptions.
The first is that if consensus does exist in a group, responses should
tend to fall into a modal category. The second is that measurement
error will cause some of the consensual responses to fall into the categories immediately adjacent to the "true" modal category. Therefore, one
is justified in comparing the number of responses actually falling into
the mode and two adjacent categories with the number that would
be expected to do so if there was an equal distribution of answers
in each magnitude of the scale. This leads to the formula:

$$\text{Consensus} = \left(\frac{\text{Frequency observed} - \text{Frequency expected}}{N - \text{Frequency expected}}\right)$$

The consensus score takes on values bounded by +1.0 and

$$\left(\frac{n - f_e}{N - f_e}\right)$$

where n is the minimum number of responses that could be in a modal
category. A value of +1.0 occurs when there is complete consensus—
that is, when all the responses fall into the mode and two adjacent

TABLE A-4

Republicans

	Dominant Group	Conservative Libertarians	Economic Managers	Republican Moderates	Isolates
Dominant Group	.51	.43	.32	.40	.24
Conservative Libertarians		.46	.31	.33	.18
Economic Managers			.45	.30	.20
Republican Moderates				.49	.19
Isolates					.12

Democrats

	Dominant Group	Liberal Pacifists	Liberal Internationalists	Cautious Liberals	Thrifty Liberals	Democratic Moderates	Coercive Individualists	Isolates
Dominant Group	.53	.43	.41	.35	.36	.38	.19	.17
Liberal Pacifists		.52	.28	.31	.33	.29	-.01	.12
Liberal Internationalists			.51	.40	.35	.23	.19	.15
Cautious Liberals				.49	.36	.32	.29	.21
Thrifty Liberals					.52	.32	.22	.17
Democratic Moderates						.47	.27	.17
Coercive Individualists							.44	.14
Isolates								.04

categories. A value of 0 occurs when the number of cases in the mode and two adjacent categories is just that expected if the answers were equally distributed among all categories. Negative values occur when there is disagreement. This would take place if one subgroup agreed with a statement while another subgroup disagreed, thus causing a bimodal rather than a unimodal distribution.

A-14.1 INFORMATION-LEVEL MEASURE

The measure of information level is a simple count of the number of responses given to the series of open-ended questions about parties and candidates. The Center for Political Studies usually codes up to 10 responses (that is, five likes and five dislikes) for each party and candidate. This gives the measure a theoretical range from 0 to 40. The actual range in 1976 was from 0 to 31.

The 1976 distribution of the measure is portrayed in Figure 14-1, and the data are presented in Table A-5. The mean value is 7.1, and the standard deviation is 5. The categories for Table 14-1 (and subsequent cross-tabulations) started at the mean value. A new category began at each standard deviation (except for the highest, where there were very few cases).

This measure makes the same assumption that is made for open-ended questions: that the better-informed person will say more about a topic than a less-informed person. It is open to the challenge that a garrulous person will say more than a taciturn person even though the latter may know more. In order to check the validity of this information-level measure, correlations were run between it and a host of other variables with which it might be related. The highest correlation (Tau-c = .44) was with the interviewer's own estimate of the respondent's level of political information. Other high correlations are shown in Table A-6. Since all of these variables should be correlated with a true measure of political information, this measure appears to be valid.

TABLE A-5

Information-Level Category	Number of Responses	Percent of Electorate
Low	0–1–2	17.5%
Average minus	3–4–5–6–7	41.2
Average plus	8–9–10–11–12	25.5
High	13–14–15–16–17	11.7
Very high	18–19–20–21–22	3.2
Extremely high	23 through 31	0.9

TABLE A-6

Related Variable	Kendall's Tau-c
Interest in the campaign	.40
Reads about national politics in newspapers	.40
Reads magazines	.39
Follows public affairs	.37
Tries to influence another person's vote	.35
Reads about international affairs in newspapers	.35
Interviewer's estimate of respondent's intelligence	.34

A-15.1 PROBIT ANALYIS

Probit analysis is a technique first developed in biology, and then extended to economics. It was introduced in political science by Gerald H. Kramer (1965, 1971), and more recently has been employed by a number of others (McKelvey & Zavonia, 1969; Aldrich & Cnudde, 1975; Rosenstone & Wolfinger, 1978; Fiorina, 1981). It was developed to handle the problem of a dichotomous dependent variable. It has since been extended to other applications, but it is the dichotomous dependent variable that makes it particularly appropriate for voting analyses.

The problem can be visualized with a single independent and a single dependent variable. If both are free to vary, then a relationship is shown by drawing a regression line that minimizes the distance of any data point from the line. If the relationship is as shown in the figure ($y = bx + u$ where $b = 1$), then one would say that the two variables are related because a unit change in x would be associated with a unit change in $y \pm$ an error term, u.

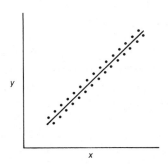

Now consider what happens if y, the dependent variable, can take on just two values. No matter what kind of straight line one draws, as in (A) or (B), many of the data points are going to be far from the line. A line also "predicts" that many of the data points should fall in the middle of the two values or outside of the values. Since the dependent variable is restricted to the two values, this is impossible. If, however, one draws an S curve as in (C), then a great many of the data points are going to be located close to the curve, and few "impossible" predictions will be made.

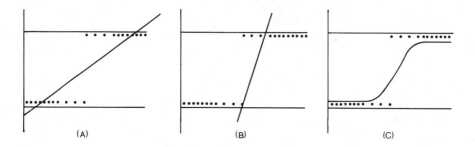

(A)   (B)   (C)

There are several functions in the mathematical literature that produce an S curve of the desired form. All of these rely on some assumed underlying distribution. If the two values are 1 and 0, then the basic model is:

$$P = \text{Prob}(Y_i = 1) = F(\beta' X_i) \text{ and } P = \text{Prob}(Y_i = 0) = 1 - F(\beta' X_i)$$

One of the functions that can be used to estimate these probabilities is to assume that $F(\beta' X_i)$ has a cumulative normal distribution. In this case, a change in one unit of the independent variable will produce a change in the probability that $Y_i = 1$ by an amount that is directly proportional to $\beta' F(\beta'X_i)$. Unlike simple linear regression, these equations cannot be solved. They can only be estimated. Therefore the interpretation is altered from a statement that a unit change in x will produce a change of so many units in y, to a maximum likelihood estimate that a unit change in X_i will produce a change in the *probability* that Y_i will take on one value rather than the other. (The word probit in probit analysis is an abbreviation for probability unit. It is also sometimes called "normit" by way of reference to the cumulative normal distribution.) It is obviously more complex than regression analysis, but its assumptions make it a superior form of analysis for voting data. Its increased power can be shown by comparing the probit solutions used in Chapter 15 with regression solutions using identically coded independent variables. Using 1976 data, the regression solution explained 47 percent of the variance in the vote, while the probit solution explained 73 percent of the variance. The 1980 regression solution for the major party candidates explained 51 percent of the variance in the vote, whereas the comparable probit solution explained 80 percent of the variance. (For further information about probit analysis, see Hanushek & Jackson, 1977, chap. 7; Aldrich & Cnudde, 1975; Nelson, 1976; Nelson & Olson, 1978; and Fiorina, 1981, Appendix A.)

The maximum likelihood estimates in Chapter 15 were reported as MLE* to denote the fact that they had been standardized. The computer program written (and kindly made available) by Richard McKelvey does not contain any standardization. Indeed, it is questionable if one should do this at all. The computer program does supply the sample variance for the independent and dependent variables. This made it possible to standardize by multiplying by the ratio of the square roots of the sample variances. In other words, the maximum likelihood estimate is standardized by multiplying it by the standard deviation of the independent variable divided by the standard deviation of the dependent variable.

The reason for standardizing can be seen from an example. The maximum likelihood estimates for economic management and agriculture in 1976 were .29 and .52, respectively. This suggests that attitudes about agriculture were more important in 1976 than attitudes about economics. Now recall that a unit change in any independent variable produces a change in the probability that the dependent variable will take on one value rather than the other. This is important because the variance for economic management was 3.52 and the variance for agriculture was .05. This means that attitudes on economics vary across more units than attitudes on agriculture, and therefore have more opportunities to affect vote. It is this consideration that one takes into account when standardizing. In this example, standardization increases the maximum likelihood estimate for economics from .29 to 1.10, and decreases the MLE for agriculture from .52 to .25, thereby reflecting the much greater range through which economic attitudes vary, and the restricted range for attitudes on agriculture.

Another reason for standardizing in this particular way is related to a goal of the analysis. By controlling for the effects of variance, standardization allows a better comparison between the effects of the attitude components in a given election. But we also want to be able to make comparisons across elections—and it happens that the variance for vote has been remarkably stable (see Table A-7). The variance was slightly depressed in the one-sided elections of 1964 and 1972, but even including those years, the variance in the dependent variable (i.e., vote) has been relatively steady. This means that when one uses this method of standardization for any one election, the denominator of the ratio is quite similar for other years, allowing us to make comparisons across elections.

TABLE A-7

Year	Sample Variance for Vote
1952	.244
1956	.241
1960	.250
1964	.219
1968	.248
1972	.230
1976	.250
1980	.246

A-15.2 ATTITUDE CATEGORIES FOR VOTING ANALYSES

The Center for Political Studies master code categories in 1976 are shown in Table A-8. For the three broad attitude categories, the master

TABLE A-8

Candidate, general	0009, 0036, 0201, 0223–0224, 0427–0430, 0443–0455, 0457, 0497–0498, 0505, 0701–0711, 0721–0722, 0797
Record—incumbency	0217, 0553, 0554, 0611
Experience	0211–0212, 0215–0216, 0218–0221, 0297, 0313, 0314, 0425–0426, 0456
Management	0311–0312, 0407–0408, 0601–0602, 0605–0610, 0612, 0697, 0841–0842
Intelligence	0413–0422
Trust	0213–0214, 0307–0308, 0309–0310, 0401–0404, 0431, 0432, 0603, 0604, 1010–1020
Personality	0301–0306, 0315–0320, 0411–0412, 0423–0424, 0433–0442, 0459–0460
People in party	0001–0008, 0010–0035, 0037–0097, 0502–0504, 0508, 0541–0542
Party affect	0101–0197, 0500–0501, 0506, 0507, 0597
Issues—general	0509–0512, 0515–0518, 0531–0536, 0551–0552, 0720, 0801–0828, 0843–0897, 0900, 0934–0935, 0997, 1297
International involvement	0513–0514, 0519–0520, 1101–1172, 1175–1177, 1179–1197
Economic management	0901–0904, 0911–0913, 0926–0933, 0936–0941, 0952–0958, 1007–1009, 1201–1214
Social benefits	0905–0910, 0914–0925, 0965–0967, 0994–0996 1001–1003, 1219, 1222, 1227–1228, 1233–1234
Civil liberties	0405–0406, 0946–0951, 0968–0993, 1173–1174, 1178, 1217–1218, 1223–1226, 1229–1232
Natural resources	0959–0964, 1004–1006
Agriculture	0942–0945, 1215–1216
Missing data	9001–9002, 9996–9999, 0000

codes in the seven candidate categories, the two party categories, and the seven issue categories were simply combined. Parallel coding decisions were made for the other years.

A-16.1 INDICES OF PARTISAN ISSUE CONSISTENCY AND PARTISAN ATTITUDE CONSISTENCY

Both of the indices were based on the assumption that partisans would have more favorable perceptions of their own party than of the opposition. Strong Republicans, Weak Republicans, and Independent Republicans were regarded as consistent if they evaluated the Republican party more highly than the Democratic party. The opposite convention applied to Strong Democrats, Weak Democrats, and Independent Democrats. Independents were excluded from these scales.

The Index of Partisan Attitude Consistency was constructed from the responses to five issue items and the associated perceptions of the candidates. The issue items included were:

Welfare payments ought to be increased.

The police ought to be given more authority.

America should spend whatever is necessary to have a strong military force.

We must have peace in Vietnam.

Busing should not be used to desegregate schools.

Each respondent answered these questions by placing a card containing the statement in one of seven positions ranging from Strongly Agree to Strongly Disagree on a sort board. Each of the five items was adapted so the respondents could similarly indicate their perceptions of the two presidential candidates. For example:

McGovern as president would increase welfare payments.

Nixon as president would increase welfare payments.

For each item, a respondent was given a score of 1 if their own party's candidate was perceived as being closest to their preferred position, a score of 0 if the opposition candidate was perceived as being closest to their preferred position, and a score of .5 if the candidates were perceived as being equidistant from their preferred position. The respondent's score on the Index of Partisan Issue Consistency was the average of these item scores for the items on which the respondent expressed a preference and reported perceptions of both presidential candidates.

The Index of Partisan Attitude Consistency is based on the open-ended questions that were used to analyze information level and presidential vote choice. A score of +1 was assigned to each comment that favored the respondent's own party or criticized the opposition party. A score of −1 was assigned to each comment that criticized the respondent's own party or favored the opposition party. The sum of these scores was divided by the total number of comments. This produced a raw index that varied between +1 for complete partisan consistency and −1 for complete partisan inconsistency. The raw scores were then adjusted to bounds of 1 for complete consistency and 0 for complete inconsistency so as to be comparable to the Index of Partisan Issue Consistency.

BIBLIOGRAPHY

Abramson, Paul R. (1975) *Generational Change and the Decline of Party Identification.* Lexington, Mass.: Lexington Books.

————. (1983) *Political Attitudes in America: Formation and Change.* San Francisco: W. H. Freeman.

Abramson, Paul R., and Aldrich, John H. (1982) "The Decline of Electoral Participation in America." *American Political Science Review* (September) pp. 502–521.

Abramson, Paul R., Aldrich, John H., and Rhode, David W. (1982) *Change and Continuity in the 1980 Elections.* Washington, D.C.: Congressional Quarterly Press.

Adrian, Charles, and Press, Charles. (1968) "Decision Costs in Coalition Formation." *American Political Science Review* (June) pp. 556–563.

Aldrich, John H. (1980a) *Before the Convention: A Theory of Campaigning for the 1976 Presidential Nomination.* Chicago: University of Chicago Press.

————. (1980b) "A Dynamic Model of Pre-Convention Campaigns." *American Political Science Review* (September) pp. 651–669.

Aldrich, John H., and Cnudde, Charles. (1975) "Probing the Bounds of Conventional Wisdom: A Comparison of Regression, Probit, and Discriminant Analysis." *American Journal of Political Science* (August) pp. 571–608.

Aldrich, John H., Gant, Michael, and Simon, Dennis. (1978) "To the Victor Belong the Spoils: Momentum in the 1976 Nomination Campaigns." Paper prepared for the 1978 Meeting of the Public Choice Society.

Alexander, Herbert E. (1972) *Political Financing.* Minneapolis, Minn.: Burgess.

————. (1976) *Financing the 1972 Election.* Lexington, Mass.: D. C. Heath.

————. (1980) *Financing Politics: Money, Elections, and Political Reform.* 2d ed. Washington, D.C.: Congressional Quarterly Press.

————. (Forthcoming) "Making Sense about Dollars in the 1980 Presidential Campaign." In Michael J. Malbin, ed., *Parties, Interest Groups, and Money in the 1980 Elections.* Washington, D.C.: American Enterprise Institute.

Anderson, Patrick. (1968) "The New Defense Secretary Thinks Like the President" in *The New York Times Magazine,* January 28, pp. 20–21, 70, 72–75.

Apple, R. W., Jr. (1976) "The Ethnics

Vote in the States that Really Count." *New York Times,* October 10, p. E1.

Arrington, Theodore S. (1975) "Some Effects of Political Experience on Issue Consciousness and Issue Partisanship among Tucson Party Activists." *American Journal of Political Science* (November) pp. 695–702.

Arterton, F. Christopher. (1978) "Campaign Organizations Confront the Media-Political Environment" in James D. Barber, ed., *Race for the Presidency: the Media and the Nominating Process.* Englewood Cliffs, N.J.: Prentice-Hall.

————. (1984) *Media Politics: The News Strategies of Presidential Campaigns.* Lexington, Mass.: Lexington Books.

Asher, Herbert B. (1984) *Presidential Elections and American Politics: Voters, Candidates and Campaigns since 1952.* 3d ed. Homewood, Ill.: Dorsey Press.

Axelrod, Robert. (1972) "Where the Votes Come From: An Analysis of Electoral Coalitions, 1952–1968." *American Political Science Review* (March) pp. 11–20.

————. (1982) "Communication." *American Political Science Review* (June) pp. 393–396.

Balch, George. (1974) "Multiple Indicators in Social Research: The Concept of Political Efficacy." *Political Methodology* (Spring) pp. 1–43.

Barber, James David. (1974) *Choosing the President.* Englewood Cliffs, N.J.: Prentice-Hall.

————. (1978) *Race for the Presidency: The Media and the Nominating Process.* Englewood Cliffs, N.J.: Prentice-Hall.

Barrett, Laurence I. (1983) *Gambling with History: Reagan in the White House.* New York: Doubleday Publishing.

Beck, Paul Allen. (1974) "Environment and Party: The Impact of Political and Demographic County Characteristics on Party Behavior." *American Political Science Review* (September) pp. 1229–1244.

Bennett, W. Lance. (1977) "The Growth of Knowledge in Mass Belief Systems: An Epistomological Critique." *American Journal of Political Science* (August) pp. 465–500.

Berman, Larry. (1979) *The Office of Management and Budget and the Presidency 1921–1979.* Princeton, N.J.: Princeton University Press.

Bibby, John F. (1981) "Party Renewal in the National Republican Party." In Gerald M. Pomper, ed., *Party Renewal in America: Theory and Practice.* New York: Praeger Publishers.

————. (1983) *Congress Off the Record: The Candid Analyses of Seven Members.* Washington, D.C.: American Enterprise Institute.

Bibby, John F., Cotter, Cornelius P., Gibson, James L., and Huckshorn, Robert J. (1982) "Parties in State Politics." In Herbert Jacob and Virginia Gray, eds., *Politics in the American States.* Boston: Little, Brown.

Bishop, George E., Tuchfarber, Alfred J., and Oldendick, Robert W. (1978) "Change in the Structure of American Political Attitudes: The Nagging Question of Question Wording." *American Journal of Political Science* (May) pp. 250–269.

Bone, Hugh A. (1971) *American Politics and the Party System.* New York: McGraw-Hill.

Brams, Steven J. (1978) *The Presidential Election Game.* New Haven, Conn.: Yale University Press.

Brams, Steven J., and Fishburn, Peter C. (1978) "Approval Voting." *American Political Science Review* (September) pp. 831–847.

————. (1983) *Approval Voting.* Cambridge, Mass.: Birkhauser Boston.

Broder, David S. (1970) "Reporters in Presidential Politics." In Charles Peters and Timothy J. Adams, eds., *Inside the System.* New York: Praeger Publishers.

————. (1980) *Changing of the Guard: Power and Leadership in America.* New York: Simon & Schuster.

————. (1981) "Diary of a Mad Majority Leader." *Washington Post* (December 13) pp. C1, C5.

Brody, Richard A. (1977) "Stability and Change in Party Identification: Presidential to Off-Years." Paper prepared for delivery at the 1977 Annual Meeting of the American Political Science Association, Washington, D.C.

Bunce, Valerie. (1981) "Policy Cycles and the American Presidency." Paper prepared for the Annual Meeting of the Midwest Political Science Association, Cincinnati, Ohio.

Burnham, Walter Dean. (1970) *Critical Elections and the Mainsprings of American Politics.* New York: W. W. Norton.

————. (1975) "American Politics in the 1970s beyond Party?" In William N. Chambers and Walter Dean Burnham, eds., *The American Party Systems: Stages of Political Development.* 2d ed. New York: Oxford University Press, pp. 308–357.

Caddell, Patrick and Wirthlin, Richard. (1981) "Face Off: A Conversation with the President's Pollsters." *Public Opinion* (December/ January) pp. 2–12, 63–64.

Campbell, Angus, Converse, Philip E., Miller, Warren E., and Stokes, Donald E. (1960) *The American Voter.* New York: John Wiley & Sons.

Campbell, Angus, Gurin, Gerald, and Miller, Warren E. (1954) *The Voter Decides.* Evanston, Ill.: Row, Peterson.

Cannon, James M. (1960) *Politics, U.S.A.: A Practical Guide to the Winning of Public Office.* New York: Doubleday Publishing.

Cannon, Lou. (1982) *Reagan.* New York: G. P. Putnam's Sons.

Carmines, Edward G., and Stimson, James A. (1981) "Issue Evolution, Population Replacement, and Normal Partisan Change." *American Political Science Review* (March) pp. 107–118.

Cartwright, Dorwin. (1965) "Influence, Leadership, Control." In James G. March, ed., *Handbook of Organizations.* Skokie, Ill.: Rand McNally.

Cattani, Richard J. (1983) "The 'Big Bang' Theory of '84 Politics." *Christian Science Monitor,* February 17, pp. 1–9.

Chester, Lewis, Hodgson, Godfrey, and Page, Bruce. (1969) *An American Melodrama: The Presidential Campaign 1968.* New York: Viking Press.

Clarke, James W. (1970) Personal communication.

Clausen, Aage R. (1972) "State Party Influence on Congressional Party Decisions." *Midwest Journal of Political Science* (February) pp. 70–101.

————. (1973) *How Congressmen Decide: A Policy Focus.* New York: St. Martin's Press.

Clausen, Aage R., and Cheney, Richard B. (1970) "A Comparative Analysis of Senate and House Voting on Economic and Welfare Policy: 1953–1964." *American Political Science Review* (March) pp. 138–152.

Clausen, Aage R., and Van Horn, Carl E. (1977) "The Congressional Response to a Decade of Change: 1963–1972." *Journal of Politics* (November) pp. 624–666.

Cochran, James L. (1981) "Carter Energy Policy and the Ninety-Fifth Congress." In Craufurd D. Goodwin, ed., *Energy Policy in Perspective: Today's Problems, Yesterday's Solutions.* Washington, D.C.: Brookings Institution.

Comparative State Election Project. (1973) *Explaining the Vote: Presidential Choices in the Nation and the States.* Chapel Hill, N.C.: Institute for Research in Social Science.

Congressional Quarterly Weekly Report (various issues).

Congressional Quarterly. (1979) *Energy Policy.* Washington, D.C.: Congressional Quarterly Press.

Converse, Philip E. (1964) "The Nature of Belief Systems in Mass Publics." In David E. Apter, ed., *Ideol-*

ogy and Discontent. New York: Free Press.

————. (1972) "Change in the American Electorate." In Angus Campbell and Philip E. Converse, eds., *The Human Meaning of Social Change.* New York: Russell Sage Foundation.

————. (1975) "Public Opinion and Voting Behavior." In Fred I. Greenstein and Nelson W. Polsby, eds., *Handbook of Political Sciences.* Vol. 4. Reading, Mass.: Addison-Wesley Publishing.

————. (1976) *The Dynamics of Party Support: Cohort Analyzing Party Identification.* Beverly Hills, Calif.: Sage Publications.

Converse, Philip E., and Markus, Gregory B. (1979) "Plus ca change . . . : The New CPS Election Study Panel." *American Political Science Review* (March) pp. 32–49.

Corwin, Edward S. (1948) *The President Office and Powers, 1787–1948: History and Analysis of Practice and Opinion.* 3d rev. ed. New York: New York University Press.

Costain, Anne N. (1978) "An Analysis of Voting in American National Nominating Conventions, 1940–1976." *American Politics Quarterly* (January) pp. 375–394.

Cotter, Cornelius P., and Hennessy, Bernard C. (1964) *Politics without Power: The National Party Committees.* New York: Atherton.

Cotter, Cornelius P., and Bibby, John F. (1979) "The Impact of Reform on the National Party Organizations: The Long-Term Determinants of Party Reform." Paper prepared for delivery at the 1979 Annual Meeting of the American Political Science Association, Washington, D.C.

Crewe, Ivor. (1981) "Electoral Participation." In David Butler, Howard R. Penniman, and Austin Ranney, eds., *Democracy at the Polls: A Comparative Study of Competitive National Elections.* Washington, D.C.: American Enterprise Institute.

Cronin, Thomas E. (1980) *The State of the Presidency.* 2d ed. Boston: Little, Brown.

Cross, Christopher T. (1981) "If the White House Calls to Offer a Top Job, Hang Up." *Washington Post,* March 26, pp. C1–C3.

Crotty, William J. (1980) *The Party Symbol: Readings on Political Parties.* San Francisco: W. W. Freeman.

Crotty, William J., and Jacobson, Gary C. (1980) *American Parties in Decline.* Boston: Little, Brown.

David, Paul T., Goldman, Ralph M., and Bain, Richard C. (1960) *The Politics of National Party Conventions.* Washington, D.C.: Brookings Institution.

Davidson, Roger H. (1981) "Subcommittee Government: New Channels for Policy Making" in Thomas E. Mann and Norman J. Ornstein, eds., *The New Congress.* Washington D.C.: American Enterprise Institute.

Davis, Eric L. (1983) "Legislative Liaison: The People and the Institutions." In Anthony King, ed., *Both Ends of the Avenue.* Washington, D.C.: American Enterprise Institute.

Dennis, Jack. (1981) "On Being an Independent Partisan Supporter." Paper prepared for delivery at the 1981 Annual Meeting of the Midwest Political Science Association, Cincinnati, Ohio.

Destler, I. M. (1974) *Presidents, Bureaucrats, and Foreign Policy: The Politics of Organizational Reform.* Princeton, N.J.: Princeton University Press.

————. (1975) "National Security Advice to Presidents." Paper prepared for a Conference on Presidential Advising sponsored by the Princeton University Politics Department and the Woodrow Wilson School, Princeton, N.J.

Dexter, Lewis A. (1969) "Congressmen and the Making of Military Policy." In Robert L. Peabody and Nelson W. Polsby, eds., *New Perspectives on the House of Representatives.* 2d ed. Skokie, Ill.: Rand McNally.

Dodd, Lawrence C., and **Oppenheimer, Bruce I.** (1981) *Congress Reconsidered.* 2d ed. Washington, D.C.: Congressional Quarterly Press.

Downs, Anthony. (1957) *An Economic Theory of Democracy.* New York: Harper & Row.

Drew, Elizabeth. (1977) *American Journal: The Events of 1976.* New York: Random House.

―――. (1981a) "Early Days." *New Yorker* (March 16).

―――. (1981b) *Portrait of an Election: The 1980 Presidential Campaign.* New York: Simon & Schuster.

Edwards, George C., III. (1983) *The Public Presidency: The Pursuit of Popular Support.* New York: St. Martin's Press.

Eldersveld, Samuel J. (1964) *Political Parties: A Behavioral Analysis.* Skokie, Ill.: Rand McNally.

―――. (1982) *Political Parties in American Society.* New York: Basic Books.

Epstein, Leon D. (1974) "Political Parties." In Fred I. Greenstein and Nelson W. Polsby, eds., *Handbook of Political Science.* Vol. 4. Reading, Mass.: Addison-Wesley Publishing.

Erikson, Robert S. (1971) "The Electoral Impact of Congressional Roll Call Voting." *American Political Science Review* (December) pp. 1018–1032.

Everson, David H. (1980) *American Political Parties.* New York: New Viewpoints.

Fallows, James. (1979) "The Passionless Presidency." *Atlantic* (May) pp. 33–48 (June) pp. 75–81.

Farah, Barbara G. (1982) "Political Ambition: An Enduring Quest among Political Activists." Paper prepared for delivery at the 1982 Annual Meeting of the American Political Science Association, Denver, Colo.

Farah, Barbara G., Jennings, M. Kent, and **Miller, Warren E.** (1982) *Report to Respondents: The 1980 Convention Delegate Study.* Ann Arbor, Mich.: Institute for Social Research.

Fenno, Richard F. (1973) *Congressmen in Committees.* Boston: Little, Brown.

―――. (1978) *Home Style: House Members in their Districts.* Boston: Little, Brown.

―――. (1983) *The United States Senate: A Bicameral Perspective.* Washington, D.C.: American Enterprise Institute.

Ferber, Mark F. (1971) "The Formation of the Democratic Study Group." In Nelson W. Polsby, ed., *Congressional Behavior.* New York: Random House.

Fiorina, Morris P. (1977) "An Outline for a Model of Party Choice" in *American Journal of Political Science* (August) pp. 601–625.

―――. (1981) *Retrospective Voting in American National Politics.* New Haven, Conn.: Yale University Press.

Fishel, Jeff. (1977) "Agenda Building in Presidential Campaigns: The Case of Jimmy Carter." Paper prepared for delivery at the 1977 Annual Meeting of the American Political Science Association, Washington, D.C.

Flanigan, William H., and **Zingale, Nancy H.** (1979) *Political Behavior of the American Electorate.* 4th ed. Boston: Allyn & Bacon.

Fogel, Norman J. (1974) *The Impact of Cognitive Inconsistency on Electoral Behavior.* Ph.D. dissertation, Ohio State University, Columbus.

Ford, Gerald R. (1979) *A Time to Heal.* New York: Harper & Row.

Fortune. (1935) "The Democratic Party" (April) p. 136. Cited in Herring (1940) p. 265.

Frankel, Max. (1965) "The Importance of Being Bundy." *New York Times Magazine,* March 28, pp. 32–33, 94–98.

―――. (1968) "Seek to Counter Survey's Impact." *New York Times,* October 9, p. 34.

Gatlin, Douglas. (1973) "Florida." In Comparative State Election Project, *Explaining the Vote: Presidential Choices in the Nation and the*

States, 1968. Chapel Hill, N.C.: Institute for Research in Social Science.

Gelb, Leslie H. (1980) "Muskie and Brzezinski: The Struggle over Foreign Policy." *New York Times Magazine,* July 20, pp. 26–27, 32, 34–40.

George, Alexander L. (1972) "The Case for Multiple Advocacy in Making Foreign Policy." *American Political Science Review* (September) pp. 751–785.

————. (1980) *Presidential Decisionmaking in Foreign Policy: The Effective Use of Information and Advice.* Boulder, Colo.: Westview Press.

Gerston, Larry N., Burstein, Jerome S., and **Cohen, Stephen S.** (1979) "Presidential Nominations and Coalition Theory." *American Politics Quarterly.*

Gertzog, Irwin N. (1976) "The Routinization of Committee Assignments in the U.S. House of Representatives." *American Journal of Political Science* (November) pp. 693–712.

Gibson, James L., Cotter, Cornelius P., Bibby, John F., and **Huckshorn, Robert J.** (1981) "Assessing Institutional Party Strength. Paper prepared for delivery at the 1981 Annual Meeting of the Midwest Political Science Association, Cincinnati, Ohio.

————. (1982) "Whither the Local Parties?: A Cross-Sectional and Longitudinal Analysis of Party Organizations. Paper prepared for delivery at the 1982 Annual Meeting of the Western Political Science Association, San Diego, Calif.

Goodwin, George, Jr. (1970) *The Little Legislatures: Committees of Congress.* Amherst: University of Massachusetts Press.

Graber, Doris A. (1976) "Press and TV as Opinion Resources in Presidential Campaigns," *Public Opinion Quarterly* (Fall) pp. 285–303.

————. (1980) *The Mass Media and Politics.* Washington, D.C.: *Congressional Quarterly Press.*

————. (1982b) "Hoopla and

Horse-Race in 1980: Campaign Coverage: A Closer Look." Paper prepared for delivery at the 1982 Annual Meeting of the Midwest Association for Public Opinion Research, Chicago.

————. (1982a) *The President and the Public.* Philadelphia: Institute for the Study of Human Issues.

Greeley, Andrew M. (1974) *Building Coalitions: American Politics in the 1970's.* New York: Franklin Watts.

Greenstein, Fred I. (1974) "What the President Means to Americans." In James David Barber, ed., *Choosing the President.* Englewood Cliffs, N.J.: Prentice-Hall.

————. (1978) "Change and Continuity in the Modern Presidency." In Anthony King, ed., *The New American Political System.* Washington, D.C.: American Enterprise Institute.

————. (1982) *The Hidden-Hand Presidency: Eisenhower as Leader.* New York: Basic Books.

————. (1983) *The Reagan Presidency: An Early Assessment.* Baltimore: The Johns Hopkins Press.

Grossman, Michael Baruch, and **Kumar, Martha Joynt.** (1981) *Portraying the President: The White House and the News Media.* Baltimore: The Johns Hopkins Press.

Guylay, L. Richard. (1960) "Public Relations." In James W. Cannon, ed., *Politics, U.S.A.: A Practical Guide to the Winning of Public Office.* New York: Doubleday Publishing.

Hanushek, Erik A., and **Jackson, John E.** (1977) *Statistical Methods for Social Scientists.* New York: Academic Press.

Hart, Gary W. (1973) *Right from the Start: A Chronicle of the McGovern Campaign.* New York: Quadrangle/New York Times.

Harwood, Richard. (1980) *The Pursuit of the Presidency.* New York: Berkley Books.

Heard, Alexander. (1960) *The Costs of Democracy.* Chapel Hill: University of North Carolina Press.

Heclo, Hugh. (1978) "Issue Networks

and the Executive Establishment." In Anthony King, ed., *The New American Political System*. Washington, D.C.: American Enterprise Institute.

Hermann, Charles F. (1972) International Crises: Insights from Behavioral Research. New York: The Free Press.

Herring, Pendleton. (1940) *The Politics of Democracy: American Parties in Action*. New York: Rinehart & Co.

Hershey, Marjorie R. (1977) "A Social Learning Theory of Innovation and Change in Political Campaigning." Paper prepared for delivery at the 1977 Annual Meeting of the American Political Science Association, Washington, D.C.

Hess, Stephen. (1974) *The Presidential Campaign: The Leadership Selection Process after Watergate*. Washington, D.C.: Brookings Institution.

————. (1976) *Organizing the Presidency*. Washington, D.C.: Brookings Institution.

————. (1983) "The Golden Triangles: Press Relations at the White House, State Department and Department of Defense." Paper prepared for a Conference on War, Peace, and the News Media, New York University, New York.

Hinckley, Barbara. (1971) *The Seniority System in Congress*. Bloomington: Indiana University Press.

————. (1981) *Coalitions and Politics*. New York: Harcourt Brace Jovanovich.

Hinckley, Barbara, Hofstetter, Richard, and Kessel, John H. (1974) "Information and the Vote: A Comparative Election Study." *American Politics Quarterly* (April) pp. 131–158.

Hoagland, Henry W. (1960) "The Advance Man." In James W. Cannon, ed., *Politics, U.S.A.: A Practical Guide to the Winning of Public Office*. New York: Doubleday Publishing.

Hofstetter, Richard. (1976) *Bias in the News: Network Television Coverage of the 1972 Election Campaign*. Columbus: Ohio State University Press.

Holcombe, Arthur N. (1950) *Our More Perfect Union: From Eighteenth Century Principles to Twentieth Century Practice*. Cambridge, Mass.: Harvard University Press.

Holsti, Ole R., and George, Alexander L. (1975) "The Effects of Stress on the Performance of Foreign Policy-Makers." In Cornelius P. Cotter, ed., *Political Science Annual*. Vol. 6. Indianapolis, Ind.: Bobbs-Merrill.

Howell, Susan E. (1976) "The Psychological Dimension of Unity in American Political Parties." Paper prepared for delivery at the 1976 Annual Meeting of the American Political Science Association, Chicago.

Huckshorn, Robert J. (1976) *Party Leadership in the States*. Amherst: University of Massachusetts Press.

————. (1980) *Political Parties in America*. North Scituate, Mass.: Duxbury Press.

Huckshorn, Robert J., and Bibby, John F. (1983) "National Party Rules and Delegate Selection in the Republican Party." *PS* (Fall) pp. 656–666.

Ivins, Molly. (1976) "Liberal from Goldwater Country." *New York Times Magazine*, February 1, pp. 12–33.

Jackson, John E. (1975) "Issues, Party Choices, and Presidential Votes." *American Journal of Political Science* (May) pp. 161–185.

Jenkins, Ray. (1968) "Wallace Team Gears National Effort toward Election Day." *Christian Science Monitor*, September 17, p. 3.

Jennings, M. Kent. (1966) Personal communication.

Jennings, M. Kent, and Zeigler, Harmon. (1966) *The Electoral Process*. Englewood Cliffs, N.J.: Prentice-Hall.

Jewell, Malcolm E., and Chu Chi-Hung. (1974) "Membership Movement and Committee Attractiveness in the U.S. House of Representatives, 1963–1971." *American Journal of Political Science* (May) pp. 433–441.

Johnson, Loch K., and Hahn, Harlan. (1973) "Delegate Turnover at National Party Conventions, 1944–68." In Donald R. Matthews, ed., *Perspectives on Presidential Selection*. Washington, D.C.: Brookings Institution.

Johnson, Lyndon B. (1971) *The Vantage Point*. New York: Popular Library.

Jones, Charles O. (1961) "Representation in Congress: The Case of the House Agriculture Committee." *American Political Science Review* (June) pp. 358–367.

———. (1968) "The Minority Party and Policy-Making in the House of Representatives." *American Political Science Review* (June) pp. 481–493.

———. (1970) *The Minority Party in Congress*. Boston: Little, Brown.

———. (1979) "Congress and the Making of Energy Policy." In Robert Lawrence, ed., *New Dimensions in Energy Policy*. Lexington, Mass.: Lexington Books.

———. (1981a) "Congress and the Presidency." In Thomas E. Mann and Norman J. Ornstein, eds., *The New Congress*. Washington, D.C.: American Enterprise Institute.

———. (1981b) "Nominating 'Carter's Favorite Opponent': The Republicans in 1980." In Austin Ranney, ed., *The American Elections of 1980*. Washington, D.C.: American Enterprise Institute.

———. (1982) *The United States Congress: People, Place, and Policy*. Homewood, Ill.: Dorsey Press.

———. (1983) "Presidential Negotiation with Congress." In Anthony King, ed., *Both Ends of the Avenue*. Washington, D.C.: American Enterprise Institute.

Jordan, Hamilton. (1982) *Crisis: The Last Year of the Carter Presidency*. New York: G. P. Putnam's Sons.

Keech, William R., and Matthews, Donald R. (1976) *The Party's Choice*. Washington, D.C.: Brookings Institution.

Kelley, Stanley, Jr. (1956) *Professional Public Relations and Political Power*. Baltimore: The Johns Hopkins Press.

Kelley, Stanley, Jr., Ayers, Richard E., and Bowen, William G. (1967) "Registration and Voting: Putting First Things First." *American Political Science Review* (June) pp. 359–377.

Kemeny, John G., Snell, J. Laurie, and Thompson, Gerald L. (1957) *Introduction to Finite Mathematics*. Englewood Cliffs, N.J.: Prentice-Hall.

Kessel, John H. (1968) *The Goldwater Coalition: Republican Strategies in 1964*. Indianapolis, Ind.: Bobbs-Merrill.

———. (1974) "The Parameters of Presidential Politics." *Social Science Quarterly* (June) pp. 8–24.

———. (1975) *The Domestic Presidency: Decision-Making in the White House*. North Scituate, Mass.: Duxbury Press.

———. (1977) "The Seasons of Presidential Politics." *Social Science Quarterly* (December) pp. 418–435.

Key, V. O., Jr. (1949) *Southern Politics in State and Nation*. New York: Alfred A. Knopf.

———. (1964) *Politics, Parties, and Pressure Groups*. 5th ed. New York: Crowell.

King, Anthony. (1978) *The New American Political System*. Washington, D.C.: American Enterprise Institute.

———. (1983) *Both Ends of the Avenue: The Presidency, the Executive Branch, and Congress in the 1980s*. Washington, D.C.: American Enterprise Institute.

Kingdon, John W. (1968) *Candidates for Office: Beliefs and Strategies*. New York: Random House.

Kirkpatrick, Jeane. (1976) *The New Presidential Elite: Men and Women in National Politics*. New York: Russell Sage Foundation and Twentieth Century Fund.

Kramer, Gerald H. (1965) *Decision Theoretic Analysis of Canvassing and other Precinct Level Activities in Political Campaigning.* Ph.D. dissertation, Massachusetts Institute of Technology, Cambridge.

————. (1971) "The Effects of Precinct-Level Canvassing on Voter Behavior." *Public Opinion Quarterly* (Winter 1970–1971) pp. 560–572.

Kraus, Sidney. (1962) *The Great Debates: Kennedy vs. Nixon 1960.* Bloomington: Indiana University Press.

————. (1979) *The Great Debates: Ford vs. Carter 1976.* Bloomington: Indiana University Press.

Kruskal, Joseph B., and **Wish, Myron.** (1978) *Multidimensional Scaling.* Beverly Hills, Calif.: Sage Publications.

Lacy, Alex B., Jr. (1967) "The Development of the White House Office." Paper prepared for delivery at the 1967 Annual Meeting of the American Political Science Association, Chicago.

Ladd, Everett Carll, and **Hadley, Charles D.** (1978) *Transformations of the American Party System.* 2d ed. New York: W. W. Norton.

————. (1982) *Where Have All the Voters Gone?: The Fracturing of American Political Parties.* 2d ed. New York: W. W. Norton.

Lamb, Karl A. (1966) "Under One Roof: Barry Goldwater's Campaign Staff." In Bernard Cosman and Robert J. Huckshorn, eds., *Republican Politics: The 1964 Campaign and Its Aftermath.* New York: Praeger Publishers.

Lane, Robert E. (1973) "Patterns of Political Belief." In Jeane M. Knutson, ed., *Handbook of Political Psychology.* San Francisco: Jossey-Bass.

Lazarsfeld, Paul F., Berelson, Bernard, and **Gaudet, Hazel.** (1944) *The People's Choice.* New York: Duell, Sloan & Pearce.

LeLoup, Lance T., and **Shull, Steven A.** (1979) "Dimensions of Presidential Policy Making." In Steven A. Shull and Lance T. LeLoup, eds., *The Presidency: Studies in Policy Making.* Brunswick, Ohio: King's Court Communications.

Lelyveld, Joseph H. (1976a) "The Selling of a Candidate." *New York Times Magazine,* March 28, p. 16ff.

————. (1976b) "President's New TV Commercials." *New York Times,* October 29, p. 22.

————. (1976c) "Iowa Woman, 79, Who Met a 'Nobody' in '75, Is Tickled by Carter Victory." *New York Times,* November 4, p. 51.

Lengle, James I., and **Shafer, Byron E.** (1976) "Primary Rules, Political Power, and Social Change." *American Political Science Review* (March) pp. 25–40.

————. (1983) *Presidential Politics: Readings on Nominations and Elections.* 2d ed. New York: St. Martin's Press.

Levin, Eric. (1977) "How the Networks Decide What Is News." *TV Guide,* July 2, pp. 4–10.

Levinson, Daniel J. (1977) *The Seasons of a Man's Life.* New York: Alfred A. Knopf.

Light, Paul C. (1980) "The President's Agenda: Notes on the Timing of Domestic Choice." Paper prepared for delivery at the Annual Meeting of the American Political Science Association, Washington, D.C.

————. (1982) *The President's Agenda: Domestic Policy Choice from Kennedy to Carter.* Baltimore: The Johns Hopkins Press.

Loomis, Burdette A. (1981) "Congressional Caucuses and the Politics of Representation." In Lawrence C. Dodd and Bruce I. Oppenheimer, eds., *Congress Reconsidered.* 2d ed. Washington, D.C.: Congressional Quarterly Press.

Luce, R. Duncan, and **Raiffa, Howard.** (1957) *Games and Decisions: Introduction and Critical Survey.* New York: John Wiley & Sons.

Lydon, Christopher. (1972) "How McGovern Rose to Top in Long

Campaign." *New York Times,* June 11, p. 40.

Mackenzie, G. Calvin. (1981a) *The Politics of Presidential Appointments.* New York: Free Press.

————. (1981b) "Cabinet and Sub-cabinet Personnel Selection in Reagan's First Year: New Variations on Some Not-So-Old Themes." Paper prepared for delivery at the 1981 Annual Meeting of the American Political Science Association, Chicago.

MacRae, Duncan, Jr. (1970) *Issues and Parties in Legislative Voting.* New York: Harper & Row.

Malbin, Michael J. (1980) *Unelected Representatives: Congressional Staff and the Future of Representative Government.* New York: Basic Books.

————. (1981) "The Conventions, Platforms, and Issue Activists." In Austin Ranney, ed., *The American Elections of 1980.* Washington, D.C.: American Enterprise Institute.

————. (1983) "Rhetoric and Leadership: A Look Backward at President Carter's Energy Plan." In Anthony King, ed., *Both Ends of the Avenue: The Presidency, the Executive Branch, and Congress in the 1980s.* Washington, D.C.: American Enterprise Institute.

Mann, Thomas E., and **Ornstein, Norman J.** (1981) *The New Congress.* Washington, D.C.: American Enterprise Institute.

Markus, Gregory B. (1982) "Political Attitudes during an Election Year: A Report on the 1980 NES Panel Study." *American Political Science Review* (September) pp. 538–560.

Marvick, Dwaine. (1973) "Party Organizational Behavior and Electoral Democracy: The Perspectives of Rival Cadres in Los Angeles from 1963 to 1972." Paper prepared for delivery at the Ninth World Congress, International Political Science Association, Montreal, Canada.

————. (1983) "Stability and Change in the Views of Party Activists: Findings from Los Angeles Surveys, 1968–1980. Paper prepared for the 1983 Annual Meeting of the American Political Science Association, Chicago.

Matthews, Donald R. (1973) *Perspectives on Presidential Selection.* Washington, D.C.: Brookings Institution.

————. (1978) "Winnowing: The News Media and the 1976 Presidential Nominations." In James David Barber, ed., *Race for the Presidency: The Media and the Nominating Process.* Englewood Cliffs, N.J.: Prentice-Hall.

Matthews, Donald R., and **Prothro, James W.** (1966) *Negroes and the New Southern Politics.* New York: Harcourt Brace Jovanovich.

McClosky, Herbert, Hoffman, Paul J., and **O'Hara, Rosemary.** (1960) "Issue Conflict and Consensus among Party Leaders and Followers." *American Political Science Review* (June) pp. 406–427.

McGinniss, Joe. (1969) *The Selling of the President 1968.* New York: Trident Press.

McGregor, Eugene B. (1978) "Uncertainty and National Nominating Coalitions." *Journal of Politics* (December) pp. 1011–1042.

McKelvey, Richard, and **Zavonia, William.** (1969) "A Statistical Model for the Analysis of Legislative Behavior." Paper prepared for delivery at the 1969 Annual Meeting of the American Political Science Association, New York.

McPherson, Harry. (1972) *A Political Education.* Boston: Little, Brown.

McPherson, J. Miller, Welch, Susan, and **Clark, Cal.** (1977) "The Stability and Reliability of Political Efficacy: Using Path Analysis to Test Alternative Models." *American Political Science Review* (June) pp. 509–521.

Michelson, Charles. (1944) *The Ghost Talks.* New York: G. B. Putnam's Sons.

Miller, Arthur H. (1974) "Political Issues and Trust in Government: 1964–1970." *American Political Sci-*

ence Review (September) pp. 951–972.

Miller, Arthur H. (1983) "Is Confidence Rebounding?" *Public Opinion* (June/July) pp. 16–20.

Miller, Arthur H., and Wattenberg, Martin P. (1983) "Measuring Party Identification: Independent or No Partisan Preference?" *American Journal of Political Science* (February) pp. 106–121.

Miller, Arthur H., and Miller, Warren E. (1977) "Partisanship and Performance: 'Rational' Choice in the 1976 Elections." Paper prepared for delivery at the 1977 Annual Meeting of the American Political Science Association, Washington, D.C.

Miller, Warren E., and Levitin, Teresa E. (1976) *Leadership and Change: Presidential Elections from 1952 to 1976.* Cambridge, Mass.: Winthrop Press.

Mitofsky, Warren J., and Plissner, Martin. (1980) "The Making of the Delegates, 1968–1980." *Public Opinion* (October/November) pp. 37–43.

Moley, Raymond E. (1960) "Collaboration in Political Speech Writing." In James W. Cannon, ed., *Politics, U.S.A.: A Practical Guide to the Winning of Public Office.* New York: Doubleday Publishing.

Moore, Jonathan. (1981) *The Campaign for President: 1980 in Retrospect.* Cambridge, Mass.: Ballinger.

Moore, Jonathan, and Fraser, Janet. (1977) *Campaign for President: The Managers Look at '76.* Cambridge, Mass.: Ballinger.

Mueller, John E. (1973) *War, Presidents, and Public Opinion.* New York: John Wiley & Sons.

Munger, Frank J., and Blackhurst, James. (1965) "Factionalism in the National Conventions, 1940–1964: An Analysis of Ideological Consistency in State Delegation Voting." *Journal of Politics* (May) pp. 375–394.

National Journal (various issues).

Naughton, James M. (1976) "Ford Hopes Linked to Catholic Vote." *New York Times,* September 5, pp. 1, 26.

Neisser, Ulrich. (1976) Cognition and Reality. San Francisco: W. H. Freeman.

Nelson, Forrest D. (1976) "On a General Computer Algorithm for the Analysis of Models with Limited Dependent Variables." *Annals of Economic and Social Measurement,* pp. 493–509.

Nelson, Forrest D., and Olson, Lawrence. (1978) "Specification and Estimation of a Simultaneous-Equation Model with Limited Dependent Variables." *International Economic Review* (October).

Neustadt, Richard E. (1960) *Presidential Power: The Politics of Leadership.* New York: John Wiley & Sons.

————. (1968) *Presidential Power: The Politics of Leadership with an Afterword on JFK.* New York: John Wiley & Sons.

————. (1980) *Presidential Power: The Politics of Leadership from FDR to Carter.* New York: John Wiley & Sons.

Nexon, David. (1971) "Asymmetry in the Political System: Occasional Activists in the Republican and Democratic Parties, 1956–1964." *American Political Science Review* (September) pp. 716–730.

Nie, Norman H., and Andersen, Kristi. (1974) "Mass Belief Systems Revisited: Political Change and Attitude Structure." *Journal of Politics* (August) pp. 540–591.

Nie, Norman H., Verba, Sidney, and Petrocik, John R. (1976) *The Changing American Voter.* Cambridge, Mass.: Harvard University Press.

Niemi, Richard G., and Jennings, M. Kent. (1968) "Intraparty Communication and the Selection of Delegates to a National Convention." *Western Political Quarterly.*

Niemi, Richard G., and Weisberg, Herbert F. (1976) *Controversies in American Voting Behavior.* San Francisco: W. H. Freeman.

Nimmo, Dan, and Savage, Robert L. (1976) *Candidates and Their Images: Concepts, Methods and Findings.* Santa Monica, Calif.: Goodyear Publishing.

Nivola, Pietro. (1979) "The Natural Gas Policy Act of 1978: The Politics of Enactment." Paper prepared for the 1979 Annual Meeting of the American Political Science Association, Washington, D.C.

Ogden, Daniel M., and Peterson, Arthur L. (1968) *Electing the President.* Rev. ed. San Francisco: Chandler.

Ogul, Morris S. (1976) *Congress Oversees the Bureaucracy.* Pittsburgh, Penn.: University of Pittsburgh Press.

————. (1981) "Congressional Oversight." In Lawrence C. Dodd and Bruce I. Oppenheimer, eds., *Congress Reconsidered.* 2d ed. Washington, D.C.: Congressional Quarterly Press.

Oppenheimer, Bruce I., and Peabody, Robert L. (1977) "The House Majority Leadership Contest, 1976. Paper prepared for delivery to the 1977 Meeting of the American Political Science Association, Washington, D.C.

Ornstein, Norman J. (1983) "The Open Congress Meets the President." In Anthony King, ed., *Both Ends of the Avenue,* Washington, D.C.: American Enterprise Institute.

Ornstein, Norman J., Mann, Thomas E., Malbin, Michael J., and Bibby, John F. (1982) *Vital Statistics on Congress.* Washington, D.C.: American Enterprise Institute.

Orren, Gary R. (1978) "Candidate Style and Voter Alignment in 1976." In Seymour Martin Lipset, ed., *Emerging Coalitions in American Politics.* San Francisco: Institute for Contemporary Studies.

Page, Benjamin I. (1978) *Choices and Echoes in Presidential Elections: Rational Man and Electoral Democracy.* Chicago: University of Chicago Press.

Page, Benjamin I., and Brody, Richard A. (1972) "Policy Voting and the Electoral Process: The Vietnam War Issue." *American Political Science Review* (September) pp. 979–995.

Panning, William H. (1982) "Blockmodels: From Relations to Configurations." *American Journal of Political Science* (August) pp. 585–608.

Parker, Glenn R., and Parker, Suzanne L. (1979) "Factions in Committees: The U.S. House of Representatives." *American Political Science Review* (March) pp. 85–102.

Parris, Judith H. (1972) *The Convention Problem.* Washington, D.C.: Brookings Institution.

Parry, James M. (1977) "AMDAHL Speaks: Carter Really Won the Election." *National Observer,* February 12.

Patterson, Samuel C. (1978) "The Semi-Sovereign Congress." In Anthony King, ed., *The New American Political System.* Washington, D.C.: American Enterprise Institute.

Patterson, Samuel C., and Caldeira, Gregory A. (1983) "Getting Out the Vote: Participation in Gubernatorial Elections." *American Political Science Review* (September) pp. 675–689.

Patterson, Samuel C., Davidson, Roger H., and Ripley, Randall B. (1982) *A More Perfect Union: Introduction to American Government.* Rev. ed. Homewood, Ill.: Dorsey Press.

Patterson, Thomas E., and McClure, Robert D. (1976) *The Unseeing Eye: The Myth of Television Power in National Politics.* New York: G. P. Putnam's Sons.

Patterson, Thomas E. (1978) "Assessing Television Newscasts: Future Directions in Content Analysis." In William Adams and Fay Schreibman, eds., *Television Network News: Issues in Content Research.* Washington, D.C.: George Washington University.

Peabody, Robert L. (1976) *Leadership in Congress: Stability, Succession, and Change.* Boston: Little, Brown.

Penner, Rudolph G., and Heclo,

Hugh. (1983) "Fiscal and Political Strategy in the Reagan Administration." In Fred I. Greenstein, ed., *The Reagan Presidency: An Early Assessment.* Baltimore: The Johns Hopkins Press.

Petrocik, John R. (1974) "Intransitivities in the Index of Party Identification." *Political Methodology* (Summer) pp. 31–48.

————. (1981) *Party Coalitions: Realignments and the Decline of the New Deal Party System.* Chicago: University of Chicago Press.

Pika, Joseph A. (1979) "White House Boundary Roles: Linking Advisory Systems and Presidential Publics." Paper prepared for the 1979 Annual Meeting of the Political Science Association, Washington, D.C.

Plissner, Martin, and Mitofsky, Warren. (1981) "What If They Held an Election and Nobody Came?" *Public Opinion* (February/March) pp. 50–51.

Polsby, Nelson W. (1969) "Goodbye to the Inner Club." *Washington Monthly* (August) pp. 30–34.

————. (1971) *Congressional Behavior.* New York: Random House.

————. (1978) "Presidential Cabinet Building: Lessons for the Political System." *Political Science Quarterly* (Spring) pp. 15–25.

Polsby, Nelson W., and Wildavsky, Aaron. (1980) *Presidential Elections.* 5th ed. New York: Charles Scribner's Sons.

Pomper, Gerald M. (1979) "New Rules and New Games in the National Conventions." *Journal of Politics* (August) pp. 784–805.

————. (1981) *The Election of 1980: Reports and Interpretations.* Chatham, N.J.: Chatham House.

Pomper, Gerald M., and Lederman, Susan S. (1980) *Elections in America: Control and Influence in Democratic Politics.* 2d ed. New York: Dodd, Mead.

Porter, Roger B. (1980) *Presidential Decision Making: The Economic Policy Board.* New York: Cambridge University Press.

————. (1981) "The President and Economic Policy: Problems, Policies, and Alternatives." In Hugh Heclo and Lester M. Salamon, eds., *The Illusion of Presidential Government.* Boulder, Colo.: Westview Press.

Rabinowitz, George B. (1975) "An Introduction to Non-Metric Multidimensional Scaling." *American Journal of Political Science* (May) pp. 343–390.

Ranney, Austin. (1975) *Curing the Mischiefs of Faction: Party Reform in America.* Berkeley: University of California Press.

————. (1978) "The Political Parties: Reform and Decline." In Anthony King, ed., *The New American Political System.* Washington, D.C.: American Enterprise Institute.

————. (1981) *The American Elections of 1980.* Washington, D.C.: American Enterprise Institute.

Raskin, A. H. (1972) "All Over Lot in '72 Campaign." *New York Times,* August 20, pp. E1–E2.

Ray, Bruce A. (1982) "Committee Attractiveness in the U.S. House, 1963–1981." *American Journal of Political Science* (August) pp. 609–613.

Reichley, A. James. (1981) *Conservatives in an Age of Change: The Nixon and Ford Administrations.* Washington, D.C.: Brookings Institution.

Republican National Committee Chairman's Report. (1979) Washington, D.C.: By the Committee.

Republican National Committee Chairman's Report. (1980) Washington, D.C.: By the Committee.

Rhode, David W., and Shepsle, Kenneth A. (1973) "Democratic Committee Assignments in the House of Representatives: Strategic Aspects of a Social Choice Process." *American Political Science Review* (September) pp. 889–905.

Riker, William H. (1962) *The Theory of Political Coalitions.* New Haven, Conn.: Yale University Press.

Ripley, Randall B. (1969) *The Major-*

ity Party in Congress. Boston: Little, Brown.

—————. (1983) *Congress: Process and Policy.* 3d ed. New York: W. W. Norton.

Robinson, Michael J. (1976) "Television News and the Presidential Nominating Process: The Case of Spring." Unpublished manuscript.

Rosenstone, Steven J. (1983) *Forecasting Presidential Elections.* New Haven: Conn.: Yale University Press.

Rosenstone, Steven J., and **Wolfinger, Raymond E.** (1978) "The Effect of Registration Laws on Voter Turnout." *American Political Science Review* (March) pp. 22–45.

Rubin, Richard L. (1976) *Party Dynamics: The Democratic Coalition and the Politics of Change.* New York: Oxford University Press.

Safire, William. (1975) *Before the Fall: An Inside View of the Pre-Watergate White House.* New York: Doubleday Publishing.

Schick, Allen. (1981a) "The Three-Ring Budget Process: The Appropriation, Tax and Budget Committees in Congress." In Thomas E. Mann and Norman J. Ornstein, eds., *The New Congress.* Washington, D.C.: American Enterprise Institute.

—————. (1981b) *Reconciliation and the Congressional Budget Process.* Washington, D.C.: American Enterprise Institute.

—————. (1983) "Politics through Law: Congressional Limitations on Executive Discretion." In Anthony King, ed., *Both Ends of the Avenue.* Washington, D.C.: American Enterprise Institute.

Schlesinger, Joseph A. (1965) "Political Parties." In James G. March, ed., *Handbook of Organizations.* Skokie, Ill.: Rand McNally.

—————. (1975) "The Primary Goals of Political Parties: A Clarification of Positive Theory." *American Political Science Review* (September) pp. 840–849.

Schneider, William. (1983) "Party Unity on Tax, Spending Issues: Less in House, More in Senate in 1982." *National Journal* (May 7) pp. 936–952.

Schram, Martin. (1977) *Running for President 1976: The Carter Campaign.* New York: Stein & Day.

Sears, David O. (1977) "The Debates in the Light of Research: An Overview of the Effects." Paper prepared for delivery at the 1977 Annual Meeting of the American Political Science Association, Washington, D.C.

Sears, David O., and **Chaffee, Steven H.** (1979) "Uses and Effects of the 1976 Debates: An Overview of Empirical Studies." In Sidney Kraus, ed., *The Great Debates, 1976: Ford vs. Carter.* Bloomington: Indiana University Press.

Semple, Robert B. (1968) "Two Nixons Emerge in '68 Race: Stump Sloganeer, Radio Thinker." *New York Times,* October 17, p. 38.

Shafer, Byron D. (1983a) "Continuity and Change, Predictability and Change in the Politics of Presidential Selection." *PS* (Fall) pp. 648–655.

—————. (1983b) "Projecting the Outcome in 1984." *PS* (Fall) pp. 689–694.

Shaffer, Stephen D. (1981) "A Multivariate Explanation of Decreasing Turnout in Presidential Elections, 1960–1976." *American Journal of Political Science* (February) pp. 68–95.

Shields, Currin V. (1954) "A Note on Party Organization: The Democrats in California." *Western Political Quarterly* (December) pp. 673–683.

Shively, W. Phillips. (1977) "Information Costs and the Partisan Life Cycle." Paper prepared for delivery at the 1977 Annual Meeting of the American Political Science Association, Washington, D.C.

—————. (1979) "The Development of Party Identification in Adults." *American Political Science Review* (December) pp. 1039–1054.

Simon, Herbert A. (1952) "Comments on the Theory of Organizations." *American Political Science Review* (December) pp. 1130–1152.

Simon, Herbert A., Smithburg, Donald W., and Thompson, Victor A. (1950) *Public Administration.* New York: Alfred A. Knopf.

Sinclair, Barbara D. (1972) "State Party Delegations in the U.S. House of Representatives." *Journal of Politics* (February) pp. 199–222.

————. (1976) "Electoral Marginality and Party Loyalty in House Roll Call Voting." *American Journal of Political Science* (August) pp. 469–481.

————. (1981) "The Speaker's Task Force in the Post-Reform House of Representatives." *American Political Science Review* (June) pp. 397–410.

————. (1982) *Congressional Realignment, 1925–1978.* Austin: University of Texas Press.

Smith, Hedrick. (1978) "Problems of a Problem Solver." *New York Times Magazine,* January 8, pp. 30–34, 36, 40, 44–45.

————. (1979) "Carter's Race against Time." *New York Times Magazine,* September 2, pp. 12–15, 26, 28.

Smith, Richard Norton. (1982) *Thomas E. Dewey and His Times.* New York: Simon & Schuster.

Smith, Steven S. (1981) "The Consistency and Ideological Structure of U.S. Senate Voting Alignments, 1957–1976." *American Journal of Political Science* (November) pp. 780–795.

Sorauf, Frank J. (1984) *Party Politics in America.* 5th ed. Boston: Little, Brown.

Sorenson, Theodore. (1965) *Kennedy.* New York: Bantam Books.

Soule, John W., and Clarke, James W. (1970) "Amateurs and Professionals: A Study of Delegates to the 1968 Democratic National Convention." *American Political Science Review* (September) pp. 888–898.

Soule, John W., and McGrath, Wilma E. (1975) "A Comparative Study of Presidential Nominating Conven-

tions." *American Journal of Political Science* (August) pp. 501–517.

Sperlich, Peter W. (1971) *Conflict and Harmony in Human Affairs: A Study of Cross-Pressures and Political Behavior.* Skokie, Ill.: Rand McNally.

Sperling, Godfrey, Jr. (1972) "Steelworkers Wary on McGovern." *Christian Science Monitor,* September 20, p. 3.

————. (1983) "As Jimmy Carter Sees It." *Christian Science Monitor,* August 4, pp. 12–13.

Stein, Herbert. (1981) "Presidents and Economics." *AEI Economist* (January).

Sterling, Christopher, and Haight, Timothy. (1979) *The Mass Media: Aspen Institute Guide to Communication Industry Trends.* Queenstown, Md.: By the Institute.

Stevenson, Robert L. (1978) "The Uses and Non-Uses of Television News. Paper prepared for the International Society of Political Psychology Meeting, New York.

Stimson, James A. (1976) "Public Support for American Presidents: A Cyclical Model." *Public Opinion Quarterly* (Spring) pp. 1–21.

Stokes, Donald E., Campbell, Angus, and Miller, Warren E. (1958) "Components of Electoral Decision." *American Political Science Review* (June) pp. 367–387.

Sullivan, Dennis G., Pressman, Jeffrey L., Page, Benjamin I., and Lyons, John J. (1974) *The Politics of Representation: The Democratic Convention 1972.* New York: St. Martin's Press.

Sullivan, John L., Piereson, James E., and Marcus, George E. (1978) "Ideological Constraint in the Mass Public: A Methodological Critique and Some New Findings." *American Journal of Political Science* (May) pp. 250–269.

Sundquist, James L. (1968) *Politics and Policy: The Eisenhower, Kennedy and Johnson Years.* Washington, D.C.: Brookings Institution.

Tillett, Paul. (1962) *Inside Politics:*

The National Conventions, 1960. Dobbs Ferry, N.Y.: Oceana Press.

Truman, David B. (1956) "The State Delegations and the Structure of Party Voting in the United States House of Representatives." *American Political Science Review* (December) pp. 1023–1045.

————. (1971) *The Governmental Process.* 2d ed. New York: Alfred A. Knopf.

Tufte, Edward R. (1978) *Political Control of the Economy.* Princeton, N.J.: Princeton University Press.

Van Doren, Peter. (1981) "The Causes of Public Policy: State Intervention in Energy Markets." Paper prepared for delivery at the 1981 Annual Meeting of the American Political Science Association, New York.

Van Wingen, John R., and **Valentine, David C.** (1978) "Partisanship, Independence, and the Partisan Identification Index. Paper prepared for delivery at the 1978 Annual Meeting of the Midwest Political Science Association, Chicago.

Verba, Sydney, and **Nie, Norman H.** (1972) *Participation in America: Political Democracy and Social Equality.* New York: Harper & Row.

Walker, Jack L. (1977) "Setting the Agenda in the U.S. Senate: A Theory of Problem Selection." *British Journal of Political Science* (October) pp. 423–445.

Watson, Richard A., and **Thomas, Norman C.** (1983) *The Politics of the Presidency.* New York: John Wiley & Sons.

Wayne, Stephen J. (1978) *The Legislative Presidency.* New York: Harper & Row.

————. (1984) *The Road to the White House.* 2d ed. New York: St. Martin's Press.

Weaver, Warren, Jr. (1976) "Political Fever Is Causing Washington Mallaise" in *New York Times,* August 15.

Weisberg, Herbert F. (1978) "Evaluating Theories of Congressional Roll Call Voting." *American Journal of Political Science* (August), pp. 554–577.

————. (1979) "The Validity of Voter Registration and Turnout Reports in Surveys." Paper prepared for delivery at the Conference on Voter Turnout, San Diego, Calif.

————. (1980) "A Multidimensional Conceptualization of Party Identification." *Political Behavior* (No. 1) pp. 33–60.

Weisman, Steven R. (1982) "Reaganomics and the President's Men." *New York Times Magazine,* October 24, pp. 24–29, 82–85, 89–92, 109.

White, F. Clifton. (1967) *Suite 3505: The Story of the Draft Goldwater Movement.* New Rochelle, N.Y.: Arlington House.

White, Theodore H. (1961) *The Making of the President 1960.* New York: Atheneum Publishers.

————. (1965) *The Making of the President 1964.* New York: Atheneum Publishers.

————. (1969) *The Making of the President 1968.* New York: Atheneum Publishers.

————. (1973) *The Making of the President 1972.* New York: Atheneum Publishers.

————. (1975) *Breach of Faith: The Fall of Richard Nixon.* New York: Atheneum Press, Reader's Digest.

————. (1982) *America in Search of Itself: The Making of the President 1956–1980.* New York: Harper & Row.

Williams, Daniel C., and others. (1976) "Voter Decisionmaking in a Primary Election." *American Journal of Political Science* (February) pp. 37–49.

Wilson, James O. (1980) *American Government: Institutions and Policies.* Lexington, Mass.: D. C. Heath.

Wilson, Woodrow. (1884) *Congressional Government, Meridian Edition.* New York: Meridian Books, 1956.

Wirthlin, Richard, Breglio, Vincent, and **Beal, Richard.** (1981) "Campaign Chronicle." *Public Opinion* (February/March) pp. 43–49.

Witcover, Jules. (1977) *Marathon: The Pursuit of the Presidency.* New York: Viking Press.

Wolfinger, Raymond E. (1972) "Why Political Machines Have Not Withered Away and Other Revisionist Thoughts." *Journal of Politics* (February) pp. 365–398.

Wolfinger, Raymond E., and others. (1977) "The Myth of the Independent Voter." Paper prepared for delivery at the 1977 Annual Meeting of the American Political Science Association, Washington, D.C.

Wolfinger, Raymond E., and **Rosenstone, Steven J.** (1980) *Who Votes?* New Haven, Conn.: Yale University Press.

Wood, Robert C. (1970) "When Government Works." *The Public Interest* (Winter) pp. 39–51.

Wooten, James T. (1976) "Carter Strategy from the Start: 1976 Was the Year for a Gambler." *New York Times,* June 10, p. 42.

Yarnell, Steven. (1975) "The Measurement of Perceptual Accuracy: A Methodological Note." Unpublished paper, Ohio State University.

Young, James Sterling. (1966) *The Washington Community 1800–1828.* New York: Harcourt Brace Jovanovich.

INDEX

This book has been set VideoComp in 10 and 9 point Vermilion, leaded 2 points. Part numbers and titles are 20 point Spectra Extra Bold; chapter numbers and titles are 18 point Spectra Extra Bold. The size of the type page is 27 by 47 picas.